MW00996841

WORLD WAR II
LAW AND LAWYERS

ISSUES, CASES, AND CHARACTERS

THOMAS J. SHAW

WORLD WAR II
LAW AND LAWYERS

ISSUES, CASES, AND CHARACTERS

Defending Liberty
Pursuing Justice

Printed in the United States of America.

17 16 15 14   5 4 3

Library of Congress Cataloging-in-Publication Data

Shaw, Thomas J. (Attorney)
  World War II law and lawyers : issues cases and characters / Thomas J. Shaw.
     pages cm
  Includes bibliographical references and index.
  ISBN 978-1-61438-872-2 (alk. paper)
  1. Lawyers—History. 2. Practice of law—History. 3. World War, 1939-1945—Law and legislation. I. Title.
  K124.W37S53 2013
  340.09'044—dc23

                                    2013014100

DEDICATION

My inspiration for my deep involvement with the subject of World War II and the writing of this book is my late father, Dr. Keith Wesley Shaw. His experiences as the very young copilot of a bomber plane in the Pacific theater led to a long fixation with this war, a fixation that he naturally passed on to me and later to my young daughter Ayaka, whom he never had the opportunity to meet. Ayaka carried on the family connection to this most global of conflicts with her kindly intended (but unsolicited) inputs during her summer break while I wrote the first chapters of this book. May they get to know each other better through this writing, as viewed respectively from heaven and from earth.

Dr. Keith Wesley Shaw
Courtesy of Alan J. Shaw and Carol M. White

CONTENTS

FOREWORD

One of my first memories in life was watching a World War II (WWII) drama at a drive-in movie theater in our family station wagon. Not just once but multiple times amidst the large buckets of popcorn, glass Coke bottles, and window-mounted speakers, I watched intently through the windshield as John Wayne and his costars reenacted the invasion of Normandy.

The reason for my father's focus on this movie and WWII became a little clearer as I heard of talks with former army buddies and saw his old war photos. The story came together slowly, as my father was a man of few words on this topic: like many of his generation, he did not discuss his war experiences with those who were not involved. His was the tale of a high school senior who volunteered for military service when he turned eighteen; entered the U.S. Army Air Forces (Air Corps); was deployed to the Asian theater; and flew many missions as a bomber copilot, the last over the USS *Missouri* in Tokyo Bay during the formal signing of the instrument of surrender.

I have spent my life attached to this war. As a child I was surrounded by imagery of the "Good War," where good and evil were so clearly in opposing camps. This was reinforced by numerous heroic movies and television shows (think *Twelve O'Clock High*, *The Guns of Navarone*, and *To Hell and Back*). It was only much later that the complexities of the war began to enter my consciousness. This may have started with the debates about the need for additional nuclear weapons testing or the apologies to Japanese-American citizens interned during the war but it continues right up to the present-day debates on the use of military trials for enemy combatants and the disputed ownership of islands in the Pacific.

My reasons for wanting to write this book, though, actually emanate from a distant point on a very long arc stretching almost a century—from my daughter's Canadian great-grandfather fighting in the trenches dug in Europe during

World War I to her Asian ancestors fighting in the name of an emperor to her American grandfather flying bombing missions in the Pacific during WWII. She wants to know how the country of her father's ancestors and the country she has grown up in, such strong allies today, could have ever been involved in fighting each other in such a terrible conflict. My reply, in part, is this book.

More recent events have brought me to the actual writing of this book. As I was authoring my third legal book, I came across a book written by a fellow author/lawyer that mixed law and history. Art Downey's *Civil War Lawyers*, which arrived while I was reading several other works about that same time period, was proof that perhaps I could marry many of my passions in life: writing, the law, history, and educating my daughter. When the American Bar Association presented me with the opportunity to write about legal history during wartime, I knew exactly which war I wanted to document and so set out on the journey to research and write this book. It has consumed most of five months of my life.

Why another book about WWII, especially more than seventy years after it was first fought? There are clearly hundreds, if not thousands, of books on this war. Although my goals here are modest, what hopefully makes this book unique is its focus on the three main areas suggested by the subtitle of the book: legal issues, cases, and characters. First, it brings together in a single volume the major legal issues surrounding this conflict. Second, it takes a global view, looking at the laws and cases in as many countries as necessary to describe these major issues. And third, it introduces many lawyers and judges from around the world involved with these issues, some of whom may be little known or long forgotten today. The legal issues and the laws passed to address them set the stage for what I find most interesting—the legal cases and their actors.

SCOPE

When tackling a subject as big as the second World War, it is necessary to find a scope appropriate for the niche served. Scope involves many dimensions, including topic, time, geography, viewpoint, and language.

The overall topic of this work is the legal issues that arose from actions taken prior to and during the war. Of course, every action taken during a war potentially can be an issue analyzed for legal implications. The many acts that are now termed *crimes against humanity* and *war crimes* could and do fill up whole volumes by themselves. So, the question is how to draw a line between what is manageable and what is not manageable in a single-volume survey. What I have decided to do is to try to limit the discussion, as necessary, to large-scale or systemic acts carried out by agents of the various governments, instead of individual or nonsystemic acts.

This book is neither a general history of WWII nor a legal treatise. Instead, it is a legal history lying somewhere in between. Because I do not claim to be a professional historian, I defer in the broader themes of this global conflict to those who have written much more ably and in greater detail. I present significant wartime events to briefly set the stage for the legal issues that arose from them. I assume that readers are familiar enough with the general story of the war that a repeat telling is unnecessary. I strongly encourage readers who want more background to turn to the many available sources for deeper understandings of this conflict, its origins and resolutions, and the detailed events and timelines. Likewise, many of the cases, lawyers, and judges featured in this work have been the focus of entire books. So, it is clear that in a survey of such a broad subject as this, I can merely introduce the individual topics and take them to a certain level of depth, which then can serve as a jumping-off point for further reading and research. I do not intend to be the final citation source, only a starting point for further inquiry into a vastly deep pool of facts and events.

From a time perspective, this war was primarily fought from 1939 to 1945, but the legal issues themselves extend back farther, to some incidents or laws from WWI and to cases that took place several years after that war (during the various trials and the attempts to reclaim properties). While the seeds of the any war are clearly sown in the preceding one, I will leave those connections for another volume. The laws and cases from WWI are presented only tangentially, but the key laws in the interwar period are covered in more detail.

With a world war, there are few geographic limits; but in practical writing terms, there must be a geographical center. In this book, that center is in western and central Europe, East Asia, and the United States, the areas that encompass the seven countries that I have chosen to represent the major legal issues of the war. It does not mean that nothing of legal significance happened in Scandinavia, South America, North Africa, Southeast Asia, Australasia, Russia, the Baltics, eastern Europe, Canada, or southern Europe during the war. Perhaps these geographies will be included in a future edition of this book.

I have tried to bring a global viewpoint to this book. Truly understanding the legal issues that arose within each country requires an understanding of the culture within which those issues arose. Having lived outside the United States for almost twenty years now, I believe that I have an understanding of how other (non-American) cultures function and can articulate the perspectives of those who are not American (i.e., the majority of those involved in this conflict), even when their native language is not English. Having said that, however, I do expect that an American viewpoint of what occurred may seep through. Storytellers must originate from somewhere.

Writing in any one language obviously disadvantages those whose points of view are most clearly expressed in their native tongue. Research in a foreign language can be broader than the language of writing through the translation of important documents. But there are inherent limitations to research in a foreign language: the researcher may never find the proper documents; may not have a clear understanding of all meanings, synonyms, and possible references; and may not do a good job of translating the original. Despite these limitations, foreign language sources were used throughout this book, although in some cases I translated the titles to English for ease of reader understanding.

PRESENTATION

This book is organized around legal issues that arose from significant events in the major geographical areas mentioned earlier. Each chapter opens with a brief introduction and a "Prominent Lawyers and Judges in This Chapter" section, which previews the names of the lawyers and judges discussed in the various sections of that chapter. The individual sections of the chapters typically identify one of the major legal issues; and the related statutes, executive orders, decrees, regulations, relevant cases, subsequent events, and modern applicability (where appropriate) are discussed. Almost every section concludes with biographies of the lawyers and judges featured in that section, except when the events are not part of the WWII era.

Because the book centers around legal issues, it follows each issue from beginning to end and, as such, is not in chronological order from the first chapter to the last. The historical author would normally follow a strict time-sequence order. However, because the legal issues typically take many years to play out, from statute to violation to trial to appellate review, it is not possible to follow a precise timeline. What I have chosen to do is present each legal issue on the date that it was identified in a statute, executive order, or decree and then follow it through to its end, often taking the reader many years into the future, even after the conclusion of the war. I believe that this works better than trying to weave together many story lines on an exact calendar presentation or working backward from when the court cases were decided. After all, the enactment of laws closely follows the sentiment that was present at the time and so clearly presents the historical atmosphere that brought on particular issues.

Legal Issues

I have highlighted fifty-two major legal issues from WWII, spread across the chapters of this book. The following is a consolidated list of those issues, mostly in the order in which they are described. Those with an asterisk are linked to a discussion of modern applicability.

Sedition	Espionage★
Conscientious Objectors	Desegregation/Integration
Lend–Lease	Export Controls★
Declaration of War★	Rationing and Supply Controls
Price Controls	Labor Disputes
Seizure of the Means of Production	Enemy Assets★
Military Tribunals★	Martial Law
Revocation of Citizenship	Treason/Treachery
Citizen Internment	Freedom of Expression
Official Secrets★	National Registration
Emergency Powers	Contract Failure
Friendly Fire	Anschluss (Annexation)★
Collaboration★	Neutrality
Military Internment	Refugees★

Looted Assets★	Destruction of Democratic Institutions
Subversion of Judicial Integrity	Conspiracy or Common Plan
Crimes Against Humanity★/ War Crimes★	Crimes Against Peace/ Aggressive War
Medical Experimentation	Slave Labor
Murder of POWs	Privacy Violations★
Plunder and Exploitation of Occupied Countries	Systematic Destruction of Cultural Life★
Genocide★/Mass Murder of Civilians	Creation of a Divine Military★
Aggressive War/Preemptive Military Strikes★	Mass Rape★
Mistreatment of POWs	Narcotics Trafficking
Biological Warfare	Sexual Slavery
Use of Nuclear Weapons★	Occupation/Rehabilitation★
Peace Treaties★	Return of Cultural Assets★

I have written about each issue as it occurred in only a single country. As the United States is presented first and in greater detail, this makes the book a bit America-centric. Clearly, many of the same issues repeat themselves in many countries, e.g., controlling prices was important to all of the warring nations. While I could have discussed, for example, how the United Kingdom dealt with inflation and perhaps contrasted and compared it to how the United States, Japan, and Germany did so, I felt that the incremental value of that was less than the value of covering more issues. Internationally, I discuss only those issues unique to a region's situation.

Cases

Some cases were chosen for their historical significance; others were chosen because they seemed historically more interesting. I have selected both well-known and obscure cases in order to present the bigger themes of each issue as well as fill in with additional situations to which the themes would naturally extend. In order to keep the length of the book reasonable, however, I have not featured every relevant case; where possible, I have given preference to those that have been reviewed by at least two courts. My intent is to help readers understand the broad strokes of legal history, not the minutiae, so I have not gone into the trifling details of each issue raised in each case. There are myriad articles available that do provide such a level of examination for those so interested.

Several of these cases were (and remain) controversial. Former enemies are now allies and friends. Some of those convicted later presented a case of possible innocence. I have tried to take a neutral approach, focusing on these issues as seen through the eyes of those adjudicating them in their own time period. This is a not a book designed to reinterpret old issues but to relate them as understood then. I am fully aware that a few of those convicted were later exonerated. However, as evidenced by the trial records at that time, most judges and attorneys involved (with obvious exceptions) attempted to mete out justice and balance interests as best they could against the backdrop of a dangerous and unstable world, one that could have possibly imploded around them based on the outcome of the next battle.

Characters

The characters are the lawyers, judges, and law school graduates involved with drafting or influencing statutes, executive orders, decrees, and subsequent litigation or implementation. While I could not discuss every lawyer involved in each issue, I have tried to identify a representative group across gender, nationality, race, fame, and geography, with the understanding that during this time in history, not all groups were allowed to fully participate in the legal world. Although some are as well known as presidents and Supreme Court justices, others are not as well known. I have tried to find as many people who may not be known to the reader as people who will be instantly recognizable (although perhaps in a role early in their careers). I hope to bring them all, famous and obscure, to the attention of a new generation of readers.

At the end of most sections in each chapter, a "Legal Profiles" section displays a brief biography of one or more characters in that section. The brief bios of the approximately 300 featured lawyers, judges, and law school graduates are just that—brief. They are not meant to be in-depth analyses, nor do they contain the legal philosophies particular to these different people. These are merely

introductions to the profiled individuals. I intend these bios to be only a starting point, and I highly encourage the reader to move on to full biographies of
this infinitely interesting cast of characters (to further this end, I have tried to
provide at least one external citation for each character). (See the Appendix for
a composite list of the legal personalities discussed in this book.)

Subsequent Events

I have also tried to link the legal events that occurred during this war to subsequent events and, where it makes sense, to modern applications. Some of these
matters were essentially settled legally long ago, while others still resonate as
unsettled even today. The subsequent events typically occurred within a few
years of the end of the war, while modern applicability covers events that
happened long after the war or may be happening now. Because the modern
applicability sections feature characters outside the era of this war, I decided
not to provide profiles of lawyers and judges for these sections.

   While I find history in and of itself sufficiently fascinating, linking it to
the search for answers to current problems not only provides the necessary
perspective but also makes it practical. Some of the legal matters arising from
this war are still with us today and can easily arise in the next conflict. My
goal here is not only to educate and entertain those new to these issues, cases,
and characters from seventy years ago but also to provide a brief historical
foundation for those still dealing with these complex issues. I hope that I have
accomplished all of this.

Thomas J. Shaw, Esq.
March 2013

ABOUT THE AUTHOR

Thomas J. Shaw, Esq., Attorney at Law,
CPA, CRISC, CIP, CIPP, CISM, ERMP, CISA, CGEIT, CCSK

Thomas J. Shaw, Esq., is an attorney in Asia and frequent author and speaker on legal topics from a global perspective. He is the author of the 2012 book *"Children and the Internet: A Global Guide for Lawyers and Parents,"* author of the 2011 book *"Cloud Computing for Lawyers and Executives: A Global Approach,"* and lead author/editor of the 2011 book *"Information Security and Privacy: A Practical Guide for Global Executives, Lawyers and Technologists."* He is the author of the forthcoming companion book *"World War I Law and Lawyers: Issues, Cases and Characters."* Mr. Shaw writes extensively on the law and has published dozens of legal articles in many periodicals. He is also the editor/founder of two American Bar Association periodicals: the *Information Security & Privacy News* and the *EDDE Journal.* In addition to legal authoring and publishing and raising his daughter, Mr. Shaw works with organizations on Internet, information, and international law, compliance, information governance, audit, contracts, new technologies, and risk. He runs CloudRisk Asia, which provides risk assessment services for private and public-sector organizations and cloud service providers (www.cloudriskasia.com). He also spends significant time helping to make children safe on the Internet. He can be reached at thomas@tshawlaw.com.

CHAPTER 1

BEFORE THE WAR

The "Good War" was also good for lawyers. In the United States and its allied countries and initially in the countries that would be their enemies, the rule of law was a centering tendency. Lawyers and judges controlled many aspects of what was done, how it was legally implemented, and how it was later interpreted. They tried to follow their respective countries' guiding legal principles while balancing the demands of governmental and military institutions and civilian populations—in effect, stretching but trying not to break those core beliefs in responding to the urgent needs of wartime. In some countries, the rule of law held up throughout the war, providing a vast amount of new legal direction on issues not previously addressed and also on issues left over from the last global conflict. In other countries, the rule of law tottered and eventually broke down as various forms of totalitarianism took over.

In America, where the rule of law prevailed throughout the conflict, events arose creating relatively novel legal issues (e.g., citizen internment). Other legal issues had been around for some time (e.g., segregation) but were tested anew. Some issues were domestically focused, and others looked overseas to allies or enemies; some were economic, and others were military; some dealt with loyalty, some with the right of religious choice, and some with the right of free speech. In common with many countries, the extra powers given to the executive branch and military were among the key legal issues. While these issues arose in preparation for or during this conflict, many were not ultimately resolved until after the war concluded.

In other countries that were able to maintain a rule of law, such as the United Kingdom and Switzerland, the legal principles similarly went back and forth between wartime exigencies and long-held traditions, always with a wary eye on the military situation abroad. In countries annexed or overrun by the Axis powers, like Austria and France, there were legal issues regarding the responsibility for turning over the country to the enemy and then collaborating with it. In the leading Axis powers, Germany and Japan, where effectively the rule of law collapsed and gave way to totalitarianism, the important legal issues were often addressed subsequently by new laws written by former enemies applied in some cases retroactively to those who had been the initial aggressors in this conflict. These new laws were created to deal with atrocities previously unimaginable.

Regardless, in all situations and countries, lawyers were involved. They were involved in writing statutes as part of legislatures, executive orders as part of countries' political leadership, and even decrees as part of totalitarian regimes. They were, of course, involved as judges, attorneys, solicitors, barristers, advocates, and amici curiae in resolving cases about violations of these laws. In many cases, though, as wartime is a fountain springing forth new career opportunities, they temporarily or permanently left their legal roles behind to take on new roles in politics or the military. There were times when their legal training and experience were able to temper extreme actions and assist them in getting their constituents' desires expressed, but in other cases their training and experience were abandoned in the bloodlust of wartime extravagance. While the lawyers and judges profiled herein on balance had a positive impact, that cannot be said to be true with all lawyers and judges of this time period. Some had a truly negative or malicious impact. The only consistency in this conflict was their wide-ranging presence and influence.

This influence started decades earlier: much of the basis for what happened legally in WWII evolved from developments during WWI, including what worked well (selective service), what did not work well (censorship), and the laws that were still on the books (espionage). This chapter sets the basis for WWII legal issues by looking at some of the significant legal steps that happened after WWI and in the interwar period.[1]

---

1. An overview of applicable laws from WWI will be referenced as necessary in each of the following chapters, but a deeper analysis of the WWI laws can be found in the forthcoming companion book to this work: THOMAS J. SHAW, WWI LAW AND LAWYERS: ISSUES, CASES, AND CHARACTERS (2014).

WWI was completed with a series of treaties among the various warring parties that in large part did not satisfy the participants, leading to ongoing strife and feelings of mistreatment or mistrust. As postwar good economic times turned bad during the Depression, totalitarianism of different kinds came to the fore in Germany, Japan, and Italy and in other smaller countries that were overrun by the Axis powers. The difficult global economy, lingering issues from WWI, and the lack of strong international institutions, along with a number of other country-specific factors, helped set the stage for the re-armaments and national justifications for expansion beyond domestic borders that eventually led to WWII.

This chapter focuses on two major areas of legal activity in the period between the wars that impacted the coming conflict of WWII: treaties ending WWI and U.S. neutrality laws of the 1930s. (The legal activities occurring between the wars in the other countries described in this book are explained in each of their respective sections and chapters.)

PROMINENT LAWYERS AND JUDGES IN THIS CHAPTER

Treaties Ending WWI:

- Robert Lansing (U.S. secretary of state)
- David Lloyd George (British prime minister)
- Ellis Dresel (U.S. commissioner to Germany)
- V. K. Wellington Koo (Chinese treaty representative)
- John William Salmond (New Zealand treaty representative)
- Robert Laird Borden (Canadian treaty representative)
- Charles G. Dawes (reparations plan sponsor)
- Frank B. Kellogg (international treaty author)
- Aristide Briand (international treaty author)
- Edvard Benes (president of Czechoslovakia)
- Edward Bernard Raczynski (Polish treaty signatory)
- Leon Blum (French prime minister)

U.S. Neutrality Laws:

- Franklin Delano Roosevelt (president)
- John Nance Garner (vice president)

- Alger Hiss (Senate committee legal counsel)
- William B. Bankhead (Speaker of the House)
- Homer S. Cummings (U.S. attorney general)
- James E. Major (court of appeals judge)
- John T. Cahill (intervenor's attorney)
- Claude A. Swanson (secretary of the navy)

1.1 TREATIES ENDING WWI

A. Versailles Treaty

The First World War was supposed to be the "war to end all wars," but, in fact, its termination sowed some of the seeds of the next war. This unanticipated result was rooted in the legal treaties that ended the conflict, particularly the Versailles Treaty.[2]

WWI had started after a decades-long series of minor conflicts, territorial realignments, colonial additions, and shifting allegiances through (often-secret) treaties, stretching back to the Napoleonic Wars of the early nineteenth century. Once begun, it pitted modern weapons technology (e.g., tanks, submarines, chemical weapons, machine guns, aircraft) against antiquated tactics (e.g., charges en masse, the use of cavalry), resulting in well more than thirty-five million casualties.[3] Not only the military and civilian populations but also the natural and economic resources of the principal combatants were significantly depleted. Many of these powers were empires—Austro-Hungarian, Russian, and Ottoman—that were long in decline and did not survive the war. Against this backdrop of political, human, and economic exhaustion, the process of structuring peace began.

The Versailles Treaty was the agreement between Germany and the winners of the war. (The other losers—Austria, Bulgaria, Hungary, and Turkey—signed separate agreements giving up land and implementing various other restrictions: the Treaty of Saint-Germain-en-Laye,[4] the Treaty of Neuilly-sur-

---

2. Treaty of Peace Between the Allied and Associated Powers and Germany, June 28, 1919 [hereinafter Versailles Treaty].
3. U.S. DEP'T OF JUSTICE, WWI CASUALTY AND DEATH TABLES.
4. Treaty of Peace Between the Allied and Associated Powers and Austria, Sept. 10, 1919.

Seine,[5] the Treaty of Trianon,[6] and the Treaty of Sevres,[7] respectively. Germany also signed the Treaty of Rapallo with Russia.[8]) The winning powers—the British Empire, France, Italy, and the United States—dictated the terms of the Versailles agreement but could not necessarily agree among themselves. France wanted vengeance and protection from future invasions because it had lost two wars with the Germans/Prussians in the previous one-hundred-plus years and was wounded badly by its losses in the recent conflict: more than six million men killed, wounded, held as prisoners, or missing (more than 70 percent of the total men it deployed); and natural (e.g., coal mines) and artificial (e.g., factories and bridges) resources. The British Empire, with casualty rates about half that of France and not geographically contiguous with Germany, could afford to be more lenient. However, it did not have the ability to be as magnanimous as the United States, which had a 7 percent casualty rate and a wide oceanic separation from Germany.

U.S. President Woodrow Wilson took what he believed to be a forward-looking view to the peace talks after the war and presented his Fourteen Points as the basis for peace for all nations. These points were as follows:

I.   *Open Political Agreements*: no private international understandings of any kind

II.   *Absolute Freedom of Maritime Navigation*: freedom outside territorial waters, in peace and war

III.   *Free Trade*: removal of all economic barriers and equality of trade conditions

IV.   *Mutual Arms Reductions*: reduction to the lowest point consistent with domestic safety

V.   *Colonial People*: equal weight for their interests in questions of sovereignty

VI.   *Russia*: self-determination of her political development and national policy

VII.   *Belgium*: restoration to its prewar condition

---

5. Treaty of Peace Between the Allied and Associated Powers and Bulgaria, Nov. 27, 1919.
6. Treaty of Peace Between the Allied and Associated Powers and Hungary, June 4, 1920.
7. Treaty of Peace Between the British Empire and Allied Powers and Turkey, Aug. 10, 1920.
8. Treaty of Rapallo, Germany-Russia, Apr. 16, 1922.

VIII. *France*: restoration of Alsace-Lorraine and other invaded portions of France

IX. *Italy*: adjustment of borders along clearly recognizable lines of nationality

X. *Austria-Hungary*: autonomous development

XI. *Romania, Serbia, and Montenegro*: restoration, provision of outlet to the sea, and Balkan relations determined along historically established lines of allegiance and nationality

XII. *Ottoman Empire*: grant to Turks of their own country, grant of autonomous development to other nationalities under Ottoman rule, and permanent passage through Dardanelles for all nations

XIII. *Poland*: independent state with passage to the sea

XIV. *League of Nations*: formation for the purpose of affording mutual guarantees of political independence and territorial integrity to great and small states alike

As negotiated in the early months of 1919, the Versailles Treaty did not contain most of the ideas that Wilson had presented. Instead, the French and British teamed up to produce a more vengeful document that was a very long and detailed (440 articles and annexes). It was presented to Germany, which was given a matter of weeks to respond. Although the Germans objected to many of the provisions,[9] the Allied counterresponse was not positive: "The protest of the German Delegation shows that they utterly fail to understand the position in which Germany stands today.... The conduct of Germany is almost unexampled in human history.... Germany has despoiled her neighbours of everything she could make use of or carry away."[10] In the end, only a few changes were made, and Germany's request to immediately join the League of Nations was denied.

It is easiest to understand the Versailles Treaty by looking at its various parts and what they entailed. The first twenty-six articles covered the creation and management of the League of Nations. As stated in its preamble, the League of

---

9. Letter from Count von Brockdorff-Rantzau, German Delegation Head, to Georges Clemenceau, Peace Conference President (May 1919).

10. Letter from Georges Clemenceau, Peace Conference President, to Count von Brockdorff-Rantzau, German Delegation Head (May 1919).

Nation's objective was to "promote international co-operation and to achieve international peace and security by the acceptance of obligations not to resort to war by the prescription of open, just and honourable relations between nations by the firm establishment of the understandings of international law as the actual rule of conduct among Governments. . . ."[11]

Invited to join were the following signatory countries:

- United States
- Europe: Belgium, Czechoslovakia, Denmark, France, Greece, Italy, the Netherlands, Norway, Poland, Portugal, Romania, Serb-Croat-Slovene State (Yugoslavia), Spain, Sweden, and Switzerland
- British Empire: Canada, Australia, South Africa, New Zealand, and India
- Latin America: Argentina, Bolivia, Brazil, Chile, Colombia, Cuba, Ecuador, Guatemala, Haiti, Honduras, Nicaragua, Panama, Paraguay, Peru, El Salvador, Uruguay, and Venezuela
- Asia: China, Japan, and Siam (Thailand)
- Middle East and Africa: Hedjaz (part of Saudi Arabia), Liberia, and Persia

Not invited at the beginning were the losers of WWI: Germany, Turkey, Austria, Hungary, Bulgaria, and Russia. However, these countries did eventually join, along with Abyssinia (Ethiopia), Afghanistan, Albania, Costa Rica, Dominican Republic, Ecuador, Egypt, Estonia, Finland, Iraq, Ireland, Latvia, Lithuania, Luxembourg, and Mexico.

Following the League of Nations provisions were articles describing how political boundaries would be drawn in postwar Europe. The first set described the boundary of Germany and East Prussia vis-à-vis its neighbors.[12] Germany would lose a significant amount of its pre-WWI land mass, estimated at more than 13 percent. Then were land transfers to be made within Europe, including to Belgium,[13] Luxembourg,[14] Czechoslovakia, and Poland.[15] France received the Saar Basin, in compensation for the destruction of its coal mines, and

---

11. Versailles Treaty, *supra* note 2, preamble.
12. *Id.* arts. 27–30.
13. *Id.* arts. 31–39.
14. *Id.* arts. 40–41.
15. *Id.* arts. 81–93.

Alsace-Lorraine, which had been ceded to Germany after the Franco-Prussian war fifty years earlier.[16] The treaty also placed East Prussia under international control and addressed the Baltics,[17] respected the independence of Austria[18] and Russia,[19] demilitarized the left (west) bank of the Rhine,[20] and established a military occupation of the Rhine for fifteen years as a guarantee against further aggression.[21]

The treaty forced Germany to give up her overseas colonies[22] and renounce her rights, titles, and privileges in China, Siam, Liberia, Morocco, Cameroon, Turkey, and Bulgaria, among others. In addition, the treaty mandated demobilization of the German military; reductions in armaments, fortifications, and recruiting; restrictions on the size and number of naval ships that could be built; and a prohibition on an air force.[23] It called for war crime trials, mentioning, specifically, the former emperor of Germany.[24] Germany was required to pay significant reparations based on its admission: "Germany accepts the responsibility of Germany and her allies for causing all the loss and damage."[25] Finally, the treaty specified the return of unique items, such as "the original Koran of the Caliph Othman" and "[t]he leaves of the triptych of the Mystic Lamb painted by the Van Eyck brothers."[26]

Primarily because it included the League of Nations, which a majority of the U.S. Senate opposed due to its potential impact on U.S. sovereignty, the United States never ratified this treaty and its counterparts with Austria and Hungary. Instead, the United States signed separate peace treaties in 1921 with

---

16. *Id.* arts. 45–79.
17. *Id.* arts. 94–115.
18. *Id.* art. 80.
19. *Id.* arts. 116–17.
20. *Id.* arts. 42–44.
21. *Id.* arts. 428–32.
22. *Id.* arts. 118–58.
23. *Id.* arts. 159–213.
24. *Id.* arts. 227–30. However, none occurred except for the Leipzig trials before the German Supreme Court in 1921.
25. *Id.* arts. 231–63. Initially, the amount was 269 billion gold marks, but this was later substantially reduced. The bonds on loans taken out to pay reparations were finally retired in 2010.
26. *Id.* arts. 246–47.

Germany,[27] Austria,[28] and Hungary[29] that included most of the terms of the Versailles Treaty but excluded the League of Nations provisions, the specific land settlements, and the references to an international labor organization.

LEGAL PROFILES

Robert Lansing was the U.S. secretary of state during WWI and a lawyer. He was born in New York in 1864 and started his legal practice there. As a lawyer in his father's law practice, he became interested in international law. He was involved in a number of international arbitrations, often working for the U.S. government, and in 1914 was named counsel for the State Department. After William Jennings Bryan's resignation the following year, Lansing was appointed as the U.S. secretary of state. During the war, he negotiated a treaty with Japan. After the Paris Peace Conference, he resigned and returned to private practice. He died in 1928.[30]

David Lloyd George was the British prime minister during WWI and a solicitor. Born in England in 1863, he started his practice in Wales (he also spoke Welsh as a first language) but eventually moved his practice to London. He was first elected to the British Parliament in 1890. He joined the cabinet of the government in 1906; became the chancellor of the exchequer in 1908, a position he retained until 1915; and then held positions as minister of munitions and secretary of state for war. In late 1916, he became the prime minister, a position he would hold through the rest of the war, until 1922. After the war, he remained in Parliament but never again held the position of prime minister. He died in 1945.[31]

---

27. Treaty of Peace Between Germany and the United States, Aug. 25, 1921.
28. Treaty of Peace Between Austria and the United States, Aug. 24, 1921.
29. Treaty of Peace Between Hungary and the United States, Aug. 29, 1921.
30. *See Robert Lansing*, N.Y. TIMES (Nov. 1, 1928).
31. *See Earl Lloyd George Dies in Sleep*, ASSOCIATED PRESS (Mar. 28, 1945).

Ellis L. Dresel was the U.S. politician who signed the peace treaty with Germany; he was also a lawyer. He was born in 1864 in Massachusetts and started his legal practice there. When the war broke out, he was already in Europe (his father was a German pianist), so he volunteered to serve in a position for the U.S. Embassy in Germany and France, from 1915 until 1917, helping Americans stranded by the war. He then moved to Switzerland and worked on prisoner of war (POW) issues with the American Red Cross, the American Legation, and the War Trade Board. From 1919 to 1921, he was the U.S. commissioner (later, chargé d'affaires) for Germany, returning to the United States the following year. He died in 1925.[32]

B. Agreements of the 1920s

There were several other notable follow-up global agreements during the 1920s. These included the Nine-Power Treaty in 1922, agreements based on the Versailles Treaty in 1924 and 1925, and the Kellogg-Briand Pact in 1928.

1. The Nine-Power Treaty

The purpose of the Nine-Power Treaty was to stabilize conditions in the Far East, to safeguard the rights and interests of China, and to promote relations on a "basis of equality of opportunity" between China and the other eight countries that were parties to the treaty.[33] In this agreement, the other eight powers agreed to respect the sovereignty, independence, territorial integrity, and administrative integrity of China and allow her to develop an effective and stable government. There was also agreement on the Open Door policy, i.e., that there would be equality of trade in China for all nations, that nations would not create "spheres of influence or secret agreements among themselves," and that nations would respect Chinese neutrality in times of war.

---

32. *See Ellis L. Dresel, Diplomatist, Dead; Signer of Peace Treaty with Germany,* N.Y. TIMES (Sept. 21, 1925).
33. Treaty Between the United States of America, Belgium, the British Empire, China, France, Italy, Japan, the Netherlands, and Portugal, Feb. 6, 1922.

LEGAL PROFILES

V. K. Wellington Koo (Ku Wei-chun) was one of the representatives of the Republic of China at the Washington Naval Conference, where the Nine-Power Treaty was signed. He was born in 1887 in China but graduated with a degree in international law from Columbia University. He then returned to China in 1912 to serve the Chinese government. In 1915, he became minister to the United States. In 1919, he was part of the Chinese delegation at the Paris Peace Conference and served as China's first representative to the League of Nations. He briefly served as the premier of the Republic of China twice in the 1920s. Between 1936 and 1946, he served as Chinese ambassador to first France and then Britain. After the war, he served as ambassador to the United States and was one of the signers of the United Nations charter. In 1956, he became a judge at the International Court of Justice at The Hague, serving until 1967. He died in 1985.[34]

John William Salmond was the New Zealand representative at the Washington Naval Conference and a judge. He was born in England in 1862, but his family moved to New Zealand while he was young, where he started his practice as a barrister and solicitor. In 1897, he was appointed as a law professor in Australia at the University of Adelaide. He returned to New Zealand as a law professor in 1906 and was appointed as the solicitor-general in 1911. He produced many well-regarded legal texts, including those on torts, contracts, and jurisprudence. He was then appointed as a judge on the Supreme Court of New Zealand in 1920. He continued to serve in this role until his death in 1924.[35]

Robert Laird Borden was the Canadian representative to the Washington Naval Conference and a lawyer. He was born in 1854 in Nova Scotia, Canada, where he started his legal practice (without having attended a formal law school). He continued his practice and was elected in 1896 to Parliament, where he was in and out of power until 1911. In

---

34. *See V. K. Wellington Koo Dies; A Former Premier of Chine*, N.Y. TIMES (Nov. 16, 1985).
35. *See Sir John William Salmond*, THE MAIL (Sept. 20, 1924).

that year he became the prime minister of Canada, a position he held throughout WWI, until 1920. At the Paris Peace Conference, he was able to procure for Canada (and other major British Empire nations) a separate seat at the table (prior to that, Canada was represented as part of the British Empire). He took the role of chancellor of Queen's University from 1924 to 1930. He died in 1937.[36]

2. Agreements Based on the Versailles Treaty: Dawes Plan, Young Plan, and Treaty of Locarno

The Inter-Allied Reparations Commission, established under Versailles Treaty Article 233, looked into the ability of Germany to repay her war-related debts, resulting in reduced reparation obligations, currency stabilization, foreign loans, and central bank reorganization under the Dawes Plan of 1924. This plan was later replaced by the Young Plan of 1929, which further significantly reduced Germany's reparation payments.

The Treaty of Locarno, 1925, was actually a series of agreements that normalized relations between Germany, France, and Belgium by agreeing to set their national borders as they had been set in the 1919 Treaty of Versailles, to respect the demilitarized zone on the Rhine, and to repudiate the use of war to solve disputes among each other.[37] The other parties to the treaty, including Great Britain and Italy as guarantors, were to come to the aid of any party that was the victim of a flagrant violation of this agreement.

LEGAL PROFILE

Charles G. Dawes was head of the reparations commission and a lawyer. He was born in Ohio in 1865 but began his legal practice in Nebraska. After many years in private practice, he became the president of two midwestern utility companies. This business prominence and work in a

36. *See Empire Grief, Sir Robert Borden,* Winnipeg Free Press (June 11, 1937).
37. Treaty of Mutual Guarantees Between Germany, Belgium, France, Great Britain, and Italy, Oct. 16, 1925.

presidential campaign led to his being named the U.S. comptroller of the currency in 1898. In 1901, he resigned to pursue an unsuccessful run for the U.S. Senate, after which he returned to the business world in banking. He served in the U.S. Army during WWI heading up supply efforts and after the war was the first director of the Bureau of the Budget. This led to an appointment on the Inter-Allied Reparations Commission, where he proposed the Dawes Plan to help Germany deal with its war reparation payments. For this he was awarded the Nobel Peace Prize in 1925. He was nominated for the position of vice president of the United States and won election to that office in 1924. In 1929, he became the U.S. ambassador to Great Britain. He then returned to the business world. He died in 1951.[38]

3. The Kellogg-Briand Pact

The Kellogg-Briand Pact of 1928 included the United States, France, Australia, Belgium, Canada, Czechoslovakia, Germany, Great Britain, India, Ireland, Italy, Japan, New Zealand, Poland, and South Africa.[39] The parties committed their countries to renouncing war as an instrument of national policy, to condemning war as a solution for international controversies, and to solving conflicts through peaceful means. Besides these parties, forty other countries ratified this treaty, including, eventually, Austria, Hungary, China, and Russia.

LEGAL PROFILES

Frank B. Kellogg was one of the authors of this international agreement and a lawyer. He was born in New York in 1856 but moved as a child to Minnesota, where he began his legal practice. He worked as a city and county attorney from 1878 to 1887. He was then appointed by President Theodore Roosevelt to work for the U.S. Department of

---

38. *See Charles G. Dawes*, United States Senate Historical Office.
39. International Treaty for the Renunciation of War as an Instrument of National Policy, Aug. 27, 1928.

Justice prosecuting antitrust suits. In 1916, he was elected to the U.S. Senate, where he served only a single term. From 1923 to 1925, he was U.S. ambassador to Britain; and in 1925 he served as the U.S. secretary of state, the position he held during the negotiations for this treaty. Due to his work on this treaty, he was awarded the Nobel Peace Prize in 1929. From 1930 to 1935, he served as a judge on the International Court of Justice. He died in 1938.[40]

Aristide Briand was the other author of this international agreement. He was born in 1862 in France, where he studied and practiced law. He preferred writing and was involved in the labor union movement in France. In 1902, he was elected to the French Chamber of Deputies. He served as prime minister first in 1909 and then again for periods in 1913, 1915–1917, 1921, 1925–1926, and 1929. He was often simultaneously either the interior minister or the minister of foreign affairs, the role he held during this conference. He was the longest-serving foreign minister in France since Charles Maurice de Talleyrand. He was also a recipient of the Nobel Peace Prize, but for a separate agreement he had negotiated several years earlier (the Treaty of Locarno) with Germany and other European countries to truly settle outstanding WWI issues. He died in 1932.[41]

C. Agreements of the 1930s

The 1930s saw the first conflicts that eventually led to WWII. These included significant military actions in China, Spain, Czechoslovakia, Abyssinia, Indochina, and finally Poland and eastern Europe. Such conflicts led to a flurry of agreements among potential adversaries and allies.

1. London Naval Treaties of 1930 and 1936

The London Naval Treaty of 1930 included the countries of Japan, Italy, France, the United Kingdom, and the United States.[42] Stemming from the

---

40. *See Kellogg, Frank Billings*, BIOGRAPHICAL DIRECTORY OF THE UNITED STATES CONGRESS.
41. *See Death of M. Briand, Peace Apostle 11 Times Premier of France*, DAILY TELEGRAPH (Mar. 7, 1932).
42. Treaty for the Limitation and Reduction of Naval Armament, Apr. 20, 1930.

Washington Naval Treaty in 1922,[43] this new agreement placed limits on the replacement of capital ships from 1931 to 1936. It specified certain ships for decommissioning; established limits on building or fitting out aircraft carriers; limited the size and number of submarines; instituted rules for decommissioning; set limitations on tonnage and numbers of naval cruisers for the United States, Japan, and the United Kingdom; and placed submarines under the same international law as surface ships, including the requirement for safety of their crews. It also required communication of such information to the other parties to the agreement.

In the follow-up London Naval Conference, concluding in early 1936, Japan withdrew and Italy would not sign after its invasion of Abyssinia in 1935. The agreement finally signed by France, the United Kingdom, and the United States limited the displacement and armaments of new naval vessels (including capital ships, aircraft carriers, submarines, and light surface ships) and the arming of merchant ships.[44] Capital ship specifications regarding the armament caliber were allowed to increase if all of the parties to the 1922 agreement did not sign this agreement (i.e., Japan and Italy). The agreement allowed for suspension of the treaty if one of the parties became engaged in a war. It was to be in effect until the end of 1942.

2. Anglo-German Naval Agreement of 1935

Separately, the United Kingdom signed a naval agreement with Germany in 1935 because the two parties plus France could not come to an agreement.[45] This agreement specified that in total tonnage, Germany's navy was not to exceed 35 percent of that of the Royal Navy, including the Commonwealth nations. These limits were to be applied across each category of naval vessels, but submarines could be up to 45 percent of the Royal Navy.

3. France-Soviet Mutual Assistance Treaty of 1935

In 1935, France and the Soviet Union agreed to provide each other aid in the face of unprovoked aggression by another European state.[46] It did not need to be an actual attack, only "threatened with, or in danger of, attack." This was

---

43. Treaty for the Limitation of Naval Armament, Feb. 6, 1922.
44. Treaty for the Limitation of Naval Armament, Fr.-U.K.-U.S., Mar. 25, 1936.
45. Exchange of Notes Between His Majesty's Government in the United Kingdom and the German Government Regarding the Limitation of Naval Armaments, June 18, 1935.
46. Franco-Russian Mutual Assistance Pact, May 2, 1935.

in response to Germany publicizing in 1935 its previously secret rearmament efforts. This agreement signaled a possible two-front war if Germany continued on its aggressive path. Germany used this agreement as justification to reoccupy the Rhineland in early 1936, in violation of the Versailles Treaty.

4. Anti-Comintern Pact of 1936

In 1936, Japan and Germany signed the Anti-Comintern Pact, which was an anti-Communist cooperation agreement.[47] It was nominally directed against the Communist International (discussed further in Chapter 2's sedition trials) but in actuality against potential conflicts with the Soviet Union. Italy and a number of other European dictatorships or puppet governments joined the pact as well.

5. Munich Agreement of 1938 and Subsequent Riom Trial

In 1938, France and the United Kingdom attempted to appease German aggression and met in Munich. The resulting agreement covered the evacuation of the Sudetenland area of Czechoslovakia, home not only to those of German ancestry but also to Czechoslovakia's most significant defensive positions, raw materials, and industry.[48] This is the area where German troops first entered Czechoslovakia, which was soon completely taken over and dismembered among Germany and Nazi client states (see Chapter 6).

After the war in Europe had started, a trial was held in Riom, France, involving one of the signers of the Munich agreement, former prime minister Edouard Daladier, as well as former prime minister Leon Blum and leaders of the French army and air force. The French Vichy government (see Chapter 5), which controlled southern France under Nazi oversight, put these prewar leaders on trial before the French Vichy Supreme Court of Justice. They were ostensibly charged with betraying their offices by undermining the military capabilities of France from 1936 to 1940, leading to France's defeat by Germany in 1940. These were crimes that did not exist at the time of their supposed commission.

The trial was also intended to show that "war guilt" belonged to France instead of Germany for starting the war, possibly to later demand reparations

---

47. Agreement Guarding Against the Communist International, Japan-Ger., Nov. 25, 1936.
48. Agreement Concluded at Munich Between Germany, Great Britain, France and Italy, Sept. 29, 1938.

from France during peace negotiations. This issue did not end up being adjudicated in the trial. Instead, the Vichy leader, Marshal Philippe Pétain, convened a separate closed trial with a separate court where the evidence found by the supreme court was considered. In October 1941, Pétain pronounced that the maximum penalty under this charge, which was confinement to a fortress, was to be applied to these same defendants. This took the "war guilt" aspect out of the public trial.

The public trial began in February 1942 in the French city of Riom near Vichy, and was open to the press and public. Pierre Caous presided over the trial, which included not only judges but an admiral in the French (Vichy) navy and a general in the French (Vichy) army. Preliminary proceedings for the trial had taken eighteen months, with an examining commission collecting evidence and taking witness testimony. The charges against the former prime ministers included not preparing the army, nationalizing the defense industry, and emphasizing leisure over labor (instituting a forty-hour work week). The defendants who testified refuted the charges, claiming that they had indeed carried out their assigned political roles; rather, they said, it was the French military and the industrialists who had failed the country. The defense contended, among other things, that the creation of the court was beyond Vichy's mandate and that the criminal law under which they were being charged was retroactive and therefore unconstitutional. It also claimed that the period of time examined was arbitrary and should include periods during which current Vichy leaders were in control of France and its military. Numerous military officers testified about a lack of modern military equipment, a lack of personnel and training, and low morale in the military ranks. The defendants strongly refuted this testimony, as well. Not making the progress they expected, the Vichy government recessed the trial and then indefinitely suspended it in April 1942 while imprisoning the defendants. The trial was never resumed.

LEGAL PROFILES

Edvard Benes was the president of Czechoslovakia at the time of the Munich Conference and a doctor of law. He was born in Bohemia in 1884 and taught at a university there. During WWI, he attempted to obtain recognition for an independent Czechoslovakia from the Austro-

Hungarian Empire and to raise an army to fight on the side of the Allies. Independence for Czechoslovakia finally occurred at the end of WWI. He then served as the first foreign minister of the new country, until 1935. He also was a member of the Czechoslovakian Parliament and represented the country at many of the international conferences described earlier. He became president of the country in 1935, and served until the crisis brought on by the Munich agreement and the ceding of the Sudetenland region to Germany in 1938. He then set up a government in exile during the war; he was also was a visiting lecturer at the University of Chicago at the time, furthering his cause. He returned to Czechoslovakia in 1945 and was elected president again but soon stepped down for political and health reasons. He died shortly thereafter in 1948.[49]

Leon Blum was one of the defendants in the Riom trial and a lawyer by training. He was born in France in 1872 and studied law in the country. Well-known early in his career for writing as a social critic, he became involved in the Socialist Party and in 1919 was elected to the French National Assembly. He went on to lead the Socialist Party and was again elected to the National Assembly in 1929. An alliance of several political parties in the Popular Front led to an electoral majority in 1936 and his election as prime minister of France. He was both the first Socialist and first Jewish prime minister of the country but only served a year in this position. During his short term, his coalition passed a number of popular employment-related laws, including the forty-hour work week and paid vacations. He was briefly prime minister again in 1938. After Germany invaded France in 1940, he was arrested and later placed on trial. He eventually was sent to concentration camps during the war and was ultimately rescued by Allied forces. After the war, he spent a brief time as prime minister (for the third time) and also helped France secure international financial credits. He died in 1950.[50]

---

49. *See The Tragedy of Benes*, N.Y. TIMES (Sept. 4, 1948).
50. *See Leon Blum Is Dead of a Heart Attack*, N.Y. TIMES (Mar. 31, 1950).

6. German Agreements of 1939: Pact of Steel and Molotov-Ribbentrop Pact

Germany signed additional agreements with its allies to clear the way for aggression. In the spring of 1939, Italy and Germany signed the ten-year Pact of Steel, which tied the two countries to mutual aid and to military, economic, and foreign policy coordination.[51] The Molotov-Ribbentrop Pact, which was signed later in 1939, not only stipulated nonaggression between Germany and the Soviet Union but also divided eastern Europe into various spheres of influence, providing Germany and the Soviet Union the necessary framework to attack these smaller countries without interference from the other.[52]

7. Agreements with Poland in 1939: Kasprzycki-Gamelin Convention and Anglo-Polish Mutual Assistance Agreement

To protect against German aggression, France had earlier updated their long-standing military alliance with Poland via the Kasprzycki-Gamelin Convention by promising military assistance if Poland was attacked by Germany.[53] The United Kingdom and Poland then signed the Anglo-Polish Mutual Assistance Agreement, promising to provide "all the support and assistance in its power" to the other if engaged in hostilities with a European power.[54] Unfortunately, neither agreement was successful as Germany and the Soviet Union began their invasion of Poland and eastern Europe and so officially started WWII.

LEGAL PROFILES

Edward Bernard Raczynski was the Polish ambassador to the United Kingdom who signed the mutual assistance treaty; he was also a doctor of law. He was born in Poland in 1891 and studied law there and in Great Britain. Upon Poland winning its independence from Russia after WWI, he served in the diplomatic service of the country in several European nations. He was appointed Poland's ambassador to the League of Nations in 1932 and to the United Kingdom in 1934. He remained

---

51. Pact of Friendship and Alliance Between Germany and Italy, May 22, 1939.
52. Treaty of Non-Aggression Between Germany and the Soviet Union, Aug. 23, 1939.
53. Kasprzycki-Gaemelin Convention, Fr.-Pol., May 19, 1939.
54. Agreement of Mutual Assistance Between the United Kingdom and Poland, Aug. 25, 1939.

in London during WWII and was part of the Polish government in exile as its foreign minister. Following the Soviet takeover of his country and move toward Communism, he remained abroad as part of a new government in exile. He served as the president of this government in exile from 1979 to 1986. He died in 1993.[55]

---

8. Tripartite Pact of 1940

After the war in Europe had started but before the war in the Pacific, the three Axis powers signed the ten-year Tripartite Pact in 1940.[56] This agreement recognized among the parties German and Italian influence in Europe and Japanese influence in Greater East Asia. If any of the parties was attacked by a nation not already involved in the European or Second Sino-Japanese wars, then the parties were to "assist one another with all political, economic and military means."[57] Hungary, Romania, Bulgaria, Slovakia, Yugoslavia, and Croatia eventually joined the agreement.

1.2 U.S. NEUTRALITY LAWS OF THE 1930s

A. Statutes

1. Events Leading Up to Neutrality Acts

As the 1920s turned to the 1930s, the Great Depression, festering issues from the last war in Europe, the ongoing fight against Communism, and the expanding aspirations of Japan were to have impacts globally over the coming decade and a half. In the United States, the most immediate impact was the emergence of Franklin Delano Roosevelt as the new U.S. president, elected in 1932. Roosevelt's influence on the next twelve years would be outsized, unlike

---

55. *See Count Raczynski, 101, Diplomat Who Served Poland in Wartime*, N.Y. Times (Aug. 2, 1993).
56. Tripartite Pact Between Japan, Germany, and Italy, Sept. 27, 1940.
57. *Id.*

that of any other American president since Abraham Lincoln and for a much longer period of time. He loomed large over the world's conflicts, officially on the sidelines during the 1930s but very active in doing what he could legally and politically at the time and always preparing for what was to come. Much like Lincoln during the American Civil War but on a global stage for a conflict that not only consumed his life but also ended up taking it, Roosevelt was the nexus of the American and global efforts to hold back totalitarianism in two vastly different arenas. He did this while setting the table for a future different than what had come out of the last global war.

The large U.S. involvement and cost in both financial and human terms during WWI left a great distaste in political America for any future involvement in foreign wars. As such, America entered a period of isolationism and noninterventionist policies, fed by publications claiming that the United States entered the war to help bankers and arms merchants. The most influential of these was the report of the U.S. Senate Special Committee on Investigation of the Munitions Industry (Nye Committee), which conducted investigations aimed at tying munitions companies to extensive foreign bribes and efforts to defeat any attempts at disarmament.[58]

Against this backdrop of American isolationism and nonintervention in the 1930s was a world where conflicts began to rage. Japan invaded Northern China (Manchuria) in 1931 and again in 1937. Italy invaded Abyssinia (Ethiopia) in 1935, and the Spanish Civil War broke out in 1936. Contrary to the terms of the Versailles Treaty, Germany remilitarized the Rhineland in 1936, took over the Sudetenland in 1938 from Czechoslovakia, and annexed Austria in the Anschluss before taking over the rest of Czechoslovakia in 1939. In 1937, Japan, Germany, and Italy signed the Anti-Comintern Pact; and in 1939, the Treaty of Non-Aggression Between Germany and the Soviet Union was signed. The invasion of Poland in 1939 by Germany and the Soviet Union finally led to the declaration of war by France and Britain against Germany. Further aggression followed, including the Soviet Union invading Finland.

---

58. *See* REPORT OF THE SPECIAL COMMITTEE ON INVESTIGATION OF THE MUNITIONS INDUSTRY, 74th Cong. (Feb. 24, 1936).

LEGAL PROFILES

Franklin Delano Roosevelt was the president of the United States before and during WWII; he was also a lawyer. Born in New York in 1882, he started his legal practice there in 1908. He was elected to the New York Senate in 1910 and 1912 but then resigned to take the position of assistant secretary of the U.S. Navy under Woodrow Wilson, a position that he held until 1920. In that year, he was nominated to be the U.S. vice presidential candidate on a ticket headed by James M. Cox but lost out as Warren Harding won the presidency. He then returned to law practice and the next year contracted the paralyzing disease that immobilized his lower body. He was then elected as the governor of New York in 1928 and again in 1930. It was in 1932 that he was first elected to what would be an unprecedented four-election victory as a U.S. president, the only person ever elected more than twice to that office. He led the United States throughout the rest of the Depression and during the lead up to, the commencement of, and most of WWII, until his death toward the end of the war in the spring of 1945.[59]

John Nance Garner was the vice president under Franklin Delano Roosevelt and an attorney. He was born in Texas in 1868 and began his legal practice there. He was an elected county judge from 1893 to 1896. In 1898, he was elected to the Texas House of Representatives and reelected two years later. In 1902, he was elected to the U.S. House of Representatives. He was subsequently elected fourteen more times, keeping his seat until 1933 and spending the last two years as the Speaker of the House. In 1932, he campaigned for the U.S. presidency but did not have enough votes, so he gave his support to Roosevelt and became his vice presidential candidate. He served two terms in this office; but in 1940, he ran again for the presidential nomination and lost overwhelmingly to Roosevelt. After this, he retired from politics. He died in 1967.[60]

---

59. *See Roosevelt, 31st President, Led U.S. Through Critical Era*, WASH. POST (Apr. 13, 1945).
60. *See Garner, John Nance*, BIOGRAPHICAL DIRECTORY OF THE UNITED STATES CONGRESS.

Alger Hiss was a legal assistant on the Nye Committee. He was born in Maryland in 1904 but started his legal practice in Massachusetts. He then worked for the U.S. government in various roles in the Justice Department, supporting the Nye committee and defending the Agricultural Adjustment Administration. In 1936, he began a series of positions in the U.S. State Department. He was involved in early discussions for what became the United Nations and attended the Yalta Conference in 1945. After the war, he became president of the Carnegie Endowment for International Peace, a position that he held until 1949. In 1948, he was accused of being a Communist trying to infiltrate the U.S. government, and the investigation was pursued intensely by Congressman (and future U.S. president) Richard Nixon. He was eventually tried for and convicted of perjury, which led to his disbarment.[61] When the evidence from his trial was finally declassified many years later, it led to his reinstatement by the Massachusetts bar in 1975. He died in 1996.[62]

2. Neutrality Acts of 1935-1939

To stay out of the conflicts in other hemispheres, the U.S. Congress passed a series of neutrality laws but took the cautious steps of limiting the effective time periods of each law so that it would have to look afresh at the current situation before renewal. In actuality, neutrality laws were passed four times between 1935 and 1939, sometimes adding and sometimes not renewing what was previously enacted.

The Neutrality Acts of 1935[63] and 1936[64] described their purposes as a prohibition on the exportation of "arms, ammunition, and implements of war" to belligerent countries (or to neutral countries for transshipment) or the use of U.S. vessels to ship such; a restriction on travel by Americans in belligerent ships during war; and a requirement for the registration and licensing of people who manufactured, exported, or imported arms, ammunition, or implements

61. United States v. Hiss, 185 F.2d 822 (2d Cir. 1950).
62. *See Alger Hiss Dead at 92*, BOSTON GLOBE (Nov. 16, 1996).
63. Pub. Res. 74-67 (1935).
64. Pub. Res. 74-74 (1936).

of war. Whenever the president found that a state of war existed between two foreign states, he was required to issue a proclamation of these prohibitions, restrictions, and requirements. (A presidential proclamation, noting a condition or event triggering statutory compliance, is legally equivalent to an executive order.) He also was to periodically issue an enumerated list of prohibited items. Violators were subject to criminal penalties. The Neutrality Act of 1935 expired at the end of February 1936 but was extended to April 30, 1937, through the passage of the Neutrality Act of 1936, which also prohibited loans to belligerents.

In September 1935, President Roosevelt issued the enumerated list of what he considered to be the arms, ammunition, and implements of war that applied under the Neutrality Act of 1935.[65] Shortly thereafter, with the outbreak of the Italian invasion of Ethiopia, he issued a proclamation prohibiting the shipment of arms and ammunition to Italy or Ethiopia, demonstrating that these restrictions applied to both the aggressors and the victims in any conflict.[66] This prohibition banned the export of rifles, pistols, machine guns, howitzers, mortars, ammunition, grenades, flame throwers, mustard gas, bombs, mines, tanks, vessels, and aircraft. He then issued a proclamation warning Americans about travel aboard ships of either country.[67] These proclamations and prohibitions were renewed under the Neutrality Act of 1936.[68]

The Neutrality Act of 1936 did not cover civil wars, such as the one that broke out in Spain in 1936; so, at the beginning of 1937, Congress passed a resolution specifically aimed at prohibiting the export of arms, ammunition, and implements of war to that country and canceling all licenses to do so.[69] Then, at the beginning of May 1937, the Neutrality Act of 1935 as amended in 1936 was updated to include a prohibition on exports to countries in a state of "civil

---

65. Exec. Proclamation No. 2138, Defining Arms, Ammunition and Implements of War Under the Neutrality Legislation (Sept. 25, 1935).
66. Exec. Proclamation No. 2141, Prohibiting the Export of Arms and Ammunition to Ethiopia and Italy (Oct. 5, 1935).
67. Exec. Proclamation No. 2142, Warning Americans Against Travel on Ships of Belligerent Nations During Italian–Ethiopian War (Oct. 5, 1935).
68. Exec. Proclamation No. 2159, Prohibiting the Export of Arms and Ammunition to Italy and Ethiopia (Feb. 29, 1936).
69. Pub. Res. 75-1 (1937).

strife," such as was occurring in Spain.[70] It included the enumerated list of prohibited items from the presidential proclamation, excluding raw materials. The president was also able to restrict the export of "certain articles or materials" and to issue an enumerated list of such items. The purchase of belligerent state bonds or the making of loans to belligerent states was prohibited, as was travel on belligerent state vessels. Belligerent state warships and submarines could be banned from U.S. ports.

The concept of "Cash and Carry" was never created as a single piece of legislation due to the need of the administration to warily deal with both Congress and the public on aid to belligerents. There is no section in the neutrality laws titled Cash and Carry; the concept can only be pieced together from several of the provisions, including the allowance of on raw materials and the ability to exclude certain items and materials from the bans when the title passed to the foreign government, it used its own ships to transport such materials, and it used cash instead of loans to purchase the items. Arms sales to Spain were subsequently prohibited by executive proclamation, essentially banning the same list of items that were banned for export to Italy and Ethiopia two years previously, plus a long list of high explosives.[71]

Several parts of the 1937 law were to expire within two years, so once again, in 1939, it was time for Congress to pass a neutrality act. However, Congress let the law lapse until the autumn of 1939, when it was renewed after the declarations of war in Europe. The act now prohibited American vessels from carrying people, articles, or materials named in executive proclamations but again allowed for the Cash and Carry policies. Roosevelt proclaimed U.S. neutrality[72] in the European conflict and then implemented a proclamation prohibiting exports of arms to France, Germany, Poland, the United Kingdom, India, Australia, and New Zealand.[73] He later defined the areas of combat under this act.[74]

---

70. Pub. Res. 75-27 (1937).

71. Exec. Proclamation No. 2236, Forbidding the Export of Arms and Munitions to the Civil War in Spain (May 1, 1937).

72. Exec. Proclamation No. 2348, Neutrality of the United States (Sept. 5, 1939).

73. Exec. Proclamation No. 2349, Prohibiting the Export of Arms and Munitions to Belligerent Powers (Sept. 5, 1939).

74. Exec. Proclamation No. 2376, Defining Combat Areas Under the New Neutrality Act of 1939 (Nov. 4, 1939).

LEGAL PROFILES

William B. Bankhead was Speaker of the House when the Neutrality Acts were enacted; he was also a lawyer. He was born in Alabama in 1874 and started his legal practice there. In 1898, he became a city attorney and served one term in the state House of Representatives. From 1910 to 1914, he served as solicitor for one of the Alabama judicial districts. Unsuccessful in his first try at winning a seat in the U.S. House of Representatives in 1914, he was then elected in 1916. His father was a longtime member of Congress, including during WWI, and his brother served during this same time in the U.S. Senate. He was reelected numerous times and remained in the House for the rest of his life. In 1936, he was chosen as the Speaker of the House. He served in that post until his death in 1940.[75]

B. Cases

Few cases arose under the Neutrality Acts, but the following three offer a brief understanding of this issue. The first case tested the constitutionality of this type of delegation of legislative power to the president, which would be a common feature of legislation in the upcoming prewar and war periods. The second case considered the impact of these new bans on contracts. The third case again looked at the impact on contracts from a different perspective.

1. Constitutionality

United States v. Curtiss-Wright Export Corp.[76] tested the ability of Congress to delegate its power to ban munitions sales, but the case actually predated the Neutrality Act of 1935: it dealt with a prohibition put in place the year prior to the act. In 1934, there was a conflict in South America between Bolivia and Paraguay over the Chaco region and its natural resources, especially energy-related resources. Congress passed a joint resolution making it illegal for the United States to sell arms or munitions to the countries engaged in this con-

---

75. *See Bankhead, William Brockman*, BIOGRAPHICAL DIRECTORY OF THE UNITED STATES CONGRESS.
76. United States v. Curtiss-Wright Export Corp., 299 U.S. 304 (1936).

flict if the president found that, after consulting with the other governments in the Americas, such a prohibition would help reestablish peace.[77]

President Roosevelt then issued a proclamation stating that he had found that "prohibition of the sale of arms and munitions of war in the United States to those countries now engaged in armed conflict in the Chaco may contribute to the reestablishment of peace between those countries."[78] The following year, he revoked his previous proclamation, stating that the leaders of the two countries had committed not to make new purchases of war material until concluding a peace treaty.[79]

The defendant in this case was accused of selling machine guns to one of the belligerents, Bolivia. The defendant alleged that the congressional resolution was an invalid delegation of power to the president, specifically arguing the following:

- It was based upon the judgment of the president (regarding the beneficial effect upon the reestablishment of peace).
- The issuance of the proclamation was left to the "unfettered discretion" of the president.
- The ability to end the prohibition was again up to the president's discretion.
- The extent of the operations was not controlled by any standard from Congress.[80]

The Court first addressed the difference between domestic powers and foreign powers under the Constitution, finding that "powers of external sovereignty did not depend upon the affirmative grants of the Constitution."[81] Quoting Chief Justice John Marshall (while he was still a member of the House of Representatives), it said that "[t]he President is the sole organ of the nation in its external relations, and its sole representative with foreign nations."[82] The Court found that he was more capable than Congress of know-

---

77. Pub. Res. 73-28 (1934).
78. Exec. Proclamation No. 2087, Forbidding the Shipment of Arms to the Combatants in Chaco (May 28, 1934).
79. Exec. Proclamation No. 2147, Revoking the Arms Embargo at the Termination of Hostilities in Chaco (Nov. 14, 1935).
80. *Curtiss-Wright Export Corp.*, 299 U.S. at 314-15.
81. *Id.* at 318.
82. *Id.* at 319.

ing the conditions in foreign nations, some of which were based on confidential information that all members would not be privy to. The Court proceeded to review many instances, from the beginning of the Republic, where Congress gave the president the right to embargo; the Court then elaborated upon the reasons why it would not upset such a long line of precedent. It found that there was "sufficient warrant" for the broad discretion that Congress vested in the president in these matters.[83]

The defendant also claimed that the congressional resolution did not become effective because the president did not "find essential jurisdictional facts," which meant that he did not state which other countries he consulted.[84] The Court ruled that because the president stated that he did consult with other countries and secure assurances of their cooperation, this was sufficient.

Finally, the defendant claimed that the proclamation revoking the prohibition on these sales ended liability under the congressional resolution. The Court found that the president's revocation only extended to his original proclamation and not to the congressional resolution, and so the defendant's liability under the resolution remained.

LEGAL PROFILES

Homer S. Cummings was the U.S. attorney general during the 1930s responsible for enforcing the Neutrality Acts. He was born in Illinois in 1870 and started his legal practice in Connecticut. He was an elected mayor of Stamford in the early 1900s but was not successful in several attempts at higher office in the U.S. Congress. From 1914 to 1924, he was a county attorney in Connecticut as well as a leading figure on the Democratic National Committee. Upon the election of Franklin Delano Roosevelt in 1932, he was slated to be the governor-general of the Philippines; but the nominee for U.S. attorney general passed away, so he instead was nominated for that role. He was one of the longest serving attorneys general in history, keeping the position until early 1939. He was involved in defending all of the major New Deal legislation, some

83. *Id.* at 329.
84. *Id.*

of which was overturned. He was then involved in drafting the Supreme Court reorganization bill, which, although never implemented, did lead to a significant turnover in the Supreme Court membership over the next few years. After this, he returned to private practice. He died in 1956.[85]

2. Impact on Contracts, No. 1

In *Benedictus v. Sundstrand Machine Tool Co.,* the plaintiff was the agent of the defendant, tasked with selling the defendant's machines in Belgium.[86] In early 1940, the plaintiff acquired several orders from Belgium for the defendant's milling machines. The defendant had accepted the orders and had promised to pay a commission to the plaintiff, only part of which was paid. The defendant gave the German invasion of Belgium in May 1940 as the reason that the full commission was not paid. This led to the proclamations[87] and executive orders that made it both impossible and illegal to export the remaining milling machines to Belgium.

The court here cited an earlier Fourth Circuit case in which Chief Justice Taft, who was sitting as a circuit judge, ruled that "[t]he promise of the defendant was without exception or condition on this head. The contract was made during the war."[88] Because in the instant case the court found that the plaintiff had been hired to secure orders, the plaintiff had done so, the orders were accepted, and there was no provision reserving the right to nonpayment in case of wartime restrictions, the plaintiff's case should be allowed to proceed.

LEGAL PROFILES

James E. Major was one of the court of appeals judges in this case. He was born in 1887 in Illinois and started his legal practice in the state. He worked as a state's attorney from 1912 to 1920 and was then elected

---

85. *See Homer Cummings, Ex-U.S. Aide, Dies,* N.Y. TIMES (Sept. 11, 1956).
86. Benedictus v. Sundstrand Mach. Tool Co., 138 F.2d 504 (7th Cir. 1943).
87. Exec. Proclamation No. 2405, U.S. Neutrality in the War Between Germany and Belgium, Luxembourg, and the Netherlands (May 11, 1940).
88. *Benedictus,* 138 F.2d at 505.

to several terms in the U.S. House of Representatives, starting in 1923, although he was twice not reelected. He served in Congress until 1933, when President Franklin Delano Roosevelt appointed him to the federal district court in Illinois. Then, in 1937, he was appointed to a seat on the appeals court for the Seventh Circuit. In both of these court appointments, he replaced the same judge who had vacated the seat. He served on the Seventh Circuit until 1956 and as the chief judge between 1948 and 1954. He died in 1972.[89]

3. Impact on Contracts, No. 2

In *Suspine v. Compania Transatlantica Centroamericana*, S.A., the plaintiffs were seamen from the Philippines who were seeking their wages under employment contracts they signed for a ship that was to sail from Virginia to England.[90] Under their agreements, they were to be paid differing amounts, based on different reasons, if their employment on the ship was canceled; one reason was the termination of the voyage for matters outside their control, such as an embargo or a declaration of war. They would make significantly more if they were dismissed without proper grounds. When the ship was to sail in July 1940, the master of the port would not let it leave with Filipino seamen on board as this would violate the Neutrality Act of 1939. The ship was allowed to leave when the Filipino seamen were taken off the ship.

The reason had to do with the recent semi-independence of the Philippines from the United States. The Philippines had been granted commonwealth status but would not be fully independent until after the war. Under the Philippine Independence Act, Filipinos were still required to owe allegiance to the United States until they achieved full independence.[91] Under the Neutrality Act, *citizens* included anyone owing allegiance to the United States, and the United States included "the several States and Territories, the insular possessions of the United States (including the Philippine Islands), the Canal Zone, and the District of Columbia."[92]

---

89. *See Major, James Earl*, FED. JUDICIAL CTR., BIOGRAPHICAL DIRECTORY OF FEDERAL JUDGES; *Major, James Earl*, BIOGRAPHICAL DIRECTORY OF THE UNITED STATES CONGRESS.
90. Suspine v. Compania Transatlantica Centroamericana, S.A., 37 F. Supp. 268 (N.Y.S.D. 1941).
91. Pub. L. No. 73-127 (1934).
92. *Suspine*, 37 F. Supp. at 271.

The president had issued a proclamation that described all areas around the British Isles, among others, to be a combat zone and made it illegal for any American citizen or vessel to proceed into such areas.[93] The court found that it would be illegal for the seamen to enter the combat zone since they were considered American citizens for purposes of the Neutrality Act (although aliens for other laws), and thus the contract was null and void. Therefore, the court ruled against the seamen collecting wages for this voyage.

LEGAL PROFILES

John T. Cahill was the attorney for the intervenor (the United States) in this case. He was born in New York in 1903 and started his legal practice there. He joined the federal prosecutor's office as an assistant district attorney and was involved in several well-known criminal prosecutions (and lesser-known antitrust cases). These included the 1939 case of Martin T. Manton, a federal judge who was prosecuted and convicted for "selling justice" from his judicial position.[94] Cahill also was involved in the prosecution of U.S. Communist Party leader Earl Browder for passport violations.[95] Cahill was the U.S. attorney for the Southern District of New York from 1939 to 1941, after which he left to return to private practice. He died in 1966.[96]

C. Subsequent Events

President Roosevelt did not always use the legal tools given to him as they sometimes seemed to be counterproductive. For example, he did not issue a proclamation on each conflict that arose globally, such as the 1937 Japanese incursion into Manchuria. In this situation, there was a concern that Japan would be more able than China (a friend of America) to use Cash and Carry

---

93. Exec. Proclamation No. 2376, Defining Combat Areas Under the New Neutrality Act of 1939 (Nov. 4, 1939).
94. United States v. Manton, 107 F.2d 834 (2d Cir. 1938).
95. Browder v. United States, 312 U.S. 335 (1941).
96. *See John T. Cahill, 62, Lawyer, Is Dead*, N.Y. TIMES (Nov. 4, 1966).

provisions. Instead of issuing a proclamation, the president took action through the use of publicity, laying out his concerns in his Quarantine Speech of October 1937, in which he warned of a spreading "epidemic of world lawlessness" that needed to be quarantined. He then began a "moral" embargo of airplane parts to Japan. Roosevelt's actions in responding to the many threats of the decade continued to combine legalities with negotiation and public relations.

The Neutrality Act of 1939 was partly repealed by an act passed in November 1941.[97] This act repealed the following parts: section 2 (covering commerce with countries engaged in armed conflict), section 3 (defining combat areas and keeping American citizens and vessels out of them), and section 6 (prohibiting the arming of American merchant vessels). The Cash and Carry provisions of the act and their impact on the Lend-Lease program are discussed in Chapter 2. The other sections of the act remained in effect and have been used subsequently to prosecute those in violation.

LEGAL PROFILES

Claude A. Swanson was the U.S. secretary of the navy during this period of the neutrality laws, and he was also a lawyer. He was born in Virginia in 1862 and started his legal practice there. He was elected in 1892 to the U.S. Congress and reelected six more times as a representative. In 1906, he was elected governor of Virginia (after a previous unsuccessful attempt at nomination). He held that position until 1910, when he was first appointed and then elected to the U.S. Senate. He was reelected three more times, staying in the Senate until 1933. He then became the secretary of the navy in President Roosevelt's cabinet, a position that he held until his death in 1939.[98]

---

97. Pub. L. No. 77-294 (1941).
98. *See Swanson, Claude Augustus*, BIOGRAPHICAL DIRECTORY OF THE UNITED STATES CONGRESS.

CHAPTER 2

UNITED STATES: PREPARING FOR WAR

In the United States, 1940 was not only an election year but also a year in which involvement in the war was moving inevitably closer. Having twice been elected, Franklin Delano Roosevelt (FDR) decided to attempt what no other U.S. president had achieved: winning a third consecutive term in office. Dealing with the needs of an election campaign, however, did not prevent him from also addressing many of the pressing issues and taking the necessary steps in preparing for war.

The undeclared war in Europe had been going on since at least 1938 and similarly in Asia since at least 1937. Whether the United States would be drawn into direct participation was still to be seen, but allies of the United States were already involved, e.g., the United Kingdom in Europe and China in Asia. From the beginning of 1940 through the end of 1941 when war finally officially came, the Roosevelt administration and Congress took many steps to ensure that as the wars in Europe and in Asia moved closer and closer to America, the United States prepared itself for possible direct involvement.

There were many ways to prepare, both domestically and internationally, via statute and executive order. One was to address military needs in land, manpower, and organization. Another was to set the watch for saboteurs and those promoting the interests of foreign powers on American soil and to look for possible attacks on the government from subversive organizations within the country. There was also the need to assist allies with monies and materials for the war efforts in which they were already engaging and to ensure that certain key materials and instruments of war were not made available to potential adversaries. During this time, the United States moved from its long-held isolationist stance to a more internationalist posture, from moral embargoes to real embargoes, and from neutrality laws to laws that provided for direct aid.

For a country both with an isolationist outlook and a geographical isolation from the two main theaters of expected war in Europe and Asia, it is surprising how many preparations the United States took before its involvement in the conflict actually started. For example, by executive order, Roosevelt placed a number of military areas under more secure control, starting twenty months before war actually came.[1] This chapter focuses on those preparatory steps taken by the United States via statute and executive order, from which significant legal issues arose and were tried in cases during the war. The issues discussed are sedition, espionage, conscientious objectors, desegregation/integration, Lend-Lease, export controls, and declaration of war.

PROMINENT LAWYERS AND JUDGES IN THIS CHAPTER

Sedition:

- Howard W. Smith (statute sponsor)
- Albert Goldman (defendant and defense attorney)
- Osmond K. Fraenkel (defense attorney)
- Edward C. Eicher (trial judge)
- O. John Rogge (prosecutor)
- Henry H. Klein (defense attorney)
- Charles B. Sears (special examiner)
- George W. Crockett Jr. (defense attorney)

Espionage:

- Alben W. Barkley (senator)
- Stanley F. Reed (Supreme Court justice)
- Frank Murphy (Supreme Court justice)
- Newell Mecartney (defendant and attorney)

---

1. Exec. Order No. 8381, Defining Certain Vital Military and Naval Installations and Equipment (Mar. 22, 1940); Exec. Order Nos. 8680, 8682–84 (Feb. 14, 1941); Exec. Order No. 8794 (June 14, 1941); Exec. Order No. 8852 (Aug. 16, 1941).

Conscientious Objectors:

- Edward R. Burke (statute sponsor)
- Clyde W. Summers (defendant)
- Peter Woodbury (appeals court judge)
- Harlan F. Stone (Supreme Court justice)

Desegregation/Integration:

- A. Philip Randolph (executive order influencer)
- Thurgood Marshall (defense appeals attorney)
- Sadie Tanner Mossell Alexander (Civil Rights Commission member)
- Truman K. Gibson Jr. (executive order influencer)

Lend-Lease:

- Oscar S. Cox (statute drafter)
- Robert H. Jackson (Supreme Court justice)
- Cordell Hull (agreement negotiator)
- Dean Acheson (statute drafter)

Export Controls:

- Henry L. Stimson (statute implementer)
- Harrie B. Chase (court of appeals judge)

Declaration of War:

- Everett Dirksen (congressman)
- Albert B. Maris (court of appeals judge)
- Herbert F. Goodrich (court of appeals judge)

2.1 SEDITION

A. Statutes

Congress had previously passed a law requiring agents of foreign governments to register. The Foreign Agents Registration Act of 1938 supplemented the WWI-era Espionage Act (see Section 2.2) by requiring in peacetime those who are representing the political interests of foreign powers to register with the secretary of state and disclose their relevant activities.[2] The act was intended "to require the registration of certain persons employed by agencies to disseminate propaganda in the United States and for other purposes," and it applied to those engaged in public relations as well as their representatives, including attorneys for foreign principals.[3] It did not apply either to those in commerce not representing foreign entities' political interests or to diplomats. Disclosures included copies of all employment contracts, names of those represented, and compensation being paid.

The Foreign Agents Registration Act led the way, in 1940, for the passage of the Alien Registration Act of 1940, also known generally as the Smith Act.[4] Its purpose was to "prohibit certain subversive activities" and to address issues specific to aliens.[5] It had a number of titles, not necessarily related to each other.

Title I dealt with subversive activities. Section 1 prohibited encouraging disloyalty among the armed forces by direct advice or urging or distributing of written materials of that nature. Section 2 prohibited advocating the overthrow of governments in the United States utilizing force, violence, or assassination; publishing or disseminating these ideas with the intent to cause the overthrow of such governments; or organizing or joining any group advocating such overthrow by use of force. Section 3 prohibited conspiring (or attempting) to commit the acts prohibited in the first two sections.

Title II of this act allowed for the deportation of aliens who violated Title I, who were convicted of possessing an automatic or semiautomatic weapon, or who assisted other aliens in entering the United States illegally. It also amended the Immigration Act of 1917, which "exclude[d] and expel[led] from the United States aliens who are members of the anarchistic and similar classes,"[6] by making it an offense to have belonged to any of the listed classes (anarchist and those seeking to overthrow the government by force) "at any time," instead of just at the time of entering the country.[7]

Title III addressed alien registration by requiring fingerprinting and registration of all aliens entering the United States. Violators could be jailed for up to ten years and fined up to $10,000.

---

2. Pub. L. No. 75-583 (1938).
3. *Id.*
4. Pub. L. No. 76-670 (1940).
5. *Id.*
6. Pub. L. No. 65-221 (1918).
7. Pub. L. No. 76-670, § 20.

Later in 1940, Congress passed the Nationality Act, which prohibited naturalization for those who advocated anarchy ("opposition to all organized government"), the overthrow of the U.S. government, or attacks on its property or people; who wrote, published, or disseminated materials advocating such beliefs; or who belonged to organizations that advocated such beliefs.[8]

The act "to require the registration of certain organizations carrying on activities within the United States, and for other purposes," otherwise termed the Voorhis Act, also passed in 1940.[9] It required all organizations subject to "foreign control" to register if they were involved in civilian-military activities ("preparation for military action") or political activities (advocating the overthrow of the U.S. government).[10] The act required registration for all organizations not subject to foreign control that were involved in political activities, civilian-military activities, or political activities advocating the use of force or violence. All organizations subject to the registration requirement were required to provide information on finances, aims, locations, charters, bylaws, insignia, and publications, among other information.

LEGAL PROFILES

Howard W. Smith was the sponsor of the Alien Registration Act as well as an eighteen-term Democratic congressman and an attorney. Smith was born in 1883 in Virginia and started his legal practice there. In his early prepolitical years, he was involved in a variety of legal pursuits, including working in the general counsel's office for the federal Alien Property Custodian program during WWI. He worked as an attorney for the Commonwealth of Virginia from 1918 to 1922, as a corporation court judge from 1922 to 1928, and as a state circuit court judge from 1929 to 1930. He was then elected to Congress, serving for thirty-four years in the House of Representatives. Besides the Alien Registration Act, he also sponsored the Smith-Connally Act (see Chapter 3). He was eventually defeated in a primary election campaign for Congress when

---

8. Pub. L. No. 76-853, § 305 (1940).
9. Pub. L. No. 76-897 (1940).
10. *Id.* § 2.

he was more than eighty years old and so left politics to return to his law practice. He died in 1976.[11]

B. Cases

These statutes led to prosecutions against aliens and a number of antigovernment groups. Several of these prosecutions occurred during the war. This section discusses three such cases. The first major case was brought in the Minnesota federal district court against leaders of the Socialist Workers Party (SWP) in 1941, the so-called Minneapolis Sedition Trial. The second major case was the so-called Great Sedition Trial, which took place in 1944. The third case involved the government's attempts to deport a foreign-born labor leader.

1. Minneapolis Sedition Trial

There is quite a background to the Minneapolis Sedition Trial, involving not only the split between Communist and Socialist parties in the United States but also rivalries within the U.S. labor movement. The U.S. Communist Party had splintered into two parts after the death of Vladimir Lenin, with the larger group favoring Joseph Stalin and the smaller group favoring Leon Trotsky. It was this latter group that would eventually enter and take control of the U.S. Socialist Party. Through many disputes, splits, and reorganizations, this became the SWP. As WWII was starting around the world and encroaching on the United States, the U.S. Communist Party had openly supported Roosevelt, support that became even more pronounced after the Germans attacked Russia in 1941, thereby making the United States and Russia allies in the fight against Nazi Germany. The SWP, on the other hand, was not in favor of the war and was still dedicated to labor unrest to achieve its organization's goals.

As the SWP stated in an article in the *Manifesto of the Fourth International on Imperialist War and the Imperialist War,* "we do not forget for a moment that this war is not our war. . . . [Our] policy [is based] not on the military fortunes of the capitalist states but on the transformation of the imperialist war into a

---

11. *See Smith, Howard Worth*, BIOGRAPHICAL DIRECTORY OF THE UNITED STATES CONGRESS; Bruce Dierenfield, *Howard W. Smith*, ENCYCLOPEDIA VIRGINIA (Apr. 7, 2011).

war of the workers against the capitalist."[12] At the SWP's initial convention in Chicago starting on the last day of 1937, Max Shachtman, the editor of the publication *New International*, delivered a speech entitled "War Crisis Looms," part of which was as follows:

> If the working class is unable to prevent the outbreak of war, and the United States enters directly into it, our party stands pledged to the traditional position of revolutionary Marxism. It will utilize the crisis of capitalist rule engendered by the war to prosecute the class struggle with the utmost intransigence, to strengthen the independent labor and revolutionary movements, and to bring the war to a close by the revolutionary overthrow of capitalism and the establishment of proletarian rule in the form of the workers state.[13]

The SWP's policies against the war effort, including support of labor strikes and its rivalries with other parts of the labor movement, soon brought the organization legal trouble. The SWP had gained significant control over the International Brotherhood of Teamsters (IBT) Local 544 in Minnesota. The national head of the IBT was Daniel Tobin, who headed the union from 1907 to 1952. He was an ally of Roosevelt—he was offered the secretary of labor position several times but turned it down—and expected his union to support the war effort, including avoiding strikes. In the IBT's official publication, Tobin denounced the Trotskyist leaders of the SWP and their impact on Local 544.[14] Tobin determined that Local 544 was not following the IBT policies and tried to put the local into receivership under an IBT-appointed receiver, who would have the legal power to bring it back into line with national direction. The local resisted this move, instead voting to withdraw from the American Federation of Labor (AFL) and join the Congress of Industrial Organizations (CIO).

---

12. Manifesto of the Fourth International on Imperialist War and the Imperialist War: Imperialist War and the Proletarian World Revolution (adopted May 1940).

13. *Left Wing Delegates Found Socialist Workers Party at Convention in Chicago*, 2:2 Socialist Appeal 1 (Jan. 8, 1938).

14. Daniel Tobin, 38:5 Official Mag. Int'l Brotherhood of Teamsters, Chauffeurs, Stablemen & Helpers Am. (May 1941).

Tobin looked to both state officials and the administration in Washington for support, which soon came. Federal officials raided the offices of the SWP in June 1941, much material was confiscated, and indictments followed. Twenty-nine defendants were indicted, although only twenty-eight stood trial because one (Grant Dunne) committed suicide before the trial started. The defendants included James P. Cannon, the national secretary of the SWP; Vincent R. Dunne, the national labor secretary of the SWP; various labor organizers in Local 544; the editors of three publications of these organizations (the SWP's *Fourth International* and *The Militant* and Local 544's *The Industrial Organizer*); and SWP attorney Albert Goldman.

The trial started in October 1941, with the defendants charged under both the Smith Act and an 1861 law, the Sedition Act, for conspiring to forcibly overthrow the government. The government presented a great deal of the materials captured in the raid on the SWP, some witness testimony of defendants encouraging dissent in the military, and the spoken and written words of the leaders on trial.

The defense's strategy was designed mostly with propaganda, rather than exoneration, in mind. As Cannon explained in his memoir, "[at the trial], we had the opportunity, for the first time, to speak to the masses—to the people of the United States." So, "we planned to conduct our defence in court not as a 'criminal' defence but as a propaganda offensive. . . . [I]t was our aim to use the courtroom as a forum to popularise the principles of our movement." As to the result, Cannon noted that "we think . . . the policy has been amply vindicated by the results. Our principles were widely popularized. . . . The trial was by far our greatest propaganda success."[15]

For the count under the Sedition Act, none of the defendants were found guilty. For the count under the Smith Act, the jury found eighteen of the defendants guilty and five not guilty, and the court gave five defendants directed verdicts of not guilty. Among those found guilty and given prison terms of more than one but less than two years were the following:

- James P. Cannon, national secretary of the SWP
- Albert Goldman, attorney for the SWP and *The Militant*

---

15. James P. Cannon, Socialism on Trial (1942).

- Vincent R. Dunne, national labor secretary of the SWP
- Felix Morrow, editor of *The Fourth International*
- Farrell Dobbs, editor of *The Militant*
- Carlos Hudson, editor of *The Industrial Organizer*[16]

The verdicts of the eighteen were appealed to the Eighth Circuit.[17] Goldman and American Civil Liberties Union (ACLU) attorney Osmond K. Fraenkel presented the defense case to the appeals court. The court of appeals looked at three issues: the validity of the Smith Act, the sufficiency of the indictment, and the sufficiency of the evidence. It dealt quickly with the sufficiency of the indictment but expounded at length upon the other two issues.

The appellants raised arguments against the validity of sections 1 through 3 of Title I of the Smith Act. The court found that section 1's prohibition on "advis[ing], counsel[ing], urg[ing], or in any manner caus[ing] insubordination, disloyalty, mutiny, or refusal of duty by any member of the military" did not restrict free speech by limiting the issuance of opinions because it prohibited only those made with the intent to influence the military's "loyalty, morale, or discipline."[18] Appellants' arguments against section 2 attacked its vagueness, in particular in regard to the use of technical or obscure language in the publications of radical groups, most members' lack of understanding of the SWP's doctrines, guilt by association, and parties knowing whether their doctrines advocate overthrow of governments until decided by a court. The court held that this section was not inherently invalid.

Appellants also argued that the statute was not only defective as written but also invalid as applied. This was based on the "clear and present danger" doctrine from the *Schenck v. United States* case:

> The question in every case is whether the words used are used in such circumstances and are of such a nature as to create a clear and present danger that they will bring about the substantive evils that Congress has a right to prevent. It is a question of proximity and degree. When a

---

16. *How the Eighteen Were Railroaded to Penitentiary*, 5 THE FOURTH INT'L 8, (Jan. 1944).
17. Dunne v. United States, 138 F.2d 137 (8th Cir. 1943).
18. *Id.* at 140.

nation is at war, many things that might be said in time of peace are such a hindrance to its effort that their utterance will not be endured so long as men fight, and that no Court could regard them as protected by any constitutional right.[19]

The court here stated that the *Gitlow v. New York* case provided the situations where *Schenck* did not apply, i.e., where the legislature has determined that "utterances of a certain kind involve such danger of substantive evil that they may be punished."[20] Because the government may protect the integrity of the military and protect against the overthrow of the government ("a State may punish utterances endangering the foundations of organized government and threatening its overthrow by unlawful means"), prohibiting such utterances is permissible, and the act is not invalid in its application.[21]

The court then looked at the claims of invalidity of the evidence. It started with the evidence for the charges based on section 2 of the act, i.e., that it was the intention of the SWP to overthrow the government by force. Quoting from the SWP's own Declaration of Principles,[22] the court found that the SWP did not intend to use the institutions of a capitalist government (e.g., voting) to effect change. It also referenced statements of the SWP leaders as well as the training of "Defense Guards," instructed by Trotsky, and their deployment into Local 544. Furthermore, it found numerous instances in the evidence record of the SWP encouraging insubordination within the military, including the SWP instructing people to accept service if drafted under the Selective Training and Service Act but then "to do everything in their power to disrupt, hinder and impair the efficient functioning thereof, and when the appropriate time came to turn their weapons against their officers."[23]

The court handed down its ruling on September 20, 1943, finding the evidence presented to be sufficient and affirming the judgments of each appellant.

---

19. Schenck v. United States, 249 U.S. 47, 52 (1919).
20. Gitlow v. New York, 268 U.S. 652, 670 (1925).
21. *Id.* at 667.
22. SOCIALIST WORKERS PARTY, DECLARATION OF PRINCIPLES (Jan. 1938).
23. *Dunne*, 138 F.2d at 152.

LEGAL PROFILES

Albert Goldman not only was on trial as one of the defendants but also acted as a defense attorney. Goldman was born in 1897 in Illinois and went to law school there. He joined the Communist Party, for which he was chief counsel, in 1932. He represented the party in a variety of issues but left when the party splintered into the Stalin and Trotsky camps, following the latter. He worked for the SWP during the Minneapolis labor strikes in the 1930s and continued to do so right up until the SWP trials. He was a prolific writer, helping to found the newspaper for the SWP and also leaving behind documents about this trial and his speeches in it.[24] He helped to defend Trotsky's position before an informal commission while in exile in Mexico.[25] He was disbarred in 1944 after his conviction but reinstated twelve years later.[26] He died in 1960.[27]

Osmond K. Fraenkel was a New York attorney involved with the ACLU for more than forty years, serving as one of its general counsel for more than twenty years, beginning in 1954. He was born in New York in 1888 and started his legal practice in the state. Prior to his involvement with the ACLU, he was co-counsel for the New York Civil Liberties Union for more than twenty years. He was involved in a number of important issues and cases over the years, including many before the U.S. Supreme Court: the so-called Scottsboro Boys trials (sexual assault)[28] *Hirabayashi v. United States* (curfews for minorities during wartime),[29] *Draper v. United States* (evidence in criminal trials),[30] *Schneider v. State*

---

24. Albert Goldman, In Defense of Socialism: The Official Court Record of Albert Goldman's Final Speech for the Defense in the Famous Minneapolis Sedition Trial (1944).
25. *Mr. Goldman's Position: Trotsky Supporter Takes Exception to Conclusions in Dispatch*, N.Y. Times (Apr. 10, 1937).
26. *Ex-Red Again Lawyer*, N.Y. Times (Sept. 12, 1956).
27. *See Albert Goldman, Lawyer, 63, Dies*, N.Y. Times (May 24, 1960).
28. Norris v. Alabama, 294 U.S. 587 (1935).
29. Hirabayashi v. United States, 320 U.S. 81 (1943).
30. Draper v. United States, 358 U.S. 307 (1959).

(Town of Irvington) (freedom of expression and prior approval of hand-bills by municipalities),[31] *De Jonge v. State of Oregon* (freedom of expression and criminal syndicalism laws),[32] *Kunz v. New York* (city permits for religious expression),[33] and cases described in later chapters (e.g., *Korematsu v. United States*,[34] discussed in Chapter 4). He wrote a number of books on a variety of topics, including the Sacco-Vanzetti case and civil liberties,[35] and included draft resisters and Bertrand Russell among his clients. He died in 1983.[36]

2. The Great Sedition Trial

The second notable trial under the Smith Act occurred in Washington, D.C. The defendants in this trial were Nazi Germany supporters of various backgrounds and professions. Grand jury indictments were handed down in this matter beginning in 1942, but the trial did not start until 1944 because there were three separate sets of indictments covering forty-two defendants. The final indictment in *United States v. McWilliams*, in January 1944, named the thirty defendants who finally went to trial.[37] Those indicted included German supporters from the German American Bund organization, authors and publishers who supported Germany and Fascism, lobbyists in the United States for Germany, and other groups who publicly supported Germany and its aims.

The indictment was for conspiracy to incite disloyalty in the U.S. military under the Smith Act. The indictment charged that thirty defendants (although some were severed and later dismissed) had joined in a conspiracy to replace the government of the United States with one based on "a National Socialist form by causing insubordination, disloyalty, mutiny, and refusal of duty by

---

31. Schneider v. State (Town of Irvington), 308 U.S. 147 (1939).
32. De Jonge v. State of Oregon, 299 U.S. 353 (1937).
33. Kunz v. New York, 340 U.S. 290 (1951).
34. Korematsu v. United States, 323 U.S. 214 (1944).
35. Osmond K. Fraenkel, Our Civil Liberties (1944); Osmond K. Fraenkel, The Supreme Court and Civil Liberties: How the Court Has Protected the Bill of Rights (1960).
36. *See Osmond K. Fraenkel Dies at 94; Former Counsel to the A.C.L.U.*, N.Y. Times (May 17, 1983).
37. United States v. McWilliams, 54 F. Supp. 791 (D.D.C. 1944).

members of the military and naval forces of the United States."[38] As part of this conspiracy, they, in conjunction with the leaders of the Nazi Party in Germany, carried out the following acts in Washington, D.C.: "(a) cause to be printed and circulated, inter alia, 42 specified publications and (b) use, inter alia, 35 specified agencies as distributors, and (c) thereby and otherwise disseminate, inter alia, 24 specified representations and charges."[39]

Venue was set in Washington, D.C.—though many of the indictees had never even been to that city—because a resident of the District had requested and received from the defendants in that location the materials supporting the indictments. In fact, the defendants were from many different parts of the country. An attempt by defense counsel to quash jurisdiction and venue was rebuked by the court, which ruled that "assuming a conspiracy by all the defendants, no matter where entered into, then any acts done within the District in furtherance of its objectives, by any defendant, establish venue here as to all."[40]

Much has been made of the fact that this trial was motivated by Roosevelt's determination to quiet dissent against the war and by pressure from internationalist and Jewish organizations.[41] Considering the disparate situations of the defendants (some powerful voices, some already imprisoned on other charges, and others one-man limited-circulation publishing shops) and the multiple indictments, suppression of support for the Nazi cause may well have been the goal. According to authors Lawrence Dennis and Maximilian St. George:

> The pattern of the prosecution gradually emerged something like this: Our country is at war; Russia is our ally; the Russian government is communist; these defendants fight communism; they are therefore weakening the ties between the two countries; this is interfering with the war efforts; this in turn is injuring the morale of the armed forces. The indictees should therefore be sent to prison.[42]

---

38. *Id.* at 793.
39. *Id.*
40. *Id.* at 794.
41. Lawrence Dennis & Maximilian St. George, Trial on Trial: The Great Sedition Trial of 1944 (1945); David Baxter, The Great Sedition Trial of 1944: A Personal Memoir (1986); Michael C. Piper & Ken Hoop, A Mockery of Justice: The Great Sedition Trial of 1944 (1999).
42. Dennis & St. George, *supra* note 41.

The trial opened in April 1944, with Judge Edward C. Eicher presiding. The government's lead prosecutor was O. John Rogge. With so many defendants, the number of defense attorneys was quite large, with some defendants also aiding in defending themselves, which made for quite a circus-like atmosphere in the courtroom. Eighteen of the defendants were indigent, so the government had to appoint counsel for them. The most well-known of the many defense attorneys involved may have been Henry H. Klein, who originally defended Elmer Garner, a cousin of FDR's former vice president, John Nance Garner (see Chapter 1). After eighty-three-year-old Garner died during the trial, Klein defended Eugene Sanctuary. Klein himself took part in the theatrics, getting convicted of contempt for trying to withdraw from the case. Several of the lawyers and those defending themselves were likewise convicted by the judge.

During the course of the trial, Rogge presented documentary evidence variously published by the defendants. The large contingent of defense attorneys repeatedly interrupted the proceedings, causing the judge great distress. In November 1944, Rogge had only introduced part of the evidence when the trial came to a sudden end because Judge Eicher died. After almost eight months, the prosecution had not even called half of its witnesses, and the defense had not yet begun to present its case. This resulted in a mistrial.

With a successor judge in place, the government asked for more time to go to Germany, after that country's defeat, and look for additional evidence of the conspiracy.[43] Rogge eventually had to admit that the United States did not find evidence in Germany that could lead to convictions. Finally, the succeeding judge dismissed all charges due to the denial of the defendants' constitutional right to a speedy trial: it had been two years since the death of the original judge and "five years of intensive investigation."[44] The following year, the court of appeals affirmed the lower court's decision.[45]

---

43. United States v. McWilliams, 69 F. Supp. 812, 813 (D.D.C. 1946).
44. *Id.* at 814.
45. United States v. McWilliams, 163 F.2d 695 (D.C. Cir. 1947).

LEGAL PROFILES

Edward C. Eicher was the chief justice who presided over this trial. He was born in Iowa in 1878 and began to practice law in the state. He worked as an attorney for a railroad company for many years and then returned to private practice before being elected to Congress as a representative from Iowa in 1932. He was reelected twice. In 1938, President Roosevelt appointed him as a commissioner of the U.S. Securities and Exchange Commission (SEC). After being appointed chairman of the SEC and serving for four years, he was then appointed as the chief justice for the U.S. District Court for the District of Columbia, where he was serving when this trial began. The unruliness of the trial may have contributed to his death, which occurred in 1944.[46]

O. John Rogge was the government's lead prosecutor for this trial. He was born in Illinois in 1903. After several years in private practice, he began his government career in 1934. He worked for several government agencies, including the Treasury Department, the Reconstruction Finance Corporation, and the SEC. He had two stints with the Justice Department, the first of which involved dismantling the Huey Long machine in Louisiana. The second time he worked for the attorney general and was given the responsibility for this trial. He was subsequently fired by attorney general (and later Supreme Court justice) Tom C. Clark for publicly revealing some of the information he had uncovered in his investigation when he went to Europe. He returned to private practice and became involved in a number of progressive political causes, including defending those accused by the House Un-American Activities Committee in the early 1950s. He also wrote a number of books on civil liberties and was involved in civil rights and freedom of expression cases. He died in 1981.[47]

---

46. *See Eicher, Edward Clayton*, Biographical Directory of the United States Congress; Eicher, Edward Clayton, Fed. Judicial Ctr., Biographical Directory of Federal Judges.

47. *See O. John Rogge, 77, Anti-Nazi Activist*, N.Y. Times (Mar. 23, 1981).

Henry H. Klein, one of the defense attorneys, was born in 1879 in Hungary and emigrated to the United States as an infant. Spending his life in New York, he wrote a book about the city.[48] He was involved in a number of investigations, such as for the New York State Civil Service Commission in 1914 and for public utilities in 1916. In 1927, he exposed graft in city sewer projects. Among his many roles, he was a deputy commissioner of accounts in New York City from 1918 to 1923 and special counsel for utilities beginning in 1924. In 1933, he ran for the office of mayor of New York but lost.[49] Considering the nature of this sedition trial and its defendants, it is noteworthy that Klein was born into Judaism (before later converting to Christianity). Klein wrote a number of supposed exposé books[50] and was virulently anti-Communist. His contempt conviction for withdrawing from the Great Sedition Trial without the court's permission was eventually overturned.[51] Klein died in 1955.[52]

3. Bridges Trials

Both of the previous trials concerned Title I of the Smith Act. A third case, the Bridges trials, involved Title II of the act, which referenced those aliens who entered the United States and their activities. The Title II revision was Congress's reaction to the *Kessler v. Strecker* case of 1939, in which the Supreme Court would not allow the deportation of an admitted past member of the Communist Party.[53]

The Bridges trials involved Australian Harry Bridges, a labor activist who had entered the country more than twenty years before in 1920. The administration had tried to deport Bridges previously; but, under the Sedition Act, deportations were only allowed if the accused was part of one of the listed organizations upon or after entering the country, which the government could

48. HENRY H. KLEIN, MY LAST FIFTY YEARS, AN AUTOBIOGRAPHICAL HISTORY OF "INSIDE" NEW YORK (1935).
49. *H.H. Klein Ran Only Once*, N.Y. TIMES (Jan. 27, 1934).
50. HENRY H. KLEIN, DYNASTIC AMERICA AND THOSE WHO OWN IT (1921); HENRY H. KLEIN, BANKRUPTING A GREAT CITY: THE STORY OF NEW YORK (1915).
51. *Two Attorneys Lose*, N.Y. TIMES (May 1, 1945).
52. *See Henry H. Klein, 76, Lawyer, Is Dead*, N.Y. TIMES (July 18, 1955).
53. Kessler v. Strecker, 307 U.S. 22 (1939).

not prove. With the Smith Act revision to the Sedition Act now in place, the government again looked to deport Bridges, who was a leading figure in the International Longshoremen's Association, the founding of the International Longshore and Warehouse Union, and the West Coast maritime strike of a few years earlier. Although the decision was reversed by the Board of Immigration Appeals, U.S. Attorney General Francis Biddle ordered him deported, finding in accordance with Special Examiner Charles B. Sears that Bridges was a member of and affiliated with the Communist Party USA, a "group that believes in, advises, advocates, and teaches the overthrow by force and violence of the Government of the United States."[54] Bridges started a lengthy federal court appeals process before finally arriving at the Supreme Court.

a. *Ex Parte Bridges*

First, in *Ex parte Bridges*, Bridges submitted a petition for a writ of habeas corpus (which requires a person, typically one under arrest, to be brought before a court) to the local district court, demanding to go before the court to present his claims.[55]

The district court found Bridges' claim of double jeopardy invalid because the previous deportation proceedings against him in 1938 and 1939 were not subject to double jeopardy. The Supreme Court had held in another case that deportation is the "revocation of a privilege" and not "punishment for a crime."[56] The revised Sedition Act (see Section 2.2) penalized membership or affiliation with groups that advocated the violent overthrow of the U.S. government; prior proceedings against Bridges could not find active membership in or affiliation with the Communist Party.

Bridges went on to claim that the Smith Act revision was an ex post facto law that punished his prior activities. The court ruled that it was not an ex post facto law because it was not a criminal law: "[D]eportation . . . is not a punishment. . . . The right to expel aliens is a sovereign power."[57] The court also turned down his claim that the sole purpose of the revisions in the Smith Act was to deport him: "The motives of the legislators . . . will always be presumed to be to accomplish that which follows as the natural and reasonable effect of

---

54. Bridges v. Wixon, 144 F.2d 927, 934 (9th Cir. 1944).
55. *Ex parte* Bridges, 49 F. Supp. 292 (N.D. Cal. 1943).
56. Mahler v. Eby, 264 U.S. 32 (1924).
57. *Ex parte Bridges*, 49 F. Supp. at 298.

their enactments."[58] In addition, the court defined *affiliation* as that which can "reasonably be said to support the progress of proscribed organizations towards the recognition of their ultimate unlawful goal."[59]

The petition was denied.

b. *Bridges v. Wixon*

In the Ninth Circuit, the court in *Bridges v. Wixon* reiterated that it was empowered to rule only on the Fifth Amendment due process rights of the deportee petitioner and not the sufficiency and weight of the evidence.[60] The majority upheld the district court's ruling, but the dissent focused upon the meaning of the word *affiliation*. The dissenting opinion stated that Congress's meaning of the phrase was "having a substantial tendency, to further the subversive aims of the group," as opposed to sympathy or temporary association.[61] Furthermore, the court found no credibility in the testimony of two witnesses used to establish Bridges' membership in the Communist Party.

c. *Bridges v. United States*

In June of 1945, the Supreme Court in *Bridges v. United States* ruled that Bridges should not be deported.[62] It followed the lines of the dissent in the appeals court decision. Affiliation, the Court ruled, involves "those who contribute money or anything of value to an organization which believes in, advises, advocates, or teaches the overthrow of our government by force or violence"; affiliation is not cooperation in lawful activities. The court held that the attorney general had misconstrued *affiliation* per this statute. In addition, the testimony of one of the witnesses claiming that Bridges was a member of the Communist Party was inadmissible, and the other witness's testimony could not stand alone. Therefore, the Court ruled his detention for deportation unlawful and reversed the lower courts' rulings.

Bridges' troubles with the U.S. legal system were far from over, however. He subsequently became a naturalized U.S. citizen, but this status was brought under attack when he was charged with lying on his naturalization application

---

58. *Id.* at 299.
59. *Id.* at 307.
60. Bridges v. Wixon, 144 F.2d 927 (9th Cir. 1944).
61. *Id.* at 941.
62. Bridges v. Wixon, 326 U.S. 135 (1945).

by claiming that he had never been a member of the Communist Party. He was convicted and sentenced to jail, and once again his case was appealed through the federal judiciary, with the Supreme Court finally overturning the decision due to the statute of limitations.[63] Bridges later died in the United States at the age of eighty-eight.

LEGAL PROFILES

Charles B. Sears was the special examiner at Bridges' 1941 Immigration and Naturalization Service hearing. He was born in New York in 1870 and began his legal practice there. During WWI, he was first appointed and then elected to positions in the New York State judiciary. He was a member of the state's supreme court (New York's highest court is the superior court) from 1917 to 1940 and served as presiding justice from 1929 to 1940. He was then appointed to the court of appeals before finally retiring. After retirement, he was involved not only in the Bridges case but also as a presiding justice in one of the military tribunals held in Nuremberg after the war (see Chapter 7). He died in 1950.[64]

C. Subsequent Events

After the war, Communism once again replaced Fascism as the ideology in disfavor in the United States. The Smith Act was utilized as a tool to go after some of the leaders of the Communist Party USA in a trial known as the Foley Square Trial for its location in New York City. The general secretary of the U.S. Communist Party, Eugene Dennis, and ten other leaders of the party were indicted in 1948; and their trial, *United States v. Foster*, commenced later in the year and lasted until late 1949.[65] The men were charged under Title I, section 3, of the Smith Act with conspiracy to advocate the teachings of Communism,

---

63. Bridges v. United States, 346 U.S. 209 (1953).
64. *See Charles B. Sears, Jurist, Dies at 80*, N.Y. TIMES (Dec. 17, 1950).
65. United States v. Foster, 83 F.Supp. 197 (S.D.N.Y. 1949).

including the violent overthrow of capitalist governments. Their literature and that produced by the antecedents of the Communist movement (e.g., Karl Marx, Lenin, and Stalin) were introduced at trial to show that their organizations supported the use of force to bring down the U.S. government.

The defendants used the opportunity to showcase Communism—much like the SWP did with Socialism in the Minneapolis Sedition Trial—and their attorneys put on a show of their own. When told that a single objection would be sufficient for all of the defendants, the attorneys filled the air with multiple objections. There were many motions for mistrial, claims that the jury selection excluded the poor and minorities, and accusations against Judge Harold R. Medina (see Chapter 4). Many of the defense attorneys were cited for criminal contempt a number of times, with their conduct later described as "abominable," and given prison terms; their sanctions cases eventually reached the U.S. Supreme Court.[66] At the conclusion of the main trial, all eleven of the Communist Party defendants were found guilty.

The defendants appealed the decision to the circuit court.[67] In an opinion written by Chief Judge Learned Hand, the circuit court conducted an extensive analysis of prior Supreme Court decisions, looking for guidance on the test for "clear and present danger." It stated that courts must look to "whether the gravity of the 'evil,' discounted by its improbability, justifies such invasion of free speech as is necessary to avoid the danger." It asked, "When does the conspiracy become a 'present danger'?" The court looked to the current situation in Europe and the advance of Communism there and answered that "such a conspiracy creates a danger of the utmost gravity and of enough probability to justify its suppression. We hold that it is a danger 'clear and present.'" Inside a lengthy opinion, after reviewing 570 pages of briefs from defendants of their "objections and complaints," the court finally affirmed the district court's judgment.[68]

The case, *Dennis v. United States*, then reached the Supreme Court, which ruled the following year.[69] The Court looked at only two issues: (1) whether

---

66. Sacher v. United States, 343 U.S. 1 (1952).
67. United States v. Dennis, 183 F.2d 201 (2d Cir. 1950).
68. *Id.* at 234.
69. Dennis v. United States, 341 U.S. 494 (1951).

section 2 or 3 of the Smith Act violated the Bill of Rights or was indefinite and (2) the meaning of the "clear and present danger" test.

The Supreme Court held that the Smith Act did not violate the Bill of Rights nor was it vague, based on a sufficient line of cases clearly showing that advocating overthrow of the government was illegal. The Court also agreed with the circuit court's definition of *clear and present danger*, which affirmed that governments can clearly defend themselves and are not required to wait until the overthrow is about to be executed; the circuit court also stated that the "success or probability of success" is not the key criteria.[70] The judgments of conviction were affirmed.

Subsequent Supreme Court decisions did much to whittle down the power of the Smith Act. In 1957, the Court ruled in *Yates v. United States* that "advocacy and teaching of forcible overthrow of the Government as an abstract principle" is not proscribed under the Smith Act.[71] Fourteen leaders of the California Communist Party were indicted and had been convicted under the Smith Act. The Supreme Court overturned five of the convictions and ordered a retrial for the remaining defendants, stating in the majority opinion that the instructions to the jury were a misunderstanding of the *Dennis* case in that "advocacy of abstract doctrine and advocacy directed at promoting unlawful action" are different.[72]

Two cases in the 1960s further weakened the Smith Act. In 1961, the Court issued an opinion in *Scales v. United States* regarding the leader of a local Communist Party organization who was twice convicted of belonging to an organization that advocated the violent overthrow of the government.[73] The Court held that the membership clause of the Smith Act was not a violation of freedom of expression but that membership had to be active with the specific intent of achieving the organization's purpose. And in 1969, in *Brandenberg v. Ohio*, the Court, ruling on the actions of a Ku Klux Klan leader from Ohio, held that "constitutional guarantees of free speech and free press do not permit a State to forbid or proscribe advocacy of the use of force or of law violation

---

70. *Id.* at 510.
71. Yates v. United States, 354 U.S. 298 (1957).
72. *Id.* at 318.
73. Scales v. United States, 367 U.S. 203 (1961).

except where such advocacy is directed to inciting or producing imminent lawless action and is likely to incite or produce such action."[74] In concurrence, Justice Douglas added that "[c]ertainly there is no constitutional line between advocacy of abstract ideas as in Yates and advocacy of political action as in Scales. The quality of advocacy turns on the depth of the conviction; and government has no power to invade that sanctuary of belief and conscience."[75]

LEGAL PROFILES

George W. Crockett Jr. was one of the defense attorneys in the *Dennis* trial and appeal. He was born in 1907 in Florida and began his law practice there. He was involved in the leadership of the National Lawyers Guild, the founding of the first racially integrated bar association, and the creation of the first racially integrated law firm. He went to work for the U.S. Department of Labor before going into private practice for twenty years. He was jailed for contempt after this trial, and he authored a pamphlet about his summation therein.[76] He subsequently became involved with trying to prevent and then investigate the murders in 1964 in Mississippi of the young civil rights activists James Earl Chaney, Andrew Goodman, and Michael Schwerner, known as the Mississippi Burning case. He subsequently became a criminal court judge in Michigan. After retiring from practice, he ran for Congress and won a seat at the age of seventy-one. He served in Congress for ten years. During that time, he sued the Reagan administration for violation of the War Powers Act (see Chapter 3).[77] He died in 1997.[78]

74. Brandenburg v. Ohio, 395 U.S. 444 (1969).
75. *Id.* at 457.
76. GEORGE W. CROCKETT JR., FREEDOM IS EVERYBODY'S JOB: THE CRIMES OF THE GOVERNMENT AGAINST THE NEGRO PEOPLE: SUMMATION IN THE TRIAL OF THE 11 COMMUNIST LEADERS (1950).
77. Crockett v. Reagan, 720 F.2d 1355 (D.C. Cir. 1983).
78. *See Crockett, George William, Jr.,* BIOGRAPHICAL DIRECTORY OF THE UNITED STATES CONGRESS.

2.2 ESPIONAGE

A. Statutes

The Espionage Act of 1917, titled as an act to "punish acts of interference with the foreign relations, the neutrality, and the foreign commerce of the United States, to punish espionage, and better to enforce the criminal laws of the United States," required those representing the political interests of foreign powers to register and disclose their relevant activities to the U.S. government, giving the government the power to prohibit acts in support of foreign powers.[79] The Espionage Act was revised by the Sedition Act of 1918[80] to include, generally, antigovernment speech and opinion; this act was repealed after WWI ended.[81]

The Espionage Act had a number of different provisions. Title I dealt with espionage. The remainder of the act included provisions covering issues such as how the United States could deal with ships of other nations in its waters; ships engaged in foreign commerce; and, as to be discussed later, neutrality. Title I criminalized gathering, copying, obtaining, transmitting, or negligently allowing removal of information relating to the U.S. national defense that could be "used to the injury of the United States, or to the advantage of any foreign nation."[82] If the information is transmitted to a foreign power, the penalties are increased. Conspiring to perform these acts or harboring someone suspected of performing these acts is also prohibited.

The Espionage Act was amended in March 1940 under legislation with the following paragraph-long but aptly descriptive title and purpose: "To amend the Act entitled 'An Act to punish acts of interference with the foreign relations, the neutrality, and the foreign commerce of the United States, to punish espionage, and better to enforce the criminal laws of the United States, and for other purposes,' approved June 15, 1917, as amended, to increase the penalties for peacetime violations of such Act."[83]

---

79. Pub. L. No. 65-24 (1917).
80. Pub. L. No. 65-150 (1918).
81. Pub. Res. 66-64 (1921).
82. Pub. L. No. 65-150.
83. Pub. L. No. 76-443 (1940).

LEGAL PROFILES

Alben W. Barkley was the U.S. Senate majority leader during the entire
Second World War. He was born in Kentucky in 1877 and began his
practice of law in that state. He took on the roles of local prosecuting
attorney and judge until he ran for and won a seat in the House of
Representatives in the 1912 election. He remained in that seat representing Kentucky for fourteen years until he was elected to the Senate.
He held this position continuously for thirty-four years, broken only
by the four years that he resigned his seat to become the vice president
of the United States under Harry Truman from 1949 to 1953, starting
at the age of seventy-one. During his time in the House and Senate,
he helped pass varied legislation, such as the amendment establishing
Prohibition, many of the New Deal acts, wartime financing and foreign
relations such as Lend-Lease (see Section 2.5), and the United Nations
(U.N.) Charter. After an abortive run for the U.S. presidency in 1952,
he returned to the Senate in 1954, which is where he was serving when
he died in 1956.[84]

B. Cases

The Espionage Act created the groundwork to try a number of high-profile
cases, but in actuality there were not that many. The first two cases discussed in
this section are Supreme Court cases under the Espionage Act. In the first case,
the government prosecuted both a naturalized U.S. citizen who passed national
defense information to a foreign agent and the foreign agent who received the
information. In the second case, the government prosecuted a U.S. citizen and
WWI veteran who produced some rather vile materials purportedly aimed at
demoralizing U.S. military officers and potential military recruits. The third
case, which was not heard by the Supreme Court, also dealt with publishing
propaganda.

---

84. *See Barkley, Alben William*, BIOGRAPHICAL DIRECTORY OF THE UNITED STATES CONGRESS.

1. Passing Information to the Enemy

In this case, the defendant (Gorin) was a Soviet spy who was purchasing information from a worker in U.S. naval intelligence (Salich). Salich was born in Russia and had moved with his family across Russia to China and then to Japan before finally settling in the United States. He became a naturalized citizen and, after working at a local police department, took a position working for the U.S. Naval Intelligence Office in San Diego. Gorin was a citizen of the Soviet Union who moved to Los Angeles ostensibly to work on organizing tourist groups to visit the Soviet Union. Salich met Gorin originally on official business as requested by his supervisor. After an introduction from the vice consul of the Soviet embassy, Gorin asked Salich for information on Japanese activities in the United States. Although Salich originally reported the request to his supervisor, he later passed such intelligence to Gorin for money.

In 1939, the two were charged and convicted in district court of violating the Espionage Act by obtaining documents having to do with the national defense, transmitting these to Gorin as a representative of the Soviet Union, and conspiring to do so. The trial court stated that the first count required taking national defense information with the purpose of obtaining national defense information with reason to believe it would be used to injure the United States or assist the Soviet Union. The second count required disclosure of national defense information to representatives or citizens of the Soviet Union with reason to believe it would be used to injure the United States or assist the Soviet Union. The third count required a conspiracy to commit these actions. The documents that Salich and Gorin were convicted of passing involved Japanese military and civil official movements, private citizens of interest, movement of fishing boats suspected of espionage activities, and photos of American war vessels.

In a joint appeal to the circuit court, *Gorin v. United States* and *Salich v. United States*, the appellants focused on the wording of the act and whether national defense was narrowly defined as "vessels, aircraft, navy yards, submarine bases, forts, railroads, arsenals, mines, factories, telephone stations, buildings, etc." connected to places where "vessels, aircraft, arms, munitions or instruments for use in time of war are being made, prepared, repaired, or stored."[85] Their conten-

---

85. Gorin v. United States and Salich v. United States, 111 F.2d 712, 718 (9th Cir. 1940).

tion was that the information connected with national defense must also be so limited, in which case the information exchanged was not national defense information.

The court rejected this argument, stating that whether or not a piece of information concerns national defense is something for a jury to determine at the time and place—in other words, what is connected to national defense changes over time. The court used the example of a flintlock musket. It held that *national defense* is similar to *common defense* in the Constitution; thus, the court held, it was within the scope of Congress's enumerated powers to provide for national defense, and it rejected any challenge to the constitutionality of the law. The circuit court affirmed the trial court.[86]

The case then was appealed to the Supreme Court.[87] The Court found that the term *national defense*, as used in the Defense Secrets Act of 1911, "is a generic concept of broad connotations, referring to the military and naval establishments and the related activities of national preparedness."[88] This meant that information transmitted to a foreign agent does not relate to national defense solely on the connection with specific places. The Court also focused on the fact that there is to be "no distinction . . . between friend or enemy"—any foreign government could be an illegal recipient of information on national defense.[89] The Court affirmed the decisions of the lower courts.

LEGAL PROFILES

Stanley F. Reed wrote the Supreme Court's opinion in this case. He was born in 1884 in Kentucky. Although he did not graduate from law school, he established a legal practice in his home state and was elected to the state legislature. After serving in the military's intelligence division in WWI, he returned to private practice, representing, among other things, agricultural interests. His expertise in this area led to an appointment as general counsel for the Federal Farm Board in 1929. After that

---

86. U.S. CONST. art. 1, § 8.
87. Gorin v. United States, 312 U.S. 19 (1941).
88. Pub. L. No. 61–470 (1911).
89. *Gorin*, 312 U.S. at 29–30.

appointment, he served at the federal Reconstruction Finance Corporation. President Roosevelt then appointed him solicitor general of the United States, which required him to argue in front of the Supreme Court. This was especially important at this time given the many challenges that had been raised by the policies of the New Deal. He was involved in preserving many of the New Deal cornerstones, including Social Security, minimum wages, and labor bargaining rights (National Labor Relations Act). In 1938, he was appointed to the U.S. Supreme Court, on which he served for nineteen years. He died in 1980 at the age of ninety-five.[90]

2. Publications Targeting the Military

The second major case under the Espionage Act during WWII involved a WWI veteran turned economic researcher, Ray Hartzel, who published and distributed a number of pamphlets in the United States through the mail to those in the military and those eligible for enlistment in the military. They included these three: *The British: An Inferior Breed*; *The Jew Makes a Sacrifice: Forthcoming Collapse of America*; and *The Diseased Spinal Cord*, which was about President Roosevelt. Typical of the contents was a desire "to unite the white races against what I consider to be the more dangerous enemies, the yellow races."[91] The counts of the indictment were brought against Ray Hartzel and Elmer Soller under the Espionage Act for knowingly obstructing the recruiting of personnel into the military and causing insubordination, disloyalty, and mutiny in the U.S. military. They were both convicted.

On appeal to the circuit court, Hartzel, due to his attack on Roosevelt, the commander in chief of the U.S. armed forces, was found guilty of intended demoralization of the country, including both civilians and military. Without morale, "insubordination, disloyalty and mutiny would be the inevitable result."[92] Although the court believed that few adults would be naïve enough to believe the documents that were published, Hartzel still attempted to cause

90. *See Reed, Stanley Forman*, FED. JUDICIAL CTR., BIOGRAPHICAL DIRECTORY OF FEDERAL JUDGES.
91. United States v. Hartzel & United States v. Soller, 138 F.2d 169, 173 (7th Cir. 1943).
92. *Id.*

this result and so must have intended it. The court reversed the conviction against Soller, whose role was merely that of mimeographing the books and not authoring and distributing.

The case then proceeded up to the Supreme Court for a review of Hartzel's conviction.[93] The Court reversed the conviction, citing a lack of evidence to sustain the charge of attempting to cause insubordination in the military and interfere with recruiting. Though the prosecution proved that Hartzel's pamphlets had reached various military officers, up to the commander of the army air force and numerous people eligible under the Selective Training and Service Act (see Section 2.3), the government found no evidence that Hartzel had been "associated in any way with any foreign or subversive organization." While the Court believed that were "few ideas . . . more odious to the majority of the American people or more destructive of national unity in time of war" than what was stated in Hartzel's pamphlets, it could not find beyond a reasonable doubt that he had the specific intent to cause insubordination in the military.[94] It believed more likely that he wished to shape public opinion. The Court said that "the mere fact that such ideas (the futility of our war aims, the vices of our allies, and the inadequacy of our leadership) are enunciated by a citizen" is not enough for a finding of criminal intent under the Espionage Act."[95] There was a strong dissent to this opinion, and the final vote was 5-4.

LEGAL PROFILES

Frank Murphy wrote the majority opinion in this case. He was born in Michigan in 1890. He had a varied career, including military service in WWI, private legal practice, and stints as assistant U.S. district attorney and criminal court judge in Michigan. He then served as the mayor of Detroit, followed by roles as both governor general and high commissioner of the Philippines as it was transitioning from American rule to independence. Soon thereafter he became the governor of Michigan

93. Hartzel v. United States, 322 U.S. 680 (1944).
94. *Id.* at 687.
95. *Id.* at 689.

and helped mediate a labor strike between the United Auto Workers and General Motors. After losing his reelection battle, he was recruited to become the attorney general of the United States and then was appointed to the U.S. Supreme Court in 1940. He served on the Court until his death in 1949.[96]

Newell Mecartney, an Illinois attorney born around 1890, was charged and convicted in the original trial of Hartzel and Soller as a third coconspirator.[97] The trial judge set aside his conviction as he was not involved in the distribution of the materials.[98] Mecartney subsequently filed suit against both FBI Director J. Edgar Hoover and U.S. Attorney General Francis Biddle for depriving him of his constitutional rights; to prevent them from "making unfounded charges or taking illegal actions," Mecartney asked that all FBI agents and U.S. attorneys assigned to the case be made known to him.[99] He also served a complaint on Washington, D.C.–based Hoover and Biddle for illegal arrest, false imprisonment, and defamation by leaving a copy of the complaint with the U.S. district attorney in Chicago; but, upon a motion, the court of appeals set aside the service.[100]

3. Intent Versus Accomplishment

The third case, another one involving seditious publications reaching members of the military, was not as publicly prominent because the Supreme Court denied a petition for a writ of certiorari (a document asking the Court to perform an appellate review). In *United States v. Pelley,* decided in 1942 before *Hartzel,* defendants William Pelley (a longtime publisher of extremist views and founder of the Silver Shirts, modeled on the paramilitary Brown Shirts organization in Nazi Germany), Lawrence Brown (corporate officer and researcher), and their publishing company were convicted of publishing "false statements

96. *See Murphy, Frank,* FED. JUDICIAL CTR., BIOGRAPHICAL DIRECTORY OF FEDERAL JUDGES.
97. *Hoover Seizes Attorney Here as Seditionist,* CHI. DAILY TRIB. (Sept. 6, 1942).
98. *Mecartney Freed in Sedition Case,* N.Y. TIMES (Apr. 16, 1943).
99. *Chicagoan Cites Biddle, Hoover in Sedition Case,* PRX (Sept. 16, 1944).
100. Mecartney v. Hoover, 151 F.2d 694 (7th Cir. 1945).

with intent to interfere with the operation or success of the military or naval forces of the United States or to promote the success of its enemies" and "obstruct[ing] the recruiting or enlistment service of the United States."[101]

After the war started, the defendants were involved in publishing Axis propaganda in the United States, which the government categorized into fourteen different themes. These propaganda themes, partially consolidated, were as follows:

- The United States and Great Britain are internally corrupt (e.g., political and economic injustice, war profiteering, plutocratic exploitation, Communist sedition, Jewish conspiracy, and spiritual decay).
- The foreign policies of the United States and Great Britain are morally unjustifiable (i.e., selfish, bullying, imperialistic, hypocritical, and predatory).
- The president of the United States and Prime Minister Winston Churchill are reprehensible; warmongers and liars; unscrupulous; responsible for suffering; and pawns of Jews, Communists, or plutocrats.
- Nazi Germany is just and virtuous; its aims are justifiable and noble; it is truthful, considerate, and benevolent.
- The foreign policies of Japan are morally justifiable as it has been patient and long-suffering; it is not responsible for war.
- Nazi Germany, supported by Europe, and Japan are both powerful and possess the manpower, armaments, materials, and morale essential to victory.
- The United States and Great Britain (with the British Empire collapsing) are weak and lack the materials, manpower, armaments, and morale essential for victory.
- The United Nations are disunited; they distrust, deceive, envy, and suspect each other.
- The United States and the world are menaced by Communists, Jews, and plutocrats.

On appeal, one of the appellants' key contentions was that the government had not proved that the published material, although received by servicemen, had caused any actual harm to the war effort or recruiting. The court said that

---

101. United States v. Pelley, 132 F.2d 170, 172 (7th Cir. 1942).

there was no such requirement in the statute; rather, it was the intent to interfere and not the accomplishment of that objective that was essential. Another
key contention was that the publications "are not upon their faces seditious, for
they consist of opinions, criticisms, arguments and loose talk."[102] But the court
felt that these words were presented as facts, not opinions, and would be taken
as such by readers. Quoting from *Schenck*, it reiterated that "[w]hen a nation is
at war many things that might be said in time of peace are such a hindrance to
its effort that their utterance will not be endured so long as men fight and that
no Court could regard them as protected by any constitutional right."[103] The
judgment was affirmed.

C. Subsequent Events

The Espionage Act has been used quite a number of times since WWII to
prosecute those providing information to foreigners or groups the U.S. Government considers hostile. Famous cases include the following: the Rosenbergs, convicted under the act and executed for giving nuclear secrets to the
Soviets (see Chapter 7); the Pentagon Papers trials, including the *New York
Times* decision to publish secrets about U.S. involvement and intentions in the
Vietnam War (neither Daniel Ellsberg nor the *New York Times* was ultimately
convicted under the Espionage Act)[104]; Jonathan Pollard, the spy charged with
selling secrets to Israel and sentenced in 1986; Aldrich Ames, convicted for spying for the Soviets and sentenced in 1994; and Christopher Boyce, convicted
in 1977 for selling secrets to the Soviets. It is a long list.

D. Modern Applicability

The Espionage Act is still a valid statute today and is being used in the current
war on terrorism. Several recent cases brought by the government have cited
this act. Charges in the last few years under this act have been brought against
National Security Agency official Thomas Drake and nuclear non-proliferation
specialist Stephen J. W. Kim in 2010 and former CIA agent Jeffrey Sterling in
2011. U.S. Army Private Bradley Manning, who allegedly gave classified information to WikiLeaks to disclose, was charged under the Uniform Code of
Military Justice version of the same statute. Indictments under the act continue
into 2013.

---

102. *Id.* at 176.
103. *Id.* at 179.
104. N.Y. Times v. United States, 403 U.S. 713 (1971).

2.3 CONSCIENTIOUS OBJECTORS

A. Statutes

The Selective Training and Service Act, known as the Burke-Wadsworth Act,[105] was introduced in 1940 to increase the manpower of the U.S. military and created the first peacetime draft in U.S. history. Declaring that in a free society the "obligations and privileges" of military service should be "shared generally," the act required registration for male U.S. citizens and alien residents between the ages of twenty-one and thirty-six.[106] Those volunteering could do so from age eighteen. The limit of the service and training was set at twelve months, with the president able to extend that time period when the "national interest is imperiled."[107] Those conscripted for the land force were not to be deployed outside the Western Hemisphere or U.S. territories or possessions, including the Philippines. The statute prohibited discrimination based on race. Furthermore, it allowed conscientious objectors to serve in either noncombat or civilian positions.

The bill was extended in 1941 by several amendments, as requested by President Roosevelt. The first two amendments dealt with excluding from service and training requirements men who had already done sufficient service in the military, as well as any man past his twenty-eighth birthday.[108] But on August 18, 1941, Congress passed a revision to the act, declaring "that the national interest is imperiled."[109] The Service Extension Act of 1941 extended the periods of those on active duty to eighteen months—and more if the soldier consented to additional time—with the stipulation that if Congress finds it in the national interest, the president may further extend the time commitment. The president was allowed to extend these training and service commitments "for such periods of time as may be necessary in the interests of national defense," without the previous cap on the number of men who may be in active training and service at any one time.[110] It also allowed the president to recall retired military personnel to active duty.

---

105. Pub. L. No. 76-783 (1940).
106. *Id.*
107. *Id.* § 3.
108. Pub. L. No. 77-87 (1941); Pub. L. No. 77-206 (1941).
109. Pub. L. No. 77-213 (1941).
110. *Id.* § 2.

The act was further amended by removing the territorial restrictions on the training and service of the men selected.[111] The age range for registration for selective training and service was increased to eighteen to sixty-five, with active service possible for those ages twenty to forty-five.[112] Aliens in the United States who were citizens of neutral countries could opt out but then were forever banned from becoming citizens of the United States. Those citizens of declared enemy nations were not allowed to enter the training or service.

Both of these amendments were passed after the U.S. declared war in 1941.

LEGAL PROFILES

Edward R. Burke was one of the cosponsors of the Selective Training and Service Act. He was born in 1880 in South Dakota and practiced law in Nebraska. After enlisting in the military at the age of thirty-seven, he was commissioned a second lieutenant in the air service during WWI. Returning to his law practice, he was also the president of the board of education of Omaha from 1927 to 1930. He was elected to the House of Representatives in 1932 and then ran for and won the 1935 election for the U.S. Senate, representing Nebraska. He was not renominated by his party after his term ended. He then held a variety of positions, including general counsel for the Hawaiian Statehood Commission. He died in 1968.[113]

B. Cases

The issue of whether the government had the power to draft men into the military was addressed during WWI in the Selective Draft Law Cases decided by the U.S. Supreme Court at the beginning of 1917.[114] The pre-WWII cases

---

111. Pub. L. No. 77-338 (1941).
112. Pub. L. No. 77-360 (1941).
113. *See Burke, Edward Raymond*, BIOGRAPHICAL DIRECTORY OF THE UNITED STATES CONGRESS.
114. Arver v. United States, 245 U.S. 366 (1918).

challenged the draft mostly because it was started in peacetime; these cases were quickly dismissed because "[t]o attempt a distinction because the present Act applies, though no formally declared war exists, is to import a difference which does not appear in the Constitution itself."[115]

The more substantive cases that arose under this new Selective Training and Service Act included those dealing with conscientious objectors. There were two major cases involving those who objected to their participation in the war. The first case concerned a lawyer whose religious views did not permit his admittance to the bar during wartime. The second case involved a foreigner who applied for naturalization but refused to serve in the active military; this case was not decided until after the war had already come to an end.

1. Admittance to the Bar

In re Summers was initially decided early in the war by a state board of law examiners and reached the U.S. Supreme Court later in the war.[116] The Court did not rule directly on the Selective Training and Service Act but compared it to an Illinois statute, on appeal from the Supreme Court of Illinois.

Lawyers in Illinois were required to take an oath to the state to serve in the state militia as a requirement for admittance to the bar. Clyde W. Summers, the defendant, was a conscientious objector to military service. Therefore, he did not take the oath and could not obtain the necessary certificate from the Committee on Character and Fitness in 1942. The secretary for this committee stated, in part, thus:

> [Y]ou are a conscientious objector—also that your philosophical beliefs go further. You eschew the use of force regardless of circumstances, but the law which you profess to embrace and which you teach and would practice is not an abstraction observed through mutual respect. It is real. It is the result of [the] experience of man in an imperfect world, necessary, we believe, to restrain the strong and protect the weak. It recognizes the right even of the individual to use force under certain circumstances, and commands the use of force to obtain its observance.[117]

---

115. United States v. Herling, and four other cases, 120 F.2d 236 (2d Cir. 1941).
116. *In re* Summers, 325 U.S. 56 (1945).
117. *Id.* at 3.

The Illinois Supreme Court believed that this was not a case of barring Summers because of his religious beliefs; instead, it held that he was barred from practice because he could not take the prescribed oath. This upheld the state's constitution, which had provisions for service in the militia in times of war: "The militia of the state of Illinois shall consist of all able-bodied male persons resident in the state, between the ages of eighteen and forty-five."[118] The Illinois Constitution did allow conscientious objectors to avoid service in the militia during times of peace, but not in war.[119]

Summers appealed the decision of the Illinois Supreme Court to the U.S. Supreme Court on the grounds that under the Fourteenth Amendment, the state could not violate his First Amendment rights. The Supreme Court noted that the new federal Selective Training and Service Act did have provisions whereby conscientious objectors during wartime could perform alternative work, i.e., "work of national importance under civilian direction."[120] The Court noted a long tradition in Illinois of conscientious objectors being able to pay someone to fulfill their local militia obligations in the United States,[121] which the defendant had not done. The Court then looked to the fact that in *United States v. Schwimmer* and *United States v. Macintosh*, cases concerning naturalization, aliens who refused to pledge military service were denied U.S. citizenship.[122] Drawing a parallel between a requirement of military service for citizenship and a requirement of military service for bar admission, the Court did not find this a violation of religious freedom under the Constitution and affirmed the decision of the Supreme Court of Illinois.

In dissent, Justice Black noted that the Quakers, with their "long and honorable part in the growth of our nation," could qualify for the bar in Illinois.[123] He also noted Article VI of the Constitution's prohibition on religion tests. He discussed and concurred with the dissents in the *Schwimmer*, where a pacifist from Hungary was denied naturalization based on her unwillingness to take the oath to take up arms in defense of the United States, and *Macintosh*, where

---

118. ILL. CONST. art. XII, § 1, ILL. REV. STAT. (1943).
119. *Id*. art. XII, § 6.
120. Pub. L. No. 76-783, § 5(g) (1940).
121. Hamilton v. Regents of Univ. of Cal., 293 U.S. 245 (1934).
122. United States v. Schwimmer, 279 U.S. 644 (1929); United States v. Macintosh, 283 U.S. 605 (1931).
123. *In re* Summers, 325 U.S. 56, 575 (1945).

a minister from Canada on the faculty of Yale University was willing to take the oath but not take up arms unless the war was morally justified (dissents authored by Justice Oliver Wendell Holmes and Chief Justice Charles Evans Hughes, respectively). Justice Black also noted that Illinois had not drafted anyone into the militia since the Civil War era and was unlikely to do so again. He closed by stating that "[u]nder our Constitution, men are punished for what they do or fail to do, and not for what they think and believe. Freedom to think, to believe, and to worship has too exalted a position in our country to be penalized on such an illusory basis."[124]

LEGAL PROFILES

Clyde W. Summers, the defendant in this case, was born in 1918 in Montana and obtained his legal degree in Illinois. After he was turned down by the state bar for admission in 1942, he spent the next three years teaching law until the end of the war. In fact, he spent much of his long career teaching law, including at the University of Toledo, the University of Buffalo, Yale University, and the University of Pennsylvania. He became involved in the labor movement, specifically the issues of democracy in labor unions, about which he became a nationally recognized expert. He was instrumental in the drafting of the New York Labor and Management Improper Practices Act of 1958 and the federal Landrum-Griffin Act of 1959, which, among other things, required secret elections for labor union positions. He wrote a number of leading books and law review articles and was involved in cases involving these legislative acts. He died in 2010.[125]

---

124. *Id.* at 578.
125. *See Clyde Summers, Advocate of Labor Union Democracy, Is Dead at 91*, N.Y. TIMES (Nov. 11, 2010).

2. Refusal to Bear Arms

The *Girouard v. United States* case shed further light on the relationship among conscientious objectors, naturalization, and military service.[126] James Girouard was a Seventh-Day Adventist and a Canadian who in 1940 applied for U.S. citizenship after having lived in the country for seventeen years. He had wholly agreed with the required Oath of Allegiance:

> I hereby declare, on oath, that I absolutely and entirely renounce and abjure all allegiance and fidelity to any foreign prince, potentate, state, or sovereignty of whom or which I have heretofore been a subject or citizen; that I will support and defend the Constitution and laws of the United States of America against all enemies, foreign and domestic; that I will bear true faith and allegiance to the same; and that I take this obligation freely without any mental reservation or purpose of evasion: so help me God.[127]

However, he replied no to the question "If necessary, are you willing to take up arms in defense of this country?," explaining that he was a (noncombatant) Seventh-Day Adventist.

The district court looked at the fact that if it was acceptable for someone to serve in the military in a noncombatant role as permitted by the Selective Training and Service Act—like 10,000 other Seventh-Day Adventists—this should also be sufficient to grant citizenship. (One Seventh-Day Adventist medic, Desmond Doss, received the Medal of Honor for saving at least fifty soldiers during the Battle of Okinawa in 1945.)[128] The district court found it sufficient.

The appeals court did not agree and reversed, holding that the privilege of citizenship had conditions that must be strictly complied with.[129] The court quoted from *Schwimmer*: "The influence of conscientious objectors . . . is apt to be more detrimental than their mere refusal to bear arms . . . [and] does

---

126. Girouard v. United States, 328 U.S. 61 (1946).
127. United States v. Girouard, 149 F. 2d 760, 761 (1st Cir. 1945).
128. *See Desmond T. Doss, 87, Heroic War Objector, Dies,* N.Y. TIMES (Mar. 25, 2006).
129. *Girouard,* 149 F. 2d 760.

not lessen their purpose or power to influence others."[130] It then quoted from *Macintosh*: "[T]he privilege . . . to avoid bearing arms comes, not from the Constitution, but from the acts of Congress. That body may grant or withhold the exemption as in its wisdom it sees fit."[131] The court also referenced the Nationality Act of 1940, which did not change the Oath of Allegiance, as well as 1942 amendments to the act that excluded conscientious objectors from the provision omitting those who serve in the military from the requirement to state their intentions for service during the naturalization process.

In dissent, Circuit Judge Peter Woodbury stated that the court should not be required to follow previous Supreme Court decisions as he believed that the Supreme Court itself would currently not do so. His opinion turned out to be prophetic.

The Supreme Court took the case and again reversed the lower court, as it had in *Schwimmer* and *Macintosh*.[132] In agreeing with the dissents of Holmes in *Schwimmer* and Hughes in *Macintosh* and the circuit court dissent by Woodbury, the Court stated that the requirement to bear arms was not stated in the Nationality Act:

Refusal to bear arms is not necessarily a sign of disloyalty or a lack of attachment to our institutions. One may serve his country faithfully and devotedly though his religious scruples make it impossible for him to shoulder a rifle. Devotion to one's country can be as real and as enduring among noncombatants as among combatants. One may adhere to what he deems to be his obligation to God and yet assume all military risks to secure victory.[133]

The Court noted that no federal office seeker faced a similar requirement.

The Court referred to the Selective Training and Service Act and its oath "that I will bear true faith and allegiance to the United States of America; that I will serve them honestly and faithfully against all their enemies whomsoever."[134] It interpreted the changes to the Naturalization Act referred to by the appeals

130. United States v. Schwimmer, 279 U.S. 644, 651 (1929).
131. United States v. Macintosh, 283 U.S. 605, 624 (1931).
132. Girouard v. United States, 328 U.S. 61 (1946).
133. *Id.* at 64.
134. *Id.* at 66.

court as covering noncombatant applicants for citizenship. The Court then overruled the findings from *Schwimmer* and *Macintosh*. It closed its opinion by noting that the 1942 revisions were the latest actions from Congress and therefore its most recent intent on this topic. Chief Justice Harlan F. Stone wrote a dissenting opinion maintaining the status quo and affirming the circuit court even though he had dissented in *Macintosh*. He believed that Congress had indeed acted through its subsequent legislation to affirm the Court's prior rulings.

LEGAL PROFILES

Peter Woodbury wrote the strong dissent in the First Circuit decision that became the basis for the eventual Supreme Court opinion. He was born in 1899 in New Hampshire and served in the infantry in WWI. He started a private legal practice in New Hampshire, where he also served as a judge in the municipal court before joining the superior court. From there, he spent eight years serving as a judge on the New Hampshire Supreme Court. He then was appointed to the First Circuit position by President Roosevelt in 1941, where he served for almost thirty years, including a stint as the chief judge. He died while still on the court, in 1970.[135]

Harlan F. Stone was the chief justice of the U.S. Supreme Court during all of WWII. He was born in New Hampshire in 1872. He started in private practice in New York, which included lecturing at Columbia University Law School. He eventually was named the dean and served in that capacity from 1910 to 1923. During WWI, he served on a board that reviewed the status of conscientious objectors, potentially informing his views in *Girouard*. In 1924, he was appointed attorney general of the United States. One year later, he was appointed as an associate justice of the U.S. Supreme Court. During the early years of the New Deal while he was on the Court, Stone was one of the justices who tried to support

---

135. *See Woodbury, Peter*, FED. JUDICIAL CTR., BIOGRAPHICAL DIRECTORY OF FEDERAL JUDGES.

the various legislative acts. This support led Roosevelt to nominate him for the position of chief justice in early 1941. He was involved in many decisions discussed herein and also was the author of the well-known legal jurisdiction opinion in *International Shoe Co. v. Washington*.[136] On the same day that he read his opinion in *Girouard*, he suffered a cerebral hemorrhage and died.[137]

C. Subsequent Events

The Selective Service Act of 1948[138] completely revamped the selective service system of the now-repealed act of 1940. Under the 1948 act, conscientious objectors could either be assigned to noncombatant roles or could be deferred from service. It was subsequently revised in 1951[139] and 1967.[140]

The Vietnam War brought about new conscientious objector cases, one of which made it to the Supreme Court.[141] In this case, *Gillette v. United States*, the issue was not a situation of a conscientious objector who objected to war in all its forms but who instead objected to a particular war. The district court found that Guy Porter Gillette's belief that the war in Vietnam was "immoral and unjust" did not meet the criteria in the Selective Service Act for conscientious objectors, and the court of appeals affirmed.[142]

The Supreme Court focused on the operative phrase in the act: ". . . is conscientiously opposed to participation in war in any form."[143] The Court made it clear that it was not ruling on whether the petitioner's beliefs about war were "'religious' in nature" but only whether Congress intended the phrase to allow for objection to a particular war instead of "participation in war in any form."[144] The petitioner argued that not being able to differentiate between just and unjust wars discriminates against those religions that do so, in violation

136. International Shoe Co. v. Washington, 326 U.S. 310 (1945).
137. *See Stone, Harlan Fiske*, Fed. Judicial Ctr., Biographical Directory of Federal Judges.
138. Pub. L. No. 80-759 (1948).
139. Pub. L. No. 82-51 (1951).
140. Pub. L. No. 90-40 (1967).
141. Gillette v. United States, 401 U.S. 437 (1971).
142. United States v. Gillette, 420 F.2d 298 (2d Cir. 1970).
143. *Gillette*, 401 U.S. at 443.
144. *Id.* at 447.

of the First Amendment. The Court answered that the purpose of the provi-sion is "neutral and secular" and that there are valid neutral reasons for this provision, such as fairness to all religious and nonreligious people.[145] It rejected the claim of violation of the Constitution's establishment clause ("Congress shall make no law respecting an establishment of religion"). The petitioner also claimed violation of the free exercise clause ("or prohibiting the free exer-cise thereof"), which the Court answered by stating that the statute is "not designed to interfere with any religious ritual or practice."[146] The government's substantial interest in limiting the exemption to objectors to all war and thus having a fair system for determining "who serves when not all serve" justified any incidental burdens on those who object to a particular war.[147] Finding that the petitioner's claims were without merit, the Court affirmed the lower court's ruling.

2.4 DESEGREGATION/INTEGRATION

A. Statutes

The Selective Training and Service Act had allowed for the drafting of men regardless of race or color.[148] This did not mean that the military was to be desegregated; rather, in preparation for war, the net had to be cast as far and wide as possible. Beyond that, racial discrimination in the United States was still evident in both the North and the South. Leaders of African American organizations began to look for ways to achieve some kind of breakthrough on civil rights through the necessity of fighting the war.

One such effort was instituted by the head of the railroad sleeping car porters' union, A. Philip Randolph. Randolph, along with other civil rights leaders, planned to stage a march on the Capitol to get action for desegrega-tion of the armed forces and government defense contractors. They called it the March on Washington Movement, issuing a call for supporters early in 1941 after negotiations with the government failed. Preparations were made

---

145. *Id.* at 454.
146. *Id.* at 462.
147. *Id.* at 455.
148. Pub. L. No. 76-783, § 4(a) (1940).

throughout the spring to get upward of 100,000 people to march on July 1, 1941.

President Roosevelt, finally acceding to some of the demands, issued Executive Order No. 8802 on June 25, and the march was canceled.[149] The title of this executive order specified that it concerned "full participation in the defense program by all persons." Citing evidence of discrimination as the need for the order, Roosevelt instituted a policy in the defense industries and in government prohibiting discrimination based on race, creed, color, or national origin.[150] He made it the duty of employers and labor to provide "full and equitable participation of all workers in defense industries."[151] This was to be accomplished by three sets of actions: (1) oversight of vocational and training programs for defense production to ensure these were administered without discrimination, (2) the inclusion of a provision in all defense contracts obligating the defense contractor not to discriminate, and (3) a requirement that the Office of Production Management (see Chapter 3) establish the Fair Employment Practices Commission, tasked with taking complaints, redressing grievances, and providing recommendations on achieving the goals on the executive order.[152] The order did not address integrating the armed forces.

LEGAL PROFILES

A. Philip Randolph, the influence behind Executive Order No. 8802, was not a lawyer by profession but was awarded an LL.D. during his lifetime, one of his many notable achievements in championing organized labor and civil rights. He was born in Florida in 1889. He got his start in labor organizing with elevator and dockyard workers before moving on

---

149. Exec. Order No. 8802, Reaffirming Policy of Full Participation in the Defense Program by All Persons, Regardless of Race, Creed, Color, or National Origin, and Directing Certain Action in Furtherance of Said Policy (June 25, 1941).
150. *President Orders an Even Break for Minorities in Defense Jobs; He Issues an Order That Defense Contract Holders Not Allow Discrimination Against Negroes or Any Worker,* N.Y. TIMES (June 26, 1941).
151. Exec. Order No. 8802.
152. This is why Executive Order No. 8802 is sometimes referred to as the Fair Employment Practices Act.

to form the Brotherhood of Sleeping Car Porters. Through a long series of actions, reactions, negotiations, and federal laws spanning more than a decade in dealing with the antiunion Pullman Company, Randolph was finally able to get a contract for his union. After his involvement with Executive Order No. 8802, he was involved in another executive order by another president to desegregate the military (see "Subsequent Events" in Section 2.4). He continued to be involved in the civil rights movement of the 1950s and 1960s; his March on Washington Movement idea was used to great effect in the March on Washington for Jobs and Freedom of 1963 (and in Dr. Martin Luther King Jr.'s "I Have a Dream" speech). Randolph died in 1979, the recipient of many awards, including the Presidential Medal of Freedom.[153]

B. Cases

Segregation in the armed services led to many situations where African Americans, although drafted or having enlisted on their own, were not assigned to duty in combat areas. To be active in combat was the reason that many had signed up, just like other citizens. Instead, they were often given menial tasks, far from the front lines, which led to a large amount of dissatisfaction among these soldiers and sailors. One case in particular highlighted the situation: the case of the naval magazine explosion at Port Chicago, California, and its aftermath.

On July 17, 1944, there was an extremely powerful explosion at a naval station used for munitions loading for naval vessels, which lead to the deaths of more than three hundred people, primarily African American sailors, and the loss of several ships and much property damage. Although explosions were hardly unique events during the war, the site was completely destroyed and all the people directly involved in the loading on that night were killed, making it nearly impossible to know what caused the explosion.

A Naval Board of Inquiry looked into the causes and wrote an opinion exonerating the officers involved (all white) but noting the poor quality of

---

153. *See A. Philip Randolph Is Dead; A Pioneer in Rights and Labor,* N.Y. Times (May 1, 1979).

the enlisted men (all black).[154] It also blamed a lack of petty officers, a lack of training and trainability of the enlisted men, failure to provide collateral equipment to assist in loading, and a lack of preparation for the significant increase in munitions loading required by the expanding needs for the war in the Pacific. It did not blame the speed competitions (tons of munitions loaded per hour or shift) among various loading teams that their officers had set up. Possible triggers for the explosion could have been a falling boom, a turning propeller, a "supersensitive ammunition component" that had detonated either in the "ordinary course of loading operations or as a result of rough or careless handling by an individual or individuals," or sabotage.[155] The detonation of a supersensitive ammunition component and rough handling of the ordinance were listed as the two most likely causes.

The surviving men in the units were in a state of shock after the explosion and were either assigned to assist with cleanup or reassigned elsewhere. On August 9, a number of the surviving men were ordered to load a ship at a nearby pier. Not having confidence in their officers or the procedures and still not having recovered from the prior explosion (they had not received any time off), many refused to load ammunition. Throughout the next three days, questions and orders were directed toward the approximately 300 men who had refused. This was whittled down to 258 who refused, and they were placed in a navy brig. The commanding officer for the naval district, as well as others spoke to the men about the need for these munitions in the war effort raging in the Pacific, after which 208 of the enlisted men finally agreed to return to work. The 208 men who returned to work were all convicted in a summary court-martial for refusing to obey orders, docked pay, kept on active duty, sent to other locations and units in the Pacific, and later dishonorably discharged (later upgraded for many to honorable discharges).

Fifty of the enlisted men finally did not agree to obey all orders, including loading munitions, and so a court-martial was initiated. They were charged not only with disobeying orders but also with conspiracy to mutiny. Lieutenant Commander James F. Coakley was the prosecutor at this trial, and Lieutenant Gerald E. Veltmann headed the defense. When Veltmann moved to have

---

154. Naval Historical Ctr., Dep't of the Navy, Port Chicago Naval Magazine Explosion on 17 July 1944: Court of Inquiry: Finding of Facts, Opinion and Recommendations (1946).
155. *Id.* at 50.

the conspiracy charge dropped because there was no apparent intent to take over, Coakley asserted that when a group of men strike and continually refuse to perform their duties, it is equivalent to a conspiracy; the court agreed and denied the motion. The defendants and a psychiatrist testified that the men were scared that another explosion would occur, but the prosecution pointed out that so were so many men during this war, including those involved in the containment and cleanup at Port Chicago, that "fear is no excuse."[156] The court sided with Coakley and convicted all fifty of the two charges.

During the trial, National Association for the Advancement of Colored People (NAACP) counsel and future Supreme Court justice Thurgood Marshall, who witnessed some of the trial but, as a civilian, could not act as an attorney, issued a statement.[157] In this account, Marshall listed a number of concerns with the proceeding:

1. For months prior to the Port Chicago incident it was the common knowledge of experienced longshoremen and labor leaders that such a disaster was imminent. This feeling of apprehension grew out of their knowledge of the inefficiency, mismanagement, lack of safety measures in the handling of explosives and the Navy's policy of discrimination and segregation of Negro sailors.

2. There were instances prior to the Port Chicago explosion where merchant seamen, seeing accidents occur that could have resulted in devastating explosions, started to jump overboard to save themselves. These accidents were due to the inefficient handling of explosives by inexperienced workers—for example, winch-drivers. These seamen will witness the truth of this statement.

3. The C.I.O. Longshoremen's Union has a strict policy of using only experienced men to handle explosives. Winch-drivers, especially, must have a minimum of five years' experience. For this reason there has been no instance of an explosion where such men have handled explosives—whether they were Negro or white. There have been instances where longshoremen have refused to handle this type of cargo, but those who

---

156. *Exoneration Sought in Mutiny of '44,* N.Y. TIMES (Aug. 12, 1990).
157. Thurgood Marshall, Counsel, Nat'l Ass'n for the Advancement of Colored People, Statement on the Trial of Negro Sailors at Yerba Buena (Sept. 22, 1944) (exhibit A in trial).

refused were not Negroes. All loading of explosives at Port Chicago was done by inexperienced naval personnel.

4. Waterfront unions had officially warned both the Navy and the Army prior to the Port Chicago disaster that if they continued to use inexperienced workers in the loading of munitions an explosion was inevitable. This warning was disregarded.[158]

The convictions of the fifty men were appealed to the Army Judge Advocate General's Corps in Washington, with Marshall handling the appeal. He showed that the men were given the most dangerous work but no special training in loading ammunition, while being subjected to speed-loading competitions by their officers. He also reiterated some of what Veltmann had said, i.e., that much of the testimony was hearsay and inadmissible, that the definition of *mutiny* had been contorted, and that there was a lack of direct orders given to all fifty defendants. The navy ordered a retrial without admitting hearsay; all fifty men were again convicted. Eventually, the sentences of the men were reduced, and most were returned to active duty for a probationary period, after serving more than a year in jail, and dishonorably discharged (although most were eventually upgraded to an honorable discharge).[159]

LEGAL PROFILES

Thurgood Marshall, defense attorney during the appeal, was born in Maryland in 1908 and started out in private practice in that state. In one of his first cases, Marshall won a discrimination lawsuit against the University of Maryland School of Law for Donald Murray, another well-qualified African American undergraduate who, like himself, had been denied entrance. In 1936, Marshall joined the NAACP as its chief counsel, taking on numerous civil rights cases, many that were argued in front of the U.S. Supreme Court. The most famous of these was *Brown v.*

---

158. *Id.*
159. *50 Navy Sentences Reported Voided; Negro Sailors, Convicted of 'Mutiny' in 1944, Are Said to Have Been Freed*, N.Y. TIMES (Jan. 7, 1946).

Board of Education,[160] where the separate but equal education doctrine of *Plessy v. Ferguson*[161] was finally struck down. He was appointed to the U.S. Court of Appeals for the Second Circuit in 1961 and then to the position of solicitor general of the United States in 1965. In 1967, he became the first African American justice appointed to the Supreme Court. He served on the Court until 1991 and died in 1993.[162]

C. Subsequent Events

Executive Order No. 8802, which President Roosevelt issued in 1941, covered only discrimination in the defense industries—it did not address the integration of the military. There were a number of separate forces moving that issue forward in the postwar era. One was the military's own initiative, particularly that of the navy following Port Chicago and other racially charged incidents. A second was the civil rights movement emanating from the civilian population, once again led by A. Philip Randolph, who formed the Committee Against Jim Crow in Military Service and Training. A third was the threat of the Soviet Union and the potential impact on Cold War solidarity if the military—with its increasing numbers of black servicemen—were in discord. A fourth was the President's Committee on Civil Rights, which President Truman formed in 1946. A fifth was the politics of winning the presidential election of 1948. These, combined with Truman's own beliefs and revulsion at what had happened to some black veterans after the war (including lynchings, acts of assault and torture, and widespread discrimination), resulted in the issuance of Executive Order No. 9981 and the desegregation of the military in 1948.[163]

Late in the war, the navy, under Secretary of the Navy James Forrestal, initiated various experiments with integration, including having blacks serve with whites on auxiliary ships. They started special training and other programs through the Special Programs Unit and integrated existing training. There was a move to limit the percentage of blacks in certain types of more menial work

---

160. Brown v. Board. of Educ., 347 U.S. 483 (1954).
161. Plessy v. Ferguson, 163 U.S. 537 (1896).
162. *See Marshall, Thurgood*, FED. JUDICIAL CTR., BIOGRAPHICAL DIRECTORY OF FEDERAL JUDGES.
163. Exec. Order No. 9981, Establishing the President's Committee on Equality of Treatment and Opportunity in the Armed Services (July 26, 1948).

where they had been concentrated, such as stevedoring. Toward the end of the war, training for new recruits was integrated and positions such as nurses were opened to African Americans.

The President's Committee on Civil Rights was created by Truman in 1946 under Executive Order No. 9808 with the stated aims of examining the current state of civil rights in the United States, making a list of findings, and producing recommendations.[164] The recommendations of this committee included creating a civil rights division in the Department of Justice, a permanent Civil Rights Commission, and a permanent Fair Employment Practices Commission (which was first created in Roosevelt's Executive Order No. 8802); dealing federally with issues such as lynching and voting rights (e.g., poll taxes); and officially ending discrimination and segregation in the armed forces.[165]

Truman, not having been previously elected president (he assumed the office after FDR's sudden death a few months into his fourth term), faced a difficult election in 1948. The Democrats had lost control of both houses of Congress in 1946 and had held the presidency for 16 years. To encourage votes from African Americans, the Democratic platform that year had a strong civil rights component, one that called for "Congress to support our President in guaranteeing these basic and fundamental rights . . . the right of equal treatment in the service and defense of our nation."

All of these forces led to the issuance of Executive Order No. 9981, which focused on the military.[166]

Executive Order No. 9981 did not address integration or segregation directly; rather, it stated, in pertinent part, the following:

- "It is . . . the policy of the President that there shall be equality of treatment and opportunity for all persons in the armed services without regard to race, color, religion or national origin. This policy shall be

---

164. Exec. Order No. 9808, Establishing the President's Committee on Civil Rights (Dec. 5, 1946).

165. To Secure These Rights: The Report of the President's Committee on Civil Rights 139 (Oct. 1947).

166. These forces also led to the issuance of a companion executive order dealing with the federal workforce: Exec. Order No. 9980, Regulations Governing Fair Employment Practices Within the Federal Establishment (July 26, 1948).

put into effect as rapidly as possible . . . without impairing efficiency or morale."

- "There shall be created . . . an advisory committee to be known as the President's Committee on Equality of Treatment and Opportunity in the Armed Services."
- "The Committee is authorized to examine the rules, procedures and practices of the Armed Services in order to determine in what respect such rules, procedures and practices may be altered or improved with a view to carrying out the policy of this order."
- "All executive departments and agencies of the Federal Government are authorized and directed to cooperate with the Committee in its work."[167]

LEGAL PROFILES

Sadie Tanner Mossell Alexander was a member of the President's Committee on Civil Rights. She was born in Pennsylvania in 1898 and in 1921 became the first African American woman to earn a Ph.D. in economics (and the second to earn a Ph.D. of any kind). She then became the first African American woman to be admitted to and graduate from the University of Pennsylvania Law School (her father had been the first African American to do so) and became the first African American woman admitted to the bar in Pennsylvania. She entered private practice in the state and was appointed a solicitor for Philadelphia several times.[168] In addition to serving on the President's Committee on Civil Rights and on Philadelphia's Commission on Human Rights, she served as the chair of the National Council on Aging under President Jimmy Carter in 1981. She died in 1989.[169]

---

167. Exec. Order No. 9981.
168. *See Honoring Sadie Tanner Mossell Alexander: A Role Model for Future Generations of Students,* 49:2 U. Pa. Almanac 1 (Sept. 3, 2002).
169. *See Sadie T. M. Alexander, 91, Dies; Lawyer and Civil Rights Advocate,* N.Y. Times (Nov. 3, 1989).

Truman K. Gibson Jr., as an adviser to the secretary of war for issues concerning black soldiers, advised President Truman on Executive Order No. 9981. He was born in Georgia in 1912 and started his law practice in Illinois in 1935. He was responsible for helping organize the American Negro Exposition in Chicago in 1940. Also in 1940, he was appointed to the position of assistant to the chief civilian adviser to the secretary of war to address the issues of black soldiers. In 1943, he ascended to the adviser position itself. In 1946, he was the only black member appointed to President Truman's President's Advisory Commission on Universal Training, which in 1947 urged an end to segregation in the military. He also was part of the review of the eventual executive order. He returned to private practice after his governmental service and died in 2005.[170]

2.5 LEND-LEASE

A. Statutes

The springtime 1940 invasion of France, Belgium, and the Netherlands left Great Britain as the only European power standing up to Nazi Germany. German air attacks on Britain's cities and attacks against her shipping had left her in an increasingly precarious state. Therefore, Roosevelt and Churchill devised a method whereby America, despite being limited by the neutrality laws of the 1930s covered in Chapter 1, could provide substantial assistance to its erstwhile ally. However, between the neutrality laws, the isolationist mood in the country, and his reelection campaign, Roosevelt had to move carefully.

The Cash and Carry policy of the Neutrality Act of 1939 was causing Britain to run out of cash.[171] Roosevelt had declared a surplus of some munitions and sent them to Britain under an 1892 statute, but much more was needed. On September 2, 1940, the British ambassador to the United States, the Marquess of Lothian, sent a letter to the United States offering certain military bases in "in exchange for naval and military equipment and material which the

---

170. *See Truman Gibson, Who Fought Army Segregation, Is Dead at 93*, N.Y. TIMES (Jan. 2, 2006).
171. Pub. Res. 76-54 (1939).

United States Government will transfer to His Majesty's Government."[172] U.S. Secretary of State Cordell Hull, speaking for the government of the United States, replied that "[i]t therefore gladly accepts the proposals."[173] This resulted in the first major agreement concerning the United States' involvement in WWII: the Destroyers for Bases Agreement, an agreement formalized on September 2, 1940, and deemed by the U.S. attorney general to not require the approval of Congress.[174] This agreement stated that fifty antiquated warships of the U.S. Navy from WWI would be given to Britain. In exchange, the British would sign ninety-nine-year leases for a number of its bases, giving the U.S. military a presence in the British Empire across the Americas. The rent-free leases were for air or naval bases in Newfoundland, Jamaica, Trinidad, the Bahamas, Antigua, St. Lucia, British Guiana, and Bermuda.

This agreement benefited the United States in that it could more easily coordinate and defend the Western Hemisphere from the war that had broken out in Europe. It benefited Great Britain by giving it warships it desperately needed during the Battle of Britain and the Battle of the Atlantic (some of the warships were deployed to Canada to help protect supply convoys). It also relieved Britain of having to defend its Western Hemisphere bases and resulted in upgraded facilities at some point.

However, the fifty warships were not in the best of condition, and soon Britain was again in a desperate state. In a letter from Churchill to Roosevelt in late 1940, transmitted via Lord Lothian, Churchill stated thus:

> . . . The danger of Great Britain being destroyed by a swift, overwhelming blow has for the time being very greatly receded. In its place there is a long, gradually-maturing danger, less sudden and less spectacular, but equally deadly. This mortal danger is the steady and increasing diminution of sea tonnage. . . . The decision for 1941 lies upon the seas. Unless we can establish our ability to feed this Island, to import the munitions of all kinds which we need, unless we can move our armies to the various theatres where Hitler and his confederate Mussolini must be met,

---

172. Letter from Cordell Hull, U.S. Secretary of State to the Marquess of Lothian, British Ambassador (Sept. 2, 1940).
173. *Id.*
174. Destroyers for Bases Agreement, U.S.-Brit., Sept. 2, 1940.

and maintain them there, and do all this with the assurance of being able to carry it on till the spirit of the Continental Dictators is broken, we may fall by the way, and the time needed by the United States to complete her defensive preparations may not be forthcoming. It is therefore in shipping and in the power to transport across the oceans, particularly the Atlantic Ocean, that in 1941 the crunch of the whole war will be found. If on the other hand we are able to move the necessary tonnage to and fro across salt water indefinitely, it may well be that the application of superior air-power to the German homeland and the rising anger of the German and other Nazi-gripped populations will bring the agony of civilisation to a merciful and glorious end.

But do not let us underrate the task. . . .

The moment approaches when we shall no longer be able to pay cash for shipping and other supplies. While we will do our utmost, and shrink from no proper sacrifice to make payments across the Exchange, I believe you will agree that it would be wrong in principle and mutually disadvantageous in effect if at the height of this struggle Great Britain were to be divested of all saleable assets, so that after the victory was won with our blood, civilisation saved, and the time gained for the United States to be fully armed against all eventualities, we should stand stripped to the bone. Such a course would not be in the moral or economic interests of either of our countries.[175]

At this point, Roosevelt, now having won reelection, could start to take a more direct course. He knew that he had to address not only American politicians but also the American public to help Britain and defend America against the Axis powers. He dealt with the American public first in his well-known Fireside Chat of late December:

My friends:

This is not a fireside chat on war. It is a talk on national security. . . .

---

175. Letter from Winston Churchill, Prime Minister, Great Britain, to Franklin Roosevelt, President, United States (Dec. 8, 1940).

Never before since Jamestown and Plymouth Rock has our American civilization been in such danger as now. For on September 27th, 1940—this year—by an agreement signed in Berlin, three powerful nations, two in Europe and one in Asia, joined themselves together in the threat that if the United States of America interfered with or blocked the expansion program of these three nations—a program aimed at world control—they would unite in ultimate action against the United States. . . .

Some of our people like to believe that wars in Europe and in Asia are of no concern to us. But it is a matter of most vital concern to us that European and Asiatic war-makers should not gain control of the oceans which lead to this hemisphere. . . .

If Great Britain goes down, the Axis powers will control the Continents of Europe, Asia, Africa, Austral-Asia, and the high seas. And they will be in a position to bring enormous military and naval resources against this hemisphere. It is no exaggeration to say that all of us in all the Americas would be living at the point of a gun. . . .

The British people and their allies today are conducting an active war against this unholy alliance. Our own future security is greatly dependent on the outcome of that fight. Our ability to "keep out of war" is going to be affected by that outcome. . . .

The people of Europe who are defending themselves do not ask us to do their fighting. They ask us for the implements of war, the planes, the tanks, the guns, the freighters which will enable them to fight for their liberty and for our security. . . .

I want to make it clear that it is the purpose of the nation to build now with all possible speed every machine, every arsenal, every factory that we need to manufacture our defense material. . . .

We must be the great arsenal of democracy. . . .[176]

---

176. Franklin Roosevelt, President, United States, Fireside Chat (Dec. 29, 1940).

After addressing the nation via radio, Roosevelt turned his attention to getting legislation passed to support this direction, which would take America firmly out of its post-WWI isolationism and back into an international purview. With majorities in both houses, he knew he could get the legislation through, but it was appropriate to have full support from both parties for such an important piece of legislation. To that end, he agreed to a number of amendments that ensured, for example, that U.S. Navy ships were not used in the convoys. "An Act to Promote the Defense of the United States," commonly called the Lend-Lease Act, was signed into law on March 11, 1941.[177]

The act gave the president the power to authorize the government to do the following, among other things:

(1) To manufacture in arsenals, factories, and shipyards under their jurisdiction, or otherwise procure, . . . any defense article for the government of any country whose defense the President deems vital to the defense of the United States.

(2) To sell, transfer title to, exchange, lease, lend, or otherwise dispose of, to any such government any defense article [after consulting with the military leadership]. . . .

(3) To test, inspect, prove, repair, outfit, recondition, or otherwise place in good working order, . . . any defense article. . . .[178]

Defense articles included the following:

(1) Any weapon, munitions, aircraft, vessel, or boat;

(2) Any machinery, facility, tool, material, or supply necessary for the manufacture, production, processing, repair, servicing, or operation of any article described in this subsection;

(3) Any component material or part of equipment for any article described in this subsection;

(4) Any agricultural, industrial or other commodity or article for defense.[179]

---

177. Pub. L. No. 77-11 (1941).
178. *Id.* § 3.
179. *Id.* § 2.

In addition, the act also provided that "[n]othing in this Act shall be construed to" (1) "authorize or to permit the authorization of convoying vessels by naval vessels of the United States," (2) "authorize or to permit the authorization of the entry of any American vessel into a combat area in violation of section 3 of the [N]eutrality Act of 1939," and (3) "change existing law relating to the use of the land and naval forces of the United States. . . ."[180]

LEGAL PROFILES

Oscar S. Cox was considered by many to be one of the primary drafters (along with the general counsel of the Treasury Department) of the original text of the Lend-Lease Act. Cox was born in Maine in 1906. He was in private practice in New York for several years before becoming assistant corporate counsel for taxation for the City of New York. In 1938, he took a position with the Treasury Department, until the start of the Lend-Lease program, when he became general counsel to the new Lend-Lease Administration. He also served as the fourth leader of the Office of Legal Counsel, which assisted the U.S. attorney general in writing opinions and executive orders. Cox was involved in the creation of the G.I. Bill,[181] had identified the 1892 statute for surplus munitions used prior to Lend-Lease, and served as general counsel for the Foreign Economic Administration. He was also involved in the military commissions that tried Axis leaders after the war. He returned to private practice after the war and the end of Lend-Lease and died in 1966.[182]

B. Cases

While there were no significant legal cases challenging this statute, there were any number of minor commercial cases reaching the circuit courts that dealt with questions about carrying out its details, such as whether phosphates

---

180. *Id.* §§ 5(d)–(e), 10.
181. Pub. L. No. 78-346 (1944).
182. *See Oscar Cox, Lend-Lease Aide*, N.Y. TIMES (Oct. 6, 1966).

shipped under Lend-Lease were military property or naval property, which would allow the government to pay lower rail shipping rates,[183] and whether cotton sold for use under Lend-Lease was of a lower quality than required by contract.[184]

Of particular importance, however, were one judicial case and two non-judicial opinions. The case arose from damages to vessels still owned by the U.S. government under Lend-Lease. Even more significantly, there were two major legal opinions concerning the statute: one regarding the legality of the Destroyers for Bases Agreement and the other an opinion about part of the Lend-Lease Act, commissioned, interestingly, with direction from and released under the signature of President Roosevelt himself.

1. Responsibility for Damages

United States v. Caffey[185] involved the loss of a ship and cargo in a collision with a ship delivered under Lend-Lease to the British navy. The month after the signing of the Lend-Lease Act, the British government requested a naval vessel, which the U.S. government procured from a private owner, retrofitted, and then delivered to the British Admiralty. The ship was renamed *Archer* in November 1941. Two months later, while on duty, it collided with the *Brazos*, which then sank with all of its cargo.

The district court found that the *Archer* was a "public" vessel of the United States, meaning that private owners could sue the U.S. government for damages. Because under Lend-Lease "the President had found that the defense of that country was vital to the defense of the United States," it followed that its use by the Royal Navy was use by the United States.[186] In addition, the title of the *Archer* still resided with the United States and, under the Lend-Lease Act, would ultimately have been returned to the U.S. government.

However, the government filed for a writ of prohibition or mandamus—an order for a subordinate to stop doing something the law prohibits—against the district court judge to stop him from carrying out this judgment. That issue

---

183. *See, e.g.*, United States v. Powell, 152 F.2d 228 (4th Cir. 1945).
184. *See, e.g.*, Richardson v. United States, 150 F.2d 58 (6th Cir. 1945).
185. United States v. Caffey, 141 F.2d 69 (2d Cir. 1944).
186. *Id.* at 71.

reached the Supreme Court, which remanded the case back to the circuit court for further proceedings.[187] The circuit court then determined that the key issue was who was in control at the time of the accident. Because it was the Royal Navy, this meant that the *Archer* was not a U.S. public vessel and, as such, the district court did not have jurisdiction. The government's writ of prohibition against the district court judge was granted.[188]

2. Opinion on Destroyers for Bases Agreement

Roosevelt sought a nonjudicial legal opinion from Attorney General Robert H. Jackson in August 1940 in order to provide the necessary legal support for the Destroyers for Bases Agreement, which the administration planned to formalize without congressional action.[189] In Opinion on Exchange of Over-Age Destroyers for Naval and Air Bases, Jackson identified three areas of the agreement where there were questions regarding the appropriate constitutional and statutory authority:

> First. May such an acquisition be concluded by the President under an executive agreement or must it be negotiated as a treaty subject to ratification by the Senate?

> Second. Does authority exist in the President to alienate the title to such ships and obsolescent materials, and if so, on what conditions?

> Third. Do the statutes of the United States limit the right to deliver the so-called mosquito boats now under construction or the over-age destroyers by reason of the belligerent status of Great Britain?[190]

On the first question, Jackson said that the answer must look to two powers of the president given to the executive branch by the Constitution: commander in chief of the military and control over foreign relations. As commander in

---

187. *Ex parte* United States, 319 U.S. 730 (1943).

188. *Caffey*, 141 F.2d at 72.

189. Opinion on Exchange of Over-Age Destroyers for Naval and Air Bases, Op. Att'y Gen. (Aug. 27, 1940).

190. *Id.*

chief, the president has the responsibility to provide adequate air and naval bases without risking any delay. In addition, the power of president in the field of foreign relations—"the very delicate, plenary, and exclusive power"—need not rely on statutory authority, although Congress should be involved whenever possible and especially when foreign agreements involve "commitments as to the future."[191] Because this agreement created no obligation, Jackson said that the Senate was not required to ratify. He cited the method of the Louisiana Purchase, where President Thomas Jefferson decided to buy it and Congress later approved the funds and the Senate approved a treaty. Closer to the current situation, however, Jackson cited a purchase made in 1850 by then Secretary of State Daniel Webster—a reef for a lighthouse—that was subsequently funded by Congress. He also felt that there was statutory authority in government purchases of diplomatic sites and in the recent agreement to buy coaling and naval stations in Cuba. The executive agreement was deemed to be sufficient on this question.

On the second question, Jackson found support in two acts of Congress and in a Supreme Court decision. An 1883 statute allowed that "no vessel of the Navy shall hereafter be sold in any other manner than herein provided, or for less than such appraised value, unless the President of the United States shall otherwise direct in writing."[192] This was supported by a 1922 Supreme Court decision holding that "the power of the President to direct a departure from the statute is not confined to a sale for less than the appraised value but extends to the manner of the sale."[193] He did find a possible limitation in a recent statute regarding military and naval shipbuilding requiring that U.S.-owned weapons, ships, aircraft, munitions, supplies, or equipment first be certified by the leaders of the army or navy as "not essential to the defense of the United States" before any transfers, exchanges, sales, or disposals could take place. [194] However, if the chief of naval operations judged that the exchange of the destroyers in question for the naval and air bases "will strengthen rather than impair the total defense of the United States,"[195] the president did have the power to transfer title and possession of the destroyers.

---

191. *Id.*
192. Pub. L. No. 47, ch. 141 (1883).
193. Levinson v. United States, 258 U.S. 198 (1922).
194. Pub. L. No. 76-671 (1940).
195. Opinion on Exchange of Over-Age Destroyers for Naval and Air Bases, *supra note* 191.

On the third question, Jackson looked first to a WWI neutrality statute that prohibited the United States from sending out vessels of war to a belligerent nation knowing that they would be used in conflict.[196] Here, he dug deep into an analysis of international law that differentiated the "selling [of] armed vessels to belligerents [from] building them to order," the latter of which is considered a violation of neutrality.[197] As the destroyers were built originally for the U.S. Navy and not any belligerent nation, their sale to Britain was permissible under this statute and not a violation of neutrality (but the same was not true for the mosquito boats).

3. Opinion on Lend-Lease Provision

As mentioned, Roosevelt had to accept a number of revisions to the original Lend-Lease bill to get it approved by Congress. Fearing the increasing power of the president, Congress had added the following provision in the final language of the act:

> After June 30, 1943, or after the passage of a concurrent resolution by the two Houses before June 30, 1943, which declares that the powers conferred by or pursuant to subsection (a) are no longer necessary to promote the defense of the United States, neither the President nor the head of any department or agency shall exercise any of the powers conferred by or pursuant to subsection (a). . . .[198]

Jackson, in a law review article many years later, explained that Roosevelt was concerned that this provision could give Congress the means to circumvent the president's veto power.[199] Instead of following the normal procedure of passing repealing legislation that would then itself be subject to presidential veto, Congress would be allowed, under this provision, to repeal the powers under Lend-Lease by resolution without being subject to a possible veto. Drafted initially by a member of the attorney general's office, a memo to Jackson detailed Roosevelt's reasons for believing the offending provision to be

196. Pub. L. No. 65-24 (1917).
197. Opinion on Exchange of Over-Age Destroyers for Naval and Air Bases, *supra note* 191.
198. Pub. L. No. 77-11, § 3(c) (1941).
199. Robert H. Jackson, *A Presidential Legal Opinion*, 66 HARV. L. REV. 1353 (June 1953).

unconstitutional.[200] Signed by Roosevelt, an attorney himself, it stated in pertinent part:

> On March 11, 1941, I attached my approval to the bill . . . entitled "An Act to Promote the Defense of the United States." The bill was an outstanding measure which sought to meet a momentous emergency of great magnitude in world affairs. In view of this impelling consideration, I felt constrained to sign the measure, in spite of the fact that it contained a provision which, in my opinion, is clearly unconstitutional. I have reference to the clause of Section 3 *(c)* of the Act. . . . In effect, this provision is an attempt by Congress to authorize a repeal by means of a concurrent resolution of the two Houses, of certain provisions of an Act of Congress. The Constitution of the United States, Article I, Section 7, prescribes the mode in which laws shall be enacted. It provides that "Every bill which shall have passed the House of Representatives and the Senate, shall, before it become a law, be presented to the President of the United States; if he approves he shall sign it, but if not he shall return it, with his objections to that House in which it shall have originated." It is thereupon provided that if after reconsideration two-thirds of each House shall agree to pass the bill, it shall become law. The Constitution contains no provision whereby the Congress may legislate by concurrent resolution without the approval of the President. The only instance in which a bill may become law without the approval of the President is when the President vetoes a bill and it is then repassed by two-thirds vote in each House. It is too clear for argument that action repealing an existing Act itself constitutes an Act of Congress and, therefore, is subject to the foregoing requirements. A repeal of existing provisions of law, in whole or in part, therefore, may not be accomplished by a concurrent resolution of the two Houses. In order that I may be on record as indicating my opinion that the foregoing provision of the so-called Lend-Lease Act is unconstitutional, and in order that my approval of the bill, due to the existing exigencies of the world situation, may not be construed as a tacit acquiescence in any contrary view, I am requesting

---

200. Memorandum from Franklin Roosevelt, President, United States, to Robert Jackson, Attorney General, United States (Apr. 7, 1941).

you to place this memorandum in the official files of the Department of Justice. I am desirous of having this done for the further reason that I should not wish my action in approving the bill which includes this invalid clause, to be used as a precedent for my future legislation comprising provisions of a similar nature. In conclusion, I may refer to the following pertinent remarks of President Andrew Jackson:

"I deem it an imperative duty to maintain the supremacy of that sacred instrument (the Constitution) and the immunities of the Department entrusted to my care."[201]

LEGAL PROFILES

Robert H. Jackson was the attorney general in early 1941 and also soon to become a Supreme Court justice. He was born in Pennsylvania in 1892 but began his law practice in New York, where he passed the bar without having received his law school degree. He remained in private practice until joining the federal government in a series of legal positions and was named the U.S. solicitor general in 1938. He was appointed to the attorney general position in 1940, and in 1941 to the U.S. Supreme Court, where he served until 1954. While he was on the Court, he was appointed to be the chief U.S. counsel for the prosecution of war criminals at the Nuremberg Trials (see Chapter 6) from 1945 to 1946. He died while still on the Court in 1954.[202]

C. Subsequent Events

Having received funding authorization for Lend-Lease in October 1941, Roosevelt issued Executive Order No. 8926 later that month to establish the

---

201. *Id.*
202. *See Jackson, Robert Houghwout*, Fed. Judicial Ctr., Biographical Directory of Federal Judges.

Office of Lend-Lease Administration.[203] The administrator was charged with carrying out the powers provided under the act "with respect to any Nation whose defense the President shall have found to be vital to the defense of the United States." The State Department was charged with negotiating the master agreements with each such country. The order also revoked a prior order that had set up a reporting office just after the passage of the Lend-Lease Act.[204]

The Lend-Lease program ran until 1945 and provided aid to Britain, France, Russia, and China, totaling an estimated $50 billion in 1945 dollars, with the majority going to Britain. As part of Reverse Lend-Lease—whereby Britain, Australia, New Zealand, India, France, etc., provided goods and services back to America, totaling an estimated $8 billion in products, services, and technology—the United States signed an initial master agreement in 1942 with Great Britain,[205] as it would with all countries receiving such aid. This agreement stipulated that America expected Britain to return

> at the end of the present emergency . . . such defense articles transferred under this Agreement as shall not have been destroyed, lost or consumed and as shall be determined by the President to be useful in the defense of the United States of America or of the Western Hemisphere or to be otherwise of use to the United States of America.[206]

This return of what was still usable and desirable included "all property, services, information, facilities, or other benefits or considerations" that Britain (or its dominions) could provide back to the United States.[207]

Any such repayments by Britain were "not to burden commerce between the two countries." However, as a potential lever to increase postwar U.S. trade within the British Empire by eliminating the "imperial preference" from inside the commonwealth system, the agreement stipulated "agreed action" by both parties leading to the "elimination of all forms of discriminatory treatment

---

203. Exec. Order No. 8926, Establishing the Office of Lend-Lease Administration (Oct. 28, 1941).
204. Exec. Order No. 8751, Establishing the Division of Defense Aid Reports (May 2, 1941).
205. Preliminary Agreement Between the United States and the United Kingdom, Feb. 23, 1942.
206. *Id.*
207. *Id.*

in international commerce, and to the reduction of tariffs and other trade barriers."[208]

LEGAL PROFILES

Cordell Hull was the U.S. secretary of state responsible for negotiating the master agreements with recipient nations under Lend-Lease, as well as the secretary of state during almost all of Roosevelt's administration. Born in Tennessee in 1871, Hull graduated from Cumberland School of Law and was admitted to the bar in 1891. He started his political career at the age of twenty-two in the Tennessee legislature. After fighting in the Spanish-American War, he served as a judge in Tennessee for several years before being elected to the U.S. House of Representatives in 1907, where he served almost continuously until 1931. From there, he was elected to the U.S. Senate. When FDR was elected president, he asked Hull to become secretary of state. He held this position for eleven years, concurrent with Roosevelt's long tenure. He is credited with being the force behind the creation of the United Nations, for which he received the Nobel Peace Prize in 1945. He died in 1955.[209]

Dean Acheson was the primary drafter of the master agreement with Britain. He was born in Connecticut in 1893 and started his legal practice in Washington, D.C. He was appointed Under Secretary of the Treasury in 1933 but soon returned to legal practice. In 1940, he was appointed undersecretary of state, a position he held until he was appointed secretary of state in 1949. He was involved in much of the creation of the postwar world, including the Bretton Woods Conference (birthplace of the International Monetary Fund (IMF), World Bank, and the General Agreement on Tariffs and Trade–World Trade Organization (GATT-WTO)); the Marshall Plan to aid Europe; the creation of the

---

208. *Id.*
209. *See Hull, Cordell*, Biographical Directory of the United States Congress.

North Atlantic Treaty Organization (NATO); and the U.S. approach to the Cold War (the Truman Doctrine of containment, developed with George Kennan). With the end of the Truman administration in 1953, he left government to return to private practice. However, he was never far from the White House, serving as an adviser to all of the succeeding presidents. He received a Pulitzer Prize for his memoir *Present at the Creation: My Years in the State Department.* He died in 1971.[210]

2.6 EXPORT CONTROLS

A. Statutes

Besides addressing what could be done for possible allies, steps also had to be taken in the United States to keep possible enemies from being aided. And it was also imperative that the United States' military infrastructure and capabilities be strengthened. Moving from a position of international isolation to one of engagement and possibly war, the production capabilities of the United States needed to be used to create the tools of war to defend the country. To this end, An Act to Expedite the Strengthening of the National Defense was passed in 1940 to remove some of the limitations on military production capabilities.[211]

There were several distinct parts of this bill created "to expedite the building up of the national defense."[212] It gave the secretary of war the authorization to construct, rehabilitate or convert, and operate and maintain plants, buildings, facilities, etc., for the purpose of developing, manufacturing, maintaining, and storing "military equipment, munitions, and supplies, and for shelter."[213] It also provided for the development, purchase, manufacture, shipment, maintenance, and storage of same, including exchanging obsolete or surplus materials for other desired materials. Limitations on airplanes and pilots and assignments of officers and enlisted men were suspended.

---

210. *See Dean Acheson Dies on Farm at 78*, N.Y. TIMES (Oct. 13, 1971).
211. Pub. L. No. 76-703 (1940).
212. *Id.*
213. *Id.*

The second part of the bill, deemed the Export Control Act, gave the president authorization to provide for "emergencies affecting the national security and defense" and to procure strategic and critical materials.[214] Under the act, he could also prohibit or curtail by proclamation the exportation of military equipment, munitions, component parts, machinery, tools, materials, or supplies necessary for the manufacture, servicing, or operation of such.

Roosevelt immediately began to use this power through a series of executive orders and proclamations. On the same day that this law was signed, he issued a proclamation with a lengthy list of materials that would be subject to licensing. He first set up the position of Administrator of Export Control and then released a list of goods not to be exported, which included arms, ammunition, and implements of war; many materials and products from aluminum to industrial diamonds, mercury to rubber, and platinum to tungsten; certain chemicals; aircraft parts; optical elements for fire control instruments; aircraft instruments; and metal-working machine tools.[215]

By additional proclamations, this list grew to contain many more items, including petroleum products, tetraethyl lead, and steel scrap;[216] equipment used for the production of aviation motor fuel or tetraethyl lead and plans or specifications for the design of aircraft or aircraft engines;[217] iron and steel scrap;[218] iron and steel;[219] bromine, ethylene, plastics molding machines, measuring machines, gauges, testing machines, hydraulic pumps, and equipment for production of aviation lubrication;[220] copper, brass, bronze, nickel, zinc, and potash;[221] well and refining machinery, radium, and uranium;[222] belladonna, atropine, and sole and belting leather;[223] beryllium, graphite electrodes, and pilot trainers;[224] cadmium, glycerin, pine oil, and titanium;[225] jute, lead,

---

214. *Id.* § 5.
215. Exec. Proclamation No. 2413, Prohibiting Unlicensed Export of War Materials and Strategic Raw Products (July 2, 1940).
216. Exec. Proclamation No. 2417 (July 26, 1940).
217. Exec. Proclamation No. 2423 (Sept. 12, 1940).
218. Exec. Proclamation No. 2428 (Sept. 30, 1940).
219. Exec. Proclamation No. 2449 (Dec. 10, 1940).
220. Exec. Proclamation No. 2451 (Dec. 20, 1940).
221. Exec. Proclamation No. 2453 (Jan. 10, 1941).
222. Exec. Proclamation No. 2456 (Feb. 4, 1941).
223. Exec. Proclamation No. 2460 (Feb. 25, 1941).
224. Exec. Proclamation No. 2461 (Feb. 25, 1941).
225. Exec. Proclamation No. 2463 (Mar. 4, 1941).

borax, and phosphates;[226] machinery;[227] caffeine;[228] and any design, photograph, or document with a plan, specification, or technical information that could be used with the production or manufacture of articles or materials whose exporting was prohibited or curtailed.[229] Many of these items were designed to restrict the Japanese aggressions in Asia (see Chapter 7). Additional items continued to be added to the list before the war.

The Office of the Administrator of Export Control was initially headed up by a military officer, but the office was transferred to the Economic Defense Board in September 1941.[230] The Economic Defense Board, created by executive order in late July 1941,[231] was set up to address international economic activities in the interest of national defense, including those relating to

> exports, imports, the acquisition and disposition of materials and commodities from foreign countries including preclusive buying, transactions in foreign exchange and foreign-owned or foreign-controlled property, international investments and extensions of credit, shipping and transportation of goods among countries, the international aspects of patents, international communications pertaining to commerce, and other foreign economic matters.[232]

LEGAL PROFILES

Henry L. Stimson was the secretary of war who was given the responsibility to initiate this buildup of military strength and capability. He was born in Massachusetts in 1867 and started his legal practice in New York. He was appointed U.S. attorney in 1906 and U.S. secretary of war in 1911 under the Republican Taft administration. Even at his advanced

---

226. Exec. Proclamation No. 2464 (Mar. 4, 1941).
227. Exec. Proclamation No. 2475 (Apr. 14, 1941).
228. Exec. Proclamation No. 2476 (Apr. 14, 1941).
229. Exec. Proclamation No. 2465 (Mar. 4, 1941).
230. Exec. Order No. 8900, Amending the Executive Order Establishing the Economic Defense Board (Sept. 15, 1941).
231. Exec. Order No. 8839, Establishing the Economic Defense Board (July 30, 1941).
232. *Id.*

age, he served in Europe during WWI. He was appointed governor general of the Philippines in 1927 and then U.S. secretary of state in 1929. With the outbreak of war again in Europe, Roosevelt asked Stimson to be his secretary of war in 1940, at the age of seventy-three. He held this position throughout the war, where he was involved in every major military decision. He retired after the end of the war and died in 1950.[233]

B. Cases

The cases that arose from this act during the war unsurprisingly involved the export of items prohibited by the administration. What is surprising is that there were not more cases given the large number of items on the list and the dynamic nature of the act's contents, as well as the restrictions placed on those involved in international commerce and nationals who could no longer acquire the materials from America. The first case described below involved defendants challenging the constitutionality of the statute, and the second case involved defendants challenging the constitutionality of the law as it was subsequently revised.

1. Challenging the Statute

In *United States v. Rosenberg* in 1942, the seven defendants were charged in federal district court with conspiring to violate the statute by exporting platinum to Europe, via vessels, steamships, and Pan American Clipper aircraft between the United States and Portugal.[234] The defendants' response included demurrers (challenges to a plaintiff's legal basis for a suit) that

- the statute is unconstitutional in that Congress has unlawfully and illegally delegated its legislative powers to the president of the United States;
- the executive proclamation made on July 2, 1940, is null and void due to indefiniteness and uncertainty; and
- the indictment does not state a crime in that the act contains no provision making it illegal to conspire to violate a proclamation or regulation,

---

233. *See Henry L. Stimson Dies at 83 at His Home on Long Island*, N.Y. TIMES (Oct. 21, 1950).
234. United States v. Rosenberg, 47 F. Supp. 406 (E.D.N.Y. 1942).

the act does not extend beyond June 30, 1942, and the indictment does not set forth sufficient facts to constitute a conspiracy.

The first point was based upon two Supreme Court decisions overturning part of the New Deal, *L. A. Schechter Poultry Corp. v. United States*[235] and *United States v. Butler*,[236] which addressed the National Industrial Recovery Act and the Agricultural Adjustment Act, respectively. The court differentiated those acts in two ways: (1) those two acts turned "the making of the plan, establishment of standards" over to the president, while the Export Control Act established the plan and standards, leaving only the list of commodities and timing to be determined by the president; and (2) those two acts dealt with the president's powers for "internal control" as opposed to his powers in foreign relations.[237] The court referred to *United States v. Curtiss-Wright Export Corp.* as being on point: in that case, a congressional resolution decreed that the president could proclaim that if it would contribute to the peace between certain combatants, the president could limit weapons sales to those combatants in the United States.[238] The court also stated that the description of platinum clearly included all metals and alloys; and as Congress eventually extended the act for an additional two years, it was still in effect. As such, each of the demurrers was overruled.

The appeals court supported both the district court's analysis of the powers of the president and the finding that the statute was properly in effect at the date of the trial.[239] Judge Harrie B. Chase, in a concurring opinion, stated that the president's role in foreign affairs was sufficient for the delegation of powers given him under the statute. After a discussion on whether there was one conspiracy or three (the shipments aboard the vessels, the shipments aboard the airplanes, and an aborted attempt to sell platinum in Canada), the court affirmed the lower court's decision, and the Supreme Court denied a petition for a writ of certiorari.[240]

---

235. L. A. Schechter Poultry Corp. v. United States, 295 U.S. 495 (1935).
236. United States v. Butler, 297 U.S. 1 (1936).
237. *Rosenberg*, 47 F. Supp. at 408.
238. United States v. Curtiss-Wright Export Corp., 299 U.S. 304 (1936).
239. United States v. Rosenberg, 150 F.2d 788 (2d Cir. 1945).
240. United States v. Rosenberg, 66 S. Ct. 90 (1945).

LEGAL PROFILES

Harrie B. Chase issued the brief concurring opinion in *Rosenberg*. He was born in Vermont in 1889 and entered private practice in the state. He then took a role as a state's attorney in 1919. He served on the Vermont Superior Court for eight years before joining the Vermont Supreme Court in 1927 at age thirty-eight, the youngest judge ever appointed to that court. From there, he was nominated by the outgoing President Calvin Coolidge to a seat on the U.S. Court of Appeals for the Second Circuit in 1929, again the youngest such appointee. He served on this bench for forty years, including a stint as chief judge. His cases included those of Alger Hiss and the disbarment of a Communist Party lawyer.[241] He died in 1969.[242]

2. Challenging the Revised Statute

The revised statute of 1942, besides extending the period of applicability, authorized the president to "prohibit or curtail the exportation of any articles, technical data, materials or supplies, except under such rules and regulations as he shall prescribe."[243] The five defendants in *United States v. Bareno* were accused of trying to ship platinum outside the country to Spain without a license.[244] They demurred that this new provision, allowing the export restriction on "anything" even if unrelated to the war effort, delegates to the president an "unlimited power" in violation of the Constitution.[245]

The court looked to the recent *Opp Cotton Mills, Inc. v. Administrator of the Wage & Hour Division of the Department of Labor* Supreme Court decision for the appropriate test of how much power Congress can delegate to the

---

241. *See Harrie Chase, 80, on Appeals Court*, N.Y. TIMES (Nov. 18, 1969).
242. *See Chase, Harrie Brigham*, FED. JUDICIAL CTR., BIOGRAPHICAL DIRECTORY OF FEDERAL JUDGES.
243. Pub. L. No. 77-638 (1942).
244. United States v. Bareno, 50 F. Supp. 520 (D. Md. 1943).
245. *Id.* at 523.

president.[246] If the standards and procedures are set by legislation and sufficient records are kept to confirm adherence to those standards, then "there is no failure of performance of the legislative function," the *Bareno* court ruled.[247] While acknowledging that "the delegation of power to the President under the Act now before us is broader than any heretofore given to a President by Congress," the court noted that "its unlimited character does not, per se, render the delegation invalid."[248] The court pointed to the "plenary and exclusive" powers in international relations that the Constitution bestows upon the president.[249] It then stated that "If . . . broad authority may be delegated to the President as a necessary incident to the exercise of his constitutional authority with respect to international relations when our country is itself at peace, a fortiori must the same principle apply when our country is at war."[250] The court overruled the demurrer.

After failing to win that case, the defendants pleaded guilty and were appropriately fined. Then one, Juan Tomas Bareno, legally attempted to recover the platinum, which was seized first by the arresting FBI agents and eventually turned over to the collector of customs. The district court directed that the platinum should be returned to Bareno because the government had failed to timely apply for a warrant of detention to retain the seized goods. Under the Espionage Act, goods can be seized and forfeited to the United States if the property appears to have been "about to be so unlawfully exported."[251] Nevertheless, if the Espionage Act's requirements are not strictly followed, defendants can get the goods back even if those goods are being held as evidence against them.

The appeals court, however, looked differently at the Espionage Act and the meaning of the term *seizure*.[252] The court ruled that the legal seizure for purposes of the act took place not when the FBI physically seized the platinum but when it was transferred from the FBI to the collector of customs, who, unlike the FBI agents, was charged with initiating the appropriate condemna-

---

246. Opp Cotton Mills, Inc. v. Administrator of the Wage & Hour Div. of the Dep't of Labor, 312 U.S. 126 (1941).
247. *Bareno*, 50 F. Supp. at 523.
248. *Id.* at 525.
249. *Id.* at 524.
250. *Id.* at 525.
251. United States v. 21 Pounds, 8 Ounces, of Platinum, 147 F.2d 78 (4th Cir. 1945).
252. *Id.*

tion proceedings against the goods. The collector of customs had timely begun the condemnation proceedings. The seizure for criminal proceedings was not the same as the seizure for purposes of forfeiture, the court noted. The court reiterated that "statutes to prevent frauds upon the revenue are . . . not to be construed, like penal laws generally, strictly in favor of the defendant; but they are to be fairly and reasonably construed, so as to carry out the intention of the legislature."[253] The appeals court reversed and remanded, and Bareno did not get his platinum back.

C. Subsequent Events

This act of Congress has been rewritten and renewed a number of times since 1940, but the essential idea of the need for export controls remains. Besides the revisions introduced during the war as previously discussed, a new act was created in 1949, the Export Control Act,[254] which was repeatedly renewed through a variety of revisions and amendments until the creation of the Export Administration Act in 1969.[255] The Export Administration Act was rewritten in 1979[256] and revised in 1985[257] and remains to this day a principal mechanism for the control of exports. In addition, the Arms Export Control Act was passed in 1968 to address military items for export.[258]

The Export Control Act of 1949 gave the president the ability to restrict the export of articles, materials, supplies, or technical data (except agricultural commodities in excess of domestic requirements), based on a policy with three prongs:

- Protecting the domestic economy from the excessive drain of scarce materials and to reduce the inflationary impact of abnormal foreign demand
- Furthering the foreign policy of the United States and to aid in fulfilling its international responsibilities
- Exercising the necessary vigilance over exports from the standpoint of their significance to the national security

---

253. *Id.* at 83.
254. Pub. L. No. 81-11 (1949).
255. Pub. L. No. 91-184 (1969).
256. Pub. L. No. 96-72 (1979).
257. Pub. L. No. 99-64 (1985).
258. Pub. L. No. 94-329 (1976).

D. Modern Applicability

The export control system has become very complex with all of the materials under regulation. The current U.S. export control regime for dual-use (civilian and military) goods and technology is controlled by the Export Administration Act (run by the Commerce Department under the Export Administration Regulations (EAR)) and the International Emergency Economic Powers Act (which provides a mechanism to renew the regulations under the now-expired Export Administration Act, by declaring their expiration to be an emergency).[259] The EAR has ten categories on its Commerce Control List: nuclear materials, facilities, and equipment; materials, organisms, microorganisms, and toxins; materials processing; electronics; computers; telecommunications and information security; lasers and sensors; navigation and avionics; marine (systems, equipment, materials, and software); and propulsion systems, space vehicles, and related equipment.

The Arms Export Control Act (run by the Department of State) uses the International Traffic in Arms Regulations policy to allow for the licensed sale of defense items and services designed primarily for military use (as listed on the U.S. Munitions List) to friendly nations for legitimate self-defense purposes. Nuclear goods and technologies are controlled by the Atomic Energy Act[260] (under the Nuclear Regulatory Commission controls) and the Nuclear Non-Proliferation Act,[261] as well as subject to compliance with several multilateral nonproliferation agreements. Trade sanctions are also part of export controls.

2.7 DECLARATION OF WAR

A. Statutes

When war finally came to the United States with the Japanese attack on Pearl Harbor and numerous other U.S. facilities in the Pacific on December 7, 1941, the government had to legally declare that a state of war existed between the United States and the Empire of Japan. Within days of this U.S. declaration

---

259. Pub. L. No. 95-223 (1977).
260. Pub. L. No. 83-703 (1954).
261. Pub. L. No. 95-242 (1978).

of war, the other major Axis powers, Germany and Italy, declared war on the United States. As such, there was not just one but several declarations of war that were required. As obvious as it may seem to declare what is evident, there were numerous legal implications of these declarations of war.

In response to the attacks on U.S. military installations in the Pacific, President Roosevelt addressed both Congress and the nation the next day. In one of the most famous speeches given by an American politician, Roosevelt said in part:

Yesterday, December 7, 1941—a date which will live in infamy—the United States of America was suddenly and deliberately attacked by naval and air forces of the Empire of Japan.

The United States was at peace with that nation, and, at the solicitation of Japan, was still in conversation with its government and its emperor looking toward the maintenance of peace in the Pacific. . . . [T]he Japanese government has deliberately sought to deceive the United States by false statements and expressions of hope for continued peace. . . .

The attack yesterday on the Hawaiian Islands has caused severe damage to American naval and military forces. I regret to tell you that very many American lives have been lost. . . .

The Japanese government also launched an attack against Malaya . . . Hong Kong . . . Guam . . . the Philippine Islands . . . Wake Island . . . Midway Island. . . .

No matter how long it may take us to overcome this premeditated invasion, the American people, in their righteous might, will win through to absolute victory...

Hostilities exist. There is no blinking at the fact that our people, our territory and our interests are in grave danger. With confidence in our armed forces, with the unbounding determination of our people, we will gain the inevitable triumph, so help us God.

I ask that the Congress declare that since the unprovoked and dastardly attack by Japan on Sunday, December 7, 1941, a state of war has existed between the United States and the Japanese Empire.[262]

The groundswell of patriotism in response to this speech and the events leading up to it were demonstrated when Congress shortly thereafter, in a joint resolution, used their constitutional powers to declare war as follows:

Whereas the Imperial Government of Japan has committed unprovoked acts of war against the Government and the people of the United States of America: Therefore be it Resolved by the Senate and House of Representatives of the United States of America in Congress assembled, That the state of war between the United States and the Imperial Government of Japan which has thus been thrust upon the United States is hereby formally declared; and the President is hereby authorized and directed to employ the entire naval and military forces of the United States and the resources of the Government to carry on war against the Imperial Government of Japan; and, to bring the conflict to a successful termination, all of the resources of the country are hereby pledged by the Congress of the United States.

Approved, December 8, 1941, 4:10 p. m., E.S.T.[263]

This resolution passed both houses with only a single dissenting vote. Interestingly, this belonged to Representative Jeannette Rankin, a Republican and the first woman elected to the U.S. Congress, who had similarly cast a dissenting vote against entry into WWI twenty-four years before and later stated, "As a woman I can't go to war, and I refuse to send anyone else."[264]

Besides its physical attacks on U.S. military installations, Japan had the previous day declared war on the United States. The Axis powers of the Tripartite Pact soon all declared war on the United States, so Congress formally declared

---

262. Presidential Address to Congress, Franklin D. Roosevelt, Dec. 8, 1941.
263. Pub. L. No. 77-328 (1941).
264. Representative Jeannette Rankin of Montana, Dec. 11, 1941.

war on Germany[265] and Italy[266] (followed by Bulgaria, Romania, and Hungary in June 1942, six months after they had declared war on the United States).

LEGAL PROFILES

Everett Dirksen was the U.S. House member who convinced Representative Rankin to vote "present" instead of "no" during the vote to declare war on Japan.[267] He was born in Illinois in 1896 and was attending law school when WWI broke out, at which point he enlisted in the U.S. Army. He won his first term as a U.S. representative in 1932 and continued in the House for sixteen years, until health issues forced his resignation. During that time, he was purportedly the person who added—while the majority of the House Democrats were attending a luncheon—the clause to Lend-Lease that Roosevelt found unconstitutional (see earlier subsection, "Opinion on Lend-Lease Provision").[268] In 1936, he was admitted to the bar and in 1950 was elected to the U.S. Senate, where he served for eighteen more years, the last ten years as the Senate minority leader. He was influential in getting the Civil Rights Act of 1964 out of filibuster and through the Senate for eventual passage. He died in office in 1969.[269]

B. Cases

A declaration of war impacts a number of what might otherwise be ordinary situations and transactions. The six cases highlighted here each involved an issue of particular interest: (1) the implications of an undeclared state of war, (2) the legality of a selective service system without a declared state of war, (3) the

---

265. Pub. L. No. 77-331 (1941).
266. Pub. L. No. 77-333 (1941).
267. Office of the Clerk, U.S. House of Representatives, Historical Highlights: The House Declaration of War Against the Axis Powers (Dec. 11, 1941).
268. *The Congress: 260-to-165,* TIME (Feb. 17, 1941).
269. *See Dirksen, Everett McKinley,* Biographical Directory of the United States Congress.

seizure of a previously neutral merchant vessel belonging to what became an enemy alien, (4) what happens to contracts between parties who are citizens of countries that subsequently go to war, (5) payment of life insurance proceeds for a sailor killed at Pearl Harbor, and (6) the rights of friendly enemy aliens.

1. Undeclared State of War

In 1941, in *Verano v. De Angelis Coal Co.*, Verano filed suit against the De Angelis Coal Company for damages suffered as a miner in the defendant's mines.[270] The plaintiff was an Italian national, and the defendant asked for a dismissal or stay of the action due to the inability of an enemy alien to use the courts of the United States as a plaintiff. This was based on the presumption that there was an undeclared state of war between the United States and Italy in November 1941. The court pointed out that a state of war could exist without a formal declaration of war, based on a number of precedents, but the requirement was a determination of such by the government. The court reviewed several of the recently passed statutes discussed in this chapter, such as the Alien Registration Act, the Selective Training and Service Act, and the Lend-Lease Act, and termed these as "defensive" and not directed at Italy.[271] Verano was therefore allowed to proceed with his suit.

2. Draft Without Declared State of War

In *United States v. Lambert*, Lambert was convicted in district court of failing to register for the draft, although his failure to register occurred before the war had been declared.[272] The argument put forward on appeal was that although the Selective Draft Law Cases of WWI had settled the constitutional issue of whether Congress had the power to institute a draft, what was not settled was whether there must be a declared state of war as there had been when those cases were decided.

The appeals court, quoting from Alexander Hamilton in *The Federalist*, noted that "if the presence of any enemy within our territories must be awaited before the legal warrant for self-protective measures was received 'we

---

270. Verano v. De Angelis Coal Co., 41 F. Supp. 954 (M.D. Penn. 1941).
271. *Id.* at 955.
272. United States v. Lambert, 123 F.2d 395 (3d Cir. 1941).

must receive the blow before we could even prepare to return it'"[273] and that the Constitution did not restrict the draft to times when there was a declared state of war. The court then turned to very recent events—the appeals trial occurred just after the declarations of war in December 1941—and affirmed the finding of the district court, stating, "Instances where a nation at peace has found an invader within its gates without warning are fresh in the minds of all."[274]

LEGAL PROFILES

Albert B. Maris was one of the court of appeals judges who decided the *Lambert* case. He was born in Pennsylvania in 1893 and joined the army in WWI immediately after law school. He then spent a number of years in private practice and as a borough auditor and councilman. He also found time to receive an engineering degree. He was appointed to a federal district court position in 1936, which was followed two years later by appointment to the U.S. Court of Appeals for the Third Circuit. He served on this court for more than fifty years, until his death. He also taught law at Temple University and was instrumental in the revisions of the federal criminal and judicial codes. He wrote the appeals court opinion in *Minersville School District v. Gobitis*[275] (see Chapter 4) and helped write the judicial code and laws for U.S. island territories such as Guam and the Virgin Islands. He died in 1989.[276]

Herbert F. Goodrich was the author of the *Lambert* opinion. He was born in Minnesota in 1889. He spent much of his career in legal education, holding positions as a lecturer, professor, and dean of several law schools in Iowa, Pennsylvania, and Michigan, starting in 1914. He con-

---

273. Alexander Hamilton, The Federalist XXIV (1787).

274. *Lambert*, 123 F.2d at 396.

275. Minersville Sch. Dist. v. Gobitis, 310 U.S. 586 (1940).

276. *See Maris, Albert Branson*, Fed. Judicial Ctr., Biographical Directory of Federal Judges.

tinued to lecture throughout his judicial career.[277] He was appointed by President Roosevelt to the Third Circuit to fill a vacancy created by Francis Biddle, who would eventually become the U.S. attorney general under Roosevelt. Goodrich served on the federal appeals bench for twenty-two years and was involved in the U.S. Bethlehem Steel strike case (see Chapter 3). He also chaired the drafting committee for the original version of the Uniform Commercial Code. He died in 1962.[278]

3. Seizure of Neutral Vessel Before Declaration of War

In *Villarperosa*, the U.S. Maritime Commission seized a ship belonging to an Italian company in October 1941.[279] By statute, the commission can "purchase, charter or requisition the use of, or take over the title to, or the possession of . . . any foreign merchant vessel which is lying idle in waters within the jurisdiction of the United States" as necessary for the national defense.[280] The legal action came after the vessel was sabotaged by the crew, with the prior knowledge and assumed consent of its owners, so that it would not fall into the hands of the United States and so be subject to forfeiture under the Espionage Act. More than two dozen similar acts of sabotage had occurred on German and Italian owned ships situated in U.S. waters. But between the seizing of the boat and the court decision, war was declared against Italy, which meant that the owner of the vessel, now being an enemy alien, was not eligible for compensation for use of the vessel during the war or able to pursue such.

4. Contracts and Declarations of War

In *Strauss v. Schweizerische Kreditanstalt*, a foreign plaintiff, Strauss, sued a foreign financial institution for the return of a deposit placed there for a contract to ship goods to New York over the succeeding ten years.[281] Although the federal court eventually held that there was no federal question and remanded the case

---

277. *See Judge Goodrich of U.S. Bench Dies*, N.Y. TIMES (June 26, 1962).
278. *See Goodrich, Herbert Funk*, FED. JUDICIAL CTR., BIOGRAPHICAL DIRECTORY OF FEDERAL JUDGES.
279. *The Villarperosa*, 43 F. Supp. 140 (E.D.N.Y. 1942).
280. Pub. L. No. 101-77 (1941).
281. Strauss v. Schweizerische Kreditanstalt, 45 F. Supp. 449 (S.D.N.Y. 1942).

back to the state court, it elucidated several rules on what happens to contracts upon the start of a war. Quoting from Williston and English and U.S. case precedent, the court stated thus:

> The effect of war upon an existing contract between belligerents will vary with the nature of the obligation that is yet to be fulfilled. If the contract has been fully executed by the enemy before the outbreak of hostilities, if all that is left is a unilateral obligation for the payment of a debt, the obligation is suspended. . . . The citizen must pay his debt when the war is at an end. On the other hand, if the contract is still executory at the beginning of the war, if there are mutual obligations that are yet to be fulfilled, the contract will be terminated when the essential purpose of the parties would be thwarted by delay, or the business efficacy or value of their bargain materially impaired.[282]

5. Life Insurance Proceeds Before Declaration of War

In *Savage v. Sun Life Assurance Co. of Canada* in 1944, Savage sued the Sun Life Assurance Company to compel it to pay out additional proceeds on a life insurance policy for "accidental death by external and violent means" suffered by the insured as a member of the U.S. Navy at Pearl Harbor on December 7, 1941.[283] The policy excluded this additional payment due to "death resulting from war or any act incident thereto."[284] The plaintiff insisted that there was no war because it had not yet been declared. The court looked to other incidents, such as the German submarine attacks on U.S. shipping that happened before war was declared. In its analysis, the court also considered the hypothetical situation of a fifth columnist who killed in advance of the planes attacking Pearl Harbor, wondering if that could be considered a circumstance in which the country was at war. The court held that both sides must formally acknowledge that they are at war even though a formal declaration is not required for other

---

282. *Id.* at 451.
283. Savage v. Sun Life Assur. Co. of Can., 57 F. Supp. 620 (W.D. La. 1944).
284. *Id.*

purposes. As that was not the case when the Pearl Harbor attack started, the court held for the plaintiff.

6. Impact on Friendly Enemy Aliens

In *Bernheimer v. Vurpillot*, the plaintiffs brought suit against Vurpillot to recover damages suffered by the negligent operation of the defendant's automobile in February 1941.[285] The defendant sought to dismiss or stay the suit because the plaintiffs were German nationals. The plaintiffs, citing the precedence of *Krachanake v. Acme Manufacturing Co.*[286] and others, responded that the Trading with the Enemy Act[287] does not deny "the processes of our courts to a peaceful, law-abiding citizen of an enemy nation resident in the United States."[288] The court looked back to English common law and also to the lack of a proclamation under the Trading with the Enemy Act applicable to the plaintiffs. Then, the court noted that by proclamation, the U.S. government had made all German citizens residing within the United States enemy aliens.[289] In the proclamation made in WWI for the same purposes, the government had stated that "so long as they shall conduct themselves in accordance with law, they shall be undisturbed in the peaceful pursuit of their lives and occupations and be accorded the consideration due to all peaceful and law-abiding persons."[290] The recent proclamation, though, had not included such language, and its absence required the court to stay the plaintiffs' cause of action during the war.

C. Subsequent Events

The declaring or nondeclaring of war by the United States has been a recurring issue from the end of WWII through the present time. For the many uses of the U.S. military internationally since 1945, Congress has not passed a declaration of war: the Korean War; the Vietnam War; the Gulf War; the invasions of Panama, Grenada, Afghanistan, and Iraq; and the bombings/interventions in Libya, Lebanon, El Salvador, Somalia, and Serbia. Instead, a number of other legal mandates have been used to support some of these actions, including the

---

285. Bernheimer v. Vurpillot, 42 F. Supp. 830 (E.D. Penn. 1942).
286. Krachanake v. Acme Mfg. Co., 175 N.C. 435 (1918).
287. Pub. L. No. 65-91 (1917).
288. *Vurpillot*, 42 F. Supp. at 831.
289. Exec. Proclamation No. 2526, (Dec. 8, 1941).
290. *Vurpillot*, 42 F. Supp. at 832.

Gulf of Tonkin Resolution for Vietnam,[291] the U.N. resolution for Korea,[292] the U.N. resolution[293] and congressional joint resolutions[294] for the Gulf War, and a joint resolution for the invasion of Afghanistan.[295]

D. Modern Applicability

In modern times, it is typical to use (or claim the need not to use) the War Powers Resolution in times of military conflict.[296] This act was passed into law in 1973 over the veto of President Richard Nixon during the latter stages of the Vietnam War, with the goal of honoring the intent of the framers of the Constitution by ensuring that "the collective judgment of both the Congress and the President will apply to the introduction of United States Armed Forces into hostilities."[297] Under the act, the president must act pursuant to a declaration of war, specific statutory authority, or a national emergency in order to commit the military.

The act requires the president to consult with Congress prior to and during involvement of the armed forces in hostilities. The president is required to report to Congress in any situation where there are hostilities or imminent hostilities; before going into a foreign nation "while equipped for combat"; and before sending in a number of troops that would substantially enlarge the military's presence in a foreign country.[298] The president must present his report within forty-eight hours of the introduction of the troops (and periodically thereafter) and state the circumstances that led to their introduction, the duration and scope of their involvement, and the constitutional and statutory authority supporting their introduction.

The president is then required, within sixty days of submitting the report to Congress, to terminate use of the armed forces in the related action unless Congress has declared war, given specific statutory authorization, or extended the sixty-day period. The president must remove troops if Congress so directs.

---

291. Pub. L. No. 88-408 (1964).
292. S.C. Res. 84, U.N. Doc. S/1588 (1950).
293. S.C. Res. 678, U.N. Doc. S/RES/678 (1991).
294. Pub. L. No. 102-1 (1991).
295. Pub. L. No. 107-40 (2001).
296. Pub. L. No. 93-148 (1973).
297. *Id.* § 2.
298. *Id.* § 4.

Authority is not to be inferred from existing legislation that does not specifically authorize this introduction.

The War Powers Resolution is not intended to alter the president's constitutional powers or provide new ones. In the military actions since 1973, presidents have reported under it on conflicts including Iran, Lebanon, Grenada, Libya, Panama, Iraq, Somalia, Haiti, the former Yugoslavia, East Timor (peace-keeping), Afghanistan, and Iraq.[299] When presidents have not strictly complied, courts found any dispute between Congress and the president to be a nonjusticiable political matter as Congress has the ability through its legislative function to act to resolve the matter.[300]

299. CONG. RESEARCH SERV., THE WAR POWERS RESOLUTION: AFTER THIRTY-SIX YEARS (2010).
300. Campbell v. Clinton, 203 F.3d 19 (D.C. Cir. 2000).

CHAPTER 3

UNITED STATES: MANAGING THE WAR ECONOMY

A total commitment from the country and its citizens and a rapid emergence from the isolationist policies of the 1930s was needed in order to address the war that was now upon the United States on two fronts. Even though there had been ongoing efforts for several years to prepare for what was now occurring, a large ramp-up in military armaments and a corresponding expansion of economic activity to support military needs was imperative. As such, Congress began passing laws almost immediately that gave the administration unprecedented powers to deal with both the economy and the government apparatus to oversee it.

Addressing the material and manpower needs of supporting the military while at the same time ensuring that the domestic economy provided sufficiently for those still at home was a delicate balancing act. Congress first gave the president a significant amount of power to deal with resource allocation and then proceeded to give him more, all the while fine-tuning these controls. Empowered by recent statutes and constitutional powers, President Roosevelt himself issued a number of executive orders to create various executive bodies to oversee the issue of resource allocation and then continued to reorganize and reform these executive bodies until he found a more satisfactory mixture. Some of the laws used dated back to WWI and were reactivated by this later conflict, and others were entirely new.

The domestic economy provided the production base for military armaments and supplies as well as consumer needs. The ramp-up in military needs meant that the inputs for the production of those armaments—raw materials, human labor, machine tools, and power—needed to be allocated appropriately between the military and consumers, that more factories needed to be built and/or converted to military use, that land had to be acquired for all of these new activities, and that training on a massive scale had to occur. Obviously, the result of such an increase in spending while simultaneously increasing demand for scarce resources ensured that inflation would increase the prices of both the inputs to armaments production and consumer goods, so various controls had to be implemented.

In dealing with the increase in defense production, the government tried to funnel the spike in organized labor actions, caused by the shift away from the mass unemployment of the 1930s, into the war effort. But some labor leaders were not willing to wait for the end of the war to get results, and some employers were not ready for the demands of collective bargaining. Therefore, the federal government was forced to take drastic steps in support of the war effort, such as taking over the domestic means of production.

Beside purely domestic economic considerations, the administration had to concern itself with the impacts of commerce on its enemies. It did not want to be put in the position of funding the war activities of its opponents. So, beyond the export controls discussed in Chapter 2, it initiated a series of financial controls to handle the assets of and trading with the Axis powers.

These various economic concerns led to much legal activity. This chapter focuses on five major economic steps from which significant legal issues arose in the United States: rationing and supply controls, price controls, labor disputes, seizure of the means of production, and enemy assets.

PROMINENT LAWYERS AND JUDGES IN THIS CHAPTER

Rationing and Supply Controls:

- John Lord O'Brian (WPB counsel)
- Manly Fleischmann (WPB assistant general counsel)
- Learned Hand (court of appeals judge)
- Augustus Noble Hand (court of appeals judge)
- Owen J. Roberts (Supreme Court justice)
- James F. Byrnes (OWM director)

- Walter F. George (statute sponsor)

Price Controls:

- Prentiss M. Brown (OPA head)
- William L. Prosser (Minnesota counsel for OPA)
- Arthur T. Vanderbilt (appellant's counsel)
- Thomas I. Emerson (appellee's counsel)
- Paul A. Freund (appellant's counsel)
- Henry M. Hart Jr. (appellants' counsel)
- Irene Kolin Lichtman (OPA lawyer)
- Charles H. Fahy (solicitor general)
- Fred M. Vinson (OES director)

Labor Disputes:

- William H. Davis (NWLB chairman)
- Hugo L. Black (statute sponsor)
- Francis M. Shea (appellee's attorney)
- Alvin J. Rockwell (appellant's attorney)
- Nathan P. Feinsinger (NWLB associate general counsel)
- Lloyd K. Garrison (NWLB head)
- Robert A. Taft (statute sponsor)

Seizure of the Means of Production:

- Tom T. Connally (statute sponsor)
- Joseph B. Eastman (ODT chairman)
- Joseph A. Padway (AFL attorney)
- Thomas A. Goldsborough (judge)
- Harry A. Schulman (head of panel hearing United Steelworkers' case)
- Arthur J. Goldberg (United Steelworkers' counsel)

Enemy Assets:

- John R. Mitchell (APC attorney)
- A. Matt Werner (APC general counsel)
- Thomas W. Swan (court of appeals judge)
- A. McNeil Kennedy (APC solicitor)
- John Foster Dulles (APC consulting committee member)

3.1 RATIONING AND SUPPLY CONTROLS

A. Statutes

The First War Powers Act 1941 was executed "to expedite the prosecution of the war effort."[1] It was passed just a week after the declaration of war on Germany and Italy. Spread over three titles, it gave the president the power to redistribute the functions of the executive agencies as he saw fit for a "more efficient concentration of the government," including entering into contracts or modifying existing contracts as needed to accomplish these goals.[2] The largest section of the act, the Trading with the Enemy Act[3] from WWI, included modifications that allowed the president to regulate, investigate, or prohibit banking transactions involving gold or silver or investigate, regulate, compel, or prohibit transactions in which foreign countries had a property interest; the rest of the Trading with the Enemy Act remained in force.

Within three months, Congress passed the more elaborate Second War Powers Act 1942, which contained thirteen titles.[4] Among these titles was the government's ability to condemn land as needed for military purposes and to acquire naval vessels and aircraft and the Federal Reserve's ability to purchase up to $5 billion of U.S. government bonds. The act also amended the Nationality Act (discussed in Chapter 2) to permit easier naturalization of aliens who served in the armed forces during this war, allowed for the five-cent coin to contain materials other than silver, and authorized the inspection of plants and the audit of the books of war contactors. The president was empowered to prioritize the military's material needs as "necessary or appropriate in the public interest and to promote the national defense"—even if this resulted in a shortage for domestic use or export.[5]

These "priority powers" led to rationing on the home front, a policy that was first mentioned in an amendment to the act to expedite the national defense.[6] This policy began with the rationing of rubber. After the Japanese had overrun the Indonesian rubber sources, the United States did not have

---

1. Pub. L. No. 77-354 (1941).
2. *Id.* § 1.
3. Pub. L. No. 65-91 (1917).
4. Pub. L. No. 77-507 (1942).
5. *Id.* § 301.
6. Pub. L. No. 77-89 (1941).

another substantial source for this material. To effect rationing in the domestic economy, thousands of local War Price and Rationing Boards were set up to make decisions on which American consumers qualified for what types of rationed goods. After rubber, items on the rationing list continued to grow—due to both limited supplies and the need to convert factories over to war production—until it included tires (January 1942); cars (February); typewriters (March); gasoline and sugar (May); bicycles (July); fuel oil/kerosene and rubber footwear (October); coffee (November); stoves (December); shoes (February 1943); processed foods, cheese, butter, meats, and canned foods (March); canned milk (June); and jams and jellies (November).

Three agencies were initially responsible for deciding what, when, and where to ration. The Office of Production Management (OPM), created by executive order in January 1941, had a mandate that included the following: "Plan and take all lawful steps necessary to assure the provision of an adequate supply of raw materials essential to the production of finished products needed for defense."[7] The Supply Priorities and Allocations Board (SPAB) was created by executive order in August 1941 and similarly directed the OPM to "exercise all the power, authority, and discretion conferred upon the President . . . in order to extend the power to establish priorities and allocate material."[8] The SPAB was charged with "[d]etermin[ing] policies and mak[ing] regulations governing allocations and priorities . . . of materials, articles, power, fuel, and other commodities among military, economic defense, defense aid, civilian, and other major demands of the total defense program."[9] The Division of Civilian Supply, originally created by executive order in April 1941 as part of the Office of Price Administration and Civilian Supply (OPACS) but later shifted to the auspices of the OPM (at which time the OPACS became, simply, the Office of Price Administration (OPA)), was charged with "formulat[ing] plans and programs providing for the equitable distribution among competing civilian demands of the materials, articles, power, fuel, and other commodities made available by the SPAB for civilian use."[10]

---

7. Exec. Order No. 8629, Office of Production Management and the Office for Emergency Management (Jan. 7, 1941).
8. Exec. Order No. 8875, Establishing the Supply Priorities and Allocations Board (Aug. 28, 1941).
9. *Id.* § 6.
10. Exec. Order No. 8734, Establishing the Office of Price Administration and Civilian Supply (Apr. 11, 1941).

The War Production Board (WPB) was created by executive order in early 1942.[11] It was established to perform the functions and exercise the powers of the SPAB, which was abolished, and to supervise and reorganize the OPM, which was soon abolished.[12] Also in early 1942, as explained further in the next section, the OPA was given responsibility for rationing, first under the Emergency Price Control Act[13] and then by executive order.[14] It implemented rationing for food at the direction of either the secretary of agriculture[15] or the War Food Administration[16] for food or the WPB for all other commodities.

LEGAL PROFILES

John Lord O'Brian was general counsel to the WPB. He was born in New York in 1874, where he started his practice. He became a member of the New York State Assembly in 1907. In 1909, he was appointed by President Theodore Roosevelt as the attorney general for the Western District of New York. He joined the U.S. Department of Justice in WWI, heading the War Emergency Division, which prosecuted espionage and sabotage cases. He later joined the antitrust division of the Justice Department, frequently arguing before the Supreme Court. He worked for the Tennessee Valley Authority (TVA) as special counsel and defended TVA's constitutionality before the Supreme Court. He served on the WPB and its predecessor (the SPAB) from 1941 to 1944. After the war, he returned to private practice. He died in 1973.[17]

---

11. Exec. Order No. 9024, Establishing the War Production Board (Jan. 16, 1942).
12. Exec. Order No. 9040, Defining Additional Functions and Duties of the War Production Board (Jan. 24, 1942).
13. Pub. L. No. 77-421 (1942).
14. Exec. Order No. 9125, Vesting the WPB and OPA with Additional Responsibilities (Apr. 7, 1942).
15. Exec. Order No. 9280, Delegating Authority over the Food Program (Dec. 5, 1942).
16. Exec. Order No. 9322, Centralizing and Delegating Authority with Respect to the Production and Distribution of Food (Mar. 26, 1943); Exec. Order No. 9334, Establishing the War Food Administration (Apr. 19, 1943).
17. *See* Stanford Univ., Register of the John Lord O'Brian Papers, 1916–1962.

Manly Fleischmann was the assistant general counsel of the WPB. Born in New York in 1908, he started his practice in the state. Based on his father's friendship with John Lord O'Brian, he was named to the WPB, where he stayed until 1943, when he joined the Office of Strategic Services (the predecessor to the Central Intelligence Agency). He returned to private practice after the war but with the outbreak of the Korean War was named as the general counsel to WPB in 1950. The next year, he took on the roles of administrator for both defense production and national (civilian) production. He was involved in conferences leading to the founding of the North Atlantic Treaty Organization and returned to private practice after the Korean War. He died in 1987.[18]

B. Cases

The War Powers Acts (especially the second), the related executive orders that set up the administrative structure that carried out rationing, and the rationing orders themselves caused a significant amount of litigation during the war. Because there was no single big case that set the standard for considering the constitutionality of rationing (amidst many administrative bodies), a number of cases are discussed below that capture different aspects of the impacts of rationing. The first cases looked at the discussion about rationing as provided by the War Powers Acts: the constitutionality of rationing, whether rationing powers can be used to suspend the activities of violators, and the duties of those involved in rationing to keep and produce evidence. The last two cases looked at another aspect of the War Powers Acts—condemnations.

1. Rationing: Constitutionality

The Supreme Court did not rule directly on the constitutionality of the War Powers Acts, but the circuit courts did. *O'Neal v. United States*, a typical case, involved a set of retread tires sold by a police officer without the necessary rationing certificate.[19] The tire rationing order was effective beginning February 1942. The appellants attacked the acts' unconstitutionality "because the

---

18. *See Manly Fleischmann, Lawyer Who Led Panel on Education*, N.Y. TIMES (Mar. 27, 1987).
19. O'Neal v. United States, 140 F.2d 908 (6th Cir. 1944).

statutes delegate pure legislative power to the President. . . . [N]o standards are established to which the President must conform in the exercise of the statutory powers."[20] In reviewing the Second War Powers Act, the court found those standards in the requirement that when the president identifies the existence of a shortage, he then must make allocations based not only on conditions but also as necessary or appropriate "in the public interest and to promote the national defense."[21] The court identified this as a "drastic limitation" set by Congress, not the president.[22] It also found that there were so many problems in allocation that Congress could not possibly deal with them all, so the speedy and efficient use of rationing was appropriate. Likewise, the court ruled that the broad discretion given the president under the statute does not invalidate it, citing statutes and opinions going back to the beginning of the Republic. The court affirmed.

2. Rationing: Penalties

L. P. Steuart & Bros., Inc. v. Bowles, a rationing case that did reach the Supreme Court, did not attack the War Powers Acts on the constitutionality of rationing; instead, it focused on a more narrow aspect of rationing.[23] The OPA issued Rationing Order No. 11, which focused on fuel oil because it was needed not only for military use but for industrial and agricultural use as well.[24] As stated in the order, consumers were targeted for this rationing because the "reduction of demand to the available supply is sought to be achieved largely by a curtailment of the use of fuel oil for heating premises and for hot water, virtually the only classes of uses which can be uniformly reduced without directly impeding the war effort."[25]

Fuel oil that was sold to consumers required the surrender of ration coupons, which the dealer had to then provide to his supplier within a limited amount of time. The appellants here were alleged to have delivered fuel oil to their customers without receiving valid ration coupons in return, to not have provided such coupons to the supplier, and to not have kept accurate records of

---

20. *Id.* at 911.
21. *Id.* at 912.
22. *Id.* at 913.
23. L. P. Steuart & Bros., Inc. v. Bowles, 322 U.S. 398 (1944).
24. OPA Rationing Order No. 11, 7 Fed. Reg. 8,480 (Oct. 21, 1942) (effective Oct. 22, 1942).
25. L. P. Steuart & Bros., Inc., 322 U.S. at 400.

these transactions. The rationing order stated that violators would be subject to a suspension order, so the appellants were served with such a suspension order to prohibit receipt of fuel oil for resale to consumers for the following year.

The appellants argued that the ability to allocate materials as defined in the Second War Powers Act did not also include the ability to issue suspension orders. While the Court agreed that it was the role of Congress to prescribe penalties, it viewed the dishonest middleman as an inefficiency in the very necessary system of rationing scarce resources during the war. As such, the president was not issuing a suspension order to punish an individual but "to protect the distribution system and the interests of conservation."[26] The power to allocate could also be used as a "basis of reallocation of fuel oil into more reliable channels of distribution," according to the Court.[27]

3. Rationing: Evidence

United States v. Davis involved a gasoline station operator who was found to have in his possession ration coupons for five hundred gallons of gasoline.[28] The defendant sold gasoline without coupons (for cash) to two undercover policemen. The police found that the coupons in the containers next to the gas pumps were insufficient to explain the inventory sold and then asked to enter the locked office of the gas station. The defendant may have given his consent to enter (the issue was whether the consent was voluntary); regardless, the appeals court found that this subsequent search of the office that turned up the illicit ration coupons was reasonable. The court noted that Ration Order No. 5C not only required production upon demand for any gasoline ration document but also stated that all coupons are the property of the OPA and their return can be demanded if "in the public interest."[29] The court ruled that the coupons were not records of the crime but fruits of it and as such a wider search was permissible, to "that part of the premises over which the offender's control and unlawful activities likely extended."[30] The court affirmed the conviction while not agreeing with the U.S. attorney's primary contention, i.e., when a regulated business such as this one that is required to produce records

---

26. *Id.* at 406.
27. *Id.* at 407.
28. United States v. Davis, 151 F.2d 140 (2d Cir. 1945).
29. *Id.* at 142.
30. *Id.* at 143.

refuses to do so, it automatically authorizes police to enter the business and seize the appropriate records.

LEGAL PROFILES

Learned Hand wrote this opinion, joined by his cousin Augustus Noble Hand. Learned Hand was born in New York in 1872 and started his legal practice there. He continued with this endeavor until being named to a federal judicial position in the Southern District of New York in 1909. He held this position until 1924, when he was named to the federal appeals court for the Second Circuit. He served there, part of the time as the chief judge, until assuming senior status in 1951. During his time there, he was involved in a number of well-known decisions, such as *United States v. Carroll Towing Co.*[31] and *United States v. Aluminum Co. of America.*[32] He died in 1969.[33]

Augustus Noble Hand was born in New York in 1869. He also started his practice in New York and remained in practice until likewise being named to the U.S. District Court for the Southern District of New York in 1914. He served there until he was elevated to the appeals court for the Second Circuit in 1928. He assumed senior status in 1953, shortly before his death in 1954.[34]

4. Condemnations
The Second War Powers Act gave the government the right to condemn property that was necessary for "war purposes" and to take immediate possession

31. United States v. Carroll Towing Co., 159 F.2d 169 (2d Cir. 1947).
32. United States v. Aluminum Co. of Am., 148 F.2d 416 (2d Cir. 1945).
33. *See Hand, Learned*, FED. JUDICIAL CTR., BIOGRAPHICAL DIRECTORY OF FEDERAL JUDGES.
34. *See Hand, Augustus Noble*, FED. JUDICIAL CTR., BIOGRAPHICAL DIRECTORY OF FEDERAL JUDGES.

upon filing the condemnation petition.[35] In *United States v. Merchants Transfer & Storage Co.*, the military moved to condemn a waterfront warehouse on the West Coast to use in storing and shipping naval supplies to the Pacific theater.[36] The owner, who used the warehouse for commercial shipping, opposed the condemnation, citing a lack of public necessity; the court agreed with the owner and denied immediate possession. The War Department then seized the warehouse and posted guards. The same court then held the government in contempt and demanded return of the property to the owner. The court of appeals ruled that the district court did not have jurisdiction to issue such an order. It found that there is no ability to sue the United States without its own consent; and without it, via statute, the court had no jurisdiction. In addition, it stated that the decision of the secretary of war as to the need for condemnation was final and not subject to judicial oversight.

The Supreme Court also got involved in a case concerning condemnation under the War Powers Acts. In this case, *United States v. General Motors Corp.*, the secretary of war condemned, under the Second War Powers Act, a building used for the storage and distribution of auto parts in Chicago; the court granted the temporary condemnation petition. The tenant, General Motors (GM), which was leasing this space under a long-term lease, timely removed its personal property and fixtures. GM then sought from the government the costs incidental to vacating the property, such as additional rent in a new location, labor costs, and damage to fixtures and equipment, in addition to the market rent on the building. The Court reiterated that, in general, the government does not compensate for consequential damages resulting from a government taking. However, because this was a temporary taking, the Court ruled that the government should compensate for any property damaged or destroyed in addition to rents paid. Furthermore, the Court ruled that the other items of cost incurred by GM should be part of the calculation when a short-term lease is carved out of such a long-term lease, instead of merely relying on long-term lease costs as the appropriate basis for compensation.[37]

---

35. Pub. L. No. 77-507, § 201 (1942).
36. United States v. Merchants Transfer & Storage Co., 144 F.2d 324 (9th Cir. 1944).
37. United States v. General Motors Corp., 323 U.S. 373 (1945).

LEGAL PROFILES

Owen J. Roberts wrote this decision. He was born in Pennsylvania in 1875 and started his law practice there. He spent several years as a district attorney in Philadelphia before returning to private practice. During the next twenty-five years in private practice, he also was involved in several special investigations, including the Teapot Dome scandal. He taught at the University of Pennsylvania Law School for more than twenty years. In 1930, President Herbert Hoover nominated him to the U.S. Supreme Court, where he served until resigning in 1945. He wrote an opinion in 1935 striking down one of the New Deal programs, the Agricultural Adjustment Act. He also led the commission investigating the attack on Pearl Harbor. He died in 1955.[38]

C. Subsequent Events

Rationing of various commodities persisted throughout much of the war, differing somewhat in timing and in parts of the country affected. The other resource supply focus of the War Powers Acts—addressing the control of materials beyond just consumers to military and industrial planning, allocation, and use of the resources—continued to be pressed. The earliest focus of much activity during the war concerned the supply of rubber. Given a loss of its principal source of natural rubber imports, the United States turned to a crash program of developing synthetic rubber as a substitute. The rationing and recycling programs targeting rubber, beyond the specific rubber initiatives, included the gasoline and automobile rationing programs. Rubber was so important to control that the WPB had its own rubber director.[39]

The various attempts at centralized planning and procurement control were usually not as successful as hoped for due to various reasons, many having to do with the agendas of the various stakeholders on the executive committees

---

38. *See Roberts, Owen Josephus*, FED. JUDICIAL CTR., BIOGRAPHICAL DIRECTORY OF FEDERAL JUDGES.
39. Exec. Order No. 9246, Coordination and Control of the Rubber Program (Sept. 17, 1942).

appointed by the president, including the military and industrial representatives. To finally overcome this, Roosevelt issued another executive order in May 1943, this one setting up the Office of War Mobilization.[40] Referring to his constitutional roles as commander in chief of the United States and executor of the First War Powers Act to "provide for the more effective coordination of the mobilization of the Nation for war," this office had a director and included on its committee the heads of the Department of War, the U.S. Navy, the Department of Munitions and Supply, the WPB, and the Office of Economic Stabilization (discussed in Section 3.2).[41]

The two principal functions of the Office of War Mobilization were as follows:

(a) To develop unified programs and . . . policies for the maximum use of the Nation's natural and industrial resources for military and civilian needs, for the effective use of the national manpower not in the armed forces, for the maintenance and stabilization of the civilian economy, and for the adjustment of such economy to war needs and conditions;

(b) To unify the activities of Federal agencies and departments engaged in or concerned with production, procurement, distribution, or transportation of military or civilian supplies, materials, and products and to resolve and determine controversies between such agencies or departments. . . .[42]

More than one year later, Congress passed the War Mobilization and Reconversion Act, the so-called George Bill.[43] This act created the Office of War Mobilization and Reconversion to make "such plans as are necessary to meet the problems arising out of the transition from war to peace."[44] This was a successor organization to the Office of War Mobilization. The act also dealt with other expected postwar issues, such as unemployment, public works, war

---

40. Exec. Order No. 9347, Establishing the Office of War Mobilization (May 27, 1943).
41. *Id.*
42. *Id.*
43. Pub. L. No. 78-458 (1944).
44. *Id.* § 101.

contract termination, and retraining, changing the emphasis from a ramp-up of industrial capability for munitions production back to one focused primarily on civilian goods production.

The WPB was abolished at the end of the war and its functions transferred to the new Civilian Production Administration.[45] The intent of this agency was "to further a swift and orderly transition from wartime production to a maximum peacetime production in industry free from wartime Government controls, with due regard for the stability of prices and costs."[46] Its functions and powers included the following:

- "Expand[ing] production of materials which are in short supply"
- "Limit[ing] the manufacture of products for which materials or facilities are insufficient"
- "Control[ling] the accumulation of inventories so as to avoid speculative hoarding and unbalanced distribution which would curtail total production"
- "Grant[ing] priority assistance to break bottlenecks which would impede the reconversion process"
- "Facilitat[ing] the fulfillment of relief and other essential export programs"
- "Allocat[ing] scarce materials or facilities necessary for the production of low-priced items essential to the continued success of the stabilization program"[47]

LEGAL PROFILES

James F. Byrnes was the first director of the Office of War Mobilization and a lawyer. He was born in South Carolina in 1882, where he first practiced law after an apprenticeship (he did not attend college or law school). He won election to the U.S. House of Representatives in 1911 and served there for the next fourteen years. He first lost and then subse-

---

45. Exec. Order No. 9638, Creating the Civilian Production Administration and Terminating the War Production Board (Oct. 4, 1945).
46. *Id.*
47. *Id.*

quently won a seat in the U.S. Senate, where he served for ten years, until he was nominated by President Roosevelt to the U.S. Supreme Court. He only served a little more than a year on the Court before he resigned to become the first director of the Office of Economic Stabilization (see Section 3.2). Thereafter, he was appointed as the first director of the Office of War Mobilization. President Harry Truman then appointed him secretary of state in 1945. After that, he returned to South Carolina to run for and win the office of governor. He died in 1972.[48]

Walter F. George was the sponsor of the George Bill focusing on reconversion of U.S. industry after the war, and he was also an attorney. He was born in Georgia in 1878 and started legal practice there. He was named solicitor general in 1907 and served in that office until 1912, when he became a superior court judge in Georgia. In 1917, he became an associate justice on that state's supreme court for five more years. In 1922, he was elected to the U.S. Congress as a senator and served in that position until he died in 1957.[49]

3.2 PRICE CONTROLS

A. Statutes

The war economy saw a large increase in the Gross Domestic Product of the United States—from $92 billion in 1939 to $223 billion in 1945.[50] With the economy expanding at such a rate in such a short period of time, unemployment decreasing significantly over the same period (from 17.2 percent in 1939 to 1.9 percent in 1945),[51] supply constraints imposed on raw materials, and the lack of availability of finished goods for the consumer market due to the prioritization of munitions production, prices naturally moved upward quite sig-

---

48. *See Byrnes, James Francis*, FED. JUDICIAL CTR., BIOGRAPHICAL DIRECTORY OF FEDERAL JUDGES.
49. *See George, Walter Franklin*, BIOGRAPHICAL DIRECTORY OF THE UNITED STATES CONGRESS.
50. BUREAU OF ECON. ANALYSIS, U.S. DEP'T OF COMMERCE, NATIONAL INCOME AND PRODUCT ACCOUNT TABLES (2012).
51. *Employment Status of the Civilian Population: 1929 to 2002*, U.S. CENSUS (2003).

nificantly. With an eye firmly on this issue, Congress and the president enacted several laws, executive orders, and regulations to control prices.

President Roosevelt made the first move by creating the Office of Price Administration and Civilian Supply by executive order in April 1941.[52] (After the civilian supply function was moved to the OPM by another executive order in August 1941,[53] the name was changed to the Office of Price Administration (OPA)). With respect to prices, the office was created for the purpose "of avoiding profiteering and unwarranted price rises . . . finding that the stabilization of prices is in the interest of national defense."[54] Its committee consisted of the administrator, treasury and agriculture secretaries, the federal loan administrator, the chairman of the Tariff Commission, the Federal Trade Commission chairman, and the heads of the OPM. Regarding prices, the office and committee were tasked with the following:

- "Tak[ing] . . . steps . . . to prevent price spiraling, rising costs of living, profiteering, and inflation resulting from market conditions caused by the diversion of large segments of the Nation's resources to the defense program, by interruptions to normal sources of supply, or by other influences growing out of the emergency"
- "Determin[ing] and publish[ing] . . . such maximum prices, commissions, margins, fees, charges, or other elements of cost or price of materials or commodities"
- "Advis[ing] and mak[ing] recommendations" on the prices paid for purchases or "acquisition of materials and commodities by the Government"
- "[D]evelop[ing] programs with the object of stabilizing rents"
- "[M]ak[ing] findings and submit[ting] recommendations . . . in respect to the establishment of maximum prices, commissions, margins, fees, charges, and other elements of cost or price of materials or commodities"[55]

---

52. Exec. Order No. 8734, Establishing the Office of Price Administration and Civilian Supply (Apr. 11, 1941).
53. Exec. Order No. 8875, Establishing the Supply Priorities and Allocations Board (Aug. 28, 1941).
54. Exec. Order No. 8734.
55. *Id.*

This was followed by the passage of the Emergency Price Control Act in early 1942, extensive legislation created in the interest of national defense and security and "necessary to the effective prosecution of the present war."[56] Its many purposes were as follows:

- "[S]tabilize prices"
- "[P]revent speculative, unwarranted, and abnormal increases in prices and rents"
- "[E]liminate and prevent profiteering. hoarding, manipulation, speculation, and other disruptive practices resulting from abnormal market conditions or scarcities caused by or contributing to the national emergency"
- "[A]ssure that defense appropriations are not dissipated by excessive prices"
- "[P]rotect persons with relatively fixed and limited incomes, consumers, wage earners, investors, and persons dependent on life insurance, annuities, and pensions, from undue impairment of their standard of living"
- "[P]revent hardships to persons engaged in business, to schools, universities, and other institutions, and to the Federal, State, and local governments, which would result from abnormal increases in prices"
- "[A]ssist in securing adequate production of commodities and facilities"
- "[P]revent a post-emergency collapse of values"
- "[S]tabilize agricultural prices"
- "[W]ork toward a stabilization of prices, fair and equitable wages, and cost of production"[57]

If the price of a commodity rose or threatened to rise to a level that would undermine the purposes of the act, the price administrator could set a "fair and equitable" maximum price for the commodity by order, regulation, or price schedule.[58] To do so, the administrator was to use a baseline of October 1941 prices or other generally representative prices. To stabilize or reduce rents in defense-area housing accommodations, the administrator was permitted to set

---

56. Pub. L. No. 77-421 (1942).
57. *Id.* § 1.
58. *Id.*

maximum rent using April 1941 as a baseline. In either case, the maximum commodity price or maximum housing rent could be set below prevailing levels. The administrator was also allowed to regulate or prohibit "speculative or manipulative practice" or hoarding, which was deemed likely to result in price or rent increases.[59] Furthermore, he could buy, sell, store, use, or subsidize in order to obtain the "maximum necessary production."[60] Agricultural and fishery products had special price-level protections. The act did not require the sale of any particular commodity or the rental of any particular accommodation. The administrator was allowed to require licenses for those selling regulated commodities. The act did not allow for the regulation of employee compensation paid by an employer, common carrier or public utility rates, insurance, newspapers, radio, movies, advertising, or professional services.[61]

The Emergency Court of Appeals was created to handle pricing protests, drawing from existing circuit and district court judges; appeals from this court went to the Supreme Court via a writ of certiorari. This court's domain was exclusive: no other courts were given jurisdiction to review regulations, orders, or price schedules.[62] This court was not granted the powers to issue interlocutory orders.

On April 28, 1942, the OPA issued the General Maximum Price Regulation Act.[63] This required that henceforth no person was to buy or deliver a commodity or buy or supply a service, and no business was to buy or receive a commodity or service for more than the maximum price in the regulation. The maximum price was generally set at the March 1942 levels. This only applied to domestic sales; exports were handled separately. Lower prices could be charged without limitation. There were quite a number of exceptions, including certain agricultural products; used automobiles; books, magazines, and movies; logs; stamps; coins; precious stones; securities; bars, hotels, and restaurants; merchants selling used supplies; utilities; insurance; professional services; and real property services. Sellers had to keep both base-period and current-period records and file prices with the local War Price and Rationing Board.

---

59. *Id.* § 2.
60. *Id.*
61. *Id.* § 302(c)(1).
62. *Id.* § 204(d).
63. O.P.A. Reg. 1, General Maximum Price Regulation (Apr. 28, 1942).

In October 1942, Congress passed the Stabilization Act, also called the Inflation Control Act, to "aid in preventing inflation."[64] It authorized the president to issue an order that stabilized prices, wages, and salaries affecting the cost of living. There were also limits on agricultural products and on wage and salary reductions, but the president was allowed to adjust agricultural prices, within limits, "to the extent that he finds necessary to correct gross inequities" and to adjust wages or salaries, within limits, "to the extent that he finds necessary in any case to correct gross inequities and also aid in the effective prosecution of the war."[65] He was also allowed to suspend the provisions from § 302(c)(1) of the Emergency Price Control Act, whose provisions exempted a series of businesses from regulation. Furthermore, private companies could reduce the salaries of those making more than $5,000 a year.

The next day, Roosevelt issued an executive order to establish the Office of Economic Stabilization (OES).[66] To prevent increases in the costs of labor or the "unnecessary" migration of labor (workers moving between geographic regions or across or within industries to find the best-paying positions), the director was given the mandate to develop a national policy concerning the control of "civilian purchasing power, prices, rents, wages, salaries, profits, rationing, subsidies."[67] In detail, the executive order went on to explain separate titles addressing wages and salaries, agricultural commodities, profits, and subsidies. Agricultural commodities were to be stabilized at September 1942 levels. The price administrator was directed to set price ceilings to prevent "unreasonable or exorbitant" profits.[68] The director could also direct other federal agencies to subsidize and purchase commodities for resale, to ensure maximum necessary production and distribution of a commodity, to maintain ceiling prices, or to prevent price increases.

In terms of wages and salaries, wage rates could not be increased or decreased without the approval of the National War Labor Board (see Section 3.3), which would not approve increases unless they were necessary to "correct maladjustments or inequalities, to eliminate substandards of living, to correct gross

---

64. Pub. L. No. 77-729 (1942).
65. *Id.* § 1.
66. Exec. Order No. 9250, Establishing the Office of Economic Stabilization (Oct. 3, 1942).
67. *Id.*
68. *Id.*

inequities, or to aid in the effective prosecution of the war."[69] Any increases in wage rates that would trigger a change in the price ceiling of a commodity also required the director's approval, and decreases that lowered wages or salaries below the highest wages or salaries paid in 1942 would not be approved unless necessary to "correct gross inequities and to aid in the effective prosecution of the war."[70] Unless a person took on more difficult or responsible work, no salary increases of more than $5,000 were allowed; likewise, no salaries in excess of $25,000 were allowed.

LEGAL PROFILES

Prentiss M. Brown was the second administrator of the OPA and an attorney. He was born in Michigan in 1889 and began his legal practice there. He was both a prosecuting county attorney and a city attorney between the years of 1914 and 1928. Although he ran unsuccessfully for the U.S. House of Representatives in 1924, he was successful in 1932 and served for four years. He then won a seat in the U.S. Senate, where he served until he was defeated in November 1942 (as were many Democrats that year). In 1943, President Roosevelt selected him to be the administrator of the OPA. He served for a short time at the OPA, where his deputy was the well-known economist John Kenneth Galbraith. He then returned to private practice. He died in 1973.[71]

William L. Prosser was the Minnesota counsel for the OPA. He was born in Indiana in 1898 but started his legal practice in Minnesota. He moved to the law school at the University of Minnesota as a professor in 1931, serving until 1940. It was there that he wrote his well-known legal book, *Prosser on Torts*. He then joined the OPA as counsel in Minnesota. In 1943, he returned to private practice for several years until joining Harvard University as a professor and then the University of California,

---

69. *Id.*
70. *Id.*
71. *See Brown, Prentiss Marsh*, BIOGRAPHICAL DIRECTORY OF THE UNITED STATES CONGRESS.

Berkeley as the law school dean in 1948. He remained in that position until 1961, when he took a position at the University of California Hastings College of the Law. He was known for the theory of strict product liability; and as a reporter for the *Restatement (Second) of Torts* in the 1950s, he was able to get this codified. He also worked on the Uniform Commercial Code in the 1940s. He remained in his last position in California until his death in 1972.[72]

B. Cases

An extremely large number of cases were brought during the war because of the complexity of the rules created, the intrusive amount of regulation into an area previously unregulated, and the fact that the area regulated directly concerned money. Several of these cases made their way up to the Supreme Court during that time, involving issues such as (1) which courts could review the pricing regulations, (2) the ability to regulate the prices of utilities and the definition of *public utility*, (3) the constitutionality of price controls, (4) the constitutionality of rent controls, (5) how baseline-period prices were to be set, and (6) when fair and equitable prices remain valid.

1. Exclusive Jurisdiction

The Emergency Price Control Act had given judicial review authority exclusively to the Emergency Court of Appeals, followed by appellate review in the U.S. Supreme Court. In *Lockerty v. Phillips*, that exclusivity was challenged by a wholesaler accused of violating price regulations.[73] The appellant was in the wholesale meat business and subject to Price Regulation No. 169, which it alleged did not consider a whole range of factors regarding the pricing and availability of meats and would essentially force it out of this business. Furthermore, the appellant argued, the pricing regulation violated due process and was an unconstitutional delegation of legislative power to the price administrator.

---

72. *See* Univ. of Cal., In Memoriam—William Lloyd Prosser, Law: Berkeley and Hastings (July 1975).
73. Lockerty v. Phillips, 319 U.S. 182 (1943).

Instead of raising a protest and following the designated procedure through the Emergency Court of Appeals, the appellant brought its case in district court, which dismissed for lack of jurisdiction. The Supreme Court answered that the Constitution gives Congress the power to establish (or not) inferior courts. The appellant contended that beyond merely withholding equity relief powers from other courts, the act restricted the ability of other courts to review the constitutionality of the act or orders, regulations, and price schedules; however, the Court felt that the Emergency Court of Appeals could perform this function. The Court did not rule on the appellant's contention that it was unconstitutional to not provide the Emergency Court of Appeals the power to issue temporary injunctions on orders, regulations, and price schedules. The Court affirmed the district court's dismissal.

LEGAL PROFILES

Arthur T. Vanderbilt was the counsel for the appellant in this case. He was born in 1888 in New Jersey and began his practice there. He began teaching as an adjunct professor in 1914 and eventually served as the dean of the New York University School of Law. From 1921 until 1947, he was a county counsel in New Jersey. He was involved in drafting the Federal Rules of Criminal Procedure and creating the Administrative Office of the U.S. Courts. He was president of the American Bar Association and wrote a number of legal books. He then helped to set the direction for the change to the New Jersey Constitution's judicial provisions, replacing the outdated system whereby each court in the state had its own rules. He was named the first chief justice of the newly revamped Supreme Court of New Jersey, a position that he held until his death in 1957.[74]

Thomas I. Emerson presented the case for the appellee. He was born in New Jersey in 1908 and became involved early in his career as part of the defense team that appealed the convictions in the Scottsboro Boys trials. He then went to work in Washington, D.C., in 1933 for a

---

74. *See Arthur T. Vanderbilt*, N.Y. TIMES (June 18, 1957).

number of government organizations, including the National Recovery Administration, the National Labor Relations Board (NLRB), the Social Security Board, and the U.S. Attorney General's Office. During the war, his roles included deputy administrator for enforcement of the OPA and general counsel of the OES and Office of War Mobilization and Reconversion. After the war, he became a professor at Yale, where he taught for thirty-one years. In 1965, he successfully argued the *Griswold v. Connecticut* case before the U.S. Supreme Court, which overturned the ban on selling contraceptives and established a right to privacy.[75] He died in 1991.[76]

2. Regulation of Utility Prices

In *Davies Warehouse Co. v. Bowles*, a public warehouse regulated as a public utility by the Railroad Commission of California was granted a rate increase effective in May 1942.[77] The General Maximum Price Regulation Act in late April 1942 prohibited this increase unless the warehouse fell under the exemption of a public utility. The appellant's appeal was turned down by both the price administrator and the Emergency Court of Appeals.

The Supreme Court noted that the act did not define the term *public utility* and that the Emergency Court of Appeals had split over whether to define it as a traditional utility (e.g., power, water) or all regulated businesses or to defer to what the state considered a public utility. Furthermore, the Court noted that twenty-one (of the then forty-eight) states regulated public warehouses and that forty-seven states had adopted the Uniform Warehouse Receipts Act. The legislative history was inconclusive. The Court, quoting from the first price administrator, asserted that the reason utilities were excluded from the act was that there was already sufficient state control from regulators who also wanted to ensure there were no unwarranted price increases. Given that Congress likely intended to not intrude on this area already under state control, the Court agreed that the public warehouse was to be considered a public utility and so exempted from regulation under the act. The Court, although sympa-

75. Griswold v. Connecticut, 381 U.S. 479 (1965).
76. *See Thomas I. Emerson, 83, Scholar Who Molded Civil Liberties Law*, N.Y. TIMES (June 22, 1991).
77. Davies Warehouse Co. v. Bowles, 321 U.S. 144 (1944).

thetic to a degree, was not swayed by the price administrator's objections that it would be a burden for the administrator to ascertain the constitutionality of each state's laws and consider the status of each such utility, many only partially regulated, under state law and that it was necessary to give the act uniform application in all states. The dissenting opinion felt that the Court's decision would place an "unwarranted burden" on those responsible for controlling inflation.[78]

3. Price Controls and Constitutionality

In *Yakus v. United States*, a case challenging the constitutionality of price controls, the Court affirmed the lower courts' rulings.[79]

From the beginning of the opinion, the Court laid out four questions that it needed to answer concerning the Emergency Price Control Act as amended by the Stabilization Act:

- Was there an unconstitutional delegation of legislative authority?
- Did the lack of district court review of maximum price regulations provide a defense to a criminal charge?
- Did the exclusive review procedure meet due process requirements?
- If the lack of district court review was not a defense, did the exclusive review process contravene the Sixth Amendment or interfere with judicial power?[80]

The appellants were convicted in district court of selling beef in excess of the maximum price set by Revised Maximum Price Regulation No. 169. They had never challenged the price through the accepted procedure (i.e., through the price administrator and the Emergency Court of Appeals). At trial, they attempted to introduce evidence that the regulation they violated did not conform to the act and was a taking. The district court determined that such evidence was not relevant and found the appellants guilty, which the appeals court affirmed.

The Court began by noting that Congress did have the power to set commodity prices "as a war emergency measure."[81] It ruled that Congress had

---

78. *Id.* at 156.
79. Yakus v. United States, 321 U.S. 414 (1944).
80. *Id.* at 418.
81. *Id.* at 422.

achieved the legislative function when it stated its legislative objective (the control of inflation), specified the method to use to achieve it (maximum price controls), and provided the standards of when to use the method and the particular prices to be used. The Court believed that the standards plus the statement of considerations required by the price administrator upon issuing the regulations was enough for "Congress, the courts and the public" to determine if those standards were being met.[82] Providing some flexibility to the administrator was reasonable; and for all of the above reasons, this was not an unconstitutional delegation of legislative powers.

In answer to the second question, the Court delineated that in a criminal prosecution in a district court, the court could consider the constitutionality of the statute but not of the regulations. The validity of the regulations must be considered by the established process.

For the third question, the Court looked back at the urgent need for the act and the efficiency of a single process. If the procedure allowed a reasonable opportunity to be heard and to present evidence, the Court ruled that it did not violate due process. As the appellants did not use this process, the Court could not rule on it further. The proscription of a temporary injunction until the matter could be heard was viewed as a matter of the public interest prevailing over private interests.

In answer to the fourth question, the Court ruled that there is no constitutional requirement that the test of the validity of the regulation and the trial for violation of the regulation be held in a single tribunal, as long as due process is served. The fact that the appellants did not avail themselves of the established procedure should be viewed no differently than forfeiting rights in trials by not taking timely advantage of them. For an analogy, the Court looked to the example of common carriers, where rates protests and violations are handled separately. There was no Sixth Amendment violation, and the case was properly submitted to the jury.

4. Rent Controls and Constitutionality

In *Bowles v. Willingham*, a case about rent controls, the lower courts found the act unconstitutional.[83] The appellee had originally sued to block the rent controls when her area was designated as one of twenty-eight defense-rent areas

---

82. *Id.* at 426.
83. Bowles v. Willingham, 321 U.S. 503 (1944).

in the country. After the declaration by the price administrator that the rents in these areas had increased, it followed up sixty days later as allowed under the act and issued Maximum Price Regulation No. 26, which ordered that because rents had not stabilized or decreased, as of July 1, 1942, rents should be no more than they were on April 1, 1941. In June 1943, the rent director notified the appellee that she must reduce the maximum rent of three of her apartments as it was higher than what was generally prevailing on April 1, 1941.

The Supreme Court pointed to its *Yakus* decision,[84] which had been issued the same day, noting that the act did not grant the delegation of the power of Congress to the price administrator. The Court pointed out that Congress had set the policy and determined when it was to be used and the methods to implement it, which are the steps that "constitute the performance of the legislative function in the constitutional sense."[85] Congress had not given unlimited discretion to the price administrator to fix rents—where, when, or what levels—but had set specific types of areas and a base period. The Court rejected the appellee's argument that fair and equitable pricing in rent controls required that the rents be fair and equitable to each landlord instead of generally to all landlords as a class. It also rejected the idea that landlords must be given notice and a hearing before the regulations are set, deeming judicial review to be sufficient for due process.

LEGAL PROFILES

Paul A. Freund presented the case for the appellant. He was born in Missouri in 1908. He moved to Washington, D.C., to clerk for Supreme Court Justice Louis Brandeis and then served in a series of federal government positions. He worked at the U.S. Treasury and at the Reconstruction Finance Corporation from 1933 to 1935 and in the U.S. Solicitor General's Office from 1935 to 1939 and again from 1942 to 1946. He eventually turned down an offer from President John F. Ken-

---

84. *Yakus*, 321 U.S. 414.
85. *Willingham*, 321 U.S. at 514.

nedy to serve as solicitor general. He taught at Harvard Law School from 1939 to 1976 and was the editor of the multivolume *History of the Supreme Court*, as appointed by President Dwight D. Eisenhower. He died in 1992.[86]

---

5. Baseline Prices

Bowles v. Seminole Rock & Sand Co. was a disagreement about how to determine the baseline price and whether there was a violation of Maximum Price Regulation No. 188.[87] The regulation concerned crushed stone, which the appellee manufactured. The appellee contracted in October 1941 to deliver crushed stone at 60 cents per ton, which was delivered in March 1942. In January 1942, it contracted to deliver crushed stone at 150 cents per ton, which was not delivered until August 1942 due to some delays, except for a small delivery under the agreement for crushed stone of a different grade. Thereafter—and after the price regulation became effective—the appellee contracted a delivery for 85 cents per ton. The price administrator brought an action, claiming that the appellee could not charge more than 60 cents per ton. The district court dismissed, holding that 150 cents per ton was the benchmark rate to use. The appeals court affirmed.

The Court looked at the wording in the price regulation in question to determine if the baseline price should be established based on a delivery or a sale/contract during the baseline month. The operative section of the price regulation gave the following details:

The maximum price for any article which was delivered or offered for delivery in March, 1942, by the manufacturer, shall be the highest price charged by the manufacturer during March, 1942 for the article. "Highest price charged during March, 1942" means (i) the highest price which the seller charged to a purchaser of the same class for delivery of the article or material during March, 1942 or (ii) If the seller made no such

---

86. *See Paul A. Freund, Authority on Constitution, Dies at 83*, N.Y. TIMES (Feb. 6, 1992).
87. Bowles v. Seminole Rock & Sand Co., 325 U.S. 410 (1945).

delivery during March, 1942, such seller's highest offering price to a purchaser of the same class for delivery of the article or material during that month.

The issue was interpretation of the final clauses. The Court focused on the word *delivery* and found that the baseline price should be based on the actual delivery of the item in the baseline month, not a scheduled—but possibly delayed—delivery in that month or a sale/contract in that month. As such, the lower price of 60 cents per ton was appropriate, and the Court reversed the decisions of the lower courts.

LEGAL PROFILES

Henry M. Hart Jr. presented the case for the appellants. He was born in 1904. He did postgraduate work for Felix Frankfurter, future Supreme Court justice, and then began his legal career by clerking for Supreme Court Justice Louis Brandeis. He spent most of his legal career as a professor at Harvard, starting in 1932 and continuing until his death. During the war, he worked for the federal government, including as a special assistant to the Immigration and Naturalization Service in the U.S. Attorney General's Office in 1940 and 1941 and at the OPA. He authored many important and influential legal works, including *The Legal Process and Federal Courts and the Federal System*. He died in 1969.[88]

6. Maintenance of Fair and Equitable Pricing

Gillespie-Rogers-Pyatt Co. Inc. v. Bowles discussed the process used by the Emergency Court of Appeals in evaluating prices: the court was asked to determine the validity of the process for determining if prices remained fair and equitable and the proffered evidence to prove such.[89] The complainants contended

---

88. *See Henry M. Hart Jr., Harvard Teacher; Professor of Law, 64, Dead—Authority on Judiciary*, N.Y. TIMES (Mar. 25, 1969).
89. Gillespie-Rogers-Pyatt Co. Inc. v. Bowles, 144 F.2d 361 (Emer. Ct. App. 1944).

that the maximum pricing for bleached shellac, issued under Maximum Price Regulation No. 245 in October 1942, was no longer appropriate one year later. Increased costs and decreased profit margins since then made these no longer generally fair and equitable. The price administrator had turned down the protests, leading to this appeal.

To make adjustments to the October 1941 prices, the price administrator looked to relevant factors of general applicability, including speculative fluctuations and general increases or decreases in costs or profits since then. Standards used included industry earnings compared to base years (typically 1936–1939) and product standards (for multiproduct industries). If the industry's costs had increased more than the industry's gross income, the price administrator would "consider[] an increase in the industry's maximum prices."[90] The maximum prices were deemed to be "generally fair and equitable" if the industry

- was "receiving over-all earnings on all its operations equaling or exceeding its peacetime earnings" and
- was "not, except for the highest-cost fringe of producers, incurring an out-of-pocket loss on any particular line or product."[91]

The complainants contended that the industry income standard was not fixed in law and did not achieve the goal of maximum prices "for each individual product" regardless of the other earnings of the respective industry. The court did not agree, referring to its earlier decisions that an increase in the cost of a single commodity does not by itself entitle the industry to an increase in the maximum price. Rather, it was also necessary to show that increases in costs had not been offset by decreases in costs elsewhere and that an unreasonable industry profit decrease had actually resulted. The standard may apply not to a single commodities price but to those of a group of commodities used in the industry.

The court rejected the practicality of product-by-product profit margin maintenance and noted that it would be inflationary. "The Administrator has never taken the position that any price for a particular product is fair, no matter how low, so long as overall peacetime earnings are equaled."[92] The court held

---

90. *Id.* at 363.
91. *Id.*
92. *Id.* at 364.

that the use of the industry earnings standard was a valid use of the discretion of the price administrator. Based on its analysis of the validity of the industry standard, the court held that the complainants' evidence of raw material price increases was insufficient because the evidence did not also include company net earnings information for the base or current periods; as such, the court dismissed the complaint.

LEGAL PROFILES

Irene Kolin Lichtman was one of the OPA attorneys who were part of the defense team for the price administrator in these types of cases. Born in Connecticut in 1911, she went to work at the U.S. Soil Conservation Service in the early 1930s. In 1940, she graduated from law school and passed the Washington, D.C., bar exam, one of only twenty women to do so in that year. After her work with the OPA's Washington, D.C., office, in which she appeared before the Emergency Court of Appeals, she turned to private practice with a focus on helping juveniles stay off the streets, out of jail, and employed. Practicing into her seventies, she died in 2005.[93]

Charles H. Fahy was the U.S. solicitor general responsible for all of these cases presented to the Supreme Court. Born in Georgia in 1892, he started practice in Washington, D.C. He served as an aviator in WWI and returned to private practice. In 1924, he moved his practice to New Mexico, where he also served as a city attorney. In 1933, he returned to Washington as a counsel for the Department of the Interior, followed by a stint at the Petroleum Administrative Board. In 1935, the same year as the passage of the Wagner Act (see Section 3.3), he joined the NLRB as general counsel. In 1940, he was named assistant solicitor general for the United States and solicitor general in 1941, serving until 1945. After several immediate postwar roles with the State Department and the mili-

---

93. *See Irene Kolin Lichtman Lawyer,* WASH. POST (Mar. 20, 2005).

tary, he served on the President's Committee on Equality of Treatment and Opportunity in the Armed Forces from 1948 to 1950. He was then appointed to the court of appeals in the D.C. district in 1950, serving until his death in 1979.[94]

C. Subsequent Events

Despite all of the actions taken, inflation kept increasing during the war years. Based on the consumer price index (CPI), consumer inflation rose from -1.4 percent in 1939 to 10.9 percent in 1942[95] and was still rising at an annual rate of 8 percent in April 1943.

On April 8, 1943, Roosevelt issued his "Hold the Line" executive order.[96] In a statement released with this order, he said that "we cannot tolerate further increases in prices affecting the cost of living or further increases in general wage or salary rates. . . . All items affecting the cost of living are to be brought under control. No further price increases are to be sanctioned unless imperatively required by law."[97] The order was designed to reduce excessively high, inequitable, or unfair prices, including those that were excessively high when the Stabilization Act was passed. It also applied to stopping increases in wages and in utilities and common carrier rates. Roosevelt noted that

[s]ome groups have been urging increased prices for farmers on the ground that wage earners have unduly profited. Other groups have been urging increased wages on the ground that farmers have unduly profited. A continuance of this conflict will not only cause inflation but will breed disunity at a time when unity is essential. . . . We cannot stop inflation solely by wage and price ceilings. We cannot stop it solely by rationing. To complete the job, Congress must act to reduce and hold in check the excess purchasing power. We must be prepared to tax ourselves more, to spend less and save more.[98]

---

94. *See Fahy, Charles*, Fed. Judicial Ctr., Biographical Directory of Federal Judges.
95. U.S. Bureau of Labor Statistics, Table of Historical Inflation Rates (2012).
96. Exec. Order No. 9328, Price and Wages (Apr. 8, 1943).
97. *Id.*
98. *Id.*

In the order, the price administrator and the food administrator were directed to take immediate steps to place ceiling prices on all commodities that affected the cost of living; to prevent further increases; and to reduce excessively high, unfair, or inequitable prices. To assist in this, the order transferred the powers of the Secretary of Agriculture to the food administrator. The National War Labor Board (see Section 3.3) was directed to not authorize further increases in wages or salaries. The War Manpower Commission was directed to forbid employment to any new employee in order to prevent job migration to positions with higher salaries (unless the change of employment would aid in the effective prosecution of the war). Common carrier and utilities rate approvals were to be rejected and rate reductions implemented.

These price control programs seemed to be successful. War munitions production began to peak in late 1943, so direct causal relationships may not be easily found between these programs and inflation; however, the CPI was down to 3.0 percent by December 1943 (a 6.1 percent annual rate) and down to 1.7 percent for the full year of 1944,[99] even as the annual U.S. GDP was still increasing and annual U.S. unemployment rates were still falling. The government was seemingly victorious in its battle against domestic consumer inflation.

Price controls and rent controls continued for a while right after the war terminated in hopes of maintaining stability in the transition to a peacetime economy,[100] but they and their administrative agencies were eventually wound down[101] and the OES was abolished.[102] The Emergency Court of Appeals

---

99. U.S. BUREAU OF LABOR STATISTICS, *supra* note 94.

100. Exec. Order No. 9599, Providing for Assistance to Expanded Production and Continued Stabilization of the National Economy During the Transition from War to Peace, and for the Orderly Modification of Wartime Controls over Prices, Wages, Materials and Facilities (Aug. 18, 1945); Exec. Order No. 9651, Amending Executive Order 9599, Providing for Assistance to Expanded Production and Continued Stabilization of the National Economy During the Transition from War to Peace, and for the Orderly Modification of Wartime Controls over Prices, Wages, Materials and Facilities (Oct. 30, 1945).

101. Exec. Order No. 9737, Revoking Section 3 of Executive Order 3928 of April 8, 1942, Relating to the Stabilization of Wages, Prices, and Salaries (June 17, 1946); Exec. Order No. 9745, Providing for the Interim Administration of Certain Continuing Functions of the Office of Price Administration (June 30, 1946); Exec. Order No. 9809, Providing for the Disposition of Certain War Agencies (Dec. 12, 1946).

102. Exec. Order No. 9620, Abolishing the Office of Economic Stabilization and Transferring Its Functions to the Office of War Mobilization and Reconversion (Sept. 20, 1945).

remained in operation for many years after the war, hearing cases as late as 1961.[103]

LEGAL PROFILES

Fred M. Vinson was the second director of the OES, as well as a future Supreme Court justice. He was born in Kentucky in 1890 and started his legal practice there. After serving in WWI for two years, he was elected the Commonwealth's Attorney for the Thirty-Second Judicial District of Kentucky. He then ran for Congress and, with a one-term interruption, served from 1924 to 1938. He was then appointed by President Roosevelt to a seat on the court of appeals for the D.C. Circuit. He served there for five years before leaving to head up the OES, including more than a year as the chief judge on the Emergency Court of Appeals. After the OES and a short time as the director of the Office of War Mobilization and Reconversion, he was appointed as secretary of the treasury in 1945, where he served for about one year before being appointed by President Truman as the chief justice of the U.S. Supreme Court in 1946. He served in this role until his death in 1953.[104]

3.3 LABOR DISPUTES

A. Statutes

From the administration's perspective, labor as a focus had several tracks. One was the productivity of the labor force, i.e., the proper allocations of labor where and when it was needed. Another was the imperative to control the impact of wages and salaries on general inflation levels, as discussed in the

---

103. *See* Rosenzweig v. General Servs. Admin., 299 F.2d 22 (Emer. Ct. App. 1961).
104. *See Vinson, Frederick Moore*, BIOGRAPHICAL DIRECTORY OF THE UNITED STATES CONGRESS; *Vinson, Frederick Moore*, BIOGRAPHICAL DIRECTORY OF FEDERAL JUDGES.

previous section. A third was protecting the rights of workers, including the relatively nascent legal support for collective bargaining and minimum work hours. A fourth was facilitating some degree of labor-management harmony and therefore averting strikes in essential defense industries. The latter is discussed further in the next section ("Seizure of the Means of Production") because strikes often lead to a government takeover of the means of production.

Prior to the war, labor had gained significantly from the New Deal. Workers had gained legal protections through the passage of the National Labor Relations Act (also known as the Wagner Act) in 1935 and the Fair Labor Standards Act in 1938. The National Labor Relations Act dealt with collective bargaining rights.[105] The act specified that it was an unfair labor practice to interfere with the rights of employees to self-organize, bargain collectively, and engage in concerted activities or the creation and maintenance of a labor organization; it also specified that it was illegal to discriminate in hiring, promotion, or termination or to so interfere or to refuse to bargain collectively. It did not interfere with the right to strike. The NLRB was the enforcement mechanism under this act. The law was found constitutional in a significant victory for the New Deal legislation,[106] around the time of the court-packing threats from the administration.[107]

The Fair Labor Standards Act provided for a minimum wage of twenty-five cents an hour (rising to forty cents an hour within seven years) and a maximum workweek of forty-four hours (decreasing to forty hours within two years) with overtime at 1.5 times the base rate.[108] Certain industries (e.g., agriculture) and job types (e.g., salesman) were exempted, "oppressive" child labor was banned, and compliance with the act was overseen by the Department of Labor. The law was upheld in *Tennessee Coal, Iron & Railroad Co. v. Muscoda Local No. 123*,[109] although the workweek was later extended during the war by executive order[110] and wages suppressed due to inflationary concerns.

---

105. Pub. L. No. 74-198 (1935).
106. National Labor Relations Bd. v. Jones & Laughlin Steel Corp., 301 U.S. 1 (1937).
107. This was part of a bill, the Judiciary Reorganization Bill of 1937, to add an additional justice to the Court for each justice over the age of 70, in response to the Court's earlier rulings striking down parts of the New Deal, such as the Agricultural Adjustment Act.
108. Pub. L. No. 75-718 (1938).
109. Tennessee Coal, Iron & R.R. Co. v. Muscoda Local No. 123, 321 U.S. 590 (1944).
110. Exec. Order No. 9301, Establishing a Minimum Wartime Work Week of Forty-Eight Hours (Feb. 9, 1943).

To help shape legislation and to deal with the disparate positions of management and labor, Roosevelt appointed Frances Perkins as secretary of labor in 1933, and she continued in that office for the whole period of the war. Not only was she the first female cabinet-level officer in U.S. history (thereby placing her in the line of succession to the presidency), but she was a strong advocate for labor.

In addition to Perkins, Roosevelt counted on the skills of labor leader Sidney Hillman in helping the administration negotiate with the burgeoning union movement. In the constant reorganization of federal administrative agencies that occurred in the early prewar and war years, labor-focused entities were no exception. Political infighting and resultant ineffectiveness led to increasingly stronger agencies. In 1940, Roosevelt reactivated the Advisory Commission of the Council of National Defense, a WWI emergency agency,[111] with Sidney Hillman leading the Labor Division within it. When the OPM was created in early 1941 (see Section 3.1), Sidney Hillman was named associate director; he brought the Labor Division with him, which then became part of the War Production Board in 1942. Initially quite effective at averting strikes, Hillman, due to personal illness and other political reasons, became less so, which led to a new administrative organization.

The National Defense Mediation Board was created by executive order in March of 1941.[112] It was structurally independent of the OPM and the Department of Labor. Its stated aim was that work for national defense must go forward "without interruption and with all possible speed."[113] This board was comprised of eleven members, three from the public and four each from labor and employers. If a dispute (as certified by the secretary of labor) between employers and employees impacted the production or transportation of equipment or materials essential to national defense (with the exception of railroad labor disputes), the board could facilitate settlement negotiations, initiate arbitration, or establish dispute resolution techniques. The board was also empowered to investigate, conduct hearings, take testimony, make findings of fact, and formulate recommendations or ask the NLRB's assistance in matters of collective bargaining. In addition, both employers and employees involved with

---

111. Pub. L. No. 64-242 (1916).
112. Exec. Order No. 8716 Establishing the National Defense Mediation Board (Mar. 19, 1941).
113. *Id.*

national defense were required to give notice of any disputes and possible interruptions to "permit exploration of all avenues of possible settlement of such controversies so as to avoid strikes, stoppages, or lockouts."[114] Initially successful, the National Defense Mediation Board was eventually undone by a number of strikes in 1941, including those involving Bethlehem Steel, the United Mine Workers, North American Aviation, railway workers in Michigan, Allis-Chalmers, International Harvester, and the Federal Shipbuilding and Drydock Company in New Jersey.

The month after the declaration of war, Roosevelt created the stronger National War Labor Board (NWLB) by executive order to succeed the National Defense Mediation Board.[115] Similar to the same-named entity that had existed during WWI, the NWLB referred to the labor-industry conference called by Roosevelt in mid-December 1941, which resulted in a "pledge" that there were to be no strikes or lockouts during the war (although this pledge was not fully kept). The new board had twelve members (one more public member). Similar to the National Defense Mediation Board, the NWLB took responsibility for any disputes after certification from the secretary of labor, but it could also enter disputes on its own accord. The methods open to it included mediation, voluntary arbitration, and arbitration by its rules.

Later, when the OES was created, the executive order required that the NWLB approve all wage increases for all industries and employees, except in cases where "such increase is necessary to correct maladjustments or inequalities, to eliminate substandards of living, to correct gross inequities, or to aid in the effective prosecution of the war."[116] This function of dealing with wage increases greatly increased the workload of the NWLB, which set up a number of regional and specialized industry offices to handle it.

To address labor utilization, Roosevelt created the War Manpower Commission in April 1942.[117] This executive order was the first labor-related one to refer to a specific statute for support, i.e., the First War Powers Act. Designed for the "effective mobilization and utilization of the national manpower,"[118]

---

114. *Id.*
115. Exec. Order No. 9017, Establishing the National War Labor Board (Jan. 12, 1942).
116. Exec. Order No. 9250, Establishing the Office of Economic Stabilization (Oct. 3, 1942).
117. Exec. Order No. 9139, Establishing the War Manpower Commission (Apr. 18, 1942).
118. *Id.*

it consisted of the federal security administrator and representatives from the Departments of War, Navy, Agriculture, and Labor; the WPB; the Selective Service System, and the Civil Service Commission. The responsibility of the commission included the following:

- Creating plans, programs, and policies to ensure the most effective mobilization and maximum utilization of the country's manpower
- Estimating industry manpower requirements while reviewing military, agricultural, and civilian manpower requirements and directing government agencies "as to the proper allocation of available manpower"[119]
- Coordinating federal programs for recruitment, vocational training, and placement of workers to meet the needs of industry and agriculture

The next major step was the passage of the War Labor Disputes Act (also called the Smith-Connally Act) in June 1943.[120] After the bitter United Mine Workers strike of 1943, Congress wanted more power for the NWLB in dealing with strikes impacting the war effort. Passed over Roosevelt's veto, the act, besides its relationship to addressing strikes (discussed in Section 3.4), gave additional powers to the NWLB. When a labor dispute affecting the war effort existed, the NWLB, either on its own or by certification from the Department of Labor, could summon both parties to appear before it; in addition, the act gave the NWLB (under the president's Second War Powers Act) subpoena power as to attendance of witnesses and production of books, papers, and records. In reaching settlements and issuing orders, the NWLB was required to comply with the Fair Labor Standards Act, the National Labor Relations Act, the Emergency Price Control Act, and the Stabilization Act.

Orders issued by the NWLB were not always followed. Therefore, the president issued an executive order in August 1943 to assist the NWLB.[121] This order allowed the director of the OES to issue "such directives as he may deem necessary" to contend with noncompliers:

---

119. *Id.*
120. Pub. L. No. 78-89 (1943).
121. Exec. Order No. 9370, Action in Connection with the Enforcement of Directives of the National War Labor Board (Aug. 16, 1943).

- For noncomplying employers, directives included restricting/withdrawing priority, benefits or contracts from the government.
- For noncomplying unions, directives included restricting/withdrawing benefits, privileges, or rights under the terms of employment where the government is operating a plant, mine, or facility.
- For noncomplying individuals, directives included having the War Manpower Commission modify/cancel draft deferments or employment privileges.[122]

LEGAL PROFILES

William H. Davis was the chairman of the NWLB during most of WWII; he was also a lawyer. He was born in Maine in 1879. Because he worked as a patent examiner before starting his practice in New York, he did some work for the U.S. Patent and Trademark Office and later the War Department during WWI. President Roosevelt appointed him as the deputy administrator for the National Recovery Administration, where he remained until its creation was ruled unconstitutional and the agency was disbanded. He was appointed to New York's Labor Mediation Board by Frances Perkins, which led to his appointment to the National Defense Mediation Board and the NWLB as its head. In early 1945, he took on the role of director of the OES after Fred Vinson left to join the Supreme Court, but the office was soon closed down. He was involved in the Atomic Energy Commission and became the New York commissioner of transit after the war. He died in 1964.[123]

Hugo L. Black was the primary drafter of the Fair Labor Standards Act while a senator; he was also a future Supreme Court justice. Born in Alabama in 1886, he started his legal practice there, including a stint as a police court judge. In 1914, he became a county prosecuting attorney. He resigned during WWI to join the army. In 1926, he was elected

---

122. *Id.*
123. *See William Hammatt Davis is Dead; Chairman of the War Labor Board*, N.Y. TIMES (Aug. 15, 1964).

to the U.S. Senate, where he remained until 1937. In that year, he was appointed by President Roosevelt to the U.S. Supreme Court; he filled a seat made vacant by retirement but perhaps influenced by the introduction of the Judicial Procedures Reform Bill (the court-packing plan) the same year. He was involved in a number of key opinions over the years and remained on the Court as one of its longest-serving justices until his death in 1971.[124]

B. Cases

The courts looked at both of the functions of the NWLB, i.e., mediating labor disputes and approving wage rate changes. The first case dealt with the enforceability of NWLB orders. The second case analyzed the additional reach of NWLB orders. The third case considered the legality of the NWLB's role in reviewing wage rate increases. The fourth case examined the effect of orders from the War Manpower Commission.

1. Effect of NWLB Orders, No. 1

Employers Group of Motor Freight Carriers, Inc. v. National War Labor Board looked at the ability of NWLB orders to be enforced on their own.[125] The complainant represented more than three hundred trucking companies in the New England area that could not reach agreement with their employees. This was certified by the secretary of labor. The NWLB then reached the conclusion that, among other things, the employees should receive an increase of about three dollars a week. The complainant disputed the findings, alleged an incorrect interpretation of statutes and executive orders, and stated that it would be "impossible for the plaintiffs to absorb the said award, and the industry is confronted with outright failure and dissolution."[126] The companies felt that they needed to comply, though, because other firms that had not done so had faced government seizure of their businesses.

The court dismissed the complaint, stating that the NWLB order was not reviewable by the courts because there was no statute authorizing such review.

---

124. *See Black, Hugo Lafayette*, FED. JUDICIAL CTR., BIOGRAPHICAL DIRECTORY OF FEDERAL JUDGES.
125. Employers Group of Motor Freight Carriers, Inc. v. National War Labor Board, 143 F.2d 145 (D.C. Cir. 1944).
126. *Id.* at 146.

Because no administrative or judicial proceedings could be maintained based upon this order, there was no need for review. The court also ruled that these orders are not mandatory and therefore not enforceable. The legislative history showed the lack of a desire to give the NWLB enforcement powers, so instead its orders provide a "moral obligation of employers and workers to abide by the no-strike, no-lock-out agreement."[127]

The court held that, in concurrence with a letter from the Director of Economic Stabilization, the effect of support from his office for NWLB issues applied only to actions brought under the War Labor Disputes Act. The appellants were concerned that if noncompliance was reported to the president, he might then move to seize their plants and facilities. The court dismissed that concern as being both speculative and also unrelated to the NWLB's order, which was merely advisory. The court noted that the president had seized plants and facilities, but such seizure was independent of NWLB orders. The court added that it had no right to enjoin the NWLB from giving advice to the president, which would be akin to enjoining any of his other advisers from giving advice.

LEGAL PROFILES

Francis M. Shea was the lawyer for the appellee in this case. He was born in New Hampshire in 1905 and started his legal practice in New York. He worked for the firm of John Lord O'Brian (see Section 3.1) before moving on to federal government positions with the Agricultural Adjustment Administration in 1933 and the Puerto Rico Reconstruction Administration two years later. He then became the dean of the law school at the University of Buffalo. In 1939, he was recruited by Robert H. Jackson (see Chapter 2) to become the assistant attorney general in the Claims Division, where he remained for the course of the war, arguing many cases before the U.S. Supreme Court. After the war, he was a chief assistant to Jackson in the lead-up to the Nuremberg Trials in Germany, and then founded his own law firm. He died in 1989.[128]

---

127. *Id.* at 149.
128. *See Francis M. Shea, 74, Legal Firm Founder,* N.Y. TIMES (Aug. 10, 1989).

2. Effect of NWLB Orders, No. 2

In *Paris v. Metropolitan Life Insurance Co.*, the court acknowledged the effect of these orders but went further.[129] This matter dealt with the effect of an NWLB ruling requiring retroactive payment of wages that were contrary to state insurance laws by which the defendant was bound. The court determined that the federal laws under which the NWLB operated superseded the state insurance laws. However, before that, it analyzed the legal validity of NWLB orders in general. Although noting their advisory nature, the court found that the orders cannot "be disregarded or that they are legal nullities" as they are enforceable by government agencies other than courts; it noted in particular the enforcement based on executive sanction, such as the power to take over plants or the power of the OES director to order certain benefits and privileges withheld. The court ordered that the NWLB order be followed and the retroactive payments made. (This decision was later overturned on other grounds,[130] but eventually payments were ordered.)[131]

3. Approval of Wage Increases

National Labor Relations Board v. Indiana Desk Co. examined the requirement to obtain NWLB approval for wage increases.[132] The NLRB sought to obtain enforcement of its order against the respondent for engaging in unfair labor practices, including dismissing those involved in a strike.

After employees demanded increased wages and the employer refused, the employees went on strike. The strike was illegal because the wage increase had to be approved by the NWLB first as it contravened the Stabilization Act and related executive orders and would have subjected the employer to criminal sanctions if it granted such a wage increase without approval. Thus, the court ruled, the situation did not give rise to a labor dispute; and, as such, the employer was within its rights to fire the workers who went on strike. The court, also taking into account further illegal actions by the strikers who shut down the plant, denied the NLRB's enforcement of its order.

---

129. Paris v. Metropolitan Life Ins. Co., 68 F. Supp. 64 (S.D.N.Y. 1946).
130. Paris v. Metropolitan Life Ins. Co., 167 F.2d 834 (2d Cir. 1948).
131. Paris v. Metropolitan Life Ins. Co., 94 F. Supp. 356 (S.D.N.Y. 1950).
132. National Labor Relations Bd. v. Indiana Desk Co., 149 F.2d 987 (7th Cir. 1945).

LEGAL PROFILES

Alvin J. Rockwell was the lawyer for the appellant in this case. He was born in Michigan in 1908 and began to practice law in Massachusetts before moving to Washington, D.C. to work as a labor lawyer in the federal government. He worked with the NLRB from 1937 to 1940 and then for the Department of Justice in both the Tax Division and the Office of the Solicitor General from 1940 to 1943. He returned to the NRLB as general counsel from 1943 to 1945. In 1945, he was the associate legal director for the Office of the Military Government for Germany, United States, where he was instrumental in rebuilding the legal system in Germany. He also played a role in educating the German populace about the differences between the totalitarianism with which they had become familiar and democracy. He then moved to San Francisco and returned to private practice. He died in 1999.[133]

4. Effect of War Manpower Commission Orders

In *San Francisco Lodge No. 68 of International Ass'n of Machinists v. Forrestal*, the court analyzed the effects of the powers of the War Manpower Commission.[134] In this case, the plaintiff union's labor dispute was referred to the NWLB, which ordered the union to drop its specific demands and return to work. Upon the union's refusal, the matter was referred to the president, who ordered the navy to take over and operate the machine shops, which were considered essential to the war effort. Besides requesting withdrawal of the NWLB order, the union asked that its members not be subject to the War Manpower Commission's freezing orders. These orders stop "clearance and referrals," which are essential to enable employees to obtain employment in other war plants.[135] The plaintiff held that such orders are a penalty and outside the powers of an administrative agency. The court held that in this case there was no judiciable

---

133. *See Alvin Rockwell, 90; Lawyer Helped Mold a Postwar Germany*, N.Y. Times (May 20, 1999).
134. San Francisco Lodge No. 68 of Int'l Ass'n of Machinists v. Forrestal, Sec'y of the Navy, 58 F. Supp. 466 (N.D. Cal. 1944).
135. *Id.* at 467.

controversy presently before it because these actions had not yet occurred; however, it noted that if it did rule, it would find the denial of clearance not a penalty but rather a "remedial" action, which an administrative agency was allowed to issue.[136]

LEGAL PROFILES

Nathan P. Feinsinger was associate general counsel of the NWLB under Jesse Freidin. He was born in New York in 1902 and joined the law school faculty at the University of Wisconsin in 1929, where he taught for forty-three years. In 1937, he was appointed general counsel for the Wisconsin Labor Relations Board, where he served for two years. President Roosevelt appointed him as associate general counsel of the NWLB in 1942 and as director of National Disputes in 1943, and eventually chairman. Both during and after the war, he was involved in mediating a number of major strikes. In 1951, President Truman nominated him to lead the National Wage Stabilization Board during the Korean War. He was soon involved in the strike of United Steelworkers of America, which led Truman to seize the steelworks (see Section 3.4). He continued to work on mediating strikes the rest of his life, including the 1966 New York City transit strike. He died in 1983.[137]

C. Subsequent Events

The NWLB was disbanded in late 1945 by executive order, with its duties given to the NLRB and the Department of Labor.[138] Statistics reflect the extent of the work it accomplished: the NWLB was involved in the settling of approximately 18,000 disputes covering more than 12 million employees (more than 80 percent were wage-related disputes) and handling more than 400,000 appli-

---

136. *Id.* at 469.
137. *See Nathan P. Feinsinger, 81, Dead; U.S. Labor Mediator Taught Law,* N.Y. TIMES (Nov. 4, 1983).
138. Exec. Order No. 9672, Establishing the National Wage Stabilization Board and Terminating the National War Labor Board (Dec. 31, 1945).

cations for wage adjustments affecting more than 26 million employees.[139] The vast majority of cases were wage related and handled by the regional offices using wage formulas such as the Little Steel approach of giving a 15 percent increase over early 1941 wages, based on a major NWLB decision.[140] Other disputes often centered around the open shop versus closed shop issue, which was compromised by a maintenance-of-membership agreement, i.e., those in unions had to remain, while those not in unions were not required to join.

Both the experiences and the frustrations of the wartime labor laws, processes, and disputes shaped the after-war period. Frustrated by the lack of significant progress due to their no-strike pledge during the war, labor caught up almost as soon as the war ended. There were many significant strikes in 1946 involving, e.g., coal workers, electrical workers, autoworkers, steelworkers, meatpackers, railway workers, and longshoremen.

When the Republican Party gained more than fifty seats and control of the House of Representatives in the elections in late 1946, they not only were able to get legislation passed to deal with the strikes, they were able to overcome Truman's veto in June 1947 and pass the Taft-Hartley Act. The purpose of this new law, also called the Labor-Management Relations Act of 1947,[141] was

> to promote the full flow of commerce, to prescribe the legitimate rights of both employees and employers in their relations affecting commerce, to provide orderly and peaceful procedures for preventing the interference by either with the legitimate rights of the other, to protect the rights of individual employees in their relations with labor organizations whose activities affect commerce, to define and proscribe practices on the part of labor and management which affect commerce and are inimical to the general welfare, and to protect the rights of the public in connection with labor disputes affecting commerce.[142]

---

139. 1-3 U.S. Nat'l War Labor Bd., The Termination Report of the National War Labor Board, January 12, 1942–December 31, 1945: Industrial Disputes and Wage Stabilization in Wartime (1947).

140. National War Labor Bd., Case Nos. 30, 31, 34, 35 (July 16, 1942), involving "Little Steel" companies Bethlehem Steel, Republic Steel, Youngstown Sheet & Tube, and Inland Steel (but not giant U.S. Steel).

141. Pub. L. No. 80-101 (1947).

142. *Id.* § 1.

The changes are primarily modifications to the National Labor Relations Act to give the law more balance by having it focus on the actions of labor unions instead of just the actions of employers. Unfair labor practices now included union actions that violated § 7 rights, certain types of strikes, refusal to bargain collectively, extortion, or coercion of employees. Secondary boycotts (boycotts of other companies' products or services), solidarity strikes (strikes with other unions), strikes over assignment of certain types of work, and wildcat strikes (strikes not approved by union leaders) were all prohibited. Employees were allowed to not join unions (open shop), and states could pass right-to-work laws. The government could seek an injunction to enjoin a strike that affected most of an industry and imperiled "the national health or safety."[143] Labor unions as well as employers could now be sued for violations of contracts and were required to give advance notice of strikes. Union officials had to sign affidavits that they were not members of the Communist Party. The impacts of this law were felt keenly in the next war (see Section 3.4), when organized labor and industry would again interact with the successors to the NWLB, OES, and OPA.

LEGAL PROFILES

Lloyd K. Garrison was the head of the NWLB at its termination; he was also a lawyer. Born in New York in 1897, he left the university he was attending to enter the navy during WWI. He started out in practice in New York and in 1929 was named dean of the law school at the University of Wisconsin. He assisted the U.S. attorney general in a 1930 investigation into bankruptcy fraud. Roosevelt appointed Garrison as the first chairman of the NLRB in 1934 (influencing the following year's statute) and as a mediator for the Little Steel Strike of 1937. Garrison was named chief counsel of the NWLB in 1942 and chairman in 1945. After the war, he returned to private practice in New York and was involved in a number of high-profile cases, including defending J. Robert Oppenheimer and Arthur Miller against accusations of Communist sympathies

---

143. *Id.* § 206.

and litigating a seminal environmental law case.[144] From 1947 to 1952, he was the president of the National Urban League. His wife was a descendant of Supreme Court Chief Justice John Jay. Garrison died in 1991.[145]

Robert A. Taft was the cosponsor of this legislation and an attorney. He was born in Ohio in 1889, the son of the future U.S. president and U.S. Supreme Court chief justice William Howard Taft. He entered private practice in Ohio in 1913 and, after unsuccessfully trying to enlist in the army in WWI, worked during the war years for the U.S. Food and Drug Administration and the American Relief Administration in Europe. He returned to Ohio to run for the state house in 1920, served until 1926, and then won a seat in the state senate in 1930. In 1938, he was elected to the U.S. Senate, where he won three terms and became the Senate majority leader in 1953. He ran for president as a conservative Republican in three different elections but never won his party's nomination. He died in 1953.[146]

3.4 SEIZURE OF THE MEANS OF PRODUCTION

A. Statutes

President Roosevelt had been dealing with the problem of labor-management discord at munitions plants even before the war had officially begun. As mentioned above, 1941 had been a particularly strike-prone year in the defense industry, and he was forced to intervene in several of these strikes.

For instance, the federal government intervened in the strike at North American Aviation, for which the president issued an executive order stating that "[c]ontinuous production . . . is essential to national defense."[147] Much of the property in that plant was owned, "directly or indirectly," by the govern-

144. Scenic Hudson Preservation Conference v. Federal Power Comm'n, 354 F.2d 608 (2d Cir. 1965).
145. *See Lloyd K. Garrison, Lawyer, Dies; Leader in Social Causes Was 92*, N.Y. TIMES (Oct. 3, 1991).
146. *See Taft, Robert, Jr.*, BIOGRAPHICAL DIRECTORY OF THE UNITED STATES CONGRESS.
147. Exec. Order No. 8773, Seizure of the North American Aviation Company Plant at Inglewood, California (Jun. 9, 1941).

ment, including aircraft in the course of production, raw material, machinery, and other property.[148] Because a labor dispute had stopped production (contrary to agreement), conciliation had failed, and the National Defense Mediation Board had not been successful in a "situation seriously detrimental to the defense of the United States,"[149] Roosevelt had to act. He relied on not only his role as commander in chief but also the 1941 proclamation declaring "an unlimited national emergency"[150] for authority to have the secretary of war take charge of the plant and operate it until normal production resumed.

The government typically returned seized plants as soon as it could (e.g., North American Aviation was returned in less than a month).[151] But that was not always possible. On May 1, 1943, Roosevelt was forced to issue an executive order to take control of the coal mines.[152] He said that he had tried to get John L. Lewis and the United Mine Workers to stop their strikes, which were "directly interfering" with the prosecution of the war and would have the same effect "as a crippling defeat in the war."[153] To avoid a "grave peril" but at the same time appealing to the patriotism of any mine workers who wanted to return to work, he ordered the secretary of the interior to take possession of and operate the striking coal mines "in such manner as he deems necessary for the successful prosecution of the war, and to do all things necessary for or incidental to the production, sale, and distribution of coal."[154] Possession and operation was to be terminated if no longer needed "for the furtherance of the war program."[155]

Shortly thereafter, at the end of June 1943, Congress passed the War Labor Disputes Act (see Section 3.3), further empowering the NWLB.[156] Another part of this act revised § 9 of the Selective Training and Service Act of 1940,[157] which had given the president the power to take immediate possession of

---

148. *Id.*
149. *Id.*
150. Exec. Proclamation No. 2487, Proclaiming That an Unlimited National Emergency Confronts This Country, Which Requires That Its Military, Naval, Air and Civilian Defenses Be Put on the Basis of Readiness to Repel Any and All Acts or Threats of Aggression Directed Toward Any Part of the Western Hemisphere (May 27, 1941).
151. Exec. Order No. 8814, Directing the Secretary of War to Relinquish Possession of the Inglewood Plant of North American Aviation, Inc. (July 2, 1941).
152. Exec. Order No. 9340, Seizure of Coal Mines (May 1, 1943).
153. *Id.*
154. *Id.*
155. *Id.*
156. Pub. L. No. 78-89 (1943).
157. Pub. L. No. 76-783 (1940).

any plant either involved with or capable of producing munitions that did not agree to manufacture or to furnish these at a reasonable price, thereby allowing the government to manufacture the required items. The new revision extended "to any plant, mine, or facility equipped for the manufacture, production, or mining of any articles or materials which may be required for the war effort or which may be useful in connection therewith."[158] The act applied if there was a strike or other disturbance that impeded the war effort and seizure was necessary in order to operate the plant, mine, or facility in the "interest of the war effort."[159] The act also made it illegal to interfere with any government-run plant, including facilitating a labor strike there.

In 1941, there were three executive orders whose purpose was to take over defense-related plants;[160] in 1942, four such executive orders;[161] and in the first half of 1943, just two such executive orders.[162] After the passage of the War Labor Disputes Act, this number increased substantially. The impact of this act, in combination with the increased war effort and some amount of weariness with unrelenting conflict between employers and labor unions, was significant. In the second half of 1943, there were seven executive orders taking over defense-related plants;[163] and in 1944, there were twenty-seven such orders.[164]

In late 1943, Roosevelt issued an executive order for the seizure of the railroads.[165] In doing so, he did not invoke the authority of War Labor Disputes Act

158. War Labor Disputes Act, Pub. L. No. 78-89.
159. *Id.*
160. Exec. Order No. 8773 (Jun. 9, 1941); Exec. Order No. 8868 (Aug. 23, 1941); Exec. Order No. 8928 (Oct. 30, 1941).
161. Exec. Order No. 9141 (Apr. 18, 1942); Exec. Order No. 9220 (Aug. 13, 1942); Exec. Order No. 9225 (Aug. 19, 1942); Exec. Order No. 9254 (Oct. 12, 1962).
162. Exec. Order No. 9340 (May 1, 1943); Exec. Order No. 9351 (June 14, 1943).
163. Exec. Order No. 9375 (Sept. 3, 1943); Exec. Order No. 9393 (Nov. 1, 1943); Exec. Order No. 9395-B (Nov. 20, 1943); Exec. Order No. 9399 (Nov. 25, 1943); Exec. Order No. 9400 (Dec. 3, 1943); Exec. Order No. 9408 (Dec. 19, 1943); Exec. Order No. 9412 (Dec. 27, 1943).
164. Exec. Order No. 9416 (Jan. 21, 1944); Exec. Order No. 9420 (Feb. 7, 1944); Exec. Order No. 9426 (Feb. 23, 1944); Exec. Order No. 9435 (Apr. 13, 1944); Exec. Order No. 9436 (Apr. 13, 1944); Exec. Order No. 9438 (Apr. 25, 1944); Exec. Order No. 9443 (May 20, 1944); Exec. Order No. 9459 (Aug. 3, 1944); Exec. Order No. 9462 (Aug. 11, 1944); Exec. Order No. 9463 (Aug. 12, 1944); Exec. Order No. 9466 (Aug. 19, 1944); Exec. Order No. 9469 (Aug. 23, 1944); Exec. Order No. 9473 (Aug. 29, 1944); Exec. Order No. 9474 (Aug. 31, 1944); Exec. Order No. 9475-A (Sept. 2, 1944); Exec. Order No. 9476 (Sept. 3, 1944); Exec. Order No. 9477 (Sept. 5, 1944); Exec. Order No. 9478 (Sept. 6, 1944); Exec. Order No. 9480 (Sept. 9, 1944); Exec. Order No. 9481 (Sept. 12, 1944); Exec. Order No. 9482 (Sept. 14, 1944); Exec. Order No. 9483 (Sept. 19, 1944); Exec. Order No. 9484 (Sept. 23, 1944); Exec. Order No. 9493 (Oct. 24, 1944); Exec. Order No. 9496 (Nov. 3, 1944); Exec. Order No. 9505 (Dec. 6, 1944); Exec. Order No. 9508 (Dec. 27, 1944).
165. Exec. Order No. 9412, Seizure and Operation of the Railroads (Dec. 27, 1943).

but instead referred to a WWI-era statute[166] that allowed the president, during a war, to take possession and assume control of any system of transportation of "troops, war material and equipment, or for such other purposes connected with the emergency as may be needful or desirable."[167] However, when he took over the coal mines in 1944,[168] it was the Selective Training and Service Act as amended by the War Labor Disputes Act (along with the Constitution) that provided the legal authority for these actions of seizure.

LEGAL PROFILES

Tom T. Connally was one of the two sponsors of the War Labor Disputes Act and a lawyer. Born in Texas in 1877, he started his legal career there. He served in the army in both the Spanish-American War and WWI. He was first elected to the Texas legislature in 1900 and became a county attorney in 1906. In 1917, he was elected to Congress, where his first vote was to declare war on Germany. After that, he resigned to join the army even though he was forty years old. He returned to his position in the House, serving there until 1928. He then was elected to the U.S. Senate, where he remained until 1953. He was involved in the conference leading to the creation of the United Nations and helped procure approval for its charter in the Senate. He died in 1963.[169]

B. Cases

As would be expected when the subject is the takeover of the production facilities of a company and the replacement of any number of workers at that facility, there were a number of lawsuits brought against the government for takeovers during the war. The ability to take over munitions plants was clear

---

166. Pub. L. No. 64-242 (1916).
167. *Id.*.
168. Exec. Order No. 9474, Authorizing the Secretary of the Interior to Take Possession of and Operate the Mines, Collieries, and Preparation Facilities of the Ford Collieries Company of Curtisville, Pennsylvania, and Rochester and Pittsburgh Coal Company (Aug. 31, 1944).
169. *See Connally, Thomas Terry (Tom)*, BIOGRAPHICAL DIRECTORY OF THE UNITED STATES CONGRESS.

enough, but other situations were not as clear-cut. The first case involved the prospective government takeover of a retailer. The second case involved the takeover of a transportation company and the subsequent labor strikes aided by the company. The third case involved the takeover of a railroad. The fourth case concerned changes to collective bargaining recognition that occurred while the government was operating a mine. The fifth case dealt with penalties imposed for interfering with government control.

1. Retailers

United States v. Montgomery Ward & Co.[170] concerned the government takeover of a large retailer. There had been many problems concerning Montgomery Ward and its refusal to follow the orders of the NWLB related to labor issues referred to that board. Numerous labor strikes ensued, and the government feared that these constant labor disputes would spread to other locations both inside and outside the company, thereby impeding the war effort. The president issued an executive order to take over Montgomery Ward's plants and facilities in eight locations, but not the three factories over which Montgomery Ward still had control (the government was already operating one Montgomery Ward factory, but that factory made less than 2 percent of its products).[171]

The district court was asked to declare that the government was rightly in possession and to enjoin the defendant from interfering with the plaintiff. The defendant responded that the government had no power (from the Constitution, statutes, or the War Labor Disputes Act) to take these actions. The court ruled that the act itself was constitutional but looked at whether the government could take over a retail establishment engaged solely in distribution. The court looked at the following text from the act: "take over any mine, plant or facility which is *equipped* for the manufacture, mining or *production* of any article or material necessary or useful in the war effort."[172] Focusing on the italicized words, the court found that distribution was not covered by the act, and so the president did not have the power to seize the facilities. The court then looked at whether the president had such power under the Constitution as commander in chief. Looking back to Civil War–era cases, the court found that the president did not have the power because the retailing plants and facil-

---

170. United States v. Montgomery Ward & Co., 58 F. Supp. 408 (N.D. Ill. 1945).
171. Exec. Order No. 9508, Authorizing the Secretary of War to Take Possession of and to Operate Certain Facilities of Montgomery Ward & Co., Incorporated (Dec. 27, 1944).
172. War Labor Disputes Act, Pub. L. No. 78-89 (1943).

ities were not in the theater of war and there was no immediate public danger. Although chastising the selfishness of the disputants, the court dismissed the complaint.

The court of appeals took a different approach.[173] It noted that Montgomery Ward had filed "35,466 applications for priority distribution of articles. . . . Ward's requires the articles for the war effort"; in addition, Montgomery Ward had received contracts under Lend-Lease for apparel in liberated countries. Furthermore, the court noted, the NWLB had certified only 31 of 362,000 cases for further action (0.0086 percent). The court also noted the government's success in holding down wartime wage inflation via the Little Steel Strike formula (discussed in Section 3.3) combined with the "laborers' agreement not to strike and the employers' agreement to abide by the Board's rulings."[174] The court then reviewed each of the seized locations and found that in every one of these locations the defendant had refused to comply with an NWLB order regarding settlement of a local labor dispute. The referral to the president and seizure order had followed.

The court then analyzed the act, looking again at whether "production" included "distribution." It looked at prior, related acts, such as the Fair Labor Standards Act—where *production* included "handled, or in any other manner worked on" and "transporting"[175]—as well as a Supreme Court interpretation of the statute. It also looked to the defendant's own words in its many priority applications for materials, i.e., statements that those materials were vital for the war effort and were being shipped to "vital defense areas."[176] Finally, the court quoted from the affidavit of the head of the NWLB, who said thus:

> The persistent refusal of the (Ward) company to settle its disputes in the manner provided for in the Board's orders will, in my opinion, unduly impede and delay the war effort for the following reasons:
>
> 1. It threatens the disintegration of the wartime structure of labor relations which depends upon the peaceful settlement of disputes by the Board and which can not survive successful repudiation by a company of the size and economic importance of Ward.

---

173. United States v. Montgomery Ward, 150 F.2d 369 (7th Cir. 1945).
174. *Id.* at 372-373.
175. Fair Labor Standards Act, Pub. L. No. 75-718, § 3 (1938).
176. *Montgomery Ward*, 150 F.2d at 378.

2. It has already precipitated a strike of the company's employees in Detroit, which threatens to affect the maintenance of uninterrupted war production and the national no-strike pledge there and elsewhere.

3. It endangers the hold-the-line national stabilization program by rendering the government incapable of bringing about wage adjustments necessary "to correct gross inequities or aid in the effective prosecution of the war."

In summary, the wartime labor policy cannot, in my opinion, continue to function effectively if large groups of workers are compelled to resort to the strike and picket line because of the refusal of their employers to accept the procedures established by the President and Congress for the peaceful adjustment of disputes. Nor can the fight against inflation be successfully administered if employees are deprived of the minimum adjustments allowable under the stabilization law.[177]

The court then reversed the lower court and directed that the relief sought by the government be granted.

2. Transportation Systems

United States v. McMenamin concerned the government takeover of the transportation systems of the Philadelphia Transportation Company.[178] Via an executive order,[179] the government took over the system and subsequently charged the company with interfering with the workers and inciting them to strike.

In dealing with a motion to quash the indictment, the court was confronted with two questions: Was there power under the act to deal with labor disputes involving a transportation system? Could the government take over a transportation system? On the first question, the court felt it was clear that § 3 of the act only allowed the takeover of those facilities, etc., dealing with the production of munitions; as such, a transportation system was not covered. However, § 6, dealing with the interference of any plant, mine, or facility operated by the

---

177. *Id.* at 381.
178. United States v. McMenamin, 58 F. Supp. 478 (E.D. Penn. 1945).
179. Exec. Order No. 9459, Possession and Control of the Philadelphia Transportation Company by the Secretary of War (Aug. 3, 1944).

government, was not similarly limited to war-materials production. Because the court determined that a transportation system was a facility, the company could be charged with a violation under § 6. Furthermore, noted the court, the legality of taking over the transportation system can be found in the authority of the previously discussed WWI-era statute allowing the president to take over transportation systems during wartime.[180]

3. Railroads

Toledo, Peoria & Western Railroad v. Stover concerned the government takeover of a railroad and the railroad company's attempts to regain control of it.[181] There had been labor-management problems for some time (several years) involving the National Mediation Board. After the attack on Pearl Harbor in December 1941, the board convinced the employees to not strike and to agree to arbitration, but the employer refused to join arbitration. Thus, a strike ensued, and the employer sought injunctive relief, and the district court granted the relief. The U.S. Supreme Court eventually overturned the district court action, holding that before seeking such relief a party must make every reasonable effort to settle, which included entering arbitration.[182]

In March 1942, long before the *Toledo, Peoria & Western Railroad* decision was handed down, the president had issued an executive order to take over the railroad and put it under the management of the Office of Defense Transportation (ODT),[183] which had been created by executive order in late 1941.[184] The seizure of this railroad was followed in December 1943 with an executive order issued for the secretary of war to take control of all common carriers in the continental United States in order to avoid impending strikes.[185] In mid-January 1944, when this danger seemed to be averted and when the secretary of war determined that his control was "no longer required to prevent interruption of transportation service," he terminated that control as the executive order allowed.[186] The plaintiff's railroad was returned to the ODT.

---

180. Pub. L. No. 64-242 (1916).
181. Toledo, Peoria & W. R.R. v. Stover, 60 F. Supp. 587 (S.D. Ill. 1945).
182. Brotherhood of R.R. Trainmen, Enter. Lodge, No. 27 v. Toledo, Peoria & W. R.R., 321 U.S. 50 (1944).
183. Exec. Order No. 9108, Directing the Director of the Office of Defense Transportation to Take Control of the Toledo, Peoria, and Western Railroad Company (Mar. 21, 1942).
184. Exec. Order No. 8989, Establishing the Office of Defense Transportation (Dec. 18, 1941).
185. Exec. Order No. 9412, Possession and Operation of Railroads (Dec. 27, 1943).
186. *Id.*

The plaintiff contended that (1) the later executive order voided the first and so control should be returned to it and (2) the first executive order was void because it was not handled by the secretary of war. To the latter claim, the court agreed that it was the secretary of war who was required to take control under the authority of the first order, the WWI-era law. The court examined several laws to determine if the president was authorized to use another person to take control of a railroad and found that under the First War Powers Act (discussed in Section 3.1), the ability to redistribute functions and transfer powers among executive agencies empowered him to give to the ODT the secretary of war's power regarding a railroad's operation. However, when the second executive order was issued, the secretary of war regained possession of the railroad; and when the secretary issued the termination order on January 18, 1944, the United States gave up legal possession and control of the railroad, and it was not legally transferred back to the ODT. As such, the court sided with the railroad.

LEGAL PROFILES

Joseph B. Eastman was the first director of the ODT and a lawyer. He was born in New York in 1882 and started his legal practice in Massachusetts. From 1906 to 1913, he was part of a group called the Public Franchise League, which supported future Supreme Court justice Louis Brandeis in actions against railroads and later in wage arbitrations with railroads. Eastman was named to the Massachusetts Public Service Commission in 1915; and in 1919, President Woodrow Wilson appointed him to the Interstate Commerce Commission, where he remained until 1941, serving as the chairman beginning in 1939. In 1933, Roosevelt appointed him to the position of federal coordinator of transportation, and he remained in that capacity until 1936. He was appointed as director of the ODT in 1941, a position that he held until his death in 1944.[187]

---

187. *See The Man Who Makes the Wheels Go Round*, N.Y. TIMES (June 7, 1942).

4. Labor Changes Under Government Control

The government took control of coal mines on a number of occasions. In *Glen Alden Coal Co. v. National Labor Relations Board*,[188] the government seized control of the Glen Alden Coal Company mines based on an executive order in November 1943.[189] During the government's control, a small American Federation of Labor (AFL) union was recognized by the NLRB as the negotiating unit for the mine's foundry workers. The company refused to bargain with this union due to the company's agreement with the United Mineworkers, a non-AFL but locally much larger union, which represented almost all other workers at the mine. The company sued the NLRB to block recognition of this union while the government controlled the mine.[190] The court noted that the executive order gave the secretary of the interior, who had taken over the mines, authority under the War Labor Disputes Act to apply to the NLRB for approval of the labor contract with this now-recognized AFL union. Even though the government was in control, the court ruled that NLRB approval was binding upon the coal company.

LEGAL PROFILES

Joseph A. Padway was the AFL general counsel during this time. He was born in England in 1891. He moved to the state of Wisconsin, and it was there that he began his legal practice. One of his first jobs was working for the Wisconsin State Federation of Labor beginning in 1915, and he eventually became general counsel for all AFL unions in the state. He was elected to the Wisconsin state senate in 1924 but later resigned in 1926 to take an appointment as a civil court judge, where he was involved in much of the labor-related legislation that was ahead of what was occurring on the federal level, including unemployment compensation and the minimum-wage and -hour laws. During the strike at the Kohler factory in 1934, he was the counsel for the Wisconsin State Federation of Labor. He was then appointed as the first general counsel of

---

188. Glen Alden Coal Co. v. National Labor Relations Bd., 141 F.2d 47 (1944).
189. Exec. Order No. 9393, Possession and Operation of the Coal Mines (Nov. 1, 1943).
190. *Glen Alden Coal Co.*, 141 F.2d 47.

the national AFL in 1938 and argued a number of times before the U.S. Supreme Court.[191] He was also defense counsel for the United Mineworkers and John L. Lewis in the U.S. case against them (see next case discussion). He died in 1947.[192]

5. Penalties for Interference

Bituminous coal represented more than 40 percent of all energy produced in the United States,[193] so it was essential for the national economy. The government again had to take over the coal mines by executive order shortly after the war ended.[194]

In *United States v. United Mineworkers of America*,[195] the government had reached agreement with the United Mineworkers union on changes to their contract in the seized coal mines. Several months later, the union announced that it was going to break its agreement in an attempt to get much higher wages and benefits from the government-controlled mines. The government applied for and won a restraining order against the union, which subsequently went out on strike.

In court, the union argued that the Norris–La Guardia Act, which forbid temporary injunctions during peaceful labor disputes, applied.[196] The court, however, held that the act did not apply because the government had not agreed to be sued under it. Estimating that even a sixty-day mine work stoppage would cause the unemployment of five million people, a $20 billion GDP decrease, and a tax revenue loss of $280 million, the court found the union and its leader in criminal contempt of court for interfering with the government's

191. *See, e.g.*, Hill v. Florida *ex rel.* Watson, 325 U.S. 538 (1945); International Ass'n of Machinists v. National Labor Relations Bd., 311 U.S. 72 (1940).

192. *See Padway of AFL Dies Soon After Speech; General Counsel, 56, Stricken at Convention While Assailing the Taft-Hartley Act*, N.Y. TIMES (Oct. 9, 1947).

193. *United States v. United Mineworkers of America et al.*, 70 F. Supp. 42 (D.D.C. 1946).

194. Exec. Order No. 9728, Authorizing the Secretary of the Interior to Take Possession of and to Operate Certain Coal Mines (May 21, 1946).

195. *U. S. v. United Mineworkers of America.*

196. Pub. L. No. 72- 65 (1932).

operations of the mines and for leading the miner's strike. It fined the union $3.5 million and John L. Lewis $10,000.

LEGAL PROFILES

Thomas A. Goldsborough was the judge in this case. Born in Maryland in 1877, he started his legal practice there in 1901. From 1904 to 1908, he was a state's attorney before returning to private practice for the next thirteen years. In 1921, he was elected to the House of Representatives, where he remained until 1939. In presenting the *United Mineworkers* opinion, he stated that he had served in Congress with Representative Fiorello La Guardia at the time of the passage of the Norris–La Guardia Act and so felt that he knew the intent of its drafters sufficiently well to pass judgment upon it. After his long time in Congress, he was nominated by President Roosevelt to the district court in the District of Columbia. He served on this court until his death in 1951.[197]

C. Subsequent Events

The issue of the impact of strikes during wartime and the government's subsequent ability to take over production facilities arose again in 1952 during the Korean War when the United Steelworkers of America went on strike. In the lead-up to this strike, Nathan Feinsinger (see Section 3.3), head of the National Wage Stabilization Board (the successor to the NWLB), appointed a panel to hear the steelworkers' case. However, no agreement could be reached. At this time, there was no Congress-declared war or national emergency (only a United Nations mandate). Powers under the Taft-Hartley Act (see Section 3.3) allowed for a way to prevent the strike in case of a national emergency.

---

197. *See Goldsborough, Thomas Alan*, Fed. Judicial Ctr., Biographical Directory of Federal Judges; *Goldsborough, Thomas Alan*, Biographical Directory of the United States Congress.

Instead of using these tools, President Truman decided to implement an executive order to have the secretary of commerce take over the steelworks.[198] The steel companies went to the district court, stating that the government had no power to seize the plants. An initial injunction was eventually granted against the government taking over the steel plants, but the Supreme Court quickly granted certiorari.

The Supreme Court case, *Youngstown Sheet & Tube Co. v. Sawyer*, produced many different opinions by the justices.[199] The Court's opinion started out with the basic premise that the president's power must derive from either the Constitution or a congressional act. No statute was used to support the president's act, although two such statutes were then available. The Court also pointed out that in the recent Taft-Hartley Act (see Section 3.3), Congress had decided not to provide such powers. Moreover, the president could not point to any specific express powers but relied instead on an "aggregate of his powers" under the Constitution.[200] The Court ruled that pursuant to his commander-in-chief role, he could not "take possession of private property in order to keep labor disputes from stopping production. This is a job for the Nation's lawmakers, not for its military authorities."[201] It also could not find any authority under the sum of his constitutional powers, and his executive order both created law and then had it carried out. As such, the Court affirmed the lower court's decision.

Five concurring opinions were filed in this 6-3 decision. Examples of these opinions show the justices' desire to check unlimited presidential powers:

- Justice Douglas: "Today a kindly President uses the seizure power to effect a wage increase and to keep the steel furnaces in production. Yet tomorrow another President might use the same power to prevent a wage increase."
- Justice Burton: "The foregoing circumstances distinguish this emergency from one in which Congress takes no action and outlines no govern-

---

198. Exec. Order No. 10340, Directing the Secretary of Commerce to Take Possession of and Operate the Plants and Facilities of Certain Steel Companies (Apr. 8, 1952).
199. Youngstown Sheet & Tube Co. v. Sawyer, 343 U.S. 579 (1952).
200. *Id.* at 587.
201. *Id.*

mental policy. In the case before us, Congress authorized a procedure which the President declined to follow."

- Justice Clark: "In the absence of such action by Congress, the President's independent power to act depends upon the gravity of the situation confronting the nation."[202]

Justice Jackson's concurring opinion highlighted the two ends of the power spectrum for presidents:

When the President acts pursuant to an express or implied authorization of Congress, his authority is at its maximum. . . . When the President takes measures incompatible with the expressed or implied will of Congress, his power is at its lowest ebb, for then he can rely only upon his own constitutional powers minus any constitutional powers of Congress over the matter.[203]

Jackson compared the administration's request to another power situation well known in American history: "The example of such unlimited executive power that must have most impressed the forefathers was the prerogative exercised by George III, and the description of its evils in the Declaration of Independence leads me to doubt that they were creating their new Executive in his image."[204] In defining the president's power, Justice Jackson said,

[t]he Constitution expressly places in Congress power "to raise and *support* Armies" and "to *provide* and *maintain* a Navy." . . . [T]he Constitution did not contemplate that the title Commander in Chief *of the Army and Navy* will constitute him also Commander in Chief of the country, its industries and its inhabitants.[205]

The steelworker's strike continued for almost two more months before it was finally settled, both by the severe economic impacts on the steel companies and the nation and from President Truman's final push.

---

202. *Id.* at 662.
203. *Id.* at 637.
204. *Id.* at 641.
205. *Id.* at 644 (emphasis added by Court).

LEGAL PROFILES

Harry A. Shulman was the leader of the panel who heard the steel-workers and steel industry case. He was born in the Russian Empire in 1903 but moved to the United States when he was young. He started his private practice in New York but then began to clerk for Louis Brandeis, future Supreme Court justice, in 1929. In 1930, he started teaching at Yale University's law school, where he taught the rest of his life and was named dean in 1954. He served as special counsel for the U.S. Railroad Retirement Board from 1934 to 1936 and was a reporter on the *Restatement of Torts* from 1937 to 1939. He was involved in many labor arbitrations, from maritime to autos, and wrote the first casebook on arbitration of collective bargaining disputes. During WWII, he was involved with the U.S. attorney general's committee on administrative procedure and served on the NWLB. He was also involved in administrative and tort law and authored a number of books, including one with Felix Frankfurter, soon-to-be Supreme Court justice. He died in 1955.[206]

Arthur J. Goldberg was the amicus curiae counsel for the United Steelworkers; he was also a future Supreme Court justice. He was born in 1909 in Illinois and started his practice there. During WWII, he was involved with the Office of Strategic Services. After the war, he became the general counsel for the United Steelworkers in 1948, general counsel for the Congress of Industrial Organizations (CIO) the same year, and eventually the general counsel for the merged AFL-CIO from 1955 to 1961. In 1961, President Kennedy appointed him as secretary of labor. The following year, he was appointed as a justice on the Supreme Court. He only remained there for three years until resigning and taking on the role of U.S. ambassador to the United Nations, where he remained until 1968. He then returned to private practice and died in 1990.[207]

---

206. *See Harry Shulman, Yale Dean, Dead*, N.Y. TIMES (Mar. 21, 1955).
207. *See Goldberg, Arthur Joseph*, FED. JUDICIAL CTR., BIOGRAPHICAL DIRECTORY OF FEDERAL JUDGES.

3.5 ENEMY ASSETS

A. Statutes

There were a number of laws and executive orders in the early 1940s created to deal with the assets of enemy aliens, transactions with the enemies, and dealings with enemy economies. The control of exports was discussed in Chapter 1. Beyond this, there was Title III of the First War Powers Act, a revision to the WWI Trading with the Enemy Act.[208] It gave the president the ability to regulate or prohibit transactions involving foreign exchange, gold or silver, transfers of credit, or foreign-owned property. Prior to this, under the authority of the Trading with the Enemy Act, the assets of certain countries in Europe[209] and Asia[210] were frozen by executive orders. In Europe, the effective dates of the freezes on countries corresponded to the dates that these countries fell under Axis control:

- April 8, 1940: Norway and Denmark
- May 10, 1940: the Netherlands, Belgium, and Luxembourg
- June 17, 1940: France (including Monaco)
- July 10, 1940: Latvia, Estonia, and Lithuania
- October 9, 1940: Romania
- March 4, 1941: Bulgaria
- March 13, 1941: Hungary
- March 24, 1941: Yugoslavia
- April 28, 1941: Greece
- June 14, 1941: Albania, Andorra, Austria, Czechoslovakia, Danzig, Finland, Germany, Italy, Liechtenstein, Poland, Portugal, San Marino, Spain, Sweden, Switzerland, and the Union of Soviet Socialist Republics

The order freezing the assets of certain Asian countries included not only Japan but also China. The effect of the order was to bring the "financial and import and export trade transactions in which Japanese interests are involved

---

208. Pub. L. No. 77-354 (1941).
209. Exec. Order No. 8785, Freezing the Assets of Certain European Countries (June 14, 1941).
210. Exec. Order No. 8832, Freezing Japanese and Chinese Assets in the United States (July 26, 1941).

under the control of the Government."[211] The government wanted to prevent trade and U.S. financial facilities being used "in ways harmful to national defense and American interests, to prevent the liquidation in the United States of assets obtained by duress or conquest, and to curb subversive activities in the United States."[212] To assist China, Chinese assets were frozen at the "specific request of Generalissimo Chiang Kai-shek, and for the purpose of helping the Chinese Government."[213]

By executive order, the Office of Alien Property Custodian (APC) was established in 1942.[214] It delegated to the APC all of the powers that the president had received (except for certain functions performed by the Treasury Department and Federal Reserve). The order was quickly amended to transfer to the APC functions similar to those of the Department of Justice's Office of Alien Property[215] and to differentiate the APC's role from that of the Treasury.[216] (Treasury dealt with financial assets such as cash, securities, and bullion that did not require active management; and APC dealt with assets that did require active management, such as real and intellectual property, ships, and businesses.) The APC actively sought a return on vested assets that it did not liquidate, including the licensing of enemy patents. It was very busy because the amount of foreign-owned property at the beginning of the war was more than $7 billion ($500 million owned by individuals from the Axis powers, $4.0 billion by individuals from countries occupied by the Axis powers, and $2.7 billion by other blocked countries).[217]

---

211. *Id.*
212. *Id.*
213. *Id.*
214. Exec. Order No. 9095, Establishing the Office of the Alien Property Custodian (Mar. 11, 1942).
215. Exec. Order No. 9142, Transferring Certain Functions, Property, and Personnel from the Department of Justice to the Alien Property Custodian (Apr. 21, 1942).
216. Exec. Order No. 9193, Amending Executive Order No. 9095 Establishing the Office of Alien Property Custodian and Defining the Functions and Duties and Related Matters (July 6, 1942).
217. OFFICE OF ALIEN PROPERTY CUSTODIAN, ANNUAL REPORT FOR THE PERIOD MARCH 11, 1942, TO JUNE, 30, 1943 (1943).

LEGAL PROFILES

John R. Mitchell was an attorney in the Office of Alien Property Custodian during the war. He was born in Tennessee in 1877 and started his legal practice there. Between 1908 and 1925, he served as assistant attorney general and attorney general for a state judicial circuit. He then spent the next six years as a judge in the same circuit. He was elected to Congress in 1931 and spent the next eight years in the House, after which he ran unsuccessfully for the U.S. Senate and returned to private practice. He worked for the Office of Alien Property Custodian from 1943 to 1945 under James E. Hartman, a lawyer who was first the assistant director and then the director of the APC. Mitchell then worked in the antitrust division of the Department of Justice until 1951. He died in 1962.[218]

B. Cases

A number of different types of cases dealt with situations involving enemy assets. The first case examined when a U.S. citizen might be considered a national of an enemy nation. The second case discussed when a U.S. citizen might not be considered a national of an enemy nation. The third case, which involved several Supreme Court decisions, looked at the effect of Congress only partially modifying the prior law after the start of the current war.

1. Enemy National

In *Draeger Shipping Co. v. Crowley*, the question was whether the appellant was an enemy or allied with one.[219] The appellant corporation was owned by a naturalized U.S. citizen who was born in Germany. He had merged his firm with a Germany company owned by the German state railway, which had

---

218. *See Mitchell, John Ridley*, Biographical Directory of the United States Congress.
219. Draeger Shipping Co. v. Crowley, 55 F. Supp. 906 (S.D.N.Y. 1944).

transferred its shares to a Dutch national. After the Netherlands was overrun, it became a blocked country, and its share of the U.S. entity was subject to takeover by the APC. An investigation of the naturalized U.S. citizen determined that he was a German national, so the entire company was subject to seizure by the U.S. government. The capital stock of the company was then vested in (i.e., its title was transferred to) the APC "to be held, used, administered, liquidated, sold, or otherwise dealt with in the interest of and for the benefit of the United States."[220]

The court said that the appellant had to prove that he was not a "national" of an enemy country, as defined under the act. A national is one who is controlled by or acting on behalf of a designated enemy country; is domiciled in or is a subject, citizen, or resident of an enemy nation; or is an ally of an enemy or a blocked country. Furthermore, a person could be designated as a national if it is in the interest of the United States that such person be treated as a national of an enemy country. Because there was sufficient evidence that the naturalized American was fronting for the interests of the German firm, the court found that he was a national under the definition of the statute; and, as such, the vesting by the APC was proper.

LEGAL PROFILES

A. Matt Werner was general counsel for the APC. He was born in Wisconsin in 1894 and started his legal career there. He served in the U.S. Navy during WWI. In 1937, he joined the local newspaper and in 1939 became a regent at the University of Wisconsin. He went to work for the federal government during the war. After the war, he returned to the *Sheboygan Press*, a newspaper his wife's father had helped found. He became editor and president by 1951 and then chairman in 1964. He was involved in local and national politics and was president of a radio station. He died in 1977.[221]

---

220. *Id.* at 910.
221. *See A. Matt Werner*, N.Y. TIMES (Nov. 5, 1977).

2. Not Enemy National

In *Josephberg v. Markham*, the appellant was a naturalized U.S. citizen from Italy.[222] He had since been diagnosed with a mental disease and was told to return to Italy to convalesce. He did so and had never returned to America after leaving, but then he inherited a significant sum in the United States. As he was judged to be legally incompetent, he was represented by guardians; when his property was seized by the U.S. government, they interceded.

The question for the court was whether he was a national of an enemy. This depended on where he was a resident. The representatives said that he was in Italy only temporarily for health reasons and had to remain there against his will after the war began; the government said that he had expatriated, was a Fascist supporter, and had voted again in Italy.

The court said that the issue of his residence was not decisive because he was incompetent and could not reach his money and neither could anyone from Italy, and in any event the Treasury Department could have frozen his funds. The purpose of the statute was to deprive the enemy of the ability to make war, and in this case the funds could not be used by the enemy. The court found that the appellant had not expatriated as he had gone overseas for health reasons, so the statute did not apply to him. It was concerned that if the court ruled in favor of the government, even U.S. soldiers stationed overseas could then be considered residents of enemy nations and have their assets seized. The court reversed the lower court, ruling that the appellant should not have been subject to a vesting of his U.S. assets.

LEGAL PROFILES

Thomas W. Swan was a judge in this case. He was born in Connecticut in 1877 but started his legal practice in Illinois, where he was in private practice until 1916. During this time, he lectured at the law school at the University of Chicago. In 1916, he was named the dean and a professor at Yale Law School. He held this position until 1927, focusing on bank-

---

222. Josephberg v. Markham, 152 F.2d 644 (2d Cir. 1945).

ruptcy and corporation law and modernizing the law school. President Calvin Coolidge then appointed him to a seat on the court of appeals for the Second Circuit. He served on this bench until 1953, the last two years as chief judge. He died in 1975.[223]

3. Conflict Between Provisions

In a case that reached the Supreme Court, *Markham v. Cabell*, the issue involved how a provision of the WWI-era Trading with the Enemy Act operated in the current war.[224] This statute went back into effect due to the declaration of war on December 8, 1942. A creditor for services provided to an Italian insurance company whose assets had been seized by the APC filed suit against the APC to recover under § 9(a). Changes made to the statute's § 9(e) in the 1920s restricted claims under § 9(a) to those assets that were seized by 1917 or those claims made by 1928. The government wanted § 9(e) to be used to block suits filed under § 9(a) because it would allow payment of the vested assets of enemy nationals only to nonenemy creditors. The new § 5 wording added by the First War Powers Act allowed the vesting and freezing of assets of any foreign nationals, including enemies; and, thus, disallowing the application of § 9(e) would give preference to creditors of enemies over creditors of other nationals whose assets had been vested or frozen, unbalancing the statute.

The Court disagreed, ruling that § 9(e) applied only to claims arising from WWI and that claims under § 9(a) could proceed. Its role was not to judicially rebalance the statute as that was a duty for Congress to undertake. In the concurring opinion, the original statute was analyzed as having both permanent and temporary provisions, the latter being those using phrases such *the present war*. Section 9(a) was considered a permanent provision, while § 9(e) was considered a temporary provision. The continuity of the APC, made part of the Justice Department in the 1930s and then reinvigorated by the several executive orders in 1942 described above, proved the permanence of the statute.

The Supreme Court was again confronted by the discrepancies between these two provisions in 1947. In *Clark v. Uebersee Finanz-Korporation, A.G.*,[225]

---

223. *See Swan, Thomas Walter*, FED. JUDICIAL CTR., BIOGRAPHICAL DIRECTORY OF FEDERAL JUDGES.
224. Markham v. Cabell, 326 U.S. 404 (1945).
225. Clark v. Uebersee Finanz-Korporation, A.G., 332 U.S. 480 (1947).

a claimed neutral company wanted to use § 9(a) to recover its property. As previously stated, the Court knew that there would be a disadvantage to the creditors of nonenemies (this case involved a Swiss company) as the unbalanced ability to make a claim left them no recourse. The Court held that it would allow the claim of this neutral, assuming that it was "free of all enemy taint . . . where no enemy, ally of an enemy, nor any national of either has any interest of any kind whatsoever."[226] Interestingly, the same corporation was before the Court five years later, having been exposed in further proceedings as being almost completely controlled by a German national.[227] Quoting the lower court that it would be "difficult to find a stronger case of enemy taint in vested property short of full ownership by an enemy than exists in this case," the Court did not allow the petitioner to recover.[228]

LEGAL PROFILES

W. McNeil Kennedy was the solicitor for the APC. He was born in New York in 1909. He began work for the Commerce Clearing House in 1930. From 1935 to 1942, he was the regional administrator for the Securities and Exchange Commission. During this time, he also lectured at the University of Chicago. From 1942 to 1944, he was the solicitor for the APC before returning to private practice. He was active in the Chicago and American Bar Associations. He died in 1970.[229]

C. Subsequent Events

During the war, the APC issued more than five thousand vesting orders to take ownership; took over hundreds of businesses, thousands of pieces of property, and tens of thousands of items of intellectual property;[230] and was also involved

---

226. *Id.* at 482.
227. Uebersee Finanz-Korporation, A.G. v. McGrath, 343 U.S. 205 (1952).
228. *Id.* at 212.
229. *See W. M. Kennedy, Lawyer, Bar Officer, Dies*, CHI. TRIBUNE (May 6, 1970).
230. OFFICE OF ALIEN PROP., CIVILIAN AGENCY RECORDS: RECORDS OF THE OFFICE OF ALIEN PROPERTY.

in Latin America (to prevent Axis assets from being hidden there). After the war, efforts at locating the ownership of foreign assets required investigations overseas.[231] The Office of Alien Property Custodian was terminated by executive order in 1946,[232] but its functions were transferred back to the Justice Department's Office of Alien Property. Due to the vast number of outstanding issues to resolve (thousands of lawsuits and tens of thousands of claims), the APC's successor was not formally abolished for twenty more years.[233] Cases continued to be litigated, such as the Standard Oil case to retrieve certain patents that were tied up with international entities[234] and especially the long, drawn-out case of Interhandel and its claim to have severed all ties to the notorious I.G. Farben before the war.[235]

LEGAL PROFILES

John Foster Dulles was a member of the consulting committee that assisted in formulating the basic policies of the APC. He was born in Washington, D.C., in 1888 but started his legal practice in New York. In WWI, he served in army intelligence and worked on the War Industries Board. After the war, he was legal counsel for the U.S. delegation to the Paris Peace Conference (his uncle was the U.S. secretary of state) and was involved initially with the Allied Reparations Commission. He returned to private practice after the war but stayed involved in international legal matters. During WWII, he was also involved as a lawyer for the War Trade Board. After the war, he was involved with the creation of the United Nations. For a few months in 1949, he was a U.S. senator by appointment. He was responsible for negotiating the Treaty of San Fran-

---

231. *See, e.g., Markham Goes Abroad*, N.Y. TIMES (June 17, 1945).

232. Exec. Order No. 9788, Terminating the Office of Alien Property Custodian and Transferring Its Functions to the Attorney General (Oct. 14, 1946).

233. Exec. Order No. 11281, Transferring Jurisdiction over Certain Blocked Assets from the Attorney General to the Secretary of the Treasury (May 13, 1966).

234. Standard Oil v. Clark, 163 F.2d 917 (2d Cir. 1947).

235. Societe Internationale Pour Participations Industrielles et Commerciales, S.A. v. Rogers, 357 U.S. 197 (1958).

cisco, signed in 1951, officially ending the war with Japan (see Chapter 8). In 1953, he was appointed as the U.S. secretary of state and, among other accomplishments, built up the North Atlantic Treaty Organization, helped to form the Southeast Asia Treaty Organization, and secured international mutual security agreements. He held this position until his death in 1959.[236]

D. Modern Applicability

Seizing the assets of enemy nations is still practiced in modern times, although the enemy may not be one upon which war has been declared. For example, the United States has recently frozen assets of the Iranian government and its central bank that are held either in the United States or by a foreign branch of a U.S. firm.[237] The United Kingdom has seized the assets of those involved in a terror plot.[238] Individuals as well as nations have endeavored to seize assets of terrorists and those who have assisted terrorists.[239] And violations of the Trading with the Enemy Act continue to be relevant, as a recent $619 million settlement demonstrates.[240] The Office of Foreign Assets Control in the U.S. Treasury Department administers a series of laws that support both U.S. foreign policy and national security objectives. This responsibility covers approximately a dozen countries and thousands of foreign firms and individuals with whom transactions are regulated or prohibited.[241]

236. *See Foster, John Dulles*, BIOGRAPHICAL DIRECTORY OF THE UNITED STATES CONGRESS.
237. *Obama Freezes Iranian Government, Central Bank Assets*, BLOOMBERG (Feb. 6, 2012).
238. *Iranian U.S. Terror Plot Accused Assets Seized in U.K.*, BBC (Oct. 18, 2011).
239. *Judge Nails Iran, Al Qaeda for 9/11 with $6 Billion Penalty in Lawsuit*, N.Y. DAILY NEWS (July 30, 2012).
240. *Dutch Bank Pays Steep Price for Ignoring U.S. Sanctions on Iran and Cuba*, CHRISTIAN SCI. MONITOR (June 12, 2012).
241. U.S. TREASURY DEP'T, OFAC REGULATIONS FOR EXPORTERS AND IMPORTERS (Jan. 24, 2012).

CHAPTER 4

UNITED STATES: MILITARY AND HUMAN RIGHTS ISSUES

In his State of the Union address in January 1941, President Roosevelt stated that there are four fundamental freedoms that people everywhere in the world should enjoy and that should be "attainable in our own time and generation":

- Freedom of speech and expression
- Freedom of every person to worship God in his own way
- Freedom from want ("secure to every nation a healthy peacetime life for its inhabitants")
- Freedom from fear ("no nation will be in a position to commit an act of physical aggression against any neighbor")[1]

These freedoms became incorporated in the Universal Declaration of Human Rights in 1948,[2] but it wasn't easy in a time of intense global war to always maintain such ideals.

In addition to the economic issues, the war brought on a host of other legal issues that affected both civilians and those involved with the military. Legal military jurisdiction affected not only those directly engaged in combat but also captured enemies and those supporting the military. Civilians had to deal with new restrictions imposed for national security reasons, including off-limit

---

1. Franklin D. Roosevelt, President, United States of America, Annual Message to Congress on the State of the Union (Jan. 6, 1941).
2. Universal Declaration of Human Rights, U.N. G.A. Res. 217 A III, U.N. Doc. (1948).

areas and times and the implications of being tried by military courts for what might previously have been civilian matters. In dealing with issues of loyalty to the United States, the government could revoke the American citizenship of those who displayed disloyalty. Others chose to renounce their U.S. nationality of their own volition. Loyalty issues became much more serious when actions were treasonous. Not used since the Civil War, treason prosecutions arose from the actions of those in the American population who supported the cause of wartime enemies. To prevent acts of possible sabotage, the government, in a then- (and still-) controversial decision, determined that it was in the national security interest to move the Japanese-American citizen population away from the West Coast into relocation camps (along with Japanese nationals, but that was a different matter). In addition, the extent of free speech during wartime was tested in a number of cases.

The tension between the rights of citizens and aliens and the security needs of the country was very high during the war. This chapter focuses on six major areas of such tension from which significant legal issues arose in the United States: military tribunals, martial law, revocation of citizenship, treason, citizen internment, and freedom of expression.

PROMINENT LAWYERS AND JUDGES IN THIS CHAPTER

Military Tribunals:

- Francis B. Biddle (U.S. attorney general)
- Kenneth C. Royall (defense attorney)
- A. Frank Reel (defense attorney)
- Myron C. Cramer (JAG Corps)

Martial Law:

- Sam T. Rayburn (speaker of the house)
- Minoru Yasui (defendant)
- A. L. Wirin (appellant's attorney)
- Bert E. Haney (circuit court judge)
- Earl Warren (amicus curiae attorney)
- Edward J. Ennis (respondents' attorney)

- Arthur G. Hays (amicus curiae attorney)
- Thomas H. Green (military attorney general)

Revocation of Citizenship:

- Harold H. Burton (senator)
- Carol Weiss King (petitioner's attorney)
- Wendell L. Willkie (petitioner's attorney)
- Pearl M. Hart (amicus curiae attorney for petitioner)
- Felix Frankfurter (Supreme Court justice)
- Beatrice Rosenberg (appellee's attorney)
- Frederick Bernays Wiener (appellee's attorney)
- Tom C. Clark (defendant)

Treason:

- Xenophon Hicks (circuit court judge)
- Harold R. Medina (petitioner's attorney)
- Irving S. Shapiro (respondent's attorney)
- Walter L. Pope (circuit court judge)
- Wayne M. Collins (appellant's attorney)
- Calvert Magruder (circuit court judge)
- Oscar H. Davis (U.S. government attorney)

Citizen Internment:

- John J. McCloy (assistant secretary of war)
- Philip M. Glick (WRA counsel)
- Robert R. Reynolds (senator)
- Nanette Dembitz (Justice Department attorney)
- Saburo Kido (appellant's attorney)
- William Denman (court of appeals judge)
- Ernest Besig (Northern California ACLU leader)
- William O. Douglas (Supreme Court justice)
- Herbert Weschler (assistant attorney general)
- Ralph F. Fuchs (assistant to attorney general)
- Albert L. Stephens Sr. (court of appeals justice)
- Fred Okrand (ACLU attorney)
- Warren Magnuson (statute sponsor)

Freedom of Expression:

- Frank C. Walker (U.S. postmaster general)
- Hayden C. Covington (respondents' attorney)
- Abe Fortas (amicus curiae attorney for appellees)
- Zechariah Chafee Jr. (amicus curiae attorney for appellees)
- Basil O'Connor (amicus curiae attorney for appellees)
- Wilbur V. Keegan (defendant)
- Wiley B. Rutledge (Supreme Court justice)
- William H. Timbers (petitioners' attorney)
- Morris L. Ernst (respondent's attorney)
- Harriet F. Pilpel (respondent's attorney)
- Charles A. Horsky (amicus curiae attorney for respondent)

4.1 MILITARY TRIBUNALS

A. Statutes

Military as well as civilian law needed to be established in the war undertaking. The Articles of War used by the military stretched back to the Revolutionary War. Those articles in effect when this war began were established right after WWI. In June 1920, the act to amend an act entitled "An Act for making further and more effectual provision for the national defense, and for other purposes," approved June 3, 1916, and to establish military justice was passed, setting out the revised Articles of War.[3] Consisting of 121 articles, the act detailed who was subject to military justice (all officers, cadets, camp retainers, and soldiers (drafted or enlisted)); general justice (required at least five officers and provided for any type of punishment); special justice (required at least three officers and provided up to six months imprisonment); or summary court-martial (required only a single officer and provided imprisonment of up to one month). Jurisdiction was not exclusive to courts-martial.

The list of crimes subject to court-martial included those applicable at any time: fraudulent enlistment, false muster, desertion, aiding another to desert, absence without leave, disrespecting the president, disrespecting a superior officer, refusing orders, mutiny, and sedition. Specific wartime offenses included

---

3. Pub. L. No. 66-242 (1920).

misbehavior before an enemy, compelling a commander to surrender, improper use of countersign, forcing a safeguard, dealing in captured enemy property, corresponding or aiding the enemy, and spying. Other offenses included misuse of military property, being drunk on duty, selling provisions, a sentinel leaving his post, conduct unbecoming an officer, conduct that brings discredit upon the military, and dueling. Civilian criminal crimes were included and subject to court-martial.

To further clarify who was subject to these articles, President Roosevelt issued a proclamation in mid-1942 concerning the ability of enemies to use civilian courts in the United States.[4] Relying on his constitutional powers and unspecified statutory authority, he said that enemies who entered the United States through its defenses "as part of an invasion or predatory incursion, or who have entered in order to commit sabotage, espionage, or other hostile or warlike acts," were subject to the jurisdiction of military tribunals.[5] These enemies would not have the privilege of utilizing the U.S. civilian courts to seek remedies unless allowed by the attorney general.

LEGAL PROFILES

Francis B. Biddle was the U.S. attorney general for much of the war and presented *Ex parte Quirin*, the first case discussed below.[6] He was born in France in 1886, and his first legal position was working for Supreme Court Justice Oliver Wendell Holmes in 1911. He practiced law in Pennsylvania and served in WWI. He was appointed special assistant to the U.S. Attorney of the Eastern District of Pennsylvania in 1922, and in 1934 was nominated to head the National Labor Relations Board. In 1938, he was chief counsel to the congressional committee investigating the Tennessee Valley Authority; and in 1939, he was appointed to the court of appeals for the Third Circuit. One year later, he was appointed as U.S. solicitor general and also the director of the Immigration and

---

4. Exec. Proclamation No. 2561, Denying Certain Enemies Access to the Courts (July 2, 1942).
5. *Id.*
6. *Ex parte* Quirin, 317 U.S. 1 (1942).

Naturalization Service. This was followed in 1941 by his appointment as U.S. attorney general, a position that he held until 1945. After the war, he was appointed as one of the judges for the Nuremberg Trials (see Chapter 6). He died in 1968.[7]

B. Cases

The types of cases that arose from the use of the Articles of War concerned not only the application of these articles to specific offenses but clarification of the appropriate jurisdiction of these articles, i.e., where and to whom they applied. The first case involved German saboteurs and the use of a military commission to try them. The second case concerned a Japanese military commander in charge during a brutal occupation and the use of a military commission to try him. The third case examined the question of whether army rules or navy rules applied to a court-martial defendant. The fourth case determined whether a defense worker returning home from overseas was subject to a court-martial.

1. Military Tribunals and Saboteurs

Ex parte Quirin, a case involving the trial and conviction of German agents, reached the U.S. Supreme Court in 1942.[8] The eight agents, actual or in essence German nationals, were all at one time residents of the United States but returned to Germany at various times and received training on various activities regarding sabotage of U.S. defense facilities. In mid-June 1942, they were brought ashore by U-boats, half in New York and half in Florida. In their possession were explosives and related equipment. Although they were wearing military uniforms on their arrival, they soon discarded those uniforms. Two of the eight gave up their plan to the Federal Bureau of Investigation (FBI), and all eight were apprehended.

Pursuant to his 1942 proclamation, President Roosevelt set up a military commission to try the men, from which this appeal arose and traveled through the federal courts. The Army Judge Advocate General's (JAG) Corps charged the men with violating the law of war as well as two articles from the Articles

---

7. *See Biddle, Francis*, Fed. Judicial Ctr., Biographical Directory of Federal Judges.
8. *Ex parte Quirin*, 317 U.S. 1.

of War, spying and giving intelligence to the enemy and conspiracy. The appellants contended in federal court that the president did not have the authority to try them in a military court and that they should be tried in a civilian court. Additionally, they contended that the president's proclamation was contrary to a number of the articles in the Articles of War, specifically Articles 38 (rule setting), 43 (death sentences), 46 (approval of sentences), 50 (board of review), and 70 (thorough and impartial investigation).

The Supreme Court, in a per curium opinion, noted that the courts where the defendants went ashore and were arrested and the courts in the nation's capital were all open and functioning normally. It also noted that even though the defendants were enemy aliens, the courts could still consider whether U.S. law and the Constitution "forbid their trial by military commission."[9]

The Court then reviewed the respective constitutional war powers of Congress and the president and examined how the Articles of Wars, passed by Congress, affected the military tribunal. Looking to Articles 38 (setting rules) and 46 (approval by convening authority), it found the president's authority to establish military commissions. The articles containing the charges also allowed the military commission, and Article 15 did not exclude trying by military commission those offenders who are subject to court-martial for violations of the law of war.

As to the first charge, violating the law of war, the Court looked at what the law of war was and noted that Congress, instead of being overly specific, had incorporated by reference all offenses that could constitutionally be included. Under the accepted law of war, lawful combatants could be captured and detained; and unlawful combatants, even U.S. citizens fighting with enemies, could also be tried before military tribunals. Spies and saboteurs fall into the latter category. The Court cited the Revolutionary War (Major John André, British officer executed for spying for assisting Benedict Arnold's plans to capture West Point), the Mexican War, the U.S. Civil War (many examples), and the Hague Convention for support of this position.[10] As such, the Court found that the first count, violating the law of war as unlawful combatants intent on destroying war supplies and production, had sufficient foundation. The fact that the appellants did not actually commit or attempt any sabotage was not

---

9. *Id.* at 25.
10. Hague Convention IV: Respecting the Laws and Customs of War on Land, Oct. 18, 1907.

relevant, only that they did without appropriate uniforms enter the United States with explosives planning such.

After going back to the Revolutionary War era to justify why enemy aliens did not have a right to a jury trial instead of a military tribunal, the Court noted that the *Ex parte Milligan* case from the Civil War should apply here.[11] In the *Ex parte Milligan* case, the defendant was convicted by a military commission organized in a state (Indiana) not engaged in rebellion, in which the federal courts were open and functioning. The ruling was that the military commission did not have jurisdiction to try, convict, or sentence for any criminal offence, a citizen who was neither a "resident of one of the rebellious states nor a prisoner of war," nor a person in the military or naval service.[12] Because Milligan was a nonbelligerent not subject to the law of war, that case was not applicable to these facts.

As this first count was sufficient, the Court did not review the other two counts relating to the Articles of War; the Court held that the president did have the power to convene the military commission, and so the writ of habeas corpus was denied. The Court's decision was handed down on July 31, 1942. The seven-member military commission concluded its deliberations a few days later, and all eight defendants were then convicted and sentenced to death. On August 8, the six men who did not turn themselves in were electrocuted. The two remaining men eventually had their life sentences commuted and were returned to Germany after the war.

LEGAL PROFILES

Kenneth C. Royall was one of the defense attorneys, along with Lauson Stone (son of Harlan Stone, then chief justice of the United States),[13] assigned to argue the case for the appellants from the trial and district courts and finally to the Supreme Court. He was born in North Carolina in 1894 and started his legal practice there. He served in WWI in the army, returning to private practice afterward. He was elected to the state

---

11. *Ex parte* Milligan, 71 U.S. 2 (1866).
12. *Id*. at 118.
13. *See L. H. Stone, 94, Defender of 8 in '42 Trial for Sabotage*, N.Y. TIMES (Nov. 12, 1999).

legislature as a senator in 1927. He returned to the military as a colonel in the army in 1942, managing the War Department's legal services. In 1943, he was promoted to brigadier general and became an assistant to the secretary of war and then undersecretary of war in 1945. From 1947 to 1949, he served as the secretary of the army. After the war, he returned to private practice. He died in 1971.[14]

2. Military Tribunals and Enemy Commanders

In re Yamashita involved a Japanese general in charge of the army forces in the Philippines who surrendered there in September 1945.[15] He was subsequently charged with violations of the law of war. The charge was for his failure to discharge his duty to control his forces, which committed "brutal atrocities and other high crimes against people of the United States and of its allies and dependencies, particularly the Philippines; and he . . . thereby violated the laws of war."[16] The particulars included "a deliberate plan and purpose to massacre and exterminate" the civilian population of one province and destroy property "wantonly and without military necessity," which led to the killing or "brutal mistreat[ment]" of more than 25,000 unarmed civilian noncombatants, including women, children, and POWs.[17]

Yamashita was tried before a military commission of five officers. The defense team consisted of six lawyers, all military officers. The court heard from 286 witnesses to the acts described above before finally determining that the defendant was guilty and sentencing him to death.

The defense then appealed (first to the Philippine Supreme Court, which denied his writ based on the same claims[18]), claiming the following:

- "[T]he military commission . . . was not lawfully created."
- "[N]o military commission . . . for violations of the law of war could lawfully be convened after the cessation of hostilities."
- "[T]he charge . . . fails to charge him with a violation of the law of war."

14. See Kenneth Royall of Truman Cabinet Dies, N.Y. TIMES (May 27, 1971).
15. In re Yamashita, 327 U.S. 1 (1946).
16. Id. at 14.
17. Id.
18. Yamashita v. Styer, G.R. No. L-129 (Phil. Sup. Ct. 1945).

- The admission of depositions, affidavits, hearsay, and opinion evidence violated the Articles of War, the Geneva Conventions, and Fifth Amendment due process.
- The commission failed "to give advance notice of petitioner's trial to the neutral power representing the interests of Japan as a belligerent."[19]

The Court started out by restating what it had said in *Ex parte Quirin*, i.e., that its role was not to determine the guilt or innocence of the defendants or to review that sentence, which is reserved for military authorities, but to ensure the authority of the military commission to try them. The Court had no trouble in identifying the proper legal authority for the military commission, so it turned to the question of whether the commission's mandate extended beyond the cessation of hostilities. The Court found that the power, without a peace agreement, was not limited to winning the war "but carries with it the inherent power to guard against the immediate renewal of the conflict, and to remedy, at least in ways Congress has recognized, the evils which the military operations have produced."[20] In addition to that, the Japanese government had accepted the Potsdam Declaration (see Chapter 7), which included the provision that "justice shall be meted out to all war criminals, including those who have visited cruelties upon our prisoners."[21]

By detailing the acts described above, the Court had no trouble finding that the acts violated the law of war as the commander was responsible for the acts of those in his charge. It also ruled that the Articles of War allowed two types of defendants under military commissions: (1) those who are members of the U.S. military being tried under the Articles of War and who receive its benefits and (2) enemy combatants who were tried under the "common law of war," not the U.S. Articles of War and as such do not receive its benefits.[22] The provisions of the Geneva Conventions applied to any acts committed by a person while a POW, not during the war, and so were not applicable.

Having addressed all of the points raised by the petitioner, the Court denied the writ. Yamashita was executed in the Philippines a few weeks later.

---

19. *In re Yamashita*, 327 U.S. at 6.
20. *Id.* at 12.
21. *Id.* at 10.
22. *Id.* at 20.

LEGAL PROFILES

A. Frank Reel was part of the defense team that included attorneys Colonel Harry E. Clarke and Masakatsu Hamamoto (acting as the personal interpreter for the defendant). Born in Wisconsin in 1907, Reel started his own legal practice in Massachusetts, involved in labor issues. He enlisted in the army when the war started, rose to the rank of captain, and was assigned to the Claims Division in the Pacific. He returned to his firm after the war and later argued a writ of habeas corpus for enemy aliens before the Supreme Court.[23] He later worked in the radio and television industries before returning once again to his legal practice. He wrote a book about this trial and also a book about network television. He unsuccessfully ran for Congress in 1962 and was involved in politics on a local (as city attorney and trustee) and national level. He died in 2000.[24]

3. Military Tribunals: Army or Navy?

McCune v. Kilpatrick presented the question of which set of articles might apply to a military person's conduct violation.[25] The counterpart to the army's Articles of War was the Articles for the Government of the United States Navy (sometimes called "Rocks and Shoals").[26] Article 2 of the Articles of War specifically stated that the Articles of War did not apply to anyone under naval jurisdiction. The defendant in this case was a chief cook, a veteran of WWI, who volunteered to serve on a ship that he thought contained seaman. When soldiers filed on board to be transported, he tried to quit even though he had signed an agreement. He was held for desertion.

The district court framed the single issue as being whether a civilian cook serving on a liberty ship used to transport troops could be subject to a U.S.

---

23. Johnson v. Eisentrager, 339 U.S. 763 (1950).
24. *See A. Frank Reel, 92, Defended Japanese General in '45 Trial,* N.Y. Times (Apr. 10, 2000).
25. McCune v. Kilpatrick, 53 F. Supp. 80 (E.D.Va. 1943).
26. U.S. Bureau of Naval Personnel, NAVPERS-100A (1930).

Army court-martial. Article 2 of the Articles of War specifically defined who was subject to the articles: "*in time of war* all such retainers and persons *accompanying or serving with the Armies of the United States in the field.*"[27] Considering that the mission was to transport five hundred troops to battle zones from an army base, the army was clearly in the field, which was defined as any place where military operations were conducted. The court determined that the cook was accompanying or serving with the army even though he had signed a contract with a civilian entity and was subject to the master's rules for the navigation and management of the ship.

The bigger question was whether the exception to the Articles of War for those "under naval jurisdiction" applied.[28] The cook was part of the merchant marine service, governed under laws separate from those of the navy. His contention was that because the merchant marine oversight function had been transferred to the coast guard[29] and in times of war the coast guard serves with the navy,[30] he was subject to the "under naval jurisdiction" exception. At the same time, because he was subject to different rules for merchant seamen, he was not under the Articles for the Government of the United States Navy. The court did not agree, ruling that the exception was only meant to place military personnel under one of the two sets of rules, not to evade both. The court also ruled that the cook was not a member of the coast guard and that navy articles did not cover his role. He was not covered by this exception, and so his application for the writ was denied.

4. Military Tribunals and Civilian Workers

Perlstein v. United States involved a civilian working for a defense contractor doing salvage work overseas to clear a port for active use.[31] Shortly after the worker's arrival in Africa, the army dismissed him; on the way back to the United States, he was apprehended at the military base in Eritrea with stolen jewelry. He was tried by court-martial in Egypt and convicted on all three

---

27. *McCune*, 53 F. Supp. at 84 (emphasis added by court).
28. Articles of War, Pub. L. No. 66-242, § 52 (1920).
29. Exec. Order No. 9083, Redistribution of Maritime Functions (Feb. 28, 1942).
30. *See* Exec. Order No. 8929, Directing the Coast Guard to Operate as Part of the Navy (Nov. 1, 1941).
31. Perlstein v. United States, 151 F.2d 167 (3d Cir. 1945).

counts. He appealed, claiming that he was not subject to military jurisdiction and that even if he was subject to military jurisdiction during his employment, he committed the act after his termination.

The court found that his work supporting the salvage of the enemy military ships clearly included him as one accompanying the army and so subjected him to the Articles of War. As the purpose of the salvage work was to clear the port for active use as a base, the defendant was "directly concerned with the movement or supply of troops."[32]

The more important issue was whether his termination meant that he was no longer accompanying the army when he committed the crime. Because he was required to leave the area of war surrounding the base and used military transport to return to the United States, he was still under the control of the military. As such, the court-martial had jurisdiction over him, and so the court of appeals affirmed the lower court's decision.

LEGAL PROFILES

Myron C. Cramer, major general in the JAG Corps, was on the brief for the appellee. He was born in Connecticut in 1881, started his legal practice in New York, and then moved to Washington State as a deputy county prosecutor. He joined the National Guard the next year. During WWI, he served in France and then joined the JAG Corps in 1920. He taught at the U.S. Military Academy beginning in 1922. In 1941, he was appointed head of the JAG Corps, a position he held until the end of the war. During the war, among many other trials, he prosecuted the defendants in the *Ex parte Quirin* trial (see earlier discussion). After the war, he was one of the judges on the International Military Tribunal for the Far East (see Chapter 7). He died in 1966.[33]

---

32. *Id.* at 169.
33. *See Myron C. Cramer; Prosecuted Nazis*, N.Y. TIMES (Mar. 26, 1966).

C. Subsequent Events

In 1950, Congress passed the Uniform Code of Military Justice (UCMJ) to provide a consolidated set of legal rules for all of the U.S. armed forces.[34] This meant that the disparate legal rules across the services, such as the Army's Articles of War and the Articles for the Government of the United States Navy, were now unified. In practice, the UCMJ took more from the army's rules than the navy's rules. The questions that were raised in the *McCune* case should not arise again as there are now no gaps between sets of rules to consider. However, many of the questions from the other cases do remain, to be tested in new wars.

D. Modern Applicability

Most recently, with the war on terror that started with the September 11, 2001, terrorist attacks on the United States, the issues from *Ex parte Quirin* have been raised again. It started with a congressional joint resolution (Authorization for Use of Military Force)[35] referencing the War Powers Resolution (see Chapter 2). This was followed by a military order[36] that is based on this joint resolution and refers to two UCMJ articles. The first is Article 21, which allows use of military commissions (Article of War 15);[37] and the second is Article 36, which allows the president to prescribe rules (Article of War 38).[38] This military order allows military commissions to try individuals subject to the order (e.g., members of Al-Qaeda or those engaged in international terrorism). In addition, the Department of Defense issued an order establishing the procedures to be used for military commission terrorism trials against non-U.S. citizens.[39]

Use of this authority led to a lawsuit regarding military commissions, *Hamdan v. Rumsfeld*, that reached the Supreme Court in 2006.[40] In finding for the appellant, the Court ruled that the military commission set up by the president violated both the UCMJ and the Fourth Geneva Convention of 1949. It

---

34. Pub. L. No. 81-506 (1950).
35. Pub. L. No. 107-40 (2001).
36. Detention, Treatment, and Trial of Certain Non-Citizens in the War Against Terrorism, 66 Fed. Reg. 57,833 (Nov. 16, 2001).
37. 10 U.S.C. § 821.
38. 10 U.S.C. § 836.
39. Dep't of Defense, Military Commission Order No. 1 (Mar. 21, 2002).
40. Hamdan v. Rumsfeld, 548 U.S. 557 (2006).

looked at the support for military commissions in *Ex parte Quirin* and said that the president's power to convene these commissions required compliance with the law of war. It described three types of military commissions: (1) those set up in occupied countries defeated in war, (2) those set up where martial law had been declared, and (3) those set up to deal with enemy combatants who violated the law of war. It believed that it could not find sufficient support for the conspiracy charge as a violation of the law of war, noting the *Ex parte Quirin* Court's silence on that charge in the opinion.

However, the main focus of the Court's decision was the military commission order; its withholding of classified evidence from the defendant; and its admissibility of any evidence, including hearsay and coerced confessions. It noted the changes since the *Yamashita* decision in that the UCMJ and the Geneva Convention of 1949 now applied to such prisoners. The Court agreed with the appellant's contention that the rules set up under military order were not uniform (they did not comply with the *Manual for Courts-Martial*[41]), which they were required to be unless impractical. The Court did not find such impracticality. For this and noncompliance with the Geneva Convention of 1949, it reversed the lower court.

Hamdan was followed in 2006 by Congress's passage of the Military Commissions Act, which created a new section of the UCMJ dealing directly with unlawful enemy combatants.[42] Combatant Status Review Tribunals determine whether enemy combatants are lawful or unlawful. The act also does not allow the Geneva Convention of 1949 to be invoked during writs of habeas corpus before the courts. The law apparently applies to alien unlawful enemy combatants, not U.S. citizens. It prohibited habeas corpus challenges by alien unlawful enemy combatants, but this was challenged and the Supreme Court overruled this part of the statute (while again quoting from *Yamashita* and *Ex parte Quirin* regarding the limits of the court's review of these writs).[43] This issue continues to be contentious, but *Ex parte Quirin* is also cited modernly in piracy cases for its openness in relying on international norms for the precise definition of *piracy*.[44]

---

41. MANUAL FOR COURTS-MARTIAL (2005).
42. Pub. L. No. 109-366 (2006).
43. Boumediene v. Bush, 554 U.S. 723 (2008).
44. *See, e.g.*, United States v. Dire, Case Nos. 11-4310 et al. (4th Cir. 2012).

4.2 MARTIAL LAW

A. Statutes

There are three kinds of military jurisdictions: military law, used during times of war and peace, such as the Articles of War and UCMJ; martial law, used during an invasion within the boundaries of the United States; and occupation or military government, used in a foreign war outside the boundaries of the United States. Martial law is the subject of this section. (Occupation/military government will be discussed in Chapter 8.)

In defending its territory, the United States had to designate appropriate rules for those areas subject to invasion. After the attack on Pearl Harbor, both Hawaii and later the American West were placed under various types of restrictions. As mentioned above, before the war, a number of areas, especially in the west, were withdrawn from public use and placed under the control of the military or designated as defense areas. Immediately after the attack on Hawaii, many areas were designated as prohibited and restricted, and the attorney general was given power to exclude enemy aliens from such;[45] and the president authorized special precautionary measures for military guards and patrols around national defense materials, premises, and utilities.[46]

With war now fully engaged, Congress and the president created additional legal measures to aid in the defense of the country. Drawing on a WWI-era statute,[47] President Roosevelt issued an executive order to protect against espionage and sabotage to national defense materials (e.g., arms, munitions, food); premises (e.g., factories, forts, prisons); and utilities (e.g., railroads, electric lines, dams).[48] As commander in chief, he gave the secretary of war and designated military commanders the authority to designate the military areas that would be prohibited or restricted to any and all people. The secretary and the military commanders could determine appropriate restrictions on who could enter, leave, or remain in these areas and could enforce compliance with

---

45. Exec. Proclamation Nos. 2525, 2526, 2527 (Dec. 7–8, 1941).
46. Exec. Order No. 8972, Authorizing the Secretary of War and the Secretary of the Navy to Establish and Maintain Military Guards and Patrols, and to Take Other Appropriate Measures to Protect Certain National-Defense Material, Premises, and Utilities from Injury or Destruction (Dec. 12, 1941).
47. Pub L. No. 65-135 (1918) (as amended by Pub. L. Nos. 76-886 (1940), 77-234 (1941)).
48. Exec. Order No. 9066, Authorizing the Secretary of War to Prescribe Military Areas (Feb. 19, 1942).

these restrictions. This superseded the authority given to the attorney general to designate prohibited or restricted areas. Provisions were to be made for those so excluded. Congress then passed a statute making it a misdemeanor to violate any of the military areas if the person knew or should have known of such regulations.[49]

LEGAL PROFILES

Samuel T. Rayburn was the Speaker of the House of Representatives during the entire war period and thus responsible for ensuring the passage of all of these statutes. He was born in Tennessee in 1882 but started his legal practice in Texas. He won a seat in the Texas house in 1908, where he served two terms, including as the speaker the last two years. He was then elected to the U.S. House of Representatives, where he served from 1913 to 1961, during the terms of eight U.S. presidents. He was first voted speaker of the house in 1940 when William Bankhead (see Chapter 1) died; and over three terms broken by two spells as the minority party, he served in this role for seventeen years, the longest of any speaker in the history of Congress. He died in 1961.[50]

B. Cases

The restrictions on travel within what had heretofore been a free and open country were not easily digested. As residents of the United States became used to these prohibitions, several individuals decided to try to make a point about these restrictions, leading to litigation. The first case involved an individual who knowingly walked into a restricted area in the continental United States because he did not agree with the regulation. The second case dealt with the martial law imposed in Hawaii. The third case also concerned the martial law in Hawaii, but the U.S. Supreme Court did not hand down a decision until after the war had ended.

---

49. Pub. L. No. 77-503 (1942).
50. *See Rayburn, Samuel Taliaferro*, BIOGRAPHICAL DIRECTORY OF THE UNITED STATES CONGRESS.

1. Restricted Mainland Areas

On December 11, 1941, the secretary of war designated the Western Defense Command as a theater of operations made up of the states of Oregon, Washington, Idaho, Nevada, Utah, and Arizona and the territory of Alaska. Via public proclamations, the commander of the area designated certain military areas and zones within his command as restricted or prohibited in order to limit attempts at espionage and sabotage. The next public proclamation limited such access by enemy aliens and people of Japanese ancestry.

In *United States v. Minoru Yasui*, the defendant was a Japanese American who tested these laws by walking into a police station in a designated area.[51] He claimed that because he was a citizen of the United States, the statute as applied to him was unconstitutional and void.

The court defined the question that it needed to answer as one of "whether a military commander has the right to legislate and pass statutes defining crimes which will be enforced by the civil courts."[52] The court noted that military power was the power to act, not to legislate future action, because the power to legislate the conduct of citizens, even in times of war, lies with Congress. The court quoted President Lincoln in saying that it is only from military necessity that martial law has a basis.

The court differentiated martial law in a case of civil disturbance and in a case where the military is assisting the civil power. The court quoted *Ex parte Milligan*[53] in noting that the proper place for martial law was during foreign invasion or civil war, when the courts are closed. Although it is military necessity that drives the need for martial law, during a war the issue of what is a necessity is not a justiciable one. The court found no declaration of martial law. As such, the civil courts had power over citizens, and the proclamation based on race was void as to citizens but valid as to enemy aliens.

The question then was whether the defendant was a citizen or an enemy alien. The defendant was not only a native-born U.S. citizen but also a citizen of Japan, so he was a dual citizen under international law. The court said that the choices he made were mental ones, so it looked to his activities as an adult. After college, he was employed by the Japanese consulate, responsible

---

51. United States v. Minoru Yasui, 48 F. Supp. 40 (D. Or. 1942).
52. *Id*. at 46.
53. *Ex parte* Milligan, 71 U.S. 2 (1866).

for propaganda for the Empire of Japan. He even registered as a foreign agent, as required by law (see Chapter 2), and he was still employed in that capacity when Pearl Harbor was attacked. From this, the court determined that he had made a choice in favor of Japan and as such was an alien who had violated the laws; thus, the court found him guilty.

This case was appealed to the Supreme Court,[54] which had just held in the *United States v. Gordon Kiyoshi Hirabayashi* case (see Section 4.5) that the curfew did apply to citizens and, as such, the issue of nationality was not relevant.[55] Given the appellant's insistence on his U.S. citizenship and the one-year sentence handed down, the Court vacated the judgment to give the district court the chance to resentence and to strike its findings about the loss of his U.S. citizenship, which the district court did.[56]

LEGAL PROFILES

Minoru Yasui was the defendant in this case and an attorney. He was born in Oregon in 1916 and started his legal practice in the state. He then worked at the Japanese consulate in Chicago, a position from which he resigned on December 8, 1941. His efforts to enlist with the U.S. military were unsuccessful. After he served time in jail for this initial conviction, he was freed by the district court's second decision and eventually forced into an internment camp (see Section 4.5). Freed during the war, he moved to Colorado, passed the bar, and practiced there. In 1984, a federal court in Oregon finally vacated his criminal conviction and dismissed his indictment, but his motion for a writ of coram nobis (setting aside an erroneous judgment) was dismissed and the appeal from that ruling held as untimely.[57] He died in 1986.[58]

---

54. Yasui v. United States, 320 U.S. 115 (1943).
55. United States v. Gordon Kiyoshi Hirabayashi, 46 F. Supp. 657 (W.D. Wash. 1942).
56. United States v. Yasui, 51 F. Supp. 234 (D. Or. 1943).
57. Yasui v. United States, 772 F.2d 1496 (9th Cir. 1985).
58. *See Minoru Yasui, 70, Activist in Japanese-American Rights*, N.Y. TIMES (Nov. 15, 1986).

A. L. (Abraham Lincoln) Wirin was one of Yasui's attorneys for the Supreme Court appeal. He was born in Russia in 1901. His family moved to Massachusetts, but he started his legal practice with the American Civil Liberties Union (ACLU) and was the first full-time lawyer for the ACLU. He moved to Los Angeles in 1931 and worked for the Congress of Industrial Organizations (CIO) but was eventually fired when he could not back the CIO's war position of complete support for the national effort. His many experiences in supporting civil liberties included being kidnapped and left in the desert after filing suit for immigrant farm laborers. Besides *Minoru Yasui*, he was involved in several other Japanese American cases (see Section 4.5) and causes, some reaching the Supreme Court. He died in 1978.[59]

---

2. Martial Law in Hawaii, No. 1

Unlike on the mainland, martial law was declared in Hawaii. On December 7, 1941, the governor of Hawaii (still a U.S. territory at that time) invoked the provisions (section 67) of the Hawaiian Organic Act to implement martial law and suspended the writ of habeas corpus as so provided "in case of rebellion or invasion, when the public safety requires it."[60] The U.S. president approved this declaration. The military governor took over and established military commissions and provost courts to deal with civilians. The civilian courts were closed.

In *Ex parte Zimmerman*, the provost marshal of Honolulu took the appellant, a U.S. citizen, into custody in 1942.[61] This was based on an order of the Board of Officers and Civilians, which inquired into potential subversive activities, detained those who were found not loyal to the United States, and then removed them from the jurisdiction. The defendant was not formally charged. The district judge did not grant the application for a writ of habeas corpus because "the court is forbidden to issue a writ of habeas corpus."[62]

The appeals court only looked to the fact that the declaration of martial law was proper and that there were no allegations that the detention was in bad faith. It believed that the military authorities were best organized to

---

59. *See A. L. Wirin, First Counsel to Civil Liberties Union*, N.Y. Times (Feb. 5, 1978).
60. Pub. L. No. 56-331, § 67 (1900).
61. *Ex parte Zimmerman*, 132 F.2d 442 (9th Cir. 1942).
62. Haw. Military Governor, Gen. Order No. 57 (Jan. 27, 1942).

deal with proactive threats through precautionary measures, while the civilian courts responded to committed crimes in a punitive manner; thus, "the courts, in circumstances like the present, ought to be careful to avoid idle or captious interference."[63] The appeals court affirmed the lower court's ruling.

A strong dissent (citing, among other sources, *Ex parte Milligan* and *Ex parte Quirin*) held that the courts always had the power to review a writ of habeas corpus as these powers cannot be taken away by the other branches of government; but if public safety required it, the privilege of habeas corpus could be suspended as appropriate.

Certiorari was later denied as moot because Hans Zimmerman was released before his case could be tried before the Supreme Court.[64]

LEGAL PROFILES

Bert E. Haney was the judge who dissented in this case. He was born in Oregon in 1879 and started his legal practice there. From 1904 to 1908, he served as a deputy district attorney in Oregon before returning to private practice. He was the chairman of the Oregon Democratic Committee from 1910 to 1915. In 1918, he became the U.S. attorney for Oregon, a position in which he served for two years. In 1922, he became chairman of the state's Board of Pardons and Paroles. The next year, he became a member of the U.S. Shipping Board, where he remained until 1926. In that year, he unsuccessfully ran for the U.S. Senate and returned to private practice. In 1935, President Roosevelt appointed him to a seat on the court of appeals for the Ninth Circuit. Haney remained in this seat until his death in 1943.[65]

Earl Warren was California's attorney general and an amicus curiae for the government in this case and *Minoru Yasui*; he was also a future chief justice of the U.S. Supreme Court. He was born in California in 1891 and started his private practice there. He served in WWI and then held a

---

63. *Ex parte Zimmerman*, 132 F.2d at 446.
64. Zimmerman v. Walker, 132 F.2d 442 (9th Cir. 1942), *cert. denied.*
65. *See Haney, Bert Emory*, Fed. Judicial Ctr., Biographical Directory of Federal Judges.

variety of deputy district attorney positions in Alameda County between 1919 and 1925 before becoming the district attorney in 1925, a position he held until 1938. In that year, he was named as the attorney general for California, a position in which he served until 1942. In that year, he ran for and was elected governor of California, an office he held until 1953. He was then nominated by President Eisenhower to be chief justice of the United States. On the Supreme Court, he served until his retirement in 1969, overseeing a large number of seminal decisions, beginning in his first term with *Brown v. Board of Education*.[66] He died in 1974.[67]

3. Martial Law in Hawaii, No. 2

The defendants in *Ex parte Duncan* were convicted of two separate crimes in Hawaii—White, a civilian businessman, for embezzlement in 1942; and Duncan, a civilian working for the navy, for assault on military sentries in 1944—but their cases were consolidated on appeal due to the similarity of the issues before the appeals court, i.e., whether the petitioners were unlawfully imprisoned and whether the court could review this due to the suspension of the writ of habeas corpus.[68] The district court had overturned these convictions, stating that the provost court was without authority because the civil courts were open and there was no military necessity for trial by the military courts.

The appeals court first took issue with the district court's interpretation of the Hawaiian governor's proclamation of February 8, 1943, which partially lifted some aspects of martial law, including the suspension of the writ of habeas corpus. Although the appeals court did not concur with this, it felt that this was not essential to its decision. It noted that the reopening of civil courts in January 1942 precluded them from jurisdiction in criminal cases. The proclamation of February 1943 had restored civil and judicial proceedings except for civil suits or criminal prosecutions involving members of the armed forces or for violations of military orders. Because Duncan's conduct as a civilian involved members of the military, the appeals court reversed the lower court.

---

66. Brown v. Board of Educ., 347 U.S. 483 (1954).
67. *See Warren, Earl*, Fed. Judicial Ctr., Biographical Directory of Federal Judges.
68. *Ex parte Duncan*, 146 F.2d 576 (9th Cir. 1944).

The Supreme Court then heard this case.[69] The Court's opinion did not look at the types of military powers dealing with members of the armed forces, enemy belligerents, those accompanying armed forces, POWs, occupied enemy territory, regained territory, insurrections, curfew rules, or blackouts (most discussed elsewhere in this chapter). Instead, its only concern was whether the Hawaiian Organic Act gave the power of trying civilians to the military.

The Court tried to start with the term *martial law* as defined in the Organic Act but could not, quoting the attorney general from just before the Civil War: "[C]ommon law authorities and commentators afforded 'no clue to what martial law . . . really is.'"[70] The Court then found that Congress intended to give Hawaiians the same protections under the Constitution as those of inhabitants of the forty-eight states. However, not finding the answers in either the language of the act or in the legislative history, the Court turned to legal history, quoting back to English kings James I and Charles I and the resultant Petition of Right (1628), the Declaration of Independence, Shay's Rebellion (1787), and the Whiskey Rebellion (1794) to demonstrate the nonsubservience of the courts to military power. The Court stated that the courts are "indispensable to our Government" while military tribunals are not. Congress had only a single time authorized the supplanting of courts by military tribunals (during the Civil War), and to do so Congress tried to take away the Court's power to review this legislative act.[71] The Court reversed the court of appeals and ordered both defendants released from custody.

LEGAL PROFILES

Edward J. Ennis argued this case for the respondents in front of the Supreme Court. He was born in New Jersey in 1907 and started his legal practice working for the federal government as an assistant U.S. attorney. His many positions over fourteen years with the Justice Department included defending the New Deal programs, serving as general counsel of the Immigration and Naturalization Service, as director of the Alien

---

69. Duncan v. Kahanamoku, 327 U.S. 304 (1946).
70. *Id.* at 315.
71. *Ex parte McCardle*, 73 U.S. 318 (1868).

Enemy Control Program, defending internment, and as administrator of foreign travel control. After the war, he joined the ACLU, of which he was general counsel from 1955 to 1969 and then president from 1969 to 1977. He died in 1990.[72]

Arthur G. Hays was amicus curiae for this case, *Yasui*, and *Zimmerman*. He was born in New York in 1881, where he started his legal practice. He formed a law firm that assisted German interests in WWI (both of his parents were of German ancestry). He became general counsel for the ACLU in 1920. He was involved in a number of high-profile cases there, including the 1925 John Scopes "Monkey Trial" and the Ossian Sweet segregation-violence case in Detroit (both with famed attorney Clarence Darrow), the Sacco-Vanzetti anarchists' trial, the American Mercury censorship case, the Scottsboro Boys trials, and the 1933 Leipzig trials for the burning of the German Reichstag. He died in 1954.[73]

C. Subsequent Events

From the start of martial law until the end in 1944, the military governor of Hawaii and his subordinates issued more than five hundred orders of different types.[74] These involved oversight of rationing, censorship, tracking residents, running utilities, handling labor issues, and imposing curfews and blackouts. Food, alcohol, movie houses, and the use of cash (a special currency was mandated) were regulated. Fingerprinting and identification cards were implemented. Special restrictions on travel and assembly and possession of firearms, cameras, and radios were imposed on resident aliens and those of Axis powers ancestry.

After a partial relaxation in 1943, the state of martial law was finally terminated in late 1944 and the privilege of the writ of habeas corpus restored.[75] The proclamation stated that "public safety no longer requires that the privilege of

---

72. *See Edward Ennis, 82, Ex-Prosecutor and Head of Civil Liberties Union*, N.Y. TIMES (Jan. 9, 1990).

73. *See Arthur Garfield Hays*, N.Y. TIMES (Dec. 15, 1954).

74. MARTIAL LAW IN HAWAII, THE PAPERS OF MAJOR GENERAL THOMAS H. GREEN, JUDGE ADVOCATE GENERAL'S CORPS, U.S. ARMY (1941–1943).

75. Exec. Proclamation No. 2627 (Oct. 19, 1944).

the writ of habeas corpus remain suspended or that martial law continue in the said Territory."[76] The governor of the territory of Hawaii subsequently issued a companion proclamation on October 24, 1944.[77] The island became a defense area, similar to what was on the mainland (described earlier).

Subsequently, martial law was briefly declared in Alabama to control rioting during the Freedom Rides in 1961, and a similar procedure (although legally not martial law) was used in response to Hurricane Katrina in 2005; but the same issues of suspension of the courts were not raised in either situation. However, the issue of military control of areas in the United States was raised after the passage of the Defense Authorization Act in 2007.[78]

LEGAL PROFILES

Thomas H. Green, military attorney general, was assigned to oversee the legal aspects of martial law in Hawaii. He was born in Massachusetts in 1889 and started his legal practice there. He served in the army in WWI and remained in the military, transferring to the JAG Corps in 1924. He held a variety of different posts in the JAG Corps until he was assigned to Hawaii in 1940. After the attack on Pearl Harbor, he became an executive to the military governor of Hawaii as the military attorney general, whereby he was heavily involved in all of the legal aspects of the martial law period. After the partial return to civilian rule in 1943, he returned to Washington, D.C., as assistant judge advocate general, taking on new roles such as intervening in domestic labor disputes in industrial plants (see Chapter 3). In 1944, he was named deputy judge advocate general. He was then promoted in late 1945 to lead the JAG Corps. He retired in 1949 and died in 1971.[79]

---

76. *Id.*
77. Proclamation by Governor of Hawaii, Ingram M. Stainback (Oct. 24, 1944).
78. Pub. L. No. 109-364 (2007).
79. *See Meet General Green*, THE JUDGE ADVOCATE JOURNAL, VOL. II No. 3 (Fall-Winter, 1945).

4.3 REVOCATION OF CITIZENSHIP

A. Statutes

The Nationality Act of 1940 was discussed in Chapter 2 with regard to its provisions against naturalization for those engaging in seditions.[80] It also included a section on revocation of naturalization.[81] Upon an affidavit showing good cause, the government could bring an action to revoke the order of admittance to citizenship and to cancel the certificate of naturalization on the grounds of fraud or the illegal procurement of the order and certificate. Leaving the country and returning to one's native country within five years of gaining citizenship was considered prima facie evidence of a lack of intent to become a permanent U.S. citizen.

This act superseded the 1906 Act to Establish a Bureau of Immigration and Naturalization and to Provide for a Uniform Rule for the Naturalization of Aliens throughout the United States,[82] based on Congress's constitutional power to do so. Section 15 of the 1906 act was essentially the same in important details as § 338 of the 1940 act.

LEGAL PROFILES

Harold H. Burton served on the Senate Committee on Immigration responsible for the revisions to the Naturalization Act of 1940; he was also a lawyer. Born in Ohio in 1888, he started his legal practice in the state. He worked for several power companies before serving in WWI in the army, and then he returned to private practice. In 1929, he was elected to the state legislature; and in 1935, he was elected mayor of Cleveland, an office that he held until 1940. In that year, he was elected to a seat in the U.S. Senate. He served until late 1945, when President Truman appointed him to the U.S. Supreme Court as an associate justice

---

80. Pub. L. No. 76-853 (1940).
81. *Id.* § 338.
82. Pub. L. No. 59-338 (1906).

even though he was a Republican. Burton served on the Court until his resignation in 1958. He died in 1964.[83]

B. Cases

The need to ensure loyalty to the country during the war led to efforts to minimize the prominence of possibly disloyal citizens and, in the most extreme cases, to try to strip them of their citizenship. Naturalized citizens originally from Germany who still supported Germany were frequently under investigation. The first case involved the attempt to revoke the citizenship of a Communist Party leader. The second case concerned the revocation of a German nationalist's citizenship. The third case dealt with the revocation of citizenship from a member of the German American Bund, taking into account how the two previous cases were decided.

1. Communist Party Leader

In *Schneiderman v. United States*,[84] the action against petitioner William Schneiderman, secretary of the Communist Party in California, began in 1939 and so proceeded under the 1906 act. The lower courts revoked Schneiderman's naturalization twelve years after it was granted in 1927. He was charged with illegal procurement of his naturalization because the organizations to which he belonged (Communist) did not espouse views compatible with the principles of the Constitution.

The Supreme Court noted that immigration was a privilege; but because it was such a valuable commodity, it "should not be taken away without the clearest sort of justification and proof."[85] The Court noted that it chose not to consider two key questions, i.e., whether the courts could retract a decision considered to be a final judgment and whether the government could have a "*de novo* re-examination of a naturalization court's finding and judg-

---

83. *See Burton, Harold Hitz*, Biographical Directory of the United States Congress; *Burton, Harold Hitz*, Fed. Judicial Ctr., Biographical Directory of Federal Judges.

84. Schneiderman v. United States, 320 U.S. 118 (1943).

85. *Id.* at 122.

ment that an applicant for citizenship was attached to the principles of the Constitution."[86]

Instead, the key issue was the applicant's behavior. The Court noted that in the five years before the application for citizenship, the petitioner had not been arrested or connected to any disorder or made any statements advocating the overthrow of the government (this was a disqualifying factor in 1927, but membership in the Communist Party was not). His behavior had shown attachment to the principles of the Constitution. In addition, his behavior had shown that he was "well disposed to the good order and happiness of the United States," which was the ultimate test as applicants can have differing opinions about the need for changes to the Constitution (as did the applicant).[87] His words or actions since his application were not pertinent to the application period itself, and the policies of the Communist Party were not clearly contrary to the Constitution. As the government had not proved its case by "evidence which does not leave the issue in doubt," the Court reversed the rulings of the lower court, letting the petitioner's citizenship stand.[88]

LEGAL PROFILES

Carol Weiss King was an attorney for the petitioner. She was born in New York in 1895 and started her legal career there. She was from a family of lawyers but became involved early in labor issues. She was involved in the Scottsboro Boys trials, the 1939 Harry Bridges deportation case (see Chapter 2), and the defense of national and international Communist leaders. In addition, she worked with the ACLU and was involved with many immigration and naturalization cases, leading to well-accepted rulings, including bail for aliens. In 1942, she took a position as general counsel for the American Committee for Protection of Foreign Born and worked on many immigration cases. Widowed in 1930, she raised her son during her legal career. She died in 1952.[89]

---

86. *Id.* at 124.
87. *Id.* at 129.
88. *Id.* at 135.
89. See *Mrs. Carol King, 56, Noted Lawyer, Dies; Expert on Deportation and Civil Rights Cases Had Defended Bridges, Browder, Eisler,* N.Y. TIMES (Jan. 23, 1952).

Wendell L. Willkie was the attorney presenting for the petitioner. He was born in Indiana in 1892 of two lawyer parents (his mother was the first female lawyer in Indiana) and started practice there. He enlisted in the army in 1917 and was later involved in legal support for enlisted men in Europe. After returning from the war, he worked as a corporate lawyer for a tire company in Ohio and then entered private practice. He moved to New York in 1929 and became the president of one of the largest utility companies in 1933. He opposed the creation of the Tennessee Valley Authority, which would compete directly with a subsidiary of his company. This was one more factor that led him to switch from his long-time Democratic Party allegiance to the Republican Party for the 1940 election. He won the party's nomination somewhat surprisingly over the more established Thomas Dewey and Robert Taft (see Chapter 3). After losing that election, he returned to private practice and traveled the globe for Roosevelt, supporting programs such as Lend-Lease and other international-oriented initiatives and meeting leaders. He gave up another presidential bid after losing an early primary in 1944 and died that year.[90]

Pearl M. Hart was an amicus curiae attorney for the petitioner. She was born in Michigan in 1890 and started practice in Illinois. She began her career as a defense attorney, working as a probation officer for several years. She represented a number of then–socially disadvantaged clients, including children, women, gays, and lesbians, and drafted legislation to defend children. In addition, she defended immigrants and also joined the American Committee for Protection of Foreign Born, which she was representing in this case. Furthermore, she argued before the Supreme Court on alien rights during deportation matters. Hart practiced in Chicago for more than sixty years before her death in 1975.[91]

---

2. German Nationalist

Baumgartner v. United States was brought under the Nationality Act of 1940.[92] The lower courts had revoked Baumgartner's certificate of naturalization, first

---

90. *See Willkie, International Figure, Started His Political Career Late in Life,* N.Y. Times (Oct. 8, 1944).
91. *See Pearl M. Hart,* Chi. Trib. (Mar. 23, 1975).
92. Baumgartner v. United States, 322 U.S. 665 (1944).

214 WORLD WAR II LAW AND LAWYERS

issued in 1932, almost ten years later. The charge was falsity and illegal procurement in that he had renounced his allegiance to Germany. Originally born in Germany, he had been captured by the British in WWI and was forced to spend two years in England. After returning to Germany after the war and starting a career, he emigrated to the United States in 1927. He found gainful employment, but over the years he consistently extolled the virtues of Adolf Hitler and the German way of doing things to those around him and in public speeches, even attending a meeting where the Nazi salute was given.

The Court clearly spelled out the requirement that the evidence must be strong enough to denaturalize a citizen. Naturalization required a person to give up allegiance to his prior country and give it to the United States. At Baumgartner's 1932 naturalization, the Court noted, his allegiance was to the Weimar Republic in charge of Germany, so Baumgartner's current statements of support for Hitler did not mean that he was not sincere in giving up allegiance to the prior regime in Germany. The Court said that the few incidents of "proof" that occurred after he took the oath could not be used to conclusively demonstrate his beliefs at the time of the oath. Because Baumgartner claimed to be still as loyal to the United States as when he took the oath in 1932 and because the utterance of "silly or even sinister-sounding views . . . [are no different than those] which native-born citizens utter with impunity," there was not sufficiently compelling evidence to strip away his citizenship.[93] Thus, the Court reversed the lower courts' decision to revoke Baumgartner's U.S. naturalization.

In concurrence, Justice Frank Murphy clearly articulated the Court's standard on denaturalization:

> American citizenship is not a right granted on a condition subsequent that the naturalized citizen refrain in the future from uttering any remark or adopting an attitude favorable to his original homeland or those there in power, no matter how distasteful such conduct may be to most of us. He is not required to imprison himself in an intellectual or spiritual strait-jacket; nor is he obliged to retain a static mental attitude. Moreover, he does not lose the precious right of citizenship because he subsequently dares to criticize his adopted government in vituperative or defamatory terms. . . . The naturalized citizen has as much right as the

---

93. *Id.* at 677.

natural-born citizen to exercise the cherished freedoms of speech, press, and religion, and, without "clear, unequivocal, and convincing" proof that he did not bear or swear true allegiance to the United States at the time of naturalization he cannot be denaturalized.[94]

LEGAL PROFILES

Felix Frankfurter wrote the Court's opinion. He was born in Austria in 1882 and moved to New York at a young age, where he started his legal practice. He went to work for Henry Stimson (see Chapter 2), who at the time was a U.S. district attorney. When Stimson was named secretary of war in 1911, Frankfurter took a position as legal counsel at the Bureau of Insular Affairs (which oversaw the Philippines, Cuba, and Puerto Rico) until 1914. He then went to work for Harvard Law School until 1917; after the war, he returned to this position until 1939. In WWI, he ran the JAG Corps and dealt with, among other issues, labor disputes that impacted war production. Afterward, he helped found the ACLU. In 1939, he was appointed by President Roosevelt to a seat on the U.S. Supreme Court, where he served until 1962. He died in 1965.[95]

3. German American Bund Leader

Knauer v. United States was argued before the Supreme Court soon after the war had ended.[96] The appellant was born in Germany, served in WWI, and moved to America in 1925 at the age of thirty. He was naturalized in 1937 while Hitler was in power. Proceedings to revoke that citizenship were initiated in 1943; the district court found that he had fraudulently obtained his naturalization certification as he had not been and was not "attached to the principles of the Constitution" and had taken a false oath of allegiance.[97] The

---

94. *Id.* at 678.
95. *See Frankfurter, Felix*, FED. JUDICIAL CTR., BIOGRAPHICAL DIRECTORY OF FEDERAL JUDGES.
96. Knauer v. United States, 328 U.S. 654 (1946).
97. *Id.* at 656.

evidence against Knauer included the following: meeting Hitler in person and consistently praising him; raising money for the Nazis; retaining membership in the German American Bund, which advocated allegiance to Hitler over obligations to the United States; leading Bund-related organizations; pushing the use of the swastika flag within German American organizations; promoting Nazi propaganda within America; owning Bund property; using the Nazi salute; recruiting skilled workers in America to send to Germany; and many other ties to the Bund.

As in *Baumgartner*, the Court noted how compelling the evidence must be for the government to win a denaturalization case against the undercurrent of typical human relationships:

> Human ties are not easily broken. Old social or cultural loyalties may still exist, though basic allegiance is transferred here. The fundamental question is whether the new citizen still takes his orders from, or owes his allegiance to, a foreign chancellery. Far more is required to establish that fact than a showing that social and cultural ties remain.[98]

In reviewing the evidence in this case, though, the Court found that there was compelling evidence presented that the appellant was before, during, and after his naturalization a "thoroughgoing Nazi and a faithful follower of Adolph Hitler."[99] It found that his allegiance at the time of his oath was to Hitler. Thus, the Court found that his oath must then have been fraudulent and so affirmed the lower courts' revocation of his naturalization.

LEGAL PROFILES

Beatrice Rosenberg was an attorney for the appellee in this case. She was born in New Jersey in 1908. She worked for the U.S. Justice Department from 1943 to 1972, ending up as the chief of the appellate section in the Criminal Division, arguing about thirty cases before the U.S.

---

98. *Id.* at 659-660.
99. *Id.* at 660.

Supreme Court in the 1950s and 1960s, which was the most for any woman until very recently. She then headed up the appellate litigation section of the Equal Employment Opportunity Commission. After her retirement in 1979, she worked as a mediator in the District of Columbia. She died in 1989.[100]

Frederick Bernays Wiener was an attorney for the appellee in this case. He was born in New York in 1906 and started his practice in Rhode Island. In 1933, he went to work for the federal Public Works Administration. The following year, he began working for the Department of the Interior. In 1937, he joined the Justice Department. He had joined the U.S. Army Reserve in the JAG Corps and was called to active duty in 1941. He held a variety of positions in Asia and Washington, D.C., during the war. After the war ended, he worked for the U.S. Solicitor General's Office until 1948, when he went into private practice. He argued a number of cases, including *Reid v. Covert*, the only instance where a rehearing changed the result of a published opinion (without a change in the Court's composition).[101] He wrote several books on topics such as military justice and appellate law. He died in 1996.[102]

C. Subsequent Events

The Nationality Act of 1940 contained a section for loss of nationality. In 1944, Congress amended § 401 of the act to mandate loss of nationality for those who made a formal written renunciation of nationality when the country was in a state of war.[103] This led to a number of such renunciations—followed by litigation after the war to restore the renounced citizenship, with the litigants alleging that their renunciations were forced.

In the first case, *Yuichi Inouye v. Clark*, the plaintiff, a Japanese American, was a teenager when his family was moved to a war relocation center in the U.S.

---

100. *See Beatrice Rosenberg; Prominent Attorney for the U.S. Was 81*, N.Y. TIMES (Dec. 2, 1989).
101. Reid v. Covert, 345 U.S. 1 (1957).
102. *See* U.S. ARMY JAG SCHOOL ORAL HISTORY (1987).
103. Pub. L. No. 78-405 (1944).

west (see Section 4.5).[104] He had never lived anywhere except in the United States and evidenced no disloyalty to America. But at the age of seventeen, he renounced his U.S. citizenship while in the war relocation camp. The next month, however, he tried to retract his renunciation. Subsequent to the war, he enlisted in the U.S. military, where he was serving at the time this case was tried. He claimed that his parents influenced his renunciation. The court said that his renunciation was void because he was still a minor; and the influence of his parents, who were subject to deportation, was sufficient to make his renunciation null and void.

There were three other plaintiffs attached to this lawsuit with common experiences. All were Japanese Americans who were married to Japanese nationals and who had renounced their citizenship. While at the Tule Lake Relocation Center, they were subject to constant threats, abuse, assaults, and purported "stabbings in the dark" from the pro-Japanese faction and their own husbands to renounce their U.S. citizenship. This was contrary to their desires, and they were found free of suspicions of disloyalty to America. The court said that the terror groups engaged in "violent activities of assaults, beatings, threats of murder and murder of those Japanese who opposed their policies. . . . Those Japanese who spoke against the pro-Japanese were . . . in mental fear, intimidation and coercion when they applied for their renunciation."[105] The court held that these three did not exhibit a full and voluntary will to renounce and thus restored their U.S. citizenships.

In the next case, *Tadayasu Abo v. Clark*, about 2,300 of more than 5,000 people who signed U.S. citizenship renunciations at the Tule Lake Relocation Center sued to void their renunciations.[106] They claimed that they were also in a state of duress, that the renunciation law was unconstitutional, and that the renunciation hearings were unfair. The court dismissed the latter claim because hearings were not even statutorily required and would not take up the constitutional issue. As for the factors to consider on duress, the court noted that the actions of the pro-nationalist factions, parental influence, fear of loss of community, the inevitability of deportation, and mass hysteria "cast the taint of incompetency" upon these renunciations.[107] As such, the court ordered the

---

104. Yuichi Inouye v. Clark, 73 F. Supp. 1000 (S.D. Cal. 1947).
105. *Id.* at 1004.
106. Tadayasu Abo v. Clark, 77 F. Supp. 806 (N.D. Cal. 1948).
107. *Id.* at 808.

renunciations canceled, with the government given ninety days to present evidence proving that any individuals freely revoked their U.S. citizenship.

In the third case, *Acheson v. Murakami*, plaintiffs brought suit against the secretary of state due to the State Department's refusal to issue passports to the plaintiffs on account of their renunciations at the Tule Lake Relocation Center.[108] As there were some four thousand such cases pending, the appeals court agreed to examine the underlying facts. It recounted the conditions in the camps; the enormous difficulties in evacuations; the attitude of the military general responsible for this, who did not give any preference to Nisei (U.S.-born Japanese) or to those who were WWI veterans; and the threats from mobs when the Japanese Americans returned to civilian life. The court held that all of the renunciations were null, void, and canceled and that the secretary of state must treat the appellees as U.S. citizens.

LEGAL PROFILES

Tom C. Clark was the named party in two of these lawsuits and the assistant attorney general during the latter part of the war. He was born in 1899 in Texas and started his legal practice there. He served as a district attorney for the City of Dallas from 1927 to 1932 and then returned to private practice. In 1937, he joined the U.S. Justice Department's Bureau of War Risk Litigation and was later the civilian coordinator for the relocation of Japanese Americans (see Section 4.5). He served in the Justice Department's Antitrust and Criminal Divisions for the rest of the war. After the war, he served as the attorney general from 1945 to 1949, when he was appointed by President Truman to a seat on the U.S. Supreme Court. He served on the Court until 1967, when he retired (the same year, his son was appointed as U.S. attorney general). He died in 1977.[109]

---

108. Acheson v. Murakami, 176 F. 2d 953 (9th Cir. 1949).
109. *See Clark, Tom C.*, Fed. Judicial Ctr., Biographical Directory of Federal Judges.

4.4 TREASON

A. Statutes

The crime of treason was not based upon new law but old law that was rein-terpreted. Its seriousness is such that it is the only crime specified in the U.S. Constitution. *Treason* is defined in the Constitution as follows:

> Treason against the United States shall consist only in levying War against them, or in adhering to their Enemies, giving them Aid and Comfort. No person shall be convicted of Treason unless on the Testimony of two Witnesses to the same overt Act, or on Confession in open Court. The Congress shall have Power to declare the Punishment of Treason, but no Attainder of Treason shall work Corruption of Blood, or Forfeiture except during the Life of the Person attainted.[110]

Adhering means to change allegiances from one's country to another and also requires the act of giving aid and comfort—one without the other is not treasonous.[111]

The Criminal Code of 1909 made it a crime for

> [w]hoever, owing allegiance to the United States, levies war against them or adheres to their enemies, giving them aid and comfort within the United States or elsewhere, is guilty of treason. Whoever is convicted of treason shall suffer death; or, at the discretion of the court, shall be imprisoned. . . . Whoever, owing allegiance to the United States and hav-ing knowledge of the commission of any treason against them, conceals and does not, as soon as may be, disclose . . . is guilty of treason.[112]

In addition, a treasonous intent was required.[113]

B. Cases

The crime of treason had not been in evidence since the Civil War but was resurrected during WWII. Those convicted under treason laws included those

---

110. U.S. Const. art. 3, § 3.
111. *See* Cramer v. United States, 325 U.S. 1, 29 (1945).
112. Pub. L. No. 60-350 (1909).
113. *Cramer*, 325 U.S. at 54.

U.S. citizens involved in aiding enemies from within the United States and later those who did so from outside the country. The first case involved the charge of treason for aid to an escaped German POW. The second case concerned aid to the German saboteurs who came to America in 1942 (see Section 4.1). The third case also dealt with aid given to these saboteurs, but the defendant in this case was the father of one of the saboteurs.

1. Aid to a POW

In *Stephan v. United States*, the appellant was charged with assisting a German air force officer who had escaped from a POW camp in Canada in 1942.[114] The specifics included harboring and sheltering; providing sustenance, money, and transportation; giving false information; and not reporting the escaped German POW. The indictment listed in detail twelve overt acts. Stephan, the appellant, was a U.S. citizen naturalized in 1935 who had come from Germany but had sworn an oath of allegiance to acquire U.S. citizenship as follows:

> I hereby declare on oath that I absolutely and entirely renounce and abjure all allegiance and fidelity to any foreign prince, potentate, state or sovereignty, and particularly to Germany of whom (1) I have heretofore been a subject or citizen; that I will support and defend the Constitution and laws of the United States of America against all enemies foreign and domestic; that I will bear true faith and allegiance to the United States of America, and that I take this obligation freely without any mental reservation or purposes of evasion, so help me God.[115]

Stephan met the POW in the apartment of a Canadian citizen of German ancestry whom the POW had originally contacted. The Canadian woman and the since-recaptured POW officer witnessed and testified to several of the overt acts, such as providing clothing, money, and transportation. Stephan then transported the POW to several restaurants, buying his food and drinks and covering up his true identity. Witnesses at these restaurants identified the POW and testified to the appellant's actions in each location. The appellant also arranged a hotel stay for the POW and the purchase of a bus ticket the fol-

---

114. Stephan v. United States, 133 F.2d 87 (6th Cir. 1943).
115. *Id.* at 91.

lowing morning from Detroit to Chicago. The trial court convicted Stephan and sentenced him to be executed. The conviction was appealed.

Beyond the question of overt acts was the question of whether there was intent to give aid to the enemy, i.e., "the subject of a foreign power in a state of open hostility with us."[116] The appeals court said that this does not require proof by two witnesses as it can be proved by "by one or more witnesses, or by circumstances, or by a single fact."[117] Because Stephan knew of the POW's position in the military and his intent to escape and return to Germany to fight again, the finding of treasonable intent was substantially supported. The court also addressed the contentions—and disagreed with them—that the POW was incompetent to testify, being "so infamous," and that his whole testimony should be struck as he had not answered several questions because he contended that they concerned military secrets.[118] The court found no reversible errors and affirmed the conviction. Certiorari was denied[119] and the execution later rescheduled,[120] but at the last moment President Roosevelt commuted Stephan's death sentence to life imprisonment.[121] Stephan died in jail in 1952.

LEGAL PROFILES

Xenophon Hicks was the judge who wrote the opinion in this case. He was born in Tennessee in 1872 and started his private practice there. He was a city attorney and then a county attorney between 1892 and 1896. In 1898, he joined the army and thereafter became the mayor of a city in Tennessee. He was elected to the state senate in 1911, after which he was appointed as an assistant state attorney general. In 1913, he was appointed as a judge on the criminal court in Tennessee until 1918, when he became a circuit court judge in the state. In 1923, President Warren G. Harding appointed him to the Tennessee district court, where he served until 1928, when he was appointed to a seat on the court of

---

116. *Id.* at 94.
117. *Id.*
118. *Id.* at 95.
119. Stephan v. United States, 318 U.S. 781 (1943).
120. United States v. Stephan, 50 F. Supp. 738 (E.D. Mich. 1943).
121. *Max Stephan, Traitor, Has Life Saved by Mr. Roosevelt*, STAR & SENTINEL (July 10, 1943).

appeals for the Sixth Circuit. He served there, including as a chief judge, until his death in 1952.[122]

2. Aid to Saboteurs, No. 1

Cramer v. United States was a treason case that reached the Supreme Court.[123] Anthony Cramer, the defendant/appellant, was a German-born naturalized U.S. citizen who had given aid to the group of saboteurs that had landed in America in 1942 and were later captured, tried, and executed as spies (see Section 4.1). One of the two members of that group not executed in 1942 testified to Cramer's aid to the saboteurs. Cramer, a veteran of WWI for Germany, had known and socialized with the since-executed spy Werner Thiel for more than a decade in the United States, and they had belonged to the same pro-German organizations. After receiving a cryptic note in June 1942, Cramer met Thiel, who had returned to America on his sabotage mission. Thiel was eventually caught and convicted of treason.

Noting that "not one execution on a federal treason conviction" had occurred since the founding of the country, the Court focused on what constituted an overt act and whether these acts were similar to conspiracy in that they were acts in furtherance of the crime of treason even though on their face they might be innocuous.[124] To answer this, the Court looked back at the framing of the Constitution and, further, to the Treason Act in the reign of King Edward III, finding that the Constitution's treason clause "was framed by men who, as we have seen, were taught by experience and by history to fear abuse of the treason charge almost as much as they feared treason itself."[125] In addition to what was taken from English, Mosaic (based on biblical law), and other legal traditions, the founders had added two new wholly American provisions, i.e., that Congress could add no new causes for treason and that each overt act had to have two witnesses.

The Court found that treasonous intent could possibly be inferred from the overt acts themselves and other evidence as long as the overt acts had the necessary two witnesses. But applying these rules on overt acts to the facts

---

122. *See Hicks, Xenophon,* FED. JUDICIAL CTR., BIOGRAPHICAL DIRECTORY OF FEDERAL JUDGES.
123. Cramer v. United States, 325 U.S. 1 (1945).
124. *Id.* at 24.
125. *Id.* at 21.

in this case, the Court noted that the government could only prove that FBI agents witnessed, but didn't overhear, meetings between the defendant and Thiel. These acts did not really provide any aid or comfort to the enemy. Other overt acts had to be withdrawn due to the lack of two testifying witnesses, such as Thiel giving a large sum of money to the defendant for safekeeping. The Court felt that other evidence, such as the testimony of a single witness to the appellant's knowledge, the confession to FBI agents (not in open court), and the appellant's prewar utterances, was not sufficient proof. As such, the Court reversed the conviction of the lower court 5-4, over a strong dissent that the two-witness proof requirement should be restricted only to the overt acts themselves and not to proving the treasonable character of those overt acts (based on the fact that treasonable intent only required a single witness).

LEGAL PROFILES

Harold R. Medina was the attorney for the petitioner. He was born in New York in 1888 and started his legal practice there. He was involved in private practice from 1912 to 1947. During that time, he founded and taught a well-known bar review course for thirty years and from 1915 to 1940 taught at Columbia University Law School. In 1947, President Truman appointed him a federal judge in the Southern District of New York. Here, he oversaw the 1947 Foley Square Trial of Communist Party leaders (see Chapter 2). In 1951, the president appointed him to a seat on the court of appeals for the Second Circuit, the seat that was vacated by Learned Hand. He served in that seat full-time until 1958. He died in 1990.[126]

3. Aid to a Saboteur, No. 2

The petitioner in *Haupt v. United States*, Hans Max Haupt, a naturalized citizen originally from Germany, was the father of one of the saboteurs caught

---

126. *See Medina, Harold Raymond*, Fed. Judicial Ctr., Biographical Directory of Federal Judges.

and executed in 1942.[127] The government alleged three types of overt acts by Haupt: sheltering the saboteur, helping him acquire an automobile, and helping him gain employment at the plant that manufactured parts for the Norden bombsight so important in Allied bombing missions.

The Court ruled that these acts clearly gave aid and comfort to the enemy, his son. The Court also said that while witnesses must testify to the same overt act, their testimony does not need to be identical. The Court used this example: one witness might hear a gunshot and see a smoking gun in the hand of the accused and the victim falling; the other witness might be deaf but see the accused raise and point the gun and see a puff of smoke emanate from it.

One other consideration was that Haupt might not have adhered to the enemy but was merely assisting his son. The Court felt that the jury was adequately instructed that

if they found that defendant's intention was not to injure the United States but merely to aid his son as an individual, as distinguished from assisting him in his purposes, if such existed, of aiding the German Reich, or of injuring the United States, the defendant must be found not guilty.[128]

The Court affirmed the conviction of the petitioner (who had been previously convicted along with his wife and other relatives and friends of the same charge but whose convictions were reversed on appeal for technical reasons[129]). Haupt was eventually released from prison and deported in 1957.

LEGAL PROFILES

Irving S. Shapiro was on the brief for the government. He was born in Minnesota in 1916 and went to work for the federal government in 1941 in the Office of Price Administration, concentrating on the rationing program (see Chapter 3). He moved to the Justice Depart-

127. Haupt v. United States, 330 U.S. 631 (1947).
128. *Id.* at 641.
129. Haupt v. United States, 136 F.2d 661 (7th Cir. 1943).

ment as a trial lawyer, practicing before the Supreme Court. After the war, in 1951, he worked for E. I. DuPont in the legal department. In 1974, he became chairman of the DuPont Corporation, leading it through a number of transformations. Eventually, he returned to private practice. He later led the Howard Hughes Medical Institute. Shapiro died in 2001.[130]

C. Subsequent Events

After the war, there were a number of treason prosecutions. The first type was for the acts of propaganda broadcasters who turned against their own country and facilitated the war efforts of the enemy. The second type involved the difficulties of dual nationality.

1. Propaganda Broadcasters

a. Tokyo Rose

Perhaps the most well-known of the propaganda broadcast treason prosecutions in the United States was *Iva Ikuko Toguri D'Aquino v. United States*, the trial of Iva Ikuko Toguri (adding D'Aquino after a 1945 marriage), commonly called "Tokyo Rose" in her broadcasting capacity.[131] An American citizen of Japanese descent, she had gone to Japan in the summer of 1941 and was there when the war broke out. Unable to return, she worked at various jobs until she joined the broadcast program Zero Hour under the stage name "Orphan Ann," from which her conviction arose.

The appellant was convicted of treason by a district court for spending almost two years as an announcer and scriptwriter on a Japanese government propaganda show targeting American military in the Pacific. This was one of the most expensive trials on record at that time, including the cost to the government to obtain dozens of affidavits from people in Japan.

---

130. *Irving S. Shapiro, 85, Lawyer and Ex-Chairman of DuPont*, N.Y. TIMES (Sept. 15, 2001).
131. Iva Ikuko Toguri D'Aquino v. United States, 192 F.2d 338 (9th Cir. 1951).

The conviction centered on one specific overt act during a program airing in October 1944. In an attempt to demoralize Allied troops in the Pacific, she significantly overstated the number and impact of Allied ships lost in the Battle of Leyte Gulf in the Philippines. She said, "Now you fellows have lost all your ships. You really are orphans of the Pacific. Now how do you think you will ever get home?"[132] This act provided aid and comfort to the enemy. The government produced five witnesses to this broadcast.

The purported aim of the *Zero Hour* program was "news and commentaries containing propaganda which was to be used as an instrument of psychological warfare. Their object was to cause the Allied troops to become homesick, tired and disgusted with the war."[133] The court cited other examples of the demoralizing nature of these broadcasts, which witnesses testified were in her voice:

- "Joe Brown was out with Sally Smith. He is a rejectee who is getting the cream of the crop while you Joes are out there knocking yourselves out."
- "What are your wives and sweethearts doing?"
- "Wouldn't it be nice to be home now, driving down to the park and parking and listening to the radio a while[?]"
- "Why don't you kick in now? There's no hope."
- "There is no sense in being out there in those mosquito infested islands, perhaps getting yourselves killed."
- "The Island of Saipan was mined with high explosives."
- "I wonder who your wives and girlfriends are out with tonight? Maybe a 4F. Maybe someone working in a war plant making big money, while you are out here fighting, knowing you can't succeed."
- "Haven't you heard? Your fleet is practically sunk."
- "You know the boys at home are making the big money and they can well afford to take your girl friends out and show them a good time."[134]

D'Aquino appealed, raising numerous objections, which the court considered in turn. The most serious may have been her contention that she per-

---

132. *Id.* at 352.
133. *Id.*
134. *Id.* at 376.

formed her work under duress and coercion. She did not claim that there were any physical threats or coercion, mostly just talk with a few POWs with whom she worked. The trial court allowed this to show her state of mind. But it did not allow the wholesale introduction of the atrocities committed by the Japanese military that had no connection to D'Aquino and had not even been communicated to her at that time, lest "the jury were given the impression that appellant was undertaking to prove that all Japanese were cruel, savage and sadistic and hence that she had the right to fear them all."[135]

The appeals court stated that it did not know of a

> rule that would permit one who is under the protection of an enemy to claim immunity from prosecution for treason merely by setting up a claim of mental fear of possible future action on the part of the enemy. We think that the citizen owing allegiance to the United States must manifest a determination to resist commands and orders until such time as he is faced with the alternative of immediate injury or death. Were any other rule to be applied, traitors in the enemy country would by that fact alone be shielded from any requirement of resistance. The person claiming the defense of coercion and duress must be a person whose resistance has brought him to the last ditch.[136]

The appeals court found that "there is no evidence that the appellant ever so conducted herself as to bring about a demonstration that death or serious and immediate bodily harm was to be apprehended for a refusal."[137]

The court considered in detail the appellant's briefs listing twenty-three major groups of contended errors by the trial court but in the end found no reversible error and affirmed the trial court's conviction. The Supreme Court denied a writ of certiorari. The appellant remained in prison until 1956.

---

135. *Id.* at 363.
136. *Id.* at 359.
137. *Id.* at 360.

LEGAL PROFILES

Walter L. Pope wrote the decision in the Tokyo Rose case. He was born in Indiana in 1889 but began private practice in Nebraska in 1912. He taught at the University of Nebraska from 1913 to 1916 and the University of Montana from 1916 to 1948. He remained in private practice from 1917 to 1949. In 1923, he served in the state legislature in Montana. He worked as a special assistant to the U.S. attorney from 1937 to 1941. In 1949, President Truman appointed him to the court of appeals for the Ninth Circuit. He served full-time until 1961. He died in 1969.[138]

Wayne M. Collins was the appellant's attorney in the Tokyo Rose case, along with Ted Tomba. Collins was born in California in 1900 and practiced there. He represented a number of Japanese Americans in a variety of cases related to the war, including the *Korematsu v. United States* case (see Section 4.5),[139] cases involving the release of citizens from internment camps (see Section 4.5), and cases involving the renunciation of citizenship (see Section 4.3). For many years, he worked on both a mass and an individual basis on resolving citizenship issues for those who renounced their citizenship during this period. His practice also focused on other deportation matters, loyalty oaths, and free speech issues. He died in 1974.[140]

b. Other Propaganda Broadcast Cases

There were a number of other treason trials involving those who were broadcasting propaganda. In the United Kingdom, "Lord Haw-Haw" (William

---

138. *See Pope, Walter, Lyndon*, FED. JUDICIAL CTR., BIOGRAPHICAL DIRECTORY OF FEDERAL JUDGES.
139. Korematsu v. United States, 140 F.2d 289 (9th Cir. 1943).
140. *See Wayne Collins, 74, Tokyo Rose Lawyer*, N.Y. TIMES (July 20, 1974).

Joyce) was convicted of treason for broadcasting English-language propaganda from Germany between the years 1939 and 1945, and he was executed after the war (even though he was a U.S. citizen and a naturalized German).[141] This is discussed further in Section 5.1. In Italy, the poet Ezra Pound, who had broadcast anti-American propaganda from there during the war, was captured but eventually deemed unfit to stand trial for treason and confined to a mental institution for more than a decade.

There were at least four Americans who were arrested for propaganda activities in Europe. The first of these involved Douglas Chandler, who voluntarily did short-wave radio propaganda broadcasts for many years for the Nazi Ministry of Public Enlightenment and Propaganda under the direction of Dr. Joseph Goebbels.[142] The purpose was to support the Nazi war effort by "creating disunity in other peoples by undermining the morale, by splitting up the people in different parties, different social and radical parties, political parties, so that the land who is doing this psychological warfare may aim their war objects."[143] In terms of the United States, the objective was "to build up racial controversies, to create unrest regarding the economic inequalities in the country, to work on minority problems . . . with the purpose of ultimately driving a wedge between the people and the Roosevelt Administration."[144] Chandler was convicted on all ten overt acts. The court of appeals affirmed, rejecting attempts not only to introduce free speech or foreign location factors into elements considered in treason charges but also to introduce the results of the broadcasts, which it found to be immaterial once the treason was committed. Certiorari was denied. Additional European-based treason convictions included "Axis Sally,"[145] "BBB,"[146] and "Captain Martin Wiethaupt."[147]

141. Rex v. Joyce, 173 L.T. 377 (1945).
142. Chandler v. United States, 171 F.2d 921 (1st Cir. 1948).
143. *Id.* at 926.
144. *Id.* at 927.
145. Gillars v. United States, 182 F.2d 962 (D.C. Cir. 1950).
146. Best v. United States, 184 F.2d 131 (1st Cir. 1950).
147. United States v. Monti, 100 F. Supp. 209 (E.D.N.Y. 1951).

LEGAL PROFILES

Calvert Magruder wrote the opinion in the *Chandler* case. He was born in Maryland in 1893 and started his legal practice clerking for Supreme Court Justice Louis Brandeis in 1916. The next year he joined the army to serve in WWI. After the war, he joined the faculty at Harvard Law School, where he would serve in various roles until 1959. In 1934 he became general counsel to the National Labor Relations Board and in 1938 general counsel for the U.S. Department of Labor. In 1939, he was nominated by President Roosevelt to a vacant seat on the U.S. Court of Appeals for the Second Circuit. He remained on the bench until 1959, serving the last eleven years as chief judge. He died in 1968.[148]

2. Difficulties of Dual Nationality

A different type of treason case involved Kawakita, a U.S. citizen in Japan. In *Kawakita v. United States*, the appellant had gone to Japan upon turning eighteen in 1939 and remained there.[149] He was a dual national but registered in Japan as a U.S. citizen (alien) and traveled under his U.S. passport. He remained in Japan after the war started. Upon finishing his schooling, he went to work as an interpreter in a plant that utilized American POWs as slave labor. After the war, he applied to renew his U.S. passport. Upon returning to the United States, he was arrested in 1946 for treason for his acts against POWs in the plant.

At his trial, evidence was presented of eight overt acts of brutality to American POWs who were survivors of the Bataan Death March, sick and emaciated from lack of food. In the factory and mine at the plant, Kawakita far exceeded his role of interpreter by beating and kicking POWs, who were forced to labor at increasing levels of productivity to support the war efforts of Japan even though

---

148. *See Magruder, Calvert*, FED. JUDICIAL CTR., BIOGRAPHICAL DIRECTORY OF FEDERAL JUDGES.
149. Kawakita v. United States, 343 U.S. 717 (1952).

most of them were physically ill. In addition, there was significant evidence presented of his acts of extreme cruelty toward POWs on numerous occasions that had nothing to do with being an interpreter. Finally, his own words on numerous occasions during this period showed his adherence to the enemy.

While not denying the acts, Kawakita claimed that he had lost his U.S. citizenship during this period in Japan, renouncing it in accordance with the Nationality Act of 1940 (see Section 4.3). He had registered locally in 1943 as a Japanese citizen, bowed daily to the emperor, uttered denunciations of the United States, and changed his registered address from California to Japan. The trial court instructed that he was to be found not guilty if that was true or even if he believed it was true because then he could not have formed treasonable intent.

The court determined that he had not renounced his American citizenship, and he was found guilty. The appeals court affirmed, and the Supreme Court agreed to review the case.

The Court stated that his acts were merely those announcing his Japanese citizenship but not renouncing his American citizenship. In his application for his passport after the war, Kawakita had claimed that he was only temporarily residing in Japan and that he had never taken an "oath of allegiance . . . as a foreign citizen or subject."[150] The officer who handled his passport application stated that he overcame the presumption of expatriation in the Nationality Act because his local registration was extracted under extreme pressure from the police and from his uncle on whom he was financially dependent.

The Court also did not allow Kawakita to utilize any of the four renunciation clauses under the Nationality Act: obtaining naturalization in a foreign state (he already was a Japanese citizen), taking an oath of allegiance to a foreign state (which he denied, as noted), serving in the armed forces of a foreign state (he was never in the Japanese military), or performing the duties of employment under the government of a foreign state (although the government restricted wartime labor movement, he worked for a private company). Where there was ambiguity in the facts, the Court did not want to create an additional exception for renunciation because the "[r]ights of citizenship are not to be destroyed by an ambiguity."[151]

---

150. *Id.* at 726.
151. *Id.* at 728.

The Court recognized the difficulties in allegiance where dual nationality was concerned, noting that dual nationality could lead to situations where the dual national would be required under compulsion of one country's laws to do things contrary to the laws of the other country. The trial court's instructions indicated that the "petitioner was held accountable by the jury only for performing acts of hostility toward this country which he was not required by Japan to perform."[152] However, the Court rejected what it called his "fair-weather citizenship, retaining it for possible contingent benefits but meanwhile playing the part of the traitor. An American citizen owes allegiance to the United States wherever he may reside."[153]

The Court thus affirmed Kawakita's treason conviction. President Eisenhower commuted his death sentence, and he remained in prison until 1963, when he was deported.

LEGAL PROFILES

Oscar H. Davis argued this case for the United States. He was born in New York in 1914 and started his legal practice there in 1937. He then joined the U.S. Department of Justice in 1939 but left in 1942 to serve in the U.S. Army Air Corps as a captain. After the war he returned to the Justice Department. In 1950, he became an assistant to the U.S. solicitor general, the position he held when this case was argued. In the 1950s, he represented the government in efforts to deport aliens who had been members of the Communist Party. In 1962, he was nominated by President John Kennedy to the federal Court of Claims. In 1982, he was reassigned to a new seat on the U.S. Court of Appeals for the Federal Circuit. He died in 1988.[154]

---

152. *Id.* at 735.
153. *Id.* at 736.
154. *See Davis, Oscar Hirsh*, FED. JUDICIAL CTR., BIOGRAPHICAL DIRECTORY OF FEDERAL JUDGES.

4.5 CITIZEN INTERNMENT

A. Statutes

After the declarations of war, the government acted quickly to confine certain alien enemies using the old Alien Enemies Act from 1798.[155] In addition, the president issued an executive order to establish military defense areas and zones within areas (see Section 4.2).[156] Based on the need to prevent espionage and sabotage, that authority led to additional actions by the administration and the military first to specify who could be in those defense areas and then to relocate those residing in them to other areas.

A new order from President Roosevelt in 1942 established the War Relocation Authority (WRA), authorizing the "war relocation" of civilians.[157] Based on the president's authority as commander in chief, this order, in the interests of national security, allowed the removal of certain people from designated areas. The director of the WRA could implement a program to remove people to "appropriate places"; to provide for the needs, including employment, of relocated people; to supervise their activities; and to assist with the management and disposal of their property.[158]

The military commander for the Western Defense Command simultaneously issued a number of proclamations.[159] The first of these described Military Area No. 1 as the coastal areas of the three U.S. states touching the Pacific (Washington, Oregon, and California) plus part of Arizona and described Military Area No. 2 as the remainder of these states. These areas were considered a theater of operations subject to attack, attempted invasion, espionage, and acts of sabotage, which required "the adoption of military measures necessary to establish safeguards against such enemy operations."[160] This proclamation stated that future proclamations may exclude people from certain zones in the military areas and that enemy aliens (Germans, Italians, and Japanese) and citizens of Japanese ancestry had to execute a change of residence notice when they moved. A second proclamation then created Military Areas Nos. 3 to 6 in

---

155. Pub. L. No. 5, Sess. II, ch. 66 (1798).
156. Exec. Order No. 9066, Authorizing the Secretary of War to Prescribe Military Areas (Feb. 19, 1942).
157. Exec. Order No. 9102, Establishing the War Relocation Authority (Mar. 18, 1942).
158. *Id.*
159. Headquarters Western Defense Command & Fourth Army, Presidio of S.F., Cal., Pub. Proclamation No. 1 (Mar. 2, 1942).
160. *Id.*

Idaho, Montana, Nevada, and Utah, respectively.[161] Congress then passed the statute mentioned in Section 4.2 penalizing those entering or remaining in the restricted areas.[162]

A third proclamation was then issued, creating regulations for enemy aliens and "all persons of Japanese ancestry" living within the military areas.[163] This included a curfew between 2000 and 0600 hours and restricted travel to places of employment or residences. Limitations were placed on those of Japanese ancestry regarding possession and use of firearms, bombs, shortwave radios, signaling devices, codes, and cameras.

Other proclamations covered the topic of evacuation and exclusion. The fourth proclamation stated that to "provide for the welfare and insure the orderly evacuation of Japanese voluntarily migrating from Military Area No. 1," the Japanese must remain in the area until further notice.[164] A series of civilian exclusion orders was also issued, detailing who specifically was to be excluded and from where. A fifth public proclamation exempted from exclusion and evacuation certain people, including hospital patients, orphans, the aged, those related to a U.S. serviceman (except Japanese), and the handicapped.[165] A sixth proclamation barred further voluntary migrations;[166] and the seventh proclamation confirmed Civilian Exclusion Order Nos. 1–99, which had the effect of excluding all Japanese aliens and nonaliens from Military Area No. 1.[167] The eighth public proclamation removed to war relocation centers those who had been evacuated from the military areas for "their relocation, maintenance, and supervision"; it also confined the evacuees to the relocation centers subject to criminal penalties.[168]

---

161. Headquarters Western Defense Command & Fourth Army, Presidio of S.F., Cal., Pub. Proclamation No. 2 (Mar. 16, 1942).

162. Pub. L. No. 77-503 (1942).

163. Headquarters Western Defense Command & Fourth Army, Presidio of S.F., Cal., Pub. Proclamation No. 3 (Mar. 24, 1942).

164. Headquarters Western Defense Command & Fourth Army, Presidio of S.F., Cal., Pub. Proclamation No. 4 (Mar. 27, 1942).

165. Headquarters Western Defense Command & Fourth Army, Presidio of S.F., Cal., Pub. Proclamation No. 5 (Mar. 30, 1942).

166. Headquarters Western Defense Command & Fourth Army, Presidio of S.F., Cal., Pub. Proclamation No. 6 (June 2, 1942).

167. Headquarters Western Defense Command & Fourth Army, Presidio of S.F., Cal., Pub. Proclamation No. 7 (June 8, 1942).

168. Headquarters Western Defense Command & Fourth Army, Presidio of S.F., Cal., Pub. Proclamation No. 8 (June 27, 1942).

LEGAL PROFILES

John J. McCloy was the assistant secretary of war responsible for initiating the military areas; he was also a lawyer. He was born in Pennsylvania in 1895 and served in WWI. After the war, he turned to private practice, where he was involved for a decade with the well-known Black Tom case (representing corporations who had suffered losses in the 1916 bombings of munitions headed for Europe that was blamed on German agents trying to sabotage U.S. efforts to supply Britain during WWI). He served as assistant secretary of war under Henry Stimson from 1941 to 1945. After WWII, he returned again to private practice but in 1947 was appointed to head the new World Bank. He then served as the high commissioner for Germany from 1949 to 1952, when the Federal Republic of Germany was founded. He served as chairman of Chase Bank from 1952 until 1960 and then went back to private practice. He also held prestigious positions atop foundations and headed the Council on Foreign Relations for almost two decades. Throughout his career, he advised seven U.S. presidents. He died in 1989.[169]

Philip M. Glick was the counsel for the WRA and assisted the Justice Department in these trials. He was born in the Russian Empire in 1905 and moved to America at a young age. He started his legal career with the Department of the Interior, where he was responsible for land policy, helped establish conservation districts, and acted as solicitor. He then became WRA's solicitor. After the war, he worked as general counsel to the Federal Housing Administration (1946–1948), the Institute of Inter-American Affairs (1948–1953), and the State Department's Technical Cooperation Administration (1951–1953). He then entered private practice and later served as legal adviser to the federal Water Resources Council and to the National Water Commission. He died in 2003.[170]

---

169. *See John J. McCloy, Lawyer and Diplomat, Is Dead at 93*, N.Y. TIMES (Mar. 12, 1989).
170. *See* U.S. DEP'T OF AGRIC., PREPARATION OF THE STANDARD STATE SOIL CONSERVATION DISTRICTS LAW (Feb. 1990).

B. Cases

The impact of these orders on law-abiding citizens was immediately obvious, and several challenges were mounted. There were challenges based on individuals doing what they believed to be the right thing and also a concerted action led by the ACLU to challenge these edicts through a series of test cases. The initial individual cases, rebuffed by district court judges, included challenges in Washington State, where a habeas corpus challenge was denied because the petitioner was not in actual custody and her lack of dual citizenship and her marriage to a Philippine national were deemed sufficient to avoid the orders applying to those of Japanese ancestry,[171] and in Wisconsin, where the court would not "declare what is a necessary or proper military area."[172]

Three subsequent cases that reached the Supreme Court, either directly on appeal or certification from the court of appeals on questions of law, were then initiated. The first case centered on the violation of the curfew law as applied to those of Japanese ancestry. The second case involved the violation of the evacuation orders. The third case concerned the detention of loyal citizens in relocation camps. The fourth type of case was different from the other three: it examined whether those interned in war relocation camps had to serve in the U.S. military.

1. Curfew Order

The defendant in *United States v. Gordon Kiyoshi Hirabayashi*, Gordon Kiyoshi Hirabayashi, was a college student who knowingly violated the laws to which he was opposed.[173] He was convicted by the trial court on two counts: violating a civilian exclusion order and violating the curfew in Public Proclamation No. 3.

The trial court, commenting that "[i]t must be realized that civilization itself is at stake in this global conflict," noted the incursions that had already occurred on the West Coast (e.g., Alaska, California, and Canada).[174] The court expressed its opinion that "parachutists and saboteurs, as well as the soldiers, of

171. *Ex parte Ventura*, 44 F. Supp. 520 (W.D. Wash. 1942).
172. *Ex parte Lincoln Seiichi Kanai*, 46 F. Supp. 286 (E.D. Wis. 1942).
173. United States v. Gordon Kiyoshi Hirabayashi, 46 F. Supp. 657 (W.D. Wash. 1942).
174. *Id*. at 659.

Japan make diabolically clever use of infiltration tactics. They are shrewd masters of tricky concealment among any who resemble them."[175]

Reviewing various Bill of Rights claims, the court started with a reminder that "in time of war a technical right of an individual should not be permitted to endanger all of the constitutional rights of the whole citizenry."[176] In particular, the Fifth Amendment due process claim was denied as not existing (at that time), and equal protection claims were rejected by comparing similar differences that existed under the Selective Service Act and the Social Security Act. The court said that the Fifth and Sixth Amendments, which were "perfectly adapted to conditions of peace, do not have the same complete and universal application in time of war."[177] Noting that "extraordinary reasons [are necessary] to justify curfew for or any removal, even from a military area, of American citizens residing therein," the court found that such extraordinary reasons existed since the Pearl Harbor attack and convicted the defendant on both counts.[178]

The appeals court sent the case to the Supreme Court.[179] The Court determined that there were two questions: Was the curfew an unconstitutional delegation of legislative powers? Does the curfew discriminate unconstitutionally against citizens of Japanese ancestry?

Looking at the long list of orders, laws, and proclamations involved, the Court noted the legislative history and the concern within the U.S. Senate of suspected fifth-column activities due to "the system of dual citizenship which Japan deemed applicable to American-born Japanese, and in the propaganda disseminated by Japanese consuls, Buddhist priests and other leaders, among American-born children of Japanese."[180] The Court, noting the extensive cooperation between the executive and legislative branches on the statutes and executive orders and the constitutional war powers of those two branches, felt that it was reasonable to allow the military commander to appraise conditions and determine the time and place of orders to protect against espionage and sabotage of national defense materials, premises, and utilities. Furthermore,

---

175. *Id.* at 661.
176. *Id.*.
177. *Id.* at 662.
178. *Id.*
179. Hirabayashi v. United States, 320 U.S. 81 (1943).
180. *Id.* at 91.

reviewing the extensive Imperial Japanese activities in the Pacific in late 1941 and early 1942, the Court ruled that it was reasonable for the government to be taking defensive measures against invasion.

As to the appellant's contention that in fairness the government must apply the curfew against all citizens or none, the Court stated that such a choice meant "inflicting obviously needless hardship on the many, or sitting passive and unresisting in the presence of the threat."[181] Noting that the states involved had a high percentage of the major government military aircraft and shipbuilding contracts, the Court found that protecting war production against sabotage and espionage at that time in early 1942 was a reasonable response by defense officials.

The Court also noted the espionage that occurred at Pearl Harbor by those sympathetic to Imperial Japan, the lack of assimilation by Japanese into the larger American culture, the large number of citizens sent back to Japan for education, and the dual-citizenship system used by Japan that considered those born of Japanese parents to be Japanese citizens even though they may never have been to Japan, spoken the language, or professed any loyalty to the emperor. The Court also noted that about one-third of the approximately 120,000 people of Japanese ancestry in the country at that time were aliens, many in influential community positions and in consulates, who would be a ready conduit of Imperial Japanese propaganda. The Court believed that Congress and the president could "reasonably have concluded that these conditions have encouraged attachment of members of this group to Japan and Japanese institutions."[182]

The Court then noted that despite the Fifth Amendment's lack of an equal protection clause, "distinctions between citizens solely because of their ancestry are by their nature odious to a free people."[183] However, it continued, although equal treatment was a controlling consideration in times of peace, Congress and the president were not precluded from taking into account the loyalty of citizens in times of war and threatened invasions. The fact that Japan was the enemy threatening invasion meant, not unreasonably, that Japanese citizens were the focus of these internal activities.

---

181. *Id.* at 95.
182. *Id.* at 98.
183. *Id.* at 100.

Because the two sentences were to run concurrently, the Court focused only on the curfew violation, not the first count of not reporting to the civilian control station. Noting the executive order and the first two public proclamations that were in place before the statute was enacted, the Court found that Congress had not delegated its legislative powers. For all of these reasons, it affirmed the district court's conviction.

The unanimous Court issued three concurring opinions, all agreeing to the military expediency argument but feeling great discomfort in doing so. For example, Justice William O. Douglas noted that "guilt is personal under our constitutional system. Detention for reasonable cause is one thing. Detention on account of ancestry is another."[184] And Justice Murphy said, "Distinctions based on color and ancestry are utterly inconsistent with our traditions and ideals. They are at variance with the principles for which we are now waging war."[185]

LEGAL PROFILES

Robert R. Reynolds was the chairman of the Senate Committee on Military Affairs, which was instrumental in the passage of the curfew legislation involved in this case; he was also a lawyer. He was born in North Carolina in 1884 and started his legal practice there. From 1910 to 1914, he served as a prosecuting attorney for the state. He ran unsuccessfully for lieutenant governor and then the U.S. Senate before finally being elected to the Senate in 1932. He was a known isolationist and apologist for the Nazi cause. He remained in his Senate seat until 1944, when he was pushed out by his own party in the primaries. He was defeated in another Senate run in 1950. After that, he returned to private practice. He died in 1963.[186]

Nanette Dembitz was on the government's legal team, along with John Burling, of the Justice Department's Alien Enemy Control Unit under Edward Ennis. She was born in Washington, D.C., in 1912. Even though

---

184. *Id.* at 108.
185. *Id.* at 110.
186. *See Reynolds, Robert Rice*, Biographical Directory of the United States Congress.

she was the niece of Louis Dembitz Brandeis, the Supreme Court justice, she could not get a legal job on Wall Street. So, she first worked for the New York State Constitutional Convention Committee and then joined the Justice Department. She then worked for the National Labor Relations Board before taking a position at the New York Civil Liberties Union from 1955 to 1967. In 1967, she was appointed to the family court in Manhattan, where she focused on children's issues. She lost a bid to be elected to the New York Court of Appeals in 1972. She wrote a book about Japanese internment cases in 1945 (*Racial Discrimination and the Military Judgment*) and other books about property claims arising from the war. She died in 1989.[187]

2. Exclusion Order

In *Toyosaburo Korematsu v. United States*, the appellant, Toyosaburo Korematsu, was convicted of violating a civilian exclusion order.[188] The court of appeals affirmed without much comment, based on the *Hirabayashi* decision.

In a separate opinion, Judge William Denman examined much of what the appellant had argued that was not being considered, highlighted what the Supreme Court did not decide in *Hirabayashi* (the constitutionality of the evacuation orders), and then went on to show that the proliferation of orders required the defendant to both stay where he was and to evacuate. The only choice that remained open for the defendant was to be arrested. Judge Denman ended by noting his dissent from the *Hirabayashi* certification of questions to the Supreme Court and his belief that those on the court of appeals, who lived among the Japanese Americans on the West Coast, were much better situated to answer these issues than those on the Supreme Court. Another opinion in this case recalled the trip of Commodore Matthew Perry to Japan starting in 1852, specifically refuting the idea that some proffered that it was the cause of Japanese aggression against America.

The Supreme Court began its opinion by stating that "all legal restrictions which curtail the civil rights of a single racial group are immediately suspect" but that "[p]ressing public necessity may sometimes justify the existence of

---

187. *See Judge Nanette Dembitz, 76, Dies; Served in New York Family Court*, N.Y. TIMES (Apr. 5, 1989).
188. Toyosaburo Korematsu v. United States, 140 F.2d 289 (9th Cir. 1943).

such restrictions."[189] Basing its reasoning on an extension of the curfew order in *Hirabayashi*, the Court justified the exclusion order, which admittedly was more severe in that it prevented access to homes instead of just forcing people to remain inside them, on the grounds of prevention of sabotage and espionage.

The Court only examined the exclusion order, which it upheld, and not the orders regarding assembly and relocation centers because this was not what the defendant was convicted for. It noted that the military, whose role was legally justified in the *Hirabayashi* decision, had concluded that a curfew was not sufficient for defense reasons and had then resorted to exclusion. Because of military expediency and the impossibility of "bring[ing] about an immediate segregation of the disloyal from the loyal," the curfew was previously upheld, as the exclusion was now.[190] For support, the Court noted that five thousand citizen evacuees refused to pledge unconditional allegiance to the United States, and several thousand requested repatriation to Japan.

However, unlike in *Hirabayashi*, there were dissenting opinions. Justice Owen Roberts felt that "the indisputable facts exhibit a clear violation of Constitutional rights," and Justice Murphy noted that "[s]uch exclusion goes over 'the very brink of constitutional power' and falls into the ugly abyss of racism."[191] Finally, Justice Robert Jackson said, "[He] has been convicted of an act not commonly a crime. It consists merely of being present in the state whereof he is a citizen, near the place where he was born, and where all his life he has lived."[192]

LEGAL PROFILES

Saburo Kido filed a brief on behalf of the Japanese American Citizens League in this case. He was born in Hawaii in 1902 but moved to California to practice law. He helped form the Japanese American Citizens

---

189. Korematsu v. United States, 323 U.S. 214 (1944).
190. *Id.* at 219.
191. *Id.* at 233.
192. *Id.* at 243.

League (JACL), wrote numerous articles for its publication, and became the JACL president in 1941. The group tried to work with the government during the evacuation to war relocation camps and in regard to the management of the camps and supported the drafting of U.S. citizens of Japanese ancestry. This set him against the direction of some other camp residents, and he was twice physically assaulted there, the second time quite severely, but he would not testify against his attackers. After the war, he joined with A. L. Wirin (see Section 4.2) in a law firm that took to the Supreme Court cases on prohibitions against aliens receiving fishing licenses and against alien land ownership.[193] He died in 1977.[194]

William Denman was a court of appeals judge with strong opinions in both the *Hirabayashi* and *Korematsu* cases. He was born in California in 1872 and started his legal practice there. In addition to his legal practice, he lectured at the law school at the University of California. In 1935, he was appointed by President Roosevelt to a seat on the court of appeals for the Ninth Circuit. He served on this bench full-time until 1957, including as chief judge from 1948 to 1957. He died in 1959.[195]

Ernest Besig was the leader of the ACLU in Northern California and behind the scenes lined up the test cases; he was also a lawyer. He was born in New York in 1905 and moved to California. He immediately became involved in longshoreman strikes in San Francisco in 1934. After the war, he remained involved in issues such as labor strikes, free speech, racial discrimination, immigration, loyalty programs, and obscenity cases. He stayed involved with the ACLU in California for almost forty years, until retiring in 1971. He taught university courses until 1985 and died in 1998.[196]

---

193. Oyama v. California, 332 U.S. 633 (1948).
194. *See Saburo Kido*, DENSHO ENCYCLOPEDIA (2012).
195. *See Denman, William*, FED. JUDICIAL CTR., BIOGRAPHICAL DIRECTORY OF FEDERAL JUDGES.
196. *See Ernest Besig, 94, ACLU Legal Crusader*, S.F. CHRON. (Nov. 18, 1998).

3. Detention Orders

Decided the same day as *Korematsu*, *Ex parte Endo*, a case challenging the evacuation of citizens, finally made it to the Supreme Court.[197] As with *Hirabayashi* and *Korematsu*, the Supreme Court received *Ex parte Endo* from the court of appeals on certification for questions of law, but the Court took on the whole decision instead. The defendant/appellant Mitsuye Endo, an American citizen of Japanese ancestry, was evacuated to a war relocation center and then filed a writ of habeas corpus. It was denied by the district court. For the first time, the courts had to examine the executive order that set up the WRA.

The Supreme Court noted that the responsibilities of the WRA were to maintain the relocation centers, separate loyal and disloyal evacuees, detain the disloyal, and relocate the loyal. The appellant contended that she was a loyal citizen and was being unlawfully held at a relocation center against her will. The WRA countered that it could hold people against whom there were no charges only long enough to ensure that their resettlement was handled appropriately, through its leave process. The Court rejected this, saying that Endo should be released immediately and not be subjected to the leave process.

The Court found that the legal orders and laws that led to Endo's situation did not provide for detention; rather, that policy developed later based on community hostility to the returning or immigrating evacuees. These laws and orders were created on the premise of preventing sabotage and espionage, not avoiding community hostility. Because there were no laws to support this latter purpose, the Court ruled that the appellant was being illegally detained and must be released. Justice Murphy concurred: "[D]etention in Relocation Centers of persons of Japanese ancestry regardless of loyalty is not only unauthorized by Congress or the Executive but is another example of the unconstitutional resort to racism inherent in the entire evacuation program."[198] Similarly, Justice Roberts said, "[T]he court is squarely faced with a serious constitutional question,—whether the relator's detention violated the guarantees of the Bill of Rights of the federal Constitution and especially the guarantee of due process of law."[199]

---

197. *Ex parte Endo*, 323 U.S. 283 (1944).
198. *Id.* at 307.
199. *Id.* at 310.

LEGAL PROFILES

William O. Douglas wrote the opinion in this case. Born in Minnesota in 1898, he followed his family out to Washington State but started his legal practice in New York. In 1926, he began teaching law at Yale University. In 1934, he was offered a position at the Securities and Exchange Commission, and he subsequently became its chairman in 1936. In 1939, at the age of only forty, he was appointed to the seat vacated by Louis Brandeis on the U.S. Supreme Court. He served on the Court for more than thirty-six years, setting numerous records for court longevity, opinions written, and dissents written; he was noted for his support of civil liberties and the environment. He died in 1980.[200]

Herbert Wechsler was the assistant attorney general when this case was tried. Born in New York in 1909, he started his legal practice there by teaching at his alma mater, Columbia Law School. He took a year off to clerk for Supreme Court Justice Harlan Fiske Stone and then returned to teaching. In 1940, he started working for the U.S. Justice Department, arguing cases in front of the Supreme Court. After the war, he took part in the Nuremberg Trials (see Chapter 6). He then returned to teaching. In 1963, he delivered the official draft for the Model Penal Code, after which he was named director of the American Law Institute. He remained in that position until 1984, overseeing a number of restatements, including the *Restatement of Contracts* and the *Restatement of Torts*. He argued for the petitioner in the seminal case *New York Times Co. v. Sullivan*.[201] In addition, he wrote a number of casebooks, including one on the federal courts, and was an expert on constitutional law. He died in 2000.[202]

---

200. *See Douglas, William Orville*, FED. JUDICIAL CTR., BIOGRAPHICAL DIRECTORY OF FEDERAL JUDGES.
201. N.Y. Times Co. v. Sullivan, 376 U.S. 254 (1964).
202. *See Herbert Wechsler, Legal Giant, Is Dead at 90*, N.Y. TIMES (Apr. 28, 2000).

Ralph F. Fuchs, an assistant to the attorney general, was on the brief for the government. Born in Missouri in 1900, he began teaching law there. He began working for the government in 1941 and for the solicitor general's office in 1943, where he argued before the Supreme Court and contributed the briefs on many other cases. He returned to teaching law after the war and was considered an expert on administrative law, authoring a number of books on this topic and shaping the Administrative Procedure Act. He was involved in the local civil liberties union and in international legal matters. He was a president of the American Association of University Professors, whose members he defended against congressional accusations of Communist affiliations in the 1950s. He died in 1985.[203]

---

4. Conscription for Internees

Another issue that arose from the relocation camps was whether evacuees of the right age and gender should be required to serve in the U.S. military. There were several such cases, three of which are discussed here.

The first case, *United States v. Masaaki Kuwabara*, involved an American citizen of Japanese descent who was evacuated to a war relocation center and then later to the segregation camp for disloyal citizens, where he was confined.[204] Upon being required under the Selective Service Act to report for military service, the defendant refused to report for his preinduction physical exam, citing among other reasons that he could not willingly consent due to his internment in the camp and the fact that he had applied for repatriation to Japan. The court did not agree that repatriation before the fact had anything to do with military induction in the United States. But it did find that "[i]t is shocking to the conscience that an American citizen be confined on the ground of disloyalty, and then, while so under duress and restraint, be compelled to serve in the armed forces, or be prosecuted for not yielding to such compulsion."[205] The court noted that the Selective Service System was set up to be "fair and just" but did not find it so in this case.[206] Because the confinement was contrary

---

203. *See Ralph Fuchs Is Dead; Retired Law Professor*, N.Y. TIMES (Feb. 21, 1985).
204. United States v. Masaaki Kuwabara, 56 F. Supp. 716 (N.D. Cal. 1944).
205. *Id.* at 719.
206. *Id.*

to due process, the indictment against the defendant was quashed, as were similar indictments against twenty-five other defendants similarly charged.

In the second case, *Shigeru Fujii v. United States*, the appellant was one of sixty-three young U.S. citizens of Japanese ancestry located in the Heart Mountain Relocation Center who had refused induction and was then tried and convicted of such.[207] The appellant was loyal to the United States and had made no application to repatriate to Japan. The court found that if indeed his detention in the camp as a loyal citizen violated due process, he should have initiated a habeas corpus motion, which he did not do. Instead, he refused the lawful order to report for selective service. He had also not exhausted his administrative remedies to seek reclassification for selective service, as required before seeking redress in the courts. Stating that "two wrongs don't make a right," the court affirmed his case and those of the other sixty-two similarly convicted.[208]

The third case, *Hideichi Takeguma v. United States*, involved three potential inductees in relocation centers who had refused to report for military induction.[209] Two had requested repatriation, which was granted, and they were segregated as enemy aliens, with the only difference being that one received an order for induction before segregation in the camp and one after. The third had not requested repatriation. All were convicted of refusing to report. The appeals court ruled that relocation does not relieve a citizen of the obligation for selective service and, as such, affirmed the conviction of the third inductee. With regard to the other two, their granted repatriation requests did not relieve them from U.S. military service, so the court affirmed their convictions as well. Judge Denman urged clemency due to the mitigating factors behind the actions of these young men.

LEGAL PROFILES

Albert L. Stephens Sr. wrote the opinion in the *Takeguma* case. Born in Indiana in 1874, he started his legal practice in California in 1899. He was a justice of the peace from 1906 until 1910 in Los Angeles and

---

207. Shigeru Fujii v. United States, 148 F.2d 298 (10th Cir. 1945).
208. *Id.* at 299.
209. Hideichi Takeguma v. United States, 156 F.2d 437 (9th Cir. 1946).

then a civil service commissioner for the state of California beginning in 1911. In 1913, he was appointed city attorney for Los Angeles. He was then appointed as a judge on the superior court in Los Angeles County in 1919, a position that he held until 1932. He was then named to the state court of appeals, serving as presiding justice the final two years. In 1935, President Roosevelt appointed him to a district court seat in the Southern District of California. Two years later, he was appointed to a seat on the court of appeals for the Ninth Circuit. He held this position full-time until 1961 and was the chief judge for several years. He died in 1965.[210]

C. Subsequent Events

In late 1944, a new public proclamation, citing the substantial improvement in the military situation, withdrew the 1942 orders and proclamations.[211] Stating that it was now possible to determine on an individual basis the dangers of sabotage and espionage, the new proclamation rescinded all mass civilian exclusion orders, Public Proclamations Nos. 3–7 and 11, and paragraph 5 (change-of-residence notices) of Public Proclamations Nos. 1 and 2. Unless subject to an individual exclusion order, all people of Japanese ancestry were exempted from exclusion orders beginning in January 1945. The Western Defense Command was allowed to issue identification cards to allow free movement and residence within the area of the Western Defense Command. All people of Japanese ancestry, noted the proclamation, "should be accorded the same treatment and allowed to enjoy the same privileges accorded other law abiding American citizens or residents."[212] However, the confinement of enemy aliens during wartime was upheld in a 1948 Supreme Court decision.[213]

The treatment of those associated with an Asia-based enemy differed greatly from the treatment of those associated with an Asia-based wartime ally. In 1943, in response to efforts by the Chinese to assist in the war and become

---

210. *See Stephens, Albert Lee Sr.*, Fed. Judicial Ctr., Biographical Directory of Federal Judges.
211. Headquarters Western Defense Command & Fourth Army, Presidio of S.F., Cal., Pub. Proclamation No. 21 (Dec. 17, 1944).
212. *Id.*
213. Ludecke v. Watkins, 335 U.S. 160 (1948).

an official ally, Congress passed the Chinese Exclusion Repeal Act of 1943 (the Magnuson Act).[214] This allowed Chinese immigration for the first time in more than sixty years as well as naturalization of Chinese immigrants already in the country. However, the act still provided restrictions on the numbers of immigrants, and straight racial restrictions on immigration were not abolished until the 1952 Immigration and Nationality Act.[215]

Many decades later, based on newly uncovered information, federal courts overturned the convictions of both Korematsu and Hirabayashi. In the first case, decided in 1984, the district court granted Korematsu's unopposed writ of coram nobis correcting errors of fact, based on the report of the Commission on Wartime Relocation and Internment of Civilians and on allegations of suppressed or inaccurate information (e.g., alleged use of radio transmitters and ship-to-shore signaling) regarding the threat posed by Japanese citizens in 1942.[216] In the second case, decided in 1987, the appeals court overturned both counts on a writ of coram nobis.[217] The district court had overturned one of the two counts on which Hirabayashi was convicted, holding that the exclusion order was a violation of due process based not on military grounds but on the difficulty in determining loyal from disloyal citizens of Japanese descent and likely on racist feelings of the commanding general.[218] It also ruled that the curfew order was a less significant infringement on Hirabayahi's freedom and that the Supreme Court would have upheld it. The appeals court ruled that the curfew order did not rest on a different legal foundation than the exclusion order and so overturned that conviction as well and granted the writ.

LEGAL PROFILES

Fred Okrand was an ACLU attorney involved in the Japanese internment cases and the later cases on fishing and land rights with A. L. Wirin and Saburo Kido. He was born in 1917 in California and started his first

214. Pub. L. No. 78-199 (1943).
215. Pub. L. No. 82-414 (1952).
216. Korematsu v. United States, 584 F. Supp. 1406 (N.D. Cal. 1984).
217. Hirabayashi v. United States, 828 F.2d 591 (9th Cir. 1987).
218. Hirabayashi v. United States, 627 F. Supp. 1445 (W.D. Wash. 1986).

legal job with Wirin's firm. He was immersed in many cases that the ACLU litigated, including cases involving conscientious objectors during the war. After serving in the U.S. Army in Europe from late 1942 until the war's end, he returned to Wirin's firm and became involved in the cases named in this section as well as the citizenship renunciation cases. He served as the counsel for the ACLU in southern California, involved in every type of civil liberties action and arguing a number of times before the Supreme Court, until his retirement in 1984. He died in 2002.[219]

Warren Magnuson was the sponsor of the Magnuson Act and a lawyer. He was born in Minnesota in 1905 but started his practice in Washington State. He was a local prosecuting attorney in 1931, elected to the state house in 1933, and then elected as a local prosecuting district attorney in 1934. In 1936, he was elected to the U.S. House of Representatives. He served during the war in the U.S. Navy in the Pacific. He was appointed to the U.S. Senate in 1944 after his predecessor took a seat on the U.S. Court of Appeals for the Ninth Circuit. He was thereafter elected to the Senate five times, serving until 1981. He was involved in many important Senate committees, including commerce and appropriations. Upon leaving Congress after forty-four years, he returned to the practice of law until his death in 1989.[220]

4.6 FREEDOM OF EXPRESSION

A. Statutes

During the war, the administration's numerous attempts to support the war effort included suppressing the voices of those who spoke against it or in support of the country's enemies. This suppression was effected through pros-

---

219. *See Fred Okrand, 84; Fought Key ACLU Battles*, L.A. TIMES (Mar. 21, 2002).
220. *See Magnuson, Warren Grant*, BIOGRAPHICAL DIRECTORY OF THE UNITED STATES CONGRESS.

ecutions or threatened prosecutions for sedition, as described in Chapter 2. Further seditious activities, such as urging on the cause of Imperial Japan as beneficial to African Americans, were similarly prosecuted.[221]

The Office of Facts and Figures,[222] established in 1941 and soon to become part of the Office of War Information,[223] and the Justice Department monitored other isolationist critics, such as the Hearst and McCormick newspapers, which were considered to be "divisionists" driving a wedge between America's allies and people; the government hoped to make a potential case for sedition against these major newspapers but eventually gave up. The government did, however, take the case to a grand jury when McCormick's *Chicago Tribune* published an article disclosing information that the U.S. Navy knew about Japanese plans before the Battle of Midway,[224] but it eventually decided that the publicity of a trial could expose the breaking of Japanese encryption codes and declined to prosecute.

The administration also used the post office to block the circulation of postal mail by organizations promoting disunity. Under the Espionage Act of 1917,[225] any publication that violated this act (publishing false statements to interfere with the military, promote the success of enemies, or cause insubordination in the military) or advocated "treason, insurrection or forcible resistance to any law" was deemed nonmailable. Relying on Supreme Court approval holding that use of subsidized reduced-rate classes of mail was a privilege granted via a permit that could be revoked,[226] the administration was able get the second-class permit revoked for *Social Justice*, a newspaper founded by the virulently anti-Semitic, pro-Fascist Father Charles E. Coughlin.[227] The administration also removed this privilege from dozens of other less popular subversive publications as well as dozens of publications it considered obscene or indecent, such as *Esquire*. The Supreme Court upheld these wiretapping-based convictions.[228]

---

221. United States v. Gordon, 138 F.2d 174 (7th Cir. 1943).
222. Exec. Order No. 8922, Establishing the Office of Facts and Figures (Oct. 24, 1941).
223. Exec. Order No. 9182, Establishing the Office of War Information (June 13, 1942).
224. *Navy Had Word of Jap Plan to Strike at Sea,* CHI. TRIB. (June 7, 1942).
225. Pub. L. No. 65-24, tit. XII (1917).
226. United States *ex rel.* Milwaukee Social Democratic Publ'g Co. v. Burleson, 255 U.S. 407 (1921).
227. *Mails Barred to "Social Justice,"* PITTSBURGH POST-GAZETTE (Apr. 15, 1942).
228. *See, e.g.,* Goldman v. United States, 316 U.S. 129 (1942).

LEGAL PROFILES

Frank C. Walker was the U.S. postmaster general responsible for issuing second-class publication-mailing permits; he was also an attorney. He was born in 1886 in Pennsylvania but started his legal practice in Montana. He was elected to the state legislature in 1913 and later served in the army during WWI, after which he returned to private practice. He moved east as general counsel for a theater firm and became the treasurer for the Democratic National Committee. He then joined the new administration in 1933 on the National Emergency Council but was also a close adviser to the president. In 1940, he became the postmaster general, a position he held until 1945. After the war, he was a member of the first U.S. delegation to the new United Nations. He died in 1959.[229]

B. Cases

There were few significant war-related freedom of expression cases that arose during the war, apart from the sedition cases already described. This was true despite widespread military censorship and the activities of the Office of Censorship.[230] The first freedom of expression case was a Supreme Court decision involving the Pledge of Allegiance. The second freedom of expression case revisited the Pledge of Allegiance after the start of the war. The third case dealt with freedom of expression involved in resistance to the selective service system.

1. Pledge of Allegiance, No. 1

Minersville School District v. Gobitis involved two children who refused to recite the Pledge of Allegiance: "I pledge allegiance to my flag, and to the Republic for which it stands; one nation indivisible, with liberty and justice for all."[231] According to their family's religious beliefs, they could not extend their hands

229. *See Frank C. Walker, Ex-Aide, Dies*, N.Y. TIMES (Sept. 14, 1959).
230. Exec. Order No. 8985, Establishing the Office of Censorship (Dec. 19, 1941).
231. Minersville Sch. Dist. v. Gobitis, 310 U.S. 586 (1940).

to salute the flag. A gesture of respect for the flag, according to their beliefs as Jehovah's Witnesses, was forbidden. Their refusal to take part in this brief daily routine led to their expulsion from the public school they attended. Not wanting to pay for a private school, the family brought suit to recover their free education. The district court and the appeals court ruled in favor of the family.

The Supreme Court, however, stated that "[c]onscientious scruples have not, in the course of the long struggle for religious toleration, relieved the individual from obedience to a general law not aimed at the promotion or restriction of religious beliefs."[232] It continued by noting that "[n]ational unity is the basis of national security."[233] The Court saw the flag as a symbol of national power, the "emblem of freedom . . . the unifying sentiment" that provides the basis for all freedoms enjoyed.[234] The Court did not want to be "the school board for the country."[235] As long as practices that served to unify citizens to a common loyalty did not interfere with religious beliefs, the Court found them acceptable; it therefore reversed the relief granted by the lower courts. The dissent argued that states may pass laws that conflict with religious practice for public safety, health, and order but not to educate and inspire loyalty.

2. Pledge of Allegiance, No. 2

In *West Virginia State Board of Education v. Barnette*, the state of West Virginia had legally mandated that students in all schools take courses in history, civics, and the Constitution "for the purpose of teaching, fostering and perpetuating the ideals, principles and spirit of Americanism."[236] Students were also required to take part in the salute to the flag; failure to do so could result in the students being expelled and their parents then prosecuted for keeping their children out of the mandatory education system. The Jehovah's Witnesses believed that the flag was a graven image that they were biblically forbidden to salute, and as such their children were expelled from the schools maintained by the appellant.

In contrast to *Gobitis*, the Supreme Court, noting that school attendance was mandatory, found in this case a distinction between educating children "to inspire patriotism and love of country" and requiring that they declare a

---

232. *Id.* at 594.
233. *Id.* at 595.
234. *Id.* at 597.
235. *Id.* at 598.
236. West Virginia State Bd. of Educ. v. Barnette, 319 U.S. 624, 625 (1943).

belief through the salute to the flag.[237] It did not find a clear and present danger where students instead remained still and silent. This was not a case involving freedom of religion even though the appellant's religious convictions brought this matter to litigation. The Court looked back at the *Gobitis* decision and took apart some of its framework, such as those ideas involving the necessary strength of government needed to compel this salute, the Court being the school board of the nation, and courts having controlling competence in these matters.

The Court then focused strongly on the *Gobitis* notion that "national unity is the basis of national security."[238] The Court did not hold with this notion, stating that "[t]hose who begin coercive elimination of dissent soon find themselves exterminating dissenters. Compulsory unification of opinion achieves only the unanimity of the graveyard."[239] The Bill of Rights prohibits those in power from coercing consent, the Court stated, noting that "[a]uthority here is to be controlled by public opinion, not public opinion by authority."[240] The Court believed that the appeal of American institutions is such that compulsion was not required and so affirmed the lower courts and overruled *Gobitis*.

Justices William Douglas and Hugo Black, who joined the majority in *Gobitis*, explained in a concurring opinion that "[l]ove of country must spring from willing hearts and free minds."[241] Noting the current situation, they stated that "[n]either our domestic tranquility in peace nor our martial effort in war depend on compelling little children to participate in a ceremony which ends in nothing for them but a fear of spiritual condemnation."[242] Justice Murphy, quoting from the Virginia Statute for Religious Freedom, noted that "[i]t is in that freedom and the example of persuasion, not in force and compulsion, that the real unity of America lies."[243] *Gobitis* opinion author Justice Frankfurter dissented, noting that despite his sensitivity based on Jewish faith as "the most vilified and persecuted minority in history," he did not believe that the due

---

237. *Id.* at 631.
238. *Id.* at 640.
239. *Id.* at 641.
240. *Id.*
241. *Id.* at 644.
242. *Id.*
243. *Id.* at 646.

process clause gave the Court the ability to override the state's legitimate leg-islative goals.[244]

LEGAL PROFILES

Hayden C. Covington was on the brief for the respondents in *Gobitis* and *Barnette* and presented the *Barnette* case to the Court. He was born in Texas in 1911 and started his legal practice there. Besides handling insurance cases, his practice found him defending cases for Jehovah's Witnesses, and he was invited to join the organization as general counsel in 1939. Over the years, he defended dozens of Jehovah's Witness cases before the Supreme Court, including those for door-to-door solicita-tions and street preaching. His winning record in front of the Supreme Court is among the best in the history of that institution. After leaving the Jehovah's Witness legal team in 1969, he was involved with invest-ment brokers. In the 1960s, he assisted Muhammad Ali in his dispute with the Selective Service System. He died in 1978.[245]

Abe Fortas was on the amicus curiae brief for the appellees in the *Barnette* case; he was also a future Supreme Court justice. He was born in Tennessee in 1910 but went to Washington, D.C. to work first at the Agricultural Adjustment Administration in 1933 and then at the Securi-ties and Exchange Commission the following year with future Supreme Court justice William Douglas. He also taught law at Yale. In 1939, he joined the Public Works Administration and then the Interior Depart-ment, where he became the undersecretary in 1942. After the war, he returned to private practice, where was involved in two seminal cases: *Durham v. United States* ("product test" on mental state of accused, i.e., the accused is not criminally liable if the illegal act was the product of a

---

244. *Id.*
245. *See* Resume and Death Certificate of Hayden C. Covington (1978).

mental disease or defect)[246] and *Gideon v. Wainwright* (indigent's right to appointed counsel).[247] He was appointed to the U.S. Supreme Court by President Lyndon B. Johnson in 1965, where he authored several seminal opinions, including *Tinker v. Des Moines Independent Community School District*.[248] He only served on the bench until 1969, when he resigned and returned to private practice. He died in 1982.[249]

Zechariah Chafee Jr. was on the amicus curiae brief for the appellees in the *Barnette* case. He was born in Rhode Island in 1885 and practiced in Massachusetts from 1913 to 1916. He then became a law professor at Harvard, where he remained for the next forty years. During that time, he authored many works on civil liberties, including *Freedom of Speech* in 1920. Between two 1919 Supreme Court cases from WWI, *Schenck v. United States* and *Abrams v. United States*,[250] he influenced the thinking of Justice Oliver Wendell Holmes such that Holmes joined Justice Brandeis in dissent in the second case. Chafee later authored more books, and was involved in drafting the Federal Interpleader Act of 1936 (for those having custody of money or property upon which there are multiple claimants). In 1952, he was named by Sen. Joseph R. McCarthy as one of the seven people "dangerous to the United States" for supporting the prison release of the U.S. Communist Party leader.[251] He died in 1957.[252]

Basil O'Connor was on the amicus curiae brief for the appellees in the *Barnette* case. He was born in Massachusetts in 1892 but started his legal practice in New York and Boston. He met and started a law firm with Franklin Roosevelt in 1924, which lasted until the latter's inauguration as U.S. president in 1933. In 1927, O'Connor worked with Roosevelt in founding the Georgia Warm Springs Foundation, where Roosevelt went for treatment of his polio symptoms. In 1938, they founded the National

246. Durham v. United States, 214 F.2d 862 (1954).
247. Gideon v. Wainwright, 372 U.S. 335 (1963).
248. Tinker v. Des Moines Indep. Cmty. Sch. Dist., 393 U.S. 503 (1969).
249. *See Fortas, Abee*, FED. JUDICIAL CTR., BIOGRAPHICAL DIRECTORY OF FEDERAL JUDGES.
250. Schenck v. United States, 249 U.S. 47 (1919); Abrams v. United States, 250 U.S. 616 (1919).
251. U.S. Senate Permanent Subcommittee on Investigations (July 2, 1952).
252. *See Zechariah Chafee Jr., 71, Dead; Lawyer, Civil Liberties Champion*, N.Y. TIMES (Feb. 9, 1957).

Foundation for Infantile Paralysis (later the March of Dimes Foundation), which O'Connor led for more than three decades. O'Connor was also appointed to head the American Red Cross from 1944 to 1949. He returned to private practice and was chiefly responsible for raising significant sums of money for medical research, which led to funding for polio pioneers Dr. Jonas Salk and Dr. Albert Sabin, among others. He died in 1972.[253]

---

3. Selective Service

In *Keegan v. United States*, a conspiracy was alleged against members of the German American Bund to evade military service in violation of the Selective Training and Service Act (see Chapter 3).[254] Using a large amount of background information about the Bund from many years before the alleged conspiracy, twenty-four of the twenty-five defendants were convicted under the act. There was no evidence that members of the Bund were opposed to the act; however, a late-added provision to the statute precluded Bund members (or those of the Communist Party) from being hired by employers when a vacancy opened up due to an employee being drafted. The members of the Bund met to discuss how to respond to this provision but at no time discussed resisting military service.

Bund Command No. 37, part of a series of such commands published by the organization, was issued in October 1940. It stated that there must be compliance with registration under the act. However, it also stated that the Bund believed that induction into military service was not justified for Bund members based on the discriminatory provision in the act and members should refuse military service until the act was changed. This command was read out to members but was not discussed further, and then the Bund disbanded in December 1941.

The Court looked at the differences in translation from German to English regarding the meaning of the words *evade*, *refuse*, and *resist*. It also looked at the exact wording of the conspiracy section. This section made it a criminal

---

253. *See Basil O'Connor, Polio Crusader, Dies*, N.Y. TIMES (Mar. 10, 1972).
254. Keegan v. United States, 325 U.S. 478 (1945).

offense to "knowingly *counsels,* aids, or abets another to *evade* registration or service."[255] Contrary to the indictment, the Bund had strongly encouraged registration; it had only called on members to refuse service, and counseling only refusal to serve was not listed as an offense anywhere in this section.

Additional testimony noted that the Bund leaders had essentially repeated their antimilitary urgings in meetings, discussing how a test case was appropriate regarding the constitutionality of this provision. The Court did not find evidence of a national conspiracy to evade registration or service, noting that the government's case was limited to the following: "That these men were partisans of Germany; were against our going to war with Germany, and might be disposed, therefore, to counsel evasion of military service, and were all familiar with Bund Command No. 37."[256] Not liking the trial judge's jury instructions any better, the Court summarized these as follows: "If defendants had innocent motives they are nonetheless guilty; if they had guilty motives they, of course, are guilty."[257] The Court reversed the convictions. In concurrence, Justice Wiley B. Rutledge found this "no more than vehement protest against § 8(i), sheer political discussion."[258]

LEGAL PROFILES

Wilbur V. Keegan was one of the defendants and a lawyer. He was born in Pennsylvania in 1889. He was general counsel for the Bund, defending free speech cases[259] and practicing before the Supreme Court.[260] He was disbarred in 1942 after the original conviction was handed down. He had originally submitted a separate petition to the Supreme Court based on the conviction depriving him of his livelihood as an attorney.[261] After being released from prison after his sentence was overturned, he reap-

255. *Id.* at 499 (emphasis in original).
256. *Id.* at 484.
257. *Id.* at 494.
258. *Id.* at 498.
259. *See, e.g.,* State of New Jersey v. Klapprott, 22 A.2d 877 (N.J. 1941).
260. Schwinn v. United States, 311 U.S. 616 (1940).
261. *Supreme Court to Rule on Bund Convictions,* ASSOCIATED PRESS (May 15, 1944).

plied for and was reinstated to the bar in New Jersey.[262] He attempted to have his innocence declared in court but was denied.[263] After the war, he continued to defend the German cause.[264] He died in 1952.

Wiley B. Rutledge wrote one of the concurring opinions in this case. He was born in Kentucky in 1894 but started his legal practice in Colorado. He taught at several law schools beginning in 1924, including appointments as dean at Washington University in 1930 and the University of Iowa in 1935. He was appointed to the court of appeals for the District of Columbia in 1939. President Roosevelt then appointed him to succeed James Byrnes (see Chapter 3) on the U.S. Supreme Court in 1943. He was still serving on the bench when he died in 1949.[265]

William H. Timbers was one of the attorneys presenting for the petitioners in this case. He was born in New York in 1915, where he started in private practice. He left private practice to serve as general counsel for the Securities and Exchange Commission in 1953. In 1956, he returned to private practice. In 1960, President Eisenhower appointed him to a seat on the federal district court in Connecticut, where he was chief judge beginning in 1964 and among other cases ruled the Lindbergh kidnapping statute unconstitutional, as it restricted a defendant's right to trial by jury. In 1971, President Nixon appointed him to the court of appeals for the Second Circuit, where he served full-time until 1981. Timbers died in 1994.[266]

C. Subsequent Events

The various efforts to control most information and to suppress points of view that did not support the war efforts stopped with the end of the war, except for the sedition trials described in Chapter 2. The Office of War Information was

---

262. *Jersey Jigsaw*, RARITAN TOWNSHIP—FORDS BEACON (Dec. 6, 1945).
263. United States v. Keegan, 71 F. Supp. 623 (S.D.N.Y 1947).
264. Von Moltke v. United States, 189 F.2d 56 (6th Cir. 1951).
265. *See Rutledge, Wiley Blount*, FED. JUDICIAL CTR., BIOGRAPHICAL DIRECTORY OF FEDERAL JUDGES.
266. *See Timbers, William Homer*, FED. JUDICIAL CTR., BIOGRAPHICAL DIRECTORY OF FEDERAL JUDGES.

terminated (although certain functions like the *Voice of America* continued),[267] as was the Office of Censorship.[268] Issues of freedom of expression continued to be a focus, especially with the next war and the Communist hunting that occurred in the early 1950s.

One case that arose in the immediate postwar period concerned the powers of the postmaster general to use second-class postage permits to censor the mail. *Hannegan v. Esquire, Inc.*, examined the decision during the war to attack morally questionable periodicals even though such periodicals were not directly related to the war effort.[269] In that case, the issue was the postmaster general's ability to make a subjective decision on whether *Esquire* magazine complied with postal regulations. Those regulations specified that there were four requirements for second-class mail sent under permit. The fourth specified that the mailing "must be originated and published for the dissemination of information of a public character, or devoted to literature, the sciences, arts, or some special industry, and having a legitimate list of subscribers."[270]

The Supreme Court noted that *Esquire's* second-class mail permit was not revoked because its material was deemed to be obscene, which would have made it nonmailable. Instead, its permit was revoked because the postmaster general found that it did not meet the fourth requirement. His opinion was that "[w]ritings and pictures may be indecent, vulgar, and risqué and still not be obscene in a technical sense . . . (but) they are morally improper and not for the public welfare and the public good . . . [especially if they are] not making the 'special contribution to the public welfare.'"[271] To receive the second-class mailing privilege, a publication had a "positive duty to contribute to the public good and the public welfare."[272] The Court was concerned that the privilege might be used politically, "granted on condition that certain economic or

---

267. Exec. Order No. 9608, Providing for the Termination of the Office of War Information, and for the Disposition of Its Functions and of Certain Functions in the Office of Inter-American Affairs (Aug. 31, 1945).

268. Exec. Order No. 9631, Termination of the Office of Censorship (Sept. 28, 1945).

269. Hannegan v. Esquire, Inc., 327 U.S. 146 (1946).

270. *Id.* at 148.

271. *Id.* at 149-150.

272. *Id.* at 150.

political ideas not be disseminated."[273] It ruled that Congress did not intend to set up censorship standards, and the postmaster general did not have the power to revoke permits based on such.

LEGAL PROFILES

Morris L. Ernst was on the brief for the respondent. He was born in Alabama in 1888 but started his legal practice in New York. He helped found the National Civil Liberties Bureau in 1917, which became the ACLU in 1920, and served as co-general counsel of the ACLU for twenty-five years. Among his cases, he defended books against obscenity charges, including James Joyce's *Ulysses* in 1933. He then won the right for newsmen to organize under the Wagner Act (see Chapter 3) in 1937. From 1933 to 1945, he served on the New York state banking board. During the war, he was special counsel to the War Production Board (see Chapter 3). He died in 1976.[274]

Harriet F. Pilpel was also on the brief for the respondent. She was born in New York in 1911 and started her practice in the state. During her career, she appeared before the U.S. Supreme Court more than two dozen times. She was on the 1960s Presidential Commission on the Status of Women and was a founder of the Women's Forum. She was involved in copyright, abortion, marriage, birth control, and civil liberties issues. In addition, she was the legal counsel for the Planned Parenthood Federation of America and served on the board of several organizations, including the National Abortion Rights Action League, and as general counsel of the ACLU. She also defended Dr. Benjamin Spock in a free speech suit. Pilpel died in 1991.[275]

---

273. *Id.* at 156.
274. *See Morris Ernst, "Ulysses" Case Lawyer, Dies,* N.Y. TIMES (May 23, 1976).
275. *See Harriet Pilpel, 79, Lawyer, Dies; An Advocate of Women's Rights,* N.Y. TIMES (Apr. 24, 1991).

Charles A. Horsky was on the amicus curiae brief for the respondent. Born in Montana in 1910, he started his career as a law clerk for Augustus N. Hand (see Chapter 3). He then worked for the U.S. Solicitor General's Office until 1937, when he left for private practice. He was involved in the *Korematsu* case (see Section 4.5) and the Nuremberg Trials right after the war (see Chapter 6). After the war, he returned to private practice. From 1962 to 1967, he served as the adviser to the president for national capital affairs and was influential in getting "home rule" started for District of Columbia residents, including locally elected representatives, and in building the Metro transit system. He died in 1997.[276]

---

276. *See Charles A. Horsky, 87, Dies; Left Imprint on U.S. Capital*, N.Y. TIMES (Aug. 24, 1997).

CHAPTER 5

EUROPE: DIFFERING
NATIONAL SCENARIOS

In Europe leading up to and during the war, there were both legal issues similar to those raised in the United States as well as those unique to the region. Just as America had to deal with sedition, espionage, selective service, and wartime economic issues, the countries in Europe were forced to confront similar problems. However, as the continent where the conflict was initially triggered, Europe also experienced a number of legal issues that were unique to it. In addition to the many countries whose legal systems were overrun along with their territory and replaced by Fascist dictatorships, the remaining countries were either taken over and became part of the Axis, were functioning as client states of the Axis powers, were trying to maintain neutrality even though surrounded by belligerents, or, in a few cases, remained independent during the entire war. All, however, were impacted by laws originating from the Fascist states.

This chapter focuses on four of the five types of legal regimes in Europe during the war and a nation that represented each of these different models: the independent state (United Kingdom), the annexed state (Austria), the client state (Vichy France, also simply called Vichy), and the neutral state (Switzerland). The fifth type of legal regime, the Fascist state (Nazi Germany), will be covered in the next chapter. Within those nations arose a long series of legal issues, including official secrets, national registration, emergency powers, treachery, contract failure, friendly fire, Anschluss (annexation), collaboration, neutrality, military internment, refugees, and looted assets.

PROMINENT LAWYERS AND JUDGES IN THIS CHAPTER

Independent State (United Kingdom):

- Donald Somervell (attorney general of England and Wales)
- Rayner Goddard (lord justice of appeal)
- Frank Douglas MacKinnon (lord justice of appeal)
- James Atkin (law lord)
- Frederic Maugham (law lord)
- Anthony Marlowe (prosecutor)
- Cyril Asquith (judge)
- Travers Humphreys (judge)
- Valentine Holmes (respondent's attorney)
- Thomas Inskip (lord chief justice of England and Wales)
- Roger J. Bushell (assistant counsel)
- Frank Soskice (attorney general of England and Wales)

Annexed State (Austria):

- Engelbert Dollfuss (chancellor of Austria)
- Kurt Schuschnigg (chancellor of Austria)
- Artur Seyss-Inquart (defendant)
- John W. Davis (amicus curiae attorney for appellant)
- Karl Renner (president of Austria)
- Adolf Schärf (vice chancellor of Austria)

Client State (Vichy France):

- Léon Noël (French ambassador)
- Raphaël Alibert (Vichy minister of justice)
- Jules Jeanneney (PGFR minister of state)
- Jacques Isorni (defendant's attorney)
- André Mornet (prosecuting attorney general)
- Pierre Laval (defendant)
- Pierre Paul Mongibeaux (president of the court)
- Fernand de Brinon (Vichy secretary of state)
- René Cassin (head of court of honor)

Neutral State (Switzerland):

- Philipp Etter (president of Swiss Confederation)
- Johannes Baumann (head of Federal Department of Justice and Police)
- Eduard von Steiger (head of Federal Department of Justice and Police)
- Florian Imer (head of internment legal team)
- Lloyd A. Free (member of U.S. military attaché's office)
- Allen W. Dulles (OSS agent in Switzerland)
- Heinrich Rothmund (director of the federal Police Division)
- Jean-Marie Musy (former president of Switzerland)
- Dietrich Schindler Sr. (expert opinion drafter)
- Samuel Klaus (Safehaven project attorney)
- Georges Sauser-Hall (drafter of decree)
- Randolph E. Paul (U.S. negotiator)
- Walter Stucki (Swiss negotiator)

5.1 INDEPENDENT STATE: UNITED KINGDOM

A. Statutes

The United Kingdom remained politically independent of the Axis powers during the war, although certain of its overseas domains were overrun (e.g., Malaya, Channel Islands). With its own legal regime and functioning government, laws were enacted as necessary to fight the war. Like the United States, the United Kingdom had several laws left over from WWI that it reinstated for this new conflict. In addition, it passed several new laws, primarily in the beginning phases of the war. The many laws dealing with the war included the Essential Commodities Reserves Act (1938);[1] Civil Defence Act (1939);[2] Import, Export and Customs Powers (Defence) Act (1939);[3] Official Secrets Act (1939);[4] Trading with the Enemy Act (1939);[5] National Registration Act (1939);[6] Military

---

1. Essential Commodities Reserves Act, 1938, 1 & 2 Geo. 6, c. 51 (U.K.).
2. Civil Defence Act, 1939, 2 & 3 Geo. 6, c. 31 (U.K.).
3. Import, Export and Customs Powers (Defence) Act, 1939, 2 & 3 Geo. 6, c. 69 (U.K.).
4. Official Secrets Act, 1939, 2 & 3 Geo. 6, c. 121 (U.K.).
5. Trading with the Enemy Act, 1939, 2 & 3 Geo. 6, c. 89 (U.K.).
6. National Registration Act, 1939, 2 & 3 Geo. 6, c. 91 (U.K.).

Training Act (1939);[7] National Service (Armed Forces) Act (1939);[8] Liability for War Damage (Miscellaneous Provisions) Act (1939);[9] Emergency Powers (Defence) Act (1939);[10] Compensation (Defence) Act (1939);[11] Treachery Act (1940);[12] Allied Forces Act (1940);[13] Allied Powers (Maritime Courts) Act (1941);[14] National Service Act (1941);[15] and Treason Act (1945).[16]

Many of these had a similar intent to already discussed U.S. laws, such as preservation of essential commodities, export controls, selective service, and trading with enemies. Others were uniquely aimed at U.K.-specific needs. For example, the Allied Forces Act addressed the situation of the armed forces of several countries that had been overrun by that point. National governments were expected to maintain their own independent military forces under their own military rules based on and allied to the United Kingdom. This initially included the countries of Poland, the Netherlands, Norway, Czechoslovakia, France, and Belgium. The Allied Powers (Maritime Courts) Act provided for naval courts for Allied countries that had merchant ships in the United Kingdom. The National Service Act of 1941 addressed the labor shortage by conscripting women into war work; it initially applied to single women between twenty and thirty years old but was later expanded to older and married women. War work included work in munitions factories, civil defense, nursing, transportation, and even manning anti-aircraft guns.

Five of these acts are highlighted below.

1. Official Secrets Act

The Official Secrets Act in effect during the war was based on the same-titled act from 1911,[17] which had reenacted one from 1889. This act penalized entering or approaching a "prohibited place" or creating, communicating, or

---

7. Military Training Act, 1939, 2 & 3 Geo. 6, c. 25 (U.K.).
8. National Service (Armed Forces) Act, 1939, 2 & 3 Geo. 6, c. 81 (U.K.).
9. Liability for War Damage (Miscellaneous Provisions) Act, 1939, 2 & 3 Geo. 6, c. 102 (U.K.).
10. Emergency Powers (Defence) Act, 1939, 2 & 3 Geo. 6, c. 62 (U.K.).
11. Compensation (Defence) Act, 1939, 2 & 3 Geo. 6, c. 75 (U.K.).
12. Treachery Act, 1940, 3 & 4 Geo. 6, c. 21 (U.K.).
13. Allied Forces Act, 1940, 3 & 4 Geo. 6, c. 51 (U.K.).
14. Allied Powers (Maritime Courts) Act, 1941, 4 & 5 Geo. 6, c. 21 (U.K.).
15. National Service Act, 1941, 4 & 5 Geo. 6, c. 15 (U.K.).
16. Treason Act, 1945, 8 & 9 Geo. 6, c. 44 (U.K.).
17. Official Secrets Act, 1911, 1 & 2 Geo. 5, c. 28 (U.K.).

obtaining information that would be "useful to an enemy," directly or indirect-ly.[18] It was not necessary to prove any specific act against the interests or safety of the country; rather, it was sufficient to establish circumstances, conduct, or "known character."[19] It was also an offense to attempt any prohibited act; to incite, aid, or abet a prohibited act; or to harbor someone who committed an offense under the act. In 1920, the act was revised, adding offenses for the use of fraudulent uniforms, documents, and reports; impersonations; and forgery to obtain information in violation of the act.[20] In 1939, the act was revised again to fully describe the conditions under which a citizen must give information about a violation.[21]

2. National Registration Act

As war was being declared, Parliament passed the National Registration Act to create a national register of all people within the United Kingdom.[22] In addi-tion, everyone in the register was required to be in possession of a national identity card. If challenged by a constable in uniform, a person had to present this card on demand or within forty-eight hours at a police station. It was a criminal offense to make false representations or to forge an identity card. The National Register contained each person's name, age, gender, marital sta-tus, occupation, residence, and armed forces membership status. This law was passed in order to keep track of the vast numbers of people relocating around the country, to obtain information on residents since it had been ten years since the last census, and to deal with the new rationing scheme.

3. Emergency Powers (Defence) Act

The Emergency Powers (Defence) Act gave the government the ability to implement Defence Regulations that it felt were "necessary or expedient for securing the public safety, the defence of the realm, the maintenance of public order and the efficient prosecution of any war."[23] Specifically, it allowed the

---

18. *Id.* § 1(1).
19. *Id.* § 1(2).
20. Official Secrets Act, 1920, 10 & 11 Geo. 5, c. 75 (U.K.).
21. Official Secrets Act, 1939, 2 & 3 Geo. 6, c. 121 (U.K.).
22. National Registration Act, 1939, 2 & 3 Geo. 6, c. 91 (U.K.).
23. Emergency Powers (Defence) Act, 1939, 2 & 3 Geo. 6, c. 62 (U.K.).

punishment of those violating these regulations, the detention of people if it was believed to be in the best interest of public safety or defense of the realm, the possession of any property, the entering and searching of any premises, and the amendment or suspension of any law. The law was set to last for one year. It was later extended by the Emergency Powers (Defence) Act of 1940 until the end of hostilities.[24]

4. Treachery and Treason Acts

The Treachery Act prescribed the death penalty for anyone who, while intending to help an enemy, performed, attempted to perform, or conspired to perform an act that impeded the country's armed forces, gave assistance to the military of the enemy, or endangered life.[25] Enemy aliens could be tried under a court-martial. This act applied to anyone in the United Kingdom and to British subjects located anywhere.

Treachery was a criminal offense separate from treason because there was some doubt as to whether the treason law applied to spies who might not be resident within the United Kingdom and did not owe any allegiance to the country; and in any event, the treason law specified more difficult rules of evidence, making convictions more difficult. Treachery could be proved under the same rules as murder. Because the treason law stretched back more than five hundred years and contained some antiquated rules, the government passed a new law toward the end of the war that modernized it (e.g., abolished corroboration requirements): The Treason Act of 1945.[26]

LEGAL PROFILES

Donald Somervell was the U.K. (England and Wales) attorney general for the entire period of the war. He was born in England in 1889 and started his practice there. Early on, he was involved in commercial interpretations of the Versailles Treaty (see Chapter 1). He was elected to the

---

24. Emergency Powers (Defence) Act, 1940, 3 & 4 Geo. 6, c. 20 (U.K.).
25. Treachery Act, 1940, 3 & 4 Geo. 6, c. 21 (U.K.).
26. Treason Act, 1945, 8 & 9 Geo. 6, c. 44 (U.K.).

British Parliament in 1931, a position that he held until the end of the war. In 1933, he became the solicitor general for England and Wales. In 1936, he became the attorney general for England and Wales and served in that capacity until the end of the war and the general electoral loss by the Conservative Party. After the war, he held a series of judicial positions, concluding with appointment as a law lord. He died in 1960.[27]

B. Cases

There were several different cases that arose under these wartime legislative acts, some during the war and some many years later. The first two cases involved the use of emergency wartime powers. The third case concerned the new treachery statute. The fourth case looked at the use of the treason law after its revision. The fifth case analyzed the impact of the war on preexisting contracts. The sixth case concerned friendly fire accidents that arose in the earliest days of the war.

1. Emergency Powers: Habeas Corpus

Under the Defence Regulations allowed under the Emergency Powers (Defence) Act described above, Regulation 18B was promulgated. This regulation specified that the secretary of state could, based on reasonable cause, detain people if they were "of hostile origin or association"; if they were involved in instigating, preparing, or carrying out acts contrary to public safety or defense of the realm; or if they were members of an organization subject to foreign influence or control or associated with enemies and there was a danger that the organization would be used contrary to public safety, defense of the realm, maintenance of public order, prosecution of the war, or maintenance of essential supplies or services.[28] In lieu of detention, the secretary of state could prohibit certain activities, impose employment or business restrictions, require reporting of movements, and restrict travel. Upward of one thousand people were detained, both naturalized citizens from Fascist countries and those belonging to or supporting Fascist organizations, including a member of Parliament.

---

27. *See Donald Somervell*, OXFORD DICTIONARY OF NATIONAL BIOGRAPHY 101036189.
28. Defence Regulation 18B of the Defence (General) Regulations 1939 (U.K.).

R v. Secretary of State for Home Affairs ex parte Greene, decided in 1941, concerned a writ of habeas corpus issued under Regulation 18B.[29] The appellant was detained in May 1940 on an order stating that he was a "person of hostile associations."[30] The home secretary stated that he had reviewed the reports of "persons in responsible positions" before making his decision to issue the detention order.[31]

The court noted that Parliament had given "almost plenary discretion" to the Cabinet in its executive role in carrying out this act.[32] The court ruled that reasonable cause was not an objective condition precedent that the appellant could challenge. Instead, it was a subjective condition based on confidential information that could not in any case be disclosed. After reviewing a similar regulation from WWI and other cases from the current war presented by counsel, the court dismissed the appeal for a writ of habeas corpus.

LEGAL PROFILES

Rayner Goddard was one of the lord justices of appeal in this decision. He was born in England in 1877, where he began his legal practice. He took on several judicial positions, known as recorders, between 1917 and 1929. In 1925, he was appointed as a king's counsel (a designation of seniority and accomplishment). After a failed run for Parliament, he was appointed to the High Court of England and Wales in the King's Bench Division in 1932. In 1937, he became a lord justice of appeal, in which capacity he served during this case. In 1944, he became a law lord. In 1946, he was appointed as the lord chief justice. He held this position for twelve years, until 1958, and then heard cases on the House of Lords Judicial Committee until 1963, when he fully retired. He died in 1971.[33]

---

29. R v. Sec'y of State for Home Affairs *ex parte* Greene, [1941] 1 K.B. 87 (C.A.) (U.K.).
30. *Id.*
31. *Id.*
32. *Id.*
33. *See Goddard, Rayner*, Oxford Dictionary of National Biography 101031152.

Frank Douglas MacKinnon was one of the lord justices of appeal in this decision. He was born in England in 1871 and began his practice there, focusing on commercial matters. In 1914, he was appointed as a king's counsel. In 1924, he was appointed to the High Court of England and Wales in the Commercial Division. In 1937, he became a lord justice of appeal, the role in which he served during this case. This meant that he was also appointed to the Judicial Committee of the Privy Council (the highest court of appeal for certain Commonwealth countries and other internal matters from, for example, church and maritime courts). He died in 1946.[34]

2. Emergency Powers: Damages

While most cases for those detained under Regulation 18B involved habeas corpus, *Liversidge v. Anderson*, decided in 1942, involved a request for damages for false imprisonment.[35] The government's position was that this was an executive decision not available for review by the court. The statute had set up a procedure for review by the home secretary and an advisory committee upon complaint, and the secretary had to report monthly to Parliament. The appellant's position was that the powers of the home secretary were limited; and, as such, the home secretary should be required to provide the grounds for the confinement decision. Similar to the *Greene* court, the court here determined that the home secretary did not need to explain his good faith determination that a person must be detained under the regulation but only needed to provide the actual order, again citing the difficulties of confidentiality, among other reasons. The appellant had to prove that there was no reasonable cause.

In dissent, Lord James Atkin noted that the decision made by the home secretary "is not made after any inquiry as to facts to which the subject is party, . . . cannot be reversed on any appeal, and there is no limit to the period for which the detention may last."[36] He then stated that "[i]t is an absolute power which, so far as I know, has never been given before to the executive."[37]

---

34. *See MacKinnon, Frank Douglas*, Oxford Dictionary of National Biography 101034761.
35. Liversidge v. Anderson, [1942] A.C. 206 (H.L.) (U.K.).
36. *Id*. at 226.
37. *Id*.

Disagreeing with the court in *Greene*, Atkin said that reasonable cause is and has been an objective test. He examined both common law and statutory powers to arrest and the requirement of the arrester to show reasonable cause; he noted that this remained the case in the Defence Regulations, pointing out many cases in various regulations where extra wording was added when it was intended that the executive officer have "unqualified discretion."[38] He then looked at Regulation 18B itself to show this difference and additionally looked at its initial and final versions to again prove the difference. He could not understand why the grounds and particulars for reasonable cause must be furnished in a complaint before the advisory committee but not so in a court. He noted that such grounds and particulars were provided in the Greene advisory committee session and that confidentiality of sources was maintained.

Atkin added that "[i]n this country, amid the clash of arms, the laws are not silent. They may be changed, but they speak the same language in war as in peace." After referencing Humpty Dumpty, he said that "one of the pillars of liberty is that in English law every imprisonment is prima facie unlawful and that it is for a person directing imprisonment to justify his act."[39] While he did vote for accepting the appeal in this case, he agreed with dismissing the appeal in the *Greene* case as sufficient evidence had been presented to justify reasonable cause.

LEGAL PROFILES

James Atkin was the law lord who wrote the dissenting opinion in this case. He was born in Australia in 1867, but he moved with his mother to Wales when he was a child. He started his legal practice in England, focusing on commercial matters. He was appointed as a king's counsel in 1906. In 1913, he was appointed to the High Court of England and Wales in the King's Bench Division. Six years later, in 1919, he became a lord justice of appeal. After nine more years, he was appointed as a law lord, the position in which he served during this case. He died in 1944.[40]

---

38. *Id.* at 236.
39. *Id.* at 244.
40. *See Atkin, James*, OXFORD DICTIONARY OF NATIONAL BIOGRAPHY 101030492.

Frederic Maugham was one of the law lords in this decision. He was born in France in 1866 but began his legal career in London. He was appointed as a king's counsel in 1913. In 1928, he was appointed to the High Court of England and Wales in the Chancery Division, where he served for six years. In 1934, he became a lord justice of appeal and was appointed to the Judicial Committee of the Privy Council. The following year, he became a law lord. In 1938, he became lord chancellor and, among other responsibilities, oversaw the courts. With the change in government in 1940, he returned to his role as a law lord, retiring in 1941. His brother was the English writer Somerset Maugham. Frederic Maugham died in 1958.[41]

---

3. Treachery

More than a dozen cases involving treachery were tried during and immediately after the war. The majority involved enemy aliens from Germany, Belgium, the Netherlands, and Switzerland caught violating the Treachery Act. Some were recruited by foreign intelligence and sent into Britain on clandestine missions before being apprehended. Others were involved in spying on convoy movements. Several were British subjects or were born in Britain. A few were tried by courts-martial, but all were tried in secret and all executed except one.

Some of the more noteworthy cases included the following:

- The court-martial of Josef Jakobs, decided in 1941, involved a German intelligence officer who had parachuted into England wearing civilian clothes under his flying suit and carrying forged papers and a wireless set. Jakobs, a WWI veteran, broke an ankle when parachuting and was apprehended. Because he was wearing a military flying suit when captured, he was given a military trial. He was convicted and executed by firing squad at the Tower of London.
- The court-martial of Duncan Scott-Ford, decided in 1941, centered on a member of the merchant navy who collected information for an enemy agent. He had originally joined the Royal Navy at the age of sixteen, but when he falsified his bank records to withdraw funds that he did not have,

---

41. *See Maugham, Frederic*, Oxford Dictionary of National Biography 101034946.

he was convicted and cashiered out of the navy. He was able to subsequently join the merchant navy and was approached by German intelligence officers for various types of information when he was in port in Portugal. On a subsequent trip to Portugal, he was again approached and blackmailed by the German intelligence agents when he did not produce any of the required information. Thus, he took some notes on the convoy's route on the trip back to Britain. This information was found by British intelligence and used to convict him. He was executed by hanging.

- In the last trial for treachery, the court-martial of Theodore Schurch occurred in 1945 just after the end of the war. A British national of Swiss parentage, he was captured during the desert campaigns in North Africa and began to work for Axis intelligence services. He was charged with ten counts, which included numerous instances of posing as a British POW to befriend other POWs and extract information that would be passed on to the enemy. In addition, he went absent without leave to join the enemy and on several occasions crossed over to the British side of the battle lines to obtain information and then returned to the Axis side to pass on this information. He was convicted and executed by hanging.

LEGAL PROFILES

Anthony Marlowe was the prosecutor in the Jakobs trial. He was born in England in 1904 and started practice in London. He first enlisted in the army reserve in the late 1930s, rising to the rank of major, and later joined the Office of the Judge Advocate General full-time during the war, where he was serving during this trial. In 1941, he became a member of Parliament, remaining an elected member until 1965. He was appointed as a king's counsel in 1945 and was involved in the Nuremberg Trials after the war (see Chapter 6). He returned more fully to his parliamentary duties after the war. Marlowe died in 1965.[42]

---

42. *See Obituary,* TIMES OF LONDON (Sept. 10, 1965).

Cyril Asquith was the judge before whom several of the trials under the Treachery Act were heard. He was born in England in 1890, and his father became one of the longest-serving British prime ministers. After serving in WWI, Cyril Asquith began his legal practice. In 1936, he was appointed as a king's counsel. In 1938, he was appointed to the High Court of England and Wales in the King's Bench Division, a position that he held for eight years. In 1946, he became a lord justice of appeal and was appointed to the Judicial Committee of the Privy Council. He served in this role for five years before becoming a law lord in 1951. He died in 1954.[43]

4. Treason

After the revision to the Treason Act, a handful of cases were prosecuted.

R. v. Joyce, a case briefly discussed in Chapter 4, involved a radio broadcaster named William Joyce ("Lord Haw-Haw").[44] Joyce, born in America of Irish parents, was a British passport holder. He was heavily involved in Fascist organizations in the United Kingdom. Just before war was declared against Germany, Joyce fled the United Kingdom for Germany to avoid arrest. While still holding his British passport, he became involved in radio broadcasts from Germany propagandizing the war effort. He was arrested and tried after the war; the court ruled that he owed an allegiance to the United Kingdom and had violated that allegiance through the broadcasts. He was convicted of treason, whose mandatory penalty was execution. His case was appealed up to the law lords without change.[45] He died by hanging at the beginning of 1946.

Another case that lacked an extensive trial involved John Amery, another British Fascist who made propaganda broadcasts from overseas and also urged the creation of the British Legion of St. George (later called the British Free Corps). Amery was in France when it was overrun and he befriended the Nazis. This led to his radio broadcasts from Germany, public speeches in occu-

43. *See Asquith, Cyril*, OXFORD DICTIONARY OF NATIONAL BIOGRAPHY 101030481.
44. R v. Joyce, [1945] 173 L.T. 377 (U.K.).
45. Joyce v. DPP, [1946] A.C. 347 (H.L.) (U.K.).

pied countries, and attempts to convince British POWs to fight with the Nazis against Britain and Russia. Arrested after the war, he was to be tried on eight counts of treason but instead decided to plead guilty. Despite the fact that he was the son and brother of members of Parliament, he was executed in December 1945.

One situation that never became an actual court case dealt with the famous English writer P. G. Wodehouse. The creator of Jeeves the butler, among many other characters, was living in France when the war started after having spent much of the previous decades in the United States. Interned as an enemy alien, he was eventually brought before the German propaganda broadcasters, who suggested that he reach out to his many fans in America through their programs. Not thinking through the consequences, he did half a dozen broadcasts before he finally was informed of their propaganda nature and stopped. Prosecutors after the war determined that there was no malicious intent and did not pursue charges. The son of a British judge, Wodehouse became a citizen of the U.S. after the war and lived there for the remainder of his life.

LEGAL PROFILES

Travers Humphreys was the judge in the *Amery* case and heard the appeal of the *Joyce* case. He was born in England in 1867, the son of a lawyer father. One of his earliest cases involved the noted playwright Oscar Wilde. He spent much of his time on criminal matters and was involved in a number of high-profile cases. He held several recorder positions before being appointed to the High Court of England and Wales in the King's Bench Division. He was then promoted to the Court of Criminal Appeal, where he continued to hear high-profile cases. After the war, he joined the Privy Council. He retired in 1951 and died in 1956.[46]

---

46. *See Humphreys, Travers*, OXFORD DICTIONARY OF NATIONAL BIOGRAPHY 101034053.

5. Contract Failure

One case was not related to a specific wartime statute but arose from the impact of the war on commercial matters. In *Fibrosa Spolka Akcyjna v. Fairbairn Lawson Combe Barbour Ltd.*, a Polish firm ordered milling machinery, for which it advanced about 60 percent of the purchase price.[47] Due to the outbreak of the war and the overrunning of Poland, the British firm believed that, under an older case involving the sudden cancellation of the coronation of Edward VII (*Chandler v. Webster*),[48] it was not responsible for returning the funds. This case held that under frustration of contract, "the loss lies where it falls."[49] The law lords in *Fairbairn Lawson* held that "the rule in *Chandler v. Webster* is wrong" as recovery of prepaid monies arising from frustration should not be treated differently from frustration by destruction of the subject matter.[50] There should be no unjust enrichment, and the appellant was entitled to the return of its prepaid funds.

LEGAL PROFILES

Valentine Holmes presented the case for the respondent. He was born in England in 1888 and started his legal career there. After serving in the military during WWI, he became involved in a number of well-known libel cases. He also served as senior treasury counsel prosecuting spies. He became a king's counsel and also was part of the respondent's counsel in the *Liversidge* case. He died in 1956.[51]

Thomas Inskip was the lord chief justice during the war. The son of a lawyer, he was born in England in 1876 and started his legal career there. In 1914, he became a king's counsel and during WWI ran the Admiralty's naval law branch. In 1918, he was elected to Parliament. In 1922, he was appointed as the solicitor general for England and Wales, a

---

47. Fibrosa Spolka Akcyjna v. Fairbairn Lawson Combe Barbour Ltd., [1942] H.L. 4 (U.K.).
48. Chandler v. Webster, [1904] 1 K.B. 493 (U.K.).
49. *Fairbairn Lawson*, [1942] H.L. at 12.
50. *Id.* at 7.
51. *See Holmes, Valentine*, Oxford Dictionary of National Biography 101033959.

position he held for six years until being appointed the attorney general in 1928. He lost that position when the government changed the next year but returned to it in 1932. In 1936, he was appointed as the newly created minister for coordination of defence. He also served as secretary of state for dominion affairs and as lord chancellor before becoming lord chief justice of England and Wales in 1940, a position he held until 1946. He died in 1947.[52]

6. Friendly Fire

A case involving a lawyer who later became well-known addressed the deadly impact of friendly fire. In the very early days of the war in September 1939, a British fighter pilot trainer was killed when he was mistakenly shot down by his own forces during an air raid alert. When the newly minted pilots were forced to scramble, they were not yet experienced enough to distinguish German planes from their own. The pilot who shot down and killed the other pilot was John Freeborn, who along with his commander and a second pilot, Paddy Byrne, who had shot down but did not kill another pilot trainer, were court martialed. The court acquitted the defendants, recognizing the inadequate state of training and the chaos of the early days of the war, deeming this incident as a rather unfortunate accident.

LEGAL PROFILES

Roger J. Bushell was the assistant counsel for the pilots in this court martial. He was born in South Africa in 1910. He moved to the U.K. to join the RAF and also pursued a legal career within the RAF for criminal cases. Becoming a squadron commander, he was shot down in 1940 and became a POW. As a POW, he escaped several times but was recaptured before making it to freedom. He was finally sent to a camp

---

52. *See Inskip, Thomas*, OXFORD DICTIONARY OF NATIONAL BIOGRAPHY 101034107.

for those who were frequent escapees, Stalag Luft III. It was here that he was reunited with his former client Byrne and led the planning for a massive escape of hundreds of POWs, in what would later be chronicled in the movie *The Great Escape*. Acting as "Big X," he had several tunnels dug and eventually got 76 POWs out in the spring of 1944, including himself. But again he was recaptured and this time there would be no further chances for escape, as he along with 49 other escapees who were also recaptured were executed by the Gestapo.[53]

C. Subsequent Events

A number of these wartime laws were discontinued at various periods after the war such as the Emergency Powers (Defence) Act, while others remained in effect to deal with continuing issues such as rationing.

One case dealt with the continuing effect of the National Registration Act. *Willcock v. Muckle* challenged the national registration system several years after the war had ended.[54] The defendant was stopped while driving in 1950 and required to produce an identity card. Saying he was a liberal, he refused to do so, and charges were brought under the National Registration Act.

The appellant's first contention was that the emergency necessitating this law had ended, as indicated by several Orders in Council (a decree issued by the government) had been issued to terminate other wartime emergency acts. The court ruled that because there were different aspects to each act passed to deal with the wartime emergency, a specific order had to be issued terminating each. As there was no termination order for this act, it remained in effect, and so the conviction stood.

As to the issue of demanding identity cards from each person detained by police, the court stated that this was overstepping the intention of the act, which was created for purposes of national security. While use of the cards for those suspected of a crime might be appropriate, demanding an identity card "from all and sundry, for instance, from a lady who may leave her car outside

---

53. *See Love, betrayal and courage: Private letters reveal the story behind the mastermind of The Great Escape Roger Bushell*, THE DAILY MAIL (Nov. 26, 2011).
54. Willcock v. Muckle, [1951] 2 All E.R. 367 (U.K.).

a shop longer than she should, or some trivial matter of that sort, is wholly unreasonable."[55] Regarding the impact of such practices, the court noted that "[t]o use Acts of Parliament, passed for particular purposes during war, in time when the war is past . . . tends to turn law-abiding subjects into law breakers."[56] The law was subsequently revoked by the incoming government.

LEGAL PROFILES

Frank Soskice was the attorney general for England and Wales and appeared on the amicus curiae brief for the prosecution in this case. He was born in England in 1902 and started his legal career there. After serving in the military during the war, he was elected to Parliament in 1945, where he remained a member for more than twenty years. The new government appointed him as solicitor general for England and Wales, a role he served in for six years. He was then appointed as the attorney general for England and Wales in 1951. In 1964, he was appointed as home secretary in the new Labour Party government and then in 1965 as the Lord Keeper of the Privy Seal. He retired the next year and died in 1979.[57]

D. Modern Applicability

The Official Secrets Act was subsequently revised several times after the war up to 1989 and invoked quite frequently.[58] In 1985, a jury did not convict Clive Ponting, the Ministry of Defence clerk accused of giving information to the military police on an Argentine warship sunk during the Falklands War.[59] The act was not able to stop the overseas publication of the book *Spycatcher* by former MI5 agent Peter Wright or disclosures of secret documents to a British newspaper by former MI5 agent David Shayler. Using the act, the government

---

55. *Id.* at 368.
56. *Id.*
57. *See Soskice, Frank*, OXFORD DICTIONARY OF NATIONAL BIOGRAPHY 101031703.
58. Official Secrets Act, 1989, c. 6 (U.K.).
59. R v. Ponting, [1985] Crim. L.R. 318 (Crown Ct.) (U.K.).

was able to obtain guilty pleas in 1984 from Sarah Tisdall, a Foreign and Com-monwealth Office clerk who passed information on American cruise missiles to a newspaper in 1983;[60] and in 1997 from Richard Tomlinson, a former MI6 agent who disclosed information to an overseas publisher about a potential tell-all book. In 2007, Leo O'Connor and David Keogh were both convicted under the act for disclosing a memo recording discussions between U.S. and U.K. officials on offensive steps against a Middle East broadcaster.[61] In 2011, the act was considered for use in the United Kingdom's phone hacking scandal.[62]

5.2 ANNEXED STATE: AUSTRIA

A. Statutes

The combination of Germany and Austria (along with the Sudetenland and other German-speaking areas) into a Greater Germany was a concept with roots in both ancient history and recent events. Supposedly, Germany and Aus-tria were united in the First Reich of Charlemagne more than one thousand years before WWI. Although Germany (more precisely, Prussia) had defeated Austria in the Austro-Prussian war in 1866 and subsequently founded the Ger-man/Prussian Empire (the Second Reich), this did not diminish the drive for a larger combination, but it did place the northern Germanic states in a more dominant position vis-à-vis the southern Germanic states. As WWI was draw-ing to a close, new governments in Austria and Germany both planned for "German-Austria" to become a part of the new Germany.

But after WWI, the Versailles Treaty (see Chapter 1) prohibited Germany from combining with Austria.[63] Based on Allied concerns about such a combi-nation and future wars, the treaty stated that

> Germany acknowledges and will respect strictly the independence of Austria, within the frontiers which may be fixed in a Treaty between that State and the Principal Allied and Associated Powers; she agrees that

---

60. R v. Tisdall, [1984] 6 Crim. App. R. 155 (S.) (U.K.).
61. Keogh v. R, [2007] EWCA (Crim.) 528 (U.K.); Times Newspapers Ltd. v. R, [2007] EWCA (Crim.) 1925 (U.K.).
62. *Phone Hacking: Scotland Yard Drops Official Secrets Act Bid Against Guardian*, TELEGRAPH (Sept. 20, 2011).
63. Treaty of Peace Between the Allied and Associated Powers and Germany, June 28, 1919.

this independence shall be inalienable, except with the consent of the Council of the League of Nations.[64]

The Treaty of Saint-Germain-en-Laye[65] between the Allies and Austria similarly prohibited political and economic union with Germany unless approval was received from the League of Nations. Specifically, it stated that Austrian independence was "inalienable" and so the country should "abstain from any act which might directly or indirectly . . . compromise her independence."[66] However, the concept of political union was strong among the German and Austrian nationalists, from the principles of the German and Austrian Nazi Parties to Hitler's goals listed in *Mein Kampf* to the feelings of average Austrian citizens.

In the early 1930s, political Austria was focused internally. In 1933, the Republic of Austria gave way to Fascist (though non-Nazi) authoritarian leadership. The federal chancellor, looking to the Italian Fascist model, took over power and proceeded to rule by decree under a WWI-era law.[67] This led to a short civil war and the banning of other political parties. In April 1934, the national parliament, in a rump form, passed a law that gave the government many of the National Assembly's powers.[68] This allowed a new constitution to be promulgated in May 1934 that consolidated power in the chancellor and the president who appointed him, which was approved by another law.[69] This eventually led to an attempted Austrian Nazi coup and the assassination of the federal chancellor, Engelbert Dollfuss. The strong stand by Mussolini, whom Dollfuss was trying to imitate, against the coup by bringing Italian military units to the border, perhaps saved Austria for the time being from invasion.

Dollfuss's successor as federal chancellor, Kurt Schuschnigg, under pressure from Nazis in both Austria and Germany, was forced into signing the Austro-German Agreement with Germany in 1936.[70] This agreement, in "making a valuable contribution . . . in the direction of peace," began with Germany recognizing the full sovereignty of Austria. It also stated the neither coun-

---

64. *Id.* art. 80.
65. Treaty of Peace Between the Allied and Associated Powers and Austria, Sept. 10, 1919.
66. *Id.* art. 88.
67. Wartime Economy Authority Law (1917) (Austria).
68. Empowering Act (1934) (Austria).
69. Constitution Transition Act (1934) (Austria).
70. Austro-German Agreement, Austria-Ger., July 11, 1936.

try would influence the political order, including the Austrian Nazi Party, of the other. However, Austria declared that she regarded herself as a "German State."[71]

By early 1938, in an attempt to keep out Nazi influence and remain independent, Schuschnigg scheduled a national referendum on the possible unification that was being forced. The ballot said, "With Schuschnigg for Austria, we want a free and a German Austria, an independent and a social Austria, a Christian and a united Austria." But the vote was not held because the chancellor was forced to resign and German troops marched into Austria in March 1938. A law was then passed approving the union of Austria and Germany.[72] This required a follow-on vote of the people, which passed with more than 99 percent approval the following month. In essence, an independent legislative function in Austria vanished until after the war.

These actions violated the Treaty of Versailles, the Treaty of Saint-Germain-en-Laye, and the 1936 Austro-German Agreement, but there was no significant response internationally. Previously, in 1935, France, the United Kingdom, and Italy had supported Austrian independence in the Final Declaration of the Stresa Conference (also called the Stresa Front), an agreement made in response to German rearmament announcements.[73] However, Allied response to the Anschluss at the time of its occurrence was muted, perhaps because it was expected or because France and the United Kingdom were not ready for war, as the Munich agreement soon demonstrated (see Chapter 1).

By 1943, however, the Allies were ready to make a stronger statement against the Anschluss and did so in the Moscow Declaration on Austria:

> The governments of the United Kingdom, the Soviet Union and the United States of America are agreed that Austria, the first free country to fall a victim to Hitlerite aggression, shall be liberated from German domination. They regard the annexation imposed on Austria by Germany on March 15, 1938, as null and void. They consider themselves as in no way bound by any charges effected in Austria since that date. They declare that they wish to see re-established a free and independent

---

71. *Id.*
72. Federal Constitutional Law for the Reunion of Austria with the German Reich (Mar. 13, 1938) (Austria).
73. Final Declaration of the Stresa Conference, Fr.-U.K.-It., Apr. 14, 1935.

Austria and thereby to open the way for the Austrian people them-selves, as well as those neighboring States which will be faced with simi-lar problems, to find that political and economic security which is the only basis for lasting peace. Austria is reminded, however, that she has a responsibility, which she cannot evade, for participation in the war at the side of Hitlerite Germany, and that in the final settlement account will inevitably be taken of her own contribution to her liberation.[74]

LEGAL PROFILES

Engelbert Dollfuss was the chancellor of Austria before Schuschnigg and a lawyer. He was born in part of the Austro-Hungarian Empire in 1892 and completed his legal studies there. He fought in WWI. After the war, he was involved in agricultural positions, which led to his appoint-ment as the minister of agriculture and forests in 1931. The following year, surprisingly, he was offered the position of chancellor of Austria, which he accepted. He essentially closed down the National Assembly to rule by decree and introduced the new constitution in 1934. Veering more toward the Italian model of government instead of the German model, he became a target of the Nazis. After surviving an assassination attempt in 1933, he died by assassination in 1934.[75]

Kurt Schuschnigg was the chancellor of Austria leading up to the Anschluss; he was also a lawyer. Born in part of the Austro-Hungarian Empire in 1897, he started his legal career in Austria. He fought in WWI. He was first elected to the Austrian National Assembly in 1927 as a member of the Christian Social Party, the one party that later was still allowed. He served in the government as the minister of justice and the minister of education before being named as chancellor following Dollfuss's assassination in 1934. After Hitler forced him to resign as chancellor just before the Anschluss in March 1938, Schuschnigg was

---

74. Joint Four-Nation Declaration, Moscow Conference, Oct. 1943.
75. *See Dr. Dollfuss Killed*, ARGUS (July 28, 1934).

imprisoned in concentration camps until freed at the end of the war. He spent much of the rest of his life teaching in the United States. He died in 1977.[76]

B. Cases

Given the state of semianarchy within the country due to assassinations of political figures, civil wars, and constant tensions between the Austrofascist government and the local and German Nazis, judicial settlement of issues was not an expected path. Much of the Austrian Supreme Court had previously resigned years before the Anschluss. But the impact of the Anschluss was seen in at least two court cases. One was the trial after the war of the new leader of Austria after the Anschluss. The second one was a U.S. court case concerning how to categorize the citizenship of Austrians after the Anschluss.

1. Responsibility for the Anschluss

There were two trials after the war that delved into responsibility for the Anschluss. One involved the German ambassador to Austria, Franz von Papen (see Chapter 6). The other involved the new post-Anschluss Austrian leader, Artur Seyss-Inquart. tried before the International Military Tribunal, in 1945 (see Chapter 6).[77]

Seyss-Inquart had briefly become president and chancellor of Austria as the Germans were invading the country and then was appointed the Reich governor of the Austrian state within Germany. He then took on a very significant role in the Nazi regime. Among the charges against him was the first count of using his position and influence to promote the German seizure of and consolidation of control over Austria. This consisted of the following aspects:

(1) He "was a member of the Nazi Party and held the rank of General in the SS."

(2) "[E]ven before he became a member of the Nazi Party," he "belonged to an organization conceived and founded upon principles which later became those of the Nazi Party."

---

76. *See Obituary*, TIMES OF LONDON (Nov. 19, 1977).
77. Trial of the Major War Criminals Before the International Military Tribunal, IMT (1945).

(3) "[A]fter the Austrian Nazi Party was declared illegal in July 1934," he "posed as a non-member of the Nazi Party but continued to support it in its activities, principles, and objectives in a subversive manner."

(4) He "derived personal benefits and political power as the result of the subversive manipulations and terroristic activities of his fellow Nazi collaborators."

(5) He "used his affiliation with the Nazis to promote the absorption of Austria into the Greater German Reich according to plan as conceived by his fellow Nazi conspirators."

(6) His activities and those of "his fellow Nazi conspirators and collaborators forced the then Austrian government into a critical situation and a struggle for survival."

(7) "Chancellor Schuschnigg determined to go before the people for a decision on the question of Austrian independence."

(8) He "then proceeded to carry out Hitler's orders and to fulfill the plans" that he and his fellow Nazi conspirators had made.

(9) "Having infiltrated the Austrian government of Chancellor Schuschnigg according to plan," he "exploited his opportunities to carry out the plan to its ultimate conclusion, i.e.[,] German annexation of Austria."

(10) "Despite [his] modesty since arrest and indictment, his fellow Nazi conspirators recognized the importance of his part in the Austrian Anschluss."

(11) "The Nazi conspirators within the German Reich evidenced their intentions of annexing Austria in many ways."

(12) "Hitler and the Nazi conspirators completed the annexation of Austria by decree."[78]

Some of the evidence of this was his long-standing relationships with Nazis on both sides of the border regarding the Anschluss and the steps required to achieve it. He had contacted Hitler by phone before the invasion "inviting" him to Austria, met Hitler when he crossed the border into Austria from Germany, and made a speech welcoming the German forces and advocating the reunion of Germany and Austria. The next day, he obtained the passage of a

---

78. Indictment, Artur Seyss-Inquart, IMT (1945).

law providing that Austria should become a province of Germany (see Section 5.2, "Statutes") and signed the law as the new president of the country.

His lawyer was Dr. Gustav Steinbauer, who refuted the charges vis-à-vis the Anschluss by attesting that it was Josef Bürckel, the mayor of Vienna, who was in charge of reunification of the two countries and that Seyss-Inquart was only a "docile tool in the hands of the big two, Hitler and Goering."[79] Seyss-Inquart was only "actuated by his enthusiasm for the Anschluss," and the "wish to bring about the national unification of a nation was not a crime; criminal, however, was the introduction of a system that has presumably blocked its realization forever."[80] Steinbauer continued thus:

> Herein lies Seyss-Inquart's mistake. He thought Hitler and Berlin would pursue a joint policy. Berlin, however, did not wish to pursue a joint policy. Is this mistake punishable . . . ? . . . As a political aim, the annexation of Austria to the German Reich is nowhere indicted, and the defendant pursued no other aim. Here . . . the prosecution goes beyond the limits of the Charter.[81]

The tribunal found Seyss-Inquart not guilty on this count of the indictment regarding the Anschluss.

LEGAL PROFILES

Artur Seyss-Inquart was the defendant in this trial and a lawyer. He was born in part of the Austro-Hungarian Empire in 1892 and started his legal career in Austria. He served in WWI and began practicing law. This led to his position as a state councillor in 1937 and as minister of the interior and security in 1938, at the demand of Hitler. After the Anschluss, he officially joined the Nazi Party and the German SS and eventually the Reich cabinet. He served as the governor of this new state

---

79. Closing Presentation by Dr. Gustav Steinbauer, IMT (July 19, 1946).
80. *Id.*
81. *Id.*

of Germany. After the invasion of Poland, he became the deputy governor-general there and then the Reich commissar of the Netherlands after Poland was fully occupied. For his involvement in committing war crimes, crimes against humanity, and crimes against peace, especially in those latter two positions, he was convicted and then executed in 1946.[82]

2. Impacts of the Anschluss

In *United States ex rel. Schwarzkopf v. Uhl*, the appellant, a citizen of Austria, was detained as an enemy alien and pursued a writ of habeas corpus.[83] The U.S. government claimed that he, Schwarzkopf, was a citizen of Germany, but the appellant said that he was an Austrian citizen and therefore not an enemy alien. Schwarzkopf had quite an extensive citizenry. Born in Prague in the Austro-Hungarian Empire, he became a Czechoslovakian citizen upon the creation of that country after WWI. He then became a German citizen in 1925 because he was in business there. In 1927, he moved to Austria and became a citizen in 1933, which terminated his German citizenship. In 1936, he relocated to the United States and applied for citizenship. His application was pending when he was taken into custody on the present charge in December 1941.

Under the Alien Enemies Act of U.S. law, if invasion is threatened against U.S. territory and the president so proclaims, then "all [adult] natives, citizens, denizens, or subjects of the hostile nation or government . . . who shall be within the United States and not actually naturalized, shall be liable to be apprehended, restrained, secured, and removed as alien enemies."[84] President Roosevelt made such a proclamation on December 8, 1941, in regard to Germany (see Chapter 4),[85] and Schwarzkopf was detained the following day.

The government's case rested on three points: (1) the appellant was an Austrian citizen when the Anschluss took place because all Austrian citizens were granted German citizenship under a German decree on July 3, 1938; (2) the United States recognized "de facto sovereignty" of Germany over Austria; and

---

82. *See Four-Power Statement on the Execution of 10 Nazis*, N.Y. TIMES (Oct. 16, 1946).
83. United States ex rel. Schwarzkopf v. Uhl, 137 F.2d 898 (2d Cir. 1943).
84. Alien Enemies Act, 50 U.S.C.A. § 21.
85. Exec. Proclamation No. 2526 (Dec. 8, 1941).

(3) the German decree of November 25, 1941, depriving Jews (of which the appellant was one) residing abroad of German citizenship was not to be considered for these matters.[86] The government did not claim de jure recognition of the Anschluss, as the State Department had publicly denied such a position.

The de facto claim was based upon the closure of the American Legation in Vienna and the opening of a consulate general, the expectation that Germany would continue paying Austrian indebtedness to the United States, the mandate that immigration quotas from Germany were to include Austrians, the need for Austrians seeking U.S. citizenship to renounce allegiance to the Third Reich, and Selective Service inclusion of Austria as an enemy nation. The court ruled that U.S. recognition of the Anschluss was irrelevant; the relevant point was whether the appellant was a German citizen under the act.

The court noted that *natives, citizens, denizens, or subjects* was an "all inclusive description" to capture all of those who by whatever ties of allegiance might support the enemy and "commit acts dangerous to our public safety if allowed to remain at large."[87] The court ruled, however, that under international law, Germany could impose German citizenship only on those who were resident in Austria at the time of the Anschluss and then only with their explicit or implicit consent. "In our view an invader cannot under international law impose its nationality upon non-residents of the subjugated country without their consent."[88]

In addition, even if the court were to recognize Schwarzkopf as a German citizen after the Anschluss, the subsequent stripping of citizenship from all German Jews further removed him from such citizenship. As such, the court ruled that he was not a German citizen for purposes of the Alien Enemies Act, and the writ of habeas corpus was granted.

In this case, the amicus curiae position was presented by Austrian Action, Inc., an organization established to direct the struggle for Austria's rebirth as an independent nation.[89] It was run by Count Ferdinand Czernin, the son of Count Ottokar von Czernin, Austria-Hungary's foreign minister during much of WWI.

86. *Schwarzkopf*, 137 F.2d at 901.
87. *Id.* at 902.
88. *Id.*
89. *What Hitler Has Done to My Country*, ST. PETERSBURG TIMES (Nov. 7, 1941).

LEGAL PROFILES

John W. Davis was the amicus curiae attorney for the appellant in this case. He was born in West Virginia in 1873 and started his legal career there. He was elected to the state legislature in 1899 and to the U.S. Congress in 1910. He resigned to become the U.S. solicitor general in 1913, a position he held through WWI. President Woodrow Wilson appointed him as the U.S. ambassador to the United Kingdom, a role in which he served until 1921. Davis ran unsuccessfully as the Democratic candidate for U.S. president in 1924. During his legal career, both as solicitor general and in private practice, he argued more than one hundred cases before the U.S. Supreme Court, including in the 1950s *Youngstown Sheet & Tube Co. v. Sawyer*, a case involving seizure powers of the president (see Chapter 3),[90] and *Briggs v. Elliott*, a case involving separate but equal schools.[91] He died in 1955.[92]

C. Subsequent Events

The government of Austria ceased to exist independently until after the war. The Anschluss was declared null and void on April 27, 1945, by a new Austrian provisional government. Actual independent sovereignty took a decade longer as the country was under Allied occupation from April 1945 until 1955. During that time, there was a national government, but it was under the control of the occupying forces.

In 1945, the four major Allied powers (France, the United Kingdom, the Soviet Union, and the United States) agreed on how they would occupy and control Austria after the war. The Agreement on Control Machinery in Austria of July 1945 established the Allied Commission for Austria. This consisted of a military commander from each Allied country overseeing occupation zones,

90. Youngstown Sheet & Tube Co. v. Sawyer, 343 U.S. 579 (1952).
91. Briggs v. Elliott, 342 U.S. 350 (1952).
92. *See Davis, John William*, BIOGRAPHICAL DIRECTORY OF THE UNITED STATES CONGRESS.

included four in the city of Vienna itself. Among the primary purposes for the commission was separating Austria from Germany and establishing a freely elected government in Austria. In 1946, the national government was allowed to engage in foreign relations negotiations.

In 1955, the Austrian State Treaty finally restored Austria as an independent and democratic country.[93] It stipulated that Germany would recognize Austrian sovereignty and renounce all territorial and political claims to her. Article 4 was titled "Prohibition of Anschluss" and prohibited political or economic union between Austria and Germany. Austria was prohibited from concluding any agreement or acting to achieve these ends, allowing any acts or organizations with these goals, or allowing any "pan-German propaganda that favored union with Germany."[94]

It took ten years for Austria to gain independence after the war due to some intransigence on the part of the Soviet Union, and it was only with the death of Stalin in 1953 that negotiations could finally take place. As President Eisenhower noted in his transmittal of the treaty to the U.S. Senate in June 1955,

> [t]he Austrian State Treaty represents the culmination of an effort by the Western Powers extending over a period of more than eight years to bring about Soviet agreement to grant Austria its freedom. The restoration of Austria's freedom and independence has been a major objective of United States policy since the pledge of Austrian liberation . . . in the Moscow Declaration of November 1, 1943. Until last April, the Soviet Union, while professing a desire for Austrian independence, by its actions and policies blocked the redemption of that pledge. The reversal in policy by the Soviet Government following its failure to prevent ratification of the Paris Pacts has now permitted the conclusion of an Austrian treaty.[95]

---

93. State Treaty for the Re-Establishment of an Independent and Democratic Austria, May 15, 1955.
94. *Id.* art. 4.
95. President Dwight D. Eisenhower, Message to the Senate Transmitting the Austrian State Treaty (June 1, 1955).

LEGAL PROFILES

Karl Renner was a leading political figure in Austria before and after the war. He was born in part of the Austro-Hungarian Empire in 1870 and undertook his legal studies in Austria. He was elected to the National Assembly in 1907, where he held a position until the end of WWI. After the war, he became the chancellor of the new country of Austria and represented his country in the Treaty of Saint-Germain-en-Laye (see Chapter 1). After several years as chancellor and also foreign affairs minister, he returned to the National Assembly and also served as the leader of that body from 1931 to 1934. His Social Democratic Party was banned in the mid-1930s, and he was arrested and imprisoned. After the war, he led a provisional government that separated Austria from Germany. He was then elected as the first president of postwar Austria in 1945, serving in this role until his death in 1950.[96]

Adolf Schärf was a leading political figure in Austria before and after the war; he was also a lawyer. He was born in part of the Austro-Hungarian Empire in 1890 and completed his legal studies in Austria. He then served in WWI. After the war, he joined the Social Democratic Party, serving as secretary. He then was elected to the National Assembly in 1933, before the subsequent banning of his party the next year. He spent the war years alternately as a political prisoner and practicing law. He returned to politics after the war in the National Assembly and also served as vice chancellor of the country from 1945 to 1956. In 1957 and again in 1963, he was elected president of Austria. He served in that office until his death in 1965.[97]

---

96. *See President Renner of Austria Dies; Socialist, Foe of Dollfuss, Was 80*, N.Y. TIMES (Dec. 31, 1950).
97. *See Dr. Adolph Scharf Is Dead at 74; President of Austria Since '57*, N.Y. TIMES (Mar. 1, 1965).

D. Modern Applicability

Annexation of neighboring nations has happened in recent times. Two prominent examples are East Timor and Kuwait. In 1975, East Timor was invaded by Indonesia and annexed, becoming the twenty-seventh province of Indonesia. It was not until the intervention of the United Nations that East Timor was able to vote on and then achieve its independence again in 2002. In 1990, Iraq invaded Kuwait and annexed it as the nineteenth province of Iraq. This led to the Gulf War, in which a U.S.-led coalition in 1991 forced Iraq out of Kuwait and restored the latter's sovereignty. Finally, although not technically annexations, Israel has occupied the Golan Heights and East Jerusalem since 1967.

5.3 CLIENT STATE: VICHY FRANCE

A. Statutes

1. The Armistice

After the declarations of war by France and the United Kingdom following the invasion of Poland in September 1939, the so-called Phoney War period of eight months lasted until the German invasions of France and the Low Countries in May 1940. These countries were quickly overrun and occupied. The military presence was often followed with the installation of a collaborationist government in the occupied territories. France was one country where this occurred, although it also occurred to varying degrees in Belgium, the Netherlands, Luxembourg, Denmark, Norway, Yugoslavia, Greece, and elsewhere.

Upon the victory of the German forces over the French, an armistice was signed—in the same location (and railway carriage) as the armistice ending WWI.[98] With a vow in the preamble that it did not intend to use the armistice as a "form of humiliation against such a valiant opponent," Germany listed the following main objectives for its demands under the armistice: to prevent France from resuming combat, to give Germany "full security" for continuing the war with England "into which it had been forced," and to set precondi-

---

98. Armistice Agreement Between the German High Command of the Armed Forces and French Plenipotentiaries, Compiègne, Ger.-Fr., June 22, 1940.

tions for a new peace treaty to remediate "the injustice that was forced" upon Germany after the last war.[99]

Under this agreement, German troops occupied the territory of France north and west of a line beginning at the French-Swiss border at Geneva to twenty kilometers east of Tours and then to the Spanish border. This effectively included the northern part of the country plus all Atlantic ports; the west coast areas, however, were to be occupied only until cessation of the hostilities with England. Germany administered Alsace-Lorraine (and the Italians administered a buffer zone in the Alps). France administered the unoccupied parts of the country.

The armistice detailed certain rights or requirements for each side. The Germans, in the occupied areas, would be able to "exercise all rights of an occupying power."[100] French officials were to "cooperate" with German military commanders "in a correct manner" and were obligated to "support with every means the regulations resulting from the exercise of these rights and to carry them out with the aid of French administration."[101] French troops were to stop fighting; be demobilized and imprisoned for the duration of the war; and be disarmed, with armaments stored, secured, or handed over. France was required to hand over, undamaged, railways, harbors, industrial facilities, docks, canals, roads, fortifications, and communications networks. France was to stop its people, soldiers, armaments, provisions, and valuables from leaving the occupied territories or going overseas. The French government was required to bear the cost of maintaining German troops on French soil and to hand over German nationals, including any refugees who had fled Germany.

This agreement was to last until the implementation of a peace treaty.

LEGAL PROFILES

Léon Noël was the French ambassador representing the Ministry of Foreign and European Affairs who signed the armistice with Germany. He was born in France in 1888 and undertook his legal studies there.

---

99. *Id.* pmbl.
100. *Id.*
101. *Id.*

He became a deputy commissioner of the government in 1920; held a variety of positions in the cabinet between 1921 and 1924, including minister of the interior and minister of justice; and became a councillor of state. From 1927 to 1930, he was a delegate of the high commissioner to the French Republic in Rhineland. Through the 1930s, he served in a department in Alsace and in ministry functions in Czechoslovakia until 1935 and then in Poland until 1940. After the war, he returned with the new government in foreign affairs roles, and he served in the French Parliament from 1951 to 1955. He was the first president of the new Constitutional Council (ruling on the constitutionality of statutes) from 1959 to 1965. He died in 1987.[102]

2. Full Powers to Pétain

There was to be no peace treaty, but following this armistice and the related agreement with Italy, the remainder of the French Parliament met in Vichy in 1940. Prime Minister Paul Reynaud had resigned over the armistice and been replaced by eighty-four-year-old WWI hero Marshal Philippe Pétain. Parliament was under a number of differing influences, including those members who favored collaboration; those who favored government reform; and those who merely reacted to current events, pressure, and promises from Pétain's deputy (Pierre Laval), and the absence of some senior leaders who had sailed into exile in Casablanca. Despite the fact that a significant number of members did not vote, the French Parliament voted overwhelmingly to give full powers to Pétain, in essence ending the Third Republic in France.[103] This violated, at the least, the 1875 law that reserved for the National Assembly itself the power to pass laws revising the constitution[104] and the 1884 law that did not allow the republican form of government to become the subject of a proposal for revision.[105]

---

102. *See Léon, Philippe, Jules, Arthur Noël*, Assemblée Nationale, Biographies des Députés de la IVe République.

103. Constitutional Law of July 10, 1940 (Fr.).

104. Law of Feb. 25, 1875, on the Organization of Government art. 8 (Fr.); Loi du 25 février 1875 relative à l'organisation des pouvoirs publics, art 8.

105. Law of August 14, 1884, Partially Revising Constitutional Laws art. 2 (Fr.); Loi du 14 août 1884 portant révision partielle des lois constitutionnelles, art 2.

The law giving full powers to Pétain had a single article, which stated that

[t]he National Assembly vests in Marshal Pétain all powers in the Government of the Republic in order that he may, by his authority and under his signature, promulgate a new constitution for the French State by one or several acts. This constitution shall guarantee the rights of labor, of the family, and of the fatherland.[106]

This statute was far removed from the traditional French values of freedom, equality, and brotherhood.

The next day, Pétain, in his first constitutional act "[i]n consideration of the Constitutional Law of July 19, 1940," assumed the role of chief of the French state and then decreed that Article 2 of the Constitutional Law of 1875 (dealing with the election of the president of the republic) was abrogated.[107]

In his second act, Pétain defined his position as having "full governmental powers."[108] He could appoint and revoke ministers and secretaries, "who shall be responsible only to him."[109] He could exercise legislative power in the Council of Ministers. He could issue budgetary or fiscal regulations, promulgate laws and assure their execution, make appointments to civil and military posts, have full power over the armed forces, have the right to grant pardons and amnesty, receive envoys and ambassadors, and negotiate and ratify treaties. However, he could not declare war unilaterally. In essence, Vichy France was controlled now through Pétain and those he appointed, in collaboration with the German occupiers.

Several more constitutional acts followed. The third act adjourned the National Assembly without assigning any specific date for it to reconvene.[110] The seventh act required ministers to swear a personal oath to Pétain.[111]

---

106. Constitutional Law of July 10, 1940 (Fr.).
107. Constitutional Act No. 1 of July 11, 1940, Appointment of the Head of State (Vichy Fr.).
108. Constitutional Act No. 2 of July 11, 1940, Establishing the Powers of the Head of the French State (Vichy Fr.).
109. *Id.*
110. Constitutional Act No. 3 of July 11, 1940, Extending and Adjourning the House (Vichy Fr.); Acte constitutionnel n° 3 du 11 juillet 1940, prorogeant et ajournant les Chambres.
111. Constitutional Act No. 7 of January 27, 1941, Status of Secretaries of State, Dignitaries, and Officials (Vichy Fr.); Acte constitutionnel n° 7 du 27 janvier 1941, statut des secrétaires d'État, hauts dignitaires et hauts fonctionnaires.

In October 1940, the Vichy government passed a law called the Statute on Jews.[112] Across ten articles, this law defined Jewishness (three Jewish grandparents), prohibited Jews from holding many public positions, and established certain requirements (fighting in WWI or winning a Legion of Honor Medal) for holding other public positions. In addition, Jews were not allowed to serve in judicial positions or as directors or managers of newspapers, films, or broadcasting. However, those who had given outstanding service in the literary, scientific, or artistic areas might be exempt from these rules. In June 1941, this law was revised, further tightening definitions and prohibiting more categories of employment.[113] In addition, penalties were prescribed for participating in the prohibited activities or misrepresenting such.

LEGAL PROFILES

Raphaël Alibert was the Vichy minister of justice when the statute giving full powers to Pétain was passed; he was also one of its signatories. He was born in France in 1887 and undertook his legal studies there. He joined the Council of State as a specialist in administrative law and became chief of staff to a member of the cabinet in 1917. In 1924, he left the government for the private sector. When Pétain was named prime minister of France in 1940, Alibert joined the cabinet as undersecretary of state. In his role in the Vichy government, he was responsible for setting up the appropriate constitutional documents, including drafting the first three constitutional acts described above. He also reviewed recent naturalizations and denaturalized fifteen thousand French citizens. He was eventually dismissed from the Vichy government, fled overseas, and was convicted and sentenced to death in absentia but ultimately given amnesty. He died in 1963.[114]

---

112. Law of Oct. 3, 1940, on the Status of Jews (Vichy Fr.), Loi du 3 octobre 1940 portant statut des Juifs.
113. Law of June 2, 1941, Replacing the Law of Oct. 3, 1940, on the Status of Jews (Vichy Fr.); Loi du 2 juin 1941 remplacant la loi du 3 octobre 1940 portant statut des juifs.
114. *See Alibert, Petain Aide, Condemned to Death*, N.Y. TIMES (Mar. 8, 1947).

B. Cases

After the war, reprisals against collaborationists by nonjudicial means led to the execution of approximately ten thousand people in France. Once a semblance of judicial order was imposed by the new French government, several of the Vichy leaders were tried, including Pétain and Laval. Their trials brought out much of the underside of the collaboration between Vichy France and Nazi Germany. The first two cases discussed here involved men tried under expurgation and national indignity ordinances passed near the end of the war: one case dealt with Pétain and his collaboration with the occupying forces; and the other case dealt with Laval and his role in the occupation, both in his collaboration and in his attempts to further the cause of the Reich. The other set of cases discussed here concern the impact of Vichy France on the outside world, specifically as seen in the U.S. courts from several aspects.

1. Expurgation and National Indignity Cases

The first two cases grew out of a set of procedures set up by Charles de Gaulle's government in exile for courts of expurgation (purging, purification) to deal with collaborators after the war and help French society heal. In August 1943, an ordinance created the commission on expurgation. This was followed in June 1944 with an ordinance that set up courts to address crimes of collaboration with the enemy committed from June 1940 until liberation under the laws that existed in June 1940 (pre-Vichy).[115] The French Resistance and the Allied troops were made equivalent to the French army, so the crimes of treason and intelligence with the enemy applied to those working with others such as the militia or Gestapo. Those following orders were absolved, but those working under personal initiative were not.

Further ordinances, including one in November 1944,[116] created the crime of national indignity, which was punishable by national degradation. The crime included providing assistance to Nazi Germany, undermining the unity or freedom of France, and not performing the expected national duty. Membership in certain organizations (e.g., the militia), in certain positions (notorious

---

115. Ordinance of June 26, 1944, on the Suppression of Acts of Collaboration (Fr.).

116. Ordinance of Nov. 28, 1944 (Amendment and Codification of Texts Relating to the Suppression of Acts of Collaboration), Repealing the Law of June 26 (Fr.); L'ordonnance du 28 novembre 1944 (« portant modification et codification des textes relatifs à la répression des faits de collaboration ») abroge celle du 26 juin.

government roles supporting racial policies), and other roles (e.g., propaganda) were clear candidates for this charge. The punishment for national indignity included imprisonment or removal from the military or the right to wear military decorations; prohibition on certain management, professional, trade, and other positions; loss of pension, loss of voting privileges, prohibitions on residence and travel, restrictions on possessing weapons, and forfeiture of property.

LEGAL PROFILES

Jules Jeanneney was the minister of state for the Provisional Government of the French Republic (PGFR) and a lawyer who signed the expurgation ordinances. He was born in France in 1864 and obtained his legal education there, focusing on private international law. He was elected mayor of Rioz in 1896 and then deputy to the National Assembly in 1902. He was first elected a senator in the National Assembly in 1909 and continued to be elected to this body until 1944. In WWI, he served on a senate commission and as an undersecretary of state. After that war, he returned to the senate, becoming, in turn, vice president in 1924, speaker, and president from 1932 to 1940. A supporter of the republican cause, he served in the provisional government during WWII but then left public life. He died in 1957.[117]

a. Pétain Trial

In July 1945, Pétain was brought to trial on charges of plotting against the internal security of the state and of intelligence with the enemy. The eleven-page indictment categorized the charges as material, moral, and political. The first category included the charges that he signed the armistice, suppressed the presidency, assumed full powers, and adjourned and never recalled the National Assembly. Under the second category, the charges included "abhorring the Republic"; wanting the hereditary monarchy to return; and maintaining rela-

---

117. *See Jules Jeanneney*, ASSEMBLEE NATIONALE BIOGRAPHIES DES DÉPUTÉS FRANÇAIS DEPUIS 1789.

tionships with the head of the Vichy police (Joseph Darnand), Nazi propagandist (Fernand de Brinon), and head of government (Laval), all of whom were later executed for their crimes against France. Under the third category, Pétain was charged with resigning himself to and accepting defeat; meeting with Hitler; accepting a degrading collaboration with the Nazis; copying German legislation regarding Jews, Freemasons, and Communists; placing French industry at Germany's disposal; and engaging in military collaboration. He was also charged with a number of foreign policy actions, including turning over bases to Axis powers and scuttling ships.

The court, led by president of the court Pierre Paul Mongibeaux, heard from a number of witnesses, including prior prime ministers Reynaud, Léon Blum, Édouard Daladier; former Supreme Commander of the military General Maxime Weygand; Resistance victims of Vichy police; mothers whose sons had died; de Brinon, Darnand; Laval; and others. The prosecuting attorney asked for the death penalty on the charges. Pétain claimed that he was only protecting France from worse by his actions. The defense attorney pointed out that Mongibeaux and André Mornet, the prosecutor, had both sworn loyalty to Pétain under Vichy France. The jury, including fighters from the Resistance and delegates from the National Assembly who did not vote to give Pétain full powers, voted for the death penalty 20-7 but also voted 14-13 in recommending that the death penalty not be carried out due to the advanced age of the defendant and his service during WWI. Pétain was also sentenced for the crime of national indignity and his property confiscated as a national degradation. His sentence was commuted to life imprisonment by de Gaulle, and he died in prison six years later.

LEGAL PROFILES

Jacques Isorni was one the lawyers for the defendant in this case. He was born in France in 1911 and began practicing law at the age of twenty. A supporter of Vichy France, he was briefly debarred by the laws of that government because his parents came from Italy (he was not wholly French). In addition to Pétain, he also defended Fascist writer Robert Brasillach of collaboration charges, who was likewise sentenced to death (and actually executed). After the war, besides defending the Pétain and Vichy legacy, Isorni was elected to the National Assembly in 1951, where he remained until 1958. Later, he also defended General Raoul Salan against treason charges. He died in 1995.[118]

André Mornet was the lead prosecutor in this case. He was born in France in 1870 and completed his legal studies there. He became involved with the Ministry of Justice as a magistrate beginning in 1898. In 1912, he was appointed attorney general. During WWI, he was involved in various councils of war near the front and then prosecuted the famous espionage trial of Mata Hari in 1917. After the war, he was appointed advocate general on the French Court of Cassation in 1922. In 1930, he became a counsel in the Civil Chamber. He was also involved in the Riom trial conducted by the Vichy government (see Chapter 1). He was brought back from retirement to be attorney general for the High Court for the trials of Pétain and Laval. After the war, he was president of the commission judging collaborationist acts of the Vichy government. He died in 1955.[119]

b. Laval Trial

The pent-up national feelings that could not be fully played out in the Pétain trial due to Pétain's advanced age and prior service record were released more forcefully the trial of the deputy leader of Vichy, Pierre Laval. Laval was charged with treason by intelligence with the enemy and plotting against the security of the state. He was also charged with national indignity. The chief judge was once again Mongibeaux, and the prosecutor was Mornet. The October 1945 trial, which was actually two trials, involved a storm of accusations and insults raining down on the defendant from the jury, gallery, judges, and prosecutor countered by the no-admission-of-guilt responses and counteraccusations from the defendant. The trial began with Laval's lawyers declining to appear

---

118. *See Jacques Isorni,* Assemblee Nationale Biographies des Députés Français depuis 1789.
119. *See Andre Mornet, French Prosecutor, Dies; Led Petain, Laval, and Mata Hari Trials,* N.Y. Times (July 23, 1955).

on the first day, claiming that they had not been briefed, and ended with Laval himself, as well as his attorneys, not attending on the final days.

Mornet argued that Laval was guilty of "political treason" and "moral treason, delivering France to the invader." Witnesses included Léon Noël, whose previous testimony against Laval in the Pétain trial was used because Laval had absented himself from his own trial. But it was primarily Laval's own public acts, statements, and orders that he issued as the head of the Vichy government that constituted the evidence against him. The prosecutor listed these acts as overthrowing the Republic, establishing a dictatorial regime, starting a "criminal collaboration" with the enemy when meeting Hitler, establishing various unconstitutional acts in the Vichy government, publicly stating his desire for Germany's victory in the war, scuttling the French fleet at Toulon, establishing the Vichy racial policies, the giving of French bases for Nazi use, employing French forced labor to assist the Nazi war effort, giving up natural resources to the Germans, and forming the militia to fight against the French Resistance.

The jury was unanimous in convicting Laval under these charges and sentenced him to death. His lawyers' request for a re-trial was rejected. There was no clemency because unlike Pétain, who may have been trying to protect the country from the greater evil, Laval desired German victory. His sentence was carried out less than one week later. Laval was also penalized by national degradation with confiscation of his property.

LEGAL PROFILES

Pierre Laval was the Vichy vice president of the Council of Ministers, the defendant, and a lawyer. He was born in France in 1883 and completed his legal studies there. He began his practice defending trade unionists. In 1914, he was elected as a deputy to the National Assembly, a position that he held through WWI. He then lost his seat but won it back in 1924, holding that seat until 1927. He was part of the government as the minister of public works and minister of justice during this period. He then was elected to the Senate, a seat he held from 1927 to 1944. He was initially the minister of labor but in 1931 became the prime minister. His government lasted about a year. He joined succeeding governments as foreign minister, in which capacity he signed the Franco–Italian agreement (an attempt to give Italy concessions in Africa for support against possible German aggression) and held build the Stresa Front (see Section 5.2). In 1935, he became the prime minister again for about six months. He then took on the role of minister of state in the Vichy government. He was executed in 1945.[120]

Pierre Paul Mongibeaux was the chief judge in this trial (and the Pétain trial, as well). He was born in France in 1879 and completed his legal studies there. He became an assistant judge in 1904 and then a deputy judge. Next, he was a public prosecutor in a number of locations and in 1920 was appointed as a prosecuting attorney. He later became a prosecutor in the appellate court and a counselor in the French Court of Cassation. In 1945, he became the president of that court. He was appointed to preside at the High Court of Justice for the Pétain and Laval trials. He died in 1950.[121]

2. Impacts of Vichy France

The change in governments in France and the actions taken by the Vichy regime led to citizenship and recognition issues. The U.S. and other governments were not completely sure which representative of France was the proper one, with possible candidates being the Vichy regime in France, the Vichy regime in North Africa, or the Free French Forces clustering around General de Gaulle in the United Kingdom.

Some of this confusion can be seen in the U.S. State Department's recognition of French governments. When the French government was relocated to Vichy, the American Legation moved there with it, with the ambassador presenting his credentials to the Vichy government in January 1941. After the Allied landings in North Africa in November 1942, the Vichy government broke off diplomatic relations with the United States. In June 1943, the French Committee of National Liberation (FCNL) was formed in Algeria, combin-

120. *See Pierre Laval,* ASSEMBLEE NATIONALE BIOGRAPHIES DES DÉPUTÉS FRANÇAIS DEPUIS 1789.
121. *See Mongibeaux Dies; French Jurist, 71,* N.Y. TIMES (Sept. 24, 1950).

ing the efforts of de Gaulle and General Henri Giraud. The U.S. government recognized the FCNL "as administering those territories which acknowledge its authority."[122] After the invasion of Normandy and the push inland to liberate France, the FCNL was reconstituted as the Provisional Government of the French Republic; and in October 1944, the U.S. government recognized it as the legitimate government of France and subsequently reopened its embassy in Paris.

Government of France v. Isbrandtsen-Moller Co., which dealt with the ability of the Vichy government to pursue claims in U.S. courts after breaking off of relations with the United States in November 1942, involved shipping and maritime claims.[123] The respondent had requested verification of the libellant, which was submitted by the French ambassador on November 9, 1942, the day after the Vichy government had broken off diplomatic relations with the United States. As such, the court held that the case could not proceed because the Vichy government was now an enemy alien under the Trading with the Enemy Act (see Chapter 3) with no access to U.S. courts. The case was suspended until such time as there was a recognized French government.

Another case stemming from the impact of the changes in the French government was *Doreau v. Marshall*, which involved a U.S. national who married a French national and was in France when the war started.[124] She was advised by the U.S. consul that she could be interned as an enemy alien and, as such, should leave occupied France. She went to a Vichy-controlled area, where she became both pregnant and ill and unable to travel. She was advised that internment there might have fatal consequences for her and her unborn child, so she applied for French citizenship. Upon the reopening of the American embassy in Paris, she reapplied for her U.S. passport, but her request was denied as she had expatriated by becoming a French citizen under the Vichy regime. The court remanded the case to the trial court, pointing to the standards of two other cases which held that if in extraordinary circumstances sufficient duress can be shown, then the expatriation is involuntary and so void.

---

122. U.S. Department of State, A Guide to the United States' History of Recognition, Diplomatic, and Consular Relations, by Country, since 1776: France.
123. Government of France v. Isbrandtsen-Moller Co., 48 F. Supp. 631 (S.D.N.Y. 1943).
124. Doreau v. Marshall, 170 F.2d 721 (3d Cir. 1948).

LEGAL PROFILES

Fernand de Brinon was the Vichy secretary of state when France broke off relations with the United States; he was also a lawyer. He was born in France in 1885 and completed his legal studies there but worked more in journalism than in law. He fought in WWI but then became an advocate of reconciliation between France and Germany after meeting German Foreign Minister Joachim von Ribbentrop in 1919. Even though his wife was Jewish, his high position during the Vichy era protected her from the concentration camps: he served as the Vichy representative to the German high command in Paris in 1940 and became the Vichy secretary of state in 1942. When the Allied forces advanced into France, he fled to Germany and set up the Vichy government in exile with himself as the leader. He was eventually captured and brought to trial, where he was found guilty of treason for intelligence with the enemy. He was also convicted of national indignity and so condemned to national degradation with confiscation of his property. He was then executed in 1947 and buried in the same grave as Laval.[125]

C. Subsequent Events

The courts set up to deal with collaboration continued to work on cases long after the war. Although many thousands were sentenced to death, including some by court-martial, less than one thousand were actually executed. National degradation was a more common punishment for collaborators. In addition, beginning in April 1945, the jury d'honneur, a panel of appointed jurors made up of former Resistance members, was set up to review cases of National Assembly members who had voted to grant Pétain full powers or who had later joined the Vichy government. The jury assessed the assembly members' support for the Vichy regime and collaboration and their commitment to the Resistance and determined whether they were eligible for reelection in the

---

125. *See De Brinon Is Executed*, N.Y. Times (Apr. 15, 1947).

postwar French government. The new government that eventually took power was essentially made up of new faces.

LEGAL PROFILES

René Cassin was the head of this new court of honor and a lawyer. He was born in France in 1887 and completed his legal studies there. He was seriously injured during combat in WWI. After the war, he became involved in international law. He was the French delegate to the League of Nations from 1924 to 1938. In WWII, he joined de Gaulle's government in exile as the minister of justice. After the war, he headed both the French Council of State and the Constitutional Council and again became heavily involved in international organizations. He was a principal author of the Universal Declaration of Human Rights adopted by the United Nations in 1948. He headed the United Nations Commission on Human Rights and helped to found the United Nations Educational, Scientific and Cultural Organization (UNESCO). He became president of the European Court of Human Rights in 1965. In 1968, he was awarded the Nobel Peace Prize. He died in 1976.[126]

D. Modern Applicability

The trials of those involved in Vichy France carried on long after the war in several high-profile trials, continuing up to current times. Several high-profile cases were those of Klaus Barbie, Paul Touvier, René Bousquet, and Maurice Papon.

In 1987, Klaus Barbie, the Gestapo leader in Lyon, France, for several years during the war, was charged with crimes against humanity for numerous acts of torture and brutality against Resistance members (including Jean Moulin) and Jews (including the eventual murder of forty-four children). On the run for almost forty years, Barbie was eventually discovered. He had previously

---

126. *See Rene Cassin, Jurist, Dies; Won Nobel Peace Prize*, N.Y. TIMES (Feb. 21, 1976).

been convicted twice for many of his crimes, but that sentence could not now be carried out because it expired under the statute of limitations since it had been more than twenty years since the convictions. However, he was brought to trial for other crimes, and the entire first day of the trial was spent reading off the list of hundreds of crimes that Barbie had committed. Some fifty witnesses were called, and the jury found Barbie guilty. He was sentenced to life in prison, where he died in 1991.

Paul Touvier was a leader in the Milice, a violent Vichy militia group opposed to the French Resistance. He was tried numerous times, always escaping conviction and punishment. He even received a pardon while the Roman Catholic Church in France supported and shielded him. Like Barbie, he escaped trial for many of his war crimes under the statute of limitations. However, he was tried in 1994 for crimes against humanity, convicted, and sentenced to life in prison, where he died in 1996.

René Bousquet, the head of the police in Vichy (and a law student) was responsible for sending more than seventy thousand Jews, including significant numbers of children, to the concentration camps and death; but he was assassinated in 1994 before he could be tried for his crimes against humanity. He had originally been sentenced after the war only to national degradation as part of the postwar Vichy amnesty programs.

Maurice Papon was tried in 1998 for crimes against humanity for signing the deportation orders of almost two thousand Jewish residents, including hundreds of children. Appointed by the Vichy government, he later switched sides and rose in the French bureaucracy and political systems after the war, even being elected to the National Assembly and joining the cabinet. It was only later that his crimes were exposed, as were those of many of the Vichy officials, by the efforts of French lawyer Serge Klarsfeld. After long eluding trial after indictment, he was convicted and sentenced to ten years in prison. He died in 2007 after being released early from prison for health reasons.

5.4 NEUTRAL STATE: SWITZERLAND

A. Statutes

Switzerland had long tried to play a neutral role in European conflicts. Its policy of armed neutrality dated back almost five hundred years, to the Battle of Marignano in the early sixteenth century and the subsequent declaration of neutrality by the Old Swiss Confederacy. After the end of the Thirty Years' War in the seventeenth century, the Peace of Westphalia confirmed Swiss independence and neutrality.[127] Following the Napoleonic Wars in the early nineteenth century, the instruments signed at the Second Treaty of Paris recognized Switzerland's perpetual neutrality and the integrity and inviolability of its territory.[128] These wars two hundred years ago were the last time Switzerland was involved in a significant war outside of its own borders (although individual Swiss citizens have been involved in external wars).

In modern times, neutrality was first based upon the 1815 Congress of Vienna.[129] Neutral nations were then given a series of obligations under the Hague Convention of 1907 if they wished to be regarded as neutral by others. Hague Convention V addressed neutrality in land wars[130] (Hague Convention XIII addressed neutrality in naval wars, not applicable to land-locked Switzerland).[131] It stated that the territory of neutrals was inviolable and that belligerents were forbidden to move troops, supply convoys, or munitions across the neutral's territory or to erect or use communications networks there for war purposes (but they could use those of private companies or of the neutral country). A neutral country must ensure that these acts or recruiting for the war did not happen on its territory. A neutral country was not required to stop people from crossing its borders to offer services to the belligerents or to stop the export or transport of arms or munitions to the belligerents, but if it did, it had to do so impartially. However, efforts to stop violations of its territory were not to be regarded as hostile acts. Belligerent troops who entered neutral territory were to be interned as far away from the theater of war as possible. The neutral country was obliged to supply those interned with food,

---

127. Peace Treaty Between the Holy Roman Emperor and the King of France and Their Respective Allies art. LXIII, Oct. 24, 1648.
128. Act of Acknowledgement and Guarantee of the Perpetual Neutrality of Switzerland, Nov. 20, 1815.
129. General Treaty of the Final Act of the Congress of Vienna art. LXXXIV, June 9, 1815.
130. Convention Respecting the Rights and Duties of Neutral Powers and Persons in Case of War on Land, Oct. 18, 1907.
131. Convention Respecting the Rights and Duties of Neutral Powers and Persons in Naval War, Oct. 18, 1907.

clothing, and "relief required by humanity."[132] Escaped POWs were not to be interned. Sick or wounded troops were to be guarded by the neutral country to ensure they did not rejoin the fighting, but the Geneva Convention applied to their treatment. Providing supplies or loans to the belligerents was not considered a violation of neutrality.

Switzerland ratified the Hague Convention in 1910. Upon its entry into the League of Nations in 1920, it requested recognition of its neutrality. The League Council,

> while affirming that the conception of neutrality of the members of the League is incompatible with the principle that all members will be obliged to cooperate in enforcing respect for their engagements, recognizes that Switzerland is in a unique situation, based on a tradition of several centuries which has been explicitly incorporated in the Law of Nations.... [M]embership in the League of Nations imposes ... the duty of cooperating in such economic and financial measures as may be demanded by the League ... [and Switzerland is prepared to] make every sacrifice to defend her own territory under every circumstance ... but will not be obliged to take part in any military action or to allow the passage of foreign troops or the preparations of military operations within her territory.[133]

In 1938, the Council granted Switzerland's request for unconditional neutrality, relieving it from the obligation to participate in economic sanctions.

The Swiss Constitution itself requires a commitment to neutrality. Starting with the constitution of 1848 and described more completely in the constitution of 1874, neutrality was a mandate for the federal government. The Federal Assembly, made up of the National Council and the Council of States, listed as one of its competencies "[m]easures for the external security as well as for the preservation of the independence and neutrality of Switzerland, declaration of war and conclusion of peace."[134] The Federal Council, the supreme

---

132. Convention Respecting the Rights and Duties of Neutral Powers and Persons in Case of War on Land.
133. *Id.*
134. Constitution of 1874, art. 85 (Switz.).

executive and governing authority in the country, listed as one of its powers and obligations "watch[ing] over the external security of Switzerland and over the preservation of its independence and neutrality."[135] This was the law of the land when WWII started.

A number of laws prior to and during WWII dealt with the issue of refugees. Swiss law in regard to nonmilitary refugees only allowed refuge for those seeking asylum due to reasons of political activity, not those responding to situations such as the discriminatory racial policies of Nazi Germany. The 1931 federal Law on the Residence and Settlement of Foreigners allowed for permanent residence, temporary residence (e.g., students), and tolerance permits for short-term stays of those without valid papers,[136] but asylum only for those who were politically persecuted.[137] In April 1933, a new Federal Council decree differentiated between political and other refugees.[138] In 1939, Switzerland began rule under the Emergency Plenary Powers Decree, which transferred much of the legislative function to the Federal Council.[139] Subsequent decrees relating to refugees required police to deport illegal refugees and to intern undeportable refugees to ensure that they would not seek or gain employment or engage in political activities,[140] and required refugees to labor at selected jobs in work camps[141] or to pay a tax for their own support costs.[142] The second "solidarity" tax required refugees in the country to reveal all financial valuables or be deported.[143] Cash and valuables for those entering the country were confiscated for safekeeping (an action that had no legal support until a Federal Council decree of March 12, 1943), from which living costs and other fees were deducted.[144]

---

135. Constitution of 1874, art. 102 (Switz.).
136. Bundesgesetz über Aufenthalt und Niederlassung der Ausländer, Mar. 26, 1931, arts. 4–6 (Switz.).
137. *Id*. art. 21.
138. Federal Council Decree (Apr. 7, 1933) (Switz.).
139. Federal Council Decree on Measures for the Protection of the Country and the Maintenance of Neutrality, Vollmachtenbeschluss (Aug. 30, 1939) (Switz.).
140. Federal Council Decree (Oct. 17, 1939) (Switz.).
141. Federal Council Decree (Mar. 12, 1940) (Switz.).
142. Federal Council Decree (Feb. 20, 1939) (Switz.).
143. Federal Council Decree (Mar. 18, 1941) (Switz.).
144. Federal Council Decree (Mar. 12, 1943) (Switz.).

LEGAL PROFILES

Philipp Etter was the president of the Swiss Confederation when these acts were passed in 1939 and a lawyer. He was born in Switzerland in 1891 and completed his legal studies there, becoming a patent lawyer. In 1918, he was elected to the Grand Council in his canton and in 1922 entered the Council of State. In 1930 he was elected to the Council of States in the Federal Assembly. In 1934, he was elected to the Federal Council, where he took over the portfolio of the Department of Home Affairs. He served on the council for twenty-five years, serving as the president of Switzerland four times (1939, 1942, 1947, and 1953 (each term was for one year)). Postwar, he focused on improvements to the internal infrastructure, such as roads, and to scientific research. He died in 1977.[145]

Johannes Baumann was in charge of the Federal Department of Justice and Police in the second half of the 1930s, responsible for refugee issues federally. He was born in Switzerland in 1874 and completed his legal studies there. In 1901, he was elected to his canton's parliament. In 1905, he became a councillor for the canton's police department. In 1911, he was elected to the Federal Assembly in the Council of States, a position he held until 1934. In that year, he joined the Federal Council as head of the Federal Department of Justice and Police, a position he held until 1940. He was the president of Switzerland in 1938. He died in 1953.[146]

Edward von Steiger was in charge of the Federal Department of Justice and Police after Baumann; he was also a lawyer. He was born in Switzerland in 1881 and completed his legal studies there. He was elected to the parliament in his canton in 1914, where he remained

---

145. *See Philipp Etter,* The Federal Authorities of the Swiss Confederation.
146. *See Johannes Baumann,* The Federal Authorities of the Swiss Confederation.

until 1939. In 1940, he was elected to the Federal Council, heading the Federal Department of Justice and Police. He remained in this position until 1951. He was the president of Switzerland in 1945 and 1951. He died in 1962.[147]

B. Cases

The cases arising out of Switzerland's determined focus on neutrality covered several areas. The first involved the internment of Allied airmen whose planes were shot down and were first interned and then imprisoned in Switzerland during the war. A second concerned the civilian refugees who went to Switzerland in increasing numbers and those who tried to assist them locally in the face of official sanctions. A third dealt with assets stolen from countries and victims of the war and transferred into Switzerland.

1. Military Internment

During the war, Switzerland had to deal with foreign troops, both escaped POWs (those captured by the enemy in the course of military operations) and those combatants who were not POWs but who ended up in Switzerland through the disabling or loss of their airplane. Under the rules of the Hague Convention of 1907, Switzerland was not required to intern the POWs, who often stayed in nice hotels and resorts vacated during the war. In contrast, however, Switzerland was required to intern the combatant airmen to keep them from participating further in the war. With the war still going on and the close proximity of the fighting, many of the military internees tried to escape to return to the battles. However, the Swiss, wanting to protect their armed neutrality and with the looming threat of German invasion (Operation Tannenbaum, where the German high command, along with Italy, had drawn up plans to invade Switzerland), reacted strongly to such attempts, especially by repeat violators, who were subject to imprisonment as criminals in their subsequent confinements.

Under the Third Geneva Convention of 1929, POWs were to be "humanely treated and protected, particularly against acts of violence, from insults and

---

147. *See Edward von Steiger,* THE FEDERAL AUTHORITIES OF THE SWISS CONFEDERATION.

from public curiosity. Measures of reprisal against them are forbidden."[148] They were to be housed with others of their nationality in premises that "afford[ed] all possible safeguards as regards hygiene and salubrity" and given food rations equal to those of the troops of the detaining power.[149] Although POWs could be interned, they could not be imprisoned except as a "measure indispensable for safety or health."[150]

Acts of insubordination subjected POWs to the military laws of the detaining power. However, per the Geneva Convention, the detaining power was required to minimize the detention period during investigations for escape attempts and hold the trial as soon as possible. Those who attempted escape could be "subjected to a special régime of surveillance" but not any type of "corporal punishment, confinement in premises not lighted by daylight," or any type of cruelty.[151] Those escaping and recaptured were subject only to "disciplinary punishment" that could not exceed thirty days' imprisonment, which included time spent in detention before trial.[152] These punishments were not to be carried out in actual prisons. The Geneva Convention specified that defendants must be present at trial to have the opportunity to represent themselves. In addition, they had the right to be represented by both competent counsel and translators, and they had the right to appeal.

But military internees were not POWs. As such, the Geneva Convention technically did not apply to military internees in a neutral country. To help clarify this situation, the International Committee of the Red Cross, which dealt with POW conditions in the respective belligerent countries, notified many neutral countries in 1940 that it believed that the Geneva Convention should be applied to military internees.[153] However, in spite of Switzerland's role in inspecting POW conditions globally through the Red Cross, the Swiss believed that they were justified under international law in using the Swiss Military Penal Code to deal with escaped internees, whose punishment regime was different than that of the Geneva Convention. They were also concerned

---

148. Geneva Convention Relative to the Treatment of Prisoners of War, July 27, 1929.
149. *Id.*
150. *Id.*
151. *Id.*
152. *Id.*
153. INT'L COMM. FOR THE RED CROSS, 1 REPORT OF THE INTERNATIONAL COMMITTEE OF THE RED CROSS ON ITS ACTIVITIES DURING THE SECOND WORLD WAR: GENERAL ACTIVITIES (1948).

that failure to enforce the Hague Convention would be interpreted as a failure of neutrality, inviting possible retaliation.

Thus, those military internees in Switzerland who escaped and were captured again were often detained while awaiting trial and then sentenced to imprisonment in the Wauwilermoos camp, a prison notorious for poor hygiene, barbed wire fences, mud, and guard dogs. Brigadier General Barnwell Legge, a military attaché of the American Legation in Switzerland, described the Swiss as exhibiting "extreme severity and [an] inflexible attitude concerning the unjustified punishment of internees for having attempted to escape."[154] In a letter to the Swiss in charge of the internment, Legge quoted British POWs in saying that "the punishment meted out in Switzerland for attempting to escape is more severe than that in German prisoner of war camps."[155] And in a letter to the head of the American Legation, Legge noted that the problems in the internment camp included prisoners being held incommunicado for indefinite periods, lengthy sentences, confiscation of money and possessions, refusal to deliver Red Cross packages, and overcrowding and unhygienic facilities "worse than in enemy prison camps."[156]

A number of military internees suffered in these conditions. One was Staff Sergeant Dale Ellington, whose plane was hit by flak and crash-landed in Switzerland in April 1944.[157] He was interned until mid-September, when he tried to escape and was subsequently interned in Wauwilermoos. After forty-five days there, he was taken before a military tribunal, where the proceedings were conducted entirely in German. He was eventually sentenced to an additional thirty days for breaking Swiss military penal law by attempting to escape from military internment. A similar case involved Technical Sergeant Daniel Culler, whose plane was incapacitated by flak in March 1944 and forced down in Switzerland by Swiss fighters.[158] He was also interned and attempted to escape in July 1944. Upon becoming ill during the attempt and returning, he was interned in Wauwilermoos. After more than a month in confinement, he was

154. OFFICE OF THE MILITARY ATTACHÉ, AMERICAN LEGATION, BERN, SWITZERLAND (Dec. 12, 1944).
155. *See* Letter from Barnwell Legge, Gen., Military Attaché of American Legation in Switzerland, to Colonel Divisionnaire Dolfuss, Adjudant Général de l'Armée Suisse (Oct. 19, 1944).
156. *See* Letter from Barnwell Legge, Gen., Military Attaché of American Legation in Switzerland, to Leland Harrison, Head of American Legation (Nov. 1, 1944).
157. *See* WAR CRIMES OFFICE, JUDGE ADVOCATE GENERAL'S DEP'T, TESTIMONIES (1945); *see generally* Swiss Internees Ass'n, swissinternees.tripod.com.
158. *See* Letter from Daniel Culler, Technical Sergeant, to Will Lundy (June 9, 1986); *see generally* Swiss Internees Ass'n, swissinternees.tripod.com.

brought before a military tribunal, which sentenced him to a term of ninety days, with credit for his pretrial detention. (Culler later received both the Prisoner of War Medal and the Distinguished Flying Cross from the United States.)[159] The sentences of both Ellington and Culler, who served their extra time back at Wauwilermoos, were in excess of the thirty-day maximum specified in the Geneva Convention.

The number of Allied airmen who ended up in Switzerland increased as the bombing campaigns over Germany intensified in late 1944 and early 1945. This meant that not only more Allied airmen were interned but also more tried and failed to escape internment and were detained in Swiss prisons. General Legge reached an agreement with the Swiss to parole U.S. internees from Wauwilermoos on condition that they did not attempt to escape. And in spite of repeated Allied violations of its airspace, occasional instances of its planes being shot down (Swiss flew German-made fighters), and accidental bombings of its territory near Germany (some were deliberately targeted at munitions plants) and under pressure from the Allies with German defeat more certain, Switzerland began to limit the sentences of escaped military internees.

LEGAL PROFILES

Florian Imer, a major in the Swiss army, was head of the legal services for internment. He was born in Switzerland in 1898 and completed his legal studies there. From 1926 to 1933, he was the chief justice of a district court. He then became a judge on the canton's supreme court in Bern, a position he held until 1968. In 1950 and 1954, he was the chief judge. He also headed the local lawyers' association and authored a number of historical works. He died in 1981.[160]

Lloyd A. Free, captain, U.S. Army, was a member of the military attaché's office in Bern. He was born in California in 1908 and started his legal practice there. He decided to switch careers and found a job in international broadcasting in London. He then taught internal affairs for

---

159. *See* Letter from Dep't of the Air Force to Daniel Culler, Technical Sergeant (Apr. 15, 1996).
160. *See Florian Imer*, HISTORICAL DICTIONARY OF SWITZERLAND.

several years and became involved in public opinion surveys before joining the Foreign Broadcast Monitoring Service during the war, which
helped to predict German offensives by monitoring German broadcasts.
He then served in Switzerland in the U.S. military attaché's office. After
the war, he worked with the United Nations on mass communications
as well as with the U.S. State Department on polling techniques to
understand the political climate in countries around the world. In 1968,
he coauthored *The Political Beliefs of Americans*, demonstrating Americans'
belief in small government but big government programs. He ran the
School of Public and International Affairs at Princeton until his retirement. He died in 1996.[161]

Allen W. Dulles was the Office of Strategic Services (OSS) agent stationed in Switzerland at the American Legation during this time; he was
also a lawyer. He was born in New York in 1893 and started his legal
practice there. Prior to beginning the practice of law, he joined the U.S.
diplomatic corps, serving in Europe during and after WWI, including at
the Paris Peace Conference. The brother, nephew, and grandson of past
and future U.S. secretaries of state, Dulles joined the Council on Foreign
Relations in 1927. He then served overseas in several diplomatic posts.
He was an adviser at the Geneva Disarmament Conference from 1932
to 1933 and authored books on international neutrality. In 1938, he
unsuccessfully ran for Congress, arguing against the isolationist trend in
U.S. politics. He was in Bern, Switzerland, during the war, cultivating
contacts, creating an espionage network, and gathering intelligence on
German plans, activities, and munitions. He helped negotiate the surrender of the German army in Italy in 1945. In 1950, he became the deputy
director and in 1953 the first civilian director of the newly formed Central Intelligence Agency (CIA). He was involved in many CIA missions
during the early Cold War era, until he retired in 1961. He served on the
Warren Commission investigating the assassination of President John F.
Kennedy. He died in 1969.[162]

161. See *Lloyd A. Free, 88, Is Dead; Revealed Political Paradox*, N.Y. Times (Nov. 14, 1996).
162. See *Allen W. Dulles, CIA Director from 1953 to 1961, Dies at 75*, N.Y. Times (Jan. 31, 1969).

2. Refugees

Refugees from Germany were the subject of a 1936 international agreement assuring grace periods before deportation to their country of origin;[163] Switzerland ratified this agreement in 1937. However, after the Anschluss triggered more refugees, Switzerland issued a federal decree in March 1938 requiring a visa for Austrians entering Switzerland.[164] Later, all refugees without visas were expelled.[165] Then, in September 1938, Switzerland and Germany entered an "agreement" concerning the admission into Switzerland of German Jewish citizens: instead of a visa, these citizens would have a *J* stamped in their passports to identify them at border crossings and would only be allowed to cross the border if they had authorization to enter Switzerland.[166] On top of these many limitations on refugees, Switzerland attempted to limit the number of "undesirable" refugees by further copying some Nazi racial practices, including limitations on other German non-Aryans.[167] On the other hand, desirable refugees, such as out-of-favor German industrialist Fritz Thyssen, were allowed to remain.

As the plight of certain people worsened due to increasingly severe racial laws in Nazi Germany and a large number of countries overrun or annexed by the Nazis, several Swiss stepped in to break the rules and help refugees enter the country. Two such heroes were Paul Grüninger, the local police captain in St. Gallen, and Recha Sternbuch, who worked with Grüninger.

To address the potential issue of an escalating number of refugees entering a relatively small country surrounded by Axis powers with no country as a final destination, Heinrich Rothmund, head of the Swiss federal police, issued a directive in the late summer of 1938 to close the borders to anyone without a valid visa. Grüninger, the president of the Swiss police association and a WWI veteran, responded to the increase in Austrians leaving their country after the Anschluss by ignoring Rothmund's directive and assisting the Austrian refugees in successfully entering and remaining in Switzerland. Grüninger not only helped guide them personally but also issued them temporary and residence visas and linked them up with refugee organizations inside the country. To get around the legal limitations of the law, he changed the dates of entry

---

163. Provisional Agreement on the Legal Status of German Refugees, July 4, 1936.
164. Federal Council Decree (Mar. 28, 1938) (Switz.).
165. Federal Council Decree (Aug. 19, 1938) (Switz.).
166. German-Swiss Protocol, Ger.-Switz., Sept. 29, 1938.
167. Federal Council Decree (Oct. 4, 1938) (Switz.).

into the country so that it appeared that the refugees entered the country in advance of the August 20, 1938, deadline for closing the border. When he was finally arrested in April 1939 and ousted from his job while awaiting trial, he had saved more than two thousand refugees who would have certainly perished had they been turned back.

Grüninger was charged with altering the dates on documents to make them appear that the refugees had entered the country before the new regulations went into effect. He was formally accused of giving false information to his supervisor and forging official documents. The court found him guilty of changing the date on a single refugee's passport. He was fined a small amount plus court costs. Due to his arrest and conviction, he was not able find work during and after the legal investigation and trial and lost his pension. But toward the end of his life in the late 1960s, after articles and television shows publicized his heroics, he earned worldwide acclaim for his actions. His legal rehabilitation took much longer as it was not until 1995 that the same court in St. Gallen that had sentenced him in 1940 voided his conviction.

Another Swiss who was very active in assisting refugees was Recha Sternbuch. She helped fund and organize refugees who were trying to enter the country by working with canton officials such as Paul Grüninger. She was able to help thousands of refugees from Germany, France, and Austria enter her country, directing their escapes by organizing networks of local citizens to assist. She was arrested in 1939 and charged with bribery and accessory to a crime. She was briefly imprisoned and lost a child during this several-year investigation and trial. In the end, the case against her fell apart due to lack of evidence. She subsequently worked globally to save victims of the Holocaust, including soliciting the help of former Swiss president Jean-Marie Musy in negotiating with the Nazis in the closing days of the war to save thousands in concentration camps from extermination.

LEGAL PROFILES

Heinrich Rothmund was the director of the federal Police Division who closed the border to illegal refugees. He was born in Switzerland in 1888 and completed his legal studies there. During WWI, he was involved in federal economic efforts related to the war economy. In 1919, he was appointed to head the federal Police for Foreigners department. In 1929, he became director of the federal police division under the Federal Department of Justice and Police. He attended numerous international refugee conferences representing Switzerland, including the 1938 Evian International Refugee Conference on German refugees. He wrote the presidential decree that closed the borders to all refugees in August 1942.[168] He held these positions until 1954, except for some postwar work dealing with the Intergovernmental Committee on Refugees/U.N. International Refugee Organization. He died in 1961.[169]

Jean-Marie Musy was the former president of Switzerland who helped negotiate the release of concentration camp inmates; he was also a lawyer. He was born in Switzerland in 1876 and completed his legal studies there. He worked as attorney general in his home canton and then in private practice. In 1914, he was elected to the National Council. In 1919, he was elected to the Federal Council, where he was responsible for the Finance and Customs Department; he remained on the council until 1934. He was twice the president of Switzerland, in 1925 and 1930. It was his contacts and relationships with the Nazis, including Heinrich Himmler, that facilitated the deal for the prisoners in 1945. He died in 1952.[170]

3. Looted Assets

Switzerland provided a number of economic benefits to the belligerents during the war. Although the Hague Convention of 1907 required that Switzerland not give preference economically to either side,[171] in reality it was Swiss exports, financial credits backed by government guarantees, and currency trading that helped to facilitate the Nazi war effort.

---

168. Federal Council Presidential Decree (Aug. 13, 1942) (Switz.).
169. *See Heinrich Rothmund*, HISTORISCHES LEXIKON DER SCHWEIZ.
170. *See Jean-Marie Musy*, THE FEDERAL AUTHORITIES OF THE SWISS CONFEDERATION.
171. Hague Convention Respecting the Rights and Duties of Neutral Powers and Persons in Case of War on Land art. 9, Oct. 18, 1907.

Being surrounded geographically by Axis powers by the summer of 1940 and reliant on imports for food and exports for jobs, Switzerland turned primarily to Germany as a key trading partner (in some industries, such as aluminum, exclusively). The Swiss feeling was that as long as Switzerland did not exploit new business opportunities that were created by the war, continuing business relationships with Germany was acceptable under the spirit of neutrality. On August 9, 1940, Switzerland made an agreement with Nazi Germany for mutual economic cooperation, which included clearing loans and shipments of electricity, aluminum, machines, arms, munitions, and food to Germany in exchange for coal and steel and reducing exports to the United Kingdom. In response, the United States blocked exports into occupied Europe, including Switzerland, and froze its assets in America (see Chapter 3).

As the war turned in late 1943, Switzerland reluctantly reached agreements with the Allies to reduce arms sales to Germany. It reduced some strategic exports to Germany, closed some of its tunnels through the Alps to transshipment in late 1944, and stopped coal and iron transits in early 1945. With American demands that it stop exports and transshipments to Germany, the Swiss government finally restricted transit and froze German assets in Switzerland in early 1945, although it did not stop all commercial transactions.[172]

Despite all of its activities undertaken to maintain neutrality, Switzerland was accused of quite a number of legal and moral crimes in the economic sector due to its geographic proximity to Axis powers, its bank secrecy laws, and its continued business and financial transactions with Nazi Germany throughout the war. As documented in three major studies in the late twentieth century (commonly called the *Bergier Report*, the *Eizenstat Report*, and the *Volcker Report*), these accusations included the following:

- Buying "monetary" gold from Nazi Germany that was looted from the central banks of occupied countries
- Buying "nonmonetary" gold from Nazi Germany that included gold taken from victims of the Holocaust, including personal possessions and dental fillings
- Not returning the financial assets of Holocaust and other war victims

---

172. Federal Council Decree (Feb. 16, 1945) (Switz.).

- Selling Swiss francs and providing credit to Nazi Germany to purchase raw materials and armament, thereby prolonging the war
- Providing Germany electrical power and use of its railways for transshipments to assist with the Nazi war effort
- Receiving works of art and other cultural assets stolen from Nazi-occupied countries
- Selling securities stolen by the Nazis on the Swiss stock exchange
- Camouflaging the ownership of German companies by "Swissifying" them
- Using slave labor directly through German subsidiaries of Swiss companies or indirectly financing its use
- Not paying insurance claims on the lives of Holocaust victims[173]

This section deals with the cases involving financial assets stolen from countries and from some individual victims, including Holocaust victims, that were received, stored, and hidden in Switzerland. Although the actions occurred during the war, the resolution of these issues occurred after the war, in some cases many decades later. Swiss resistance to restitution of these assets, even though they were not material to the net worth of the institutions involved, has only recently diminished. (The *Volcker Report*, based on a detailed audit, showed that approximately 1 percent of Swiss bank accounts open during the war period probably or possibly could be related to victims of Nazi aggression, although only 60 percent of those could be identified,[174] in part because the largest Swiss commercial bank was accused of destroying evidence of such accounts—discussed below in Subsection b.)

a. Looted Assets of Countries and Individuals

To ensure that Germany could not use its assets to fund its war efforts, the United States initially froze German assets in the United States and prevented trading with that country (see Chapter 3). As the war progressed, the concern

---

173. INDEP. COMM'N OF EXPERTS SWITZ.—SECOND WORLD WAR, SWITZERLAND, NATIONAL SOCIALISM AND THE SECOND WORLD WAR (2002) [hereinafter *Bergier Report*]; U.S. DEP'T OF STATE, U.S. AND ALLIED EFFORTS TO RECOVER AND RESTORE GOLD AND OTHER ASSETS STOLEN OR HIDDEN BY GERMANY DURING WORLD WAR II (1997) [hereinafter *Eizenstat Report*]; INDEP. COMM. OF EMINENT PERSONS, U.S. AND ALLIED EFFORTS TO RECOVER AND RESTORE GOLD AND OTHER ASSETS STOLEN OR HIDDEN BY GERMANY DURING WORLD WAR II (1999) [hereinafter *Volcker Report*].
174. *Volcker Report, supra*, at 23.

changed from quarantining German assets to help pay for reparations and restitution after the war to returning any stolen assets to their owners and ensuring that that Nazism did not arise again elsewhere, funded by these stolen assets. Starting in early 1943, Allied officials sent out warnings to neutral countries that Nazi gold was looted and any purchases of it would not be recognized as valid, noting that "[t]his warning applies whether such transfers or dealings have taken the form of open looting or plunder, or of transactions apparently legal in form, even when they purport to be voluntarily effected."[175]

The Swiss National Bank commissioned Dietrich Schindler Sr. to analyze this situation. His report stated that under the Hague Convention of 1907, occupying powers were entitled to seize monetary assets and valuables that belonged to the occupied states (although not those belonging to private individuals).[176] Thus, Switzerland could buy gold looted by the Nazis as it now had legal title, if such purchases were done in good faith. The report proposed that to support good faith, a declaration was required with the purchase that it had not been acquired by any means that might be in contravention of international law.

Unofficially at first and then officially at the Bretton Woods Conference in 1944, the Safehaven project was launched to prevent Nazi assets from being transferred to and hidden in neutral countries.[177] In August 1944, Switzerland first agreed to stop selling certain key items to Germany[178] and then in March 1945 to freeze German assets in Switzerland and stop purchasing Nazi gold:[179]

> The Swiss Government . . . affirms its decision to oppose that the territory of Switzerland . . . be used for the concealment or the receiving of assets taken illegally or under duress during the war. It further declares that every opportunity will be given to dispossessed owners to claim in Switzerland . . . any property found there.[180]

---

175. *See* Inter-Allied "London" Declaration Against Acts of Dispossession Committed in Territories Under Enemy Occupation or Control (Jan. 5, 1943); Declaration on Gold Purchases (Feb. 22, 1944).
176. Dietrich Schindler Sr., Expert Opinion (July 22, 1944).
177. United Nations Monetary and Financial "Bretton Woods" Conference Resolution VI, July–Aug. 1944.
178. US-UK-Swiss War Trade Agreement, U.S.-U.K.-Switz., Aug. 14, 1944.
179. Currie Mission Agreement with Switzerland, Mar. 8, 1945.
180. *Id.*

Switzerland subsequently reneged on this agreement, purportedly because it violated its neutrality.

The Allied Control Council (see Chapter 8), which governed postwar Germany, decided to stake a claim to all external German assets.[181] At the Potsdam Conference in July 1945, the leaders of the wartime Allies agreed that German gold would be collected for return to those countries from which it had been stolen. Thus, at the Paris Conference on Reparation in late 1945, the Tripartite Gold Commission consisting of the United States, the United Kingdom, and France was created to pool the gold looted from countries and allocate to each claimant country a proportionate amount.[182]

During the war, Switzerland, under the principle of legal certainty that a good faith purchase should not later be invalidated by subsequent information, had effectively done nothing to inventory or to stop the import or export of stolen assets. Finally bowing to domestic pressure from the Swiss Bankers Association and the Swiss Art Dealers Association, the Federal Council finally issued its Decree on Looted Assets in 1945.[183] This decree allowed claims for restitution of lost property when the person had been robbed or had surrendered his property as a result of fraud or threat. However, this decree set up a short two-year window for claims, it applied only to threats during the years 1939 to 1945, it did not include nonoccupied territories such as Germany and Austria, and it required that the property be located in Switzerland. It also did not initiate any investigations, so a subsequent decree created the Swiss Clearing Office.[184]

The Swiss National Bank was accused of buying gold from Nazis that was stolen both from occupied countries and from individual victims: it was estimated that the bank received and held up to $400 million (approximately $5 billion today) of looted gold, both of its own account and for other neutral countries, by the end of the war. Subsequent negotiations with the Swiss, who strongly denied the existence of much of the looted gold and other Nazi-

---

181. Allied Control Council Law No. 5 (Oct. 30 1945).
182. "Paris" Agreement on Reparations from Germany, on the Establishment of an Inter-Allied Reparation Agency and on the Restitution of Monetary Gold, U.S.-U.K.-Fr., Jan. 14, 1946.
183. Federal Council Decree on Looted Assets Concerning Legal Actions Raised for the Return of Assets Seized in Occupied Territories, Raubgutbeschluss (Dec. 10, 1945) (Switz.).
184. Federal Council Decree (Feb. 22, 1946) (Switz.).

owned assets as well as the international basis for expropriating Swiss assets for the benefit of rebuilding Europe, were difficult.

Created in late 1945, the Inter-Allied Reparations Agency called on the lead Allied countries to open negotiations with the Swiss. The resulting agreement at the 1946 Washington Conference specified that if Switzerland made a payment to offset its gold purchase from the German Reichsbank—the original estimate of up to $400 million in looted gold was reduced to a Swiss liability of $58 million—the Allies would waive "all claims against the Government of Switzerland and the Swiss National Bank in connection with gold acquired during the war from Germany by Switzerland."[185] The Swiss also agreed to liquidate the other assets owned in Switzerland by Germans living in Germany. Half of the proceeds were to go to war reparations and half to the Swiss. In addition, the Swiss agreed to search for and use heirless assets in its possession for victims of the war. The United States agreed to lift the freeze on Swiss assets in America and to stop blacklisting Swiss companies. There was no agreement on the sale proceeds of Nazi businesses in Switzerland, estimated at $250 to $500 million.

Although the Swiss made their payment for gold to the Tripartite Gold Commission and the blacklists and asset freezes were lifted, the sale of German assets never took place for a number of reasons, including Switzerland's desire to protect the assets of its German clients. Therefore, a new agreement was created in 1952 that included the new German government.[186] This agreement required a one-time payment to the Allies of $28 million, the exact amount received by Switzerland from Germany in a parallel treaty.[187] It was not until 1962, when the Swiss Federal Council finally issued its registration decree, that its commitment regarding heirless assets was initiated.[188] This decree required the reporting of "any assets whose last-known owners were foreign nationals or stateless persons of whom nothing had been heard since 9 May 1945 and

---

185. Allied-Swiss Accord, May 26, 1946.

186. Allied-Swiss Agreement on Liquidation of German Property, Revising 1946 Washington Accord, Aug. 28, 1952.

187. German-Swiss Agreement on Financing German Debt to Switzerland, Ger.-Switz., Aug. 26, 1952.

188. Federal Council Decree, Assets Situated in Switzerland Belonging to Foreigners or Stateless Persons Persecuted for Reasons of Race, Religion, or Political Beliefs (Dec. 20, 1962) (Switz.).

who were known or presumed to have been victims of racial, religious, or political persecution."[189]

The Swiss National Bank was subsequently sued in the late 1990s for its role in the purchase of gold looted by Nazi Germany from occupied countries.[190] The suit, *Rosenberg v. Swiss National Bank*, alleged that the bank had knowingly accepted looted assets, primarily stolen gold, from Nazi Germany. Given the postwar statements by German Reichsbank deputy governor Emil Puhl at his Nuremberg trial (see Chapter 6) that the Swiss were aware that they were receiving looted gold from Germany, the charge was difficult to deny.[191] In its press release response, the bank claimed that "we contest the competence of the US courts in our case."[192] Furthermore, it said, "The Swiss National Bank is a public institution, not a commercial bank. Its gold transactions during the Second World War were the subject of a binding agreement under international law, the so-called Washington Agreement of 1946."[193] The bank did set up the Special Fund for Needy Victims of the Holocaust/Shoa in 1997 and funded it with CHF100 million but did not admit to liability beyond the Washington Agreement. The Rosenberg lawsuit was settled in conjunction with the sweeping settlement in the following Holocaust case, for which the Swiss National Bank declined to provide any funding.[194]

LEGAL PROFILES

Dietrich Schindler Sr. was the Swiss professor who analyzed the situation for the Swiss National Bank when the Allies sent warnings to Switzerland in 1943 about the invalidity of Nazi looted gold. He was born in Switzerland in 1890 and completed his legal studies there and

---

189. *Id.*

190. Rosenberg v. Swiss Nat'l Bank, Case No. 98-cv-01647 (U.S.D.C., filed June 29, 1998).

191. Press Release, Swiss National Bank, Swiss National Bank's Gold Transactions with the German Reichsbank from 1939 to 1945 (1984).

192. Press Release, Swiss National Bank, Swiss National Bank Opposes Intended Class Action in the USA (Apr. 3, 1998).

193. *Id.*

194. Press Release, Swiss National Bank, Swiss National Bank Will Not Contribute to Bank Settlement (Aug. 21, 1998).

in Berlin, including a year at Harvard. In 1927, he started teaching at the University of Zurich, where he eventually became a professor in the department of constitutional and administrative law. Later, he became a professor of international law and legal philosophy. He was the longtime legal adviser to the Swiss Federal Council. An author of several books, including one on constitutional law, Schindler was involved in local and cantonal politics and the Red Cross. He was a delegate to the Washington Conference in 1946. He died in 1948.[195]

Samuel Klaus was responsible for the Safehaven project; he was also an attorney. He was born in New York in 1904 and completed his legal studies there. He worked for the federal government, first the Treasury Department from 1934 and then the State Department. After his time on the Safehaven project, he worked on Operation Paperclip, bringing German scientists to America in order to prevent Soviet access to them, through the Joint Intelligence Objectives Agency. He was involved in the Joseph McCarthy anti-Communism hearings in the 1950s, supposedly identifying Soviet agents and Communists working in the State Department. He was also involved in trying to bring justice to surviving U.S. airmen from the air force transport that was shot down over the Soviet Union in 1958. He died in 1963.[196]

Georges Sauser-Hall helped draft the Decree on Looted Assets. He was born in Switzerland in 1884 and completed his legal studies there. After teaching law, he was the general counsel to the political department from 1915 to 1924. From 1924 to 1954, he was a professor of civil, comparative, and international private law at the University of Geneva. He served the government of Turkey between 1925 and 1931, was named a member of the Permanent Court of Arbitration in The Hague in 1946, and was named to the commission of arbitration settling financial issues between Germany and the Allies in 1956. He defended Switzerland before the International Court of Justice many times. His

---

195. *See Dietrich Schindler Sr.*, HISTORISCHES LEXIKON DER SCHWEIZ.
196. *See Samuel Klaus, 58, Legal U.S. Legal Adviser*, N.Y. TIMES (Aug. 3, 1963).

book *A Guide to Swiss Politics* has remained popular through many editions. He died in 1966.[197]

Randolph E. Paul was the lead U.S. negotiator in the 1946 Washington Conference negotiations and an attorney. He was born in New Jersey in 1890 and started his legal practice in New York. He focused on tax law, which he practiced from 1918 to 1940, advising a number of prominent clients. He also taught law at Yale. In 1940, he became a director of the Federal Reserve Bank of New York. After the war began, he joined the Treasury Department, eventually as the general counsel for the Office of Foreign Funds. He was instrumental in starting the War Refugee Board.[198] After the war, in addition to representing the United States in the negotiations with the Swiss, he returned to private practice and teaching. He died in 1956.[199]

Walter Stucki was the lead Swiss negotiator in the 1946 Washington Conference negotiations and an attorney. He was born in Switzerland in 1888 and completed his legal studies there, becoming a patent attorney. In 1917, he was the secretary general for the Federal Department of Economic Affairs. Beginning in 1924, he headed the international negotiating team for this department, negotiating many agreements and representing the country before becoming a minister. He was elected to the National Assembly in 1935. He was appointed by the Federal Council as a delegate for trade agreements. From 1938 to 1944, he was the Swiss ambassador to France, which eventually became Vichy France. Here, he was able to assist with the evacuation of Vichy upon the approach of Allied forces and the retreat of Axis forces in 1944. After the Washington Conference, he continued to represent Switzerland in international conferences. He died in 1963.[200]

---

197. *See Georges Sauser-Hall*, Historisches Lexikon der Schweiz.
198. Exec. Order No. 9417 (Jan. 22, 1944).
199. *See Randolph E. Paul Dies at Hearing*, N.Y. Times (Feb. 7, 1956).
200. *See Walter Stucki*, Historisches Lexikon der Schweiz.

b. Looted Assets of Holocaust Victims

After the end of the Cold War and the release of interim and final reports from the Bergier Commission, lawsuits were filed against Swiss financial firms, calling on them to account for their actions during and after the war. Several suits were eventually consolidated into a single action, *In re Holocaust Victim Assets Litigation*.[201] After long negotiations and threats of the loss of business licenses where these firms operated very profitably on an international basis, a settlement was finally reached. It was very comprehensive in scope, intended to potentially resolve all war-related issues at once.

This case began as four separate suits.[202] The plaintiffs' allegations were that

> before and during World War II, they were subjected to persecution by the Nazi regime, including genocide, wholesale and systematic looting of personal and business property and slave labor. . . . [I]n knowingly retaining and concealing the assets of Holocaust victims, accepting and laundering illegally obtained Nazi loot and transacting in the profits of slave labor, Swiss institutions and entities, including the named defendants, collaborated with and aided the Nazi regime in furtherance of war crimes, crimes against humanity, crimes against peace, slave labor and genocide.[203]

The plaintiffs also alleged that

> defendants breached fiduciary and other duties; breached contracts; converted plaintiffs' property; enriched themselves unjustly; were negligent; violated customary international law, Swiss banking law and the Swiss commercial code of obligations; engaged in fraud and conspiracy; and concealed relevant facts from the named plaintiffs and the plaintiff class members in an effort to frustrate plaintiffs' ability to pursue their claims.[204]

---

201. *In re* Holocaust Victim Assets Litig., 105 F. Supp. 2d 139 (E.D.N.Y. 2000).
202. Sonabend v. Union Bank of Switz., CV 96-5161 (E.D.N.Y. 1996); Trilling-Grotch v. Union Bank of Switz., CV 96-5161 (E.D.N.Y. 1996); Weisshaus v. Union Bank of Switz., CV 96-4849 (E.D.N.Y. 1996); World Council of Orthodox Jewish Cmtys. v. Union Bank of Switz., CV 97-0461 (E.D.N.Y. 1997).
203. *In re Holocaust Victim Assets Litig.*, 105 F. Supp. 2d at 141.
204. *Id.*

As a result of these acts, the plaintiffs sought "an accounting, disgorgement, compensatory and punitive damages, and declaratory and other appropriate relief."[205]

Under the settlement agreement, the defendants agreed to pay $1.25 billion and give up potential defenses, such as justiciability of the dispute, whether plaintiffs' claims are barred under foreign law, whether plaintiffs lack standing, and whether plaintiffs' claims are barred under the statute of limitations.[206] For issues of fairness, the settlement balanced the amounts to be paid against the legal uncertainties and the dwindling life spans of the victims.

Per the agreement, the settlement benefited "persons recognized as targets of systematic Nazi oppression on the basis of race, religion or personal status."[207] Thus, the settlement was explicitly designed to benefit targets of systematic Nazi persecution on the basis of race, religion, or personal status: Jews, homosexuals, Jehovah's Witnesses, the disabled, and Romani. The refugee beneficiaries included victims of Nazi persecution who did not suffer injury as a result of the conduct of the defendant banks.

The settlement beneficiaries were split into the following classes:

- *Deposited Assets Class:* Victims or targets of Nazi persecution and their heirs who had deposited assets at one of the defendants' banks and sought relief in regard to those assets
- *Looted Assets Class:* Victims or targets of Nazi persecution and their heirs whose assets were looted (stolen, expropriated, Aryanized, confiscated, or wrongly taken) or cloaked (owned by a German or German-controlled company whose identity was disguised) and who sought relief in regard to those assets
- *Slave Labor Class I:* Victims or targets of Nazi persecution and their heirs "who actually or allegedly performed slave labor for companies . . . that actually or allegedly deposited the revenues or proceeds of that labor with, or transacted such revenues or proceeds through, releasees," and who sought relief in regard to those revenues or proceeds or cloaked assets

---

205. *Id.*
206. *In re* Holocaust Victim Assets Litig., Class Action Settlement Agreement (Jan. 26, 1999).
207. *Id.*

- *Slave Labor Class II*: Individuals and their heirs "who actually or allegedly performed slave labor at any facility or work site, wherever located, actually or allegedly owned, controlled or operated by any corporation . . . headquartered, organized or based in Switzerland or any affiliate thereof," and who sought relief in regard to such labor "claims against any releasee other than settling defendants, the Swiss National Bank, and other Swiss banks"
- *Refugee Class*: Victims or targets of Nazi persecution and their heirs "who sought entry into Switzerland in whole or in part to avoid Nazi persecution and who actually or allegedly either were denied entry into Switzerland or, after gaining entry, were deported, detained, abused or otherwise mistreated," and who seek relief against any releasee "relating to or arising in any way from such actual or alleged denial of entry, deportation, detention, abuse or other mistreatment"[208]

Although the suit named only the three largest Swiss commercial banks as defendants, the settlement agreement included releases for many more parties not named as defendants, including the Swiss National Bank, the Swiss Confederation and its political subunits, and a large number of Swiss industrial firms. Apparently, all Swiss firms that had potential liabilities based on their conduct during the war wanted to ensure that they received a release. The plaintiffs agreed to release not only the defendants but also Swiss governmental and business entities. The "releasees" were to be discharged for any and all claims relating to "the Holocaust, World War II, and its prelude and aftermath, victims or targets of Nazi persecution, transactions with or actions of or in connection with the Nazi regime, treatment by the Swiss Confederation or other releasees of refugees fleeing persecution, or any related cause or thing whatever."[209] The settlement resolved not only the four cases that were consolidated into this single case but also several other cases, including the *Rosenberg* case against the National Bank of Switzerland described in the previous subsection and a case filed in California.[210]

---

208. *Id.*
209. *Id.*
210. Markovicova v. Union Bank of Switz., Case No. C98-2924 (N.D. Cal. 1998).

This settlement agreement was not the end of the matter. Several more times, the judge who helped fashion this agreement was called upon to clarify its terms. In 2004, while noting that approximately $600 million had been distributed to the victims under the settlement, the clearly irritated judge wrote that

> the bank defendants have filed a series of frivolous and offensive objections to the distribution process. . . . These objections bring to mind the theory that, "if you tell a lie big enough and keep repeating it, people will eventually come to believe it." The "Big Lie" for the Swiss banks is that during the Nazi era and its wake, the banks never engaged in substantial wrongdoing. . . . These statements continually distort and obscure the truth.[211]

Quoting a member of the Bergier Commission, the independent body of experts from several countries tasked with looking into Swiss financial transactions during the war, the judge said,

> The Swiss banks acted with an eye to their own bottom line . . . systematically put aside the interests of the clients they had so ardently solicited with assurances that their assets would be kept safe for them and theirs, in favor of business interests they perceived at that moment to be more promising.[212]

Quoting the *Bergier Report* on what happened after the Nazis overran Poland and then requested that money owned by Poles be transferred to Germany, the judge noted that

> although there were legal and moral objections to transferring the funds, the consideration that they "still had important interests in Germany, and should avoid friction and unpleasantness whenever possible" prevailed and they complied with the request and opted for the principle of carry-

---

211. *In re* Holocaust Victim Assets Litig., 302 F. Supp. 2d 59 (E.D.N.Y. 2004).
212. *Id.* at 62.

ing out legally signed orders even when they were not received directly from customers, but via the Reichsbank in Berlin. . . . These banks did not decide to order forced transfers because they thought it would serve their clients well.[213]

This was contrary to both the advice of their legal departments and Swiss court decisions, the judge added.

The court noted that stonewalling ("entrench[ing] themselves behind banking secrecy") actually benefited the Swiss banks in three ways: avoidance of liability for improper acts; an increase in their reputations as defenders of property rights; and, in particular, direct financial benefits.[214] "Unlike other countries (such as the United States) where dormant assets are transferred to state governments, in Switzerland dormant assets remain indefinitely with the banks," noted the court, quoting from the *Volcker Report*. The court added, quoting from the *Bergier Report*, that

> Unclaimed safe-deposit boxes and safeguard deposits generated income from the fees charged and—in the case of interest-bearing assets—commission earnings. The banks lost nothing if the dormancy persisted; on the contrary, the monies entrusted to them that affected the balance sheet continued to improve their interest balance—particularly as the banks usually stopped paying interest on the dormant accounts.[215]

The court noted that under Swiss law, documents could be destroyed after ten years regardless of whether the bank was open or closed. Based on the findings in the *Bergier Report*, the *Eizenstat Report*, and the *Volcker Report*, the strategy employed by the Swiss banks was to stonewall up to the ten-year limitation period, destroy the documents that would prove the existence of the bank accounts, and not retain any lists of destroyed records as required under Swiss law. In addition, as fees were continuously being charged on these dormant accounts, the accounts would eventually be reduced to a zero balance and closed. The court, referring to the *Volcker Report* of bank audits, noted that only 60 percent of the bank accounts open from 1933 to 1945 in Swiss banks

213. *Id.* at 63.
214. *Id.* at 67.
215. *Id.* at 66.

had records and many of those were minimal. In spite of a Federal Council decree in 1996 to preserve all such records, document destruction continued. (One particularly well-known case involved Christoph Meili, a Swiss security guard who saved documents illegally destined for a shredder and turned them over to a Jewish organization; he then sought asylum in the United States after becoming the object of an investigation for violating bank secrecy laws.)

Because of such activities, potential Deposited Assets Class claimants were having trouble documenting their ownership of Swiss bank accounts. The court stated that there was to be an adverse inference against the banks as the destroyers of much of the evidence that claimants would use, from the forced transfers during the war to stonewalling thereafter. In supporting the current distribution process being used, the judge noted that he had

> ignored the recurring submissions of the Swiss banks, because, as they acknowledge, the banks have "no role in the settlement distribution process." The amount of their liability is fixed and the distribution is being administered by the court. Their objections on this score are therefore legally irrelevant and their only purpose has been to burden the record with spin and distortion. The banks' last submission, however, was one too many.[216]

The 2004 memorandum and order was the judge's response.

In 2010, the judge noted that more than $1 billion had been distributed to almost half a million claimants.[217] However, in terms of the Deposited Assets Class, the banks had destroyed records on 2.8 million of the 6.8 million accounts open during the period 1933 to 1945, and most transactional records were destroyed on the other 4 million accounts. As such, to pay out to the Deposited Assets Class members, presumptive (average) account balance techniques were used. New information and new techniques became available, increasing the amounts of the average account balances; the court recognized and mandated these techniques for the Deposited Assets Class claims process and thus allocated additional funds from the settlement amounts (previously earmarked for the other classes) to the Deposited Assets Class.

---

216. *Id.* at 85.
217. *In re* Holocaust Victim Assets Litig., 731 F. Supp. 2d 279 (E.D.N.Y. 2010).

C. Subsequent Events

After the war, two individuals took their cases directly to the Swiss for resolution.

Joseph Spring (originally Josef Sprung), who was born in Berlin to a Polish Jewish family, was sent to live in Belgium with his relatives. After the German invasion, he moved to France, procuring French identity papers as Joseph Dubois. With his cousins, he tried to escape into Switzerland in November 1943. After the Swiss would not let him in, he was caught by German guards and sent to concentration camps. In 1998, he brought a legal action in Switzerland, but the Swiss Federal Council rejected his claims due to the passage of time and the lack of substantive legal foundation. The Swiss Federal Supreme Court also rejected his claims; however, it did help with his legal costs, although it refused to classify this as "compensation."

The Sonabend family likewise traveled from Belgium through France, trying to enter Switzerland to escape Nazi persecution. A watchmaker, Mr. Sonabend had the support of Swiss watchmakers in his application for refugee status. Nonetheless, the day after their arrival, the Swiss police captured the Jewish family with two small children and forced them back over the border into France. They were immediately captured by a German patrol on the French side of the border. The parents were sent to a concentration camp and murdered. The children, Charles and Sabine, survived, hidden for the remainder of the war. In 1998, they undertook legal action in Switzerland for minimal damages of CHF100,000 but the Swiss Federal Council rejected their claims, again for the passage of time and lack of substantive legal basis. Subsequently, the parties reached an out-of-court settlement.

D. Modern Applicability

Swiss secrecy is still a focus in modern times as various countries in Europe and America wrestle with the ongoing use of bank secrecy laws. That secrecy allows people to hide assets from their countries' taxing authorities. In Germany, authorities have recently purchased CDs with the names of German nationals who have used various entities and accounts in Switzerland to avoid German taxes; the CDs also contained instructions for Swiss bank employees on how to help their customers evade German taxes.[218] For years, the United States has also been pursuing information on American taxpayers who

---

218. *Swiss Banks Accused over Tax Evasions*, FIN. TIMES (Aug. 12, 2012).

use Swiss bank accounts to hide assets and therefore avoid paying American income tax on the funds.[219]

Refugee issues are another modern holdover from WWII. A major outcome of modern wars is the creation of refugees displaced by conflicts. The number of refugees fleeing conflicts globally is in the millions, with the majority currently in Somalia, Afghanistan, Sudan, Eritrea, Myanmar, Vietnam, the Democratic Republic of the Congo, and Iraq.[220] Refugees are not only victimized once by being displaced but are often then victimized again through crime and deprivation. Rules for dealing with refugees were created by the United Nations through the Convention Relating to the Status of Refugees in 1951. This convention defined a refugee as one who, "owing to well-founded fear of being persecuted for reasons of race, religion, nationality, membership of a particular social group or political opinion, is outside the country of his nationality and is unable, or owing to such fear, is unwilling to avail himself of the protection of that country."[221] Among other rights to be granted to refugees are access to courts; freedom of movement; the ability to transfer assets to a third country; nonimposition of special levies; and prohibition of expulsion "where his life or freedom would be threatened on account of his race, religion, nationality, membership of a particular social group or political opinion."[222] Various relief organizations worldwide, led by the Office of the United Nations High Commissioner for Refugees, now exist to deal with these peoples' many problems.

---

219. *Apologetic Swiss Banks Sweat It Out as U.S., Europe Mull Redress*, REUTERS (Aug. 12, 2012).
220. OFFICE OF THE UNITED NATIONS HIGH COMM'R FOR REFUGEES, UNHCR STATISTICAL ONLINE POPULATION DATABASE, 2011.
221. Convention Relating to the Status of Refugees, July 28, 1951.
222. *Id.*

CHAPTER 6

EUROPE: NAZI GERMANY

As noted in the previous chapter, there were a number of different legal regimes in WWII Europe, primarily categorized by the degree of autonomy the government had. That degree of autonomy largely was a response to the situation of the country vis-à-vis Nazi Germany. Those countries that were able to maintain a significant degree of physical inviolability were also able to maintain a good part of their prewar legal regime, but those that were overrun or annexed were not.

In Germany, the transition to Nazi Party power was essentially legally executed, but what came afterward was only partly based on the rule of law—and that soon broke down. The effective rule of law vanished, and the rule of totalitarian dictatorial powers arose in its place. This is not to say that legal issues did not arise, only that the statutes that were passed were themselves often the subjects of later trials. Although German government illegalities did not start with the Nazis (the Weimar Republic had been violating the Versailles Treaty through secret rearmament for many years), they soon became the norm. Many legal actions such as the passage of statutes and the decisions of courts were undertaken outside a normative process where laws are issued by a democratic government with inherent checks and balances.).

There were numerous legal issues that later resulted in prosecutions against members of the Nazi regime, which is not surprising given the illegal basis for much of the government's functions. The victorious Allies and the new Federal Republic of Germany conducted the postwar trials concerning Nazi actions, which occurred over the period from the 1930s to the end of the war. However, the response to these issues went on much longer, with some cases concerning war-related crimes continuing to this day.

This chapter focuses on the following legal issues: destruction of democratic institutions, subversion of judicial integrity, crimes against humanity and war crimes (medical experimentation, slave labor, murder of POWs, mass murder of civilians, plunder and exploitation of occupied countries, systematic destruction of cultural life), crimes against peace, conspiracy or common plan to commit these crimes, genocide, and privacy violations.

PROMINENT LAWYERS AND JUDGES IN THIS CHAPTER

Destruction of Democratic Institutions:

- Franz Gürtner (minister of justice)
- Wilhelm Frick (minister of the interior)
- Wilhelm Bünger (presiding judge)
- Paul Vogt (examining magistrate)
- Hans Gisevius (trial reporter)
- Roland Freisler (presiding judge)
- Fabian von Schlabrendorff (defendant)
- Klaus Bonhoeffer (defendant)
- Reinhold Frank (defendant)
- Hans John (defendant)
- Hans Koch (defendant)
- Berthold von Stauffenberg (defendant)
- Josef Wirmer (defendant)
- Thomas Dehler (chief prosecutor of political liberation ministry)

Subversion of Judicial Integrity:

- Helmuth von Moltke (defendant)
- Otto Thierack (minister of justice)
- James T. Brand (presiding judge)
- Telford Taylor (chief prosecutor)
- Charles M. La Follette (deputy chief prosecutor)
- Franz Schlegelberger (defendant)

- Egon Kubuschok (defense counsel)
- Oswald Rothaug (defendant)

Crimes Against Humanity and War Crimes:

- Wilhelm Stuckart (defendant)
- Hans Globke (assistant to Stuckart)
- Bessie Margolin (ordinance drafter)
- Robert Servatius (defense counsel)
- Walter B. Beals (presiding judge)
- Alfred Seidl (defense counsel)
- Otto Kranzbühler (defense counsel)
- Cecelia H. Goetz (associate counsel for prosecution)
- William J. Wilkins (judge)
- William Denson (prosecutor)
- Herbert Arthur (H. A.) Smith (defense expert)
- Herbert J. Strong (defense counsel)
- Josef Bühler (defendant)

Genocide:

- Rudolf Lange (Wannsee Conference participant)
- Gerhard Klopfer (Wannsee Conference participant)
- Gerhard Leibholz (former jurist)
- Bernhard Lösener (Nuremberg law drafter)
- Katherine B. Fite (drafter of London Charter)
- Geoffrey Lawrence (IMT judge)
- Hartley Shawcross (chief prosecutor)
- Henri de Vabres (IMT judge)
- François de Menthon (chief prosecutor)
- Iona Timofeevich Nikitchenko (IMT judge)
- Roman Andreyevich Rudenko (chief prosecutor)
- Benjamin Kaplan (indictment drafter)
- Robert Kempner (assistant trial counsel)
- Thomas J. Dodd (executive trial counsel)
- Franz Exner (defense counsel)
- Hermann Jahrreiß (defense counsel)
- Herbert Kraus (defense counsel)

- Hans Frank (defendant)
- Ernst Kaltenbrunner (defendant)
- Raphael Lemkin (convention drafter)

6.1 DESTRUCTION OF DEMOCRATIC INSTITUTIONS

A. Statutes

The National Socialist German Workers (Nazi) Party came fully into power in German politics in early 1933 at the very end of the Weimar Republic through a series of both legal and quasi-legal acts. Many circumstances played a significant role in making the political environment amenable for a Nazi takeover: Germany's loss in WWI; the instability of the Weimar Republic government; political incompetence; the untimely death of internationally-focused German statesman Gustav Stresemann (who helped reconcile Germany with France after WWI and was co-awarded the Nobel Peace Prize for his efforts); the overwhelming animosity between the Communists, the Social Democrats, and the Nazis; the general lawlessness surrounding political functioning; the militarist actions of the country's armed forces; industrialist complicity; intentional citizen ignorance; and the Great Depression. But it was the following legal acts that finally tipped the scales, allowing for the rapid descent from democratic to totalitarian rule.

1. Reichstag Fire Decree

Shortly before a national election and under mysterious circumstances, the building where the national parliament sat, the Reichstag, was destroyed by a fire. At that time, the Nazi Party was the largest but not the majority party in the lower house of the national legislature, and Hitler was the chancellor of Germany. The occasion of this fire gave rise to both a decree and a trial (discussed in the "Cases" subsection of this section).

The Decree of the Reich President for the Protection of the People and State was issued by the aged president of Germany, Paul von Hindenburg, but had been created by the Nazi machinery then in office.[1] Taking advantage of

---

1. Verordnung des Reichspräsidenten zum Schutz von Volk und Staat, Feb. 28, 1933 RGBI. I at 83 (Nazi Ger.).

the situation to claim that a Communist revolution was imminent, this Nazi-inspired decree was the beginning of the destruction of democratic institutions created in post-WWI Germany.

The decree called upon Article 48 of the German Constitution to defend against Communist acts of violence "that endanger that state."[2] Article 48 allowed that in the case of threats to public security and order, the president could take necessary measures to ensure their restoration, including suspending articles of the constitution that dealt with fundamental rights: Articles 114 (personal liberty), 115 (dwellings), 117 (privacy of communications), 118 (freedom of expression and the press), 123 (peaceable assembly), 124 (association), and 153 (payment for expropriation of property). Article 48 also gave the Reichstag the ability to demand the revocation of any measures taken under this article. The power of this article had been used on numerous occasions in the 1920s and 1930s to deal with the many problems of the country, especially when parliamentary majorities could not be found and it was easier to rule by presidential decree.

The first of the six sections of the Reichstag fire decree suspended those seven articles of the constitution that dealt with fundamental rights, thereby placing unlimited

[r]estrictions on personal liberty, on the right of free expression of opinion, including freedom of the press, on the right of assembly and the right of association, and violations of the privacy of postal, telegraphic, and telephonic communications, and warrants for house searches, orders for confiscations as well as restrictions on property.[3]

The decree also allowed the central government to take over the powers of any state government and required state and local governments to follow the decrees of the central government. In addition, it mandated a punishment of death instead of life imprisonment for crimes ranging from treason to damage to railways; likewise, attempts on the life of government officials or serious disturbances of the peace could be punishable by death. It was signed by von Hindenburg, Hitler, Wilhelm Frick (minister of the interior), and Franz Gürtner (minister of justice), to take effect immediately.

---

2. *Id.* art. 1.
3. *Id.*

2. Enabling Act

This decree was followed shortly by the Law to Remove the Distress of the People and the State.[4] Otherwise termed the Enabling Act, the preamble to this law stated that it met the requirements for revising the constitution and had the approval of both the Reichstag and the Reichsrat (upper house). The first article allowed the cabinet to enact national laws. The second article allowed these laws to deviate from the constitution but would not impact the Reichstag, the Reichsrat, or the office of the president. Article 3 allowed these laws to be drafted by the chancellor. Article 4 gave to the cabinet the authority to conclude and implement treaties. It was to be in effect for four years, until April 1, 1937 (although it was subsequently renewed in 1937 and 1941). It was signed by von Hindenburg, Hitler, Frick, Konstantin von Neurath (minister of foreign affairs), and Lutz von Krosigk (minister of finances), to take effect immediately.

Between the passage of this act and the Reichstag's last seating in 1942, the Reichstag passed only seven laws (the government itself passed nearly one thousand).[5] Although there were several single-party elections, the passage of this act effectively stopped the representative legislative function in Germany.

3. Treachery Decree

The Decree of the Reich President for Protection against Treacherous Attacks on the Government of the Nationalist Movement penalized anyone who wore a Nazi uniform or insignia while not a member of the party.[6] It also allowed incarceration for those who made untrue or exaggerated statements that could seriously harm the welfare or reputation of the Reich or the parties who supported the Reich. This was followed by a similar law later the following year, the Law Against Treacherous Attacks on the State and Party and for the Protection of Party Uniforms.[7]

4. Laws for the Nazi Party and Against Others' Parties

The Law Against the Establishment of Political Parties declared that the Nazi Party was the only party in the country, and it outlawed all parties except the

---

4. Gesetz zur Behebung der Not von Volk und Reich, Mar. 24, 1933 RGBl. I at 141 (Nazi Ger.).
5. DEUTSCHER BUNDESTAG, NATIONAL SOCIALISM (1933–1945).
6. Verordnung des Reichspräsidenten zur Abwehr heimtückischer Angriffe gegen die Regierung der nationalen Erhebung, Mar. 21, 1933 RGBl. I at 1933 (Nazi Ger.).
7. Gesetz gegen heimtückische Angriffe auf Staat und Partei und zum Schutz der Parteiuniformen, Dec. 20, 1934 (Nazi Ger.).

Nazi Party.[8] It was followed by the Law on Plebiscites, which gave the appearance of democratic rule to public votes that were otherwise effectively rigged.[9] These were followed by the Law to Safeguard the Unity of Party and State, which established the Nazi Party as "inseparable" from the German state and brought the SA (Sturmabteilung, a Nazi paramilitary organization) and the deputy führer into the government of the Reich.[10]

5. Laws Abolishing German Political Institutions

The German states were effectively stripped of representation through four acts. The first was the Act Establishing the Identity of the Länder with the Reich, which gave the power of the states (länder) to the central government.[11] The second was the Law Concerning the Reconstruction of the Reich, which dissolved the states' parliaments;[12] a later law, the Law on the Abolition of the Reichsrat, then dissolved their representation in the national government, the Reichsrat.[13] Then the Law Concerning the Highest State Office of the Reich was passed, which effectively merged the chancellor's office with that of the president.[14] The final three laws were passed even though they were expressly contrary to the provisions in the Enabling Act promising not to interfere with either of the national legislative chambers or the office of the president.

Upon von Hindenburg's death shortly thereafter, Hitler became the effective dictator of the country, as then confirmed by national referendum.

LEGAL PROFILES

Franz Gürtner was the minister of justice when the fire decree was passed. He was born in Germany in 1881 and completed his legal studies there. He served in WWI and then began a career in public service

---

8. Gesetz gegen die Neubildung von Parteien, July 14, 1933 RGBI. I at 479 (Nazi Ger.).
9. Gesetz über Volksabstimmung, July 14, 1933 (Nazi Ger.).
10. Gesetz zur Sicherung der Einheit von Partei und Staat, Dec. 1, 1933 RGBI. I at 1016 (Nazi Ger.).
11. Gesetz über die Gleichschaltung der Länder mit dem Reich, Mar. 31, 1933 RGBI. I at 153 (Nazi Ger.).
12. Gesetz über den Neuaufbau des Reiches, Jan. 30, 1934 (Nazi Ger.).
13. Gesetz über die Aufhebung des Reichsrats, Feb. 14, 1934 RGBI. I at 75 (Nazi Ger.).
14. Gesetz über das Staatsoberhaupt des Deutschen Reichs, Aug. 1, 1934 (Nazi Ger.).

in 1922 as the minister of justice for Bavaria. He served in this role for almost ten years, during which time he was able to influence the proceedings against Hitler for the failed 1923 Beer Hall Putsch (an attempt to overthrow the Weimar Republic) and get him released early from prison. This eventually led to Gürtner's appointment as the Reich minister for justice in 1932 and his retention by Hitler upon Hitler's ascendancy. He was involved in some attempts at limiting the atrocities around him but also was involved in giving legal support to others. He remained in this position until his death in early 1941.[15]

Wilhelm Frick was the minister of the interior who was responsible for many of these laws. He was born in Germany in 1877 and completed his legal studies there. His early legal career included working for local police departments. He worked as an assessor in Bavaria until becoming involved in the Beer Hall Putsch and serving time in prison. After being released, he was elected to the Reichstag in 1925, where he served until 1930. He was then appointed as the minister of the interior for the province of Thuringia. When Hitler rose to power, he appointed Frick as national minister of the interior. Beyond the laws described above, Frick was involved in drafting the racial Nuremberg Laws (see Section 6.4). He remained in this position until 1943, when he was replaced by Himmler, and oversaw Bohemia for the last part of the war. He was tried after the war for many crimes at the Nuremberg Trials (see Section 6.4), was found guilty, and then hanged in 1946.[16]

B. Cases

There were any number of challenges to the power of the Nazi state over the succeeding twelve years since the Nazis rose to power in 1933. Many challenges were met with the outright murder of those involved. The following are three cases that went to trial. These cannot necessarily be assumed to be fair trials, following established rules of evidence and testimony—and this lack of adherence to established rules became more true as time went on. The first

---

15. *See Franz Gürtner,* Biographie des Deutschen Historischen Museums.
16. *See Wilhelm Frick,* Biographie des Deutschen Historischen Museums.

case concerned the aftermath of the Reichstag fire, when there was still some sense of judicial normalcy in the country. The second and third cases occurred later as direct challenges to the Nazi state power and were dealt with by the People's Court, an institution created in response to the investigations and verdicts in the first trial so that judicial results in the future would align favorably with the desires of the Nazi leadership (see Section 6.2).

1. Reichstag Fire Trial

The trial that followed the burning of the Reichstag charged five defendants with the crime and attempting to overthrow the government: a Dutch anarchist, Marinus van der Lubbe; the head of the Communist Party in the Reichstag, Ernst Torgler; and three Bulgarian Communists who were in Germany, Georgi Dimitrov, Blagoi Popov, and Vassil Tanev. The pretrial investigation gathered evidence and testimony and reported by the end of August. In September, the trial commenced in Leipzig with an examination of the evidence gathered, then moved to Berlin to examine the remains of the building and interview local witnesses, and then returned to Leipzig for the final phase.

Only van der Lubbe was apprehended at the scene; admitting to the crime under interrogation; he was subsequently executed. The other four defendants, all connected to the Communist Party, had various alibis. Given the amount of accelerant used and the number of different locations where fires were started, as proved by the forensic investigation, it is clear that many people must have been involved—but who? Although this trial was part of the Nazi plot to discredit the Communists (they had been barred from the Reichstag under the fire decree discussed above), the preliminary investigation had not turned up evidence against these other four. In the end, the trial judge was forced to acquit them while at the same time accusing the Communist Party of orchestrating the burning as part of a plot to overthrow the government.

Before the trial had opened in Leipzig, the International Commission of Legal Inquiry into the Reichstag Fire, a group driven by German Communists with jurists recruited from many countries, had gathered in London to review the evidence and arrive at its own conclusion. The jurists included Arthur G. Hays of the ACLU (see Chapter 4), who also would attend the trial in Leipzig. The commission concluded that the Nazis had set the fire themselves, pointing out the underground passage into the building that could be accessed from the residence of the Reichstag president, Hermann Göring. The Communists also published the *Brown Book of the Reichstag Fire and Hitler Terror*. As part of the trial in Leipzig, Nazi officials were given a chance to respond to this book. In civil law trials like this one, the judges ask most of the questions, but defendants also can question witnesses who testify. It was defendant Dimitrov's questioning of certain witnesses that brought out many of the most interesting aspects of the trial: he intensely questioned Göring and Joseph Goebbels, who defended the regime. Such an opportunity would not avail itself until twelve years later, at Nuremberg.

At the Nuremberg postwar trials in 1946, Hans Gisevius, a young lawyer working at the time for the Gestapo and assigned to cover the trial, testified that the fire had indeed been set by the Nazis.[17] A group of up to ten men had not only set the fire but also later brought van der Lubbe to the scene to take the fall. Almost all of these men were murdered during the Night of the Long Knives, the purge of the SA the following year. Although van der Lubbe, the lone defendant convicted, had been executed for his crimes, the federal courts in Germany, in trials beginning in the 1960s and culminating in 2008, overturned his conviction due to reasons of mental incompetence. While the matter of Nazi involvement in the Reichstag fire is still being debated, the immediate beneficiary of the trial was the Nazi Party, and the loser was the Communist Party in Germany.

LEGAL PROFILES

Wilhelm Bünger was the presiding judge at this trial. He was born in Germany in 1870 and completed his legal studies there. In 1897, he became a deputy judge. In 1902, he moved to the prosecutor's office in Frankfurt. During WWI, he served in the military. After the war, he again became a prosecutor. In 1920, he was voted into the Saxony parliament, where he remained until 1931. He served many roles there, including as the minister of justice for several years, the minister of education, and the prime minister of the state. In 1931, he took a position on the state supreme court in Leipzig, where he served during this trial. He held that position until his death in 1937.[18]

---

17. 12 NUREMBERG TRIAL PROCEEDINGS 252-53 (Apr. 25, 1946).

18. *See Wilhelm Bünger*, DAS BUNDESARCHIV.

Paul Vogt was the examining magistrate responsible for gathering evidence for this case. He was born in Germany in 1877 and completed his legal studies there. In 1906, he was appointed as a deputy judge. In 1909, he became a prosecutor. During WWI, he served in the military. After the war, he returned to being a prosecutor; and in 1922, he was nominated to the bench in the regional court. He was appointed as an examining magistrate for the supreme court and then in 1932 to the Supreme Court. He became the leader of the court in 1937, where he remained until he retired in 1944. He was captured after the war and was imprisoned until 1952. He died many years later, in the 1970s.[19]

Hans Gisevius was the Gestapo assistant and lawyer assigned to report on this trial. He was born in Germany in 1904 and completed his legal studies there. He went to work for the secret State Police (the newly formed Gestapo) in 1933. He eventually moved to the Ministry of the Interior. When the war started, he joined the intelligence services. He worked under Admiral Wilhelm Canaris, who was opposed to Hitler and a leader of the July 20, 1944, plot discussed in Section 6.1B.3. This allowed him to be posted to Switzerland, where he began working with Allen Dulles of the OSS (see Chapter 5) as a liaison to the Germans in the military opposed to Hitler. As he was part of the failed plot to assassinate Hitler in 1944, he went into hiding and was able to transit through Switzerland out of the reach of the Nazis and so survive the war. In the Nuremberg Trials after the war, he was a witness for both the prosecution and the defense. He documented his experiences in a book, *To the Bitter End*. He died in 1974.[20]

---

2. White Rose Trials

The result in the Reichstag fire trial led to the creation of the People's Court, where the rules of procedure and evidence were quite different and quite slanted toward the prosecution (see Section 6.2). Convictions were preordained, and executions followed the same day. Two important sets of trials were

---

19. *See Paul Vogt*, DAS BUNDESARCHIV.
20. *See Hans Gisevius, 68, Anti-Nazi, Is Dead*, N.Y. TIMES (Mar. 27, 1974).

heard in this court. The first set was part of a student resistance movement called the White Rose. The second involved the military plot against Hitler's life and is described in the next subsection.

The White Rose was a student movement at the University of Munich that was determined to rise up against Nazi power, knowing that the war had been lost, especially after the loss at Stalingrad. Led by university students Hans and Sophie Scholl (siblings), Willi Graf, Alexander Schmorell, and Christoph Probst, they held meetings and then created and distributed six pamphlets in 1942 and 1943, calling on other Germans to resist the Nazis, and painted graffiti with similar messages on buildings. They managed to get their literature distributed all over southern Germany and into Austria. A number of the students had worked as medics on the eastern front and had seen for themselves many of the atrocities against which they were protesting. Finally caught in early 1943, they were immediately put on trial for treason before the People's Court.

Through their pamphlets, they were charged with calling for sabotage during wartime, propagating defeatist ideas, defaming the führer, and calling for the overthrow of the Nazis. After a brief trial under the grossly one-sided conditions deployed by Chief Judge Roland Freisler, and with their parents unable to attend, Hans, Sophie, and Christoph were convicted and sentenced to be executed, which was carried out the same day. In a separate trial, Graf, Schmorell and their philosophy professor Dr. Huber were also sentenced to death (and later executed), and ten others were sentenced to imprisonment of various lengths. A third trial of four others, with a different judge, only resulted in a single conviction. The students' final pamphlet, which was smuggled out of the country, was subsequently air-dropped onto Germany by Allied warplanes.

LEGAL PROFILES

Roland Freisler was the lead judge in this trial and the July 20 plot trials, discussed in the next subsection. He was born in Germany in 1893 and completed his legal studies there. During WWI, he served in the army and was captured by the Russians in 1915. He remained in Russia after the war and eventually returned home to start work as a lawyer in 1924. Shortly thereafter, he joined the Nazi Party, defending its members when they got into trouble with the law. He was later elected to the Prussian legislature in 1932 and the Reichstag in 1933. In 1934, he became secretary of state in the Reich Ministry of Justice, where he remained until 1942 and was instrumental in developing the Nazi penal code. He then took on the role of president of the People's Court, where he ruled with an audacious style of prejudging defendants, shouting them down in court, and sentencing them almost unfailingly to death. His perverted judicial role finally came to an end when an American bombing mission over Berlin bombed the People's Court and killed Freisler in February 1945.[21]

Fabian von Schlabrendorff was a defendant and purportedly the next victim of Freisler, scheduled to go on trial the day after the People's Court bombing for his role in the July 20 plot (see next subsection); von Schlabrendorff was also a lawyer. He was born in Germany in 1907 and completed his legal studies there. During WWII, he joined the army and was involved with various plots to overthrow the Nazis. It was he who planted a time-detonated bomb on an aircraft that Hitler was to use in 1943, but the bomb failed to explode. He was rounded up as part of the July 20 plot; but due to the death of Freisler, he survived the war. He eventually served as a judge on the Constitutional Court of the Federal Republic of Germany from 1967 to 1975. He died in 1980.[22]

3. July 20 Plot Trials

In a tale told in books and on film, the final major attempt (there had been numerous prior attempts) at assassinating Hitler on July 20, 1944, failed as the blast of the bomb was partly deflected by a heavy conference room table. In the aftermath, many thousands of German nationals were rounded up, and by some estimates more than five thousand people were executed. The vast majority of these murders occurred outside public view; but with the need to show its invulnerability, the Nazi regime put on several show trials of highly placed members of the German state who were involved (or presumably involved

---

21. *See Roland Freisler*, Biographie des Deutschen Historischen Museums.
22. *See Fabian von Schlabrendorff*, Das Bundesverfassungsgerichts.

or whom this was a convenient excuse to eliminate). The legality of the trials barely rose above outright murder, but appearances mattered.

These trials occurred in front of the People's Court presiding judge, Roland Freisler. There were several trials at the start involving military figures that received prominent coverage. The one military figure who was not brought up before the court was Field Marshall Erwin Rommel, who, based on his prior service, was given the choice of taking poison and being buried as a military hero, saving the honor of the Nazis for the time being. The trials started in August 1944 and continued through the end of the war. Dozens of trials were held and more than one hundred death sentences handed out involving conspirators, those who aided them, and those who did not report their knowledge in advance of the actual implementation of the plot.

A typical trial was the first: it involved eight military officers, including Field Marshall Erwin von Witzleben, and the charges and appointed defense counsel were only made available to the defendants shortly before the trial. The defendants had all been discharged from the military, subjecting them to civil instead of military courts. The trial itself, which was full of Freisler's heavy invective against any claims of innocence or explanation, was concluded within a day. Ending in death sentences for those involved, the trial offered no avenue for appeal. All of those sentenced were executed the same day in the Plötzensee Prison in Berlin. Many of those sentences were carried out via the most excruciatingly slow and painful methods.

LEGAL PROFILES

Klaus Bonhoeffer was one of the plotters and a lawyer. He was born in Poland in 1901 but completed his legal studies in Germany. In his legal career, he worked, beginning in 1937, with Lufthansa airlines and so traveled frequently, which gave him the ability to further resistance efforts. The efforts included his brother, a religious pastor, who was also rounded up. Bonhoeffer was sentenced and executed in April 1945.[23]

---

23. *See Klaus Bonhoeffer*, BIOGRAPHIE DES DEUTSCHEN HISTORISCHEN MUSEUMS.

Reinhold Frank was one of the plotters and a lawyer. He was born in Germany in 1896 and completed his legal studies there. Prior to that, he served in WWI. His legal practice included the defense of a number of Catholic priests persecuted by the Nazis. He was part of a leading resistance group but not directly active in the plot. He was sentenced and executed in January 1945.[24]

Hans John was one of the plotters and a lawyer. He was born in Germany in 1911 and completed his legal studies there. He worked at the University of Berlin in aviation law before being drafted into the military in 1940. In early 1942, he was severely wounded and returned to his legal scholarship. He and his brother Otto then became involved in the resistance movement affiliated with the military and intelligence services and thus this plot. He was sentenced and executed in April 1945.[25]

Hans Koch was one of the plotters and a lawyer. He was born in Germany in 1893 and completed his legal studies there. In 1927, he started a legal practice after a series of state roles. While working with the resistance movement, he developed a reputation such that if the plot had succeeded, he was to be named as the head of the German Supreme Court. He was arrested while hiding one of the conspirators; although he was never convicted, he was executed in April 1945.[26]

Berthold von Stauffenberg was one of the plotters and a lawyer. He was born to an aristocratic family in Germany in 1905 and completed his legal studies there. He became an assistant professor of international law at the Kaiser Wilhelm Institute in 1927. In 1931, he started a two-year stint with the Permanent Court of International Justice at The Hague. When the war started in 1939, he joined the German navy, doing legal work as a staff judge. This provided him with the opportunity to work with the resistance movement in the military. It was von Stauffenberg's brother Claus, a military officer, who was assigned to carry the bomb

---

24. *See Reinhold Frank*, GEDENKSTÄTTE DEUTSCHER WIDERSTAND: BIOGRAPHIE.
25. *See Hans John*, GEDENKSTÄTTE DEUTSCHER WIDERSTAND: BIOGRAPHIE.
26. *See Hans Koch*, GEDENKSTÄTTE DEUTSCHER WIDERSTAND: BIOGRAPHIE.

to the meeting with Hitler. In August 1944, von Stauffenberg was sentenced and executed.[27]

Josef Wirmer was one of the plotters and a lawyer. He was born in Germany in 1901 and completed his legal studies there. He worked as a lawyer in private practice in Berlin, defending those of varying political and racial backgrounds against Nazi mistreatment, for which he was kicked out of the National Socialist Bar Association. His reputation was such that he was targeted by the plotters for the position of minister of justice in the post-Hitler government. During his "trial" at the People's Court, he made it a point of confronting Freisler. He was sentenced and executed in September 1944.[28]

C. Subsequent Events

In an effort to undo the twelve years of inseparability between the state and the Nazi Party, the Allies started a program of "denazification." This began officially with a U.S. Joint Chiefs of Staff directive in April 1945,[29] whose principles were repeated in the Potsdam Agreement.[30] One of its political principles was to "destroy the National Socialist Party and its affiliated and supervised organizations, to dissolve all Nazi institutions, to insure that they are not revived in any form, and to prevent all Nazi and militarist activity or propaganda."[31] The directive went on to state that

> Nazi leaders, influential Nazi supporters and high officials of Nazi organizations and institutions and any other persons dangerous to the occupation or its objectives shall be arrested and interned. . . . All members of the Nazi party who have been more than nominal participants in its activities and all other persons hostile to Allied purposes shall be removed

---

27. *See Berthold von Stauffenberg*, GEDENKSTÄTTE DEUTSCHER WIDERSTAND: BIOGRAPHIE.
28. *See Josef Wirmer*, GEDENKSTÄTTE DEUTSCHER WIDERSTAND: BIOGRAPHIE.
29. U.S. Joint Chiefs of Staff Directive JCS 1067/6, Directive to Commander in Chief of United States Forces of Occupation Regarding the Military Government of Germany (Apr. 26, 1945).
30. Tripartite Agreement by the United States, the United Kingdom and Soviet Russia Concerning Conquered Countries, U.S.-U.K.-U.S.S.R., Aug. 2, 1945.
31. U.S. Joint Chiefs of Staff Directive JCS 1067/6, *supra* note 29.

from public and semipublic office and from positions of responsibility in important private undertakings. Such persons shall be replaced by persons who, by their political and moral qualities, are deemed capable of assisting in developing genuine democratic institutions in Germany.[32]

In early 1946, the Allies, via the Allied Control Council (see Section 6.2), which was the Allies' postwar authority to run Germany, promulgated a directive that removed Nazis from all positions of power.[33] The Allied Control Council and the respective military governments in the four occupation zones (American, British, Russian, French) promulgated several laws that abrogated Nazi laws,[34] dissolved the Nazi Party,[35] restricted Nazi employment,[36] and restricted the property holdings of Nazis.[37]

After it had initially handled the denazification efforts, screening almost 300,000 people in leading positions, the military was ready to turn over these efforts to the Germans. Thus, a new law, based on suggestions from several of the German states, was promulgated, giving this screening function to the states.[38] The law, effective from mid-1946, was adopted initially in the states of Bavaria, Greater Hesse, and Württemberg-Baden. It mandated that each adult German fill out and submit a registration form, detailing his past political history. The law created five categories detailing levels of responsibility for Nazi activities: (1) major offenders; (2) offenders, including activists (those who substantially assisted the tyranny of the Nazis), militarists (those responsible for domination, exploitation, or deportation of foreign people), and profiteers (those who extracted advantage from the tyranny of the Nazis); (3) lesser offenders, i.e., probationers (those who could be offenders but deserved special consideration or followers who had to prove themselves first); (4) followers; and (5) exonerated people, i.e., those who actively resisted Nazi tyranny.

These registrations did not preclude criminal proceedings, which were to be carried out by the minister for political liberation. The registrations were

32. *Id.*
33. Allied Control Council Directive No. 24, Removal from Office and from Positions of Responsibility of Nazis and of Persons Hostile to Allied Purposes (Jan. 12, 1946).
34. U.S. Military Gov't–Ger., Law No. 1 (1945).
35. U.S. Military Gov't–Ger., Law No. 5 (1945).
36. U.S. Military Gov't–Ger., Law No. 8 (1945).
37. U.S. Military Gov't–Ger., Law No. 52 (1946).
38. Law for Liberation from National Socialism and Militarism of 1946 (Ger.).

sent to the public prosecutor, who evaluated these along with other evidence and referred cases to and prosecuted them in front of tribunals. The tribunals determined the classifications of people and the sanctions to be imposed. Anyone falling into either of the first two categories had to prove their innocence by clear and convincing evidence. Appeals could be made to the minister for political liberation.

In reality, those who were only ordinary members of the Nazi Party wanted to be tried in order to have their names cleared so that they could get on with the recovery from the war. Those who were major offenders or offenders held back. Almost two million people were cleared of sanctions in the first six months after the registration law was enacted, while around 200,000 went through the tribunal process.[39] This still left close to four million cases, so amnesties were granted to those in the followers category and those who were in their mid-twenties or younger. By the end of the first year, around twelve million registrations produced almost one million cases that should be either tried or sanctioned without being charged.

By this time, however, the Cold War made it more important that the focus shift to Germany getting back on its feet as an ally, so eventually the West German government took over and refocused the denazification process. Whether it was ultimately successful or not is still an open question, which is perhaps best answered by the intervening seventy years.

LEGAL PROFILES

Thomas Dehler was the chief prosecutor of Bavaria's political liberation ministry. He was born in Germany in 1897 and completed his legal studies there. After serving in WWI, he started his legal practice in Munich and then practiced in Bamberg. During the war, he was arrested several times for his ties to resistance activities. Although he tried to enlist, he was not allowed to remain in the military because he was married to a woman with Jewish ancestry. After the war, he served as an

---

39. U.S. OFFICE OF THE MILITARY GOVERNMENT FOR GERMANY (U.S.), DENAZIFICATION: REPORT OF THE MILITARY GOVERNOR 4 (1948).

attorney in the state courts and was elected to the German Bundestag in 1949, remaining in that position until 1967. From 1949 to 1953, he served as the minister of justice in Konrad Adenauer's first government, although he later opposed Adenauer's direction. He became chairman of the Free Democratic Party, which was originally part of the ruling coalition. In 1960, he became vice president of the Bundestag and was in this position when he died in 1967.[40]

6.2 SUBVERSION OF JUDICIAL INTEGRITY

A. Statutes

Part of the destruction of democratic institutions in Nazi Germany was the subversion of judicial integrity. Courts were created, such as the People's Court described above, where the rules were arbitrary, sentences were predetermined, and defendants were given essentially no opportunity to vindicate themselves through testimony or presentation of evidence. In countries where democratic institutions remained intact, the courts were available to provide a check on government excess in support of the war effort. Where democracy collapsed, the judiciary rarely stood up long in the face of dictatorial rule. Nazi Germany may have been the most egregious example of that. As such, direct review of legal decisions during Nazi Germany's absence of an impartial judiciary would not be of much value.

Instead, the actions of the courts during this period can be analyzed through the postwar trials. After the war, major Nazi war criminals were tried before the International Military Tribunal (IMT), composed of the judicial capabilities of the Allies. This was called the Trial of the Major War Criminals Before the International Military Tribunal, commonly known as the Nuremberg Trials. Subsequently, there were many additional trials of war criminals before tribunals conducted individually by the United States, the other Allies, and victim countries. A particularly famous series of trials was called the Trials of War Criminals Before the Nuremberg Military Tribunals (NMT), the so-

---

40. *See Thomas Dehler*, Biographie des Deutschen Historischen Museums.

called Subsequent Nuremberg Trials, which were actually twelve trials conducted entirely by the Americans at Nuremberg. One of the twelve trials was called the Judges' Trial, also known as the Justice Trial; this trial is discussed in the "Cases" subsection.

The ability to try the judiciary of another country required a significant legal foundation. Thus, Allied Control Council Law No. 10 gave the occupying powers the ability to arrest war criminals and conduct trials in their respective zones of occupation (the United States, the United Kingdom, France, and the Union of Soviet Socialist Republics (USSR) each had their own zone in Germany).[41] The law used the same authority as the IMT but applied to defendants not tried by the IMT within Germany. Each zone commander could set the rules and procedures for tribunals in his zone. The following were designated as crimes:

- Crimes against peace, i.e., initiating invasions of other countries and wars of aggression in violation of international laws and treaties
- War crimes, i.e., atrocities or offenses against people or property constituting violations of the laws or customs of war
- Crimes against humanity, i.e., atrocities and offenses committed against a civilian population or persecutions based on political, racial, or religious grounds
- Membership in categories of a criminal group or organization (as defined by the IMT)

An official position was not a defense, nor was following orders, although it could be considered as a mitigating factor. There was no statute of limitations from 1933 forward and any pardons or amnesty granted during the Nazi regime is not a bar to prosecution or punishment.

In the United States, an executive order was issued in 1945 to give an extra layer of legal foundation for trials subsequent to the IMT trials.[42] Amending

---

41. Allied Control Council Law No. 10, Punishment of Persons Guilty of War Crimes, Crimes Against Peace and Against Humanity (Dec. 20, 1945).
42. Exec. Order No. 9679, Amendment of Executive Order No. 9647 of May 2, 1945, Entitled "Providing for Representation of the United States in Preparing for and Prosecuting Atrocities and Charges of War Crimes Against the Leaders of the European Axis Powers and Their Principal Agents and Accessories" (Jan. 16, 1946).

the prior executive order that provided for the IMT, this new executive order allowed the U.S. representative and the chief counsel to pursue prosecutions before U.S. military and occupation tribunals for atrocities and war crimes not tried before the IMT.

U.S. Military Government Ordinance No. 7 provided for the specific procedural aspects of these trials.[43] For example, the tribunals were composed of three or more members. Defendants were given a copy of the indictment in their own language, legal representation, sufficient time before the trial, and the right to present evidence and cross-examine witnesses. The tribunals were not bound by "technical rules of evidence" but could pursue evidence considered to have probative value. The determinations of the IMT in regard to crimes, aggressive acts, etc., were binding. The judgments of the tribunals as to guilt or innocence were final and not subject to review with the exception that the military governor could mitigate or otherwise change sentences.

LEGAL PROFILES

Helmut von Moltke was one more victim of the People's Court and a judge himself. He was born in Germany (in an area now part of Poland) in 1907 and completed his legal studies there and in Austria. He was the great-grandnephew of the famous Prussian military leader of the same name. Opposed to the Nazis, he turned down a judgeship in 1933 that required party membership and set up his own legal practice. He made arrangements to take on a British legal practice, training in British law during visits to the country; but the war started, and he was drafted. He worked on international legal matters in the military, trying to get the military to follow the Geneva Conventions and other international agreements. All the while he was furthering resistance through a group called the Kreisau Circle (named after his estate), looking at how to found a new Germany based on moral and democratic principles. He was arrested in early 1944 for giving information to other resistance members and was

---

43. U.S. Military Gov't–Ger., Ordinance No. 7, Organization and Powers of Certain Military Tribunals (Oct. 18, 1946).

eventually brought before the People's Court. Not having evidence that he was involved in the July 20 plot, Freisler invented the notion that a moral and democratic Germany was treasonous. So, convicted for his ideas, von Moltke was executed in January 1945.[44]

B. Cases

The Justice Trial, *United States v. Josef Altstoetter*, involved sixteen defendants whose trials were consolidated as one case.[45] All were members of the Ministry of Justice or were judges or prosecutors in the People's Court or the Special Courts. The heads of the Ministry of Justice during the war (Otto Thierack and Gürtner) died before the trial, as well as Freisler. Several of the defendants, though, had served as undersecretary or state secretary of the ministry. Of the sixteen living defendants, one committed suicide before the trial (Carl Westphal), and another had a mistrial due to illness (Karl Engert). Of the remaining fourteen, the court convicted ten and acquitted four. From indictment to judgment, the trial lasted for eleven months in 1947. Below are the general details of the prosecution and defense cases and specifics regarding two of the defendants, Franz Schlegelberger and Oswald Rothaug, whose cases particularly exemplify Nazi subversion of judicial integrity. The twelve defendants not discussed below include Josef Altstoetter, Wilhelm von Ammon, Paul Barnickel, Hermann Cuhorts, Günther Joel, Herbert Klemm, Ernst Lautz, Wolfgang Mettgenberg, Günther Nebelung, Rudolf Oeschey, Hans Petersen, and Curt Rothenberger.

LEGAL PROFILES

Otto Thierack was head of the Ministry of Justice in the last few years of the war but did not live to be put on trial. He was born in Germany in 1889 and completed his legal studies there. These studies were inter-

---

44. *See Helmuth James Graf von Moltke*, GEDENKSTÄTTE DEUTSCHER WIDERSTAND: BIOGRAPHIE.
45. United States v. Josef Altstoetter, Case No. 3 (NMT 1947).

rupted by long service during WWI. He started out as a deputy judge in 1920 and became a prosecutor the following year. In 1926, he took on the role of prosecutor on the court of appeals in Dresden. A member of the Nazi Party, he was appointed as minister of justice for Saxony after the party rose to power in 1933. In 1936, he became the president of the People's Court, a position he held until 1942. Subsequently, he served as the Reich minister of justice. In this position, he initiated the Richterbriefe, highlighting cases that the Nazi leadership believed were correctly decided. He also began evaluations of judges and cases before they were tried, all leading to the predetermination of judgments. He also worked closely with the SS on handing over "undesirables." He committed suicide before the Justice Trial in 1946.[46]

1. Justice Trial: Prosecution and Defense Cases

The indictments in the Justice Trial were based on the common format used in the Nuremberg Trials, which involved charges of crimes against peace, crimes against humanity, war crimes, and conspiracy to commit these offenses. For the defendants in this trial, the indictments specified four counts: common design and conspiracy, war crimes, crimes against humanity, and membership in criminal organizations. The details of each count were as follows:

- *Common Design and Conspiracy*: According to a common design, the defendants, between January 1933 and April 1945, illegally conspired to commit war crimes and crimes against humanity. Part of this was to "enact, issue, enforce, and give effect to certain purported statutes, decrees, and orders, which were criminal both in inception and execution."[47] This also included, through the Ministry of Justice from 1934, countrywide "total control of the administration of justice, including preparation of legislation concerning all branches of law, and control of the courts and prisons."[48]

---

46. *See Otto Georg Thierack*, Biographie des Deutschen Historischen Museums.
47. *Josef Altstoetter*, Case No. 3, at 17.
48. *Id.* at 18.

To facilitate this, the ministry set up extraordinary political courts with "wide and arbitrary" criminal jurisdiction throughout the Reich,[49] which included the following:

- The People's Court (Volksgerichtshof): This was the "court of original and final jurisdiction in cases of "high treason" and "treason.""[50] This court investigated and prosecuted the cases before it, and there was no appeal. It became notorious for "the severity of punishment, secrecy of proceedings, and denial to the accused of all semblance of judicial process."[51]

- Special Courts (Sondergerichte): Special Courts dealt with "political" cases and acts deemed inimical to either the party, the government, or continued prosecution of the war. Prosecutors could arbitrarily refer any case there. Convictions were based upon offending the "healthy sentiment of the people."[52]

The judicial process was a

> powerful weapon for the persecution and extermination of all opponents of the Nazi regime and for the persecution and extermination of races...Independence of the judiciary was destroyed. Judges were removed from the bench for political and racial reasons. Periodic letters were sent by the Ministry of Justice to all Reich judges and public prosecutors, instructing them as to the results they must accomplish.[53]

Judges and lawyers were continually spied upon and were directed to keep dispositions of their cases politically acceptable, effectively reducing them "to an administrative arm of the Nazi Party."[54]

- *War Crimes*: These irregular courts were used to create a "reign of terror" over those who opposed the Nazis, including in occupied countries,

> subject[ing] civilians . . . to criminal abuse of judicial and penal process including repeated trials on the same charges, criminal

---

49. *Id.*
50. *Id.*
51. *Id.* at 19.
52. *Id.*
53. *Id.* at 18–19.
54. *Id.* at 19.

abuse of discretion, unwarranted imposition of the death penalty, prearrangement of sentences between judges and prosecutors, discriminatory trial processes, and other criminal practices, all of which resulted in murders, cruelties, tortures, atrocities, plunder of private property, and other inhumane acts.[55]

Special Courts were used for Jews, Poles, Romani, and other groups, subjecting them to "discriminatory and special penal laws and trials, and denied them all semblance of judicial process."[56] These courts were also used under the Nazi's Night and Fog Decree to set up secret trials for resistance fighters in occupied countries without evidence, testimony, or defense counsel. The Ministry of Justice ran prisons more like concentration camps, allowing executions of untried prisoners and murdering many upon the approach of Allied troops. It was involved in Nazi racial purity programs, including those under which the insane, aged, and sick from occupied countries were systematically murdered.

- *Crimes Against Humanity*: In addition to the many war crimes related above, "special health courts (Erbgesundheitsgerichte) perverted eugenic and sterilization laws or policies regarding German civilians and nationals of other countries which resulted in the systematic murder and ill-treatment of thousands of persons."[57] And the criminal laws of Germany were expanded and "perverted" by the defendants to subjugate German citizens and exterminate nationals of occupied countries, resulting in murder, torture, illegal imprisonment, and ill-treatment for thousands.[58]
- *Membership in a Criminal Organization*: Certain defendants were leaders in the Nazi Party or were members of the Schutzstaffel (SS), organizations deemed criminal by the IMT.

In his opening statement, Telford Taylor, chief prosecutor, laid the foundation for this trial, stating thus:

Those men, leaders of the German judicial system, consciously and deliberately suppressed the law, engaged in an unholy masquerade of

---

55. *Id.*
56. *Id.*
57. *Id.* at 21.
58. *Id.* at 20.

brutish tyranny disguised as justice, and converted the German judicial system to an engine of despotism, conquest, pillage, and slaughter. . . .

The defendants and their colleagues distorted, perverted, and finally accomplished the complete overthrow of justice and law in Germany. They made the system of courts an integral part of dictatorship. They established and operated special tribunals obedient only to the political dictates of the Hitler regime. They abolished all semblance of judicial independence. They brow-beat, bullied, and denied fundamental rights to those who came before the courts. The "trials" they conducted became horrible farces, with vestigial remnants of legal procedure which only served to mock the hapless victims. . . .

This conduct was dishonor to their profession. Many of these misdeeds may well be crimes. But, in and of themselves, they are not charged as crimes in this indictment. . . .

Great as was their crime against those who died or suffered at their hands, their crime against Germany was even more shameful. They defiled the German temple of justice, and delivered Germany into the dictatorship of the Third Reich, "with all its methods of terror, and its cynical and open denial of the rule of law."[59]

To support the indictment, the prosecution laid out the following major points:

- From its inception, the Nazi Party destroyed the state justice functions and centralized all judicial functions on a national level.[60]
- The control of bar admission (i.e., exclusion of Jews, Communists, and non-Aryans),[61] judicial training, legal publications, legal associations, and law school education was Nazified.

---

59. *Id.* at 31–33.
60. First Law for the Transfer of the Administration of Justice to the Reich, Feb. 18, 1934 (Nazi Ger.); Second Law for the Transfer of the Administration of Justice to the Reich, Dec. 5, 1934 (Nazi Ger.).
61. Law Concerning Admission to the Bar, Apr. 7, 1933 (Nazi Ger.).

- Judges were removed if they did not follow the interests of the state, were Jews, or were political opponents of the Nazis.
- Criminals were those who were against the state as defined by the Nazis, with ever-expanding types of offenses includable under the crime of treason.
- The penal code was expanded significantly, proclaiming that

  [w]hoever commits an act which the law declares as punishable or which deserves punishment according to the fundamental idea of a penal law or the sound sentiment of the people, shall be punished. If no specific penal law can be directly applied to this act, then it shall be punished according to the law whose underlying spirit can be most readily applied to the act.[62]

- Precedent was not to be a barrier to any decision, based on a directive stating that "[w]hen a decision is made about a legal question, the Reich Supreme Court can deviate from a decision laid down before this law went into effect."[63]
- The survival of the state was the purpose of criminal law, stated as such:

  While making his decisions the judge is to proceed less from the law than from the basic idea that the offender is to be eliminated from the community. . . . [I]t is not so much a matter of whether a judgment is just or unjust, but only that the decision is expedient. The State must protect itself in the most efficient way. . . . One must not proceed from the law, but from the resolution that the man must be wiped out.[64]

- All criminal decisions could be retried or punishments changed if the Ministry of Justice did not think they were severe enough.
- The number of justices and attorneys was limited; and many procedural safeguards, including the right of appeal, were eliminated to speed up sentences.[65]

---

62. Law Amending Provisions of Criminal Law and Criminal Procedure, Apr. 24, 1934 (Nazi Ger.).
63. *Josef Altstoetter*, Case No. 3, at 45.
64. *Id.* at 46.
65. Decree Concerning Simplification of the Administration of Justice, Mar. 21, 1942 (Nazi Ger.); Decree for the Further Simplification of the Administration of Justice in Criminal Cases, Aug. 13, 1942 (Nazi Ger.).

- Hitler was granted the ability, outside any established process, to change the sentence of any criminal defendant as the Supreme Law Lord[66] and was eventually granted unlimited powers.[67]
- Deviation from any law was allowed in order to create a Nazi "administration of justice."[68]
- The Ministry of Justice issued briefs to judges on expected decision making.
- The Ministry of Justice protected loyal members of the Third Reich from criminal prosecution for their "innumerable atrocities."[69]
- The Nazis handed over defendants, including undesirables in occupied countries, to the SS for "protective custody" (i.e., enslavement and execution without trial).[70]
- The Nazis subverted the purpose of the court as such:

> The sentences of the People's Court can be understood only if one keeps in mind the intent underlying the penalties. This was not primarily that of imposing punishment in accordance with normal "bourgeois" conceptions of crime and punishment, but rather of annihilating an opposition which could become detrimental to the German aims.[71]

To refute the indictment, the defense presented the following points:

- German judges were not able to review the constitutionality of laws because Article 78 of the Weimar Constitution gave the Reichstag the ability to be "the majority that can amend the constitution, could abolish

---

66. Decree of the Fuehrer and Reich Chancellor Concerning Execution of the Right of Pardon, Sept. 3, 1939 (Nazi Ger.).

67. Unanimous Decision of the Greater German Reichstag Concerning Unrestricted Powers of Adolf Hitler, Apr. 26, 1942 (Nazi Ger.).

68. Decree Concerning Special Powers Authorizing the Reich Minister of Justice to Deviate from Any Existing Law in Establishing a National Socialist Administration of Justice, Aug. 20, 1942 (Nazi Ger.).

69. United States v. Josef Altstoetter, Case No. 3 (NMT 1947).

70. *Josef Altstoetter*, Case No. 3, at 21.

71. *Id.* at 85.

the republic, the federal state, democracy, even basic laws. No judge was entitled to doubt the constitutional validity of such a law."[72]

- German law, being codified, did not grow by judicial review but expected adherence to the codified law, with this inflexibility meaning that there was a separation between law and morality:

  > If it cannot even be conceded that the judge is entitled to examine the law as for its being constitutional or not, so it can be conceded even less that he may refuse obedience to a law which was passed constitutionally because according to his opinion concerning certain standards which again according to his opinion are above the legislator, that is to say, morality, ethics, natural law, they contradict these points or because they cannot stand up to certain evaluations.[73]

- No German jurist was required to interpret national laws vis-à-vis international laws because international laws were transformed into national laws, which then stood on their own without the need to reexamine the intent of the international laws.
- The Ministry of Justice was caught in a web of relationships with the police and its overseers and was merely carrying out its functions in these dynamics, including, for example, the programs of sterilization and euthanasia.
- Changes to criminal law were caused by "public distress" in Germany at the time.[74]
- Differences between common law and civil legal systems contributed to a misunderstanding of the roles played by German courts, include the People's Court and the Special Courts.
- The nullity plea and the extraordinary objection (i.e., the führer's role was that of a Supreme Law Lord who could intervene as it pleased him with an "extraordinary objection") were not based on Nazi violent intent but on maintaining uniformity of legal decision making.

---

72. *Id.* at 255.
73. *Id.* at 257.
74. *Id.* at 144.

LEGAL PROFILES

James T. Brand was the presiding judge in the Justice Trial (taking the place of the original presiding judge, who became ill). He was born in Ohio in 1886 but started his legal practice in Oregon. He served as a city attorney and then as a state circuit judge for many years. In 1941, he was appointed to and then subsequently elected to the Oregon Supreme Court, a seat he retained for seventeen years. In 1951, he became the chief justice of the court for two years. In 1947, he was appointed to the Nuremberg court by the War Department. He resigned from the court in 1958 and taught at the Stetson University College of Law. Supposedly, the Spencer Tracy character in the 1961 movie *Judgment at Nuremberg* about this very trial was based on Brand. He died in 1964.[75]

Telford Taylor, a brigadier general, was the chief prosecutor and chief counsel in the Justice Trial. He was born in New York in 1908 and started his legal work with the federal government in 1933, including the Department of the Interior, the Agricultural Adjustment Administration, the Department of Justice, and the Federal Communications Commission. He joined the military in 1942 in the intelligence services and was eventually posted as a military attaché in London. He helped to work on the London Charter of the IMT (see Section 6.4) and then worked as Robert Jackson's deputy at the IMT. After Jackson returned to his Supreme Court position, Taylor took his place as chief counsel for the IMT. He also prosecuted many of the remaining trials before the NMT. After the war, he returned to both private practice and teaching at several law schools. He oversaw small defense plants during the Korean War, at the invitation of President Truman. He was a vocal critic of McCarthyism, defending several high-profile targets and later the Vietnam War. He authored a number of books and died in 1998.[76]

---

75. *See James T. Brand*, N.Y. TIMES (Feb. 29, 1964).
76. *See Telford Taylor, Who Prosecuted Top Nazis at the Nuremberg Trials, Is Dead at 90*, N.Y. TIMES (May 24, 1998).

Charles M. La Follette was the deputy chief prosecutor and deputy chief counsel in the Justice Trial. He was born in Indiana in 1898 and started his legal practice there after serving in the army in WWI. He was a member of the Indiana legislature from 1927 to 1929 and the U.S. House of Representatives from 1943 to 1947, after which he became deputy chief counsel. However, he ran unsuccessfully for the U.S. Senate. Until early 1949, he stayed in Europe as director of the Office of Military Government in Württemberg-Baden in the American zone. He was a distant cousin of the progressive politician Robert M. La Follette. He died in 1974.[77]

2. Justice Trial: Schlegelberger Decision

In its decision about Schlegelberger, the longtime undersecretary in the Ministry of Justice, the court did not repeat many of its prior words. Instead, it focused on several specific examples while noting that after Schlegelberger's resignation from the Ministry of Justice, Hitler rewarded him for his "good and faithful service," which he rendered while committing both war crimes and crimes against humanity.[78]

One example was Schlegelberger's support for the changes to criminal law, punishing those whose deeds were not punishable under the law and basing those punishments on the "sound instincts of the people."[79] The court found no objective standard for these sound instincts and instead found that these were the desires of Hitler and the Nazis. The court found that the numerous changes to the criminal law subjected citizens to arbitrary opinions of judges as to what constituted an offense, which destroyed "the feeling of legal security and created an atmosphere of terrorism."[80] It ruled that Schlegelberger contributed to the destruction of judicial independence, including the Night and Fog Decree. He was fully aware of and acquiesced to the eradication of Jews and Poles and created the direction for criminal law in those occupied territories, including the Law Against Poles and Jews.

---

77. *See La Follette, Charles Marion*, BIOGRAPHICAL DIRECTORY OF THE UNITED STATES CONGRESS.
78. *Josef Altstoetter*, Case No. 3, at 1082.
79. *Id.*
80. *Id.* at 1083.

The court cited the case of a milk hand, sentenced in 1940, who claimed that a police officer beat him to coerce a confession. A courageous judge tried and convicted the policeman of brutality. Himmler was incensed and stated that it would hurt the morale of police to sentence them for such brutalities. Schlegelberger quashed the proceedings and issued a pardon to the policeman, who was subsequently promoted by Himmler.

Among other devices, the defense proposed the theory that if Schlegelberger had resigned, a worse person would succeed him. The court rejected this defense, stating that he and others

> took over the dirty work which the leaders of the State demanded, and employed the Ministry of Justice as a means for exterminating the Jewish and Polish populations, terrorizing the inhabitants of occupied countries, and wiping out political opposition at home. . . . The prostitution of a judicial system for the accomplishment of criminal ends involves an element of evil to the State which is not found in frank atrocities which do not sully judicial robes.[81]

In conclusion, the court said that it believed "that he loathed the evil that he did, but he sold that intellect and that scholarship to Hitler for a mess of political pottage and for the vain hope of personal security." It found the defendant guilty of war crimes and crimes against humanity. He was sentenced to lifetime imprisonment.

LEGAL PROFILES

Franz Schlegelberger was one of the defendants in the Justice Trial. He was born in Germany in 1875 and completed his legal studies there. He started his legal career as a judge in a series of positions and then was named councillor of the Berlin Court of Appeals in 1914, a position that he held until 1918. He then was appointed to the Reich Board of Justice and then as a privy government councillor. In 1922, he began to teach

---

81. *Id.* at 1086.

law at the University of Berlin and wrote several legal books. In 1927, he was appointed ministerial director in the Reich Ministry of Justice. From 1931 to 1941, he was secretary of state for the Reich Ministry of Justice. Upon the death of the head of the ministry in that year, he became the temporary head of the ministry for one and a half years. When his successor was appointed, he resigned. In 1950, he was released early from his life sentence (at the age of seventy-four). He died in 1970.[82]

Egon Kubuschok was Schlegelberger's defense counsel during this trial and the first to present his argument. He was born in Germany (in an area now part of Poland) in 1888 and completed his legal studies there. He established a criminal law practice in Breslau, which included defending resistance fighters in the People's Court as well as major industrialists. Before this NMT trial, he defended Franz von Papen[83] and the German government before the IMT. After these trials, he was involved in the defense of the head of the one the largest German banks during another of the twelve NMT trials, the Ministries Trial. In the 1960s, he continued to advise clients[84] and died after 1972.

---

3. Justice Trial: Rothaug Decision

The case against Rothaug focused on the racial policies implemented by the Special Courts. The court here cited a number of specific examples of cases that the defendant oversaw.

The first case concerned two Polish girls who were caught in the vicinity of a harmless fire at an armaments plant. After interrogation by the Gestapo, they were put on trial before the Special Courts. The indictment was drawn up right there, and the defense counsel had no time to prepare because the trial started within an hour of their arrival, with Rothaug presiding. The younger girl was seventeen years old and should not have been before the court at all, let alone subject to possible capital punishment. Rothaug did not believe the

---

82. *See Franz Schlegelberger*, Das Bundesarchiv.
83. *See Nazis Grab of Austria Told in Court*, Stars and Stripes (Nov. 29, 1945).
84. *See So Oben Rum*, Der Spiegel (Jan. 3, 1972).

recanted testimony of the girls and sentenced them to death, which was carried out within a few days of this nontrial.

In the second case, a young Polish farmhand was convicted of making indecent advances to his employer's wife and sentenced to a two-year imprisonment by a district court. The Reich Supreme Court entered a nullity plea on this sentence, and so the case was retried before the Special Courts under the more severe Decree Against Public Enemies. Rothaug did not allow the testimony of a second Pole who was present at the incident as he had never permitted a Polish witness and disbelieved the testimony of the defendant Pole. Among the reasons for sentencing this Pole to death, Rothaug stated, "The whole inferiority of the defendant, I would say, lies in the sphere of character and is obviously based on his being a part of Polish subhumanity, or in his belonging to Polish subhumanity."[85] The act of this defendant was "directed against the purity of the German blood."[86] It was "also necessary in the interest of the Reich security to deter Poles of similar mentality."[87] The defendant was subsequently executed.

In the third case, an older Jewish man was convicted of polluting the races. The law prohibited intercourse between Germans and Jews. The investigation could not prove this liaison and both parties denied it; the man was a fatherly figure who helped support the German family. When the regular court could not make the case, Rothaug transferred the case to the Special Courts. A new indictment added a second charge under the Decree Against Public Enemies. A perjury charge against the German girl was added so that she could not testify for the defendant. Rothaug stated, "It is sufficient for me that the swine said that a German girl had sat upon his lap."[88] He instructed the prosecutor to ask for the death penalty. In finding the defendant guilty, the court confirmed the second charge because the defendant had talked to the girl during the darkness caused by air raid blackouts, thereby committing a crime for which the death penalty was used. The defendant was then executed.

The court ruled that the executions of these four, both Jews and Poles, were "in conformity with the policy of the Nazi State of persecution, torture, and extermination of these races. The defendant Rothaug was the knowing

---

85. *Josef Altstoetter*, Case No. 3, at 1149.

86. *Id.*

87. *Id.*

88. *Id.* at 1166.

and willing instrument in that program of persecution and extermination."[89] The court found him guilty of crimes against humanity, for which he was sentenced to life imprisonment.

LEGAL PROFILES

Oswald Rothaug was one of the defendants in the Justice Trial. He was born in Germany in 1897 and completed his legal studies there. He served in WWI before finishing his legal education and starting his career as an assistant judge. In 1927, he became a public prosecutor. From 1929 to 1933, he was the councilor at a local court. In 1933, he served as the chief prosecutor for Nuremberg. From 1937 to 1943, he was the director of the Nuremberg District Court as well as the chairman of the Special Courts. From 1943 to 1945, he was the public prosecutor of the People's Court in Berlin. His sentence from the NMT was later reduced, and he was released in late 1956. He died in 1967.[90]

C. Subsequent Events

Nine of the ten defendants who were convicted in this trial (von Ammon, Joel, Klemm, Lautz, Mettgenberg, Oeschey, Rothaug, Tothenberger, and Schlegel-berger) applied for a writ of habeas corpus to the U.S. Supreme Court in 1949. The writ was denied on May 2, 1949. Four of the justices (Vinson, Reed, Frankfurter, and Burton) believed that "there is want of jurisdiction."[91] Four other justices (Black, Douglas, Murphy, and Rutledge) believed that arguments should be heard on the motions to settle what remedy, if any, the petitioners had. Justice Jackson took no part in the consideration or decision of these applications because he had been the chief counsel for the prosecution in the IMT trials.

---

89. *Id.* at 1155.
90. *See Na Und*, DER SPIEGEL (Oct. 9, 1967).
91. United States v. Josef Altstoetter, Case No. 3, at 1204 (NMT 1947).

The Allied Control Council took a number of initial steps after the war to reverse what the Nazis had done to the German system of justice. It proclaimed fundamental principles of judicial reform based on "democracy, civilization, and justice."[92] The first article established equality before the law regardless of race, nationality, or religion. The second article gave guarantees to the accused, including due process; criminal responsibility only for offenses defined by law; prohibition against crimes by analogy or "sound popular instinct"; the right to a speedy and public trial, to know the charges, to confront witnesses, and to have the assistance of counsel; and the quashing of unjust convictions during the Nazi era on political, racial, or religious grounds. The third article liquidated the People's Court, the Nazi courts, and the Special Courts and prohibited their reestablishment. The fourth article guaranteed independence of the judiciary, including judicial independence from the executive and "obedience only to the law," and judicial roles open to all regardless of race, social origin, or religion.[93] The fifth article required justice to be administered by ordinary German courts in accordance with these principles.

In addition, three council laws dealt with Nazi-era laws. The first, repealed many of the more odious Nazi laws, decrees, and ordinances, including the amendment to the criminal code on April 24, 1934.[94] The second, following the council proclamation of fundamental principles of judicial reform, based the reorganization of German courts on a 1924 law, which reestablished the three-level ordinary court system.[95] It required the dismissal of all judges and prosecutors who were Nazi Party members and who had "more than nominal" roles in the "punitive practices" of the Nazi regime.[96] The third repealed many criminal laws and decrees from the Nazi era, including the Law Against Poles and Jews.[97]

---

92. Allied Control Council Proclamation No. 3, Fundamental Principals of Judicial Reform (Oct. 20, 1945).
93. *Id.* art. 4.
94. Allied Control Council Law No. 1, Repealing of Nazi Laws (Sept. 20, 1945).
95. Allied Control Council Law No. 4, Reorganization of the German Judicial System (Oct. 30, 1945).
96. *Id.*
97. Allied Control Council Law No. 11, Repealing of Certain Provisions of the German Criminal Law (Jan. 30, 1946).

6.3 CRIMES AGAINST HUMANITY AND WAR CRIMES

A. Statutes

Crimes against humanity and war crimes were numerous in the European theater of operations, with most nations involved as either victim or aggressor. As such, there were many prosecutions by war crimes tribunals across many different countries in the years after the war.

The Justice Trial described in Section 6.2 was just one of the twelve trials in the series of Subsequent Nuremberg Trials. In addition, there were two medical trials, three economic trials, two military trials (Hostages Trial[98] and High Command Trial[99]), one government trial (Ministries Trial),[100] and three racial policy trials (Einsatzgruppen Trial,[101] RuSHA Trial,[102] and Pohl Trial[103]).

There were also concentration camp cases, involving most major concentration camps. The U.S. military held trials for those involved in Dachau and other camps, such as Buchenwald, Mauthausen, and Nordhausen, right at the Dachau concentration camp. The Poles held a trial for Nazis involved in the Auschwitz camp, and the British conducted the Belsen and Ravensbrück trials, among others. There were also numerous trials (some of them connected with the concentration camp trials) under military courts by Allied nations—including Canada, Norway, France, Britain, Denmark, Luxembourg, Poland, and the United States—against individuals or small groups for actions against soldiers, POWs, and civilians. For example, the Poles tried the deputy leader of the occupation for war crimes and crimes against humanity, and the United States and Britain held trials for the killing of POWs.

Generally, after a war, independent states have the necessary jurisdiction to punish war criminals in their custody regardless of the physical territory in which the crimes were committed, the citizenship (or noncitizenship) of the victims or perpetrators, or when the custodial country became engaged in the particular war (i.e., war crimes committed after the war began but before the

---

98. United States v. Wilhelm List, Case No. 7 (NMT 1947–48).
99. United States v. Wilhelm von Leeb, Case No. 12 (NMT 1947–48).
100. United States v. Ernst von Weizsaccker, Case No. 11 (NMT 1947–48).
101. United States v. Otto Ohlendorf, Case No. 9 (NMT 1947–48).
102. United States v. Ulrich Greifelt, Case No. 8 (NMT 1947–48).
103. United States v. Oswald Pohl, Case No. 4 (NMT 1947).

custodial country became a belligerent are within their jurisdiction to try). Beyond that, each country needs its own legal foundation for prosecuting war crimes.

In the United States, the legal foundation for the medical experimentation trials and the economic trials discussed in the next subsection was the same as for the Justice Trial since they were part of the NMT trials. In contrast, the U.S. POW trials, which were part of the Dachau Trials mentioned earlier, had their initial foundation in a Joint Chiefs of Staff decree.[104] This directive defined crimes to include the following:

> Atrocities and offenses against persons or property constituting viola-
> tion of international law, including the laws, rules and customs of land
> and naval warfare; Initiation of invasions of other countries and of wars
> of aggression in violation of international laws and treaties; and Other
> atrocities and offenses, including atrocities and persecutions on racial,
> religious or political grounds, committed since January 1933.[105]

This directive allowed that "appropriate military courts" could conduct tri-als of suspected criminals who were in custody and proceed with the execu-tion of sentences; these courts were to be separate from those courts trying offenses that occurred after the war but during the occupation.[106] This directive was then backed up by a directive from military headquarters in Europe to commanding generals in the eastern and western districts authorizing them to appoint military commissions for the trials of people violating the laws or customs of war, law of nations, or laws of occupied territories.[107] In addition, military government courts, established by ordinance[108] and the related Uni-form Rules of Procedure in Military Government Courts and set up in the American zone of occupation, could deal with war crimes cases. A few early

---

104. U.S. Joint Chiefs of Staff Directive JCS 1023/10, Directive on the Identification and Appre-hension of Persons Suspected of War Crimes or Other Offenses and Trial of Certain Offenders (July 8, 1945).

105. *Id.*

106. *Id.*

107. Headquarters, European Theater, U.S. Forces, Directive on Military Commissions (Aug. 25, 1945).

108. U.S. Military Gov't–Ger., Ordinance No. 2 (July 16, 1945).

war crimes cases were tried by military commissions but most by specially appointed military government courts.

The British military trials for war criminals were founded upon the authority of a Royal warrant, which stated that the king deemed it expedient to make provisions for trials for war crimes (violations of the laws and usages of war) committed after the start of the war in September 1939.[109] A Polish court conducted a case against the deputy leader of an occupied country based upon a decree of August 1944,[110] which supplemented additional decrees in terms of scope and the appropriate court; this decree, in accordance with the London Agreement (see Section 6.4), included authority for crimes such as the murder, ill-treatment, and persecution of civilians and POWs and the arrest or deportation of people of any nationality or race by the occupying powers, with the exception of established common law crimes.

LEGAL PROFILES

Wilhelm Stuckart was a defendant in the NMT Ministries Trial and a lawyer. He was born in Germany in 1902 and completed his legal studies there. In 1930, he became a district court judge and then worked for the SA and joined the SS. In the Nazi government, he held the position of state secretary in the Reich Ministry of the Interior from 1935 to 1945, where he worked on drafting racial laws. He attended the Wannsee Conference. He was involved in the incorporation of Austria (1938); the Sudetenland (1938); Bohemia and Moravia (1939); Alsace, Lorraine, and Luxembourg (1940); Norway (1941); and the occupied southeastern territories (1941). In May 1945, he briefly became the Reich minister of the interior. He was convicted on charges of slave labor, war crimes and crimes against humanity for atrocities, and membership in the Nazi

---

109. U.K. Royal Warrant, Army Order 81/45, as amended (June 14, 1945) (U.K.).
110. Polish Comm. of Nat'l Liberation, Concerning the Punishment of Fascist-Hitlerite Criminals Guilty of Murder and Ill-Treatment of the Civilian Population and of Prisoners of War, and the Punishment of Traitors to the Polish Nation (Aug. 31, 1944) (Pol.).

organizations, but he was released early from prison due to illness. He died in a car accident in 1953.[111]

Hans Globke was an assistant to Stuckart and a lawyer. Throughout his career, he served Germany under three different governments: the Weimar Republic, the Nazi regime, and the postwar Federal Republic. He was born in Germany in 1898 and completed his legal studies there. He joined the civil service in his hometown in 1925 before joining the interior ministry in Prussia in 1929. He then took a position with the Reich Ministry of the Interior, where he worked for Stuckart and wrote an official interpretation of the Nazis' many racial laws. After being interned after the war, he was called back to service with the new democratic government. From 1953 to 1963, he served the Republic as the state secretary at the German Chancellery and an assistant to Chancellor Adenauer. In this position, his past caught up with him: the fact that he had written the interpretation of racial laws led to his resignation in 1963. In the same year, he was tried in absentia in an East German court on those same charges. He then moved to Switzerland and died in 1973.[112]

Bessie Margolin was the original drafter of U.S. Military Government Ordinance No. 7 (see Section 6.2), under which the Subsequent Nuremberg Trials took place; she was also a lawyer. She was born in New York in 1909 and started her legal practice with the Tennessee Valley Authority in 1933. In 1939, she began working for the U.S. Department of Labor, where she remained for the next thirty-three years, initially in the Wage and Hour Division. She became involved in defending labor law, such as the Fair Labor Standards Act, in front of the Supreme Court, arguing more than twenty-five cases there and winning most of them (and arguing another 150 in front of circuit courts). She volunteered to go overseas after the war to work in Europe, where she drafted the ordinance under which the Nuremberg courts operated. In her career she interacted professionally with many of the leading judicial figures of

---

111. *See Nuremberg Terms Run 4 to 25 Years*, N.Y. TIMES (Apr. 15, 1949).
112. *See Hans Globke Dies; Aide to Adenauer*, N.Y. TIMES (Feb. 14, 1973).

the time, including William O. Douglas, Robert Jackson, Abe Fortas, and Earl Warren. After her retirement in 1972, she was involved with teaching law and in leading arbitrations. She died in 1996.[113]

B. Cases

Although there were hundreds of trials after the war, the following seven cases highlight significant legal issues that emanated from the charges of crimes against humanity and war crimes: medical experimentation, slave labor, plunder of occupied countries, mass murder of civilians, murder of POWs, and systematic destruction of cultural life. As with all of the cases in this chapter, the discussions are greatly condensed summaries of extensive trial records running to thousands of pages.

1. Medical Experimentation

In the Doctors' Trial, *United States v. Karl Brandt*, one of the twelve trials comprising the Subsequent Nuremberg Trials, more than twenty physicians (including one female physician) affiliated with the SS, the armed forces, or civilian health agencies were charged with carrying out a barbaric series of medical experiments.[114] These included the following types of tests on human beings: high-altitude; freezing; malaria; mustard gas; sulfanilamide; bone, muscle, and nerve regeneration; bone transplantation; seawater; epidemic jaundice; typhus; poison; incendiary bomb; phlegmon; polygal; phenol; and mass sterilization. In addition, charges included murder of tubercular patients and euthanasia. Those charged included not only the high-ranking medical officials (Rudolf Brandt and Siegfried Handloser) but also the personal physicians to Hitler (Karl Brandt) and Himmler (Karl Gebhardt) and several concentration camp doctors (Waldemar Hoven).

The counts of the indictment were for conspiracy, belonging to a criminal organization, war crimes, and crimes against humanity. The principal count describing the crimes was war crimes, i.e., the defendants were charged with "murders, brutalities, cruelties, tortures, atrocities, and other inhuman acts"

---

113. *See Obituaries*, WASH. POST (June 21, 1996).
114. United States v. Karl Brandt, Case No. 1 (NMT 1946–47).

committed by carrying out medical experiments without consent on civilians of occupied countries and POWs. In more detail, the experiments included the following:

- Placing concentration camp inmates in low-pressure chambers and reducing the pressure to simulate altitudes up to twenty thousand meters
- Freezing concentration camp inmates by placing them in freezing water for hours or leaving them without clothes totally exposed outdoors while their body parts froze.
- Infecting concentration camp inmates with the malaria virus, yellow fever, smallpox, typhus, paratyphus A and B, cholera, diphtheria, and epidemic jaundice
- Exposing concentration camp inmates to mustard gas
- Severely wounding and then infecting concentration camp inmates with bacteria (e.g., streptococcus, gas gangrene, tetanus) to test sulfanilamide treatment
- Removing sections of bone, muscle, and nerves from concentration camp inmates to test regeneration
- Making concentration camp inmates live on a diet of only seawater
- Inflicting forced sterilizations on concentration camp inmates
- Secretly poisoning concentration camp inmates and killing them in order to conduct autopsies
- Inflicting phosphorous burns from incendiary bombs on concentration camp inmates

Defendants were also charged with measuring and killing a select group of more than one hundred Jewish inmates and then carrying out, for the purposes of research and completion of a skeleton collection, "comparison tests, anatomical research and studies regarding race, pathological features of the body, form and size of the brain."[115] In addition, they were charged with the murder or mistreatment of thousands of Poles with tuberculosis and the murder of hundreds of thousands of humans (so-called useless eaters) in a "systematic and secret execution of the aged, insane, incurably ill, of deformed children,

---

115. *Id.* at Vol. I, 15.

and other persons, by gas, lethal injections, and diverse other means in nursing homes, hospitals, and asylums."[116]

The details of these experiments are beyond human belief and difficult to comprehend, let alone read; the following example from the high-altitude experiments highlights these unspeakable horrors:

> It was a continuous experiment without oxygen at a height of 12 kilometers conducted on a 37-year-old Jew in good general condition. Breathing continued up to 30 minutes. After 4 minutes the experimental subject began to perspire and wiggle his head, after 5 minutes cramps occurred, between 6 and 10 minutes breathing increased in speed and the experimental subject became unconscious; from 11 to 30 minutes breathing slowed down to three breaths per minute, finally stopping altogether.... One hour after breathing had stopped, the spinal marrow was completely severed and the brain removed. Thereupon, the action of the auricle of the heart stopped for 40 seconds. It then renewed its action, coming to a complete standstill 8 minutes later. A heavy subarachnoid oedema was found in the brain. In the veins and arteries of the brain, a considerable quantity of air was discovered. Furthermore, the blood vessels in the heart and liver were enormously obstructed by embolism.[117]

Chief prosecutor Taylor began his opening statement thus:

> The victims of these crimes are numbered in the hundreds of thousands. A handful only are still alive; a few of the survivors will appear in this courtroom. But most of these miserable victims were slaughtered outright or died in the course of the tortures to which they were subjected. For the most part they are nameless dead. To their murderers, these wretched people were not individuals at all. They came in wholesale lots and were treated worse than animals.... The defendants in the dock are charged with murder, but this is no mere murder trial.... They are not ignorant men. Most of them are trained physicians and some of them are distinguished scientists. Yet these defendants, all of whom were

116. *Id.*
117. *Id.* at Vol. I, 146.

fully able to comprehend the nature of their acts, and most of whom were exceptionally qualified to form a moral and professional judgment in this respect, are responsible for wholesale murder and unspeakably cruel tortures.[118]

The defense argued that the leaders of the medical services, starting with Brandt, should not be charged with the crimes of their subordinates; that their powers were not as great as suggested by the prosecution; and that those who were subordinates were only following orders and should not be held liable for doing so. In addition, the defense argued that Poland had been totally occupied and could be considered subject to German law; that the concentration camp inmates volunteered for the experiments; that the experiments were of military necessity; that the experiments were a substitute for sentences that were previously handed out to the concentration camp inmates; and that medical ethics should not be considered in these proceedings for a number of reasons, including different standards globally and successful experiments in the past.

Rejecting such arguments, the court ruled that the medical experiments were a systematic part of the war effort and that they were ordered or approved by "persons in positions of authority who under all principles of law were under the duty to know about these things and to take steps to terminate or prevent them."[119] In addition, the court ruled that "all of these experiments involving brutalities, tortures, disabling injury, and death were performed in complete disregard of international conventions, the laws and customs of war, the general principles of criminal law as derived from the criminal laws of all civilized nations, and Control Council Law No. 10."[120] Of the twenty-three defendants, seven were acquitted (one of these was subsequently convicted by another court) and sixteen convicted; the leaders of the "health" functions in the Nazi government, military, and SS and the personal physicians to Nazi leaders were given lengthy sentences, lifetime imprisonment, or death (Drs. K. Brandt, Gebhardt, Hoven, and Joachim Mrugowsky and officials Viktor Brack, R. Brandt, and Wolfram Sievers). The executions were carried out in June 1948 after the U.S. Supreme Court rejected a writ of habeas corpus petition.

---

118. *Id.* at Vol. I, 28.
119. *Id.* at Vol. II, 181.
120. *Id.* at Vol. II, 183.

LEGAL PROFILES

Robert Servatius was the defense counsel for Brandt in this case. He was born in Germany in 1894 and completed his legal studies there. After serving in the army in artillery units in WWI, he entered private practice but also spent years studying foreign languages (besides German, he spoke French, Russian, and English), almost letting his law license lapse in the interim. He refused to join the Nazi Party, which left him outside the power structure and suspect. Thus, he rejoined the army in an artillery unit despite his age. Besides serving as the defense counsel in this trial, he defended Fritz Sauckel and the Nazi leadership as an organization at the IMT. After his three years at Nuremberg, he returned to practice as a trial lawyer in his hometown of Cologne. Most famously, Servatius served as the defense counsel for Adolf Eichmann in 1961 in Eichmann's trial in Israel. Servatius died in 1983.[121]

Walter B. Beals was the presiding judge in this case. He was born in Minnesota in 1876 but began his legal practice in Washington State. He graduated with the first class from the University of Washington School of Law (as did his future wife). During WWI, he served in the army working in the Office of the Judge Advocate General but also saw action. He stayed in France for a while after the war serving as liaison to the French government and was one of the founders of the American Legion; he received the French Legion of Honor. From 1923 to 1926, he served as the assistant corporate counsel to the City of Seattle. He then took on the role of judge of the superior court, where he served until 1928. He then was appointed to the state supreme court, a position he held until 1946 through several reelections, and was three times the chief justice. He died in 1960.[122]

Alfred Seidl was the defense counsel for Gebhardt, Fritz Fischer, and Herta Oberheuser in this case. He was born in Germany in 1911 and completed his legal studies there. He was a member of the Nazi Party and

---

121. See *Defender of a Nazi: Robert Servatius*, N.Y. TIMES (Apr. 18, 1961).
122. See *Walter B. Beals, 84, Ex-Justice on Coast*, N.Y. TIMES (Sept. 21, 1960).

then joined the German army in WWII. After the war, he was defense counsel at the IMT for both Rudolf Hess and Hans Frank (see Section 6.4). He defended Hans Lammers in the Ministries Trial, Oswald Pohl in the Pohl Trial, and Walter Dürrfeld in the IG Farben Trial in front of the NMT, and Ilse Koch in front of a German court at Augsburg. After the war era, he defended IG Farben against a forced labor suit in 1951. In 1958, he became a member of the parliament in Bavaria; and in the mid- to late 1970s, he served in the state's Ministry of Justice and then as interior minister. He still was trying to get Rudolf Hess freed when he died in 1993.[123]

---

2. Slave Labor and Plunder

There were three economic trials under the NMT. The first was the Flick Trial, *United States v. Friedrich Flick*;[124] the second the IG Farben Trial, *United States v. Carl Krauch*;[125] and the third the Krupp Trial, *United States v. Alfried Krupp*.[126] The charges among the three were similar although not completely the same. However, in each of them, the defendants were charged with crimes against humanity for the use of slave labor and for the exploitation and spoliation of occupied countries. The Krupp case will be discussed in more detail to illustrate these common issues.

From 1903 to late 1943, the Krupp firm, which manufactured arms, among other things, was incorporated as Friedrich Krupp A.G., Essen; and thereafter it was an unincorporated firm called Friedrich Krupp, Essen. Founded in 1812, the business consisted of more than two hundred subsidiaries situated globally during the WWII era. Gustav Krupp, the leading figure in this group of companies, was indicted by the IMT, but he was not brought to trial because he was incapacitated. Thus, the defendants in the Krupp Trial were his son Alfried, who controlled the group as sole owner after it became unincorporated; eight other members of the managing board (directors after the company became unincorporated); and three company officials. The counts included crimes

123. *See Berlin Court Rejects a Bid to Free Rudolf Hess*, N.Y. TIMES (Feb. 25, 1981).
124. United States v. Friedrich Flick, Case No. 5 (NMT 1947).
125. United States v. Carl Krauch, Case No. 6 (NMT 1947–48).
126. United States v. Alfried Krupp, Case No. 10 (NMT 1947–48).

against peace, conspiracy to commit crimes against peace, and two counts of crimes against humanity.

In terms of crimes against peace, the defendants were accused of participation in starting invasions and wars of aggression in violation of international laws and treaties: Austria (March 1938); Czechoslovakia (October 1938 and March 1939); Poland (September 1939); the United Kingdom and France (September 1939); Denmark and Norway (April 1940); Belgium, the Netherlands, and Luxembourg (May 1940); Yugoslavia and Greece (April 1941); the USSR (June 1941); and the United States (December 1941). The impact from these invasions and wars was significant:

> [M]any millions of people were murdered, tortured, starved, enslaved, and robbed; countless numbers became diseased; millions of homes were left in ruins; tremendous industrial capacity capable of raising the standard of living of peoples all over the world was destroyed; agricultural land capable of feeding millions of people was laid in waste; and a large part of the world was left in economic and political chaos. The lives and happiness of two billion people were adversely affected as the result of these invasions and wars of aggression.[127]

In terms of conspiracy to commit these crimes against peace, the Krupp company was accused of facilitating German wars of aggression for generations as the "principal German maker of large caliber artillery, armor plate, and other high quality armament, the largest private builder of U-boats and warships, and the second largest producer of iron and coal in Germany."[128] It also built tanks. In violation of the Versailles Treaty (see Chapter 1), it continued research and building of armaments after WWI. It worked with the Nazi regime before it came to power and then afterward beginning in the mid-1930s to develop industrial support and plan for the forthcoming war effort. This included research into replacements for raw materials normally imported, research and developments in armaments, and restriction of exports of raw materials to potential enemies. The company also used patents and agreements in foreign countries to restrict foreign production, keep foreign prices high,

---

127. *Id.* at 10.
128. *Id.* at 11.

and gather technical information. To the vast enrichment of the family's fortune, it worked closely with the Nazis at all levels for its many aggressions into other countries.

One of the counts of war crimes and crimes against humanity involved plunder and spoliation. The defendants were involved in the plundering, "exploitation, spoliation, devastations and other offenses" against public and private property and the civilian economies of occupied countries.[129] This exploitation of occupied countries was effected "beyond the needs of the army of occupation and in disregard of the need of the local economy . . . and out of all proportion to their resources."[130] The list of plundered resources included raw materials, agricultural products, machine tools, transportation equipment, foreign securities, foreign exchange, patent rights, and commercial enterprises. Local production was curtailed in favor of production for the Nazi war effort as raw materials and equipment from occupied countries were often paid for by that country through forced loans, excessive occupation charges, and currency manipulation. This served to ensure the further Nazi domination of these countries. As Göring said,

> [T]here must be removed from the territories . . . all raw materials, scrap materials, machines, etc., which are of use for the German war economy. Enterprises which are not absolutely necessary for the meager maintenance of the bare existence of the population must be transferred to Germany, unless . . . it [is] more practicable to exploit those enterprises by giving them German orders, to be executed at their present location. . . . It makes no difference to me if . . . your people [in the occupied country] will starve.[131]

The Krupp company leadership was active in traveling through occupied countries to formulate and carry out plans to plunder them. Ownership of assets was acquired through seizures, purchases, and leases "influenced by force" and by sales of companies from the occupation government to the Krupp company; many assets were taken over as enemy or Jewish property. Early on,

---

129. *Id.* at 23.
130. *Id.*
131. *Id.* at 24.

the Krupp company drew up plans to take back assets lost in WWI and to add materials or enterprises that would be advantageous to it. These crimes occurred in France, Belgium, the Netherlands, Austria, Yugoslavia, Greece, and the Soviet Union.

The other count of war crimes and crimes against humanity involved slave labor. The defendants were part of a plan of forced labor, including women and children, that saw at least five million people sent to Germany for this purpose. The "treatment of slave laborers and prisoners of war was based on the principle that they should be fed, sheltered, and treated in such a way as to exploit them to the greatest possible extent at the lowest possible expenditure."[132] The defendants requested and recruited foreign workers, POWs, and concentration camp inmates from the SS, military, and other Reich entities and set up their own recruitment offices in occupied countries, where workers were "forced, terrorized, and misled into employment with Krupp."[133]

In deporting, exploiting, and abusing these people, the defendants forced them to work "under inhumane conditions and subjected [them] to atrocities, ill-treatment, and offenses against their persons in innumerable ways."[134] They were starved and kept under guard and behind barbed wire. Krupp employees committed many acts of violence on the foreign workers, including torture from equipment manufactured by the Krupp firm and forms of water torture. Children were often separated from parents to ensure their parents' labor. All normal working conditions were absent: clothing, medical care, shelter, and food were inadequate; rest was minimal; and workdays were excessively long. Workers were subject to minimal protection from air raid bombings and forced to work under highly dangerous conditions.

In his opening statement, chief prosecutor Taylor set the tone for the trial when he declared that "Krupp and the German militarists are the indestructible common denominator of Germany's murderous and obstinately repeated lunges at the world's throat." Taylor was not seeking to attack the armaments business but rather the Krupp company and its centuries-old armaments mentality, i.e., seeing itself as the "trustee of a historical inheritance, to safeguard the valuable experiences, irreplaceable for the armed strength of our nation."[135] In

---

132. *Id.* at 30.
133. *Id.* at 31.
134. *Id.*
135. *Id.* at 68.

other words, the Krupp firm's philosophy was that when Germany rises again by shaking off the "chains of Versailles," the Krupp firm needed to be ready.[136]

In putting this philosophy into practice, the defendants repeatedly violated the Versailles Treaty, which greatly limited German armament. These violations occurred through overseas manufacture, testing, and sale of prohibited armaments such as submarines, tanks, gun carriages, and other military vehicles. There was also significant use of front companies in foreign countries, allowing the design and manufacturing expertise to remain with the company for later use. This occurred both during the Weimar Republic and the successor Nazi regime. As the power of the Nazis rose, so rose the wealth of the Krupp firm, which was closely joined to the ruling regime.

The defense argued that Alfried Krupp was being forced to answer charges that really were applicable to his incapacitated father, that much of the evidence should not have been admitted, that the company was not involved in spoliation as it either paid for everything or in actuality received nothing, that slave labor charges could be offset by the social achievements with which the Krupp family had been credited, that the title of seized assets was not transferred to the defendants, that the acts of spoliation were authorized by the German government, and that the firm did not profit unduly in the Hitler years.

The crimes against peace and the conspiracy charges were dismissed, but the defendants were found guilty of spoliation and slave labor.

Under the spoliation charge, the court found that the defendants far exceeded what was needed under international law, disfavored the occupied countries, and acquired assets under duress. The defendants could not hide behind saying that they were authorized by the government to despoil, nor could they use the emergency of the war as a justification for spoliation. Citing numerous examples from occupied countries, the court found the Krupp firm and a number of its leaders guilty on the charges of spoliation.

Under the slave labor charge, the court, citing violations of the Third Geneva Convention on the treatment of POWs, found the use of French, Belgian, Dutch, Polish, Yugoslavian, Russian, and Italian POWs to be contrary to international law. Foreign civilian workers from occupied countries were often recruited based on mandatory labor laws, "convicted," and required to work for Krupp as their sentence; or they were captured in manhunts and

---

136. *Id.* at 125.

similarly required to work for Krupp. They were treated on a discriminatory basis depending on whether they were from western European or eastern European countries, and they were threatened with confinement in Gestapo punishment camps if they didn't continue working. The separation of children from parents led many children to die of malnutrition. Concentration camp inmates were used in special Krupp armaments factories and for construction and other projects, often handpicked by Krupp employees. For all of these reasons and those contained in the indictment and for the wholesale deportations of slave labor from occupied countries, the court found eleven of the twelve defendants guilty of the slave labor count. Ten of the defendants received sentences ranging from three to twelve years. Krupp received the longest sentence: twelve years and forfeiture of all of his property. In actuality, though, Krupp's property was never sold due to lack of buyers, and he reclaimed it upon his eventual release from prison.

LEGAL PROFILES

Otto Kranzbühler was the defense counsel for Alfried Krupp in this case. He was born in Germany in 1907 and completed his legal studies there. Following his interest in maritime law, he enlisted in the German navy in 1934. Subsequently, he became a legal adviser for the high command of the navy. During the war, he was a naval judge advocate. After the war, Admiral Karl Dönitz, the commander of the German navy and successor to Hitler as the leader of Germany, asked Kranzbühler to be his defense counsel at the IMT. In subsequent decades, he practiced corporate law, including representing firms such as Krupp against forced labor lawsuits. He died in 2004.[137]

Cecelia H. Goetz was associate counsel for the prosecution in the Krupp case. She was born in New York in 1917 and completed her legal studies there. In 1943, she started working for the U.S. Department of Justice Office of the Solicitor. She then applied to join the Nuremberg

---

137. *See* GERMANS IN THE 20TH CENTURY (Univ. of Marburg).

prosecution team but was able to do so only after intervention from the chief prosecution counsel Telford Taylor. She served on the Nuremberg prosecution team from 1946 to 1948, also working on the Flick Trial. After that, she returned home to join her father's law firm. She then worked for the federal government in the Office of Price Stabilization and the Justice Department before returning to private practice. In 1978, she became a judge in the federal bankruptcy court. She worked until retiring in 1993. She died in 2004.[138]

William J. Wilkins was a judge in this case and the author of the dissenting opinion on whether the court had jurisdiction over spoliation acts committed in Austria, France, Yugoslavia, and the USSR. He was born in Michigan in 1897 but started his legal practice in Washington State. Prior to this, he served in the army in WWI. From 1929 to 1934, he served as a deputy county prosecutor and then entered private practice. In 1940, he was appointed as a superior court judge. During the war, he served in the Judge Advocate General's Corps. After the war, he returned to the bench until his retirement in 1972. He died in 1995.[139]

3. Concentration Camps

There were many trials at the concentration camps. The section discusses two such military trials, one that was held by the Americans at Dachau and the other by the British at Belsen.

a. Dachau

United States v. Martin Gottfried Weiss was part of a larger collection of camp trials held at the Dachau concentration camp (Dachau Trials), but this one concerned the operation of the Dachau camp itself.[140] The charges were that the forty defendants operated according to a common plan to subject civil-

---

138. *See* NYU Law, Alumnus/Alumna of the Month: Cecelia Goetz (Sept. 2004).
139. *See Last of Nuremburg-Tribunal Judges, William Wilkins, Dies at 98*, Seattle Times (Sept. 12, 1995).
140. United States v. Martin Gottfried Weiss, Case No. 000-50-2 (U.S. Military Tribunal, Dachau 1945).

ians (contrary to the Hague Convention of 1907) and POWs (contrary to the Third Geneva Convention) to cruelties and mistreatments including killings, beatings, tortures, starvation, abuses, and indignities.

The prosecution presented evidence that the main camp was built for eight thousand inmates but contained thirty-three thousand upon liberation. This led to highly unsanitary conditions, leading to epidemics and death. The food and clothing was insufficient for the inmates' eighteen-hour workdays, leading to a large number of starvations. Inmates were subjected to medical experiments and discipline was strict, leading to beatings and potential executions. Ill inmates were often shipped off-site to be executed. The defense denied specific incidents and also argued that the defendants were subject to the orders of their superiors in regard to camp conditions.

The court found all forty defendants, including nine camp leaders or deputy leaders and the camp doctor, guilty. After review, death sentences stood for twenty-eight of the forty, with sentences of hard labor from ten years to life for the remainder of the defendants. Defense motions that the court did not have jurisdiction over nonenemy offenders or over non-Allied victims were rejected. The defense also made a motion that under the Third Geneva Convention the defendants who were POWs assigned as guards of other POWs had to be tried in the same manner as U.S. troops facing court-martial. The court rejected this motion because the defendants were acting as enemy combatants, not POWs.

LEGAL PROFILES

William Denson was the lead prosecutor in this case. He was born in Alabama in 1913 and started his practice there. He was commissioned into the army after graduating from West Point in 1934 but resigned his commission to attend law school. He returned to Alabama to practice law with his father and then taught law at West Point from 1942 to 1945. He then joined the Judge Advocate General's Corps and was assigned to Germany. From 1945 to 1947, he was the chief prosecutor for the concentration camp cases, including Mauthausen, Buchenwald, and Flossenbürg, and prosecuted almost two hundred defendants, more than half of whom were eventually executed. After the trials, he returned to the United States and joined the Atomic Energy Commission as chief of litigation. He subsequently returned to private practice in intellectual property. He died in 1998.[141]

---

b. Belsen

In the *Trial of Josef Kramer and 44 Others* held at the Belsen concentration camp, the forty-five defendants, including camp commandant Josef Kramer, were charged with killings and ill-treatments of Allied civilians and POWs at both the Belsen and Auschwitz concentration camps.[142] All of the defendants were staff members at one of the concentration camps, charged with the well-being of those interned there. The legal foundation for this trial limited its jurisdiction to victims from Allied countries, of which there were ten represented at this trial (Britain, Poland, France, the Netherlands, Belgium, Italy, Czechoslovakia, Greece, Russia, and Honduras).

The prosecution stated that the conditions at these camps were brought about not only by criminal neglect but also by deliberate starvation and ill-treatment. In addition, at Auschwitz there were deliberate exterminations of "thousands and probably millions of people."[143] The affidavits and testimony of many witnesses were presented, including those of concentration camp survivors as well as British soldiers and doctors who liberated the camps. The use of gassings, beatings, savage dogs, overwork, underfeeding, ill-treatment, and involuntary medical experiments was common.

The defendants' lawyers argued that the superior orders, necessity, and superiority of municipal over international law were valid defenses; that the offenses were not war crimes as the defendants were not part of the military; that some of the victims had become German nationals under occupation; that the state was responsible, not the individual; that there were discrepancies between affidavits and testimony; that a certain degree of violence was necessary to keep order and preserve food supplies; and that concentration camps were legal under German municipal law. The defense team also argued that the

---

141. *See William Denson Dies at 85; Helped in Convicting* Nazis, N.Y. TIMES (Dec. 16, 1998).
142. Trial of Josef Kramer and 44 Others (British Military Court, Lüneburg 1945).
143. *Id.*

Polish nationals who were defendants could not be charged because they were not enemies of the British. In addition, the defense served motions to separate the two concentration camp trials and requested that all of the defendants be tried separately.

The prosecution rebutted that all victims were protected under international law, that war criminals were individually responsible, that German annexations were not legal during the war, that most offenses were contrary to superior orders, that members of the SS were in the military, that the use of the gas chambers was done with the knowledge that it was wrong, and that the Polish defendants should be regarded the same as the other defendants as they had allied themselves with the Germans.

The court found thirty of the forty-five defendants guilty (one became ill and was excused). Twelve of those were sentenced to death, one to life imprisonment, and the remainder to various prison terms. The sentences were carried out shortly thereafter.

LEGAL PROFILES

Herbert Arthur (H. A.) Smith, colonel, presented the closing statement for the defense in this case. He was born in India in 1885 and completed his legal studies in England. In 1911, he was a law tutor at Oxford. He fought in WWI and was a member of the British mission to the United States from 1918 to 1919, giving lectures. He taught at McGill University in Canada from 1920 to 1928 as a professor of jurisprudence and common law. In 1928, he took a position at the University of London as a professor of international law, remaining there until his retirement in 1948 and attaining the status of professor emeritus. During the war, he was involved in official war work. He was considered an expert in international law, especially maritime law. He published a number of books on these and other subjects, including the U.S. Supreme Court, federalism in North America, the economic use of international rivers, and the law of the sea.[144]

---

144. *See* 12 ANNUAIRE CANADIEN DE DROIT INTERNATIONAL (1974).

4. Murder of POWs
Two cases pertaining to the murder of POWs involved the incidents at Malmedy and Essen.

a. Malmedy
In *United States v. Valentin Bersin*, convictions ensued after many American POWs and Belgian civilians were killed, but the case then transformed into an investigation of whether appropriate methods were used to extract the confessions upon which the convictions were based.[145]

In *Valentin Bersin*, approximately 350 American POWs were allegedly killed by the Waffen-SS in twelve locations in Belgium over a month's time during the Ardennes Counteroffensive, better known as the Battle of the Bulge. Eighty-four of the POWs were killed outside the Belgium town of Malmedy, so the entire trial was termed the Malmedy Massacre. Brought before the U.S. Military Tribunal at Dachau, the seventy-five defendants, including General Sepp Dietrich and Lieutenant Colonel Joachim Peiper of the Waffen-SS, were also charged with killing one hundred Belgian civilians. One defendant committed suicide, and another was dismissed due to French nationality, leaving seventy-three. Based largely on affidavits signed by the defense, all seventy-three were convicted; forty-three were sentenced to death and the remainder to life imprisonment or lengthy prison terms.

The defense protested the mock trials and beatings that were used to obtain the confessions on which the defendants' convictions were based. The defendants were originally housed together in prison (more than four hundred men at first), making it difficult to keep them from communicating to synchronize their stories; they were also sworn to secrecy by their leader Peiper and given false information to relay. However, the defense protestations led to a series of investigations, including by the U.S. Congress.

A congressional committee traveled to Germany, interviewed more than one hundred witnesses, and issued a report in 1949.[146] This report explained that accounts of physical abuse of defendants primarily did not surface until

---

145. United States v. Valentin Bersin, Case No. 6-24 (U.S. Military Tribunal, Dachau 1946).
146. U.S. SENATE, MALMEDY MASSACRE INVESTIGATION: REPORT OF THE SUBCOMMITTEE OF THE COMMITTEE ON ARMED SERVICES (Oct. 19, 1949).

long after the trial and convictions. The report analyzed the pretrial investigation phase and the trial itself. Despite the many claims of pretrial malfeasance, it was only able to establish that mock trials, hoods, and ruses were used on several of the defendants. Other allegations of physical abuse, starvation, fake hangings, solitary confinement, etc., generally were not borne out by corroborated evidence (e.g., subsequent physical exams).

However, regarding the trial, the committee felt that the defense was not given adequate time to prepare. Other points raised by the defense, such as severance and the inability to cross-examine witnesses without foundation, were found to be legally correct (although this committee was not serving as an appeals court). In general, the committee recommended the use of more experienced lawyers and citizens who had been naturalized at least ten years.

Besides the preliminary review by the army, the secretary of the army, Kenneth Royall, later appointed a commission of two judges to review all cases from the Dachau courts for which there were unexecuted death sentences. This committee recommended commuting the twelve sentences related to this case to life imprisonment. A justice review board was also convened to review the case, and it agreed with the previous findings on mock trials and ruses. An appeal to the U.S. Supreme Court for a writ of habeas corpus was unsuccessful for the same reasons as those emerging from the NMT. However, the army had been commuting many of the death sentences to life imprisonment (originally commuting thirty-one of the forty-three); and in the end, with the various points raised and with an eye on the Cold War and the Federal Republic of Germany as an emerging ally, all twelve remaining death sentences were commuted.

LEGAL PROFILES

Herbert J. Strong was an assistant counsel to lead defense counsel Willis M. Everett in this trial. He was born in Germany in 1904, completed his legal studies there, and began his legal practice there. However, he immigrated to America as a refugee in 1937 because he was Jewish. He began practicing law in the United States but volunteered to go back to

Germany for this trial, where he was involved in defending twelve of the accused. After the war, he continued to work in law firms in the United States until his retirement in 1984. He died in 1986.[147]

b. Essen

The *Trial of Erick Heyer & Six Others* concerned three British airmen who were killed by civilians after being captured by the German military.[148] Erick Heyer, the captain, sent the men to Luftwaffe headquarters and told his men in a loud voice in front of a crowd of civilians not to interfere if the crowd tried to harm the airmen. And that is what occurred: the crowd grew bigger as the airmen were led through a main street in Essen, and the airmen were beaten with sticks and assaulted by stones thrown by the crowd; upon reaching a bridge, the airmen were tossed over, and one was killed instantly while the other two subsequently died from beatings and shots fired.

Heyer, a private, and five civilians were brought before a British military court and charged with inciting the crowd to commit murder. The private was charged with not fulfilling his duty to protect the POWs in his custody even though he had a weapon and could have done so. The five civilians were charged with the assaults and murders. The court found Heyer and one civilian guilty and sentenced them to be executed. One of the civilians was sentenced to life imprisonment and one for ten years, and the others were found not guilty. The private was sentenced to five years' imprisonment.

5. Crimes During Occupation

In *Trial of Dr. Josef Bühler*, Poland brought charges against Josef Bühler, the deputy to the governor general of the country during its occupation.[149] The charges were that during the period of German occupation of the western part of Poland, the defendant was a member of the occupying government, a criminal organization, and he committed war crimes and crimes against humanity, specifically

---

147. *See Herbert J. Strong, 82, Attorney in War Case*, N.Y. TIMES (Oct. 16, 1986).
148. Trial of Erick Heyer & Six Others (British Military Ct. for the Trial of War Criminals 1945).
149. Trial of Dr. Josef Bühler (Sup. Nat'l Tribunal of Pol. 1948).

individual and mass murders of civilians, torturing, ill-treating, and persecuting of Polish civilians, systematic destruction of Polish cultural life and looting of Polish art treasures, germanisation, seizure of public property, and in economic exploitation of the country's resources, and of its inhabitants, and in systematically depriving Polish citizens of private property.[150]

The tribunal established that Hitler's plan for Poland after its annexation included destroying the intellectual base, destroying any means of coalescing as a nation, and forcing the people down to "the lowest standard of living and . . . allow[ing] only the minimum necessary for the sustenance, so that they become a source of cheap labour for Germany."[151] Furthermore, regarding food for the Polish population, the tribunal found that Hitler's plan was as follows: "In connection with the food supply for the population it must be attained at all costs that people engaged in concerns of vital or military importance shall maintain their efficiency, while the rest of the population shall during the food shortage be reduced to a minimum of food."[152]

By a decree of Hitler, the occupation government was effected, with the ability to legislate by decree. One such decree established the court system, including courts that dealt with matters related to German nationals and security. Special Courts were created in the country, with the power to hand out death sentences or deportations to concentration camps. Polish courts only existed where German jurisdiction did not reach and even then could be overruled by German courts.

The tribunal in *Trial of Dr. Josef Bühler* detailed the widespread police ill-treatments, torture, and murders in conjunction with the summary police courts and Special Courts; the forced labor; and the extermination of Jews. In the educational sphere, the Polish curriculum had been totally revised, restricting it to technical and professional courses to prepare a workforce for the Germans. Universities and art schools were closed or changed to work-focused schools, while libraries and laboratories were closed and their contents moved to Germany. Newspapers and periodicals were shut down. Art and cultural

---

150. *Id.*
151. *Id.*
152. *Id.*

assets were looted and sent to Germany. Public and private property was seized, with rights transferred to the Nazis. Raw materials, forests, farmland, livestock, and industrial capacity were exploited; and industrial facilities not dedicated to armaments were broken up. One million industrial and agricultural workers were deported to Germany to work in those positions. Referencing the illegality of these actions under international law, the tribunal reviewed the evidence against Bühler's boss, Hans Frank, who was tried at the IMT, and that court's pronouncement of guilt (see Section 6.4). Bühler was involved in the same activities as his boss, attending the same meetings and drafting and implementing many of these laws.

Bühler was also a willing participant in the Wannsee Conference in 1942, where the Nazis decided upon the Final Solution. This would significantly impact the three million Jews in Poland at the time, and these exterminations of human life would occur in Poland. Bühler gave orders upon his return to prepare to implement this plan and to confiscate Jewish property. He also drafted and signed many laws that carried death penalties in the Special Courts or summary police courts, often for minor offenses.

The defense argued that Bühler was merely following superior orders, of which he did not have knowledge of the consequences, and that the criminal actions were the responsibility of the state and not the individual. As with other tribunals, the tribunal in this case rejected the defenses of superior orders and lack of individual responsibility and found Bühler guilty, sentencing him to death and confiscation of his property. The sentence was carried out soon afterwards. The occupying government leadership team itself was also declared a criminal organization, after a criminal investigation. (This was in contrast to what occurred at the IMT (see Section 6.4), where the leadership of the Reich was not declared a criminal organization, but only perhaps for practical reasons (most of the defendants on trial were already dead).)

LEGAL PROFILES

Josef Bühler was a defendant in this trial before the Supreme National Tribunal of Poland. He was born in Germany in 1904 and completed his legal studies there. He began working for Hans Frank in 1933 at the inception of the Nazi government. He followed Frank to Munich, becoming the court administrator and then the district attorney in 1935. After the invasion of Poland, he followed Frank there to act as his deputy in the occupation of the country. After testifying in Frank's defense at the IMT, he was deported to Poland to face this trial. He was subsequently executed in 1948.[153]

C. Subsequent Events

After the various Allied legal proceedings through the end of the 1940s, Germany itself began to take up cases against German nationals and other surviving Nazi functionaries for war crimes and crimes against humanity. These cases targeted those who perpetrated the final acts instead of the planning, including "final phase" crimes (i.e., those committed with knowledge that the war was concluding), such as the shooting of a priest for making "derogatory" remarks about the German military situation in April 1945.[154] These occurred in both West German and East German courts, and sometimes these two countries tried the same acts. For example, both countries tried perpetrators of the liquidation of the Warsaw ghetto, mass extermination of inmates at the Treblinka concentration camp, the killing of mentally ill patients at various institutions, and the deportations to concentration camps. In total, the courts investigated more than one hundred thousand cases, handing out thousands of convictions ranging from execution to life imprisonment to varying prison terms.[155] These investigations and convictions have continued up to the current day, including the conviction in 2011 of John Demjanjuk in a German court and the investigations of still living Auschwitz concentration camp guards.[156]

D. Modern Applicability

The charge of crimes against humanity has become part of customary international law since the Nazi war criminal trials. It is now used against leaders of fallen totalitarian states, such as the leaders of the former Yugoslavia and Rwanda in their respective international criminal tribunals. Under the statute

---

153. *See Josef Bühler*, HAUS DER WANNSEE-KONFERENZ.
154. State v. Heinrich Perner, Case No. 062, LG Friedburg (1948) (Ger.).
155. *The Hunt for Nazi War Criminals*, DER SPIEGEL (May 13, 2009).
156. *Nearly 70 Years Later, a New Round of Auschwitz Prosecutions*, N.Y. TIMES (Apr. 10, 2013).

used to support the trial of the Serbian leaders,[157] tribunals may prosecute grave breaches of the Fourth Geneva Convention of 1949, violations of laws or customs of war, genocide, or crimes against humanity. The latter is defined as murder; extermination; enslavement; deportation; imprisonment; torture; rape; persecutions on political, racial, or religious grounds; or other inhumane acts. The statute also provides for individual criminal responsibility for those who plan, order, carry out, aid, and abet such crimes, without exceptions for official positions, crimes committed by a subordinate (where the leader knew or should have known), or actions pursuant to superior orders (but this may be a mitigating factor in punishment). For example, the revised indictment against Serb leader Radovan Karadžić included counts of genocide; crimes against humanity (persecutions, extermination, murder, deportation, and inhumane acts (e.g., forcible transfers)); and violations of the laws or customs of war (murder, acts of terror, unlawful attacks on civilians, and the taking of hostages).[158]

In 1998, the U.N. General Assembly adopted the Rome Statute, establishing the International Criminal Court.[159] This law further expanded and refined the definition of *crimes against humanity*, describing these as

> particularly odious offenses in that they constitute a serious attack on human dignity or grave humiliation or a degradation of one or more human beings. They are not isolated or sporadic events, but are part either of a government policy (although the perpetrators need not identify themselves with this policy) or of a wide practice of atrocities tolerated or condoned by a government or a de facto authority.[160]

The revised list included the following:

(a) Murder;
(b) Extermination;

---

157. Statute of the International Tribunal for Persecution of Persons Responsible for Serious Violations of International Humanitarian Law Committed in the Territory of the Former Yugoslavia Since 1991, S.C. Res. 827, U.N. Doc. S/RES/827 (May 25, 1993), *reaffirming* S.C. Res. 808, U.N. Doc. S/RES/808 (1993).

158. Prosecutor of the Tribunal v. Radovan Karadžić, Case No. IT-95-5.18-PT (ICTR for the Former Yugo. Feb. 27, 2009) (third amended indictment).

159. United Nations Diplomatic Conference of Plenipotentiaries on the Establishment of an International Criminal Court (July 7, 1998).

160. *Id.*

(c) Enslavement;

(d) Deportation or forcible transfer of population;

(e) Imprisonment or other severe deprivation of physical liberty in violation of fundamental rules of international law;

(f) Torture;

(g) Rape, sexual slavery, enforced prostitution, forced pregnancy, enforced sterilization, or any other form of sexual violence of comparable gravity;

(h) Persecution against any identifiable group or collectivity on political, racial, national, ethnic, cultural, religious, gender as defined in paragraph 3, or other grounds that are universally recognized as impermissible under international law, in connection with any act referred to in this paragraph or any crime within the jurisdiction of the Court;

(i) Enforced disappearance of persons;

(j) The crime of apartheid;

(k) Other inhumane acts of a similar character intentionally causing great suffering, or serious injury to body or to mental or physical health.[161]

Proving a common plan or scheme in a war crimes trial is still often elusive in modern times. The leader of the Croatian military district was convicted in 2011 for involvement in a joint criminal enterprise to remove the Serbian population from a region of Croatia by bombing a number of towns in 1995. The common plan was to remove this civilian population by force or threat of force as part of Operation Storm. This conviction was largely based upon the ruling that bombing these towns was illegal because it targeted civilians. The appeals chamber reversed the conviction, after finding that there was insufficient evidence to conclude beyond a reasonable doubt that the bombings were unlawful.[162] The trial chamber had ruled that bombardments that had impact outside a range of two hundred meters from a legitimate military target were illegal, but the appeals chamber did not find a sufficient basis for this standard. The appeals chamber found that the defendant was not a member of the joint criminal enterprise and that there was insufficient evidence in the trial record for a conviction under any other legal theory, so the defendant was acquitted.

---

161. *Id.*

162. Prosecutor of the Tribunal v. Ante Gotovina & Mladen Markač, Case No. IT-06-90 (ICTR for the Former Yugo. Nov. 16, 2012).

In terms of destruction of the cultural life of countries, a smaller version of this extreme conduct has played out modernly. In 2001, the Taliban in Afghanistan declared war on Buddhist and other cultural artifacts in the country. It destroyed the Buddhas of Bamiyan, which were two very large statues of the standing Buddha in the country that had been carved out of the sandstone cliffs during the sixth and seventh centuries. The leader of the Taliban also ordered the destruction of other artifacts that predated Islam and were thus considered idols. In 2012, similar planned attacks were made upon the Buddhist statues in the Maldives and upon ancient tombs in Timbuktu. In addition, several nonstate-directed attacks on culture have occurred with the fall of regimes, such as in Iraq in 2003 and Egypt in 2011.

6.4 GENOCIDE

A. Statutes

Originating with the 1920 Nazi Party doctrine ("[o]nly a member of the race can be a citizen")[163] and Hitler's 1923 words in *Mein Kampf* ("[the Jew must] be recognized as the most mortal enemy"),[164] the racial policies of the Nazis when they came into power were based on excluding Poles, Jews, the handicapped, and other "asocial" people (for example, those with hereditary diseases)[165] who were within Germany. To accomplish this, in addition to brute force terrorism, book burnings, and boycotts, the Nazis passed a number of laws starting in 1933 that took away the rights and livelihoods of these disfavored groups, especially Jews. Thereafter, increasingly harsh measures were passed, taking away the ability of Jewish citizens to sustain themselves and eventually denying their very existence.

As the war started, groups within occupied countries came within the scope of these laws. The plan for extermination became supreme after the Wannsee Conference in 1942, which addressed the Final Solution for eleven million Jews in Europe (more than half of whom were outside Nazi control). That genocide eliminated many millions of human lives, adding to the tens of millions killed directly through the war. In response to these and other crimes,

---

163. The Program of the National Socialist German Workers' Party, 4 (1920).
164. ADOLF HITLER, MEIN KAMPF (1925). Hitler wrote the book in 1923, but it was published in 1925.
165. Law for the Prevention of Offspring with Hereditary Diseases, July 14, 1933 (Nazi Ger.).

the Allies reached a series of agreements aimed at trying the perpetrators of these great evils after the war.

LEGAL PROFILES

Rudolf Lange was a Wannsee Conference participant who was born in Germany in 1910 and completed his legal studies there. He originally joined the SA the year that the Nazis rose to power but later joined the SS and the Gestapo. He worked in various posts within these organizations until being assigned to Latvia and the Einsatzkommandos. He led a series of massacres of Jews and created ghettos and concentration camps in the country. He was ordered to liquidate ghettos and personally murdered deportees. He died in 1945. He was never tried for his crimes.[166]

Gerhard Klopfer was a Wannsee Conference participant and a lawyer. He was born in Germany (in an area now part of Poland) in 1905 and completed his legal studies there. He began his career as a judge in 1931. After the Nazi ascendance, he joined the SS and Gestapo and became a member of the Reich Chancellery. He was responsible, among other things, for the seizure of Jewish businesses as he rose to be state secretary in the Chancellery and a general in the SS. After the war, he was not tried for war crimes due to a lack of evidence and eventually resumed the practice of law. He died in 1987, the last survivor of the fifteen principal attendees of the Wannsee Conference.[167]

1. Nazi Racial Laws

The laws and decrees categorized below depict major examples of the racial laws implemented during the Nazi regime, but it is not an exhaustive list and not necessarily in chronological order. These examples focus primarily on statutes within Germany, but many were later applied to the occupied

---

166. See *Rudolf Lange*, HAUS DER WANNSEE-KONFERENZ.
167. See *Gerhard Klopfer, General in the SS*, N.Y. TIMES (Feb. 5, 1987).

countries. There were many other examples of communications among Nazi functionaries as well as declarations that were produced at the trial, but those are not described here even though, given the Nazis' extensive use of terror and power-based hierarchy, their actual effect may have been similar to a legal decree.

a. Occupational Laws

The Law for the Restoration of the Professional Civil Service, passed in 1933, stated that non-Aryans or those unfit would not be allowed to remain in the German civil service and must retire (this included teachers and judges).[168] In a nod to veterans, those who fought, were wounded, or decorated in WWI could remain. Although this law did not define *non-Aryan* or *unfit*, it came within several days of another law regulating the civil service, in which *unfit* was defined as a Communist and *non-Aryan* was defined as anyone with more than one-quarter Jewish ancestry (one Jewish grandparent).[169] If there was any doubt, then an opinion had to be obtained from an "expert on racial research."[170] Other laws that were passed in the 1930s prohibited non-Aryans from admittance to the bar[171] and from having certain jobs, such as lawyers;[172] patent agents;[173] tax advisers;[174] physicians;[175] public officials;[176] editorial positions with German newspapers;[177] agriculture;[178] and theater, radio, creative arts, and the press.[179] Naturalizations were canceled.[180] Financial assistance was not provided to those who used Jewish doctors, lawyers, dentists, pharmacists,

---

168. Law for the Restoration of the Professional Civil Service, 1933 (Nazi Ger.).
169. First Regulation for Administration of the Law for the Restoration of the Professional Civil Service, Apr. 11, 1933 (Nazi Ger.).
170. *Id.*
171. Law Regarding Admission to the Bar, Apr. 7, 1933 (Nazi Ger.).
172. Fifth Decree to the Law Relating to the Reich Citizenship, Sept. 27, 1938 (Nazi Ger.).
173. Law Relating to the Admission of the Profession of Patent-Agent and Lawyer, Apr. 22, 1933 (Nazi Ger.).
174. Law Relating to the Admission of Tax Advisors, May 6, 1933 (Nazi Ger.).
175. Fourth Decree Relative to the Reich Citizenship Law, July 25, 1938 (Nazi Ger.).
176. Law Changing the Regulations in Regard to Public Officers, June 30, 1933 (Nazi Ger.).
177. Editorial Law, Oct. 4, 1933 (Nazi Ger.).
178. Hereditary Farm Law, Sept. 29, 1933 (Nazi Ger.).
179. Law Relating to the Reich Chamber of Culture, Sept. 22, 1933 (Nazi Ger.).
180. Executory Decree for the Law About the Repeal of Naturalizations and the Adjudication of German Citizenship, July 26, 1933 (Nazi Ger.).

funeral parlors, hospitals, etc.[181] Even prior to the passage of the civil service laws, the "Aryan paragraph" was already in use and was increasingly used by many associations and in contracts restricting membership and sales only to Aryans.

LEGAL PROFILES

Gerhard Leibholz was a German judge and an early victim of these racial laws. He was born in Germany in 1901 and completed his legal studies there. He taught at several universities in Germany but was forced out of his position due to his Jewish ancestry and then emigrated in 1938, eventually arriving in the United Kingdom. He was held as an enemy alien there when the war started but later allowed to give law lectures. He returned to Germany after the war to his previous position at the University of Göttingen. In 1951, he was appointed to the newly established constitutional court, a position he held until 1971. He was known for his equality before the law and state party doctrines. He died in 1982.[182]

b. Racial Purity Laws

The Nazi Party meeting in 1935 in Nuremberg saw the passage of two laws by the Reichstag to further defend Nazi purity: the Reich Citizenship Law and the Law for the Protection of German Blood and Honor. Together, these laws were called the Nuremberg Laws. The Reich Citizenship Law differentiated between subjects of the state and citizens who had German or kindred blood, with only the latter having full political rights.[183] The first regulation of this law allowed those of mixed Jewish blood (one or two grandparents who were fully Jewish and belonged to the religious community) to be considered

---

181. Decree of Deputy Fuehrer No. 5/37, Jan. 8, 1937 (Nazi Ger.).
182. *See Gerhard Leibholz*, Stadtarchiv Goettingen.
183. Reich Citizenship Law, Sept. 15, 1935 (Nazi Ger.).

citizens but not Jews; thus, they could not vote or occupy public office.[184] Jews were defined as having at least three Jewish grandparents or two parents who were fully Jewish. The Law for the Protection of German Blood and Honor banned marriages between German nationals and Jews.[185] It also banned relations between German nationals and Jews outside marriage, and it prohibited Jews from employing Germans and having the Reich national flag in their households.

LEGAL PROFILES

Bernhard Lösener was one of the drafters of the Nuremberg Laws, along with Wilhelm Stuckart (see Section 6.3) and Franz Medicus; he was also a lawyer. He was born in Germany in 1890 and completed his legal studies there. He worked in tax and customs offices before joining the Ministry of the Interior in 1933. Here, he became the leading expert on racial laws. Besides drafting the Nuremberg Laws, he also coauthored with Hans Globke the analysis of Nazi racial laws in 1937. He participated in follow-ups to the Wannsee Conference but later resigned from his position, purportedly due to his opposition to the extermination policies. He then worked in the administrative court. He was arrested in 1944 for his small part in a plot to assassinate Hitler. After the war, he went through the denazification program and wrote a book called *Legislating the Holocaust*. He died in 1952.[186]

c. Property Laws

A number of laws restricted the rights of Jews regarding property. As a penalty for their supposed disloyalty, Jews were ordered to pay a total of 1,000,000,000

184. First Regulation to the Reich Citizenship Law, Nov. 14, 1935 (Nazi Ger.).
185. Law for the Protection of German Blood and Honor, Sept. 15, 1935 (Nazi Ger.).
186. *See Reich Denies Jews Aid of World Law*, N.Y. TIMES (Jan. 1, 1936).

Reichsmarks to the Reich.[187] In addition, a decree mandated that every Jew report ownership of all domestic and foreign property and estates.[188] Regarding rental, Jewish tenants were prohibited by law from invoking the protection of tenancy laws if told to vacate or if a lease was terminated early.[189] Jews could only sublet to other Jews and could not rent to others with communal authority. Furthermore, by order, Jews could not operate retail shops or sell goods or services or advertise, nor were they allowed to manage a firm.[190]

An order was issued regarding Jewish businesses and real estate.[191] In another step of a process of Aryanization, owners of Jewish industrial or other enterprises could be forced to sell or liquidate an enterprise within a fixed time period. They might be forced to sell land or forests, except not to another Jew, and could not legally acquire real estate or mortgages. Jews were forced to deposit their stocks, bonds, ownership in mines, and any other securities into a foreign exchange bank; those deposits were marked as Jewish owned and could not be disposed of without the approval of the Reich minister. Jews were not allowed to acquire or sell gold, platinum, silver, pearls, or precious stones. Under a regulation added to the Reich Citizenship Law, Jews who emigrated forfeited their property to the state;[192] and under another regulation, the Reich confiscated the property of Jews after their death, and Jews lost all legal protections.[193]

d. Other

According to regulation, Jews could be restricted from appearing in certain districts or in public at certain times.[194] A police decree required Jews to wear a Jewish star in public.[195] Jews could not leave the area in which they lived without written permission of the police. A new law required all Jewish passports to be invalidated until they could be marked with a sign designating the holder

---

187. Decree Relating to the Payment of a Fine by the Jews of German Nationality, Nov. 12, 1938 (Nazi Ger.).
188. Decree on the Reporting of Jewish Owned Property, Apr. 26, 1938 (Nazi Ger.).
189. Law Concerning Jewish Tenants, Apr. 30, 1939 (Nazi Ger.).
190. Order Eliminating Jews from German Economic Life, Nov. 12, 1938 (Nazi Ger.).
191. Order Concerning the Utilization of Jewish Property, Dec. 3, 1938 (Nazi Ger.).
192. Eleventh Regulation to the Reich Citizenship Law, Nov. 25, 1941 (Nazi Ger.).
193. Thirteenth Regulation to the Reich Citizenship Law, July 1, 1943 (Nazi Ger.).
194. Police Regulation on the Appearance of Jews in Public, Nov. 28, 1938 (Nazi Ger.).
195. Police Decree on Identification of Jews, Sept. 1, 1941 (Nazi Ger.).

as a Jew.[196] The number of non-Aryans could not exceed a fixed percentage in the schools and universities.[197] Jews were required to change their first names to *Sara* for women and *Israel* for men.[198]

2. International Agreements

in 1943, the Moscow Declaration was signed by the United States, the United Kingdom, and the USSR.[199] Under this declaration, German soldiers and Nazi Party members who committed atrocities and crimes were to be returned to the country where the offenses took place and tried there.

This declaration was a precursor to an agreement signed two years later in London, commonly called the London Agreement, to prepare for the postwar trials of the major war criminals in Europe.[200] In contrast to the Moscow Declaration, the London Agreement focused on the trials of war criminals "whose offenses have no particular geographical location."[201]

Attached to the agreement, as an appendix, was the Charter of the International Military Tribunal (IMT), commonly called the London Charter. The charter called for one tribunal member from each of the four signatory countries, with a president chosen from among the tribunal members. Decisions were made by majority vote; and in case of a tie, the weight of the president would be decisive. The charter also allowed for other tribunals to be set up using this charter.

The IMT could try crimes against humanity, crimes against peace, war crimes, and conspiracy for those three crimes committed by European Axis countries. Each signatory to the agreement was required to choose a chief prosecutor responsible for investigations, collecting evidence, taking affidavits, preparing indictments, and acting as a prosecutor at the trial. The tribunal was not bound by "technical" rules of evidence. Trials were to proceed from the

---

196. Law on Passports of Jews, Oct. 5, 1938 (Nazi Ger.).

197. Law Against Overcrowding of German Schools and Higher Institutions, Apr. 25, 1933 (Nazi Ger.).

198. Second Decree for the Implementation of the Law on the Change of First and Family Names, Aug. 17, 1938 (Nazi Ger.).

199. Statement on Atrocities, U.S.-U.K.-U.S.S.R., Oct. 30, 1943.

200. Agreement by the Government of the United States of America, the Provisional Government of the French Republic, the Government of the United Kingdom of Great Britain and Northern Ireland and the Government of the Union of Soviet Socialist Republics for the Prosecution and Punishment of the Major War Criminals of the European Axis, Aug. 8, 1945.

201. *Id.*

reading of the indictment, pleas, opening statements, presentation of evidence, witness testimony, closing arguments, statements by defendants, and judgment and sentencing. Official positions or superior orders were not allowable defenses (but the latter could be a mitigating sentencing factor). The IMT could determine that whole organizations were criminal, thereby allowing charges against individuals for membership therein. Sentences could include the death penalty and confiscation of property.

LEGAL PROFILES

Katherine B. Fite was an American attorney involved with the drafting of the London Charter. She was born in Massachusetts in 1905 but started legal practice in New York. She moved to Washington, D.C., in 1935 to work with the U.S.-Mexico General Claims Commission. In 1937, she took a position with the U.S. State Department's Office of the Legal Adviser, where she was still working when the IMT was beginning to take shape. She was sent to London on loan from the State Department to assist Jackson, along many others, in shaping the London Agreement and London Charter. This included several trips to Germany, where the contingent soon moved to prepare for the Nuremberg Trials. Fite helped to prepare the brief for the case against the Reich cabinet, one of the organizations prosecuted by the IMT. She then returned to her position at the State Department. She wrote *The Nürnberg Judgment: A Summary* in 1947. She died in 1989.[202]

B. Cases

In 1945, the Trial of the Major War Criminals Before the International Military Tribunal (Nuremberg Trials) set out to try the top Nazi officials who could be found and hold them accountable for their crimes.[203] Of those, a

202. See *Woman Joins Staff of War Crimes Group*, N.Y. Times (July 11, 1945).
203. Trial of the Major War Criminals Before the International Military Tribunal, IMT (1945).

number had already died, mostly through suicide, including Hitler; Goebbels; Martin Bormann; Himmler, who committed suicide after capture; and Robert Ley, who was indicted but committed suicide before the trial started. Others, like Reinhard Heydrich, had been killed previously. Of the remaining indictees, Krupp was too ill for trial. There were twenty-one living defendants at the trial: Dönitz, Frank, Frick, Hans Fritzsche, Walther Funk, Göring, Hess, Alfred Jodl, Ernst Kaltenbrunner, Wilhelm Keitel, von Neurath, von Papen, Erich Raeder, Joachim von Ribbentrop, Alfred Rosenberg, Sauckel, Hjalmar Schacht, Baldur von Schirach, Seyss-Inquart, Albert Speer, and Julius Streicher. Several organizations were also tried: SS, Gestapo/SD, SA, Reich cabinet, Nazi Party leadership, and the military high command.

1. Tribunal Team

The prosecution was led by U.S. Supreme Court Justice Robert Jackson (see Chapter 2), who had previously been both the U.S. solicitor general and attorney general. He was appointed by President Truman under executive order.[204] The U.S. member of the tribunal was Francis Biddle (see Chapter 4), the wartime U.S. attorney general who resigned when Truman became president. The British member and president was Geoffrey Lawrence, the French member was Henri de Vabres, and the Russian member was Iona Nikitchenko. Each country also had a chief prosecutor, with the United States, the United Kingdom, France, and Russia responsible for presenting counts one through four, respectively.

LEGAL PROFILES

Geoffrey Lawrence was the presiding judge at this trial, representing the United Kingdom. He was born in England in 1880 and completed his legal studies there. He worked primarily on appellate law. During WWI, he served in the artillery. In 1927, he became a king's counsel

---

204. Exec. Order No. 9547, Providing for Representation of the United States in Preparing and Prosecuting Charges of Atrocities and War Crimes Against the Leaders of the European Axis Powers and Their Principal Agents and Accessories (May 2, 1945).

and was appointed as attorney general by the Prince of Wales. In 1932, he was appointed to the King's Bench Division as a judge. In 1944, he became lord justice of appeal. He was elevated to the House of Lords in 1947 and retired in 1957. He died in 1971.[205]

Hartley Shawcross was the chief prosecutor from the United Kingdom. He was born in Germany in 1902 but completed his legal studies in England. He was elected to Parliament in the election that brought in the Labour government in 1945. He became the attorney general, a position he held until 1951, including during this trial. He also prosecuted other war criminals, such as "Lord Haw-Haw" (see Chapter 5). He served as the United Kingdom's representative to the United Nations in its early years. After he retired from Parliament, he was made a life peer, enabling him to sit in the House of Lords. He died in 2003.[206]

Henri de Vabres was a judge at this trial, representing France. He was born in France in 1880 and completed his legal studies there. He became a professor of law at the University of Paris, where he founded the Institute of Criminology, focusing on international criminal matters. He was a longtime proponent of an international criminal court. He died in 1951.[207]

François de Menthon was the chief prosecutor from France. He was born in France in 1900 and completed his legal studies there. He became an associate professor of law in 1920 and was on the law faculty at the University of Nancy from 1929. In 1940, he volunteered for the French army, resisting the Nazi advance; he was wounded and captured but escaped and joined the Resistance movement. In 1943, he joined de Gaulle's Free French Forces as commissioner of justice. He became minister of justice and attorney general in the French government, leading the purification efforts and trials of Vichy France (see Chapter 5). He was elected to the French National Assembly in 1946, where he

---

205. *See Geoffrey Lawrence*, Oxford Dictionary of National Biography 101037661.
206. *See Hartley Shawcross*, Oxford Dictionary of National Biography 101092268.
207. *See Donnedieu de Vabres, Noted Criminologist*, N.Y. Times (Feb. 16, 1952).

remained until 1958. He was also involved in some of the early efforts at building European institutions such as the Council of Europe and the European Coal and Steel Community. He died in 1984.[208]

Iona Timofeevich Nikitchenko, major general, was a judge at this trial, representing the USSR. He was born in the Russian Empire in 1895 and completed his legal studies there. He was first appointed as a judge in 1920 for a military court and then served on the Moscow military district court in 1924. Before this trial, he had been a judge in some of the show trials conducted by Stalin in the late 1930s, and he was the vice president of the Soviet Supreme Court. He had worked on the London Charter, and his views on the judgments were less lenient than those of his colleagues. He died in 1967.[209]

Roman Andreyevich Rudenko, lieutenant general, was the chief prosecutor from the USSR. He was born in the Soviet Empire in 1907 and completed his legal studies there. He was the chief prosecutor in the Ukraine from 1944 to 1953, where he was during this trial. He then became the prosecutor general for all of the Soviet Union, a position he held until his death. He was the judge in the trial of former secret police chief Lavrentiy Beria in 1953. In 1961, he was elected to the Communist Party's Central Committee. He died in 1981.[210]

2. Indictment

The indictment against the defendants consisted of four counts.

Count 1 was for a common plan or conspiracy to commit crimes against peace, crimes against humanity, and war crimes. The specific charge included the use of the Nazi Party as the enabling mechanism, based on doctrines such as that of "German blood," to acquire totalitarian control of Germany politi-

---

208. *See Henri, Bernard, François de Menthon,* ASSEMBLÉE NATIONALE.
209. *See Iola Nikitchenko, Soviet Judge, Dies,* N.Y. TIMES (Apr. 23, 1967).
210. *See Roman A. Rudenko, 73; Soviet Chief Prosecutor,* N.Y. TIMES (Jan. 26, 1981).

cally and economically to plan for aggressive war and to use that control for foreign aggression and committing war crimes and crimes against humanity in the course of this conspiracy.

Count 2 was for crimes against peace, specifically waging wars of aggression against Poland, the United Kingdom, France, Denmark, Norway, Belgium, the Netherlands, Luxembourg, Yugoslavia, Greece, the USSR, and the United States.

Count 3 was for committing war crimes, categorized as the following:

- "Murder and ill-treatment of civilian populations of or in occupied territory and on the high seas"
- "Deportation for slave labor and for other purposes of the civilian populations of and in occupied territories"
- "Murder and ill-treatment of prisoners of war, and of other members of the armed forces of the countries with whom Germany was at war, and of persons on the high seas"
- "Killing of hostages"
- "Plunder of public and private property"
- "The exaction of collective penalties"
- "Wanton destruction of cities, towns and villages, and devastation not justified by military necessity"
- "Conscription of civilian labor"
- "Forcing civilians of occupied territories to swear allegiance to a hostile power"
- "Germanisation of occupied territories"[211]

Count 4 was for committing crimes against humanity, specifically "murder, extermination, enslavement, deportation, and other inhumane acts committed against civilian populations, before or during the war, or persecutions on political, racial or religious grounds in execution of or in connection with [the common plan]."[212]

---

211. Trial of the Major War Criminals Before the International Military Tribunal, IMT Indictment VIII (1945).
212. *Id.* at III.

LEGAL PROFILES

Benjamin Kaplan, lieutenant colonel, was the principal American drafter of the indictment against the defendants at the IMT. He was born in New York in 1911 and started his legal practice there. He worked in private practice from 1934 until 1942, when he was drafted into the military. After the war, he began teaching at Harvard, where he remained for twenty-five years, until being named to the Massachusetts Supreme Judicial Court in 1972. He served on this court for nine years, until retiring in 1981, and later served on the state court of appeals. He was a coauthor of the first casebook on copyrights. He died in 2010.[213]

3. Prosecutor's Opening Statement

In his important opening statement, Jackson set the stage for the trial:

> The privilege of opening the first trial in history for crimes against the peace of the world imposes a grave responsibility. The wrongs which we seek to condemn and punish have been so calculated, so malignant and so devastating, that civilization cannot tolerate their being ignored because it cannot survive their being repeated. That four great nations, flushed with victory and stung with injury stay the hand of vengeance and voluntarily submit their captive enemies to the judgment of the law is one of the most significant tributes that Power ever has paid to Reason.[214]

Jackson then continued by stating why this trial had to happen:

> What makes this inquest significant is that those prisoners represent sinister influence that will lurk in the world long after their bodies have returned to dust. They are living symbols of racial hatreds, of terrorism

---

213. *See Benjamin Kaplan, Crucial Figure in Nazi Trials, Dies at 99*, N.Y. TIMES (Aug. 24, 2010).
214. IMT Opening Address for the United States.

and violence, and of the arrogance and cruelty of power. They are symbols of fierce nationalisms and militarism, of intrigue and war-making which have embroiled Europe generation after generation, crushing its manhood, destroying its homes, and impoverishing its life. They have so identified themselves with the philosophies they conceived and with the forces they directed that any tenderness to them is a victory and an encouragement to all the evils which are attached to their names. Civilization can afford no compromise with the social forces which would gain renewed strength if we deal ambiguously or indecisively with the men in whom those forces now precariously survive.

Either the victors must judge the vanquished or we must leave the defeated to judge themselves. After the First World War, we learned the futility of the latter course. The former high station of these defendants, the notoriety of their acts, and the adaptability of their conduct to provoke retaliation make it hard to distinguish between the demand for a just and measured retribution, and the unthinking cry for vengeance which arises from the anguish of war. It is our task, so far as humanly possible, to draw the line between the two. We must never forget that the record on which we judge these defendants today is the record on which history will judge us tomorrow. To pass these defendants a poisoned chalice is to put it to our own lips as well. We must summon such detachment and intellectual integrity to our task that this trial will commend itself to posterity as fulfilling humanity's aspirations to do justice.[215]

Jackson then spoke about the defendants generally:

Against their opponents, including Jews, Catholics, and free labor the Nazis directed such a campaign of arrogance, brutality, and annihilation as the world has not witnessed since the pre-Christic ages. They excited the German ambition to be a "master race," which of course implies serfdom for others. They led their people on a mad gamble for domination. They diverted social energies and resources to the creation of what they thought to be an invincible war machine. They overran their

---

215. *Id.*

neighbors. To sustain the "master race" in its war making, they enslaved millions of human beings and brought them into Germany, where these hapless creatures now wander as "displaced persons." At length bestiality and bad faith reached such excess that they aroused the sleeping strength of imperiled civilization. Its united efforts have ground the German war machine to fragments. But the struggle has left Europe a liberated yet prostrate land where a demoralized society struggles to survive. These are the fruits of the sinister forces that sit with these defendants in the prisoners' dock.[216]

Although he detailed the persecution of the working class and the Catholic Church, Jackson spent the longest time talking about the persecution of the Jews:

The most savage and numerous crimes planned and committed by the Nazis were those against the Jews. . . . They were few enough to be helpless and numerous enough to be held up as a menace. Let there be no misunderstanding about the charge of persecuting Jews. What we charge against these defendants is . . . a plan and design, to which all Nazis were fanatically committed, to annihilate all Jewish people. These crimes were organized and promoted by the Party Leadership, executed and protected by the Nazi officials. . . . The persecution of the Jews was a continuous and deliberate policy. It was a policy directed against other nations as well as against the Jews themselves. . . . Anti-Semitism also has been aptly credited with being a "spearhead of terror." . . . Extermination of the Jews enabled the Nazis to bring a practiced hand to similar measures against Poles, Serbs, and Greeks.[217]

Regarding the application of law to these defendants, Jackson said thus:

I cannot, of course, deny that these men are surprised that this is the law; they really are surprised that there is any such thing as law. These defen-

---

216. *Id.*
217. *Id.*

dants did not rely on any law at all. Their program ignored and defied all law. . . . International Law, natural law, German law, any law at all was to these men simply a propaganda device to be invoked when it helped and to be ignored when it would condemn what they wanted to do.[218]

4. Trial Details

In presenting the part of its case that focused on the persecution of the Jews, the prosecution laid out the Nazis' all-out attack on Jews in the following categories:

- Hate Propaganda
- Discriminatory Decrees
- Boycotts, Raids, and Violence
- Complete Elimination

In the latter category, there were a number of phases: registration; segregation into ghettos; slave labor; and finally extermination, which was accomplished by means of starvation, annihilation, and mass disposal (murder) in concentration camps.

To illustrate the horror of the Nazis' extermination campaign, Jackson quoted a speech by defendant Hans Frank in late 1941:

> But what should be done with the Jews? . . . We must annihilate the Jews, wherever we find them and wherever it is possible. . . . The Jews represent for us also extraordinarily malignant gluttons. We have now approximately 2,500,000 of them in [Poland], perhaps with the Jewish mixtures and everything that goes with it, 3,500,000 Jews. We cannot shoot or poison those 3,500,000 Jews, but we shall nevertheless be able to take measures, which will lead, somehow, to their annihilation, and this in connection with the gigantic measures to be determined in discussions from the Reich. [Poland] must become free of Jews, the same as the Reich. Where and how this is to be achieved is a matter for the

---

218. *Id.*

offices which we must appoint and create here. Their activities will be brought to your attention in due course.[219]

Within three years, Jackson noted, Jews in Poland numbered only one hundred thousand. An estimated four million were killed in concentration camps and two million outside by police action.

The whole trial was a long one—more than ten months, generally following the format laid out in London. Alternately exciting (Jackson's opening speech), then dull (documentary evidence, which laid out irrefutable evidence against most of the defendants in their own words), then exciting again (various films, many Nazi-made), then dull again (repetitive evidence), and then exciting again (certain witness testimony and cross-examinations).

Judgments were finally pronounced by the tribunal on all of the individual defendants and organizations. The court rejected defense arguments for ex-post facto laws, victor's justice, and superior orders and convicted all but three of the defendants.

LEGAL PROFILES

Robert Kempner was assistant trial counsel for the prosecution. He was born in Germany in 1899 and completed his legal studies there. He rose to be a legal adviser to the Berlin police. Previously, he had been involved in prosecuting Hitler for the failed Beer Hall Putsch. This, along with his Jewishness, was used against him when the Nazis ascended to power, and he was stripped of his citizenship. He immigrated first to Italy and then to America. At the IMT, he presented the case against Frick, who as minister of the interior had stripped him of his German citizenship. He was credited with finding a copy of the Wannsee Protocol (minutes of the conference) in 1947. After the trials, he represented clients in Germany and the United States, including in restitution cases

---

219. *Id.*

(see Chapter 8) and in the Adolf Eichmann trial as an expert. He died in 1993.[220]

Thomas J. Dodd was the executive trial counsel for the prosecution. He was born in Connecticut in 1907 and started his career working for the Federal Bureau of Investigation in 1935. In 1937, he began working as a special assistant for the U.S. attorney general, a position he held until 1945. This included prosecuting civil rights cases against the Ku Klux Klan. Robert Jackson asked him to join the team at Nuremberg, where among other tasks he cross-examined many of the defendants. After the trials, he worked in private practice and also ran unsuccessfully for governor in 1946 and 1948. In 1952, he was elected to the U.S. House of Representatives and in 1958 to the U.S. Senate. He served two terms in the Senate before being censured by his colleagues for campaign finance abuse. He died in 1971.[221]

Franz Exner was one of the defense counsel in this trial (for defendant Jodl). He was born in Austria in 1881 and completed his legal studies there. After an initial clerkship, he held a series of legal professorships across Europe spanning a period of twenty years before taking a position at the University of Munich in 1931. He remained there through the war years. He was considered an expert in criminal law and was able to view it from numerous perspectives based on his various experiences. He authored many publications and was involved in criminologist organizations. He died in 1947.[222]

Hermann Jahrreiß was one of the defense counsel in this trial (also for defendant Jodl). He was born in Germany in 1894 and completed his legal studies there. He first worked as a judge for several years. In 1927, he became an associate professor at Leipzig and then in 1932 a full professor at Greifswald. In 1937, he transferred to the University

---

220. *See Robert Kempner, 93, a Prosecutor at Nuremberg*, N.Y. TIMES (Aug. 17, 1993).
221. *See Ex-Senator Dodd Is Dead at 64*, N.Y. TIMES (May 25, 1971).
222. *See Rene Cassin, Jurist, Dies; Won Nobel Peace Prize*, N.Y. TIMES (Feb. 21, 1976).

of Cologne, where he remained until 1962 as a professor of public law, international law, and law and political philosophy. He was considered an expert in constitutional and international law. He died in 1982.[223]

Herbert Kraus was the defense counsel for one of the defendants (Schacht). He was born in Germany in 1884 and completed his legal studies there. He then studied law in both America and France. During WWI, he worked in the Federal Foreign Office and was involved in the negotiations for the treaties ending the war (see Chapter 1). After that war, he was a professor at several universities, ending up at the University of Göttingen. He stayed involved in international law associations and taught internationally, including in the United States. He was forced out of his position for criticism of the Nazis in 1937. After the war, he was reinstated at his university and advised the new German government on the Treaty of Paris. He retired in 1953 and died in 1961.[224]

5. Individual Judgments

The following subsections focus on the judgments against the three IMT defendants with legal backgrounds: Wilhelm Frick, Hans Frank, and Ernst Kaltenbrunner.

a. Defendant Frick

Among the many crimes attributed to Wilhelm Frick (see Section 6.1) in his role as minster of the interior were writing the Nuremberg Laws, overseeing the concentration camps, and overseeing the asylums and medical institutions where euthanasia and forced sterilizations were practiced. The first of the charges against him, crimes against peace, was based on his role in bringing Germany under the "complete control" of the Nazi Party.[225] He was also responsible for legislation suppressing trade unions, the Catholic Church, and Jews and for the signing and carrying out laws in the Anschluss in Austria,

---

223. *See Hermann Jahrreiss,* DER SPIEGEL (Dec. 2, 1959).
224. *See Herbert Kraus,* MUNZINGER BIOGRAPHIE.
225. Trial of the Major War Criminals Before the International Military Tribunal, IMT Judgment: Frick (1946).

the Sudetenland, Bohemia, Moravia, and Norway. In terms of war crimes and crimes against humanity, he signed and administered laws to eliminate Jews from German life and economy, including the final decree in 1943 handing them over to the Gestapo. He extended this law to the occupied countries and introduced forced Germanization. In addition, after he took over the role of leading Bohemia and Moravia, he was responsible for terrorizing the population, forcing people into slave labor, and deporting Jews to concentration camps. In just one country (Czechoslovakia), it was estimated that almost three hundred thousand mentally deficient and aged people were subjected to euthanasia. He was convicted of crimes against peace, crimes against humanity, and war crimes and sentenced to death.

b. Defendant Frank

Hans Frank labeled himself as "the representative jurist of . . . National Socialism," noting that

> [t]he National Socialists were the first ones in the entire history of human law to elevate the concept of race to the status of a legal term. The German nation, unified racially and nationally, will in the future be legally protected against any further disintegration of the German race stock.[226]

Charges against him included that he was appointed as the leader of German-occupied Poland in 1939, implemented a plan to enslave Poles and exterminate all Jews in Poland, and attempted to destroy Poland as a national entity and to ruthlessly exploit its resources (economic and people). In addition, he established a reign of terror, with frequent summary executions, and introduced the concentration camps at Treblinka and Majdanek; attempted to starve the population; and started the deportation of slave laborers to Germany, leading to at least one million deportations. On his watch, through starvations, forced labor, and exterminations, the number of Jews in Poland decreased by two to three million. He was convicted of crimes against humanity and war crimes and sentenced to death.

---

226. IMT Judgment: Frank (1946).

LEGAL PROFILES

Hans Frank was one of the defendants and a lawyer. He was born in Germany in 1900 and completed his legal studies there. He fought in WWI and was shortly thereafter an early joiner of the Nazi Party. After passing the bar exam, he became the personal legal adviser to Hitler as well as the lawyer for the Nazi Party itself. In 1928, he founded the League of National Socialist German Jurists. He was elected to the Reichstag in 1930. In 1934, he became a Reich minister without portfolio, with the goal of creating a legal foundation for the Nazi state. In 1939, he became governor general of occupied Poland. In that capacity, he tried to annihilate not only Poland and Polish culture but also Jewish culture: a large number of extermination camps were located in that country, and Frank was responsible for massive deportations, cultural theft, and property confiscations. He was executed in 1946.[227]

c. Defendant Kaltenbrunner

A leader of the SS in Austria, Ernst Kaltenbrunner became head of the security police for the Reich (RSHA: Gestapo, SD, and criminal police) after the Anschluss. He was responsible for the Einsatzkommandos, the organization that committed mass murder of civilians in occupied countries; for establishing concentration camps; for signing "protective custody" orders committing people to concentration camps; for the torture and execution of POWs and concentration camp prisoners; for searching for and deporting people to concentration camps; and many other crimes. He was also responsible for evacuating and liquidating concentration camp inmates to cover his trail. Witnesses against him included another lawyer, SS Lieutenant General Otto Ohlendorf (who was later convicted at NMT and executed). Kaltenbrunner was convicted of crimes against humanity and war crimes and sentenced to death.[228]

---

227. *See Hans Frank*, BIOGRAPHIE DES DEUTSCHEN HISTORISCHEN MUSEUMS.
228. IMT Judgment: Kaltenbrunner (1946).

LEGAL PROFILES

Ernst Kaltenbrunner was one of the defendants and a lawyer. He was born in Austria in 1903 and completed his legal studies there. After working as a lawyer, he joined the Nazi Party and the SS in Austria, assisting Nazis who needed legal help. He was convicted of treason as part of a conspiracy to assassinate Austrian leader Dollfuss (see Chapter 5), was imprisoned for six months, and lost his law license as a result. He was involved in the Anschluss and then took on increasing roles with the SS before finally leading the RSHA in 1943. He was also the leader of the international police organization that was the predecessor of today's Interpol. He was executed in 1946.[229]

C. Subsequent Events

After the war, a United Nations convention was convened in 1948 to deal with the subject of genocide. The Convention on the Prevention and Punishment of the Crime of Genocide[230] began with the contracting parties agreeing that genocide was a crime whether committed during peace or war and whether committed by individuals, rulers, or public officials. The convention defined *genocide* as an act intended to destroy a national, ethnic, racial, or religious group. Acts included killing, causing serious bodily or mental harm to members of the group, deliberately inflicting conditions on the group calculated to bring about its physical destruction, preventing births within the group, and forcibly taking away its children. Actual or attempted genocide and conspiracy to commit or complicity in or public incitement of genocide were all punishable by a local or international tribunal.

Adolf Eichmann escaped from captivity after the war and so was not involved in a postwar trial. His role in the Nazi killing machine became clearer after the war, and he was finally identified as living in South America under an

---

229. *See Ernst Kaltenbrunner*, BIOGRAPHIE DES DEUTSCHEN HISTORISCHEN MUSEUMS.
230. Convention on the Prevention and Punishment of the Crime of Genocide, G.A. Res. 260 (III) A (Dec. 9, 1948).

assumed name. He was abducted to Israel to stand trial in 1961. Eichmann was one of the attendees of the Wannsee Conference and organized mass deportations of Jews and others to the concentration camps. He also devised a scheme to confiscate assets of those who were murdered in the camps. He was charged in an Israeli court with fifteen counts, including war crimes, membership in the SS, the SD, and the Gestapo, and:

- Being ultimately responsible for the murder of millions of Jews
- Causing the enslavement, starvation, and deportation of millions of Jews
- Deporting a half-million Poles, fourteen thousand Slovenes, and tens of thousands of gypsies and deporting and murdering one hundred Czech children
- Placing the Jews in living conditions designed to kill them and causing them grave physical and mental harm
- Sterilizing Jews
- Persecuting Jews based on national, racial, religious, and political grounds
- Confiscating Jewish property by compulsion, robbery, terrorism, and violence[231]

Rejecting many of the same defense tactics used in the various previous Nuremberg Trials (e.g., superior orders), the three-judge tribunal found Eichmann guilty on all charges and sentenced him to death. He was subsequently executed.

LEGAL PROFILES

Raphael Lemkin was instrumental in writing the genocide convention; he was also a lawyer. He was born in Imperial Russia in 1900 and completed his legal studies in Poland. He started as a prosecutor in Warsaw in 1926, working his way up until he was the public prosecutor from 1929 to 1934. From 1929 to 1935, he worked on the Committee on Codification of the Laws of the Polish Republic. In 1933, he pre-

---

231. *See The Trial of Adolf Eichmann*, Holocaust Research Project.

sented to the League of Nations the concept of a genocide crime against international law. Although forced to resign from his public position, he continued to speak at international forums. He joined the Polish army at the start of the war, was wounded, and escaped, eventually making his way to America. Based on his knowledge of international law, he was a consultant for the U.S. government's Foreign Economic Administration (see Chapter 3). He coined the term genocide in a book (*Axis Rule in Occupied Europe*) that he published in 1944; and through his continuous personal efforts, he was able to influence the passage of this convention. He stayed in the United States after the war, teaching law. He died in 1959.[232]

D. Modern Applicability

After the war, the new Federal Republic of Germany wanted to return to the family of nations, including the benefit of international credit markets to rebuild its economy. At the same time, it needed to address the vast damage done by the Nazi state to the Jews. As such, it entered into an agreement with the similarly newly established state of Israel, the so-called Luxembourg Agreement,[233] to pay reparations, including the costs of resettling Holocaust survivors. In an unprecedented legal arrangement, the Federal Republic of Germany agreed to pay these funds monetarily and in-kind to two entities: (1) a state that did not exist at the time (Israel) and (2) a private organization (the Conference on Jewish Material Claims Against Germany) that represented citizens of other countries. Besides having a significant economic impact on Israel during its early years, the Federal Republic of Germany has continued its mission of reparations and recently celebrated its sixtieth anniversary of paying monies to survivors of the Holocaust.[234]

Genocide trials are still occurring in modern times. Genocide has been charged in both the Rwandan and Yugoslavian conflicts of the 1990s. In Rwanda, the International Criminal Tribunal for Rwanda convicted several

---

232. *See Raphael Lemkin, Genocide Foe, Dies,* N.Y. TIMES (Aug. 31, 1959).
233. Agreement Between the Federal Republic of Germany and the State of Israel, Ger.-Isr., Sept. 10, 1952.
234. *For 60th Year, Germany Honors Duty to Pay Holocaust Victims,* N.Y. TIMES (Nov. 17, 2012).

people of the crime of genocide. In Yugoslavia, the International Criminal Tribunal for the Former Yugoslavia recently acquitted the former leader of Serbia, Karadžić, of the genocide charge against him (for activities before the Srebrenica massacre). In Cambodia, three of the former leaders of the Khmer Rouge are to be tried in their own country for the genocide committed during the 1970s in the "Killing Fields" of Pol Pot.

Separately, the Federal Republic of Germany has developed some of the most stringent privacy laws in the world today. The Federal Data Protection Act[235] is in part a reaction to the massive domestic spying and use of personal information to carry out racial policies during WWII. The Gestapo and SS raided the tax, voter, census, and other official records to discover who was a Jew, a Communist, or a member of other disfavored groups and to discover information about them (e.g., assets available for confiscation). The concepts of human dignity, personal liberty, the right of personality, informational self-determination, and privacy in spheres such as correspondence and the home are reflected in both national law and regional conventions[236] that support privacy in its various forms. In the early 1980s, there was a strong reaction against a census attempt by the government; this led to a decision by the German Constitutional Court defining data privacy restrictions and procedural safeguards[237] that were subsequently enacted into German and European law and that are still influential on new data protection statutes being enacted around the world.[238] Much modern good law has arisen from the ashes of rather malevolent legalities.[239]

---

235. Gesetz zum Schutz vor Mißbrauch personenbezogener Daten bei der Datenverarbeitung, Dec. 20, 1990 RGBl. I at 2924 (Ger.).
236. Convention for the Protection of Human Rights and Fundamental Freedoms art. 8, 1950 (Council of Europe).
237. Population Census Case (Volkszählungsurteil), Case Nos. 1 BvR 209/83, 1 BvR 269/83, 1 BvR 362/83, 1 BvR 420/83, 1 BvR 440/83, 1 BvR 484/83 (BVerfGE Dec. 15, 1983).
238. *See, e.g.*, Colombia, Ley 1581 por el Cual se Dictan Disposiciones Generales para la Protección de Datos Personales (Oct. 2012).
239. *See* Thomas J. Shaw, *Privacy Law and History: WWII Forward*, IAPP Privacy Advisor (Mar. 2013).

CHAPTER 7

ASIA: IMPERIAL JAPAN

In many ways, the rise of Imperial Japan as a military force temporarily dominant in its region of the world in the early stages of WWII mirrored the situation of Nazi Germany. Like Germany, Japan had begun its ascendancy in the nineteenth century leading to its defeat of a key competitor (i.e., Russia, as it was France for Germany), had lived through complex and only partly successful experiments with democracy in the 1920s, had annexed neighboring countries, and felt itself limited by international agreements it had negotiated from a position of weakness. Like Nazi Germany, Imperial Japan was determined to break off these shackles of international restraints, to be allowed to rise to its self-proclaimed position atop a regional hegemony, and to use whatever force in whatever manner necessary to accomplish its aims.

At the same time, Japan was somewhat different. Japan still retained an emperor system, which the Germans were forced to give up at the end of WWI. Japan was traditionally more comfortable with the dualism of the Shinto and Buddhist religions that dominated the culture, unlike in Germany where the Catholic and Protestant religions exacerbated regional differences. In Japan, unlike Germany, religion was tied to politics during this war. Japan, not being on the losing side in WWI, still retained its colonies in Taiwan and Korea, which it had taken over in the late nineteenth and early twentieth centuries, respectively. Unlike Germany, which had a common language with other nations or parts thereof (Austria, Switzerland, Czechoslovakia), Japan did not have a common language with another nation; however, it did have the common inheritance from China prevalent in the North Asian countries.

Like Germany since the founding of the German Empire, Japan had been a country where militarism had a close involvement with the political sphere since at least the Meiji Restoration. In the 1930s, this mirror reflection of Germany grew even sharper. Like Germany, Japanese democracy began to fade under a wave of assassinations of those who championed democracy or at least any political direction that differed from the military-influenced system. A single figure was also held out as the unifying figure for the emergent nation: Emperor Hirohito. Under the banner of being the leader of a new Asia (to be called the Greater East Asia Co-Prosperity Sphere), Japan wanted to dominate the region with its philosophy, culture, military, and technology.

Like Germany with the Jews, Japan had an "inferior race" enemy in the Chinese, based in part on a long-held insecurity concerning China (the Chinese accomplishments of previous centuries formed some part of what Japan had become, including its Confucian sensibilities and its language and script). This combined with technological advances gave Japan the confidence to rise above and now persecute the "inferior race." This history of foreign incursions into China is a very long and complex story (which explains much of the modern-day Chinese firmness in controlling its own affairs), and the Japanese had their role in that. Seeing China as the only serious threat on the Asian landmass, Japan was determined to undermine China as well as exploit it economically.

It was this desire to take over Asia that led to Japan's invasion of China, attacks on the United States, and forced occupations of many other countries in the region. This chapter focuses on the following legal issues: creation of a divine military regime; aggressive war and preemptive military strikes; crimes against humanity and war crimes (mass rape, mistreatment of POWs, narcotics trafficking, biological warfare, and sexual slavery); and use of nuclear weapons.

PROMINENT LAWYERS AND JUDGES IN THIS CHAPTER

Creation of a Divine Military Regime:

- Tatsukichi Minobe (law professor)
- Kiichiro Hiranuma (justice minister)

- Takao Saitō (member of the diet)
- Testsu Katayama (member of the diet)
- Osachi Hamaguchi (prime minister)
- Kijūrō Shidehara (finance minister)
- Kisaburo Suzuki (justice minister)
- Courtney Whitney (constitution drafter)
- Milo E. Rowell (constitution drafter)
- Toshio Shimada (cabinet member)

Aggressive War/Preemptive Military Strikes:

- Sakutaro Tachi (law professor)
- Ryōichi Kuroda (instructor in China)
- William F. Webb (presiding tribunal judge)
- John P. Higgins (tribunal judge)
- Delfin J. Jaranilla (tribunal judge)
- Ivan Michyevich Zaryanov (tribunal judge)
- William Donald Patrick (tribunal judge)
- B.V. A. Röling (tribunal judge)
- Mei Ju-ao (tribunal judge)
- Henri Bernard (tribunal judge)
- Edward Stuart McDougall (tribunal judge)
- Radhabinod Pal (tribunal judge)
- Erima Harvey Northcroft (tribunal judge)
- Kenzō Takayanagi (defense counsel)
- Haruhiko Nishi (defense counsel)
- Mamoru Shigemitsu (diplomat)

Crimes Against Humanity and War Crimes:

- Joseph B. Keenan (chief of counsel)
- Arthur Comyns-Carr (prosecutor)
- Grace Kanode Llewellyn (assistant prosecutor)
- Eleanor Bontecou (prosecution team)
- Yōsuke Matsuoka (defendant)
- Henry G. Nolan (prosecutor)
- Kōki Hirota (defendant)
- George Yamaoka (defense team)

- Ichirō Kiyose (deputy chief defense counsel)
- Somei Uzawa (chief defense counsel)
- Naoki Hoshino (defendant)
- Frank S. Tavenner Jr. (acting chief of counsel)
- Alan J. Mansfield (prosecutor)
- Lev Nicholevich Smirnov (prosecutor)
- José Laurel (Philippine president)
- Brendan F. Brown (legal assistant)

Use of Nuclear Weapons:

- John Lansdale Jr. (Manhattan Project security head)
- George L. Harrison (Interim Committee member)
- William A. Consodine (Manhattan Project security and public relations)
- William L. Laurence (newspaper science reporter)
- Shoichi Okamoto (plaintiff's counsel)
- Joseph Volpe Jr. (brief drafter)
- Brien McMahon (statute sponsor)
- Emanuel H. Bloch (defense attorney)
- Julius Tabin (physicist)
- William L. Uanna (security manager)

7.1 CREATION OF A DIVINE MILITARY REGIME

A. Statutes

1. Intertwining of Political and Military History

Japanese political and military history were intertwined in the years before WWII. Going back as far as the Meiji Restoration in 1868, the military was a significant factor in the direction of the country, both domestically and internationally. Shaken by the arrival of American naval forces in 1853 brandishing technology far beyond what Japan had, the country began to shake off its old political order and international isolation of several centuries. The new national government, led by Emperor Meiji, took over the lands and the military power of the old samurai in increasingly bolder steps. National conscription was implemented, taking manpower away from the warlords. At the same time, the Buddhist temples and priests were seized and absorbed by the native Shinto religion, which was a state-sponsored religion with the emperor at the top. Politicians were advisers to the emperor, the military swore to protect and serve the emperor, and the state religion considered the emperor a god; so in essence all were combined under a common direction through WWII.

When Japan adopted a parliamentary system, cabinet, and constitution in the 1880s, it was modeled after the German political system more than others. The same was true of a new commercial legal code. Japan's military was likewise significantly influenced by German/Prussian military methodologies, including the role of complete military devotion to the respective emperors by advisers sent over from Prussia. The conscription laws meant not only that there were additional resources available for the military but also that they could be trained and indoctrinated in the militarist philosophy that mixed with the existing samurai ethos in the country. In addition, military general staffs created for the army and navy reported not to the civilian government but directly to the emperor.

Japan had been militarily interfering in Korea against the wishes of both Korea and its imperial overlord, China, for several decades. With the Treaty of Shimonoseki ending the First Sino-Japanese War in 1895, Korea was declared to be independent of both Japan and China, and Taiwan was given to Japan. In the Treaty of Portsmouth ending the Russo-Japanese War in 1905, Japan took full control of Korea, which it fully annexed in 1910, and gained land and railway leases in Manchuria. With the outbreak of WWI, Japan joined the Allies but only used the war to gain control of Germany's holdings in China, confirming its intentions through the Twenty-One Demands document presented to the Chinese government.

The new Showa era of Emperor Hirohito beginning in 1926 saw increasing activity by Japan's military in China in the name of protecting Japanese subjects (now including Koreans and Taiwanese), legation, and commercial interests. The Japanese military stationed in Manchuria staged a series of "incidents" to escalate the conflict with the Chinese and to further add to Japan's territory and influence there. (As the postwar tribunal later noted, the Japanese governments refused to call these conflicts *war* but instead called them *incidents* as a way to assert that the rules of war did not apply.) The Mukden Incident in 1931 was typical, where the Imperial Japanese Army blew up parts of the railroad, blamed it on the Chinese, and then used that incident to move further into Manchuria. Similarly, Japan later attacked Shanghai and set up the puppet state of Manchukuo with the former emperor of China on the throne.

In 1932, a series of attempted and successful assassinations of political and business leaders in Japan culminated with the assassination of Prime Minister Inukai Tsuyoshi. The next prime minister of the country was from the military, as prime ministers would be until the end of the war. In May 1936, the new government promulgated an ordinance reviving an old rule that the navy and war ministers must be officers on the active list holding the rank of lieutenant general or above. Opposition political parties were disbanded in 1940, with only one imperial party allowed to function.

The 1930s also saw increasing preparation for additional military conflicts. Japan was already the overlord of Korea, Taiwan, and parts of China. With the establishment of the state of Manchukuo in Manchuria, the Imperial Army in China was trying to expand in all directions. Japan intended to expand in French Indochina and also to take on the Russians in parts of Manchuria and possibly elsewhere. In addition, Japan was aware that continued aggressive behavior against other nations such as China would bring potential conflicts with the United Kingdom, France, and the United States, not to mention war itself, if their territories or possessions were attacked. Thus, Japan began to bring its economy up to a war footing. Part of this plan was resource planning, i.e., ensuring that there were sufficient supplies of raw materials required for a large-scale war either by acquiring such supplies through normal commercial means before the conflict started or by expropriating them from its colonies, such as Manchuria. Japan also looked for substitutes, like synthetic fuels. The other part of Japan's plan concerned legality and direction set through several new laws.

2. Peace Preservation, Economic, and National Mobilization Laws

To maintain order, Japan had passed a series of Peace Preservation Laws in the late 1800s and early 1900s. The one still in effect in the 1930s was the Public Security Preservation Law, passed in 1925.[1] The provisions of this law included prohibitions on attacking either the private property system or "kokutai," a Japanese concept that is not easily defined that involves following the path of the emperor. In essence, this statute outlawed every type of group opposing the

---

1. Chian iji hō, Law No. 46 of 1925 (Imperial Japan).

current form of government, including the Socialists, the Communists, and, of course, the anarchists. "Thought" police sprang up everywhere, and dissension was even more ruthlessly suppressed with the increasing militarism of the country. In 1941, several laws were passed that suppressed dissension against the government: the National Defense Security Law increased the secrecy of cabinet communications and made disclosure punishable by death;[2] revisions to the public security law allowed preventive detention of those who could be a risk to public peace; the Newspaper and Publications Control Ordinance allowed for government censorship;[3] and the Press, Publications, Assembly, and Association Special Control Law prohibited threats to national security or the war effort.[4]

In 1938, as Japan was preparing for war, it passed a number of laws to focus industry and the economy on the needs of a wartime military. These included the Artificial Petroleum Manufacturing Law, the Act for the Promotion and Production of Important Minerals, the Electric Power Control Law, and the Light Metal Manufacturing Law (for airplane construction).

However, the most important law passed in 1938 was one that addressed many of the same problems that other countries entering the war were facing: the need for control of labor and goods, among other things, and the need for more military troops. As the military-leaning government became more involved in China following the Marco Polo Bridge Incident (a minor conflict that led to attacks on Beijing and the Second Sino-Japanese War) and the subsequent Nanking Massacre in 1937 (see Section 7.3.B.2.a) and had several skirmishes with the Russian military, it found that it needed more military troops. Under the guise of procuring these human resources, the military pushed for legislation that combined into a single law what had actually taken other countries multiple laws and years to accomplish. This law, the National Mobilization Law,[5] and follow-on ordinances gave the national government more control over labor, production of goods, capital, industry groups, prices, and free speech. The follow-up Citizen Draft Order allowed the drafting of citizens for the war effort.[6]

---

2. Kokubō hoan-hō, Law No. 49 of 1941 (Imperial Japan).
3. Shimbunshi to keisei seigen rei, 1941 (Imperial Japan).
4. Genron shuppan shūkai kessha tō rinji torishimari-hō, Law No. 97 of 1941 (Imperial Japan).
5. Kokka sōdōin hō, Law No. 55 of 1938 (Imperial Japan).
6. Kokumin chōyō rei, Imperial Order No. 451 of 1939 (Imperial Japan).

Under the guise of a national emergency, the cabinet could now take control over virtually any raw materials, finished products, industry, or company in support of the war effort. It could take over facilities, select personnel for both military and civilian workforces, direct the training of workers and other civilians, and prohibit any information from being disclosed. Under the new legislation, the government would control imports and exports, and war production would be prioritized over consumer production. The cabinet would control financial credit, propaganda messages sent overseas, and union actions. As in Nazi Germany, the leaders of the Japanese government (and the military) could effectively rule without consulting the legislative branch.

LEGAL PROFILES

Tatsukichi Minobe was a constitutional law professor in Tokyo who advocated belief in a constitutional emperor. He was born in Japan in 1873 and completed his legal studies there. He joined the Ministry of the Interior and undertook a multi-year mission to Europe, receiving exposure to British, French, and German legal philosophies; afterward, he returned to Japan and became a professor at Tokyo Imperial University. From 1911 through the end of the war, he drafted statutes for the government. In 1935, severe militarist and ultranationalist pressure led to his resignation from his university position and the banning of his books. After the war, he assisted efforts to draft the new constitution. He died in 1948.[7]

Kiichiro Hiranuma was the justice minister when the 1925 Peace Preservation Law was passed. He was born in Japan in 1867 and completed his legal studies there. He then joined the Ministry of Justice. He served as a prosecutor for the supreme court, with a focus on public corruption cases. This focus led to a nationalistic orientation and opposition to other political leanings. In 1923, he became the minister of justice and formed a group to combat Socialism and Communism. He joined the

---

7. *See Tatsukichi Minobe*, NATIONAL DIET LIBRARY.

Privy Council in 1926, becoming its president in 1936. In 1939, he was the prime minister for eight months; later, he served as the home minister and then adviser to the emperor. After the war, he was a defendant at the Tokyo war crimes trials tried by the International Military Tribunal for the Far East. He died in 1952.[8]

B. Cases

There were many challenges to the power of the state in the 1920s and 1930s. Some were parliamentary, such as the attacks on the military by diet member Takao Saitō, who was subsequently banned from the legislature. Other challenges were more violent attacks, some planned but never carried out, others foiled, and still others successful attacks on leaders in the government. The targets of these attacks included government leaders up to prime ministers (three Japanese prime ministers were assassinated between 1921 and 1932), military leaders whose direction was different than extreme nationalists, and even the emperor was a target of an assassination attempt. These attacks led to a number of trials, some secret, some before civilian courts, and others before military courts. These trials were typically for those who felt that legislation passed in support of a militaristic government did not go far enough and that individual actions were required to overthrow the current form of government.

LEGAL PROFILES

Takao Saitō was a diet member who bravely stood up to the ever-expanding military rule; he was also a lawyer. He was born in Japan in 1870 and completed his legal studies there. After opening a law firm, he went to the United States to study. In 1912, he was elected to the diet. After the February 26 Incident (see Section 6.1.A.2) in 1936, he rose in the diet to give his "strict military discipline" speech, criticizing the military's role in politics, for which he was roundly applauded. However,

---

8. *See Kiichiro Hiranuma*, National Diet Library.

things changed four years later: when he gave a similar speech criticizing the military, he was expelled from the diet. Despite that, he was reelected in 1942. After the war, he returned as minister of state in the government. He died in 1949.[9]

Tetsu Katayama was a Japanese politician and postwar prime minister and a lawyer. He was born in Japan in 1887 and completed his legal studies there. He opened a legal practice and then was elected to the lower house of the diet as a Socialist in 1930. He opposed the expulsion of Saitō from the diet, which caused his expulsion from his party. After the war, he was involved in advancing significant social, labor, and antimonopoly legislation during his time as prime minister, including the reform of the bureaucracy and the breakup of the Ministry of Home Affairs. He retired from politics after his election defeat in 1963. He died in 1978.[10]

1. Hamaguchi Assassination

This trial was for the attempted assassination of Osachi Hamaguchi, the prime minister, in 1930 (he died the following year, essentially of his wounds). It was Hamaguchi's government that signed the London Naval Treaty of 1930 (see Chapter 1), in which Japan agreed to unequal numbers (in comparison with the United States and the United Kingdom) of capital ships in the navies of the respective countries. This did not sit well with the ultranationalists, several of whom made speeches that incited one member of one of the secret organizations (Aikoku-sha, the Love of Country Association) to shoot the prime minister. The assassination occurred very close to where Prime Minister Hara Takashi had been killed nine years before. In this case, the killer was assisted by those exhorting him to act and supplying him with the revolver. The court sentenced the defendant Tomeo Sagoya to be executed.

---

9. *See Takao Saitō*, NATIONAL DIET LIBRARY.
10. *See Tetsu Katayama*, NATIONAL DIET LIBRARY.

LEGAL PROFILES

Osachi Hamaguchi was a prime minister who was the victim of an assassination attempt. He was born in Japan in 1870 and completed his legal studies there. He joined the national government in the Ministry of Finance, holding a variety of roles. These included head of the Monopoly Bureau in 1907, vice communications minister in 1912, and vice finance minister in 1914. He was elected to the diet in 1915, where he held finance minister positions in several cabinets between 1924 and 1927. In 1929, he became the prime minister in a new government. Here, he championed the gold standard and women's suffrage. Although he recovered from his wounds enough to lead an electoral triumph months later, he soon died of his wounds in 1931.[11]

2. May 15 Incident

This trial was for the assassination of Prime Minister Tsuyoshi Inukai (and the attempted murder of comedian Charlie Chaplin, who was visiting the prime minister) in an attempted coup d'état on May 15, 1932. In this case, junior officers of the navy attempted to overthrow the government and replace it with a military-led one devoted to the emperor. They were assisted by a group of civilians affiliated with the League of Blood Incident, a plot two months before led by a Buddhist priest to kill twenty leading political and business leaders (in actuality, only two were killed).

There were separate trials for the navy cadets, officers, and civilians. The eleven young navy officers who killed the prime minister were court-martialed; but before sentencing, hundreds of thousands of letters requesting leniency flooded the court, thousands of which were dipped in blood. The court sentences for the young naval officers were very lenient—only four years' imprisonment. Others, including more senior officers, received up to fifteen years, and the leader of the civilians received a lifetime term of imprisonment.

---

11. *See Osachi Hamaguchi*, National Diet Library.

This led to another military uprising against the government four years later, in 1936. In this situation, called the February 26 Incident, more than one thousand army officers and soldiers attempted another coup d'état, trying to get rid of the government and replace it with more direct emperor rule and to rid the country of what it saw as corrupt advisers. Again, the prime minister was targeted, but he narrowly escaped assassination (the assassins instead killed his brother-in-law by mistake, and the prime minister went into hiding). Many others were killed, including the finance minister who had decreased the military's budget. Completely cowing or killing their internal opponents, including chasing judges from the bench during trials, the military and the ultranationalists gained firm control of the Japanese government.

LEGAL PROFILES

Kijūrō Shidehara was the finance minister at the time of the assassination in the Inukai government and a lawyer. He was born in Japan in 1872 and completed his legal studies there. He joined the Ministry of Foreign Affairs and was posted to Korea in 1896. He subsequently served in Belgium, the Netherlands, the United Kingdom, and the United States before returning to Japan in 1915. In 1919, he was appointed ambassador to the United States and was Japan's representative at the Washington Naval Conference. In 1924, he became the foreign minister, advocating peaceful relations; he held that position until 1927 and again from 1929 to 1931, when the outbreak of incidents in China doomed his policies. In 1925, he was appointed to the House of Peers. After the war, he served as prime minister for a short time, as he also had after the attempted assassination of Prime Minister Hamaguchi. He was the author of the famous Article 9 of the Japanese postwar constitution (see Section 7.2), banning the waging of war by Japan (although some credit this article to American lawyer Charles L. Kades). He returned as the speaker of the lower house of the diet in 1951 and died later that year.[12]

---

12. *See Kijūrō Shidehara*, NATIONAL DIET LIBRARY.

Kisaburo Suzuki was the justice minister and then the home minister in the Inukai government; he was also a lawyer. He was born in Japan in 1867 and completed his legal studies there. He joined the Ministry of Justice, where he served variously as a judge of the Tokyo High Court, the head of the Criminal Affairs Bureau, a vice minister of the Ministry of Justice, and public prosecutor general. In 1920, he was elected to the upper house of the diet. He served as both justice and home ministers in different cabinets. In 1932, he was elected to the lower house. He died in 1940.[13]

C. Subsequent Events

After the war, the Allies voided the National Mobilization Law and the law restricting publications, and many of the ultranationalists were purged from political life. The emperor publicly declared that he was not divine and that the ties between the emperor and the people of Japan were dependent not "upon mere legends and myths. They are not predicated on the false conception that the Emperor is divine, and that the Japanese people are superior to other races and fated to rule the world."[14] Defining the role of the emperor, Article 1 of the new constitution said, "The Emperor shall be the symbol of the State and of the unity of the people, deriving his position from the will of the people with whom resides sovereign power."[15] The emperor was to be a constitutional monarch, only able to perform such acts as enumerated in the constitution and without any powers related to government.

An Allied directive banned State Shinto (as opposed to the religion of Sect Shinto), and no public funds could be used to support it. The emperor was no longer allowed to report to his ancestors on various matters of public import at Shinto shrines. Children were no longer allowed to be educated in State Shinto, and the superiority doctrines (that the emperor was superior to other nations' leaders, that the Japanese people were superior to other cultures, and that the Japanese islands were superior) were banned. The use of Shinto for

---

13. *See Kisaburo Suzuki*, NATIONAL DIET LIBRARY.
14. Ningen-sengen [Humanity Declaration], Jan. 1, 1946 (Japan).
15. JAPAN CONST. art. 1.

militarist and ultranationalist dissemination was prohibited. Any use of Shinto to expound the doctrine that extended the rule of Japan over other nations was also banned.

The National General Mobilization Law impacted not only the Japanese but also Koreans and Taiwanese. Typically, Japanese courts did not allow suits for labor under this statute since any such claims were barred by either the statute of limitations or postwar treaties. But recently, in 2012, the Supreme Court of Korea ruled in favor of a Korean who was forcibly displaced from his home country and forced to labor in Japan under the mobilization law.[16] The court said that both Japanese Supreme Court and lower Korean court rulings upholding the statute of limitations barring a suit for wartime conscripted labor were contrary to the spirit of the Korean Constitution. It deemed the Japanese occupation of the Korean peninsula to be illegal (a U.N. conference in 1963 had declared the 1910 Treaty of Protection of Korea between Japan and Korea to be legally void because it was based on coercion). As such, Japanese laws could not be legally applied to Koreans; and as such, the conscription of Korean labor was illegal. The statute of limitations did not apply due to a lack of good faith, and it also was not barred by a later 1965 treaty between the countries barring such claims.

LEGAL PROFILES

Courtney Whitney, lieutenant general, was one of two principal drafters of the new Japanese Constitution and a lawyer. He was born in Washington, D.C., in 1897 and enlisted in the military in WWI. After completing his legal studies in 1927, he opened a corporate practice in the Philippines. He returned to the military in 1940, eventually working on General Douglas MacArthur's staff. In 1944, he returned to the Philippines and organized guerilla activities there and then moved to Tokyo. He remained an assistant to MacArthur through the Korean War, until

---

16. Shin Cheon-su v. Mitsubishi Heavy Indus. Ltd. & Nippon Steel Corp. (Korea Sup. Ct. May 24, 2012).

MacArthur was recalled, whereupon Whitney also resigned his commission. Whitney died in 1969.[17]

Milo E. Rowell, lieutenant colonel, was the other principal drafter of the new Japanese Constitution and a lawyer. He was born in California in 1903 and started his legal practice there. He enlisted in the army in 1943 and was assigned to the Philippines, where he fought on the front lines. After the war, he moved to Tokyo to work with the Supreme Commander for the Allied Powers team. There, he worked with Beate Sirota Gordon, one of the translators for the Allies who grew up in Japan and influenced women's and human rights provisions in the new constitution. He died in 1977.[18]

Toshio Shimada was a cabinet member during the prewar period and also a lawyer. He was born in Japan in 1877 and completed his legal studies there. He was elected to the Tokyo assembly and two years later went to China to teach law. He returned to Japan and opened a law office. In 1912, he was elected to the lower house of the diet. He joined the cabinet in 1935 as the minister of agriculture and remained in that post through successive governments. Between June and December 1945, he became the speaker of the lower house. He was purged from politics after the war and died in 1947.[19]

D. Modern Applicability

The act of creating armies centered on religion has been going on since before recorded history and is clearly evident in many conflicts from Biblical times forward. Currently, military actions in the name of religion are most commonly found in the conflicts in the Middle East, home to three of the world's major religions; in South Asia; and in certain conflicts in Africa and Asia. Most non-Communist nations have a state religion or significant influence, with the

---

17. *See Maj. Gen. Courtney Whitney, 71, Adviser to MacArthur, Is Dead*, N.Y. TIMES (Mar. 22, 1969).
18. *See Milo E. Rowell*, NATIONAL DIET LIBRARY.
19. *See Toshio Shimada*, KODANSHA ENCYCLOPEDIA OF JAPAN.

concept of the separation of church and state a relatively recent phenomenon. In some nations, this is not a readily acceptable concept as their religion completely symbolizes and identifies the state. Where the two have been separated, as in most developed countries, offensive military conflicts have decreased significantly. Shorn of their religious pretext for invasion or expansion, nations have a more difficult time justifying war.

7.2 AGGRESSIVE WAR / PREEMPTIVE MILITARY STRIKES

A. Statutes

Japan was a party to a number of conventions and treaties that rejected war as a solution to disagreements. In particular, Japan was a member of the Hague Convention of 1907, the League of Nations, and a signatory to the Kellogg-Briand Pact. In addition, Japan was a party to numerous other bilateral agreements that objected to the use of war as a means to settle disputes.

In 1907, a number of countries agreed to give previous warning of their intent to start hostilities. The Hague Convention III of 1907 required contracting states to give notice before commencing a war. Any such notice was required to be both "previous and explicit" and could be a declaration of war, a list of reasons, or an ultimatum with a conditional declaration of war.[20] This was considered important both to maintain "pacific relations" and to advise neutral countries.[21] Before starting a war, nations were required by the Hague Convention I of 1907 to use one or more "friendly Powers" of mediation before resorting to arms to settle disputes.[22] Japan was a party to these conventions and therefore bound by them.

The Covenant of the League of Nations (see Chapter 1) in 1919 also contained several articles addressing disputes. Article 12 required members engaged in a dispute to submit their case to arbitration if so suitable (e.g., treaty interpretation, breaches of international obligations, or questions of international law) or to the Council of the League of Nations and wait at least three months to hear back from the arbitrators/council before resorting to war. If all of the

---

20. Hague Convention III: The Opening of Hostilities, Oct. 18, 1907.
21. *Id.*
22. Hague Convention I: The Pacific Settlement of International Disputes, Oct. 18, 1907.

other members unanimously agreed to the council's report, then the parties to the dispute agreed not to go to war; if agreement was not unanimous, then the parties reserved the right to "take such action as they shall consider necessary for the maintenance of right and justice."[23] Japan was a member of the League of Nations from 1920 to 1933.

The Kellogg-Briand Pact of 1928 (see Chapter 1) renounced aggressive war. The first articles stated that the contracting parties condemned the use of war as a solution to "international controversies" and that they renounced it as an instrument of national policy in their relations with other parties.[24] Only pacific means were to be used. Japan was a signatory.

LEGAL PROFILES

Sakutaro Tachi was a law professor who advocated for the war in China. He was born in Japan in 1874 and completed his legal studies there. Between 1900 and 1904, he traveled to Europe to visit France, Germany, and the United Kingdom. Upon his return, he became a professor of international law at Tokyo Imperial University. Although he attended the Paris Peace Conference and the Washington Naval Conference in the early 1920s, he was opposed to the Kellogg-Briand Pact's prohibition of war: he believed that it applied only to renouncing war as national policy and not to the actuality of war, that self-defense was still an available means of war, and that there were exceptions for areas of "immediate interest."[25] He believed that war was not illegal under international law; he was highly influential in these matters in Japan and justified Japan's invasion of Manchuria. He died in 1943.[26]

Ryōichi Kuroda was an instructor in China during this time. He was born in Japan in 1911 and completed his legal studies there. He then

---

23. League of Nations Covenant art. 15, para. 7.
24. International Treaty for the Renunciation of War as an Instrument of National Policy, Aug. 27, 1928.
25. *See Intellectual Foundation for the Road to Pearl Harbor*, KEISEN JOGAKUEN C. BULL. (Jan. 1996).
26. *Id.*

went to Manchuria to teach for a number of years. After the war, he was captured by the Soviets and spent many years in a Siberian labor camp. In 1956, he became a law professor in Osaka. He was elected as the governor of the Osaka Prefecture in 1971 and again in 1975, the first to do so solely as a Japanese Communist Party candidate. He then returned to private practice. He died in 2003.[27]

B. Cases

At the major postwar trial in Japan, the International Military Tribunal for the Far East (IMTFE) (see Section 7.3) presented an indictment against Japan with fifty-five counts in three main sections: crimes against peace, murder, and crimes against humanity and war crimes. It covered the time period from 1928 to the end of the war. Crimes against peace will be discussed here; murder and crimes against humanity and war crimes will be dealt with in Section 7.3.

The charge of crimes against peace consisted of a conspiracy or common plan to "secure the military, naval, political and economic domination" and to "wage declared or undeclared war or wars of aggression, and war or wars in violation of international law, treaties, agreements and assurances, against any country or countries which might oppose that purpose."[28] This domination was aimed at East Asia and the Pacific; the Chinese provinces of Liaoning, Kirin, Heilungkiang, and Jehol; the Republic of China; the Pacific and Indian Oceans; and all countries and islands therein or bordering thereon, including a conspiracy with other Axis countries (counts 1–5).

The next series of indictment counts (counts 6–17) were for planning and preparing wars of aggression and war or wars in violation of international law, treaties, agreements, and assurances against the Republic of China, the United States, the United Kingdom, Australia, New Zealand, Canada, India, the Philippines, the Netherlands, France, Thailand, and the USSR. Counts 18–36 were for initiating and then waging wars of aggression and war or wars in violation of international law, treaties, agreements, and assurances against the Republic of China from 1931 and 1937; the United States, the Philippines, the United

27. *See Obituary: Ryoichi Kuroda*, JAPAN TIMES (July 29, 2003).
28. International Military Tribunal for the Far East Indictment (1946) at 33 [hereinafter IMTFE].

Kingdom, Thailand, all from 1941; France from 1940; the USSR from 1938 and 1939; and Mongolia from 1939.

For ease of adjudication, the IMTFE court consolidated many of the counts (e.g., initiating and maintaining a war of aggression). Through an exhaustive review of all of Japan's actions over the previous decades, the prosecution showed and the court concurred that Japan was involved in aggressive war. The defense raised the theory that Japan had the right to initiate preemptive strikes against the countries it did because they were impacting its economic plans through embargoes. The court rejected this argument because the various embargoes were attempts to stem Japan's aggressive expansion into other nations. The court noted that Japan had undertaken these expansion plans "to the North, to the West, and to the South, at the expense of her neighbors," long before any embargoes had been undertaken by its future enemies.[29] Japan's intention to exploit its neighbors and cut off support to China drove Japan's expansion, the court ruled.

The court found that Japan's incursions into French Indochina (i.e., Vietnam) were a war of aggression based on the threats to and demands on troops stationed there in 1940 and based on the actual military action against the French troops there in 1945. The court also ruled that the attacks against the United States, the United Kingdom (in Malaya, Hong Kong, and Singapore), and the Netherlands in the Dutch East Indies (i.e., Indonesia) were unprovoked acts of aggressive war "prompted by the desire to seize the possessions of these nations."[30] The attack upon the Philippines was also an act of aggressive war. The use of Thailand to transit troops to British Malaya was not proven because there appeared to be collaboration between the two governments.

LEGAL PROFILES

William F. Webb was the presiding judge on the IMTFE. He was born in Australia in 1887 and completed his legal studies there. He started as the state public defender in Queensland in 1915 and then from 1917

---

29. IMTFE Judgment at 49,582.
30. *Id.* at 49,584.

to 1922 was a crown solicitor. In 1922, he became solicitor general of Queensland, a position he held until 1925. He became an arbitration judge as well. In 1925, he was appointed to the Supreme Court of Queensland, where he remained until 1946, becoming its chief judge in 1940. He then left for a position on the High Court of Australia, where he remained until 1958, including his time on the IMTFE. In 1943, he was responsible for investigating Japanese atrocities in Papua New Guinea. He died in 1972.[31]

John P. Higgins was one of the judges on the IMTFE. He was born in Massachusetts in 1893 and started his legal practice there. Prior to entering the practice of law, he served in the navy during WWI and after that worked as a chemist for several years. In 1929, he was elected to the state legislature, where he served for five years. In 1934, he was elected to the U.S. House of Representatives. In 1937, he was appointed chief justice of the Massachusetts Superior Court, where he remained until 1955, which included his time on the IMTFE. He resigned from the tribunal and was replaced by Myron Cramer (see Chapter 4). He died in 1955.[32]

Delfin J. Jaranilla was one of the judges on the IMTFE. He was born in the Philippines in 1883 and received his law degree in the United States. He worked as an assistant justice attorney in Manila and as an auxiliary and district judge. He became the attorney general in 1925, a city judge in 1933, and a secretary of justice before joining the Supreme Court of the Philippines in 1945. He was a prisoner on the Bataan Death March (see Section 7.3.B.1.b) and then imprisoned for much of the war. He died in 1980.[33]

The other judges on the tribunal were the following:

- **Ivan Michyevich Zaryanov**, USSR, a major general and a member of the Military Collegium of the Supreme Court of the Soviet Union and part of the Soviet show trials in the 1930s

31. *See* Weld, H. A., Webb, *Sir William Flood (1887–1972)*, Australian Dictionary of Biography.
32. *See* Higgins, John Patrick, Biographical Directory of the United States Congress.
33. *See* Supreme Court of the Philippines Associate Justice List.

- **William Donald Patrick**, United Kingdom, a WWI veteran and a lord justice (senator) in the College of Justice (Supreme Court) of Scotland
- **B.V.A. Röling**, Netherlands, a professor of law and a judge at Utrecht during the Nazi occupation
- **Mei Ju-ao**, China, an interior minister and member of the Legislative Yuan who had received a bachelor's degree from Stanford and a law degree from the University of Chicago
- **Henri Bernard**, France, a veteran of the Free French Forces and a member of the military tribunals in Paris, Austria, and Brazzaville trying collaborators and Nazis
- **Edward Stuart McDougall**, Canada, a judge on the Court of King's Bench of Quebec
- **Radhabinod Pal**, India, a member of the Calcutta High Court
- **Erima Harvey Northcroft**, New Zealand, a WWI veteran, a former member of the Supreme Court of New Zealand until retirement in 1942, and a judge advocate general of the armed forces

Kenzō Takayanagi was one of the defense counsel (for Mamoru Shigemitsu and Kisaburo Suzuki) on the IMTFE. He was born in Japan in 1887 and completed his legal studies there but also studied law at Harvard and in London. After graduating from Tokyo Imperial University, he taught law there from 1912 to 1948. Eventually, he became professor emeritus of Anglo American law. He also became a member of the House of Peers, which led to his next position. From 1957 to 1964, he was the chairman of the Commission on the Constitution, traveling abroad to gain an understanding of the constitution, and the person to whom constitution drafter Milo Rowell gave his papers. Takayanagi concluded that the drafting of the constitution was done collaboratively, not imposed on Japan.[34] He later became the president of Seikei University, where he remained until his death in 1967.[35]

Haruhiko Nishi was one of the defense counsel (for Shigenori Togo) on the IMTFE. He was born in Japan in 1893 and completed his legal

---

34. K. Takayanagi, *Some Reminiscences of Japan's Commission on the Constitution*, 43 WASH. L. REV. 961, 961 (1967–1968).
35. *See* WILLIAM D. HOOVER, HISTORICAL DICTIONARY OF POSTWAR JAPAN 302 (2011).

studies there. He then worked for the Ministry of Foreign Affairs, including significant time in the USSR. He was the vice foreign minister from 1941 to 1942, including during the Pearl Harbor attack, about which he claimed to have no knowledge. After the war, he served as the first postwar ambassador to Australia from 1952 to 1955 and then as ambassador to the United Kingdom from 1955 to 1957. He died in 1986.[36]

C. Subsequent Events

After the war, Japan completely revised its constitution. Although nominally still based on the Meiji Constitution of 1871, the new constitution focused on self-defense only. In particular, Article 9 renounced the use of its military overseas. It stated in full that

> Aspiring sincerely to an international peace based on justice and order, the Japanese people forever renounce war as a sovereign right of the nation and the threat or use of force as means of settling international disputes. In order to accomplish the aim of the preceding paragraph, land, sea, and air forces, as well as other war potential, will never be maintained. The right of belligerency of the state will not be recognized.[37]

LEGAL PROFILES

Mamoru Shigemitsu was the Japanese diplomat who signed the Instrument of Surrender. He was born in Japan in 1887 and completed his legal studies there. He joined the Ministry of Foreign Affairs, serving in a number of overseas postings in Europe and America. He brokered a cease-fire with China in 1932 and with the USSR in 1938. During the attempted assassination of the emperor in 1932, he was injured and

---

36. *See Japanese Ambassador Arrives*, CANBERRA TIMES (Jan. 8, 1953).
37. JAPAN CONST. art. 9.

lost his leg. He tried to avert the coming Japan–U.S. conflict in 1941, which led to his dismissal from power; but he was recalled to be the foreign minister, a position that lasted until the end of the war. Based on the insistence of the USSR, he was made a defendant at the Tokyo war crimes trials in front of the IMTFE but was paroled by 1950. After this, he was elected to the lower house of the diet and served as deputy prime minister and foreign minister until 1956. He died in 1957.[38]

D. Modern Applicability

The concept of being able to preemptively strike other countries in self-defense has continued beyond the Japanese attack on Pearl Harbor in 1941. In 1967, with Egyptian, Syrian, Jordanian, and Iraqi troops on its borders and under continual terrorist attacks, Israel initiated the Six-Day War and gained an immense amount of land that is the source of continuing disputes in the region. In 1981, Israel preemptively struck the Osirak nuclear reactor complex in Iraq, but that did not lead to war (Iraq was already at war with Iran). In 2003, the U.S. Republican-controlled government launched a preemptive attack on Iraq, with the purported aim of eliminating weapons of mass destruction. These weapons were never found, so the reason for the war was revised to the harboring of terrorists, etc. Finally, Israel has for several years been clamoring for an attack on Iranian nuclear facilities before they begin producing atomic weapon materials.

Article 2(4) of the Charter of the United Nations does not allow members to use threats or force against the "territorial integrity or political independence" of any member or to use threats or force inconsistent with the United Nations' purpose.[39] The United Nations has issued a report that speaks to the international legality of preemptive strikes.[40] Emphasizing the need for collective security, it first declared that no state, even the most powerful, can

---

38. *See* Mamoru Shigemitsu, Deputy Prime Minister and Foreign Minister of Japan, Address of His Excellency Mamoru Shigemitsu, Deputy Prime Minister and Foreign Minister of Japan, Before the U.N. General Assembly on the Occasion of Japan's Admission to the U.N. (Dec. 18, 1956).
39. U.N. Charter art. 2, para. 4.
40. United Nations High-Level Panel on Threats, Challenges, and Change, *A More Secure World: Our Shared Responsibility*, U.N. Doc. A/59/565 (Dec. 2, 2004).

make itself invulnerable. But it acknowledged that states are still the "front-line responders" to the threats of today because collective action "often fails, sometimes dramatically so."[41]

While encouraging the use of sanctions, preventive diplomacy, mediations, and preventive deployment in addition to reducing the supply and demand of weapons of mass destruction and increasing poverty-reduction and other programs, the report did acknowledge situations where force could be legally used. These situations included self-defense under Article 51 and Security Council–authorized actions under chapter VII. This legal use differentiated between a preemptive strike based on an imminent threat and a preventive strike based on a nonimminent threat. The panel believed that authorization for preventive strikes must be sought under Security Council action, not self-defense justifications. It provided five criteria for the Security Council to consider when determining whether to authorize (or endorse) the use of military force: (1) the seriousness of the threat, (2) whether the primary purpose of the action is to avert the threat, (3) whether all other nonmilitary options have been explored and would not succeed, (4) whether the action is proportional, and (5) whether the consequences of actions are not likely to be worse than the consequences of inaction.

7.3 CRIMES AGAINST HUMANITY AND WAR CRIMES

A. Statutes

The jurisdiction of the IMTFE was derived from a series of four agreements:

- *Cairo Declaration*: "The Three Great Allies are fighting this war to restrain and punish the aggression of Japan."[42]
- *Potsdam Declaration*: "There must be eliminated for all time the authority and influence of those who have deceived and misled the people of Japan into embarking on world conquest, for we insist that a new order of peace, security and justice will be impossible until irresponsible militarism is driven from the world. . . . We do not intend that the Japanese

---

41. *Id.*
42. Cairo Communiqué of the United States, United Kingdom and the Republic of China, U.S.-U.K.-R.C., Dec. 1, 1943.

people shall be enslaved as a race or destroyed as a nation, but stern justice shall be meted out to all war criminals including those who have visited cruelties upon our prisoners."[43]

- *Instrument of Surrender.* "We hereby undertake for the Emperor, the Japanese Government, and their successors, to carry out the provisions of the Potsdam Declaration in good faith, and to issue whatever orders and take whatever action may be required by the Supreme Commander for the Allied Powers [SCAP] or by any other designated representatives of the Allied Powers for the purpose of giving effect to the Declaration."[44]
- *Moscow Conference:* "The Supreme Commander shall issue all orders for the implementation of the Terms of Surrender, the occupation and control of Japan and directives supplementary thereto."[45]

In early 1946, SCAP established the IMTFE and provisions for its members by special proclamation.[46] The IMTFE charter established the court at Tokyo, consisting of six to eleven tribunal members, who had the power to try and punish Far Eastern defendants charged with crimes against peace, conventional war crimes, and crimes against humanity (Class A, B, and C defendants, respectively, as designated by the IMTFE charter subsection numbers[47]). The crimes against peace included conspiracy. The crimes against humanity category was slightly different than that at the IMT, lacking a religious component and fully defined as

> murder, extermination, enslavement, deportation, and other inhumane acts committed against any civilian population, before or during the war, or persecutions on political or racial grounds in execution of or in connection with any crime within the jurisdiction of the Tribunal, whether or not in violation of the domestic law of the country where perpetrated. Leaders, organizers, instigators and accomplices participating in the formulation or execution of a common plan or conspiracy to com-

---

43. Proclamation Defining Terms for Japanese Surrender Issued at Potsdam, U.S.-U.K.-R.C., July 26, 1945.
44. Japanese Instrument of Surrender, Sept. 2, 1945.
45. Communiqué on the Moscow Conference of Foreign Ministers, U.S.S.R.-U.K.-U.S., Dec. 27, 1945.
46. SCAP Special Proclamation, Establishment of an International Military Tribunal for the Far East (Jan. 19, 1946).
47. IMTFE Charter, art. 5 (1946).

mit any of the foregoing crimes are responsible for all acts performed by any person in execution of such plan.[48]

SCAP was responsible for reviewing the sentences.

LEGAL PROFILES

Joseph B. Keenan was chief of counsel for the prosecution for this trial. He was born in Rhode Island in 1888 but started his legal practice in Ohio. He served in the army in France during WWI. After this, he joined the Office of the Judge Advocate General. He worked with the Office of the U.S. Attorney General to break up criminal gangs in Ohio and then was sent to Washington, D.C., where he was assigned to deal with a wave of kidnappings and the prosecution of Prohibition era gangster "Machine Gun" Kelly. He was then promoted to head the Criminal Division in the Justice Department, where he helped to write the Lindbergh Law on kidnapping and other laws related to gangsters and racketeers. He resigned in 1939 and returned to private practice until called into service on the IMTFE. He died in 1954.[49]

Arthur Comyns-Carr was a prosecutor from the United Kingdom for this trial. He was born in England in 1882 and completed his legal studies there. He joined the army in WWI. In 1923, he was elected to Parliament, the only success in eleven elections in which he ran as a Liberal candidate. In 1924, he was appointed a king's counsel. He worked on both the IMT and IMTFE; for the latter, he was generally responsible for the Executive Committee of the prosecutor teams, drawing up the indictment and trial strategy and is credited with being the chief drafter of the IMTFE indictment. He died in 1965.[50]

---

48. *Id.* at art. 5(c).
49. *See Joseph B. Keenan, Prosecutor, Dies*, N.Y. TIMES (Dec. 9, 1954).
50. *See Carr, Sir Arthur Strettell Comyns*, OXFORD DICTIONARY OF NATIONAL BIOGRAPHY 101061800.

B. Cases

1. IMTFE Trial

The second and third sections of the IMTFE indictment concerned murder and crimes against humanity and war crimes. As with the IMT and NMT trials, these crimes were all part of a single trial with a series of charges against multiple defendants. Specifically, the trial encompassed a series of different legal issues. The crimes against peace, crimes against humanity, and war crimes included charges that the murders of soldiers and civilians of Allied nations were unlawful hostilities because Japan had not given notice as required by the Hague Convention III of 1907 so its killings were illegal (count 37) and because Japan had committed to peaceful bilateral and multilateral relations with the Allies (count 38). The indictment listed specific cases of murder at Pearl Harbor, Malaya, Hong Kong, Shanghai, and the Philippines (counts 39–43). (The other counts are discussed in later subsections.)

The trial extended from May 1946 to November 1948. The presentation of the defense cases took almost one year. Various reasons for the duration of the trial included the need for a significant amount of translation, not only between Japanese and English but also regarding the other languages of the court, such as French and Russian. Additionally, the lax evidence rules allowed for the introduction of significant numbers of documents, not all of which were necessarily relevant. Furthermore, the different legal traditions of the lawyers involved, as at the IMT, caused considerable confusion.

The twenty-eight defendants (out of eighty Class A war criminals, who were to be tried later) consisted of military leaders and political leaders, nine of whom were civilians and several of whom were former prime ministers, including wartime leader Hideki Tōjō and at least one "radical theorist." Of these, two died in prison during the trial, and the radical theorist became mentally unfit for trial. Despite the wide destruction of documents by the Japanese between the end of the war and the formal surrender, sufficient documents and testimony were presented in order for the prosecution to make its case against all of the defendants.

The tribunal was made up of representatives from eleven countries (Australia, Canada, China, France, Great Britain, India, the Netherlands, New Zealand, Philippines, United States, and the USSR) but also received evidence from the following countries/territories that were not directly represented, for various reasons: Manchuria, Korea, Mongolia, Thailand, Cambodia, Burma, and Portugal.

The defense raised several general objections to the tribunal:

- The Allies had no authority to include crimes against peace in the tribunal's charter and designate these as justiciable.
- Aggressive war was not per se illegal, and the Kellogg–Briand Pact did not enlarge the meaning of war crimes to include it.
- War was the act of a nation for which there was no individual responsibility under international law.
- The charter's provisions were "ex post facto" legislation and therefore illegal.
- The Instrument of Surrender only allowed for prosecution of conventional war crimes.
- Killings in the course of belligerent operations, unless violations of rules of warfare or the laws and customs of war, were normal incidents of war and were not murder.
- Several of the accused were POWs and thus should be tried by courts-martial as provided by the Third Geneva Convention of 1929 and not by the IMTFE.

Regarding the first four points, the tribunal looked to the rulings of the IMT on this matter. The IMTFE dismissed these challenges by quoting from that other tribunal:

The Charter is not an arbitrary exercise of Power on the part of the victorious nations but is the expression of international law existing at the time of its creation. . . . The question is what was the legal effect of the [Kellogg–Briand] Pact? The Nations who signed the pact or adhered to it unconditionally condemned recourse to war for the future as an instrument of policy and expressly renounced it. After the signing of the pact any nation resorting to war as an instrument of national policy breaks the pact. In the opinion of the Tribunal, the solemn renunciation of war as an instrument of national policy necessarily involves the proposition that such a war is illegal in international law; and that those who plan and wage such a war, with its inevitable and terrible consequences, are committing a crime in so doing.

The principle of international law, which under certain circumstances, protects the representative of a state cannot be applied to acts which are condemned as criminal by international law. The authors of these acts cannot shelter themselves behind their official position in order to be freed from punishment in appropriate proceedings. . . . The maxim "nullum crimen sine lege" is not a limitation of sovereignty but is in general a principle of justice. To assert that it is unjust to punish those who in defiance of treaties and assurances have attacked neighboring states without warning is obviously untrue for in such circumstances the attacker must know that he is doing wrong, and so far from it being unjust to punish him, it would be unjust if his wrong were allowed to go unpunished.

The Charter specifically provides . . . "the fact that a defendant acted pursuant to order of his Government or of a superior shall not free him from responsibility but may be considered in mitigation of punishment." This provision is in conformity with the laws of all nations. . . . The true test which is found in varying degrees in the criminal law of most nations is not the existence of the order but whether moral choice was in fact possible.[51]

The court addressed the fifth challenge by noting that aggressive war had already long been a war crime and that the Japanese had known about the prosecution for it. The sixth challenge was answered by the nature and volume of the killings that occurred. The seventh challenge was addressed by reference to *In re Yamashita* (see Chapter 4), which found that crimes committed while a POW (not a combatant) are subject to the Third Geneva Convention.[52]

---

51. IMTFE Judgment at 48,437–439.
52. *In re* Yamashita, 327 U.S. 1 (1946).

LEGAL PROFILES

Grace Kanode Llewellyn was an assistant prosecutor for this trial responsible for research on Japanese military and economic aggressions, including in Manchuria. After graduating from law school, she worked as a legal assistant to Justice Alfred Wheat and in private practice. She worked on the IMTFE from late 1945 into 1946, introducing evidence for the prosecution's case. Afterward, she returned to private practice. She died in 1958.[53]

Eleanor Bontecou helped prepare the case for this trial. She was born in New Jersey in 1891. The start to her legal career teaching law at the University of Chicago was abbreviated when she contracted sleeping sickness, requiring years of bed rest. She recovered enough to be able to provide legal advice for the campaign to abolish the poll tax, leading her in 1943 to join the U.S. Department of Justice's new Civil Rights Division, where she worked until 1947. She was then transferred to the War Department War Crimes Branch, where she worked on this case and later did work in Nuremberg. She died in 1976.[54]

Yōsuke Matsuoka was a former foreign minister and a defendant at the IMTFE. He was born in Japan in 1880 but completed his legal studies in the United States in Oregon. Upon his return to Japan, he joined the Ministry of Foreign Affairs. He was posted in China, in the United States, and at the Paris Peace Conference ending WWI but spent the majority of his time over a period of twenty years in Manchuria, helping to develop resources from the Japanese leases there. He also was the leader of the Japanese delegation who announced the withdrawal in 1933 of Japan from the League of Nations. In 1940, he was appointed foreign minister and was one of the people involved with the Tripartite Pact with Germany and Italy. He subsequently left government and was

53. *See Recent Deaths*, PACIFIC STARS AND STRIPES (Jan. 31, 1958).
54. *See Eleanor Bontecou*, VIRGINIA WOMEN IN HISTORY.

arrested after the war as a Class A war criminal but died in prison awaiting trial in 1946.[55]

Henry G. Nolan was a prosecutor from Canada for this trial. He was
born in Canada in 1893 and completed his legal studies there. Instead of
taking up a Rhodes Scholarship, he served in WWI. He became qualified for legal practice in both England and Canada. He then returned
to practice in Canada. In 1940, he rejoined the Canadian army during
WWII, rising to the position of vice judge advocate general. He was
appointed to the Supreme Court of Canada in 1956. He died in 1957.[56]

---

a. Mass Rape
Counts 45–50 of the indictment addressed the Nanking Massacre and the
Chinese cities of Canton, Hankow, Changsha, Hanyang, and Kweilin/Liuchow.
The court, after reviewing all of the evidence, summarized the counts of war
crimes by stating that in China, from 1931 until 1945,

> torture, murder, rape and other cruelties of the most inhumane and bar-
> barous character were freely practiced by the Japanese Army and Navy.
> . . . [W]itnesses . . . testified in detail to atrocities committed in all the-
> atres of war on a scale so vast, yet following so common a pattern in all
> theatres, that only one conclusion is possible—the atrocities were either
> secretly ordered or willfully permitted by the Japanese Government or
> individual members thereof and by the leaders of the armed forces.[57]

The court pointed out that Japan's military leaders viewed the war in China

> as a punitive war . . . fought to punish the people of China for their
> refusal to acknowledge the superiority and leadership of the Japanese
> race and to cooperate with Japan. These military leaders intended to

---

55. *See Yōsuke Matsuoka*, NATIONAL DIET LIBRARY.
56. *See Henry G. Nolan*, ARCHIVES CANADA.
57. IMTFE Judgment at 49,593.

make the war so brutal and savage in all its consequences as to break the will of the Chinese people to resist.[58]

In Nanking in late 1937, as the Japanese army took the city, the troops began to commit unlimited atrocities:

Individual soldiers and small groups of two or three roamed over the city murdering, raping, looting and burning. There was no discipline whatever. Many soldiers were drunk. Soldiers went through the streets indiscriminately killing Chinese men, women and children without apparent provocation or excuse until in places the streets and alleys were littered with the bodies of their victims. According to another witness Chinese were hunted like rabbits, everyone seen to move was shot. At least 12,000 noncombatant Chinese men, women and children met their deaths in these indiscriminate killings during the first two or three days of the Japanese occupation of the city.

There were many cases of rape. Death was a frequent penalty for the slightest resistance on the part of a victim or the members of her family who sought to protect her. Even girls of tender years and old women were raped in large numbers throughout the city, and many cases of abnormal and sadistic behavior in connection with these rapings occurred. Many women were killed after the act and their bodies mutilated. Approximately 20,000 cases of rape occurred within the city during the first month of the occupation.[59]

Later, in the city of Kweilin, Japanese troops "committed all kinds of atrocities such as rape and plunder. They recruited women labor on the pretext of establishing factories. They forced the women thus recruited into prostitution with Japanese troops."[60]

One Japanese company commander "unofficially gave instructions for raping as follows: 'In order that we will not have problems, either pay them money

---

58. *Id.* at 49,595.
59. *Id.* at 49,605-606.
60. *Id.* at 49,617.

or kill them in some obscure place after you have finished.'"[61] And the rapes and murders were particularly brutal. In Manila, after setting a building afire, "[s]ome of the women were raped and their infants bayoneted in their arms. After raping the women the Japanese poured gasoline on their hair and ignited it. The breasts of some of the women were cut off by Japanese soldiers."[62] In Indonesia, "[w]omen . . . were not killed, but were all raped several times in the presence of the commanding officer."[63]

> The German Government was informed by its representative about "atrocities and criminal acts not of an individual but of an entire Army, namely, the Japanese," which Army, later in the report, was qualified as a "bestial machinery." Estimates made at a later date indicate that the total number of civilians and prisoners of war murdered in Nanking and its vicinity during the first six weeks of the Japanese occupation was over 200,000. That these estimates are not exaggerated is borne out by the fact that burial societies and other organizations counted more than 155,000 bodies which they buried. They also reported that most of those were bound with their hands tied behind their backs. These figures do not take into account those persons whose bodies were destroyed by burning or by throwing them into the Yangtze river or otherwise disposed of by Japanese.[64]

LEGAL PROFILES

Kōki Hirota was a former prime minister and a defendant at the IMTFE trial. He was born in Japan in 1878 and completed his legal studies there. He joined the Ministry of Foreign Affairs and served in a number of overseas postings, including in the Netherlands and the

---

61. *Id.* at 49,618.
62. *Id.* at 49,640.
63. *Id.* at 49,632.
64. *Id.* at 49,608.

USSR. After returning, he became the foreign minister in 1933, where he directed policy vis-à-vis Manchuria. In 1936, he became the prime minister for a year. In 1938, he again was named as foreign minister; this position was short-lived due to disagreements with the military in Manchuria, but he was in office during the Nanking Massacre, which he took no strong action to halt. At war's end, he tried to keep the USSR out of the conflict with Japan but failed. He was tried by the IMTFE, convicted, and executed in 1948.[65]

George Yamaoka was one of the defense counsel on the IMTFE (for Hirota and Togo) and the head of the American defense team after the start of the trial. He was born in Washington State in 1903 and completed his legal studies there. He was the first Japanese American to pass the New York bar exam. He was an adviser to the Japanese at the 1930 London Naval Conference. After the war, he maintained offices in both New York and Tokyo and advised a number of Japanese firms operating in the United States. He died in 1981.[66]

---

b. Mistreatment of POWs

There were a number of statutes regarding the treatment of POWs. The Hague Convention IV of 1907 required that POWs be "humanely treated"; that the labor of nonofficer POWs "not be excessive" and not be connected with the operation of war; that POWs' food, lodging, and clothing be equivalent to the soldiers of the capturing army; that they be subject to the same laws as those of soldiers of the capturing army; and that organizations like the Red Cross be allowed access.[67] The Geneva Red Cross Convention for the Amelioration of the Condition of the Wounded and Sick in Armies in the Field, 1929, required that wounded or sick soldiers or officers be "respected and protected in all

---

65. *See Kōki Hirota*, NATIONAL DIET LIBRARY.
66. *See George Yamaoka, Lawyer Named to Post by MacArthur, Dies at 78*, N.Y. TIMES (Nov. 22, 1981).
67. Hague Convention IV: Respecting the Laws and Customs of War on Land and Its Annex: Regulations Concerning the Laws and Customs of War on Land, Oct. 18, 1907.

circumstances" and treated humanely and for the safety of those carrying out this work.[68]

The Third Geneva Convention of 1929 dictated additional requirements. For example, POWs were to be evacuated from combat zones, but "the evacuation, if on foot, shall only be effected by stages of 20 kilometers a day, unless the necessity of reaching water and food requires longer stages."[69] Regarding labor, no "physically unfit" POW was to be forced to work, the workday should not be excessively long, a twenty-four-consecutive-hour rest should be allowed weekly, and POWs were not to do "unhealthful or dangerous" work.[70] Those recaptured after escape attempts were to receive only disciplinary punishments. Trials were expected, POWs were to be able to defend themselves and tried according to the same rules as those governing the capturing country's soldiers, and no death sentence could be carried out earlier than three months. Seriously ill or injured POWs were to be sent back to their own country.

Count 44 dealt with the murder of POWs, count 53 dealt with the mistreatment of POWs, and count 54 dealt with ordering or permitting the mistreatment of POWs. These counts came into play as the court received evidence of

> Ruthless killing of prisoners by shooting, decapitation, drowning, and other methods; death marches in which prisoners including the sick were forced to march long distances under conditions which not even well-conditioned troops could stand, many of those dropping out being shot or bayonetted by the guards; forced labor in tropical heat without protection from the sun; complete lack of housing and medical supplies in many cases resulting in thousands of deaths from disease; beatings and torture of all kinds to extract information or confessions or for minor offences; killing without trial of recaptured prisoners after escape or for attempt to escape; killing without trial of captured aviators; and even cannibalism.[71]

---

68. Geneva Red Cross Convention for the Amelioration of the Condition of the Wounded and Sick in Armies in the Field, July 27, 1929.
69. Geneva Convention Relative to the Treatment of Prisoners of War, July 27, 1929.
70. *Id.*
71. IMTFE Judgment at 49,593-94.

To understand the scale of the crimes against POWs by the Japanese, the court said that the

> extent of the atrocities and the result of the lack of food and medical supplies is exemplified by a comparison of the number of deaths of prisoners of war in the European Theater with the number of deaths in the Pacific Theater. Of United States and United Kingdom forces 235,473 were taken prisoners by the German and Italian Armies; of these 9,348 or 4 per cent died in captivity. In the Pacific Theater 132,134 prisoners were taken by the Japanese from the United States and United Kingdom forces alone of whom 35,756 or 27 per cent died in captivity.[72]

The court described the mistreatment of aviators who were shot down, including those on the Doolittle raid in 1942 that landed in China and were captured. It also described numerous incidents of massacres of POWs, sometimes by the most gruesome of methods and often based on orders from higher officers. Torture of POWs was not an uncommon practice, including "water treatment, burning, electric shocks, the knee spread, suspension, kneeling on sharp instruments[,] . . . flogging," vivisection, and cannibalism.[73] The tribunal noted that it was the Japanese philosophy that POWs were "regarded as being disgraced and entitled to live only by the tolerance of their captors."[74]

The court then looked at two specific practices: death marches and death by overwork. The Bataan Death March was an example of a death march (there were many others). The surrendering general saved trucks for his men to be transported to the POW camps, but the Japanese commander would not allow their use. Instead, the POWs

> were marched in intense heat . . . [for] a distance of 120 kilometers. The sick and wounded were forced to march. Those who fell by the roadside and were unable to continue were shot or bayoneted. Others were taken from the ranks, beaten, tortured and killed. The march continued for nine days, with the Japanese guards being relieved at five kilometer

---

72. *Id.* at 49,594.
73. *Id.* at 49,663.
74. *Id.* at 49,722.

intervals by fresh guards who had been transported in the American trucks. During the first five days the prisoners received little or no food or water.[75]

Overwork was another cause of death. To facilitate communications to further their conquest of India and South Asia, the Japanese constructed the Burma-Siam Railway using POW labor. The tribunal noted that the POWs "were constantly subjected to ill-treatment, torture and privation of all kinds, commencing with a forced march of 200 miles to the area under almost indescribable hardships. As a result in eighteen months 16,000 prisoners out of 46,000 died."[76] The POWs included the sick, who were forced to work. Housing and food was insufficient, and the number of POWs who contracted diseases was staggeringly high. This did not even include the very large number of native workers who labored there and died. Near the end of the project, Japanese commanders gave the order to shorten the time to finish the railroad, and the POWs were told that "[m]en are of no importance, the railroad has to be built irrespective of any suffering or death."[77]

LEGAL PROFILES

Ichirō Kiyose was the deputy Japanese chief defense counsel (for Tōjō, Kenryo Sato, and Iwane Matsui) on the IMTFE. He was born in Japan in 1884 and completed his legal studies there. He was a longtime member of the diet, serving first from 1920 to 1945, including a stint as vice speaker of the lower house before the war from 1928 to 1930.[78] In the 1920s, he was one of the architects of the jury system in Japan (it eventually lapsed during the war), supported universal suffrage, and opposed the Peace Preservation Laws. However, he defended one of the May 15 Incident defendants and became more closely affiliated with the military. In 1938, he became a professor at Hosei University. He was among the

---

75. *Id.* at 49,647.
76. *Id.* at 49,652.
77. *Id.* at 49,662.
78. *See Warns Tokio Diet on Korean Policy*, N.Y. TIMES (Mar. 4, 1921).

strongest of the Japanese defense counsel at the IMTFE, challenging the tribunal's jurisdiction,[79] the seating of certain justices,[80] and Japan's surrender as not unconditional.[81] After the war, he was purged but then served from 1955 to 1967 and was speaker of the lower house of the diet from 1960 to 1963; in addition, in 1956, he was the minister of education. As speaker, he was responsible for getting the Japan-U.S. Security Treaty approved despite vigorous opposition. He died in 1967.[82]

Somei Uzawa was chief Japanese defense counsel (for Toshio Shiratori and Matsui) on the IMTFE. He was born in Japan in 1872 and completed his legal studies there. He was a member of the lower house of the diet, elected six times before the war and eventually to the House of Peers. He was counsel for one of the defendants in a 1936 court-martial in another coup attempt.[83] In 1934, he became president of Meiji University. He had stated that he would not defend any Japanese charged as a war criminal at IMTFE unless he believed that the defendant was innocent, so he refused to defend Tōjō as he considered him responsible for the war.[84] He died in 1955.[85]

c. Narcotics Trafficking

Although there were many treaties and conventions regulating drugs, Japan was guilty of trafficking in narcotics nonetheless.

A number of treaties and conventions in the early 1900s dealt with the issue of drugs. The Convention and Final Protocol for the Suppression of the Abuse of Opium and Other Drugs, 1912, required contracting parties to take gradual steps to suppress the "manufacturing, trafficking, and use of opium, morphine, and cocaine."[86] It also required suppressing the export of the drugs and pre-

---

79. See *Tribunal Powers Challenged at Tokyo Trials*, CANBERRA TIMES (May 14, 1946).
80. See *War Court Flurry at Japanese Challenge*, SYDNEY MORNING HERALD (May 7, 1946).
81. See *Legality of Jap Trials*, SYDNEY MORNING HERALD (May 15, 1946).
82. See *Dr. Ichiro Kiyose, Tōjō's Lawyer, 82*, N.Y. TIMES (June 28, 1967).
83. See *Tokyo Colonel Hazy on Second Restoration*, N.Y. TIMES (Feb. 7, 1936).
84. See *A Medical Exam for the Former Premier*, N.Y. TIMES (Nov. 10, 1945).
85. See *Dr. Somei Ozawa*, N.Y. TIMES (Oct. 22, 1955).
86. Convention and Final Protocol for the Suppression of the Abuse of Opium and Other Drugs, 1912.

venting the smuggling, trafficking, and use of drugs within China, including any concessions within the country. Under the Convention to the Second Opium Conference of the League of Nations of 1925, countries were required to implement laws that ensured effective control of the production, distribution, and export of opium, including limiting its use to medical and scientific purposes.[87] The Geneva Convention for Limiting the Manufacture and Regulating the Distribution of Narcotic Drugs, 1931, required estimating and not exceeding the medical and scientific needs for these drugs in any territories of a contracting state, including via imports or exports.[88]

Despite these regulations, the Japanese government, to help finance the wars in China and to undermine the resistance of the Chinese, facilitated the trafficking of opium and narcotics such as cocaine. Since Japan was bound by these international agreements to suppress the trade in opium and other illicit drugs, it used the puppet state of Manchukuo as a cover. The drugs were from facilities operated in Japanese-occupied countries or were stolen when being imported. The facilities produced a tremendous amount of revenue, so much that it was estimated by the League of Nations that 90 percent of all "illicit white drugs" in the world were of Japanese origin.[89] Several of the largest Japanese commercial trading companies were involved in the import and export of these drugs to China. Although the Chinese government had taken strides to eliminate these drugs within its borders, the tribunal found that in those areas occupied by the Japanese military, addiction increased significantly and local farmers were induced to grow opium.

LEGAL PROFILES

Naoki Hoshino was a former finance minister and a defendant at the IMTFE. He was born in Japan in 1892 and completed his legal studies there. He then joined the Ministry of Finance. Beginning in 1932, he was involved in setting up a financial infrastructure for Manchuria. In 1937, he became a finance minister for the puppet state of Manchukuo,

---

87. Convention to the Second Opium Conference of the League of Nations, 1925.
88. Geneva Convention for Limiting the Manufacture and Regulating the Distribution of Narcotic Drugs, July 13, 1931.
89. IMTFE Judgment at 49,164.

where he oversaw the large increase in opium production there, which was its chief source of revenue. In 1940, he joined the planning board; and in 1941, he joined both the Tōjō cabinet as secretary and the House of Peers. He was convicted at the IMTFE and sentenced to life imprisonment but actually was paroled in 1958. He died in 1978.[90]

d. Remaining Counts

The tribunal reviewed the remaining counts.

Count 1 of the indictment

charged that all the defendants together with other persons participated in the formulation or execution of a common plan or conspiracy. The object of that common plan is alleged to have been that Japan should secure the military, naval, political and economic domination of East Asia and of the Pacific and Indian Oceans, and of all the countries and islands [in these oceans], and for that purpose should, alone or in combination with other countries having similar objects, wage a war or wars of aggression against any country or countries which might oppose that purpose.[91]

The court found that this charge was proved.

Counts 27–36 charged the crime of waging wars of aggression and wars in violation of international law, treaties, agreements, and assurances against the countries named in those counts. The court found these charges were proved, with two exceptions: the Philippines, which it regarded as part of the United States, so it could fall under the U.S. charges; and Thailand, which, as previously discussed, may have been party to the aggression in its territory. Count 54 concerned the ordering, authorizing, and permitting the commission of conventional war crimes; and count 55 dealt with the failure to take adequate steps to secure the observance of and prevent breaches of conventions and laws of war with respect to POWs and civilian internees. The court found that counts 54 and 55 were proved.

---

90. *See Naoki Hoshino of Japan; Ex-War Criminal was 86*, N.Y. TIMES (May 30, 1978).
91. IMTFE Indictment at 33.

All twenty-five of the remaining defendants were found guilty and given sentences ranging from death to life imprisonment to two lesser prison terms for the two diplomats. Death sentences were given to the following:

- Kenji Doihara, China military expert who was responsible for POW camps
- Kōki Hirota, foreign minister in the 1930s who was part of the aggressive buildup and who did not stop the Nanking Massacre
- Seishiro Itagaki, war minister and army colonel who helped instigate the Mukden incident and later oversaw POW camps
- Heitarō Kimura, who was responsible during the building of the Burma-Siam Railway
- Iwane Matsui, the commander of the army who instigated the Nanking Massacre
- Akira Muto, who was in military positions during atrocities in Nanking, the Dutch East Indies, and the Philippines
- Hideki Tojo, wartime prime minister, war minister, and army leader in Manchuria who was responsible for the Bataan Death March, Burma-Siam Railway deaths, and many other similar atrocities

Before the executions were carried out in late 1948, the defendants appealed to the U.S. Supreme Court. In a per curium opinion, the Court noted that all of the defendants were residents and citizens of Japan.[92] It said that the IMTFE was "not a tribunal of the United States."[93] Instead, the tribunal was set up by General MacArthur as an agent of the Allied powers. As such, the U.S. courts had no power or authority "to review, to affirm, set aside or annul the judgments and sentences imposed."[94] There was one dissent and one nonvote, and of course Justice Jackson took no part in the decision. Justice Douglas issued a concurring opinion to clarify that it was possible to issue a writ of habeas corpus even though the place was not within the territorial jurisdiction of any district court (e.g., defendants held overseas could file in the district court in the District of Columbia). The Court could not review the judgment of an

---

92. Hirota v. MacArthur, Gen. of the Army, 338 U.S. 197, 198 (1948).
93. *Id.*
94. *Id.*

international tribunal but could look to the legality of the actions of an American general holding a prisoner.

LEGAL PROFILES

Frank S. Tavenner Jr. was the deputy chief of counsel for the IMTFE. He was born in Virginia in 1895 and started his legal practice there. He served in the army in France in WWI. In 1931, he became an assistant district attorney in his home state, and in 1940 the district attorney, a post he held until 1948. From late 1945 until the end of the trial, he was the acting chief of counsel for the prosecution at the IMTFE. In 1949, he was chosen to be counsel for the House Committee on Un-American Activities, a position that he held for several years. He died in 1964.[95]

Alan J. Mansfield was a prosecutor from Australia for this trial. He was born in Australia in 1902 and completed his legal studies there. He started out in private practice in Queensland, handling divorce cases. He eventually chaired the Land Appeal Court of Queensland from 1942 to 1944. In 1945, he was appointed to the commission investigating war crimes. He had been appointed to the Supreme Court of Queensland in 1940, where he served until 1966. He became chief justice of the court in 1956. In 1966, he became the governor of Queensland, a role in which he served for six years. He died in 1980.[96]

2. Non-IMTFE Trials

a. Biological Warfare
The Russian military courts, not the IMTFE, tried the crimes of biological warfare executed by the notorious Unit 731 and other similar units in the Japa-

---

95. *See F.S. Tavenner Jr., House Panel Aide*, N.Y. TIMES (Oct. 22, 1964).
96. *See Mansfield, Sir Alan James (1902–1980)*, AUSTRALIAN DICTIONARY OF BIOGRAPHY.

nese military. In a deal similar to the arrangement under Operation Paperclip for the Nazi rocket scientists who were not tried in exchange for their technical expertise and information, the leaders of Unit 731 were not tried by the IMTFE in exchange for their information. Due to the emerging Cold War with the USSR and the fact that China had become Communist, MacArthur felt that presenting this information in open court in front of the eyes of potential adversaries was a bigger national security threat than keeping it secret. Despite objections from the State Department and elsewhere, that opinion prevailed.

Japan formed Unit 731 in Manchuria in the early 1930s and gave the unit its own facility in 1936, supposedly a water purification plant. Unit 731 conducted biological warfare experiments of two major types: those carried out on individuals and those carried out on the environment, thereby affecting many people. Under the control of a Japanese doctor named Shirō Ishii, thousands of individuals were killed through experiments dealing not only with biological agents but also with freezing, amputations, burns, and pressure. Patients were vivisected to check the spread of the biological agents; a mother and daughter were asphyxiated together to time their deaths. To infect large numbers of people and record the effects, various types of biological agents were introduced into the air and drinking water, onto the open ground, and into food supplies via agriculture. These included bubonic plague, dysentery, cholera, botulism, anthrax, smallpox, and typhoid. Tens of thousands of Chinese, Russians, and others were killed in these field tests. In China, the biological agents were often deployed by airplane, sometimes using transfer agents such as fleas. Biological agents were disguised both as vaccines and candy and given to children. Plans were under way toward the end of the war to utilize balloons and kamikaze pilots to carry these diseases into the heart of the American continent. The Japanese army blew up the facility after the end of the war to hide it from the Allies and killed the last few hundred "patients" there.

The Geneva Protocol for the Prohibition of the Use in War of Asphyxiating, Poisonous or Other Gases, and of Bacteriological Methods of Warfare, entered into force in early 1928, specified that the use in war of asphyxiating, poisonous, or other gases and of all analogous liquids, materials, or devices was "justly condemned by the general opinion of the civilized world."[97] Thus, the

---

97. Geneva Protocol for the Prohibition of the Use in War of Asphyxiating, Poisonous or Other Gases, and of Bacteriological Methods of Warfare, June 17, 1925 (entered into force Feb. 8, 1928).

prohibition on such use was to be "universally accepted as part of [i]nternational [l]aw."[98] In addition, bacteriological methods of warfare were prohibited. Japan refused to sign this protocol. One line of thinking was that if something was banned under international law, "it must make a great weapon."[99]

In late 1949, a Russian court in the Khabarovsk War Crimes Trial tried twelve Japanese military, physicians, and scientists captured in Manchuria. They were charged with research into bacteriological warfare, with the intent of using it to prepare attacks on the USSR, China, and Mongolia and for experimentations upon human subjects. The Russians claimed that the evidence they gathered was available at the IMTFE but not used, so they presented it here. During this trial, the defendants admitted guilt. All twelve were given prison sentences, with the leaders receiving more than twenty years; none received capital punishment. All were eventually repatriated to Japan in the 1950s. There has been speculation that the sentences were lenient because the Russians received information from the defendants on their work.

LEGAL PROFILES

Lev Nikolaevich Smirnov was a lead prosecutor for this trial, representing the USSR; he had been an assistant prosecutor at the IMT. He was born in Russia in 1911 and completed his legal studies there. From 1934 onward, he worked in various USSR prosecutorial roles. From 1957 to 1962, he was the deputy chairman of the Supreme Court of the USSR; and from 1962 to 1972, he was the chairman of the Supreme Court of the Russian Republic. From 1972 to 1984, he was chairman of the Soviet Supreme Court. He died in 1986.[100]

---

98. *Id.*

99. *Unmasking Horror—A Special Report: Japan Confronting Gruesome War Atrocity*, N.Y. TIMES (Mar. 17, 1995).

100. *See Len N. Smirnov Dies; Leading Soviet Judge*, N.Y. TIMES (Mar. 27, 1986).

b. Sexual Slavery

The IMTFE also did not try another crime: the imposition of a system of sexual slavery on women during wartime. Because there was no significant accountability for these crimes under either the IMTFE or subsequent Japanese prosecutions, even with the reports of two different U.N. special rapporteurs, other legal approaches were taken.

The most successful approach occurred in late 2000, when a gathering of legal personnel from across the Asia–Pacific region formed the Women's International War Crimes Tribunal on Japan's Military Sexual Slavery, which arose from "the failure of states to discharge their responsibility to ensure justice," the desire to "redress the historic tendency to trivialise, excuse, marginalize, and obfuscate crimes against women," and the common philosophy that "sexual violence against women is epidemic."[101] The tribunal issued a charter and an indictment, held a trial, and issued judgments. Organized initially by women from Japan, Korea, and the Philippines, the tribunal sitting in The Hague had four judges (led by the president of the International Criminal Tribunal for the Former Yugoslavia) and prosecutors from Japan, South Korea, the People's Republic of China, East Timor, the Philippines, Indonesia, North Korea, Malaysia, Taiwan, and the Netherlands.

The issue involved the creation, approved by the leaders of the army, of sexual institutions for the military of the country. While sexual services to the military were not new, what was unique in this war was the establishment by the Japanese military of sexual services based on the involuntary services of conquered women. These women, euphemistically termed "comfort women," were coerced, lured with false promises of jobs, or outright kidnapped by the military or agents hired by the Ministry of War and forced into providing sexual services for the military. The number of females so victimized was generally estimated at two hundred thousand women and girls, largely from China and Korea but also most other Asian countries occupied by Japan. A large percentage of these women and girls were killed, and many of the survivors became infertile.

---

101. Women's International War Crimes Tribunal on Japan's Military Sexual Slavery, Case No. PT-2000-1-T (Dec. 4, 2001).

The indictment included three counts. The first two counts were charges of crimes against humanity of sexual slavery and rape inflicted across all of the occupied countries by the Japanese military. The defendants for the first two counts were Emperor Hirohito, Iwane Matsui (executed after the IMTFE), Shunroku Hata (IMTFE life sentence, paroled), Hisaichi Terauchi (died before the IMTFE), Seishiro Itagaki (executed after the IMTFE), Hideki Tojo (executed after the IMTFE), Yoshijirō Umezu (IMTFE life sentence, died in prison), Seizo Kobayashi (not tried at the IMTFE), and Rikichi Ando (committed suicide). The third count was the mass rapes inflicted upon the women of the Philippines in November 1944. It was included as "an example of the many incidents of Japanese military's mass rape of women of local populations."[102]

The tribunal noted that the defendants would make a number of arguments, including that rape during armed conflict was not prohibited by the Hague Convention IV of 1907; that the prohibition against slavery was not a customary norm at the time of the war; and that although Japan ratified the 1921 International Convention on the Suppression of the Traffic in Women and Children, that convention specifically excluded Korea and Taiwan. Regarding the first point, the tribunal found rape to be a violation of family honor as defined in the regulations of the Hague Convention IV. Regarding the second point, the tribunal looked to, inter alia, the same convention's prohibition of forced labor plus the International Labour Organization's Convention Concerning Forced or Compulsory Labour of 1930, which Japan ratified, and trafficking suppression conventions early in the twentieth century.

The tribunal sat for several days in Tokyo and took testimony and affidavits from more than thirty survivors of the sexual slavery system, who in excruciating detail revealed their horrifying experiences, including constant incidents of rape and physical and mental torture. In addition, the tribunal heard from several actual perpetrators, who noted that after raping local women, they were told to kill the women because those women could bear children—future combatants—for the enemy. The tribunal also took in documentary evidence that provided "substantial evidence of pervasive responsibility for comfort station policy-making and operation at all levels of the government hierarchy."[103] Furthermore, it found that the Japanese military and government established

102. *Id.* at 22.
103. *Id.* at 781.

"a sophisticated, heavily regulated, and unimaginably cruel system in which women and young girls were held for sexual access by Japanese soldiers" and that this military sexual slavery system was a "standard and integral part" of Japan's aggressive war in Asia/Pacific.[104]

In addition to the tribunal, another legal approach involved private lawsuits filed by the survivors from a number of countries. However, these have been without great effect. The courts have typically held that plaintiffs do not have the appropriate standing; that the statute of limitations had already passed; that Japan had sovereign immunity; that international treaties between Japan and the plaintiffs' countries settled all claims, including those of individuals; or that all claims were settled under the war-ending Treaty of San Francisco (see Chapter 8).[105] The tribunal noted that these treaties may not be the final word, for a number of reasons, including that a state cannot waive individual claims for crimes against humanity, that circumstances may change (Japan could not pay reparations at the time due to its weak economic condition), and that peace treaties are political and not legal settlements.

The Japanese believed that they resolved at least the legal matters by paying a large sum of money to settle all claims in 1965 as part of the Treaty on Basic Relations Between Japan and the Republic of Korea, commonly called the Korea-Japan Claims Settlement Agreement.[106] Furthermore, Japan set up a private (not government) fund in 1995 for comfort women, and the government issued apologies, especially in the 1990s.

C. Subsequent Events

There were numerous other trials in Asia conducted by many of the countries represented in the tribunals at the IMTFE, indicting more than five thousand Japanese and handing out almost one thousand death sentences. For example, the British tried Japanese Class B and C war criminals for acts that occurred in their territories, such as Singapore, Hong Kong, Malaya, Burma, and elsewhere. They tried almost one thousand people, and more than two hundred were sentenced to death. In another war crimes trial at Yokohama, twenty-three Japanese were convicted of the 1945 vivisection and removal of body organs

---

104. *Id.* at 797.
105. Hwang Geum Joo v. Japan, Minister Yohei Kono, Minister of Foreign Affairs, Case No. 01-7169 (D.C. Cir. 2005).
106. Treaty on Basic Relations Between Japan and the Republic of Korea, Japan-Korea, 1965.

from eight living American POWs. In addition, the Philippines tried their occupation-era president. However, the other Class A war criminals were not tried; and, unlike Germany, Japan did not follow up with its own trials of any significance. In fact, by imperial rescript, war crimes committed by the military were generally pardoned in Japan in 1946; and the Japanese government was quick to try to close the books legally on the decade and a half of conflict that it had inflicted upon the rest of Asia. Japanese citizens themselves brought lawsuits domestically for their own forced labor; however, these attempts were unsuccessful as the ability to sue the government did not exist during the wartime period.

Other conduct that could be categorized as crimes against humanity was never tried. A prominent example of this was the military's exhortation to civilians to kill themselves instead of surrender to the Allies. This was especially true in Okinawa, where Japanese citizens were told patently false information about how they would be treated by the Allied military. Thousands of these people, so close to liberation from the war, were induced to kill not only themselves but their families, many using hand grenades provided by the Japanese military or jumping off of cliffs. Parents on this island threw their children, including infants, to their deaths and then jumped after them; school classes jumped to their deaths together on their teachers' orders; and families strangled their own children with ropes.

Much later, in the early 2000s, there was a series of lawsuits filed in the U.S. state of California against Japanese firms by POWs and other forced laborers from several countries based on a new law that allowed lawsuits by victims of "the Nazi regime, its allies or sympathizers" to recover for labor performed as a WWII slave labor victim.[107]

In the first suit, Allied POWs sought damages under this law and claims for unjust enrichment, various torts including battery, and unfair business practices (not disclosing its wartime practices to current customers).[108] To give weight to the significance of the charges, the court used one POW plaintiff as an example, noting that he was about 5'11" tall and weighed 167 pounds when captured in late 1941. At war's end, after spending the war engaged in "slave labor"

---

107. *In re* World War II Era Japanese Forced Labor Litig., 114 F. Supp. 2d 1153, 1156 (N.D. Cal. 2001).
108. *Id.* at 939.

in Japan, he weighed only 98 pounds. The court held that although the claim was filed in state court under state law, it involved a matter of foreign relations and as such was properly removed to federal court. The ability to collect under these theories was restricted, the court ruled, by the 1951 peace treaty with Japan (see Chapter 8), which waived "other claims of the Allied Powers and their nationals arising out of any actions taken by Japan and its nationals in the course of the prosecution of the war."[109] The court noted that at the time of the peace treaty, Japan's economy could not sustain substantial reparations and that it was needed as a bulwark in the Cold War. However, the treaty allowed for the transfer of Japanese assets outside Japan to the Red Cross to assist POWs. The court refuted the attempt to cast this as a suit involving private parties, stating that it was not possible to "distinguish between the conduct of Imperial Japan during the Second World War and the major industry that was the engine of its war machine."[110] The court concluded by quoting from a letter written by the U.S. State Department: "Regrettably, however, it was impossible when the Treaty was negotiated—and it remains impossible today, 50 years later—to compensate fully for the suffering visited upon the victims of the war."[111]

In the second suit, Filipino forced laborers brought similar claims.[112] The main issue was whether the forced labor was for financial gain by the companies or to support the prosecution of the war. The court held that the phrase *in the course of the prosecution of the war* included activities by companies that profited financially during the war.

In the third suit, Korean and Chinese forced laborers brought similar claims under the same laws, but the issue was that their countries were not signatories to the San Francisco peace treaty with Japan.[113] China was not a signatory because it was involved in its civil war at the time; and Korea, as a colony, could not technically have been at war with Japan. The court ruled against the plaintiffs based on the unconstitutionality of U.S. state laws infringing on the powers of the federal government in international relations. States "may legislate with respect to local concerns that touch upon foreign affairs, but only

109. *Id.* at 945.
110. *Id.* at 948.
111. *Id.* at 947.
112. *In re* World War II Era Japanese Forced Labor Litig., 164 F. Supp. 2d 1153 (N.D. Cal. 2001).
113. *Id.* at 1160.

if its actions have 'some incidental or indirect effect in foreign countries.'"[114] Beyond that, claims under other laws such as the Alien Tort Claims Act would be barred by the statute of limitations.

The issue of forced sexual slavery also played out in the years after WWII. Subsequent Japanese prime ministers have backtracked from responsibility, even going so far as to deny the existence of comfort women. As such, there is still activity relating to the resolution of this issue more than seventy years later. In 2011, the Constitutional Court of Korea told the Korean government that its lack of support for Korean comfort women was a violation of the Korean Constitution.[115] In 2012, the National Assembly of South Korea adopted a resolution that called on Japan to provide an official apology and compensation for the comfort women.[116] Subsequently, unofficial talks between the countries on this subject have been held.[117]

LEGAL PROFILES

José Laurel was the president of the Philippines during the Japanese occupation and a lawyer. He was born in the Philippines in 1891 and completed his legal studies there and then in the United States. He returned to the Philippines, working at the Department of the Interior in the early 1920s. In 1925, he was elected to the Philippine Senate, where he served as majority leader from 1928 to 1931. After losing reelection, he worked on the new constitution for the Commonwealth and was then appointed to the Philippine Supreme Court in 1936. After the Japanese occupation of the country, he was selected to roles in the occupied government (the Second Republic) as minister of justice and the interior and finally president of the country between 1943 and the end of the war in 1945. Surviving an assassination attempt, he was tried after the war for treason for collaborating with the Japanese but was

---

114. *Id.* at 1173.
115. Republic of Korea, Case No. 2006Hun-Ma788 (Korea Constitutional Ct. Aug. 30, 2011).
116. *South Korea Adopts Resolutions on Takeshima, "Comfort Women,"* Asahi Shimbun (Sept. 4, 2012).
117. *"Comfort Women" Talks Being Held with South Korea,* Japan Times (Sept. 25, 2012).

pardoned as part of a general amnesty. He was once more elected to the Senate before he died in 1959.[118]

Brendan F. Brown was the legal assistant to the chief of counsel at the IMTFE. He was born in Iowa in 1898 and completed his legal studies in Nebraska, including additional studies at Oxford and Harvard. He taught law at the Catholic University of America from 1932 to 1954, including a stint as dean from 1949 to 1954. In 1954, he joined the law faculty at Loyola University of New Orleans, where he remained through 1970. He was known as a scholar in civil, canon, Roman, and common law and published numerous treatises on these subjects. He died in 1981.[119]

D. Modern Applicability

The issue of mass rapes and the systematic use of rape as a weapon of terror during wartime have survived into modern times. In a number of African conflicts over the last twenty years and in the Yugoslavian civil wars, soldiers were instructed to—or at least not restrained from—these brutalities against the female nationals of the enemy. In the *Prosecutor v. Dragoljub Kunarac* decision, the International Criminal Tribunal for the Former Yugoslavia ruled that rape was used as an instrument of terror during a conflict and that rape and enslavement were crimes against humanity.[120] Ethnics Serbs were charged with crimes against humanity and war crimes for rape, torture, enslavement, and outrages upon personal dignity in regard to numerous female Bosnian Muslims in 1992 and 1993 as part of a campaign to ethnically cleanse the area of Muslims. The defendants systematically separated detained women and girls in camps, to be taken later by both the defendants and others to whom they were "loaned." The court found the defendants variously guilty of the counts as crimes against humanity and crimes against the laws or customs of war.

---

118. *See Jose Laurel Dies, Filipino Leader; Head of Wartime Japanese Puppet Regime*, N.Y. TIMES (Nov. 6, 1959).
119. *See A Tribute to Dr. Brendan F. Brown*, 21 LOY. L. REV. 803 (1975).
120. Prosecutor v. Dragoljub Kunarac, Case Nos. IT-96-23-T, IT-96-23/1-T (IT for the Prosecution of Persons Responsible for Serious Violations of Int'l Humanitarian Law Committed in the Territory of the Former Yugo. Since 1991, Feb. 22, 2001).

7.4 USE OF NUCLEAR WEAPONS

A. Statutes
Besides new combatants such as the USSR, what finally brought this long war to an end were the atomic bombings of Hiroshima and Nagasaki.

1. The Manhattan Project
In 1945, with the Chinese and British coming from the West, the Americans from the South and the Soviets from the North, the Japanese military still refused to consider unconditional surrender. Most concerned about saving as much of their empire as possible as well as the office of the emperor, the military leaders continued to sacrifice the property and people of their country in the vain hope that the cost of taking the Japanese home islands would be larger than the Allies could bear and that a cease-fire would be called. The Allies, determined to remove the military aggression of Japan, which was compared to events in Germany, required a complete and unconditional surrender.

U.S. leaders, now with President Truman in charge after the death of President Roosevelt, wanted the help of the Russians in their aggressions against Japan if necessary but were wary of doing so. Caught in such a pincerlike movement between nations with superior manpower and military and industrial capabilities, Japan clearly would have succumbed sooner or later. But the cost to Truman and his advisers was seen as too high, in terms of both a staggering loss of life and political considerations as well since the Soviets' invasion would likely divide Japan into half, much like Korea would soon be (and remains to this day) and Germany was already.[121]

Under all of these pressures and with the complexities of many unknowns in a war-weary world, President Truman decided to turn to what he considered to be the lesser of the evils, which was based on a secret project America had begun years before. The story of the Manhattan Project, which spawned the first atomic bomb, is now well known, with famous (or soon-to-be famous) scientists Albert Einstein, Enrico Fermi, Leo Szilárd, Niels Bohr, Ernest Lawrence, Hans Bethe, James Chadwick, Edward Teller, and J. Robert Oppenheimer involved in some way. The project began in America in 1939 with a letter. Hungarian physicist Leo Szilárd spoke to Albert Einstein about

---

121. *See* Minutes of White House Meeting (June 18, 1945).

his concerns regarding the potential for other countries to develop bombs, and together Einstein drafted and Szilárd translated a letter that was delivered to President Roosevelt. It explained the new possibility of nuclear weapons and expressed concern for recent German bans on uranium exports from its only source in occupied Czechoslovakia, implying that Nazi Germany was working on developing such a weapon.

The Manhattan Project materially commenced with an executive order from President Roosevelt in mid-1941, drawing on his powers under the Constitution and other statutes for this "unlimited national emergency." [122] This executive order created the Office of Scientific Research and Development, with its director reporting directly to the president. Among its mandates were advising the president on scientific and medical research related to national defense; mobilizing scientific personnel and resources to apply the results of scientific research to national defense; and coordinating such experimental and research activities toward "creating, developing, and improving instrumentalities, methods, and materials required for national defense." [123]

Dr. Vannevar Bush was named as the first director of the Office of Scientific Research and Development. Eventually, he brought on board Brigadier General Leslie Groves to identify facilities to process the required uranium and produce plutonium and to develop and test delivery capabilities (and eventually to oversee production of the bomb itself). These included Hanford, Washington, and Oak Ridge, Tennessee, for processing and production and Los Alamos, New Mexico for the delivery mechanisms for each type of bomb. In addition, a number of laboratories around the country were in operation, working to develop the best techniques for separating uranium and creating nuclear reactors.

To speed up and build on their previously separate efforts, not to mention to gain control over global supplies of uranium, the United States and the United Kingdom signed the Quebec Agreement. [124] This agreement provided that information and research would be shared, that British and Canadian scientists would join the Manhattan Project (for which the United States was

---

122. Exec. Order No. 8807, Establishing the Office of Scientific Research and Development in the Executive Office of the President and Defining Its Functions and Duties (June 28, 1941).
123. *Id.*
124. Articles of Agreement Governing Collaboration Between the Authorities of the USA and UK in the Matter of Tube Alloys, U.S.-U.K., Aug. 19, 1943.

footing the expense), and that uranium supplies in Canada and the Belgian Congo (its government in exile was located in London) would be sold to the Americans. However, information on the design, construction, and operation of large-scale plants was to be restricted. This agreement stated that the two sides would not use these weapons against each other or against third parties without the other side's agreement; dictated secrecy; and stated that postwar commercial and industrial uses, given the United States' significant investment, were to be controlled by America. A Combined Policy Committee was to oversee the work under the agreement.

LEGAL PROFILES

John Lansdale Jr., lieutenant colonel, was the head of intelligence and security for the Manhattan Project and the Alsos Mission to capture Nazi nuclear weapons and scientists; he was also a lawyer. He was born in California in 1912 but started his legal career in Ohio. He was involved in private practice both before and after the war. Besides doing legal work and focusing on the security risks involved, he was sent to Europe to follow behind the advancing armies and locate raw materials used in nuclear production, records, equipment, and scientists. Part of his team raided suspected factories to find these raw materials, records, and equipment; and another part of the team captured German nuclear scientists such as Werner Heisenberg and Otto Hahn. He later defended J. Robert Oppenheimer, who was accused of Communist Party leanings and to whom he had accorded security clearance for the Manhattan Project, before Congress. He died in 2003.[125]

2. The Interim Committee

In 1945, the Interim Committee was set up to address wartime and postwar nuclear weapon usage issues after Truman became president. Its members

---

125. *See John Lansdale Jr., 91, Hunter of Nazi Atomic-Bomb Effort*, N.Y. TIMES (Sept. 2, 2003).

included James Byrnes (see Chapter 3) representing the president, army and navy representatives, Dr. Bush, and the presidents of the Massachusetts Institute of Technology (MIT) (Karl Compton) and Harvard (James Conant). Through a colossal collective effort over several years and at a massive financial expenditure, the various research, design, production, manpower, material, and secrecy activities overcame the many scientific, technical, procedural, and bureaucratic hurdles and eventually led to the successful Trinity test (of a nuclear device) at Alamogordo in New Mexico in July 1945.

LEGAL PROFILES

George L. Harrison was a member of the Interim Committee and a lawyer. He was born in California in 1887 but started his legal career clerking for Oliver Wendell Holmes. He joined the Federal Reserve Board in Washington, D.C., in 1914, eventually becoming general counsel. In 1920, he became deputy governor of the Federal Reserve Bank of New York. Then, in 1928, he became the president of the Federal Reserve Bank of New York, a position that he held until the end of 1940. He then became the president of the New York Life Insurance Company. During the war, he assisted Secretary of War (and fellow lawyer) Henry Stimson (see Chapter 2). After the war, he returned to his position in private industry. He died in 1958.[126]

3. The Dropping of the Bomb

The Interim Committee met several times in June and July, focusing much time on post-war control, but did concur that the bomb should be used as soon as possible.[127] With knowledge of the success of the Trinity test, President Truman was able to confidently issue the Potsdam Declaration of July 26, 1945 (see Section 7.3). The Japanese government refused to comply with this direc-

126. *See George L. Harrison*, FEDERAL RESERVE BANK OF NEW YORK HISTORY.
127. *See* Notes of the Interim Committee Meeting (June 1, 1945).

tive, so Truman gave the order to commence with the first nuclear bombing. In the official order dated July 25, 1945, the 509th Composite Group was directed to "deliver its first special bomb as soon as weather will permit visual bombing after about 3 August 1945 on one of the targets: Hiroshima, Kokura, Niigata and Nagasaki."[128] Additional bombs were to be delivered on the above targets "as soon as made ready."[129]

The bomb was dropped on Hiroshima on August 6, 1945. In a follow-up statement, President Truman stated that the United States had spent $2 billion on the "greatest scientific gamble in history—and won" and were prepared to "obliterate every productive enterprise the Japanese have . . . to completely destroy Japan's power to make war."[130] He noted the power of the bomb, the U.K.-U.S. cooperation in developing the bomb, and the good fortune that the Germans had not developed V-1 and V-2 capabilities until late in the war. He made it clear that the Japanese leaders could have spared their people from "utter destruction" but that they had rejected the proffered terms. If they did not now accept these terms, then they could expect "a rain of ruin from the air, the like of which has never been seen on this earth."[131] Truman ended his statement by noting the possible positive uses of nuclear power and expressing the hopeful intention that "atomic power can become a powerful and forceful influence towards the maintenance of world peace."[132]

Leaflets were dropped from the air all over Japan, explaining the destructive capability of the new weapon, asking the people to petition the emperor to stop the war, and telling them to evacuate their cities. When there was no further substantive response from the Japanese government, a second bomb was dropped on Nagasaki on August 9, 1945.

---

128. Order from Acting Chief of Staff to Commanding General, U.S. Army Strategic Air Forces (July 25, 1945).
129. *Id.*
130. Press Release, White House, Statement by Harry Truman, President, United States (Aug. 6, 1945).
131. *Id.*
132. *Id.*

LEGAL PROFILES

William A. Consodine, lieutenant colonel, U.S. army, was part of the security team under Lansdale and later headed the public relations efforts of the Manhattan Project, suggesting revisions to Truman's statement; he was also a lawyer. Consodine practiced law in New Jersey before starting to work for the military in 1942. He was a personal lawyer for General Groves and was part of the legal team that created briefs on the legality of resource purchases, in addition to performing security reviews. He was heavily involved in editing the statement that President Truman released after the bombing.[133] After the war, he returned to private practice and later worked as a judge in New Jersey.

William L. Laurence was a newspaper science reporter who was an observer on a mission plane during the Nagasaki bombing. He was born in Lithuania in 1888 but moved to America when he was a teenager and completed his legal studies in Massachusetts. He served in the army in WWI. He then began a career in journalism in New York, taking a job with the *New York Times* in 1930. In 1936, he won his first Pulitzer Prize for reporting on science. General Groves decided that he needed a historian for the Manhattan Project and chose Laurence as the only press witness on the blast instrumentation aircraft *The Great Artiste* at the Trinity test in July 1945 and the Nagasaki bombing in 1946. He won a second Pulitzer Prize for this and subsequent reporting on nuclear energy issues. He became science editor for the newspaper, continuing to cover nuclear weapons tests and other science issues until his retirement in 1964. He died in 1977.[134]

---

133. *See Awards to Ten Here for Atom Bomb Work*, N.Y. TIMES (Nov. 26, 1945).
134. *See William L. Laurence of the Times Is Dead*, N.Y. TIMES (Mar. 19, 1977).

B. Cases

While there was clearly not a statute prohibiting the use of atomic weapons during the war, there have been several suits filed since then. These were of several different types, against both the Japanese government and the U.S. government. The first lawsuit was a unique case seeking damages based on the illegality of the atomic bombings. The second lawsuit was initiated by a survivor of the atomic bombing against the Japanese government for survivor benefits. The third set of lawsuits involved consolidated cases against the U.S. government for U.S. nuclear weapons tests and deployments in various locations.

1. Legality of Nuclear Weapons Use

In a unique case that took almost a decade to litigate, *Ryuichi Shimoda v. State (of Japan)*, five plaintiffs from the Hiroshima and Nagasaki areas sought to have the atomic bombing of Japan declared illegal and to seek damages from both the United States and Japan.[135] The lead plaintiff lost four daughters in the bombing of Hiroshima. The plaintiffs claimed that they were injured by the illegal dropping of the atomic bombs and that because Japan waived the plaintiffs' rights under the Treaty of San Francisco to seek redress, Japan itself now stood in the place of the United States in regard to its obligation to pay damages. Under the Japanese Constitution and the State Redress Law,[136] private citizens could recover for the unlawful acts of government officials.

The plaintiffs' claims were based on the illegality of the bombing under international law. The case looked to the Hague Convention IV of 1907[137] and its accompanying regulations, the Hague Convention IX of 1907[138] and the never-adopted Hague Rules of Air Warfare of 1923. In the first convention, Article 25 stated that "the attack of bombardment, by whatever means, of towns, villages, dwellings, or buildings which are undefended is prohibited"; and Article 23 prohibited employing projectiles calculated "to cause unnecessary suffering."[139] In the second convention, Article 1 stated that "the bombardment by naval forces of undefended ports, towns, villages, dwellings, or

135. Ryuichi Shimoda v. State (of Japan) (Tokyo Dist. Ct. 1963).
136. Act No. 125 of October 27, 1947 (Japan).
137. Hague Convention IV: Respecting the Laws and Customs of War on Land and Its Annex: Regulations Concerning the Laws and Customs of War on Land, Oct. 18, 1907.
138. Hague Convention IX: Concerning Bombardment by Naval Forces in Time of War, Oct. 18, 1907.
139. Hague Convention IV, arts. 23, 25.

buildings, is forbidden"; but Article 2 allowed such bombardments of "military works."[140] In the third convention, Article 24 stated that aerial bombardments are legitimate only when directed at military objectives such as military forces or works, in the immediate neighborhood of the operations of land forces, or if they cause an indiscriminate bombardment of the civilian population. Article 22 prohibited aerial bombardment for purposes of "terrorizing the civilian population."[141] Nothing in these or any other international treaty or convention specifically addressed nuclear weapons, so the defendant asserted that the plaintiffs had no rights to violate.

The court ruled that Hiroshima and Nagasaki were not defended cities in imminent danger of attack from land forces. While there were antiaircraft guns and military objectives, there were also civilians residing therein. Because of the power of the nuclear weapons used, it was not possible to discriminate between military objectives and the civilian population; thus, such bombardments were prohibited, even under an expanded concept of a military objective in a "total war."[142] The court held that despite the fact that the Hague Rules of Air Warfare, on which it based most of its analysis, had never been adopted, the bombings were illegal under the international law that existed at the time (primarily the other Hague Conventions by analogy and conventions prohibiting poisonous materials, etc.).

Despite this finding, the court, turning next to the municipal law of the belligerents, noted no express relationship between international law and municipal law in Japan under its wartime constitution. It ruled that the municipal law must have included customary international law and treaties. It also noted the role of treaties under the U.S. Constitution and customary international law. It then went on to show that while there were clearly country-to-country claims for acts contrary to international law, individuals acting for their country, such as President Truman, could not be held liable for such damages in their roles. It also ruled that individuals only had rights under international law as provided for in treaties; and as the plaintiffs had no mechanisms to seek redress under international law, they had no rights here under international law.

---

140. Hague Rules of Air Warfare, Dec. 1922–Feb. 1923.
141. Hague Convention IX, arts. 22, 24.
142. Ryuichi Shimoda v. State (of Japan) (Tokyo Dist. Ct. 1963).

Under municipal law, the Japanese plaintiffs could not seek redress from the United States in Japanese courts due to the lack of jurisdiction of those courts over another country. In U.S. courts, this court stated, the action would be dismissed due to sovereign immunity. It also noted that under the postwar Federal Tort Claims Act, there were exceptions for executive actions, the army and navy, and what happens overseas. The court then went on to note that Japan could (under the doctrine of "diplomatic protection") and had waived all claims for itself and its nationals under the Treaty of San Francisco (see Chapter 8). The rights waived were those under the municipal law of both Japan and the Allies. This left the plaintiffs with no rights to seek redress under either international law or the municipal law of either country; thus, "the action must fail on the merits."[143]

In 1994, the U.N. General Assembly requested the International Court of Justice (ICJ) to "urgently . . . render its advisory opinion on the following question: 'Is the threat or use of nuclear weapons in any circumstance permitted under international law?'"[144] In response, the ICJ issued an advisory opinion with the following main points:

> There is in neither customary nor conventional international law any specific authorization of the threat or use of nuclear weapons . . . or any comprehensive and universal prohibition of the threat or use of nuclear weapons as such. . . . A threat or use of force by means of nuclear weapons that is contrary to [the U.N. Charter (Article 2, paragraph 4)] and that fails to meet all the requirements of Article 51, is unlawful.[145]

According to the ICJ, a threat or use of nuclear weapons should also be compatible with the requirements of the international law applicable in armed conflict, particularly those of the principles and rules of international humanitarian law, as well as with specific obligations under treaties and other undertakings that expressly deal with nuclear weapons. The threat or use of nuclear weapons would generally be contrary to the rules of international law applicable in armed conflict, and in particular the principles and rules of humani-

---

143. *Id.*
144. G.A. Res. 49/75 K, U.N. Doc. A/RES/49/75 K (1994).
145. Legality of the Threat or Use of Nuclear Weapons, Advisory Opinion, I.C.J. (July 8, 1996).

tarian law, noted the ICJ, but may not be so "in an extreme circumstance of self-defence, in which the very survival of a State would be at stake. . . . There exists an obligation to pursue in good faith and bring to a conclusion negotiations leading to nuclear disarmament in all its aspects under strict and effective international control."[146]

LEGAL PROFILES

Shoichi Okamoto was the plaintiffs' counsel in the *Ryuichi Shimoda* suit. He was born in Japan in 1891 and completed his legal studies there. He was a defense counsel (for Muto) at the IMTFE. He led the effort to put together this suit primarily on his own, without the expected assistance of Japanese lawyers in either bombed city or nationally. He had also expected assistance from the ACLU's Roger Baldwin, who had founded the Japan Civil Liberties Union, but this help was not forthcoming as there was "no legal basis" for the suit.[147] He died in 1958 before he could see the final rulings in this suit. His assistant, Yasuhiro Matsui, tried the case through to conclusion.

2. Support of Hibakusha

The victims and survivors of the atomic bombings in Japan needed significant medical care. This was not always immediately forthcoming. It was not until the crew of a Japanese fishing boat was irradiated and a crew member died as the result of a postwar U.S. test in the Marshall Islands (see next subsection) that Japanese began to demand more of their own government. In 1957, the Law on Medical Measures for the Victims of the Atomic Bomb was passed to provide medical care for the *hibakusha* (the Japanese word for A-bomb survivors).[148] In 1968, Japan passed the Law Concerning Special Measures for

---

146. *Id.*

147. *Nippon Rebuffed on A-Bomb Suit*, DESERET NEWS (Mar. 13, 1954).

148. Law No. 41 of 1957 (Japan).

A-Bomb Survivors to provide economic support for the hibakusha;[149] later, in 1994, it combined both of these into the Atomic Bomb Survivors Relief Law, which combined the two prior laws and expanded coverage.[150]

However, the expanded coverage was not sufficient for many survivors. To receive a hibakusha health certificate, a person had to be within a specified distance of the hypocenter of the blast, entered within two kilometers of the epicenter within two weeks of the blast, recognized as being affected by radiation, or in utero at the time. To receive a monthly allowance as an atomic-bomb disease sufferer, a person first had to have a hibakusha health certificate and then be certified by an expert panel as having one of a small list of recognized diseases (e.g., cancer or leukemia). Of about 250,000 hibakusha medical certificate holders, only about 1 percent were recognized as atomic-bomb disease sufferers.

In 2000, the Supreme Court of Japan handed down a ruling in the first hibakusha lawsuit, the twelve-year-old *Matsuya v. Minister of Health & Welfare* case[151] about the health and welfare minister's refusal of Hideko Matsuya's application to be recognized as an atomic-bomb disease sufferer. The ministry said that Matsuya's disease should not have been caused by atomic bomb radiation as she was 2.45 kilometers from the epicenter of the Nagasaki blast. She was three years old at the time of the blast and was hit by a roofing tile dislodged by the shock wave. Besides the problems from this injury, she also later showed symptoms of radiation exposure on her brain. Matsuya presented expert testimony about the impreciseness of radiation measurements based solely on distance and also witness testimony from another survivor with similar symptoms who was farther away from the epicenter. The court affirmed the lower court's ruling in favor of the plaintiff's claim for atomic-bomb disease sufferer status, stating that distance rules should not be mechanically applied, individual circumstances should be considered, and the usual civil causation standards should be used.

This case led to many more challenges to Ministry of Health, Labour and Welfare rulings but also led to changes in the evaluation criteria used. These changes, though, still left certain groups outside of the system, including those living overseas, such as Korean, Chinese, and Taiwanese forced laborers. More lawsuits finally brought most of these survivors into the system.

---

149. Law No. 53 of 1968 (Japan).
150. Law No. 117 of 1994 (Japan).
151. Matsuya v. Minister of Health & Welfare (Japan Sup. Ct. 2000).

3. Impact of U.S. Nuclear Weapons Tests

The United States conducted a number of nuclear weapons tests, starting with the Trinity test in 1945 and continuing with tests in both the continental United States and islands in the Pacific. Those affected by the tests sued, and the plaintiffs were of two principal types: (1) those who were in some way involved in nuclear weapons tests within the United States, either in military or civilian roles, and claimed injury caused by the radiation emitted; and (2) those involved in tests in the Marshall Islands in the Pacific.

In re Consolidated U.S. Atmospheric Testing Litigation, consolidating forty-three different legal actions, was typical of the claims of those involved in nuclear weapons tests within the United States.[152] The plaintiffs were military personnel or civilians involved in Hiroshima or subsequent experiments, which numbered twenty-one tests through 1963. The suit was treated as one brought under the Federal Tort Claims Act (FTCA), which is a "limited waiver of sovereign immunity subject to certain statutory and judicial exceptions."[153] The government moved to dismiss the suit based on several of these exceptions: the discretionary function exception, the foreign country exception, and the combatant activities exception. These exceptions materially dismissed the claims of the plaintiffs. The first exception claimed by the government was the discretionary function exception, which covered the judgment of those carrying out the government's direction. The court said that this exception addressed claims based on the failure to take adequate safety precautions and to warn of the dangers. The *Feres v. United States* doctrine stated that the FTCA does not cover "injuries to servicemen where the injuries arise out of or are in the course of activity incident to service."[154] Because there were no postservice torts proved, those claims were barred. The second claimed exception was the foreign country exception, which precluded claims that arose in a foreign country. Thus, claims relating to acts occurring in Japan, the Marshall Islands, or Christmas Island were barred. The third claimed exception was the combatant activities exception. This exception applied to activities during times of war, therefore barring claims during that period of this conflict.

Other lawsuits were based on the more than sixty nuclear tests carried out by the United States in the Marshall Islands. After many years of increasing

---

152. *In re* Consolidated U.S. Atmospheric Testing Litig., 616 F. Supp. 759 (N.D. Cal. 1985).
153. Federal Tort Claims Act, 28 U.S.C. §§ 1346(b), 2671–2680 (1948).
154. Feres v. United States, 340 U.S. 135 (1950).

funding offers and subsequent lawsuits, the governments of the Marshall Islands and the United States agreed to the Compact of Free Association, which was subsequently approved by plebiscite by the people of the Marshall Islands and the U.S. Congress.[155] Under this agreement, the U.S. government accepted responsibility, funded a trust fund (initially $150 million), and established the Marshall Islands Nuclear Claims Tribunal to handle claims. All lawsuits were settled against America, and no U.S. court would have jurisdiction to review past, present, or future claims, as subsequent claimants discovered.[156]

C. Subsequent Events

1. Atomic Energy Commission

As the meetings of the Interim Committee clearly showed, there was a strong emphasis on regulating nuclear power through legislation after the war. The main debate was whether it should be controlled by the military or by civilians. What finally emerged from Congress was the Atomic Energy Act of 1946, also known as the McMahon Bill, which favored civilian control.[157] Under the policy that development of atomic energy should, inter alia, improve the public welfare and promote world peace, the law called for both public and private research; control of technical and scientific information; and government control of the "production, ownership, and use of fissionable material."[158]

The law established the Atomic Energy Commission (AEC) to further these purposes. The AEC was designated as the sole owner of all fissionable materials (e.g., plutonium, enriched uranium), such that no individual could own any. Source materials (e.g., uranium, thorium) could only be exported under a license granted by the AEC. The AEC could distribute by-product materials from the process of making fissionable materials, giving a preference for research and development and for medical therapy uses. The AEC was also authorized to do research and conduct experiments for military uses of atomic energy and to produce atomic bombs. In addition the AEC was responsible for granting licenses for the manufacture, use, or export of equipment using fissionable materials. Control of restricted data included production and use of

155. Pub. L. No. 99-239 (1986).
156. People of Enewetak, Rongelap, & Other Marshall Islands Atolls v. United States, 864 F.2d 134 (Fed. Cir. 1988).
157. Pub. L. No. 79-585 (1946).
158. *Id.* § 1(b)(4).

fissionable materials and atomic weapons and restrictions on exchanges with other nations about nuclear energy for industrial use until safeguards could be created to control nuclear energy use "for destructive purposes."[159] The Joint Committee on Atomic Energy was created to review all related legislation.

LEGAL PROFILES

Joseph Volpe, Jr. was one of the lawyers on the Manhattan Project and later a lawyer for the AEC. He was born in New York in 1913 but was in private practice in New Jersey before joining the military in 1943. He was involved in drafting a brief on the legality of the agreement among Canada, Great Britain, and the United States to ensure that there was sufficient uranium ore for the Manhattan Project. After working on the Manhattan Project, he served as deputy general counsel (1946 to 1948) and general counsel (1948 to 1951) for the AEC. Later, he advised J. Robert Oppenheimer during his troubles with Congress in the 1950s and diplomat John Melby on his security clearance and his relationship with playwright Lillian Hellman. He died in 2002.[160]

Brien McMahon was the sponsor of the Atomic Energy Act of 1946 and a lawyer. He was born in Connecticut in 1903 and started his legal practice there. He was appointed as a judge in his hometown and started working as a special assistant for the U.S. attorney general in 1933 and as an assistant attorney general for the Justice Department's Criminal Division in 1935. Several years later, he returned to private practice. In 1944, he was elected to the U.S. Senate, where he became the chairman of the Special Committee on Atomic Energy; in this role, he held hearings and introduced this legislation. He led the subsequent Joint Committee on Atomic Energy. He was reelected in 1950 and died in office in 1952.[161]

---

159. *Id.* § 10(a)(1).
160. *See Joseph Volpe, Jr.; Aided A-Bomb Effort,* WASH. POST (Feb. 1, 2002).
161. *See McMahon, Brien,* BIOGRAPHICAL DIRECTORY OF THE UNITED STATES CONGRESS.

2. Theft of Secrets

In addition to establishing who controlled nuclear power, the government had to keep this new technology's secrets from others. This was not easily done because the Soviets had penetrated the Manhattan Project via the British team's Klaus Fuchs and others. The stakes became even greater when the United States deployed the hydrogen bomb.

The theft of these nuclear secrets led to several well-known cases. Perhaps the most well-known case in the immediate postwar period was that of the Rosenbergs. In that case, *United States v. Rosenberg*, the husband and wife defendants, along with three others, were charged with stealing secrets between 1944 and 1950 and passing them to the USSR.[162] Ethel Rosenberg was the sister of a solider (and defendant) stationed at Los Alamos.

The appeals court noted that the Espionage Act of 1917 (see Chapter 2) allowed for the death penalty even if the information was given to an ally country, not just enemy countries. In addition, it was not necessary to show that injury had befallen the home country as long as the secrets benefited the foreign nation. Furthermore, although the Rosenbergs claimed that they passed information to the USSR as an ally, they continued to do so long after the USSR became an enemy in the Cold War. In reviewing quite a long trail of evidence among all of the conspirators, amid protests by the appellants, the court upheld the conviction. The argument that the death penalty had never been given in a civil court for espionage was not something the appeals court could address as it was allowed by the statute.

In an appeal to the Supreme Court, the Rosenbergs raised the issue of whether the Atomic Energy Act removed the power of the Espionage Act to hand out capital punishment.[163] The Court, noting that the Rosenbergs had been before them seven times, found that the Atomic Energy Act had been passed two years after the overt acts in question. As these acts were committed during wartime, a sentence of death was possible. The Court turned down the appeal and lifted the stay, and the Rosenbergs were executed in 1953.

---

162. United States v. Rosenberg, 195 F.2d 583 (2d Cir. 1952).
163. Rosenberg v. United States, 346 U.S. 273 (1953).

LEGAL PROFILES

Emanuel H. Bloch was primary defense attorney for the Rosenbergs. He was born in New York in 1901 and started his legal practice there. He was known for defending left wing causes, and his clients included the leader of the Communist Party of Pittsburgh, a solider accused of Communist ties, and the Trenton Six (black defendants accused of murdering a white man and convicted by an all-white jury). At the funeral of the Rosenbergs, he laid the blame for their "murder" on the president, the attorney general, and the head of the FBI, which led to a disciplinary action by the state bar. He became the guardian for the Rosenbergs' children until their adoption. He died in 1954, seven months after the Rosenbergs' execution.[164] He was assisted in their defense by attorney Gloria Agrin.[165]

3. Treaties Against Nuclear Weapon Use

The use of nuclear weapons after the war was a constant threat. A number of countries had become declared nuclear powers, and the arms race between the USSR and the United States was an escalating concern. The "more is better" philosophy led to the Cuban missile crisis in 1962, a confrontation between the United States and the USSR/Cuba that threatened nuclear action. This, in part, spawned the notion that there should be limits to the testing and growth of nuclear weapons arsenals. A series of treaties and agreements were signed, such as the Partial Nuclear Test Ban Treaty in 1963[166] and the Strategic Arms Limitation Talks (SALT) in 1972.[167] The most important of these treaties was

---

164. *See Bloch, Attorney for Spies, Is Dead*, N.Y. TIMES (Jan. 31, 1954).
165. *See Gloria Agrin Josephson, 65, Lawyer, Dies*, N.Y. TIMES (June 22, 1988).
166. Treaty Banning Nuclear Weapon Tests in the Atmosphere, in Outer Space and Under Water, Aug. 5, 1963.
167. Treaty on the Limitation of Anti-Ballistic Missile Systems and the Interim Agreement on Certain Measures with Respect to the Limitation of Strategic Offensive Arms, U.S.-Russ. Fed., May 26, 1972.

the multilateral Treaty on the Non-Proliferation of Nuclear Weapons, ratified by the U.S. Senate in 1969.[168]

The Treaty on the Non-Proliferation of Nuclear Weapons began by noting "the devastation that would be visited upon all mankind by a nuclear war and the consequent need to make every effort to avert the danger of such a war and to take measures to safeguard the security of peoples" and continued by stating "that the proliferation of nuclear weapons would seriously enhance the danger of nuclear war."[169] Parties that were nuclear weapon states agreed not to transfer nuclear weapons to non–nuclear weapon states, and non–nuclear weapon states agreed not to receive such weapons or to transfer source or fissionable materials or specialized equipment. Parties were allowed to develop nuclear energy for peaceful purposes. The parties agreed to "pursue negotiations in good faith on effective measures relating to cessation of the nuclear arms race at an early date and to nuclear disarmament, and on a treaty on general and complete disarmament under strict and effective international control."[170] It was signed by 93 states and has been ratified by 190 to date, including the Russian Federation, United States, China, the United Kingdom, and France—but not India, Israel, or Pakistan.

LEGAL PROFILES

Julius Tabin was involved with the Manhattan Project as a scientist but later became a lawyer. He was born in Illinois in 1919 and completed his studies in physics. After working on the Manhattan Project at the University of Chicago, he joined Enrico Fermi at Los Alamos. As part of the team evaluating the results of the Trinity test, he drove a lead-lined vehicle into the blast pit, which, along with other exposure, ended his nuclear research career. He then taught at MIT and earned his law degree. He combined law with his science background and industry

---

168. Treaty on the Non-Proliferation of Nuclear Weapons, July 1, 1968.
169. *Id.*
170. *Id.* art. VI.

contacts in the early days of nuclear energy. He retired from his legal practice in 2006 and died in 2012.[171]

William L. Uanna was involved with security on the Manhattan Project and the 509th Composite Group; he later became a lawyer. He was born in Massachusetts in 1909 and completed his studies in engineering and education. In 1941, he enlisted in the army and was assigned to the counterintelligence unit. He completed his legal studies there. In 1943, he was assigned to security for the Oak Ridge plant, where uranium was being processed. After that, he was assigned responsibility for security for the 509th Composite Group, which eventually dropped the first atomic bomb, during its U.S. training and on Tinian Island. After the war, he worked in private practice for the AEC, setting up security clearance procedures; for the CIA and Commerce Department; and for the State Department, eventually becoming the chief of the Division of Physical Security. He died in Ethiopia in 1961.[172]

D. Modern Applicability

The potential use of nuclear weapons is an ongoing threat to the modern world. Even with all of the international agreements, the threat from weapons of mass destruction constitutes perhaps the most significant nonenvironmental risk to the future of humankind. As such, efforts to reach new agreements and to prosecute those who further the proliferation of nuclear weapons, legally and otherwise, are modernly very significant. Arms control agreements are still being reached, such as the New START agreement of 2010[173] between the United States and the Russian Federation, which is a further effort to reduce the number of nuclear warheads deployed on various types of delivery vehicles. Prosecutions for passing nuclear secrets continue to occur,[174] and accusations about passing nuclear secrets now fall under the auspices of the International

171. *See Julius Tabin, 1919–2012, Physicist Helped Develop Atom Bomb*, Chi. Trib. (Sept. 2, 2012).

172. *See William Uanna, Security Expert*, N.Y. Times (Dec. 23, 1961).

173. Measures for the Further Reduction and Limitation of Strategic Offensive Arms, U.S.-Russ., Apr. 8, 2010.

174. *Court Finds 3 Swiss Guilty of Aiding Nuclear Ring*, Associated Press (Sept. 25, 2012).

Atomic Energy Agency, an international oversight agency established in 1957 to further peaceful usage of nuclear energy.[175] Extrajudicial killings of nuclear scientists from undeclared nuclear states have led to lawsuits.[176] Furthermore, beyond country-level nuclear exchanges, there are threats from terrorists' simpler, not-as-heavily-regulated nuclear weapons[177] and from those without state support using such weapons.[178]

Perhaps the ultimate terror caused by the nuclear forces first unleashed during the war is not deliberate nuclear weapon use but the destructiveness of peaceful nuclear power gone awry. In 1986, an accident involving nuclear power developed for civilian use occurred in Ukraine. The Chernobyl disaster, at the time the only level 7 nuclear event, kept much of Europe in fear for months and years, killing many and unknowingly affecting many more, including children. In March 2011, the second level 7 nuclear event occurred in Japan when waves from a tsunami triggered by one of the largest earthquakes in recorded history took out the primary power and backup systems at the Fukushima Daiichi nuclear plant, resulting in partial nuclear meltdowns and emissions of radiation into the sea and atmosphere and onto land and agricultural resources. The consequences of this accident are not fully known and will not be for many years, but the fear of living under the physical and psychological clouds of radiation has had a significant impact on the local population in Japan, a country that is home to both the first victims of nuclear energy dissemination and now the most recent victims.

---

175. *Iran Accuses IAEA of Passing Nuclear Secrets to Israel*, REUTERS (Sept. 23, 2012).
176. *Families of Iranian Nuclear Scientists Assassinated in 2010 File Lawsuits*, DAILY MAIL (Aug. 15, 2012).
177. *"Dirty Bomb" Threat at Hospitals Remains, GAO Report Says*, WASH. POST (Sept. 11, 2012).
178. *Stateless Terrorists with a Dirty Bomb Now Real Threat to UK*, TELEGRAPH (Mar. 7, 2012).

CHAPTER 8

AFTER THE WAR

As the hostilities ceased, the former enemies had to now deal with each other as vanquished and vanquisher. The number of applicable legal regimes narrowed as a new type of arrangement, the multinational occupying entity, went into effect administering governments. In Germany, this entity was the Allied Control Council, and similar commissions or councils were implemented in other Axis countries. Additionally, in Germany, Austria, and elsewhere in Europe, the four victorious powers (the USSR, the United Kingdom, France, and the United States) each had their own military zone of occupation. Both before and more so after the effective demise of the Allied Control Council, the military commanders were the de facto occupying power. In Asia, Japan was nominally under the auspices of the Far Eastern Commission and the Allied Council for Japan but was primarily controlled by the United States in the role of supreme commander for the Allied powers.

Each occupying entity had to address issues that were both similar and different. In Germany, a government had to be created because the prior government had essentially collapsed with the death of Hitler; but in Japan, the national government continued to function. Besides military actions to stop all hostilities and police actions to control local unrest, the occupying entities had to deal with starving, dislocated, and bombed-out populations. With the recognition that the militarist traditions in Germany and Japan must be changed, the entities invested vast efforts in purging militarists and Nazis from these two countries. In addition, the entities had to deal with and repatriate

POWs and segregate and investigate war criminals for prosecution under the trials described in Chapters 6 and 7. The rule of law was reinstituted in both Japan and Germany, first under the military occupiers' rules, then under forms of shared responsibility, and finally under the full control of local institutions in preparation for ending the occupations.

As the two countries began to regain some semblance of order under the new political situations in their countries, peace treaties had to be worked out. Constitutions had to be written. And the war-shattered economies had to be rebuilt. All of this occurred under the shadow of the postwar movements of Communism in the countries of Western Europe, in the Soviet-controlled parts of Eastern Europe, in China, and elsewhere in Asia. The Cold War began to dictate much of what happened during the occupation as previous plans for additional purging were cut short by the need to build up allies in the fight against Communism.

There was much focus even before the end of WWII about what to do to both avoid and address the next war. The League of Nations was viewed as an insufficiently strong body given that both Japan and Germany had withdrawn from it leading up to WWII. A new forum was needed, one that had not only commitment from all nations but also power to secure peace while providing a forum for discussion. Several talks during the war among the leaders of the Allies led to the postwar creation of the United Nations, which not only served as a forum where nations could meet and agree (or not) but also included a security function to police problems that arose. In addition, many of the prewar protocols that proved inadequate during the war, such as the Third Geneva Convention (which addressed the issue of POWs), were updated for modern warfare.

After the war-torn economies started to grow and the political situation stabilized both domestically and internationally, citizens and nations who were deprived of their assets began to act to get those assets returned to them. Chapter 5 described the efforts of individuals regarding the return of their financial assets from Swiss banks. But there were also significant numbers of cultural assets stolen or lost, both from individuals and nations. Thus, internationally and in the new Federal Republic of Germany and elsewhere, conventions and laws were passed to ensure that assets taken during the war were returned to their original owners and to prevent such destruction and theft in the future.

This chapter focuses on the following legal issues: occupation/rehabilitation and the return of cultural assets.

PROMINENT LAWYERS AND JUDGES IN THIS CHAPTER

Occupation/Rehabilitation:

- Clement Attlee (British prime minister)
- John L. McClellan (senator)
- Hayato Ikeda (treaty signatory)
- Junius Richard (J. R.) Jayewardene (treaty signatory)
- John J. Sparkman (treaty signatory)
- Alexander Wiley (treaty signatory)

Return of Cultural Assets:

- Nicholas Roerich (pact sponsor)
- David E. Finley Jr. (commission vice chairman)
- Huntington Cairns (commission secretary/treasurer)
- Charles Sterling (Louvre curator)
- Keith Merrill (MFAA member)
- Erich Führer (paintings confiscator)

8.1 OCCUPATION/REHABILITATION

A. Statutes

At the Tehran Conference in late 1943, Churchill, Roosevelt, and Stalin not only coordinated the military strategy but started to work on a possible framework for the postwar world, something that had been under consideration almost as soon as the war began. The postwar framework acknowledged the deficiencies in the League of Nations, especially the lack of a meaningful enforcement capability. Based on this conference, the United States, the United Kingdom, the USSR, and China were to be the policemen of the world. At the Yalta Conference in early 1945, the leaders met again, and France was included as a fifth policeman; thus, the makeup of the future membership of the U.N. Security Council was set.

The Potsdam Conference in mid-1945 addressed the postwar occupations of Axis countries, starting with those in Europe. In the protocol from the Potsdam meetings, the military commanders in each of the four zones in Germany were to be the supreme authority, with the Allied Control Council (ACC) resolving joint problems that affected the whole of Germany.[1] The ACC was established under the November 1944 Agreement on Control Machinery in Germany, which designated the various postwar roles in Germany, including the Inter-Allied Governing Authority in Berlin;[2] and it was put into effect by the Berlin Declaration in June 1945, under which, because there was no central government or authority in Germany, the four victorious powers assumed supreme authority with respect to Germany.[3]

The Potsdam Agreement stated that the purposes of the occupation were as follows:

- "The complete disarmament and demilitarization of Germany"
- "[T]he elimination or control of all German industry that could be used for military production"
- "To convince the German people that they have suffered a total military defeat and that they cannot escape responsibility for what they have brought upon themselves"
- To destroy the Nazi Party and institutions, "to ensure that they are not revived in any form, and to prevent all Nazi and militarist activity or propaganda"
- "To prepare for the eventual reconstruction of German political life on a democratic basis and for eventual peaceful cooperation in international life by Germany"[4]

Under this accord, all Nazi laws, especially those that discriminated based on race, creed, or political opinion, were to be abolished. War criminals were to be arrested and brought to judgment, and Nazi Party members were to be removed from public and semipublic office. Nazi and militarist doctrines were

---

1. Berlin Conference of the Three Heads of Government of the USSR, U.S. and UK, Protocol of the Proceedings, U.S.S.R.-U.S.-U.K., Aug. 1, 1945 [hereinafter Potsdam Conference].
2. Agreement on Control Machinery in Germany, Nov. 14, 1944.
3. Declaration Regarding the Defeat of Germany and the Assumption of Supreme Authority with Respect to Germany and Supplementary Statements, June 5, 1945.
4. Potsdam Conference Agreement § II(3)(i)–(iv), Aug. 1, 1945.

to be removed from the education system. Freedom of speech, press, and religion were to be permitted. The overly centralized governmental structure of the Nazi regime was to be decentralized among the regions; and the judicial system was to be reorganized under principles of democracy, justice under law, and equal rights.

Under the Potsdam Declaration from the same conference, the "authority and influence of those who have deceived and misled" the Japanese people were to be ousted from Japan.[5] "Irresponsible militarism" had to be "driven from the world."[6] Japan was to be occupied until there was convincing proof that the war-making power of Japan was destroyed. War criminals would receive "stern justice."[7] The Japanese government was to allow freedom of speech, religion, and thought. War-making industries were to be prohibited.

LEGAL PROFILES

Clement Attlee was the new British prime minister who took over at the Potsdam Conference after Churchill's election defeat; he was also a lawyer. He was born in England in 1883 and completed his legal studies there. He entered the military at the start of WWI, saw extensive action in many locations, and was wounded several times. After the war, he returned to teaching at the London School of Economics, a position he had held before the war and would hold again until 1923. He was elected to Parliament in 1922, rising to leader of the Labour Party in the mid-1930s. With the outbreak of war, he and Churchill joined the Conservatives and Labour Party in a wartime coalition government, of which he became the deputy prime minister in 1942. In the July 1945 election, he became prime minister, a position he held until 1951. He remained in the House of Commons until 1955, when he retired and was appointed to the House of Lords. He died in early 1967.[8]

---

5. Potsdam Conference Declaration, Proclamation Defining Terms for Japanese Surrender, July 26, 1945.
6. *Id.*
7. *Id.*
8. *See Clement Attlee*, Oxford Dictionary of National Biography 101030498.

B. Cases

There were many types of issues that the governing bodies of the occupied territories had to deal with, including identifying, arresting, and trying war criminals; stamping out the prior militarist doctrines; purging militarists from official positions; ensuring that courts returned and overturned militarist, racial, and other suppressive laws; keeping the local populations fed; reviving the local economies; dealing with the massive numbers of displaced people, including POWs; manning checkpoints and guarding valuable installations; and policing crime originating from both the locals and the occupying forces. Many of these issues occurred in conjunction with some of the events that were covered in previous chapters, but one issue that commonly occurs when soldiers occupy a foreign country is controlling fraternization with the former enemy.

The U.S. military was very concerned about fraternization with its former enemy. It was worried that when the United States entered Germany, the retreating Nazi military machine would send out a fifth column (a group of secret sympathizers trying to undermine the conquerors) in the form of women, children, and older people—in other words, anyone who was not a soldier. In addition, the United States was apprehensive about the reactions of the people (including wives and girlfriends) back home, who had sacrificed so much for the war effort, if U.S. soldiers fraternized with the Germans. Beginning prior to the day that its troops crossed into Germany in September 1944, the U.S. Army issued publications[9] and repeatedly informed its troops that there was to be no fraternization with the occupied people in Germany. This prohibition included not only those of the opposite gender but children as well. Soldiers were not to shake hands or greet Germans, drink or socialize with them, let children climb on military vehicles, give gifts to children or play games with them, or generally communicate with Germans on matters that were unrelated to official business.

These rules ran into problems almost immediately. Local women—weary of unending war, stuck in a new cycle of poverty with destruction all around, and now significantly outnumbering the men after all of the war manpower losses (including confined POWs)—and the war-weary and suddenly liberated occupying troops found ways to work around the rules. Besides outright defiance of the rules (a common sentiment was that "it is worth the $65 [fine]"),

---

9. SPECIAL SERVS. DIV., U.S. ARMY, POCKET GUIDE TO GERMANY (1944).

there was a massive amount of deception, including soldiers employing locals in various domestic duties as a front for fraternization or claiming that the women were actually displaced people and not German nationals. The military, in increasingly vain attempts to stop fraternization, warned of the social diseases that could be (and were) contracted through such contact. It sent military personnel to arrest those who were fraternizing, which could lead to fines, loss of rank, and court-martial. But in those cases that went to trial, if they involved consensual relationships, the courts typically handed down lenient sentences, or the sentences were not fully carried out.

In the end, the military increasingly gave up, with General Dwight D. Eisenhower declaring in July 1945 that engaging in conversations in public places and on streets with German adults was no longer be prohibited.[10] Other occupying countries already allowed their troops to converse with German children. Soon, the prohibitions were dropped almost completely. What remained, for American troops, were bans on billeting with a German family and on marrying Germans.[11] But even this did not last. The number of overseas spouses increased to such an extent that Congress passed a special law at the end of 1945 admitting into America the alien spouses and minor children of American servicemen, over and above what was allowed under normal immigration rules.[12] More than ten thousand German brides and their children came to America throughout the balance of the decade, with many "occupation children" left behind. Another new law in 1946 dealt with fiancées as well, which brought thousands more to America.[13]

LEGAL PROFILES

John L. McClellan was one of a group of U.S. senators who traveled to Germany and talked to the troops about the fraternization ban;[14] he was also a lawyer. He was born in Arkansas in 1896 and started his legal

---

10. *Fraternizing Ban in Reich Modified*, N.Y. Times (July 15, 1945).
11. *Army Retains Ban on Reich Weddings*, N.Y. Times (Sept. 22, 1945).
12. Pub. L. No. 79-271 (1945).
13. Pub. L. No. 79-471 (1946).
14. *Senators Criticize Ban on Fraternizing*, N.Y. Times (June 25, 1945).

practice there at the age of seventeen in his father's office. After serving in WWI, he worked as a city attorney. He then worked as a prosecuting attorney from 1927 to 1930. He was first elected to Congress in 1934 and was elected to the U.S. Senate in 1942. He served in the Senate until 1977, leading, among others, the Committee on Appropriations and the Permanent Subcommittee on Investigations, which included looking into organized crime. He died in 1977.[15]

C. Subsequent Events

The ACC effectively stopped functioning due to disagreements among the four countries—early indications of what was to be the Cold War. The Allied military governments were eventually replaced by high commissioners and then ambassadors as the new Federal Republic of Germany began to take shape and peace treaties were signed. No peace treaty was actually signed in Germany until the decades-later reunification of the country after the fall of the Berlin Wall. The Potsdam Conference had specified that the ACC was supposed to prepare a peace settlement with Germany that was "to be accepted by the Government of Germany when a government adequate for the purpose is established."[16] Until the reunification of Germany in 1990, there was no such government.

The Two-Plus-Four Agreement between West Germany and East Germany on one side and the United States, the United Kingdom, France, and the Soviet Union on the other side occurred in 1990.[17] It specified the combination of the two separate German entities plus all of Berlin into a single country, with fixed borders and no claims to other countries. The agreement reaffirmed Germany's commitment to stability—"only peace will emanate from German soil"[18]—as well as the commitments under the Treaty on the Non-Proliferation of Nuclear Weapons. Preparation for aggressive war was prohibited and punishable under the new constitution. Germany capped its armed forces and use

---

15. *See McClellan, John Little*, BIOGRAPHICAL DIRECTORY OF THE UNITED STATES CONGRESS.
16. Potsdam Conference, *supra* note 1, § I(3)(i), U.S.S.R.-U.S.-U.K., Aug. 1, 1945.
17. Treaty on the Final Settlement with Respect to Germany, Sept. 12, 1990.
18. *Id.*

of weapons in accordance with the U.N. Charter. With these commitments, the four Allied powers terminated their rights and responsibilities and returned full sovereignty of Germany's external and internal affairs to Germany.

In Japan, the Potsdam Declaration stated that occupying forces were to be withdrawn after achieving their objectives, including a "peacefully inclined and responsible government."[19] Because Japan was not divided and still had a functioning government, its peace treaty was possible much earlier. The Treaty of San Francisco was negotiated and signed in 1951.[20] In it, Japan was given sovereignty over its own territory but renounced claims to Korea; Taiwan; the Kuril Islands and Sakhalin, which were acquired under the Treaty of Portsmouth in 1905; the Spratly Islands; Antarctica; and the League of Nations' Japanese Mandate of the Pacific Islands (e.g., Saipan, Tinian, and the Marshall Islands). In addition, Japan ceded control of Okinawa to the United States and renounced all special rights in China (it later signed separate peace treaties with China and South Korea). Furthermore, Japan accepted the judgments of the IMTFE and related courts and agreed to adhere to Article 2 of the U.N. Charter, i.e., settling international disputes by peaceful means.

The Treaty of San Francisco also included provisions concerning damages and reparations. The Allied powers agreed to waive direct reparation, except for damages done to occupied countries where Japanese assets could be seized and sold (separate reparations agreements were reached later with countries such as the Philippines). To indemnify harm done to POWs, Japanese assets in neutral or Axis countries were to be sold and the money turned over to the Red Cross (this would bar future lawsuits). Also included in the treaty were the much-litigated claim renunciation provisions (see Chapter 7): Article 19(a) "waive[d] all claims of Japan and its nationals against the Allied Powers and their nationals arising out of the war"; and Article 14(b) "waive[d] all reparations claims of the Allied Powers, other claims of the Allied Powers and their nationals arising out of any actions taken by Japan and its nationals in the course of the prosecution of the war."[21] Unresolved issues were to be referred to the International Court of Justice.

---

19. Proclamation Defining Terms for Japanese Surrender, July 26, 1945.
20. Treaty of Peace with Japan, Sept. 8, 1951.
21. *Id.* arts. 14(b), 19(a).

LEGAL PROFILES

Hayato Ikeda, the Japanese foreign minister who attended the peace treaty talks, was one of the signers for Japan. He was born in Japan in 1899 and completed his legal studies there. He then went to work for the Ministry of Finance, focusing on tax matters and rising to the position of vice minister, while also writing several books on taxation. A debilitating illness sidelined him for half a decade during his time at the Ministry of Finance. He was elected to the diet after the war and became finance minister in the Shigeru Yoshida cabinet. After his role in the peace treaty, he also served as the minister of international trade and industry. In 1960, he became prime minister, a position he held until 1964, focusing on improving Japan's postwar economy. He died in 1965.[22]

Junius Richard (J. R.) Jayewardene was the Ceylonese finance minister who attended the peace treaty talks, spoke against reparations, and signed the treaty for Ceylon; he was also a lawyer. He was born in Ceylon (Sri Lanka) in 1897 and completed his legal studies there. He joined the nationalist movement to free Ceylon from British rule. He was elected to the colonial legislature in 1943. In 1947, he became finance minister. He held many roles in Parliament before becoming prime minister in 1977. In 1978, he was elected as president of the country, a position he retained until 1989. He was in office during much of the early phase of the country's civil war. He died in 1996.[23]

John J. Sparkman was born in Alabama in 1899 and started his legal career there. He was first elected to the U.S. House in 1936 and remained there through 1946. In that year, he was elected to the U.S. Senate. He served there until 1979, representing the United States at the United Nations and relocating the Operation Paperclip scientists to Alabama.

---

22. *See Japan's Blunt Leader*, N.Y. TIMES (July 19, 1960).
23. *See J. R. Jayewardene of Sri Lanka Dies at 90; Modernized Nation He Led for 11* Years, N.Y. TIMES (Nov. 3, 1996).

He was the unsuccessful vice presidential nominee in 1952. He died in 1985.[24]

Alexander Wiley was born in Wisconsin in 1884 and started his legal career there. He worked as a county district attorney from 1909 to 1915. In 1936, he ran unsuccessfully for governor; but in 1938, he was elected to the U.S. Senate, remaining there until 1962. He died in 1967.[25]

In addition to Sparkman and Wiley, the other two signers for the United States were John Foster Dulles and Dean Acheson, profiled previously.

D. Modern Applicability

The peace treaty signed in San Francisco did not resolve all of the geographic matters in Asia, and many are still in dispute. Japan is involved in at least three different territorial disputes with Russia, China, Taiwan, and South Korea. The dispute with the Russians involves the Kuril Islands;[26] in the peace treaty, Japan ceded sovereignty, but the treaty did not say to whom. In addition, the treaty did not specifically define these islands. In addition, the Senkaku Islands[27] were not mentioned explicitly in the treaty, and it was not clear whether they should be considered part of the renounced territory in Taiwan and China. The same applies to the Liancourt Rocks,[28] which could be considered part of Korea, in which case Japan would have renounced the sovereignty to those islands as well. These issues are quite involved, spanning previous centuries and treaties, and will not be easily resolved.

The occupation of foreign nations has been revisited recently since the United States invaded both Iraq and Afghanistan. In Iraq, unlike in Germany and Japan, violence in the country continued after the cessation of the primary armed conflict. Similar to Germany and Japan, Iraq had a militaristic

24. *See Sparkman, John Jackson*, Biographical Directory of the United States Congress.
25. *See Wiley, Alexander*, Biographical Directory of the United States Congress.
26. *Russian PM Medvedev's visit to Disputed Islands Irks Japan*, BBC (July 3, 2012).
27. *China Sends Ships Back to Waters off Disputed Japanese-Controlled Islands*, Telegraph (Oct. 2, 2012).
28. *Tensions Rise Between Tokyo, Seoul over Islets*, Wall St. J. (Aug. 10, 2012).

and nationalistic ideology (Ba'athism) that had to be removed. In Japan and Germany, much of the aid was for humanitarian purposes, such as foodstuffs, due to the devastating impacts of prolonged war on their economies. In contrast, Iraq's war was relatively short-lived, so a majority of the postwar aid has been for infrastructure repair. The majority of the funds supplied to Germany and Japan "consisted of financing through loans and grants in order to enable those countries to carry out their recoveries largely on their own. In Iraq, the United States is providing not only the material assistance, but also is paying for the necessary labor."[29]

8.2 RETURN OF CULTURAL ASSETS

A. Statutes

Because of the widespread destruction and theft of cultural assets during the war (estimated at one million or more artifacts stolen or destroyed), international conventions were passed to deal with this problem.

The first postwar agreement, in 1954, was a Hague Convention that was only adopted in the Americas.[30] It stated that the way in which warfare was conducted increasingly subjected cultural property to destruction. It defined *cultural property* as

> movable or immovable property of great importance to the cultural heritage of every people, such as monuments of architecture, art or history, whether religious or secular; archaeological sites; groups of buildings which, as a whole, are of historical or artistic interest; works of art; manuscripts, books and other objects of artistic, historical or archaeological interest; as well as scientific collections and important collections of books or archives or of reproductions of the property defined above,[31]

as well as the buildings (museums, libraries, depositories) that held them and the centers containing monuments.

---

29. NINA SERAFINO, CURT TARNOFF & DICK K. NANTO, COUNCIL ON FOREIGN RELATIONS, U.S. OCCUPATION ASSISTANCE: IRAQ, GERMANY AND JAPAN COMPARED (Mar. 23, 2006).
30. Hague Convention for the Protection of Cultural Property in the Event of Armed Conflict, May 14, 1954.
31. *Id.*

This treaty drew upon the Hague Conventions of 1899 and 1907[32] and the Roerich Pact of 1935.[33] Hague Convention IV required that all necessary steps be taken in bombardments to spare, as best as possible, historic monuments and prohibited seizure or willful damage of historic monuments or works of art, which "should be made the subject of legal proceedings."[34] Hague Convention IX contained the same requirement for naval bombardments, specifying that an emblem is to be used to designate historic monuments or works of art. The Roerich Pact stated that historic monuments, museums, scientific, artistic, educational, and cultural institutions were to be "respected and protected by belligerents."[35]

The 1954 Hague Convention, which applied to both international and domestic conflicts, called on the contracting parties to prepare in peacetime for the protection of cultural assets within their borders during wartime and to establish personnel and procedures within their armed forces for protection of cultural property. Contracting parties were to respect the cultural property in their nation and that of other parties from use (unless militarily necessary), theft, pillage, misappropriation, vandalism, requisition, or reprisals. These obligations applied to those occupying the territory of another party. The convention also specified that cultural property should bear a distinctive emblem, armed guards used for special protection could not be used for military purposes, and transport of such property should be under special protection.

The first protocol to this convention[36] specified that occupying powers would not allow the export of cultural property from occupied territory and would seize any such imports into their own country. Occupying powers were to return cultural property at the conclusion of the conflict. The same applied to any property transferred from one contracting party to another to protect it during a conflict. A second protocol[37] further detailed when military necessity could be invoked, defining *enhanced protection* to apply to objects of "greatest

---

32. Hague Convention IV: Respecting the Laws and Customs of War on Land and Its Annex: Regulations Concerning the Laws and Customs of War on Land, Oct. 18, 1907; Hague Convention IX: Concerning Bombardment by Naval Forces in Time of War, Oct. 18, 1907.

33. Treaty for the Protection of Artistic and Scientific Institutions and Historic Monuments, Apr. 15, 1935 [hereinafter Roerich Pact].

34. Hague Convention IV art. 56.

35. Roerich Pact art. 1.

36. First Protocol to the Hague Convention of 1954 for the Protection of Cultural Property in the Event of Armed Conflict, May 14, 1954.

37. Second Protocol to the Hague Convention of 1954 for the Protection of Cultural Property in the Event of Armed Conflict, Mar. 26, 1999.

importance for humanity" and establishing criminal responsibility and jurisdiction for prosecuting those who violated the convention.

Germany passed its own restitution law for looted art.[38] This law allowed original owners to recover their artwork if they were improperly dispossessed of it during the Nazi era, including artwork sold while emigrating. (However, this did not apply to those who had "degenerate" art confiscated under the *entarteter Kunst* law.)[39] These restitution laws originated during the occupation but were later passed as statutes in the Federal Republic of Germany, with the stipulation that all claims had to be made by a certain date. German property law may also allow restitution for lost or stolen art, but not in the case of legally acquired art and a good faith purchaser.

LEGAL PROFILES

Nicholas Roerich was the inspiration behind the Roerich Pact. He was born in Russia in 1874 and completed his legal studies there. He then turned his life to art, directing the Imperial Society for the Encouragement of the Arts from 1906 to 1917; working with stage design (e.g., Igor Stravinsky's *The Rite of Spring*); and preserving architecture and cultural assets, using his paintings to help do so. After the revolution, he left Russia and lived in America; he also explored Asia, painting as he went and conducting archeological work, with his family in tow (his son became a well-known expert on Asia). He was nominated for the Nobel Peace Prize three times in six years, including the year of the Roerich Pact. A museum was founded in his honor, holding many of his paintings; other paintings are in museums across the world. He died in 1947.[40]

---

38. Bundesrückerstattungsgesetz, July 19, 1957 (F.R.G.).
39. Das Gesetz über die Einziehung von Erzeugnissen entarteter Kunst, May 31, 1938 (Nazi Ger.).
40. *See N. K. Roerich Dies; Artist, Explorer*, N.Y. TIMES (Dec. 16, 1947).

B. Cases

1. Roberts Commission

A number of civilian organizations, including the National Gallery of Art, the American Council of Learned Societies, the American Defense Harvard Group, and the Metropolitan Museum of Art, urged the Roosevelt administration to set up an organization that would work with the army as it invaded and moved into Europe to help preserve and protect the cultural property there. Chief Justice Harlan Stone (see Chapter 2) sent a letter to President Roosevelt asking for a government organization to coordinate civilian and military efforts to protect and conserve cultural property in war areas and to ask the Allies to set up their own groups to do so.[41] Secretary of State Cordell Hull (see Chapter 2) also suggested that a school be set up to train men to undertake this function. The result was the American Commission for the Protection and Salvage of Artistic and Historic Monuments in Europe (later renamed to include Asia as: the American Commission for the Protection and Salvage of Artistic and Historic Monuments in War Areas). The commission was dubbed the Roberts Commission after its chairman, Supreme Court Justice Owen Roberts (see Chapter 3).

LEGAL PROFILES

David E. Finley Jr. was the vice chairman of the Roberts Commission and a lawyer. He was born in South Carolina in 1890 but started his legal practice in Pennsylvania and Washington, D.C. (his father was a congressman). He served in the military in WWI. After the war, he joined the Treasury Department, where he worked closely with Treasury Secretary Andrew Mellon, including ghostwriting Mellon's publications and his speeches. He became very involved when Mellon, one of the wealthiest people in the country, started collecting art and was instrumental in

---

41. Letter from Chief Justice Harlan Stone to President Roosevelt (Dec. 8, 1942).

Mellon's planning and purchase of the National Gallery of Art, which was founded in 1941. Finley remained the art gallery's director until 1956, encouraging the donation of many works of art. He ran many of the activities of the Roberts Commission from the National Gallery of Art during the war. After the war, he was influential in founding and leading the National Trust for Historic Preservation, the U.S. Commission of Fine Arts, and the National Portrait Gallery. He died in 1977.[42]

Huntington Cairns was the secretary/treasurer of the Roberts Commission and a lawyer. He was born in Maryland in 1904 and completed his legal studies at the age of twenty. He practiced law until 1934, when he became a special adviser to the Treasury Department's Customs Bureau; his job there included, among other things, determining if imported books and art objects were "pornographic" or artistic. From 1937 to 1943, he was the assistant general counsel for the Treasury Department. While working on the Roberts Commission, he also became general counsel to the National Gallery of Art and continued as special adviser to the Treasury Department, roles in which he continued to serve until 1965. He was an author and the moderator of a radio show called *Invitation to Learning*. He died in 1985.[43]

2. Monuments, Fine Arts, and Archives Program

The Roberts Commission was able to help establish, within the War Department, the Monuments, Fine Arts, and Archives program (MFAA), through which MFAA officers followed combat troops into liberated areas to protect and preserve cultural property. From lists provided by the American Council of Learned Societies and the American Defense Harvard Group, hundreds of maps of the locations of cultural property in Europe were supplied to the MFAA. MFAA officers, working with the battle plans, tried to steer aerial and other bombardments away from cultural locations and properties, including Florence in Italy and Nara and Kyoto in Japan. MFAA teams scoured suspected

42. *See David E. Finley Dies; Art Gallery Leader*, N.Y. TIMES (Feb. 2, 1977).
43. *See Huntington Cairns; Author, U.S. Censor*, L.A. TIMES (Jan. 24, 1985).

locations and, along with the OSS, interrogated POWs and Nazi art collectors about where to find stolen art and art hidden in order to protect it from bombing raids and retreating German armies. More than one thousand storage locations were identified, including salt mines in Germany and Austria. After the war, the MFAA helped restore the cultural property to public and private owners in both Europe and Japan.

LEGAL PROFILES

Charles Sterling was a curator at the Louvre in Paris. He was born in Poland in 1901 and completed his legal studies there after fighting in the war for Polish independence. He then trained in art history in Paris and other locations. In 1929, he was offered the position of curator of the paintings department at the Louvre, where he assembled numerous catalogs. When the war started, he was heavily involved in the distribution of the paintings of the Louvre. However, he was forced to give up his position due to his religion, declining an opportunity to be declared an Aryan, so he emigrated to America. He remained there during the war, working at the Metropolitan Museum of Art (Met) and volunteering on the American Council of Learned Societies. After the war, he returned to the Louvre, remaining there until his retirement in 1968 while also working part of the year at the Met. He died in 1991.[44]

Keith Merrill was a member of MFAA responsible for shipping German artwork back to America; he was also a lawyer. He was born in Minnesota in 1887 and completed his legal studies in Massachusetts. From 1915 to 1917, he served in the National Guard, and then he joined the State Department. He worked in a variety of overseas postings until 1937, when he entered private business. He joined the navy reserve in WWII and ended up working for the Foreign Economic Administration. After that, he became involved with a shipment of 202 German-owned paintings sent to America for safekeeping. He was recalled to

---

44. *See Sterling, Charles*, DICTIONARY OF ART HISTORIANS.

active service to handle the return of the paintings several years later and then to handle the shipment of art sent to America by grateful European countries, such as Michelangelo's *David-Apollo*. He was the brother-in-law of General George S. Patton. He died in 1959.[45]

3. Restitution: Works Looted by Occupying Countries

There were many complexities in moving from the preservation of cultural property to the restitution of assets dispossessed during the war to their rightful owners. Many restitution cases in Europe used a private negotiation process and were not litigated because the national or regional governments were the holders of the art; while in the United States, private litigation often resulted when a solution could not be reached because the current possessors were more likely to be private entities. These cases arose when the provenance of the cultural assets in question could not be conclusively proven. In such lawsuits, various legal theories came into play, such as whether a good faith purchaser could be required to return an asset to its original, illegally dispossessed, owner. Private owners asserted defenses of the statute of limitations and laches against actions to return the assets. There were also cases that became cross-continental, involving at least the two legal systems of Europe and the United States. The following two modern cases illustrate the difficult issues in resolving these matters.

The first case, *Bakalar v. Vavra*, concerned a drawing by Egon Schiele, *Seated Woman with Bent Left Leg (Torso)*.[46] This was one of many owned by a victim of Dachau whose wife was required to sell his assets to pay confiscatory taxes on Jews while he was imprisoned. He and his wife subsequently died in concentration camps, and her sister (who had gained possession of the artwork in some manner) sold the drawing to a Swiss gallery, which sold it to an American gallery, which sold it to the plaintiff and current possessor of the drawing. After the successful bidder in an auction to sell the drawing withdrew his bid due to the heirs' claims to its title, the plaintiff brought an action to declare himself the rightful owner of the drawing.

---

45. *See Merrill, Keith,* YALE UNIVERSITY LIBRARY.
46. Bakalar v. Vavra, 619 F.3d 136 (2d Cir. 2010).

The trial court held in favor of the plaintiff as the judge ruled that Swiss law prevailed. Under Swiss law, a good faith purchaser can only be dispossessed within five years of the sale even if the asset was stolen (i.e., the seller did not have good title to pass). Anyone contesting the title would also have to prove a lack of good faith, and there is no heightened standard of due diligence for Nazi-era art.

The appeals court compared this to New York law, where a thief can never pass good title. The court also ruled that the statute of limitations only starts to run when the demand for replevin of the stolen item has occurred and been refused (rejecting the discovery rule, which starts the time period from when the object should reasonably have been discovered) and that the good faith purchaser has to prove good title. The court then applied a conflict of laws "interests analysis," where the law of the jurisdiction having the greatest interest in the litigation is the one applied.[47] Finding that New York State, home to a significant art market, had the larger interest in preserving the "integrity of transactions and preventing the state from becoming a marketplace for stolen goods," the court vacated the trial court's decision, requiring the trial court to apply New York law.[48]

In the second case, *Republic of Austria v. Altmann*, six paintings by the artist Gustav Klimt were confiscated by the Nazis in Austria from the fleeing Jewish owner after the Anschluss.[49] The paintings were acquired by a Nazi lawyer, who sold or gave these paintings to the Austrian Gallery, owned by the national government. After the war, when the heir tried to claim the paintings under a new Austrian law that voided coerced transactions during the war, the gallery first claimed that the paintings had been donated to it by the original owner's will. Then, using a new law that required export licenses for art important to the country's cultural heritage, the gallery worked with the relevant government agency to coerce the plaintiff's Austrian counsel to sign a statement without the plaintiff's knowledge that the donation of the Klimt paintings was legal, in return for export permits for other artwork belonging to the heir. It was not until some forty years later that a researcher discovered this, which led to a new restitution law for those so dispossessed. But the com-

---

47. *Id.* at 143.
48. *Id.* at 144.
49. Republic of Austria v. Altmann, 541 U.S. 677 (2004).

mission appointed to review the purported donation of these six paintings claimed that it was legal. Because of the high deposit requirements for filing lawsuits in Austria, the plaintiff filed the lawsuit in the United States.

The defendants alleged that they were immune to suit in the United States under the Foreign Sovereign Immunities Act (FSIA) of 1976. The trial court disagreed, holding that one of the exceptions applied, i.e., property was taken in violation of international law. On a motion to dismiss, the U.S. trial court found both that FSIA applied to cases involving pre-1976 conduct and that the defendants' conduct fell within the exception. This case made it all the way to the U.S. Supreme Court, which concurred with the original court that FSIA and its exceptions could be applied to WWII claims even though foreign countries at the time enjoyed absolute, not relative, immunity in U.S. courts.

LEGAL PROFILES

Erich Führer was the Nazi lawyer who confiscated the Klimt paintings in the second case. He was born in Austria in 1900 and completed his legal studies there. In 1932, he joined the Austrian Nazi Party and climbed to the leadership ranks by the late 1930s. After the ban on Nazi authors in 1934, he sent an open letter to all professors in the country, questioning their commitment to the Nazi Party. He joined the SS, becoming a captain. During the 1930s, he defended many Nazis who were prosecuted, including Otto Planetta, the killer of Chancellor Dollfuss (see Chapter 5). After that trial, he himself was arrested (and later released) for Nazi sympathies. During the war, he was the vice president of the Vienna Bar Association. After the war, he was sentenced to three years' imprisonment for high treason and had his assets confiscated, but he was released early. In 1965, he defended Jan Verbelen, a war criminal convicted by the Belgian courts, during his Austrian trial. Führer died in 1987.[50]

---

50. *See Drei Minuten pro Opfer*, DER SPIEGEL (Jan. 10, 1966).

4. Restitution: Works Looted by Liberating Soldiers and Survivors

The Axis powers were not the only looters of cultural assets. Soldiers liberating countries as well as survivors of the atrocities in those countries took the opportunity to steal cultural assets from Europe.

Many of these cultural assets were returned only after the deaths of the looters. For example, eleven oil paintings stored in an air raid shelter were apparently taken by a U.S. serviceman and only returned after his death to the Pirmasens museum in Germany. Another item returned was the Das Augsburger Geschlechterbuch, a sixteenth-century bound collection of drawings taken from its storage location by a U.S. soldier and eventually returned to the state of Baden-Württemberg. The most well-known case is probably the Quedlinburg medieval art theft, where the heirs of the looting soldier tried to sell these cultural items back but were instead sued by the Quedlinburg church, charged with crimes by the U.S. government,[51] and required to pay fines and penalties to the IRS. Even Holocaust survivors have been caught with looted cultural property and ordered to return it: the heirs of a survivor were recently told to return to the Vorderasiatisches Museum in Berlin a thirty-two-hundred-year-old Assyrian artifact, an inscribed gold tablet that had been in the museum since 1926.[52]

In another case, a soldier apparently sold to a New York lawyer two valuable Albrecht Duerer portraits that were painted around 1499.[53] These were stolen from what became East Germany in 1945 and sold to the soldier, who in turn sold them to the lawyer in America. Both the heir of the Grand Duke of Saxony-Weimar and the national German government (first West Germany and later East Germany) were claimants in this suit. The trial court dismissed the claims of the current possessor and the Saxony-Weimar heirs and granted summary judgment to the national German government (the successor-in-interest to predecessor sovereignties such as Saxony-Weimar).

After a fascinating discussion on the ownership dispute between the heirs of Saxony-Weimar and the national German government, the appeals court turned to whether the New York attorney could have good faith title to the

---

51. United States v. Meador, 138 F.3d 986 (5th Cir. 1998).
52. *Nazi Victim's Family Told to Return Artifact*, N.Y. TIMES (June 1, 2012).
53. Kunstsammlungen Zu Weimar v. Elicofon, 678 F.2d 1150 (2d Cir. 1982).

paintings based on his twenty years of possession. The trial court had rejected his claims that he was entitled to retain possession "either under the German doctrine of 'Ersitzung,' under which a good faith purchaser gains title to a stolen object upon 10 years' possession without notice of defect in title, or because the New York statute of limitations had run.[54] Because a lawsuit had been commenced within three years of the initial demand and refusal, the statute of limitations had not run; in addition, the statute was tolled due to the United States' nonrecognition of East Germany until 1974. The court held that New York had the greater interest in regulating its own market than Germany would in applying its doctrines to extraterritorial disputes; thus, New York law applied, meaning that a thief cannot give good title (the court ruled that the paintings had been stolen) and so the paintings properly belonged to the German government.

C. Subsequent Events

To address gaps in the Hague Conventions, a number of other rules were created. To implement a process for returning looted cultural property, the United Nations Educational, Scientific and Cultural Organization (UNESCO) established a convention in 1970 to prevent the illegal import, export, and transfer of cultural properties.[55] This included requiring export certificates, monitoring museum acquisitions, and allowing processes for recovery by rightful owners. The International Institute for the Unification of Private Law (UNIDROIT) summoned a convention in 1995 that called for the restitution of stolen cultural artifacts and the return of cultural objects that were illegally exported from their countries of origin.[56] And the Washington Conference on Holocaust-Era Assets in 1998 promulgated eleven principles, including identification of art seized by the Nazi regime but not returned to its rightful owners, publication to find prewar owners, use of a central registry, just and fair solutions in all cases, balanced commissions to identify such art, and national procedures to implement these principles.[57]

---

54. *Id.* at 1158.
55. UNESCO Convention on the Means of Prohibiting and Preventing the Illicit Import, Export and Transfer of Ownership of Cultural Property, Nov. 14, 1970.
56. UNIDROIT Convention on Stolen or Illegally Exported Cultural Objects, June 24, 1995.
57. Washington Conference on Holocaust-Era Assets, Nov. 30–Dec. 3, 1998.

D. Modern Applicability

Some of the assets taken from the WWII time period are only now being returned. During their long colonial rule in Korea from 1910 until the end of the war, Japan took a number of cultural assets from Korea. Recently, Japan returned twelve hundred of these, including the highly valued *Joseon Wangsil Uigwe*, which document and illustrate the royal protocols of the Joseon Dynasty.[58]

However, Russia has not agreed to return a number of significant cultural assets that it took when it overran Germany, e.g., Priam's Treasure, Gutenberg Bibles, Gotha book collection, and Renoir and Degas paintings. While there were some returns of cultural assets, including many to East Germany, Russia believes that it deserves compensation for the large-scale destruction of Russian cultural life that took place during the Nazi invasion, including four hundred museums and more than one million artifacts.

In the aftermath of the Iraq War in the early 2000s, the national and other museums were left unattended. That led to the large-scale looting of cultural artifacts: according to estimates, up to fifteen thousand items from antiquity were looted. Many blamed the attacking military forces for not doing more to timely protect the cultural property of Iraq at the National Museum of Iraq and Iraq National Library and Archives, especially considering that protection was provided timely to the Iraqi Ministry of Oil and that the military had been notified of this urgent need several months in advance of the looting. Subsequent recovery efforts resulted in the retrieval of many of these assets, but some still questioned whether the lack of protection was a violation of the Hague Convention requirements to protect cultural assets.

Another modern facet of the looting issue is that those attacking cultural property are being prosecuted for war crimes. For example, a Yugoslav navy admiral received a seven-year sentence for ordering an attack on the old walled city of Dubrovnik, which is on the World Heritage List, during the conflicts in the early 1990s.[59]

---

58. *Japan Returns Korean Royal Archives After a Century*, ASAHI SHIMBUN (Dec. 8, 2011).
59. *UN War Crimes Tribunal Issues Seven-Year Jail Term over Shelling of Dubrovnik*, U.N. NEWS CENTRE (Mar. 18, 2004).

AFTERWORD

The legal issues that arose from WWII were a broad reflection of the war itself. For those countries that maintained independent and functioning legislative and judicial systems, the legal issues mirrored the struggles going on inside each nation to deal with external aggression while maintaining their democratic traditions. For those countries whose legislative and judicial systems were co-opted or silenced, the legal issues represented the face of the ruling regimes, which perverted justice to attain their goals in support of aggressive war. For those countries that remained neutral, the legal issues reflected the balance between pursuing national objectives and avoiding the loss of their neutrality. In all of these situations, the use of law was an accurate barometer of the nature of the respective wartime governments.

The legal issues presented here are quite varied, from the mundane pricing of materials to the ultimate high-risk endeavor of nuclear weapons. Despite all of the effort that goes into planning and fighting military battles, the reality of war is that the larger part of it centers on supplying the armaments; finding people and material resources; keeping the wartime economy running; addressing enemies within national borders; balancing secrecy, propaganda, and openness; defending against spies and saboteurs; handling displaced people; and keeping a high level of morale and national purpose, all in addition to the usual health, welfare, and police functions of government.

Many of the issues addressed in this book were specific to this war and seem unlikely to ever arise in a new conflict. The need for instituting a new Lend-Lease program, desegregating and reintegrating the military, interning citizens, and revoking citizenships (at least in modern democracies) seems to be limited to the era of this conflict. Many of the economic issues dealing with price and supply controls, labor issues, and seizure of the means of production also would likely be handled differently in a new conflict. And with the vast publicity of and universally negative response to medical experimentation on live human beings and the murder and ill-treatment of POWs, these crimes will hopefully never be seen again.

Other issues are recurrent or even more malevolent today. Export controls on rare materials, seizure of enemy assets, military tribunals for foreign nationals, genocide of "inferior" people, annexation of neighboring countries, concealment of looted assets, destruction of cultural life, war crimes, crimes against humanity, mass rape, mass murder of civilians, plunder of occupied territories, creation of a divine military, and preemptive military strikes all are occurring currently or have occurred in the last few decades, as have the occupation and rehabilitation of militarist regimes and the lingering effects of peace treaties signed long ago.

Some issues could return in the right circumstances anywhere or in certain countries where legal protections are not prevalent. The use of forced labor/ slavery; imposition of martial law, sedition, and treason charges; loss of the freedom of expression, subversion of judicial authority; destruction of democratic institutions; biological warfare; and use of nuclear weapons are perhaps one war away from becoming a reality again, as they almost have been a reality on various occasions since WWII.

The people who represented these legal issues ran the gamut from altruistic to reasonable and pragmatic to deviant and evil. They represented the best and sometimes the worst of the respective national identities and often just spoke for the prevalent feelings in that time and place. Even when malevolence dominated the national direction, lawyers and judges at various times stood up and were counted—often leading to their own deaths—among those resisting that evil influence. It is perhaps in the examples of all of those who strongly resisted what was wrong and fought for the greater good, at the expense of their personal well-being, that hope finds a foundation for the future of the rule of law.

All of the legal personalities profiled in this book are now deceased. The memories of this conflict are ebbing from the minds of the modern world. There are fewer and fewer WWII participants around to remind us of the potential horrors of aggressive war, of ultranationalism and militaristic societies, of labeling others as inferior, of the paths to genocide. However, although on a smaller scale than world war, conflict is still all around us. Thus, occasionally, it is necessary to have a stark reminder of not only the potential for evil but also the way civilized societies should respond to evil. Occasionally, it is necessary to have a stark reminder of not only the way in which evil takes a long road to fruition but also how, with the proper reorientation, the national characteristics that lead to aggressive war can be refocused on aggressive peace. To interdict evil before it reaches the end of its path, many institutions, security arrangements, and legal conventions were established, which are still serving their functions today. Perhaps the principal understanding gained from this global war is not that conflict can be avoided but that the appropriate mechanisms need to be in place to direct, channel, and resolve the anger of real and perceived wrongs.

The intent of presenting these issues from a war finished almost seventy years ago was not only to bring back to life those legal players who so shaped the modern world but also to provide a basis for understanding what underlies some of the current problems related to conflicts—and to shine a revealing light on those problems that should have ended with this war but in many cases did not. The open question is whether, as the twenty-first century progresses, the creation of international institutions with designated policemen and the collective wisdom of humanity are sufficient to prevent future generations from enduring the evils of a global conflict. We can only hope for peace in their times.

APPENDIX

LIST OF LAWYERS AND JUDGES PROFILED

CHAPTER 1

- William B. Bankhead
- Edvard Benes
- Leon Blum
- Robert Laird Borden
- Aristide Briand
- John T. Cahill
- Homer S. Cummings
- Charles G. Dawes
- Ellis Dresel
- John Nance Garner
- David Lloyd George
- Alger Hiss
- Frank B. Kellogg
- V. K. Wellington Koo
- Robert Lansing
- James E. Major
- Edward Bernard Raczynski
- Franklin Delano Roosevelt
- John William Salmond
- Claude A. Swanson

CHAPTER 2

- Dean Acheson
- Sadie Tanner Mossell Alexander
- Alben W. Barkley
- Edward R. Burke
- Harrie B. Chase
- Oscar S. Cox
- George W. Crockett Jr.
- Everett Dirksen
- Edward C. Eicher
- Osmond K. Fraenkel
- Truman K. Gibson Jr.
- Albert Goldman
- Herbert F. Goodrich
- Cordell Hull
- Robert H. Jackson
- Henry H. Klein
- Albert B. Maris
- Thurgood Marshall
- Newell Mecartney
- Frank Murphy
- A. Philip Randolph
- Stanley F. Reed
- O. John Rogge
- Charles B. Sears
- Howard W. Smith
- Henry L. Stimson
- Harlan F. Stone
- Clyde W. Summers
- Peter Woodbury

CHAPTER 3

- Hugo L. Black
- Prentiss M. Brown
- James F. Byrnes
- Tom T. Connally

- William H. Davis
- John Foster Dulles
- Joseph B. Eastman
- Thomas I. Emerson
- Charles H. Fahy
- Nathan P. Feinsinger
- Manly Fleischmann
- Paul A. Freund
- Lloyd K. Garrison
- Walter F. George
- Arthur J. Goldberg
- Thomas A. Goldsborough
- Augustus Noble Hand
- Learned Hand
- Henry M. Hart Jr.
- W. McNeil Kennedy
- Irene Kolin Lichtman
- John R. Mitchell
- John Lord O'Brian
- Joseph A. Padway
- William L. Prosser
- Owen J. Roberts
- Alvin J. Rockwell
- Harry A. Shulman
- Francis M. Shea
- Thomas W. Swan
- Robert A. Taft
- Arthur T. Vanderbilt
- Fred M. Vinson
- A. Matt Werner

CHAPTER 4

- Ernest Besig
- Francis B. Biddle
- Harold H. Burton
- Zechariah Chafee Jr.

- Tom C. Clark
- Wayne M. Collins
- Hayden C. Covington
- Myron C. Cramer
- Oscar H. Davis
- Nanette Dembitz
- William Denman
- William O. Douglas
- Edward J. Ennis
- Morris L. Ernst
- Abe Fortas
- Felix Frankfurter
- Ralph F. Fuchs
- Philip M. Glick
- Thomas H. Green
- Bert E. Haney
- Pearl M. Hart
- Arthur G. Hays
- Xenophon Hicks
- Charles A. Horsky
- Wilbur Keegan
- Saburo Kido
- Carol Weiss King
- Warren Magnuson
- Calvert Magruder
- John J. McCloy
- Harold R. Medina
- Basil O'Connor
- Fred Okrand
- Harriet F. Pilpel
- Walter L. Pope
- Sam T. Rayburn
- A. Frank Reel
- Robert R. Reynolds
- Beatrice Rosenberg
- Kenneth C. Royall
- Wiley B. Rutledge

- Irving S. Shapiro
- Albert L. Stephens Sr.
- William H. Timbers
- Frank Walker
- Earl Warren
- Herbert Weschler
- Frederick Bernays Wiener
- Wendell L. Willkie
- A. L. Wirin
- Minoru Yasui

CHAPTER 5

- Raphaël Alibert
- Cyril Asquith
- James Atkin
- Johannes Baumann
- Fernand de Brinon
- Roger J. Bushell
- René Cassin
- John W. Davis
- Engelbert Dollfuss
- Allen W. Dulles
- Philipp Etter
- Lloyd A. Free
- Rayner Goddard
- Valentine Holmes
- Travers Humphreys
- Florian Imer
- Thomas Inskip
- Jacques Isorni
- Jules Jeanneney
- Samuel Klaus
- Pierre Laval
- Frank Douglas MacKinnon
- Frederic Maugham
- Anthony Marlowe

- Pierre Paul Mongibeaux
- André Mornet
- Jean-Marie Musy
- Léon Noël
- Randolph E. Paul
- Karl Renner
- Heinrich Rothmund
- Georges Sauser-Hall
- Adolf Schärf
- Dietrich Schindler Sr.
- Kurt Schuschnigg
- Artur Seyss-Inquart
- Donald Somervell
- Frank Soskice
- Edward von Steiger
- Walter Stucki

CHAPTER 6

- Walter B. Beals
- Klaus Bonhoeffer
- James T. Brand
- Josef Bühler
- Wilhelm Bünger
- Thomas Dehler
- William Denson
- Thomas J. Dodd
- Franz Exner
- Katherine B. Fite
- Hans Frank
- Reinhold Frank
- Roland Freisler
- Wilhelm Frick
- Hans Gisevius
- Hans Globke
- Cecelia H. Goetz
- Franz Gürtner

- Hermann Jahrreiß
- Hans John
- Benjamin Kaplan
- Ernst Kaltenbrunner
- Robert Kempner
- Gerhard Klopfer
- Hans Koch
- Otto Kranzbühler
- Herbert Kraus
- Egon Kubuschok
- Charles M. La Follette
- Rudolf Lange
- Geoffrey Lawrence
- Gerhard Leibholz
- Raphael Lemkin
- Bernhard Lösener
- Bessie Margolin
- François de Menthon
- Helmuth von Moltke
- Iona Timofeevich Nikitchenko
- Oswald Rothaug
- Roman Andreyevich Rudenko
- Fabian von Schlabrendorff
- Franz Schlegelberger
- Alfred Seidl
- Robert Servatius
- Hartley Shawcross
- Herbert Arthur (H. A.) Smith
- Berthold von Stauffenberg
- Herbert J. Strong
- Wilhelm Stuckart
- Telford Taylor
- Otto Thierack
- Henri de Vabres
- Paul Vogt
- William J. Wilkins
- Josef Wirmer

CHAPTER 7

- Henri Bernard
- Emanuel H. Bloch
- Eleanor Bontecou
- Brendan F. Brown
- Arthur Comyns-Carr
- William A. Consodine
- Osachi Hamaguchi
- George L. Harrison
- John P. Higgins
- Kiichiro Hiranuma
- Kōki Hirota
- Naoki Hoshino
- Delfin J. Jaranilla
- Mei Ju-ao
- Grace Kanode Llewellyn
- Testsu Katayama
- Joseph B. Keenan
- Ichirō Kiyose
- Ryōichi Kuroda
- John Lansdale Jr.
- José Laurel
- William L. Laurence
- Alan J. Mansfield
- Yōsuke Matsuoka
- Edward Stuart McDougall
- Brien McMahon
- Tatsukichi Minobe
- Haruhiko Nishi
- Henry G. Nolan
- Erima Harvey Northcroft
- Shoichi Okamoto
- Radhabinod Pal
- William Donald Patrick
- B.V.A. Röling
- Milo E. Rowell

- Takao Saitō
- Kijūrō Shidehara
- Mamoru Shigemitsu
- Toshio Shimada
- Lev Nicholevich Smirnov
- Kisaburo Suzuki
- Julius Tabin
- Sakutaro Tachi
- Kenzō Takayanagi
- Frank S. Tavenner Jr.
- William L. Uanna
- Somei Uzawa
- Joseph Volpe Jr.
- William F. Webb
- Courtney Whitney
- George Yamaoka
- Ivan Michyevich Zaryanov

CHAPTER 8

- Clement Attlee
- Huntington Cairns
- David E. Finley Jr.
- Erich Führer
- Hayato Ikeda
- Junius Richard (J. R.) Jayewardene
- John L. McClellan
- Keith Merrill
- Nicholas Roerich
- John J. Sparkman
- Charles Sterling
- Alexander Wiley

INDEX

Office of Lend-Lease
Administration, 94
Office of Price Administration
(OPA), 119, 122, 130, 132, 134
Office of Production Management
(OPM), 119, 149
Office of Scientific Research and
Development, 477
Office of the Administrator of
Export Control, 98
Office of War Information, 251,
259
Office of War Mobilization, 127
Official Secrets Act (U.K. 1939),
265, 266–267, 280
Ohlendorf, Otto, 420
Okamoto, Shoichi, 428, 485
Okinawa mass suicides, 472
Okrand, Fred, 187, 249–250
O'Neal v. United States (1944),
121–122
Open Door policy (China), 10
Operation Paperclip, 326, 467
Operation Storm, 399
Operation Tannenbaum, 312
*Opp Cotton Mills, Inc. v. Administrator
of the Wage & Hour Division of the
DOL (1941)*, 101–102
Oppenheimer, J. Robert, 476, 478
Orders in Council (U.K.), 279

P

Pact of Steel (1939), 19
Padway, Joseph A., 117, 169–170
Pal, Radhabinod, 427, 445
Papon, Maurice, 306, 307

Paris v. Metropolitan Life Insurance Co.
(1946), 155
Paris Conference on Reparation
(1945), 323
Paris Peace Conference, 9
Paris Treaty (1815), 308
Partial Nuclear Test Ban Treaty
(1963), 491
Patrick, William Donald, 427, 445
Paul, Randolph E., 265, 327
Peace of Westphalia (1648), 308
Peace Preservation Laws (Imperial
Japan), 430
Peace treaties. *See specific treaty by name*
Pearl Harbor attack, 238–239
Peiper, Joachim, 392
Pelley, United States v. (1942), 61–63
Pentagon Papers trials, 63
People's Court (Volksgerichtshof),
345, 347, 348, 350, 355, 360, 364,
365, 371, 372
Perkins, Frances, 149
Perlstein v. United States (1945),
196–197
Pétain, Marshal Philippe, 17, 295–
297, 298, 299–300, 301, 302, 305
Petersen, Hans, 358
Philippines
IMTFE trial, 451, 464
Japanese attack on, 443
mass rape by Japan in, 457
occupation-era president's
trial, 472
semi-independence of, 30–31
slave labor, lawsuits based on,
473